Political Systems

of

LATIN AMERICA

MARTIN C. NEEDLER

Editor

D. VAN NOSTRAND COMPANY, INC.

Princeton, New Jersey
toronto / new york / london

D. VAN NOSTRAND COMPANY, INC.
120 Alexander St., Princeton, New Jersey (*Principal office*)
24 West 40 Street, New York 18, New York

D. VAN NOSTRAND COMPANY, LTD.
358, Kensington High Street, London, W.14, England

D. VAN NOSTRAND COMPANY (Canada), LTD.
25 Hollinger Road, Toronto 16, Canada

Library of Congress Catalog Card No. 64-23962

PRINTED IN THE UNITED STATES OF AMERICA

To the Memory of

MANUEL SEOANE, OF PERU
1900–1963

". . . with love, with high resolve, with
boldness, and with the will to fight"

PREFACE

THERE ARE TWO MODES OF APPROACH TO THE POLITICS OF THE Latin American countries. One mode emphasizes similarities and discusses "Latin America" as a single entity, pointing out where this or that country deviates from the typical pattern; the other stresses variety, treating each country separately while standing prepared to make clear their common features. The present book follows the second approach, not because its editor believes that the first is inappropriate, but because he thinks that the best results are obtainable only by following both paths of understanding, and because the overwhelming preponderance of books in the field take the generalizing approach, leaving the individualizing one neglected. Something in the way of generalization is offered to the reader in the concluding chapter of the present book.

What I have done as editor has been, first, to select scholars to contribute the chapters. It has been extremely gratifying to be able to assemble as distinguished a group as the contributors to this volume are. For aid in this talent search I should like to thank David Burks, James Busey, and Milton Vanger.

In view of the wide variation among the countries treated, each author was left to his own discretion as to how closely he wished to comply with the standard format and the suggested page length. In only one instance did the length of the chapter submitted differ so markedly from the suggested length (it was somewhat over double) as to warrant revision on that account.

In two or three instances some element I thought to be of central importance to the country in question was omitted from consideration and I inserted material to remedy the lack; apart from this the changes made in the chapters submitted were confined to minor matters—uniformity of style in capitalization and the like—and to revisions made necessary by events which occurred or were likely still to occur after the chapter was submitted.

In making a book useful both for the general reader and for teaching and reference in the field of political science in United States colleges, stress must be laid on intelligibility, in all the meanings of the word. Explanatory hypotheses need to be emphasized and to control what is included. Accordingly, the chapters show parallel structure in their larger features. Bibliographies are highly selective and have been held to under a dozen items in the English language. (This rule has been bent slightly in some cases, for good reasons.)

v

For stimulating the musings which eventuated in this basic conception of the book, I should acknowledge indebtedness to Samuel H. Beer and Adam Ulam, editors of the European government text *Patterns of Government,* published by Random House, and to Professor William G. Andrews.

Thanks are due my wife, Lore, for her encouragement and forbearance. My greatest feelings of gratitude for their loyalty and cooperativeness are due my collaborators.

Ann Arbor, June 1964   M. C. N.

CONTENTS

The Contributors

MARTIN C. NEEDLER, the editor, with undergraduate and graduate degrees from Harvard is currently Assistant Professor of Political Science at the University of Michigan. His field research in Latin America has been conducted principally in Mexico and Peru. Professor Needler is the author of articles in various professional journals and of *Latin American Politics in Perspective*. He has contributed the chapter on Mexico to this volume and collaborated in chapters on Haiti and the Dominican Republic.

ROBERT J. ALEXANDER, Professor of Economics at Rutgers University, has contributed the chapter on Bolivia. Professor Alexander is easily the most prolific and versatile author in the Latin American field, having published over five hundred articles and some ten books, among them *The Bolivian National Revolution, Communism in Latin America, Today's Latin America*, and *Prophets of the Revolution*. A frequent visitor to the area, he is also noted for his active participation in inter-American labor and political affairs.

CHARLES W. ANDERSON, author of the chapters on Honduras, El Salvador, and Nicaragua, is Associate Professor of Political Science at the University of Wisconsin. He holds degrees from Grinnell, Johns Hopkins, and the University of Wisconsin and has conducted extensive field research in Latin America. Dr. Anderson is author of *The Political Economy of Mexico* (with William P. Glade, Jr.) and of the forthcoming *Politics and Economic Change in Latin America*, as well as of various articles.

JOSEPH R. BARAGER, who has contributed the chapter on Argentina, has an acquaintance with the country which goes back to his residence there as a Doherty Fellow fifteen years ago and includes several subsequent visits and a continuing research interest. Dr. Barager is at present Visiting Lecturer in Latin American History at the University of Pennsylvania and has also taught at the University of Rochester; his articles have appeared in the history journals.

GEORGE I. BLANKSTEN, author of the chapter on Ecuador, is currently Professor of Political Science and chairman of the department at Northwestern University. He holds degrees from the University of Chicago and the University of California at Los Angeles. Dr. Blanksten's extensive experience in Latin America includes missions undertaken for the United States government and a visiting professorship at the Mexican National University, as well as the research which went into his *Ecuador: Constitutions and Caudillos, Peron's Argentina,* and *United States' Role in Latin America.* Dr. Blanksten has been much in demand as a contributor to collaborative volumes, professional journals, and the *Encyclopaedia Britannica* and as a visiting professor at various institutions.

JAMES L. BUSEY, who contributed the chapter on Costa Rica, is also the author of *Notes on Costa Rican Democracy* and *Latin America: Political Institutions and Processes,* as well as a host of articles. With a degree from the Ohio State University, Dr. Busey is at present Professor of Political Science at the University of Colorado, although he has served on a visiting basis as a lecturer in universities from New Brunswick to Hawaii. His field work and writing have focused on Mexico, Central America and Panama, and Brazil.

FEDERICO G. GIL, author of the chapter on Chile, is Professor of Political Science and Director of the Institute of Latin American Studies at the University of North Carolina. Dr. Gil was born in Cuba and holds LL.D. and Ph.D. degrees from the University of Havana. An indefatigable traveler, writer, lecturer, and public servant, he holds an honorary professorship at the University of Chile and is a corresponding member of the Argentine National Academy of Law and Social Sciences. Dr. Gil's leading works are *The Governments of Latin America* (with W. W. Pierson), *Genesis and Modernization of Political Parties in Chile, La Politica Hispano-Americana,* and *Partidos Politicos en Latinoamerica.*

DANIEL GOLDRICH is currently Associate Professor of Political Science at the University of Oregon. With a doctorate from the University of North Carolina, Professor Goldrich's research interests center on political attitudes among Latin American students, especially in Panama and Costa Rica, and also on local politics in the United States, the subject of his *Comparative Community Politics* (with Robert E. Agger and Bert E. Swanson). He has contributed the chapter on Panama to the present volume.

ROSENDO A. GOMEZ is author of the chapter on Peru, where he lived
as holder of a Social Science Research Council Fellowship during
1961-62. Dr. Gomez is at present Professor of Government at the
University of Arizona, holding degrees from the Universities of
Vermont and Minnesota. He is author of *Intergovernmental Relations in Highways in Minnesota* and of *Government and Politics in
Latin America*, as well as of various articles on Latin American
politics and on Spanish immigration to the United States.

C. A. M. HENNESSY is currently a Senior Scholar of St. Antony's College, Oxford, and Lecturer in Modern History at the University
of Exeter. The history of nineteenth-century Cuba forms one of
his major research interests; he has visited Cuba since the recent
Revolution and has contributed the chapter on Cuba to this volume. Professor Hennessy is author of various articles on modern
Spanish and Latin American history and of *The Federal Republic
in Spain, 1868-1874*.

GÖRAN LINDAHL, author of the chapter on Uruguay, is head of an
Institute of Journalism in process of establishment in Sweden. With
a doctorate from the University of Stockholm, he has conducted
field research in Uruguay and is the author of *Uruguay's New Path*,
a study of politics under the first *colegiado* (1919-1933).

RAYFORD W. LOGAN is at present Chairman of the History Department at Howard University. He has written extensively on Haiti,
the subject of his contribution to this volume, and on the history
of the Negro in the United States.

LEO LOTT, author of the chapters on Venezuela and Paraguay, is an
Associate Professor of Political Science at the Ohio State University.
He has been continually concerned with problems of Venezuelan
politics since his stay in the country as a Doherty Fellow over ten
years ago and is the author of various articles on the country; he is
also the author of the sections on Venezuela and Paraguay in the
Encyclopedia Americana. His doctorate is from the University of
Wisconsin.

JOHN D. MARTZ, currently Assistant Professor of Political Science at
the University of North Carolina, and contributor of the chapters
on Guatemala and Colombia, has rapidly established himself as a

vigorous author on Latin American topics; his published works include *Central America: The Crisis and the Challenge; Colombia: A Contemporary Political Study;* and *Justo Rufino Barrios and Central American Union.* Dr. Martz has traveled and done research in most of the Latin American republics. His degrees are from Harvard, George Washington University, and the University of North Carolina.

PHYLLIS PETERSON, with a Ph.D. degree from the University of Michigan, is Assistant Professor of Political Science at the University of Indiana (Jeffersonville). Dr. Peterson's chapter on Brazil in the present volume, her first published work, is the fruit of a year of field research in the country, which included interviews with more than a hundred political figures.

FOREWORD

THE RICHNESS of the political experience of the Latin American states is still familiar only in a limited degree to those outside the area, and the insights which the assaying of that experience can contribute to the general study of politics are only beginning to be discovered.

It may well be that quite literal analogies to the characteristic features of Latin American political dynamics are displayed by other states which find themselves in comparable phases of their development—either advancing, like the new states of Africa and Asia, or regressing, like the French Republic in recent years. On a more subtle level, the attentive student can extract from Latin American experience principles which underlie political processes in general; which derive from the nature of power, interest, will, and legitimacy as categories of human experience not bound to determinate places and times; which bring one closer to an understanding of human behavior as such.

It is to this ambitious task, as well as to its more modest goal of providing the reader with descriptions and explanations of the features of Latin American political systems, that this book is dedicated.

MEXICO

REVOLUTION AS A WAY OF LIFE

Introduction: Society and Culture

An understanding of Mexican politics can be of the greatest aid in the understanding of Latin American politics. This is true not simply because Mexico is the third largest state in area or the second largest in population in Latin America—its population is now around 37,500,000—nor because Mexico in its international relations has pursued a policy of independence while remaining friendly to the United States. Mexico's importance to the student of politics lies rather in the fact that it has met and successfully surmounted many of the social, economic, and political problems which face most of the countries of Latin America—indeed most of the countries of the world. While of course each country will have to face its own problems in its own way, the experience of Mexico is nevertheless highly instructive and highly suggestive. Mexico is a country which seems to have had few of the prerequisites for a democratic system or for a high degree of economic development. Nevertheless not only does it today have a successfully developing economy, it also has a political system which respects civil liberties and is stable and, on the whole, democratic.

As in many countries of Latin America, the topography of Mexico presents formidable barriers to national unity and economic progress. Much of the country is forest or desert, and less than half of its area is suitable for agriculture. When the Spaniards came, they found Mexico, a land which had a flourishing Indian civilization of many impressive achievements, divided among speakers of over two dozen indigenous languages. Today Mexico is a mestizo rather than an Indian country. (In Mexico as elsewhere, categories like Indian or mestizo are cultural rather than racial. An Indian is defined as someone of a certain way of life, characterized by such things as going barefoot, sleeping on the floor or in a hammock, eating tortillas rather than bread, and especially speaking an Indian language rather than Spanish.) In the linguistic sense probably a maximum of 10 percent of today's Mexican population should be considered Indian. But the geographic distribution of the speakers of indigenous languages is uneven, so that some states are very heavily "Indian," especially Oaxaca, in the south, and Yucatán, home of the ancient Maya civilization, in the southeast.

1

A constant feature of Mexican life, from the time of the Aztecs on, has been the dominance of Mexico City. The city has grown extremely rapidly in recent years and together with its suburbs now has a population of some five and a half million, making it one of the great cities of the world and third largest in the hemisphere after New York and Buenos Aires. The growth in the size of Mexico City and of other urban areas in the country reflects the very high rate of population growth in the country (currently almost 3.5 percent per year); it also represents a movement of people from rural areas into the cities. In this respect Mexico is typical of the countries of the hemisphere and, like them, is showing signs of an excess of demand over supply in the provision of municipal services, housing, and jobs, especially in the Federal District.

After Mexico City, the largest population centers are Ciudad Juárez (across the Rio Grande from El Paso, Texas), Guadalajara, and Monterrey, capital of the state of Nuevo León. Fast-growing Monterrey is a center of industry and likewise of conservative and pro-clerical sentiment.

Although construction and manufacturing activities steadily increase, about half of the country's economically active population is still engaged in agricultural and pastoral pursuits and fishing.

As Mexico has become more urban—every other Mexican now being a city- or town-dweller—it has developed in other ways. Illiteracy is steadily tending downward and today stands at about 37 percent of the population of school age and over; twenty years ago it exceeded 50 percent.

The educational system of the country still falls far short of what is needed. For many years government expenditures on education were not increasing relative to need, relative to the performance of other Latin American countries, or relative to the increases in other budgetary categories. This situation began to improve during the Ruiz Cortines administration (1952-58) and education has been a subject of special attention for President López Mateos. Federal expenditures on education more than doubled during the first four years of his term (1958-64).

Public education remains essentially a matter of providing instruction in the primary grades, on the one hand, and of supporting the universities, on the other. At the secondary level, the bulk of the schools are private fee-paying institutions, predominantly Church-run.

Historical Background

In the long saga of Mexican history some recurring patterns stand out. The present-day Mexican, looking back on the history of his country, is likely to perceive certain constant themes: foreign domination, Mexican resistance, and betrayal. These themes overlay events from the time of the Conquest down to the early twentieth century. The Conquest itself set the pattern: the Spanish invaders under Cortez seized Moctezuma by treachery; heroic national resistance led by Moctezuma's successor, Cuauhtémoc, failed and Cuauhtémoc was captured and later put to death (in violation of a pledge made by Cortez). Thus the conquerors were able to establish a system in which civil, military, and religious power were combined to exploit the labor of the Indian masses. Similarly, the movement for Independence, begun in 1810 when Father Hidalgo tolled the bells of his church in the village of Dolores, was crushed temporarily with the execution of Hidalgo and later of his follower Father Morelos. Although subsequently successful when a royal officer named Iturbide went over to the rebels, the Independence movement, too, was betrayed. Begun not only in a spirit of national revolt but also as a protest against social injustices, the movement lost this second meaning as it was taken over by the creole upper classes (i.e., the locally born descendants of Spanish ancestors) who finally crowned Iturbide Emperor of Mexico. Betrayal and treachery are likewise the themes of the early history of the republic during the first half of the nineteenth century. The role of the foreigner who intervened in Mexico and exploited the Mexican people was played largely by the United States, which during this period was steadily slicing away Mexican territory, in what is now the American West and Southwest, to add to its own domain.

In the 1860's while the United States was occupied in the Civil War, the foreign intervention was that of France under Napoleon III, who tried to re-create an empire in Mexico and place on the throne Maximilian of Austria. Again (so runs the legend in the mind of the average Mexican of today) the upper classes, the Church, the landowners, rallied behind the foreign usurper. And again an indigenous hero arose to lead the national resistance, in the person of Benito Juárez. Besides leading the resistance to Maximilian, Juárez is remembered for putting through the legislation known collectively as *La Reforma*, which separated Church and State, confiscating Church lands and incidentally making it legally possible for the lands of the indigenous communities to pass into private ownership.

After Juárez left the scene, Mexican history resumed its normal pattern. The liberal principles for which Juárez had fought were, in a sense, betrayed by his lieutenant Porfirio Díaz, who established an iron rule that lasted, with one brief interval, from 1877 to 1910, giving Mexico a period of domestic tranquillity and, measured by the narrow standards of the epoch, economic progress, along with a harsh political authoritarianism. Along with Díaz came the foreign exploiters, this time British, French, Spanish, and North American investors. In the attempt to develop Mexico's economy Díaz gave substantial concessions to foreign private capitalists, and Mexico was described as "the mother of foreigners, the stepmother of Mexicans."

The Revolution

The Revolution of 1910 began with strictly political rather than social and economic goals. The limited political aims of the Apostle of the Revolution, Francisco I. Madero, were epitomized in the slogan he adopted (which also represented Díaz's announced goals when he first aspired to office). It remains today the official motto of the revolution: EFFECTIVE SUFFRAGE; NO REELECTION. That is, Madero was interested in having the votes counted the way they were cast and, by prohibiting the reelection of the president, ending the stranglehold on public office still maintained after thirty years by Díaz and his original group of political allies. But once the Revolution was under way, it took on new meanings as it progressed and as new groups flocked to its standard. What had begun as a simple movement for political reform became, as the fighting went on, a movement for land reform, economic development, the integration of the Indian international life, and the weakening or elimination of class barriers.

Madero, elected president after Díaz had left for France and exile, was betrayed, arrested, and shot "while trying to escape" by one of Díaz's generals who had sworn loyalty to Madero, Victoriano Huerta; and then the real revolution began, with general civil war that continued until 1916. The most important of the leaders of the private revolutionary armies who set out to overthrow the usurper Huerta and then continued to fight among themselves were three men: Venustiano Carranza, Pancho Villa, and Emiliano Zapata. Each of them was in his turn, like Madero, betrayed and shot. Carranza, a landowner of moderate views who had been a Díaz-era governor, was finally successful in reestablishing order, thanks largely to the strategic genius of his military commander, Alvaro Obregón, and ruled as president from 1916 to 1920.

Erratic and at times cruel, though of great personal attractiveness to his followers, Pancho Villa often behaved no better than the bandit which he was widely regarded in the United States as being. After suffering military reverses, Villa was persuaded to retire from active politics in return for a cash subsidy and a hacienda in the North of the country. Many years later he was ambushed and shot under mysterious circumstances, suggestive of Obregón's complicity, presumably to prevent his reentry into politics. Zapata differed from the other two great leaders in being motivated much more by social goals, rather than self-interest. His slogan was TIERRA Y LIBERTAD, "Land and Liberty," and he declined to lay down his arms until land should be granted to the peasant. Zapata was betrayed and shot by a colonel acting in Carranza's interest, though probably not on Carranza's orders.

The Revolutionary Presidents

Although Carranza himself was a moderate on social questions, his period as president is noteworthy for several landmarks in the development of the social consciousness of the Mexican state. During this period the present Mexican constitution, that of 1917, was adopted. Besides establishing the organization of Mexican government (including the prohibition of the reelection of the president) it was the first modern constitution in that it included detailed provisions establishing the duty of the state to advance the social welfare of the citizens. During Carranza's administration also the first land reform legislation was decreed, though little implemented until the succeeding presidential term.

At the end of Carranza's term of office there occurred something that was to become typical in succeeding years: a preelection succession crisis.[1] Carranza passed over the logical candidate to succeed him, Obregón, who felt, not unreasonably, that as the person most responsible for Carranza's success and the most popular individual in the Carranza administration, he should have been the candidate to receive Carranza's support. The Obregonist forces, fearful that Carranza's administration would rig the elections to favor the government candidate, rose in revolt. Against Obregón's orders, Carranza was—of course—betrayed and shot by someone he had trusted.

Succession crises accompanied by revolts ensued on three other occasions during the decade of the twenties—every time, in other words, that a new president was to be chosen—in 1923, in 1927, and in 1929. These revolts made a great deal of sense in the light of the experience of Mexican history, for in Mexico the candidate of the incumbent administration always wins: this has always been so and remains true today. The government, in other words, changed hands only through successful revolts. But the noteworthy thing about this series of revolts which accompanied succession crises is that each was feebler than the last. After 1929 presidential candidates of the opposition threatened and fumed but did not actually take up arms, and today the phenomenon of the predictable election-time revolt has to all intents and purposes disappeared from Mexican life. Obregón's revolt of 1920 was thus the last successful uprising in Mexican history.

This development constitutes a clear mutation in the regularities of Mexican politics and its causes are interesting and revealing. If one looks at the rising of December 1923, staged on behalf of the presidential candidacy of Adolfo de la Huerta (who had served as provisional president for six months after Carranza's assassination) one observes several very suggestive developments. Traditionally in Mexican history any revolts would be joined by legions of people, especially from the urban and rural lower classes, who believed they had nothing to fear and everything to gain from a change in government. In 1923, however, although probably the greater part of the army went over to De la Huerta, the government forces were bolstered by labor batallions from Mexico City and by irregular peasant forces: for the first time peasants and workers had something to lose by a change of administrations. This was new for Mexico. By favoring labor organization and land reform, Obregón had given peasants and workers a stake in the preservation of the regime. From that time on revolts against the regime became progressively weaker until they disappeared altogether; which surely provides a striking demonstration that the continuing stability of a political order is guaranteed only by popular acceptance, an acceptance that comes because people believe that the regime represents them and will act in their interest.

Obregón was succeeded as president by another Revolutionary general from the state of Sonora, Plutarco Elías Calles. Personally less popular than Obregón, although in his own way a very able man, Calles ruled in a firmer, indeed more ruthless, manner than his predecessor. The policies of the Calles administration differed from those of Obregón in several respects. The new president was not enthusiastic about land reform, and land distribution slowed during his administration. On the other hand, Calles showed labor great marks of favor and his right-hand man was Luis Morones, a labor leader whose early promise of greatness was unfulfilled and who grew rich and arrogant under Calles' protection.

Calles was also noted for his strongly anticlerical attitude. The bases for an anticlerical policy are laid down in the Constitution of 1917, but official attitudes towards the Church have ranged from benevolence to hostility, depending on the orientation of the incumbent president. Calles' term of office represents the high point which official anticlericalism has reached since the Revolution. The constitution had forbidden ownership of property by the Church or the celebration of religious rites in public and had established a legal basis for extensive government regulation of the clergy and of religious schools. Great opposition was aroused by Calles' attempt to implement these provisions of the constitution, culminating in a serious outbreak of acts of violence on the part of religious extremists (*cristeros*) which were repressed with great ferocity by government forces.

The Constitution had also, in line with Madero's principles, provided that no president could be reelected. Towards the end of Calles' term this was amended so that a president could not be *immediately* reelected but could come back into office after skipping a term, thus making Obregón eligible for the presidential term beginning in December 1928. The term was also extended from four years to six. Obregón was nominated to the office and elected (after the traditional preelection revolt had been overcome!) but between the election and the inauguration was assassinated by a religious fanatic.

This situation was very uncomfortable for incumbent President Calles, and led to one of the historic decisions of Mexican history. Many people expected Calles to amend the constitution and remain in office himself, as some of his supporters were urging, while some extreme agrarians even suggested that Calles himself had been responsible for Obregón's assassination. Under these circumstances Calles embarked on a course which has given the Mexican Revolution one of its most distinctive features. In the annual presidential address which opens the legislative session, he declared that the time had come for Mexico to pass from "the era of personalities" to "an era of institutions" and announced his irrevocable decision to retire forever from the presidency at the end of his legal term. Calles subsequently implemented his decision by calling for all Revolutionary forces to join in forming a political party which could assure a stable succession to office while carrying on the banner of the Revolution. Thus the National Revolutionary Party was founded. Its present-day successor, the Institutional Revolutionary Party, still rules Mexico.

As provisional president until a replacement for Obregón could be elected and inaugurated, Calles picked Emilio Portes Gil, an able lawyer and politician with a pro-labor record and acceptable to the agrarians, who had been instrumental in modifying strife between Church and State in the later days of the Calles administration. Although Calles remained the strongest political figure in the country, and the military leaders tolerated the new civilian president partly out of deference to Calles' wishes, Calles nevertheless refrained from interfering with Portes Gil's conduct of affairs, even when the new administration canceled contracts which had been given to friends of Calles on the grounds that their terms were too unfavorable to the government. In fact, Calles spent half of Portes Gil's fourteen months in office traveling outside the country. Portes Gil deviated from Calles' policies in two important ways. One was that he discontinued government favor to Luis Morones, to general popular acclaim; the other was that he stepped up the distribution of lands under the agrarian reform program. In fact more land was distributed during Portes Gil's single year of office than in any year up to that time.

The president who was elected to fill out the remainder of Obregón's term, Pascual Ortiz Rubio, proved weak and ineffectual and, after disagreements with Calles, resigned, having spent two and one-half years in office. The remainder of Obregón's six-year presidential term was completed by an able Revolutionary general, a political moderate and associate of Calles named Abelardo Rodríguez.

A young general from Michoacán named Lázaro Cárdenas was chosen as president for the 1934-40 term. Despite a previous record of loyalty to Calles, Cárdenas' policies proved too radical for the old strongman, now become fairly conservative and for some time in poor health, who found himself shipped out of the country by his erstwhile protégé when he took a position opposing the new president.

Cárdenas' presidential term seems in retrospect almost a second Revolution. Land was distributed to the peasants at a dizzy pace. Labor was shown great favor, under a new leader, an intellectual named Vicente Lombardo Toledano. The government political party was reorganized and given a new, more socialist and nationalist orientation, being rebaptized the PRM or Mexican Revolutionary Party. The railroads passed under government control, as did the oil companies, which had been foreign-owned. The oil company expropriation, hailed within Mexico as marking the economic emancipation of the nation, was not accomplished without a great deal of anguish, and even calls for military intervention, on the part of some of the North American oil companies. These were, after all, the days of the New Deal and the Popular Front movements in other countries, and Mexico shared in the enthusiasm for the radical renovation of society that was general throughout the world at the time.

The Recent Presidents

The precise nature of the process by which Mexico's presidents are actually chosen has always been shrouded in mystery. The best guess seems to be that the incumbent president does the picking, taking into account the views of senior Revolutionary figures and major interest groups. Rather strange from the point of view of ideology was Cárdenas' choice of a successor, a little known general (the "Unknown Soldier") of conservative and religious inclinations named Manuel Avila Camacho, although the two men had had close personal ties. Avila Camacho's term, 1940-1946, marked a period of relaxation from the enthusiasm of the Cárdenas days, but also a time of the conscious resumption of Calles' task of stabilizing, civilianizing, and institutionalizing the Revolution. This was the period of the Second World War, when Mexican products commanded high prices in the United States, and Mexico herself turned to manufacturing many goods which could no longer be bought from the neighbor to the north. Times were good, money was plentiful, and revolutionary enthusiasm slackened as Mexico found herself in a war for the first time on the same side as the United States.

The pendulum swung even further to the right during the term of Avila Camacho's successor, a lawyer from Veracruz named Miguel Alemán. It was a measure of how far Mexico had evolved since the great days of the Revolution that presidents no longer needed the authority of a general's rank; indeed Avila Camacho was the last Mexican president to wear a uniform. Alemán's six years in office, which ended in 1952, were marked by a business boom, with much construction and expansion of manufacturing, accompanied by the making of many fortunes (that of the president himself among them), some acquired legally, others perhaps not quite so legally. Alemán is still looked back to by conservative Mexicans as a strong president who did much for the development of the country.

By way of reaction to the lax moral tone that prevailed during the Alemán administration, the man chosen for the presidential term beginning in 1952 was an old Revolutionary with a reputation for absolute honesty, Adolfo Ruiz Cortines. During his term standards of official probity did indeed rise greatly, although they still leave much to be desired. While Ruiz Cortines made a reputation as an upright and able administrator, he was not notable for the vigorous prosecution of programs of social and economic reform. Once more a presidential candidate was chosen to succeed him whose virtues were precisely those which his predecessor most conspicuously lacked. Adolfo López Mateos, who became president in 1958, is young and vigorous (born in the year of the Revolution, 1910) and had made a progressive record as secretary of labor. He has lived up to his reputation by presiding over an administration as innovating and progressive as any since that of Cárdenas himself—a fact whose probability Cárdenas recognized by publicly endorsing López Mateos for election (and publicly praising him since that time) something which he did for neither of the two presidents immediately preceding. López Mateos moved vigorously ahead, especially in areas neglected by his predecessors. In the agrarian field, for example, he distributed land at a rate faster than any since the Cárdenas administration. He also expanded a program of distribution of food and clothing at little more than cost to low-income families begun by his predecessor. At the same time he steered a middle course between economic nationalism and favoritism to foreign interests through gradual implementation of the so-called Mexicanization program, by which a majority of stock in all companies doing business in Mexico must be held by Mexican nationals. He also made moves in the direction of far-reaching changes in the status of the labor movement by establishing a scheme for compulsory sharing by workers in the profits of the enterprise in which they work. In his foreign policy, López Mateos cooperated with the United States while assuming an independent point of view, one consonant with Mexican interests and attitudes. Past presidents of the Republic have generally advanced in some areas at the cost of neglecting others; in retrospect López Mateos may well appear the president who pushed forward in the most balanced manner, encouraging business while advancing labor, promoting industry while stimulating agriculture, and paying particular attention to the needs of those who have not shared equitably in the benefits of the progress which has been made thus far.

Looking back over the succession of presidents who have carried the Revolutionary banner forward, one can note a marked shift in the occupational skills of the chief executives as the Revolution has become institutionalized. A president of Mexico need no longer be a general of forceful personality and large personal following; today he is likely to be a career politician-administrator. This is a clear demonstration that Mexico has indeed made the transition from an era of personalities, which was also a time of political violence, to an era of institutions and a period of political stability.

The candidate nominated by the party for the presidential term 1964-70 was Gustavo Díaz Ordaz, also a career administrator-politician, who had been minister of *gobernación* under López Mateos. To judge from his previous career, it appeared likely that the new president would move the Revolution somewhat back from the more progressive position of his predecessor.

The Party System and Interest Groups

Evolution of the Government Party

The party founded over thirty years ago by Calles remains the government party, although it has seen many organizational changes since that time. Other parties exist in Mexico, of course, and there has been something of a trend in recent years for them to gain an increasing proportion of the popular vote. Nevertheless the government party, currently the Institutional

Revolutionary Party, or PRI, will continue to dominate Mexican government for the foreseeable future. Calles founded the party as a union of all "Revolutionary forces," that is, of the army, organized labor, and the peasants. In a sense, the prehistory of the party goes back before 1928, because it was these groups which had united in supporting Obregón and served as the basis for his administration. This was necessarily the case; not only was their political orientation "Revolutionary," as Calles put it, but these were also the groups whose support had to be secured if a stable basis was to be found for Mexican government. They were the groups capable of putting actual fighting forces into the field, and the alliance between them was not only a simple political alliance but in a sense also a cease-fire agreement.

President Cárdenas, who changed the party's name to Party of the Mexican Revolution, also reorganized the party so that its nature as a coalition of interest groups was given explicit recognition. The party became in its organization, as it already was in actuality, a federation of three sectors: military, labor, and agrarian. To those who objected to making the army a branch of the official party, Cárdenas replied that he did not bring the military into politics, he simply brought military political activity out into the open. Nevertheless, this move did delay the depoliticization of the military, and under Avila Camacho and Alemán this organization of the party was modified, the military sector being eliminated and most military officers who were members of the party being reabsorbed into a new sector called the "popular." But attempts to eliminate the sectoral basis of organization entirely were unsuccessful.

The political position of the military in Mexico today is interesting and is frequently misinterpreted; the army is neither totally apolitical nor the crucial factor it once was. Its political role is very greatly reduced from what it was twenty years ago. This is due to several causes, including the attrition wrought in the ranks of the old-style Revolutionary generals by time and by participation in unsuccessful uprisings, but must especially be credited to the deliberate attempts of the general-presidents—Obregón, Calles, Cárdenas, and Avila Camacho—to professionalize the army and bring it under effective civilian control. Up to a point, these attempts have been successful, and the Mexican army is no longer the collection of followers of regional *caudillos* that it once was.

The point should not be exaggerated. The military forces remain a potent lobby on their own behalf, that is, for improved pay, benefits, equipment, and so on; and President López Mateos still feels he must go out of his way, in his annual message, to pay exaggerated tribute to the armed forces. Military officers still engage in party-political activity and are still conspicuous in the affairs of the PRI, the party secretary-general frequently coming from their ranks. Moreover, the army's major function is still internal policing, and this involves it in political questions, especially at the state level. But by Latin American norms, this remains a limited degree of involvement in politics.

The "popular" sector of the party was intended to comprise supporters of the Revolution from the "bourgeois" classes, that is, professional people, small businessmen, and skilled self-employed craftsmen. But employers of labor on any except the smallest of scales are excluded from membership. Accordingly, today the popular sector includes in its membership virtually all categories of people except organized labor and peasants. For example, in the popular sector one finds the federation of government employees, lawyers' and doctors' organizations, associations of small independent farmers, and all kinds of small and petty business operators down to vendors of government lottery tickets. The popular sector is thus itself a federation of organizations, differing somewhat from the other sectors of the party in this respect. The labor sector is also a league of organizations, of labor federations and independent unions, but it is dominated by the largest national federation, the CTM (Confederación de Trabajadores Mexicanos), the Confederation of Mexican Workers. Lombardo Toledano, who had been CTM secretary-general, was dropped during the forties as too radical and replaced by the present secretary-general, Fidel Velásquez. Lombardo's present splinter labor grouping is affiliated with the international Communist labor federation; in fact Lombardo himself has been president of the latter's Latin American affiliate.

The agrarian sector of the party consists almost entirely of a single organization, the CNC (Confederación Nacional de Campesinos) of the National Confederation of Peasants, which is composed of peasants who have received land under the government's land-reform program. Organizations of agricultural laborers and other agricultural employees complete the sector's membership.

Present Organizational Structure

At present the structure of the official party is based firmly on its division into three sectors. At the national level, thus, the party statutes provide that the supreme legislative body of the party is the national assembly, which is supposed to meet normally every three years, although it may be summoned into special session. The number of delegates to the national assembly varies somewhat but is on the order of a thousand; the three sectors are represented equally. A permanent commission (Gran Comisión) acts on behalf of the assembly when the latter is not in session; it has thirty members, ten from each sector of the party. The Gran Comisión is supposed to exercise continuing control over the real directive organ of the party, the Central Executive Committee. The CEC consists of the party's president and secretary-general, one secretary representing each of the three sectors, and one representative of the party's members in each of the houses of the national legislature, chosen by the party caucuses.

This set of hierarchical relationships within the party rather resembles the formal organizational structure of the Communist Party of the Soviet Union and, as in the CPSU, while the formal lines of control and election run from the bottom to the top of the pyramid, the actual power relations run very much the other way. That is, the president and secretary-general of the national party are very much the men of the President of the Republic; although the sectors, and the groups affiliated with each sector, have a considerable importance, it is the President's men on the central executive committee who have the last word in all party matters.

Regional executive committees, similarly structured, exist in the thirty-two "federal entities" of the Republic, that is, in the twenty-nine states and two territories, and in the Federal District; they are supposed to concern themselves exclusively with regional matters, and for all intents and purposes they are the creatures of the state, territorial, or district governor. The composition of the regional executive committee mirrors that of the central committee. The president and secretary-general of the regional committee are elected at the regional party conventions, just as the president and secretary-general of the national party are elected by the national assembly, but, needless to say, this "election" is of the nature of a ratification of a decision already made elsewhere. At the local level, "municipal" committees each of five members exist for each county in Mexico, and for each election district in the federal capital. Although parity for the three sectors of the party is not stipulated for the municipal level, the members of the municipal committee, who are appointed by the CEC on advice of the regional executive committee, are supposed to be representative of the social and economic groups dominant in the county.

The Current Balance of Forces

Today the popular sector dominates the party. This has come about for various reasons. In the first place, the economic development of recent years has resulted in the steady increase as a proportion of the population of the occupational groups from which the popular organizations draw their memberships, although even today the membership of the popular sector is not very much larger than that of the other two. Nevertheless the popular sector is able today to nominate the party's candidates for public office from among its own ranks in about half of the congressional election districts, while it captures more than half of the Senate seats. Doubtless, also, professional men, especially government officials and lawyers, who are the leaders of the popular sector, possess the skills and the strategic positions requisite to success in intraparty bargaining.

In recent years it has become a truism that there are two wings of the government party, a right wing led by former Presidents Alemán and Rodríguez, taking a pro-business, pro-United States point of view, and a left wing represented especially by ex-President Cárdenas, taking a more pro-labor and pro-agrarian point of view and favoring a more "independent"

foreign policy. This left wing within the party has recently lacked leadership of dominant stature, the relationship of ex-President Cárdenas with the
party having becoming ambiguous since he agreed to head the new *fidelista*
Movement of National Liberation. It is thought that the sympathies of
President López Mateos lie more with the left wing of the party, although
in his policies he tried to be fair to both wings. It is quite likely that now that
he has left office López Mateos will become the new leader of the party's
left, a more moderate left than is represented today by Cárdenas, having more
in common perhaps with the current position of ex-President Portes Gil.

To balance the pressure brought to bear on the president by Cárdenas'
MLN, Alemán has formalized his own following within the party as the
Revolutionary Front of Civic Affirmation, or FRAC. Like the MLN, this
propagandizes for its point of view through meetings, speeches, newspaper
advertisements, etc.

Forces of the Opposition

The main opposition party to the PRI is the Partido de Acción Nacional,
Party of National Action, founded in 1939 and used in 1940 as the vehicle
for the presidential candidacy of General Juan Andreu Almazán. The PAN
has steadily built its long-term political strength and now constitutes a
permanently organized opposition party, free of dominance by any single
individual. Although the party embraces a wide range of opinion, its general principles might be characterized as essentially conservative, with a
pro-clerical and pro-business orientation. For example, the PAN takes the
position that the laws inimical to Church activities at present on the statute
books but not enforced should be repealed. It especially champions the
cause of religious education. In addition, the party favors a limited government role in the economy, and the outright private ownership of plots distributed to peasants under the government's land reform program, rather
than their collective ownership by the village under the *ejido* system. The
stronger centers of support for the PAN are so far in the middle classes in
the cities, especially in the federal capital, in Monterrey, and in Ciudad
Juárez. It is in these areas that the PAN has managed to elect some deputies
to the lower house of the federal legislature. The high point of its electoral
drawing power so far, as indicated by the official election returns,* has been
something under 20 percent of the popular vote for the party's presidential
candidate. Yet it is likely that the party's strength will continue to grow. In
the first place, the bourgeois groups on which it is based form an ever-increasing proportion of the citizens. At the same time the Catholic Church
constitutes, in a highly religious country such as Mexico is—despite the
official anticlericalism of earlier years—an important national source of
opinion formation. If the Church should ever decide that its interests were

---

* This stipulation must be made, as many Mexicans believe firmly that Almazán
actually won a majority of votes in 1940, but was "counted out" by the government, in
an era when ballots were tallied less scrupulously than today.

fundamentally threatened, it might well resume the political activity which has largely been in abeyance during recent years. At the present the Church constitutes the only national organization that can rival in effectiveness the influence of the machinery of the federal government itself, which operates to the advantage of the "official" party. There have indeed been signs of renewed Church interest and activity in politics. They represent the Church's concern over the possibility of an upsurge in Communist influence following in the wake of sympathy for the cause of Fidel Castro, and also a revival of tension over the status of religious schools stemming from a government decision to provide free textbooks to all schools, use of which would be compulsory. Part of the reason for the government's taking the position it has on the textbook question lies in its dissatisfaction with the point of view from which national history is discussed in some of the texts used in Church schools.

The PAN derives much support from business interests, especially those centered in Monterrey; but business is certainly not tied exclusively to the PAN. The national federation of Chambers of Commerce maintains a "non-partisan" position, and the views of influential business leaders are heard in government decision-making circles.

The PAN has been in some difficulty to try to avoid being identified with the forces of sheer reaction, on the assumption that a conservative and pro-clerical party must necessarily represent the traditional oligarchy which was swept from power by the Mexican Revolution of 1910. The problem is intensified by the fact that the PAN draws support from disreputably extreme right-wing elements such as the *sinarquistas*, a violent Falangist group now happily shrunk to almost negligible size. To avoid being branded as reactionary the party's leaders have tried to stress moderate elements in the party's approach to political problems and have tried to present the party as more or less a civic group interested in the purity of elections and the providing of the responsible opposition necessary to the maintenance of a healthy regime. The current leadership of the party, at any rate, has made it clear that it "accepts" the Mexican Revolution and often refers to the party as being Christian Democratic; but the PAN is certainly considerably to the right of the Christian Democrats of Chile or Peru, say.

To the left of the PRI is the PPS or Popular Socialist Party, led by Lombardo Toledano, a more or less Marxist and pro-Soviet party. Because of its support among intellectuals and students, especially at the National University, and because of Lombardo's own prominence, the party is highly visible and propagandizes energetically for its point of view. But in terms of votes the PPS is a very small-time operation, being able to attract only about 2 percent of the electorate for its legislative candidates. Very often the party does not run its own candidate in legislative or presidential elections, frequently confining itself to endorsing the PRI candidate where he proves acceptable. In fact many people regard Lombardo as something of a stooge for the PRI, coddled and perhaps even financed by the government party in an attempt to keep the opposition on the left within bounds.

A new force on the left is the Movement of National Liberation or MLN headed by ex-President Cárdenas, which has already been referred to. The MLN has made its first principle support of the regime of Fidel Castro. Relations between the MLN and the PPS have been rather ambiguous: the two groups keep criticizing each other and sent separate delegations to a recent Moscow conference. So far the MLN has taken a more intransigent attitude toward the PRI, for example endorsing candidates running against a government choice for local legislative office even where the government candidate had been endorsed by the PPS.

There have been strong indications that the small but legal Mexican Communist Party was instrumental in the organization of the MLN in the attempt to make capital from support of Fidel Castro. The Communists clearly had a hand in the organization of the Frente Electoral del Pueblo, which was formed to run candidates in the elections of 1964.

Although hopes and fears were widespread at the time of the MLN's founding that the prestige of Cárdenas would attract many supporters, especially peasants, to the new movement, this has not yet proved to be the case. It is likely that the desire to remain on good terms with the government, which has been the source of so many benefits and can be the future source of either benefits, indifference, or hostility, will prove the crucial factor in determining loyalties among the bulk of the peasantry.

University students in Mexico are not the political force they constitute in countries without a stable political order. This is perhaps just as well. In several of the faculties (i.e., schools) of the gigantic National University, students of Marxist orientation are in a majority, an effect especially notable, and true to a great extent of the professors also, in the faculties of philosophy, political science, and economics. There is actually a great affinity between a crude kind of Marxism and the traditional Mexican complaints against the United States that the Yankees exploit Mexico's weakness, establishing unfair terms of trade, and so on. As elsewhere in Latin America, students incline to a nationalism and to a "neutralism" which gives the Soviet Union the benefit of the doubt. This nationalist-Marxist orientation of so many Mexican students is, in the writer's view, one of the most disheartening features of the Mexican political scene. But as a personal orientation, this may well be transitory and change as the students grow older and as world events challenge its soundness.

Several other minor parties exist, but remain without practical significance.

Government Structure and Processes

In their general form Mexico's constitutional arrangements resemble those of the United States. That is, like the government of the United States, Mexico's government could be characterized as a federal system with separation of powers and a bicameral legislature. The two systems operate differently, however, reflecting differences in the underlying political realities. The Mexican constitution differs from that of the United States principally in its inclusion of several principles of public policy without their counterpart in the fundamental law of the neighbor to the north. Chief among these are the constitutional bases for a policy of stringent limitation of the activities of the Church given by articles 3, 4, 27, and 130, and the principle enunciated in article 27 that wealth located beneath the surface of the soil belongs to the Mexican nation; that is, title to it does not rest with the owner of title to the surface of the land.

The President

The president of Mexico differs in his constitutional lineaments from his United States counterpart in several respects, although the Mexican pattern is quite like that of other Latin American states. The president is elected for a term of six years and, since the constitutional reamendment of the late twenties, may never be reelected (article 83). The president has the usual powers to present the budget, to initiate and veto legislation, to make appointments of high officials, to conduct diplomatic negotiations, and to command the armed forces. He may also choose to delay promulgation of a law already passed by the congress and he has the power to implement legislation by decrees having the force of law.

The president's preeminence in the government of Mexico rests on more than the powers allocated to him in the constitutional document. He is also, of course, the head of the dominant party and thus has an array of informal controls over members of the legislature at his disposal. His powers of patronage (there is no merit system in the civil service) and his ability to use the vast powers of the government apparatus to reward or punish individuals and groups give another dimension to his authority. The Mexican president is also heir of an almost royal tradition that the head of government is normally above personal criticism. In view of all the foregoing it might be said that to all intents and purposes the president *is* the government of Mexico.

The president finds his task an exacting one as current custodian of the great system of compromise which is the Mexican way of government. He must be a champion to all groups and a friend to all interests. He must maintain good relations with the United States without detracting one iota from Mexico's sovereignty and prestige. He must keep business confidence high and maintain a favorable investment climate, while retaining solid labor support. Prosecution of a vigorous program of industrial development must not interfere with his zeal for land reform. If his performance in one or another of his tasks should flag; if he should fail to maintain his image as a vigorous though dignified battler for the public interest; if he becomes identified as the partisan of some interests at the expense of others; then he runs the risk of forfeiting the prestige and authority which enable him to be the great balancer of conflicting interests, the manager of the cartel of pressure groups which the Mexican Revolution has become.

The Congress

It is true in Mexico, as elsewhere (although to a greater extent), that the relationships among the organs of government are determined by the party system. Since Mexico has, in effect, a one-party system, the legislature can play only a very restricted role with relation to the head of the party to which almost all its members belong, the president of the republic; and indeed the federal legislature plays only a marginal role in the determination of national policy. Currently all 60 members of the senate are from the PRI, as are all but 5 of the 162 members of the chamber of deputies. Like the United States senate, the senate of Mexico contains two senators from each state, although in Mexico the Federal District is represented on terms of equality with the states. The senators serve for six-year terms. The chamber of deputies has 162 members, each elected in a single-member district for a three-year term.

In form, the national congress exercises the powers usually assigned to legislative bodies—that is, it passes laws, approves treaties, and monitors the acts of the executive. A permanent committee of the legislature exercises this monitoring function when the legislature itself is not in session. In actuality, however, the dominant position of the PRI in the legislative body means that the latter becomes, in effect, an instrument for the ceremonial ratification of decisions taken elsewhere, i.e., in the executive branch of the government. In view of this circumstance it makes little difference that the constitutional provision of no immediate reelection applies to the members of the legislative body, as it does to the presidency. A seat in the legislature then becomes in effect a temporary sinecure for politicians in transition from one office to the next. Accordingly, the important political figures are to be found in the president's cabinet or occasionally in the executive mansions of the states, but only accidentally in the legislature.

Cabinet and Civil Service

The country's leading figures, ex-presidents excepted, are to be found in the president's cabinet (although ex-presidents too have frequently taken cabinet posts), and it is from this group that the next president is chosen. Among the leading political figures in the cabinet are normally the occupants of the posts of minister of *gobernación* (interior) and governor of the Federal District, an office which in Mexico is appointive. The minister of the interior occupies a strategic position in that he is responsible for relations with the states, for the supervision of elections, and for the national police system. The preeminence of this position within the cabinet is suggested by the frequency with which the party's candidate for the next presidential term is the occupant of this post. This has especially been the case since the deemphasis of the role of the army in Mexican politics has decreased the strategic importance of the role of the secretary of war. In Mexico the foreign secretary does not today enjoy the *political* eminence which attaches to the occupant of that post in other countries, as it did in the Mexico of previous eras, although he may be a distinguished hemispheric figure and highly regarded in his own country. The portfolios of Foreign Affairs and Education are regarded almost as "technical" positions for intellectuals.

As was mentioned above, there is no civil service merit system in Mexico. Appointments are made by each ministry on a catch-as-catch-can basis and it remains sadly the case that nepotism as well as other forms of favoritism, and on occasion a kickback system, obtain. In all fairness, however, one should acknowledge that standards of morality in public employment have clearly improved, especially during the presidency of Ruiz Cortines and during the incumbency as governor of the Federal District of Ernesto P. Uruchurtu. Nevertheless, Mexico still has a long way to go in this regard, and the *mordida*, or petty bribe, remains a feature of Mexico's official life, as does widespread abuse of public trust by lower officials and sometimes a disregard for individual personal rights on the part of law-enforcement officers, especially at the local level. (I do not wish to imply that the United States is blameless in this regard.)

On the other hand, Mexico has been fortunate in securing the services of some extremely able and public-spirited officials, especially in the upper administrative ranks, who would do honor to the public service of any country. Part of the credit for this must go to the single-party system, which attracts able men into public service by assuring a career to policy-making officials, who need not fear going out of office with a defeated administration.

Elections

In all legislative elections, for the state legislatures as well as for the national congress, representatives are elected in single-member districts, that is, as in the United States, in districts which each return one representative to the legislative body, rather than by proportional representation, which is in effect in many of the other Latin American countries. Under proportional representation a party receiving 40 percent of the popular vote would get approximately 40 percent of the legislative seats. Under the district system a party getting 40 percent of the popular vote might receive no legislative seats at all if that 40 percent were distributed evenly in all districts so that it surpassed the 50 percent mark in none of them. In other words, although political scientists traditionally associate the single-member district election with a two-party system, it is actually just as consonant with the workings of a democratic single-party system, if not more so, as Mexican experience indicates.

Elections in the Republic today are incomparably more peaceful than they were a generation or more ago, when election-day fatalities were commonplace and pitched battles between rival groups for the control of polling places (and thus the power to determine the results of the elections in any one district) were standard procedure. However, the honesty of Mexico's elections is still regularly impugned by opposition groups, especially the PAN. The evidence which has been introduced on this point is confused and fragmentary. It is certainly true that in the early years after the Revolution wholesale irregularities in the voting process occurred. Although legislation has been passed over the last twenty years aimed at safeguarding the integrity of the elections, infractions of the law doubtless continue to occur. It is highly unlikely that the most scrupulously conducted elections could result otherwise than in a victory for the PRI, however.

At various stages of the voting process committees of supervision exist composed of representatives of all the political parties. Ultimately the members of each legislative body are the judges of the credentials of newly elected representatives, and accordingly several days of the first session after each congressional election are taken up with hearings to determine the legitimate winner in elections whose results are contested. The handful of seats in the national legislature which have been awarded to the opposition parties as a result of these hearings have been regarded by the general public as in the nature of a consolation prize or a gesture of *noblesse oblige* on the part of the PRI majority.

Early in 1963 the government announced its intention of modifying the system of congressional elections in the direction of proportional representation. Any party securing over 2½ percent of the vote nationally would be awarded five seats in the chamber of deputies, plus an additional seat for every ½ percent of the vote above that amount up to a maximum of forty seats. This seemed a clear demonstration that the president wished to be fair to the opposition parties while bypassing the problems involved in supervising, and then rehashing, the performance of the electoral authorities of each district in detail. It presumably also constituted a demonstration of his confidence that a strengthened opposition in the legislature would not threaten the continued hegemony of the PRI. One could speculate further about the president's motives: he may have intended to move Mexico in the direction of a functioning two-party system; or perhaps he simply wished to soften the bitterness of the opposition parties against the regime.

The result of the new system, which would go into effect for the first time in the legislative elections of 1964, would presumably be to guarantee the PAN between thirty and forty deputies' seats, giving the party more incentive to organize and campaign with vigor and stabilizing the party leadership. A handful of seats would also go to the Popular Socialists, or to an electoral alliance of the other left-wing groups.

Mexican Federalism

According to the constitution, Mexico has a federal system; that is, states exist, electing their own governors and legislatures, raising and spending their own funds, and legally autonomous within the spheres constitutionally assigned to their jurisdiction. Despite the constitutional position of the states, most commentators have regarded the autonomy of the states as a sham, and former President Emilio Portes Gil has gone so far as to term Mexican federalism "a great lie." It is true that the constitution itself, which establishes the autonomy of the states, at the same time gives to the central government the instrument with which it can wipe out this autonomy. Under article 76 of the federal constitution, the federal senate may make a finding that the constitutional authorities of the state have disappeared, and appoint a new governor to hold office until elections can be called. Normally, of course, the senate, when it acts under this provision, does so at the recommendation of the president and it picks the new governor from a short list which he proposes.

Translated into political terms, this means that the president can fire a state governor of whom he disapproves. Given the political system of Mexico, however, it is highly unlikely that a governor would have come to office in one of the states without the approval of the president in the first place; the governor would first have to be nominated by the PRI, which is the majority party in each of the states, just as it is on the national level, and the president as head of the national party can veto the nomination of a candidate for governor by the state branch of the party. (This is different from the United States system, in which the effective units of party organization are the states, and the national party organization, to the extent that it exists, is simply a loose alliance of the state parties.) In actual fact, the power of the national party over the state party in Mexico goes further than this and extends to outright dictation by the national party of the candidates the state party shall nominate for governor and federal senator. This has given rise to the legend of the *sobre cerrado,* the sealed envelope, in which instructions come to the state party from national party headquarters. Thus it would be quite out of the ordinary for a state administration to come into existence without at least the implicit approval of the national party leadership.

It would not be quite accurate to leave the matter at that and proceed on the assumption that the state administrations are no more than branch offices of the national administration. Given the size and complexity of the Republic of Mexico, the range of its problems, and the time and trouble it takes to travel from one part of the country to the other, it remains true that regional governments necessarily have a large degree of autonomy from the center. In fact, it has not been uncommon for state governors to erect little dictatorships and to get away with all kinds of abuses of power, for a time without the knowledge of the national leadership. This is especially the case where the governor is in collusion with the commander of the army jurisdiction in which his state lies. In fact, the real abuses of power which occur in Mexico occur—as in the United States—much more on the state than on the national level. It is still not completely unknown today for a state governor to have an opposition journalist beaten up or an opposition leader assassinated, or for the governor to use strong-arm methods to intimidate or eliminate competition in his illicit business enterprises. This situation repeats itself in miniature at the level of the *municipio*, the lowest of the three levels of government in Mexico, or of the *ejido*, the land-owning village, where some local cacique may be exercising a petty tyranny. Looked at in this light, it may be that what Mexico needs is not less central control but rather more.

Public Policy

The Land Reform

Mexico is one of the few states in Latin America or indeed in the world to conduct an extensive and thoroughgoing land-reform program in modern times. As was mentioned above, the implementation of land reform in Mexico dates from the early 1920's and Obregón's administration. During the years since, the magnitude of the program has fluctuated according to the priority set on it by the president in power. The president at the time of writing, Adolfo López Mateos, is more "agrarian" than any president since Lázaro Cárdenas, as is made evident in the table on page 22.

The land reform program has consisted essentially of distributing to landless peasants lands owned by the government or taken from owners whose holdings were greater than 5,000 hectares (a hectare is about 2½ acres). Originally land was distributed to villages despoiled of their lands by the enclosures carried on during the Díaz regime; subsequently the program was extended to give a right to receive land to almost all villages, more or less in proportion to the number of their inhabitants. Although some of the land distributed has gone to individual peasants in outright private ownership, a greater proportion has been constituted in *ejidos*. An *ejido* is a landholding village community; this form of landholding has historical antecedents both in Spain and in pre-Hispanic Mexico, and is of course quite general in precapitalist societies everywhere. This landholding village community is not to be confused with a collective farm or state farm. In most of the *ejidos* (with the exception of those in the Laguna area, which grow cotton, and those in Yucatán, which grow hemp) the *ejido* lands are not worked in common, but are divided among peasant families who farm them as though they had individual ownership. An *ejido* plot differs from an individually owned farm in that the *ejidatario* cannot sell or otherwise alienate the plot. His heir may succeed to it; alternatively the plot reverts to the village, which redistributes it. This at least is the usual legal situation, although variations and deviations from the letter of the law occur.

Considerable ideological prestige attaches to the *ejido* from a certain political viewpoint as representing a sort of middle way between individualism and collectivism. In political terms the *ejido* has an advantage in that it is not possible for the land to be reconcentrated in the hands of an individual who is luckier or perhaps more able than his fellows, thus reproducing a situation in which large landowners and landless peasants coexist.

The land distribution program has not resulted in the transformation into *ejidos* of all of the agricultural land of Mexico. At present, between 40 and 50 percent of the cropland is in *ejidos*. About 30 percent of the land is in small and medium-sized private holdings, that is, essentially family farms; but really large holdings still account for 20 or 25 percent of the cropland. Thus many latifundia still exist, despite more than forty years of land reform.

LAND DISTRIBUTION IN MEXICO, 1916-1962, BY PRESIDENTIAL TERM

YEARS	PRESIDENT	AMOUNT DISTRIBUTED (THOUSANDS OF HECTARES)	MONTHS IN OFFICE	APPROXIMATE ANNUAL RATE
1916-1920	Carranza	224	63½	43
1920	De la Huerta	158	6	316
1920-1924	Obregón	1,677	48	419
1924-1928	Calles	3,195	48	799
1928-1929	Portes Gil	2,066	14	1,770
1929-1932	Ortiz Rubio	1,204	31	466
1932-1934	Rodríguez	2,095	26	966
1934-1940	Cárdenas	20,073	72	3,345
1940-1946	Avila Camacho	5,378	72	896
1946-1952	Alemán	4,520	72	753
1952-1958	Ruiz Cortines	3,000	72	500
1958-1962	López Mateos	10,043	46	2,622

SOURCES: Emilio Portes Gil, *La Crísis Política de la Revolución y la Próxima Elección Presidencial*, Mexico, D.F., 1957; *Christian Science Monitor*, September 14, 1961; Adolfo López Mateos, *Informe*, Secretaría de Gobernación, Mexico, D.F., 1962. The figure for Ruiz Cortines is computed from the *Monitor*, and the López Mateos figure comes from the *Informe*; the rest are from Portes Gil. Figures given by different sources differ somewhat in being based on different definitions. The "approximate annual rate" is calculated by the present author.

There are various causes for this. To some extent it occurs because the large landowners divide the legal ownership of their land among many relatives so that no one person holds title to an amount of land sufficient to make him subject to expropriation proceedings. Many large landowners (some of them former Revolutionary generals) escape expropriation through the use of political pull, together with the intimidation of landless villages of the vicinity which would be entitled to land under the terms of the land-reform program. Early in 1963 López Mateos's secretary of agriculture served notice that *all* latifundia would be broken up by the end of the president's term in 1964—a goal which was in fact not reached.

With the party's swing to the right after 1940, the individual ownership of land was favored over the creation of new *ejidos*. This was done partly in the belief that the *ejidos*, while probably more productive than the old-time haciendas, are nevertheless less productive than the same land would be if farmed on a larger scale by modern techniques. This belief is in fact borne out by what statistical evidence is available. While about 44 percent of the cropland is in *ejidos* and about 53 percent of the agrarian work force work on the *ejidos*, they are credited with the production of only 37 percent of the value contributed to the economy by agriculture. One must say in mitigation of this picture that the *ejidos* frequently have the poorer land, since at the time of expropriation the landlord was permitted to retain some of his land for his own use; naturally he always chose the better land. It is also true that the *ejidos* are less mechanized than are farms in the private sector of agriculture. Moreover, *ejidos* are more likely to be located on the exhausted soil of the central plateau, and private lands have benefited more than *ejidos* from the irrigation works that have been constructed. Nevertheless, where it is possible to hold these factors constant, outright ownership of land, presumably through providing greater incentives, does seem to result in somewhat higher productivity. Counterbalancing this slight economic edge, there is on the other hand the political advantage of the *ejido* in that *ejido* land cannot be sold and therefore the reconcentration of land ownership is avoided. (In actuality some selling of *ejido* land has taken place illegally.)

The production of the *ejidos* has been principally food crops—corn and beans especially—largely for the consumption of the *ejidatarios* themselves. The figures are somewhat distorted here because the great estates of La Laguna, growing cotton, and the hemp plantations of Yucatán are categorized as *ejidos* although their form of organization is quite different.

The major increase in Mexican agricultural production which has taken place in recent years, and which has contributed much of the purchasing power with which Mexico has imported manufactured goods and machinery, has been provided by cash crops grown on larger privately owned farms, especially on newly irrigated land in the northern regions of the country. Coffee and cotton are the leading crops in this category. The *ejido* retains its ideological prestige, however, and the demand for land from those at present without it remains constant. In fact Mexico, like other Latin American countries, has in recent years seen much squatting or "parachuting," as it is called in Mexico, by landless peasants on land to which they have no legal claim. In fact there has been an organized movement of *paracaidismo* (parachuting) led initially by Jacinto López, head of a peasant union affiliated with the Popular Socialist Party. Direct action by landless peasants or by *ejidatarios* and small farmers protesting water shortages, low prices, and so on, has shown a marked increase since the organization late in 1962 of the CCI, the Independent Peasants' Central. The new farm organization shares the outlook of the MLN and is endorsed by General Cárdenas.

Members of the Mexican Communist Party appear to be active in the organization. It is ironic that there should be a heightening of peasant militancy leading to violent action against the regime of the most strongly "agrarian" president in twenty years. It was presumably at least in part in view of the increased unrest in rural areas, however, that López Mateos resolved on the policy mentioned above, to abolish the latifundia entirely by the end of his term.

Economic Policy

It is an unhappy fact of economic life that policies which may be attractive in themselves, such as the equalization of incomes, do not necessarily redound to the economic benefit of the nation as a whole. Economic growth, so long as the economy is even partly privately financed, comes about only at the cost of creating a favorable climate for foreign investors and for domestic entrepreneurs, even where this must mean the forgoing or modification of attractive domestic social programs. The presidents since Cárdenas have been pragmatic in this regard and have in general followed policies which resulted in higher levels of production, even at the expense of measures tending to equality in the distribution of the value of that production. As a result, although the lot of the poor in Mexico has tended to improve, it remains true that the middle class has been making economic gains far more rapidly, and novels of social criticism have in recent years made much of this contrast. Yet it seems impossible to dispute that the general level of life of the poorest classes in Mexico, as classes, has been raised. This can be seen clearly in the raising in levels of nutrition of *ejidatarios* over those who remain as landless laborers, for example. In addition, individuals have bettered their situations greatly by being enabled to move upward socially from one economic level to another much more readily, i.e., by leaving the stratum into which they were born.

Clearly, the central principle of the economic policy of any Mexican president must be the maintenance of a high rate of economic growth. A high rate of growth is to be hoped for in order that the standard of living of the poorer classes may be improved, of course; but its achievement has been made even more necessary by the need to keep up with Mexico's rapid rate of population growth, both to provide the means of life for the additions to the population, and to provide jobs for those who join the working force each year.

The heavy activity in construction and industrialization of the war years and the Alemán administration which followed led to a steady inflation of the currency, which government high-tariff, low-taxing, and heavy-spending policies did nothing to discourage. It was a period of high profits and a deterioration in living standards for many; one might say that the rapid economic development of the period was financed by a reduction in the purchasing power of the average Mexican.

Of course high profits provide incentives for the entrepreneur to develop new lines of business activity and for the investor to put his money into Mexican enterprises, rather than to send it, or keep it, abroad. But the López Mateos administration especially has attempted to modify economic policies which benefited the business classes disproportionately, by reducing tariffs, by moving towards workers' profit-sharing in industry, by increasing land distribution, by raising government expenditures on education, and by expanding the CEIMSA (now CONASUPO) program of retailing food and clothing in working-class neighborhoods at prices below the prevailing commercial levels.

The inflation associated with the earlier period of Mexico's economic growth died down after Alemán left office, but so for a time did the rate of increase in the gross national product, which during 1961 dropped to no more than equal the increase in population. Fright taken by foreign investors over political disturbances elsewhere in Latin America may have been more important here than misgivings over López Mateos' policies. The growth rate has started to increase again, however, owing partly to the great success which has attended Mexico's entry into the Latin American Free Trade Area, where, as an industrial state producing a wide range of goods, her products have been in demand.

López Mateos also began to enforce more seriously laws already on the books requiring the Mexicanization of businesses operating in Mexico. "Mexicanization"—not to be confused with nationalization, or government ownership—means that such businesses must be more than half-owned by Mexicans. This is clearly a nationalist policy, in the sense that it assures—at least on paper—that decisions which affect the country's economy must be made in Mexico by Mexicans. On the other hand, it constitutes very little of a burden on foreign business concerns. It may be that the program has had economic advantages in mobilizing Mexican capital which might otherwise have lain idle, by providing it with attractive investment opportunities in the possibility of combining with foreign capital in the production or marketing of established products. Perhaps it has also spread the foreign capital twice as far as it otherwise would have gone. At any rate, there seem no signs that the Mexicanization program has at all damaged Mexico's economy or the investment climate.

In recent years tourism has moved ahead to become Mexico's chief earner of foreign exchange, as more and more North Americans and others have discovered the pleasures of a visit to Mexico. This highlights one of the reasons why Mexico has advanced further than other Latin American countries in its economic development: its proximity to the United States (although a source of discomfort on many occasions in the past) has been of considerable economic benefit in recent years.

A continuing source of strength is the fact that Mexico, unlike many other Latin American countries, has not been dependent on a single product for its export earnings, although cotton and coffee (of which Mexico is one of the world's major producers) have come to constitute between them a third of the country's exports by value. The country has instead a diversified economy in which today no one product predominates.

The major characteristics of the Mexican economy today can be summarized as follows.

(1) Although there have been fluctuations from year to year, the rate of economic growth has normally been high, usually higher than that of the United States, and a long way from the stagnation of Argentina or Bolivia.

(2) Control of the economy remains mixed, in the sense that although ownership remains largely private, the government has been active in promoting development, in monitoring the performance of private business, and on occasion in taking over the ownership of firms or industries.

(3) Foreign investment is not especially favored, nor is it discriminated against; it has continued to come into the country.

(4) The rate of inflation has tapered off and the currency is now stable, in contrast with the majority of developing countries.

(5) The economy is diversified; fluctuations in the price of a single product do not spell life or death for Mexico as they do for the monocultural economies of many Latin American states.

(6) The government is at least concerned that no sector of the population should be placed at an unfair disadvantage by economic changes, although its efforts at amelioration have been faced with a formidable series of tasks which are still to be completed.

(7) Taxation is only partly related to ability to pay, but it is in general more progressive than in other Latin American states, and an income tax law is on the books.

Foreign Policy

Mexico's foreign policy has been formed ultimately by the fact of her proximity to the United States. Her relationship with the great neighbor to the north has always been ambiguous. She has been, and is today, dependent on the United States for much of her economic well-being, and the ideals and institutions of the North Americans have often been an inspiration for Mexicans; at the same time, Mexico has suffered many wrongs at the hands of her neighbor, and sources of friction and suspicion remain.

Mexican presidents thus find themselves under two imperatives: one, to remain on good terms with the Americans; the other, to maintain Mexico's independence of action, an independence implemented and demonstrated by opposing United States policies. This fundamental pattern has been elaborated in a foreign policy doctrine under which Mexico supports joint international action in the confrontation of various problems and strongly supports international organization, while at the same time insisting on national sovereignty, nonintervention in the internal affairs of other states, juridical equality of states, and national self-determination. The Mexican approach to international relations is exemplified by the Estrada Doctrine, one of the republic's leading contributions to the inventory of ideas of international law of the hemisphere, which holds that the granting or with-drawal by a state of recognition of other governments at discretion con-stitutes interference in another state's affairs, and that recognition should in essence be so automatic that both "recognition" and "nonrecognition" would cease to exist as juridical categories.

Relations with the United States have always constituted the major com-ponent of Mexico's foreign relations. At various times in the past, of course, relations have deteriorated to the point of hostilities. North Americans invaded Mexico in 1846. During the Mexican War Mexico lost about half of its territory, today the American Southwest. Texas had been lost some years earlier when North Americans who had been allowed to settle in the area rose in revolt and established an independent republic, eventually an-nexed to the United States. During the Mexican War American troops advanced into Mexico City itself, capturing Chapultepec Castle after over-coming the valiant military cadets—the *Niños Heroës*, "boy heroes"—who defended the castle.

Other military actions in which Americans violated Mexican territory took place on a smaller scale during Woodrow Wilson's administration, stemming ultimately from the facts that, on the one hand, Wilson openly took sides against Huerta after the assassination of Madero, and, on the other, that the territory of the United States was used as a sanctuary and staging area by various Revolutionary forces for operations in the north of the country. During 1914 United States naval forces shelled and occupied the port of Veracruz after a confused incident involving an alleged insult to the American flag. Two years later General Pershing was sent on what turned out to be a wild-goose chase through northern Mexico in the attempt to capture Pancho Villa, who had attacked the town of Columbus, New Mexico, and killed American citizens in retaliation for what he considered unfriendly American acts.

Since then, relations have deteriorated from time to time over unsympa-thetic North American attitudes towards acts of Revolutionary policy; tension was particularly high over the expropriation of the interests of American-owned oil companies, which represented the culmination of difficulties between the companies and the Mexican government. Some dis-gruntlement with Mexican policy was also in evidence north of the border in connection with the expropriation of land owned by United States citizens in the course of the implementation of the land reform; with the long-drawn-out and unsatisfactory negotiations over the claims of United States citizens for property damaged during the fighting which followed the Revolution; and also with the extreme anticlerical policies followed by some of the Revolutionary governments.

Some conflicts over material interests are still active today. Currently, Mexico is unhappy about the high salt content of the waters of the Colorado River which come to her from United States territory, due primarily to the dumping of saline water into the river by Arizona irrigation works engineers. This has brought great damage to crops grown in the Mexicali region. After much delay and many protestations of the unassailability of their legal position, United States authorities have undertaken to remedy this situation.

A dispute of long standing, in which the legal position of the United States was perhaps not so strong, was that over the nationality of the El Chamizal area of El Paso, Texas. The boundary treaty established the Rio Grande as the frontier between the two states, but the river had inconsiderately changed course, placing a formerly Mexican area under United States jurisdiction. In the summer of 1963, the United States agreed to settle this dispute, substantially in favor of Mexico.

A final Mexican complaint which is not legal but political is that United States cotton exports compete unfairly with Mexican, since they benefit from a government subsidy which enables them to be sold abroad at lower prices. The Mexicans are sensitive on this score since cotton has become one of the country's major earners of foreign exchange; some even suspect a plot to ruin Mexican cotton exports, since the crops grown in the Mexicali valley which were damaged by the salt water dumped into the Colorado consisted mainly of cotton.

But today Mexico finds her economic interests more often complementary to activities of the United States than competitive with them. As was noted above, tourism has become the country's principal "export," earning currently at the rate of $750 million annually. Something like 80 percent of the tourists are North Americans. The foreign investment which Mexico needs for her development, and which continues to pour into the country, comes mainly from the immediate north, too, while the United States remains Mexico's major supplier and purchaser.

Three of Mexico's leading exports depend directly on the United States government for the size of their markets. These are sugar—the volume of the importation of which is set annually by Congress as a quota for each supplying country—lead, and zinc, the latter two being stockpiled for military purposes. It is desirable that Mexico keep on good terms with the United States for the sake of the sales of each of these items; the United States price for sugar is above that of the world market, while there is much pressure from domestic United States producers of the two metals to raise tariffs, set quotas, or otherwise discriminate against foreign suppliers.

Another large-scale Mexican export to the United States is people—the *braceros*, or seasonal farm workers, who come north to pick fruit and make money to take back home. While Mexico is anxious for the program to continue—without it there would undoubtedly be a serious unemployment problem in the country—it is also concerned to safeguard the rights of the *braceros* and to assure them decent wages and working conditions. This program presents delicate problems for domestic United States politics; it is strongly supported by the fruit-growers (the wage rate for *braceros* is allowed to be lower than the domestic minimum wage level) but attacked by labor, since the Mexicans take jobs that might otherwise be filled by unemployed American workers, and keep wage levels low.

Mexico is also depending on the United States to represent her interests in negotiations with the European Common Market to assure that tariffs on Mexican goods are not made too onerous. Mexico is in a weak position to defend herself in this respect, since she has not joined the General Agreement on Tariffs and Trade (GATT), the tariff-cutting international body; Mexico still maintains tariffs to protect her developing industries which it would be politically infeasible—even if economically desirable—to eliminate. However, under López Mateos she has cautiously begun to reduce these tariffs reciprocally, under the terms of the Latin American Free Trade Area, which Mexico has joined and in which she plays a dominant role.

In her relations with other states (except for Guatemala, with whom Mexico also shares a border and with whom she occasionally experiences difficulties over fishing rights, exile activities, and so on), Mexico is freer to allow her policy to be determined by general doctrinal principles of "national self-determination"—which can serve as the dominant concept of policies on a wide range of problems, from colonialism to Berlin to Cuba —and the pursuit of peace.

Accordingly, Mexico has played an active role in the United Nations and in other international organizations. As one of the leaders of the large bloc of Latin American states, and as a country enjoying good relations with the United States though clearly not a United States satellite in any sense, Mexico has sent to the United Nations representatives who have held leading elective positions in the world organization.

On issues relating to Cuba under Castro, Mexican authorities have interpreted the requirements of respect for national self-determination and nonintervention in the sense that, although the repressive acts of the Cuban regime are to be deplored, as also is its permitting Cuban soil to be used for the stationing of Russian missiles, nevertheless neither the United States nor the inter-American organization should take hostile action toward Cuba on that account. In the first place, runs the dominant Mexican view, what the Cubans do is their own business; in the second place, Cuba does not constitute an aggressive threat to other countries of the hemisphere; in the third place, no precedent should be established for a revival of the role of policeman of the Western Hemisphere which the United States played during the days of Theodore Roosevelt.

Implicit in this approach is of course the traditional Mexican mistrust of the power of the neighbor to the north, together with a certain degree of sympathy with the domestic social goals of the Cuban Revolution. These are felt to be similar to those of the Mexican Revolution itself—which in its time was also attacked by North Americans, especially in its socialist attributes.

Further current expression of the desire to demonstrate the independence of Mexico's foreign policy is afforded by gestures of friendship towards states which are on the margins of the Soviet bloc or are neutralist in a sense implying mistrust of the United States—Poland, Yugoslavia, Indonesia —although, in the cautious and balanced style which Mexican presidents have to adopt in their domestic policy, care has been taken not to give the United States cause for misgivings by approaches to Communist China or to the Soviet Union herself.

In line with this attitude, López Mateos included Poland on the itinerary of a trip he took abroad in early 1963 (returning a visit of the Polish president to Mexico). This, taken together with frequent speeches and diplomatic initiatives Don Adolfo had favored on matters such as nuclear disarmament, prompted some observers to conclude that he was making a bid for the Nobel Peace Prize.

An Evaluation of Mexico's Course

It is easier to describe the facts of the Mexican situation than to place them in some kind of evaluative context, and indeed points of view vary widely, from those who take the position that Mexico under the PRI is hardly more than a single-party dictatorship which has not done enough to alleviate the country's economic plight to those who feel that the achievements of Mexico since the Revolution have been little short of a miracle, and that Mexico under the PRI constitutes an example which other developing countries should emulate. Clearly, a fair evaluation has to take into account both the achievements and the failures.

There are many shortcomings of the present situation to which critics of the regime can point with justice. Criticisms on the left are sound in pointing out that the benefits of Mexico's economic development have not been distributed equally throughout the population; that a class of newly rich or at least well-to-do has developed while poverty continues to exist. There is validity, too, to economic criticisms from the right such as the perennial one that the *ejido* form of organization is probably not as productive as other types of arrangement would be.

In the political field, similarly, many criticisms are in order. The fervor and dynamism of the Revolution has slackened and talk of the Revolution and its goals often degenerates into ritualistic patriotic oratory. Despite the commendable efforts which have been made by the last two presidential administrations, it remains true that petty graft and abuse of power continue to exist in Mexico. The police forces of the Republic are especially liable to criticisms on this score. Abuses of power occur especially frequently at the level of the state governments, where the erection of state dictatorships in the interest of a small clique is not uncommon. Infringements of civil liberties are not unknown, as for example in the recent imprisonment of several active leftists, among them the muralist David Alfaro Siqueiros, on nebulous charges connected with the organization of illegal strikes, and without being brought to trial within the legally specified maximum period of one year from the date of arrest (itself an overgenerous provision).

On the favorable side one must first acknowledge the gains in the economic sphere. The economy has been steadily expanding in recent years and Mexico does not face the existence of a mounting number of chronically unemployed that plagues many of the other Latin American countries. Social mobility is high and individuals do not face arbitrary barriers to their social advancement. A clear indication of what has been occurring, for example, is given by the steady decrease in the numbers of people classified as Indians in the national census. That is, while the Indians as a social class and cultural grouping still exist, proportionately fewer and fewer of the population are found in that category. So while there may not have been very spectacular improvement in the lot of the lower classes of society (yet there has certainly been a substantial amount) there has been much upward mobility of individuals *between* classes which adds up to a far higher aggregate level of individual well-being. In a sense, it is only through such individual mobility, rather than through benefits accruing to a whole population element, that substantial improvements in the real standard of living of the urban and rural proletariats can result. This is so because the structure and range of lower-class consumption patterns in Mexico are so heavily culturally determined—that is, the most important change in a lower-class Mexican's *standard* of living is the change that occurs in his *way* of living as he moves from more rural "Indian" habits to more "modern" ones.[2] Such changes are occurring increasingly with urbanization and under the influence of the mass media of communications.

Finally, Mexico has managed to avoid many of the evils which have beset other developing countries. The rate of inflation has been moderate. The rate of investment, including foreign investment, has remained high. Unemployment has remained low.

In the political realm, likewise, the achievements have been substantial. One can surely not overlook the heightened dignity and self-assurance of the lower classes, and especially of the peasantry, that has come about since the Revolution. It is an achievement worthy of some acknowledgment among Latin American states that political liberties generally exist, opposition groups are free to organize and publish, and so on. An achievement of monumental proportions in the Latin American context is that it has been possible for forty years to institute a system of peaceful succession to power in a country which not only has a long tradition of political change by violence but in whose cultural life outside of politics a high incidence of violence has been prevalent.

All this has been made possible, in the present writer's view, only by the arrangement under which all major population groups are given the opportunity to participate in the making of policy through their incorporation into the "official" party. Indeed it is on the breadth of the range of interests represented within the official party that much of Mexico's claim to be a democracy rests.

As the reader no doubt will have guessed, the present writer is inclined to strike a balance in the evaluation of the Mexican political system on the favorable side of the ledger. This is especially the case when one views Mexico against the background of the other countries of Latin America and of the developing world, especially those which started out with the same drawbacks Mexico has in cultural and economic levels. However, the final verdict on the success of the Mexican experiment cannot yet be pronounced. After all, when Calles founded the Revolutionary party thirty-five years ago, it was a two-party system he explicitly urged, a fact which commentators often forget. It remains to be seen whether the party which has ruled Mexico for two generations will be willing and able to relinquish power when it is defeated in national elections. This will be the supreme test of the maturity of the Mexican political system; although that day will not arrive for a long time to come.

NOTES FOR CHAPTER I

1. A fictional account of a typical succession crisis is presented in Martín Luis Guzmán's novel *La Sombra del Caudillo*.
2. These changes are well illustrated by the case studies in Oscar Lewis's *Five Families* and *The Children of Sánchez*.

SELECTED BIBLIOGRAPHY

Frank Brandenburg, *Mexico: An Experiment in One-Party Democracy*, doctoral dissertation, University of Pennsylvania, Philadelphia, 1956.

Anita Brenner, *The Wind That Swept Mexico*, Harper, New York, 1943.

Howard F. Cline, *The United States and Mexico*, Harvard University Press, Cambridge, 1953.

———, *Mexico: Revolution to Evolution, 1940-1960*, Oxford University Press, London, 1962.

John W. F. Dulles, *Yesterday in Mexico: A Chronicle of the Revolution, 1919-1936*, University of Texas Press, Austin, 1961.

International Bank for Reconstruction and Development, *The Economic Development of Mexico*, Johns Hopkins University Press, Baltimore, 1953.

James G. Maddox, "Mexican Land Reform," American Universities Field Staff, Mexico, D.F., July 3, 1957.

Sanford A. Mosk, *Industrial Revolution in Mexico*, University of California Press, Berkeley, 1950.

Leon Vincent Padgett, *Popular Participation in the Mexican 'One-Party' System*, doctoral dissertation, Northwestern University, Evanston, 1955.

Robert E. Scott, *Mexican Government in Transition*, University of Illinois Press, Urbana, 1959.

Frank Tannenbaum, *Mexico: The Struggle for Peace and Bread*, Knopf, New York, 1950.

William P. Tucker, *The Mexican Government Today*, University of Minnesota Press, Minneapolis, 1957.

Nathan Whetten, *Rural Mexico*, University of Chicago Press, Chicago, 1948.

GUATEMALA
Guatemala City

II   *John D. Martz*

GUATEMALA

THE SEARCH FOR POLITICAL IDENTITY

MOST POPULOUS and second largest of the Central American republics, Guatemala provides an interesting laboratory for observation. In several ways the country epitomizes problems found to a lesser degree in neighboring states. Over half of the three million Guatemalans are Mayan Indians, living outside the main stream of national life in illiteracy and poverty. The economy is basically agricultural, with national income dependent upon the uncontrollable price fluctuations of a single crop. The pattern of land use is that of extensive latifundia, with a large mass of landless peasants increasingly restive under absentee management.

Historically the dominant military power of Central America, Guatemala has been subjected to a succession of *caudillos* with minimal interest in the general welfare. Both the formal institutions of government and the realities of politics have been uncomplicated. The constants of national politics have been changing since 1945, however; society and politics have been progressing beyond the primitive state of preceding generations. Perhaps nowhere in Latin America has the search for political identity entailed greater difficulty and inherent confusion.

The contemporary effort to introduce social change and political revolution in Guatemala is far from fruition. The very direction of change is uncertain: the transitory Communist episode of the early 1950's was characteristic of the demand for progress and concomitant perplexity over the means for accomplishing it. Guatemala is not in the modern sense a nation-state, although a growing proportion of its people are developing some sense of nationality. Awareness of democratic ideals is growing, furthered by a gradual erosion of the isolation in which the conntry long slumbered. The *status quo* is reluctantly but perceptibly fading away, to be replaced by something quite different. While the precise nature of future alterations is indistinct, there is little question but that the old order is receding as the quest for social progress and political nationhood continues.

35

Social and Economic Background

A Society in Transition

Guatemalan society has traditionally followed a classically simple division of *ladinos* and Indians. The former, although not racially pure, included those of Spanish origin who constituted an aristocracy that governed the country, operated the economy, and dominated society. The Indians, more than half the population, were far removed from national affairs. Many existed in a condition of virtual servitude.

This straightforward categorization no longer suffices. In the first place, the distinction between *ladino* and Indian has become far more cultural than ethnic; social custom rather than heredity determines the social status of the individual. Those classified as "Indian" generally speak a native dialect rather than Spanish, while accepting and pursuing the values of Indian culture. The Indians reside largely in the mountainous western and north-western highlands. Many of their villages have long existed without effective contact with the outside world. The populace depends upon purely local means of subsistence. Political consciousness—if such it may be called—is circumscribed by the limits of the community. The Indian can be socially mobile, however; he may move into the *ladino* group by acceptance of appropriate social mores and customs. Adams' anthropological studies have demonstrated the facility with which an "Indian" becomes a *ladino*.

Complexities of the changing social fabric also include a proliferation of the groups composing the *ladino* class. Four components have particular political significance: the large landholders or "old families," the partially emergent middle class, the rural peasantry, and the urban labor force. The first of these champions the *status quo*, having long maintained a monopoly of wealth and political influence. Today its naturally conservative orientation is less unenlightened than in the past. Economic power and ties with the military continue to assure for this stratum of society a solid impact on national affairs. At the same time, the landholders have been challenged increasingly by those they once ignored.

The rising middle class is an important element, although not numerically large. While strongest in Guatemala City, it is becoming identifiable beyond the limits of the capital. Composed of small merchants, schoolteachers, and white-collar workers, the middle class is providing determined though sometimes frustrated leadership in the search for national progress. It is dedicated to an expansion of public services, an attack on illiteracy, and the effort to utilize the Indian as an important human element in the equation for national development. In Guatemala City its ranks are swollen by government bureaucrats. In a country where bureaucratic expertise remains in short supply, the impact of this group is greater than its numbers might suggest. In short, the middle class is prominent "in pressing its views on forms of government, on issues of social justice, and on communism and democracy." [1]

The potentialities for political exploitation have grown strong among the rural peasantry. These *campesinos,* forming the labor force operating coffee and banana plantations, have loomed ever larger in the political milieu. Promises of land ownership have gone largely unfulfilled, and squatters have multiplied to complicate the matter. Projects for land redistribution have failed to soften the cry of the peasantry for its own land. The potential strength of these *campesinos* was suggested in 1954 when President Arbenz attempted to organize and arm them as a counterweight against the military. With his precipitous fall from power, this attempt remained without result.

The role of labor is also substantial, and successive governments are grudgingly forced to include the urban workers in their calculations. Labor leaders have been frustrated by arbitrary controls and a general antilabor bias on the part of government. The returning flow to Guatemala of members of the Arbenz administration—both progressive reformers and extreme leftists of questionable commitments—is subjecting labor to stresses that are reflected in the public arena. Urban laborers wield considerable strength in the capital and can be counted upon to be in the forefront of the continuing search for progress and human dignity.

The Limitations of Economic Reality

National wealth has always been agricultural. Sugar cane, cochineal, and indigo were of major importance a century ago, but have long since given way to coffee and bananas. Coffee plantations began to flourish on hillside slopes near the turn of the century, and 70 to 80 percent of the national income from exports derives today from coffee. Planters of German origin long composed a substantial element of the owners, but confiscatory actions during World War II reduced their numbers greatly. Less lucrative is the banana industry, which contributes 10 to 12 percent of export earnings. Cultivation began on the sweltering shores of the Caribbean in 1906. Later transferred in large part to the Pacific lowlands, the industry has been dominated by the United Fruit Company of Boston. Political implications of UFCO's role are dealt with below.

Much of the country's agriculture is of the subsistence type, the Indians farming as high as 10,000 feet in some few areas. Such products as corn, potatoes, wheat, and rice have done little to reduce economic dependence on international price fluctuations, however. Susceptibility to changes in the going price of coffee has not been lessened by efforts at diversification of an essentially monocultural condition. Attempts to increase the value of mineral deposits have lagged. As far back as colonial days the Spaniards opened silver mines in the mountains near Huehuetenango, but rewards have always been minimal. More recent attempts have focused upon petroleum, which is believed to lie in the uninhabited wilderness in the northern half of Guatemala. By the start of the 1960's some sixty-five concessions had been granted to thirty-five enterprises, two-thirds of which were foreign. The rewards have not been great.

Political History

Heritage of Despotism

A sharp dividing line in Guatemalan history was drawn in 1945. All that has followed can be broadly regarded as partially "modern" and revolutionary, while what came before 1945 was traditional. During the first period, Guatemalan politics was essentially that of highly personalized, centralized, and frequently dictatorial government. Such was the setting for a long Liberal-Conservative struggle often founded more on expediency than on principle. The conflict initially involved Central American union and the position of the Church. The Liberals advocated the strengthening of regional unity while assuming a strong anticlerical position. Conservatives took the opposite stance, contributing mightily to the collapse in 1838 of the regional Confederation while gaining ascendancy in Guatemala.

From that time on, the course of traditional Guatemalan politics unfolded in the sagas of four ruthless and arbitrary leaders: Rafael Carrera, Justo Rufino Barrios, Manuel Estrada Cabrera, and Jorge Ubico. Carrera, an illiterate Indian who had led the destruction of Central American union, dominated Guatemala for nearly three decades. Serving as life president when he died in 1865, Carrera's rule brought the augmentation of ecclesiastical privilege, the protection of property rights, and a sanctification of the pre-eminence of the landowning aristocracy. The 1852 Concordat with the Vatican was the first such agreement in the former Spanish colonies.

Carrera's death brought an inevitable Liberal revival, which swept aside all opposition by 1871. The result was a major political revision under the aegis of perhaps the most influential Guatemalan of this traditional period, Justo Rufino Barrios. Dominating the country during fourteen years of drastic reform, he proved a vital and gifted ruler. His government built roads, initiated a rail system, promoted public works, balanced the budget, and encouraged the production of coffee and bananas. A new landed aristocracy was fostered through the weakening of old communal holdings and the relocation of coffee *fincas* on more productive soils. Religious privileges were withdrawn, and Church power was so thoroughly crushed that it has never fully regained its power. Property was confiscated, clerical orders were prohibited and many priests were exiled. Education was taken from the hands of the Church and civil marriage became obligatory.

Barrios' foreign policy pursued the chimera of regional reunification. Thwarted by diplomatic means, he turned to the sword in 1885 by declaring himself supreme commander of the "Army of Central America." His forces collapsed ignominiously, following his own death in battle at Chalchuapa, El Salvador. Barrios' Liberal successors retained control until 1898, when the assassination of his nephew José María Reyna Barrios led to the assumption of power by Manuel Estrada Cabrera. Thus was initiated a twenty-two-year dictatorship of the most brutal and primitive sort. Self-aggrandizement led, for example, to the declaration of national holidays on Estrada Cabrera's and his mother's birthdays, while increased revenue from coffee and bananas was funneled into the personal accounts of officials of corrupt regime. This era of savage repression, paid informers, and political assassins ended with the ouster of Estrada in 1920. An interim period gave way in 1931 to yet another dictator-president, Jorge Ubico.

Earning his authoritarian spurs as a departmental governor under Estrada, Ubico was well prepared to create his own personalistic regime. Reinstituting secret police and arbitrary rule while restoring fiscal integrity to government, he ruled what has been termed a model jail. In the absence of political democracy he extended his rule through *continuismo* while the country benefited from the growing demand for coffee. With the advent of World War II and an inevitable dissemination of democratic ideals, the regime took an aura of obsolescence. The Atlantic Charter and talk of the Four Freedoms became familiar to students and professional workers suddenly aware of the outside world. At the same time, confiscation of eighty-eight German-owned coffee plantations, affecting one-third of the industry, undermined the civilian basis of Ubico's support.

A week of protests was climaxed by a peaceful but extensive work stoppage (known as the *huelga de los brazos caídos*) in Guatemala City, forcing Ubico to resign on July 1, 1944. His legacy, as Schneider has observed, "consisted of a combination of political immaturity, an archaic social structure and economic backwardness." [2] Survivors of his regime instituted provisional leadership under a military triumvirate, but revolutionary pressures were unremitting. Attempts at sharp repression were opposed by political leaders in the capital, and the defection of a group of young military officers led to a brief battle and the triumph of revolutionary forces on October 20, 1944.

Revolution Begets Extremism

The Revolution of 1944 took on a greater meaning than the customary military uprising and turnover of dictatorial personnel. Social and political change was long overdue. A pair of elections in December chose both a president and a constituent assembly that drafted the Constitution of 1945. Juan José Arévalo, a forceful forty-year-old educator who had been teaching at Argentina's University of Tucumán, was chosen as chief of state. A man of middle-class background, his support came from intellectuals and students, many of whom belonged to the newly organized Frente Popular Libertador (FPL). His proclaimed philosophy was an imprecise doctrine termed "spiritual socialism," a vaguely appealing phrase that did little to justify his subsequent reputation as a *pensador*.

A moderate leftist in his views, Arévalo grappled but ineffectually with problems of national import. The lack of rapid progress caused a deterioration of the public support with which he entered office. His avowed program included the reduction of illiteracy, creation of a system of social security, and the drafting of a labor code. Initial impetus permitted the passage of the Social Security Law in 1946 and the Labor Code in 1947, but subsequent progress was negligible. Challenges came from landowners, merchants, and a sizable portion of the military; Arévalo was driven to rely upon the bureaucracy and the burgeoning labor movement. Lacking a substantial group on which to build an effective political organization, the president drifted without purpose.

Prospects for moderate reformism were shattered with the assassination of Colonel Francisco Arana, the emerging leader of democratic forces. Arana's death cleared the field for the rise of his longtime military rival, Lieutenant Colonel Jacobo Arbenz Guzmán. Arévalo's final period in office was dedicated primarily to a struggle to complete his term. The Law of Public Order, which gave the government authority to repress political dissension was invoked frequently to prop up the regime, and the president's survival for six years was itself an accomplishment of sorts.

In March of 1951 Jacobo Arbenz succeeded to the presidency following a government-manipulated election. During Arbenz's administration the country fell under Communist influence, culminating in the climactic hemispheric *cause célèbre* of June 1954.

The government had swung toward a radicalism that had been missing previously. Both native-born and foreign Communists came into growing prominence. The detailed account of their infiltration of the very vitals of Guatemalan life has been thoroughly documented. Labor unions were drawn increasingly into the vortex of politics under the direction of Communist sympathizers. A confiscatory agrarian reform law permitted the government to take permanent title to expropriated lands rather than granting them outright to the peasants working the land. Communist infiltration reached beyond the labor movement to penetrate the government itself. Congress felt compelled to mark the 1953 death of Joseph Stalin with a respectful moment of silence, while anti-Communist justices of the supreme court were summarily dismissed. Application of the agrarian reform included seizure with the promise of no more than nominal compensation of United Fruit Company holdings. The refusal to comply with usual standards of repayment was clouded by excoriating UFCO as a tool of alleged Wall Street imperialists.

In the latter stages of Arbenz's rule, the onslaught of economic difficulties was met by political repression, the suspension of individual rights, and the reported torture of political opponents. Fear of domestic unrest was further reflected by a mounting attack on North American "capitalists" that was climaxed by denunciatory orations at the Ninth Inter-American Conference in March of 1954 at Caracas.

The inroads of Communism had aroused great concern in Washington, although much of the hemisphere remained indifferent. In June of 1954 a raggle-taggle band of revolutionaries commanded by Colonel Carlos Castillo Armas launched a revolutionary invasion from Honduran territory. Castillo, quietly supported by the United States Central Intelligence Agency, easily won control. Arbenz, deserted in his moment of need by fleeing Communists and a disaffected military unwilling to fight, left Guatemala, soon to reappear behind the Iron Curtain. Castillo's "Army of Liberation" marched into Guatemala City, a series of executions took place, and the Colonel soon emerged as the newest Guatemalan strong man.

Counterrevolution and Conservatism

The principles of the democratic-minded reformers of 1944 had been totally betrayed by 1954. The nature and extent of Communist involvement were clearly substantiated; neither was there serious doubt about United States involvement in the Castillo invasion. The unhappy by-product was a right-wing administration directed by a man untrained to the tasks of government. Carlos Castillo Armas, almost neurotically apprehensive of leftist influence, restricted party and labor activity. His leadership was sanctioned by *imposición* through uncontested elections in October of 1954. A year later his rule was further validated by a vote in which the opposition was effectively interdicted from participation.

Strong economic support by the United States brought only slow progress, despite promises from Washington that the country would now become a "showcase of democracy." Highway construction flourished and business conditions improved, but basic social problems went unsolved. A new agrarian reform law was less confiscatory than that of Arbenz but also failed to reduce significantly the latifundia or to redistribute land to the *campesinos* in appreciable quantity. While seeking a middle-of-the-road course, Castillo failed to meet the full responsibilities of office in an inherently difficult situation. Continued interruptions of political tranquillity led to frequent resorts to the Law of Public Order. During his first eighteen months in power Castillo issued nearly six hundred decree-laws. For a time the secret Committee of National Defense enjoyed virtual immunity from constitutional restraints in rooting out alleged or suspected Communists.

Castillo's assassination by a member of his palace guard in July 1957 introduced several months of turbulence and uncertainty. National elections were reputedly won by the government-backed candidate, but balloting was patently fraudulent. Protest demonstrations were organized by supporters of General Miguel Ydígoras Fuentes, and a new vote was conducted in January of 1958. In what is generally regarded as the fairest election in Guatemalan history, Ydígoras led his three opponents by a substantial margin. In the absence of an outright majority, however, the election was thrown into congress, where the General was chosen after a brief threat of legislative irresponsibility. On March 2 he was inaugurated, bringing a firmly conservative but essentially democratic administration to power.

Ydígoras held staunchly to a democratic course, although his conservative bent was apparent from the outset. Economic policies included the stimulation of private enterprise and the institution of tax reform. A recession caused by the decline of coffee prices in 1958 and 1959 led to the adoption of stringent controls. Much of Ydígoras' program was rendered ineffective because of congressional obstructionism; economic progress was largely limited to additional public works and export diversification. Internal unrest also plagued the General, who was forced several times to suspend constitutional guarantees. An uprising came perilously close to forcing his ouster in March of 1962, when public strikes protested alleged irregularities in congressional elections the preceding December.

In the following months the president solidified his position once again and individual rights were restored. His government remained generally unpopular, however. The president's right-wing domestic policies were widely attacked, and further mistrust was engendered by his outspoken animosity toward the Cuban regime of Fidel Castro. Ydígoras was more than willing to stand up and be counted in opposition to Castro; witness to this was borne by the establishment of a training base by the United States at Retalhuleu prior to the attempted 1961 invasion of Cuba by anti-*fidelistas*. Essentially democratic, Ydígoras nonetheless was something of an anomaly. His basic conservatism was not in keeping with the times, and pressures towards change mounted during his rule.

The ambiguity of Ydígoras's exit from power was consistent with the dominant themes of his term of office. Although Ydígoras threatened to arrest Arévalo for alleged involvement in the assassination of Colonel Arana if he should return to the country, Arévalo secretly returned nonetheless during March of 1963 to begin his campaign for the presidential elections scheduled for December.

Presumably disgruntled with the president's failure to keep Arévalo out of the country and perhaps fearful that Ydígoras might allow a fair election after all—which Arévalo would probably win—the minister of war and dominant military figure of the Ydígoras government, Colonel Enrique Peralta, thereupon staged a *coup d'état* which removed Ydígoras from office.

From his exile, the new ex-president paradoxically stated that he approved of the coup, which was in the country's best interest. The only prediction one could make with assurance about Colonel Peralta's military regime was that it would not allow Juan José Arévalo to become president. Arévalo returned to his exile in Mexico and announced his retirement from politics.

The Political Process

Political Parties

During Guatemala's traditional period, party rivalry was nominally Liberal versus Conservative, but the distinction became nugatory following the reforms of Barrios in the 1880's. Power was wielded by *caudillos* whose party affiliations were largely meaningless. The final genuine issue between the classic parties disappeared with burial of the religious question, and party identification lost all meaning until the Revolution of 1944. Such alleged parties as General Ubico's Partido Liberal Progresista (PLP) were merely personal appendages. The emergence of groups resembling parties did come in the wake of the events of 1944, however. The Frente Popular Libertador (FPL) was instrumental in the wave of enthusiasm for Arévalo that swept the educator into power in the subsequent presidential election.

During that administration there was a proliferation of factions that generally fell into two groups representing varying degrees of reformism. The moderate element—by no means conservative in outlook—centered about the FPL, but slipped from its dominant position after the death of Francisco Arana in 1949. More radical parties were the Partido de Acción Revolucionario (PAR) and the smaller Renovación Nacional (RN). Both supported Jacobo Arbenz in 1950 while the FPL fragmented into smaller groups hopelessly divided in their opposition. Party activity shrank markedly in the next few years. By 1954 the only effective party was the Communist, calling itself the Partido Guatemalteco del Trabajo (PGT).

The Castillo invasion led to the outlawing of the PGT, and the complexion of party activity was colored by the harshly antileftist nature of the regime. Only Castillo's own Movimiento Democrático Nacionalista (MDN) operated with any degree of freedom.

Following Castillo's murder in 1957 it became possible for the first time to identify at least embryonic traces of what may develop into a full-blown democratic party system. Participation has increased in significance, exerting influence not only in congress but through local elections. Most groups are essentially shifting and transitory factions, but perhaps even this is a step forward. The contested elections in January of 1958, coupled with continued activity since that time, have improved the likelihood that a set of modern parties may be evolving.

Groupings are best identified in terms of a general left-right orientation, notwithstanding doctrinal imprecision and shifts based on reasons of expediency. To the right of center is Ydígoras' Partido de Reconciliación Democrática Nacional (PRDN), strongest in the rural areas. Castillo's MDN, which ran a presidential candidate in 1958, is similar in policy and popular appeal, but has floundered in the absence of sound leadership. Also to the right of center are the smaller Partido de Unión Democrática (PUD) and the Partido de Democracia Cristiana de Guatemala (PDCG). Of the four, only the last consistently opposed Ydígoras.

To the left is the Partido Revolucionario (PR), which fits in the general democratic reformist category occupied elsewhere in the hemisphere by such parties as those of Rómulo Betancourt and José Figueres. The leading leftist non-Communist party, the PR derives much of its support from urban workers and certain professional groups. Led by Mario Méndez Montenegro, it has expelled more radical elements. During elections it is customarily joined by the smaller Partido Nacional Revolucionario (PNR), a faction long identified with the fortunes of Arévalo. To the far left are the Partido de Unificación Revolucionaria (PUR) and the old Communist PGT. The latter has been illegal, while the PUR is pro-Castro in sympathy.

By no means all of these factions will survive. After nearly five years of public activity, the parties revealed an integrating tendency in the December 1961 congressional elections. Ydígoras own PRDN was joined by the MDN and the smaller PUD to form a pro-government coalition. The opposition was led by the PR and the PUR. The future of the right is thus centered on the essentially personalistic forces of Ydígoras and the deceased Castillo, with the partisans hopefully awaiting the emergence of an effective leader following the General's retirement from office. In the meantime the fortunes of both the PR and the PUR seem to be waxing. The leadership of the Partido Revolucionario includes Méndez and Luis Galich, the latter having won the "second presidency" with his 1959 victory in the Guatemala City mayoralty race. Until the military intervention, it seemed that the immediate future of party competition lay less in the outcome of the rivalry between right and left than between the moderate and extreme leftists.

Interest Groups

The role of Guatemalan labor has fluctuated tremendously in postwar years, and temporary involvement with international Communism complicates the story. The origins of the labor movement can be traced back to the nineteenth century; an important workers' organization was founded as early as 1894, the Porvenir de los Obreros. A later federation of workers associations managed to survive through the Ubico years. Following his ouster the movement boomed; a variety of unions came into being, merging in 1951 as the Confederación General de Trabajadores de Guatemala (CGTG). Communists captured the CGTG, however, and it became affiliated with the international Communist labor organization. The 1954 invasion ushered in a period of antilabor sentiment, and Carlos Castillo in particular was hostile, repeatedly suspending constitutional guarantees and pressuring labor courts to deliver pro-management decisions.

Labor activity gradually revived following Ydígoras' election. Yet a national trade union confederation was slow to develop despite the efforts of the Consejo Sindical Nacional at the start of the 1960's. The power of individual unions grew more noticeable, as for example the railway workers' organization, the Sindicato de Trabajadores Ferroviarios. Despite the somewhat retarded development of a national labor confederation, the aggregate of labor has recovered substantially after the near-disastrous hiatus of the 1950's. In conflict with labor are such employer organizations as the Asociación General de Industrias (AGI) and the Asociación General de Agricultores (AGA). The growth in membership and importance of economic organizations is also reflected in the four dozen cooperatives, which claimed some 10,000 members by 1960.

The Guatemalan military has traditionally buttressed the regime, and this has held true for the vastly different regimes of Arévalo, Arbenz, Castillo, and Ydígoras. Since 1944, however, there has been a visible division between moderate and rightist elements. The armed forces were also rent with dissension over the absorption of Castillo's irregular Army of Liberation. While it is true that a large cross section of the officer corps remains sympathetic to the principles of 1944, probably a majority of the military officers retain the more traditional conservative political orientation.

University students have been prime movers in recent Guatemalan affairs. Leading the overthrow of Ubico, later disillusioned by Arévalo's ineffectiveness, many were captivated and captured by the extreme left. Later the Asociación de Estudiantes Universitarios (AEU) applied steady pressure on Castillo in urging a reduction of arbitrary controls on political expression. Students clashed with security forces on several occasions, and some two dozen were wounded and 150 jailed in an outburst in June 1956. More recently the AEU criticized Ydígoras strongly, and the appeal of Fidel Castro among the students has grown. The AEU has thus been troublesome to several governments, but nearly always in the cause of social reform and constitutional guarantees.

Finally, attention must be directed toward the role of the Church. Gravely weakened by Justo Rufino Barrios, its influence has been augmented since 1954. The modification of official anticlericalism under Castillo was reciprocated by staunch support from Archbishop Mariano Rossell y Arellano. The Castillo-inspired Constitution of 1956 restored the right of property ownership to the Church in article 50, although the next one guaranteed "free exercise of all religions." The traditional controls having been relaxed, the importance of the Church, especially under the vigorous leadership of such a man as Rossell y Arellano, can no longer be discounted.

Governmental Institutions

The Constitution

Guatemala's checkered history of dictatorship and turbulence has not been dotted with the endless stream of basic documents that other Latin American countries have known. The first formal constitution was adopted some dozen years after Guatemala had withdrawn from the collapsing Central American Confederation. Reflecting the Conservative, clerical orientation of the Indian dictator Carrera, this basic law remained in effect until the drafting of the historic document of 1879. The latter, instituted at the bidding of the *caudillo* Barrios, sanctified Liberal principles which had emerged in the victory of 1871.

Since that time but two additional constitutions have been adopted, those of 1945 and 1956. The latter remains in effect today, resting in no small part on the framework of the 1879 document. Adopted on March 1, 1956, it declares the nation to have a unitary, republican, representative form of government. An introductory bill of rights is unremarkable, with the usual freedoms guaranteed and the sanctity of the home declared inviolable. Detention on criminal charges must be followed within 48 hours by the making public of the charge and the identity of the accuser, and concession of the right to summon defense counsel. Constitutional safeguards are thus provided for the protection of individual rights. Yet the abrogation of all such rights may be decreed by the president through use of the usual instrument of the state of siege. In Guatemala this is exercised through the *Ley de Orden Público,* or Law of Public Order.

Article 77 permits the cessation of guarantees "in case of invasion of the territory, grave disturbance of the peace, or activities against the security of the State, or public calamity." The chief executive may with the advice of his cabinet issue a decree specifying the causes of suspension and the explicit guarantees to be affected. The law is complicated by four separate stages of severity ranging from a "state of prevention" to a total state of siege and war. There is little effective check on presidential discretion. Castillo was adept at invoking the Law to harass his "Communist" critics. Ydígoras decreed varying levels of emergency status on different occasions, although with more valid justification. The Constitution provides that the congress must be convened within three days of the issuance of such a decree, and the legislators are charged with ratification or rejection of the decree. The strong tradition of executive dominance renders this constitutional precaution without practical effect.

The Executive

The chief executive serves a six-year term and is ineligible to a second incumbency until two additional terms have elapsed. Chosen by direct election, the winning candidate must receive an absolute majority. Otherwise the decision devolves upon the congress, as first happened in 1958. Presidential powers of appointment extend not only to cabinet members but also to diplomatic nominees and high-ranking military officers. The latter two categories of appointees must be confirmed by the congress. Cabinet posts customarily number ten: interior, defense, foreign affairs, economy, finance, agriculture, labor, communications, health, and education. A recent addition has been a minister for Central American economic integration affairs. The president may introduce measures into the legislature, where his power of veto is subject to reversal by a two-thirds vote.

There is no established tradition of presidential succession. In the absence of a popularly elected vice-president it remains for the president each year to submit a list of names to congress at the opening session. The legislators select first and second designates by majority vote. If the presidency is vacated the first substitute steps in, charged to conduct new elections within four months, a contest in which he himself is ineligible. Such constitutional provisions found only limited application following the assassination of Castillo. For the present, the procedure followed is determined more by the wishes of the holders of power than by constitutional precept.

The Legislature

Guatemala is among the five Central American republics with a unicameral legislature. Members of the Congreso Nacional are chosen for four-year terms, half the deputies being elected every two years. There is no bar to reelection. The country is divided into voting districts, each of which elects at least two deputies. Areas with a population above 100,000 may add a representative for each additional 50,000 or fraction exceeding 25,000. In 1962 the legislature was composed of sixty-six congressmen.

Convening annually on March 1 for a three-month session, congress may extend its meeting an additional thirty days if necessary. A *comisión permanente* composed of eight legislators continues to work while the congress is not meeting. Empowered to approve executive actions, the *comisión* may be convened by the president of the congress—who acts as its chairman—or upon the request of a majority of the committee members. Congressional powers extend to taxation, the national budget, declarations of war, and the consideration of treaties and conventions. Its subordination to the executive is customary.

The Judiciary

At the apex is the Corte Suprema, whose seven justices are elected to four-year terms by congress. The judges are eligible for reelection, after which they automatically receive tenure until compulsory retirement at age seventy. Normally the court forms two separate chambers, dealing respectively with civil and criminal appeals. The Court of Appeals is chosen similarly by the congress, and further down the pyramid are some thirty courts of first instance, with justices of the peace located in municipalities. Provisions for tenure are qualified by constitutional article 199 which permits congressional removal for cause, including "failure to perform duties." This permits a political judgment by congress that is highly detrimental to the ideal of an independent judiciary.

Local Government

Guatemalan government is unitary, although spatially divided into 22 administrative divisions commonly called departments. Each of these is ruled by a governor appointed by and responsible to the president. Dismissal on executive whim may come at any time, although recent practice has aimed at the establishment of a kind of administrative corps through the rotation of governors from one department to the other. Responsible for the smooth functioning of affairs in his department, the shrewd governor cuts a wide swath through the exercise of his essentially administrative duties. Appointment to the department of Guatemala, with a population above one-half million, means substantial political power.

Municipal government is located in some 322 subdivisions of the departments, and provides the only existing form of local rule. Town government has existed in the village since colonial days, but the degree of community autonomy depends largely on the inclinations of the president. Each *municipio* has a popularly elected council responsible for local services, taxes, and properties. Heading the council is an *alcalde* who presides over meetings and commonly acts as justice of the peace. But once again the role of the national government is overwhelming. Only the effective eradication of illiteracy and the extension of welfare measures will enable the municipalities to exercise any meaningful powers of home rule.

The Electoral System

The franchise has been limited narrowly. The 1871 constitution posited a difference in status between nationals and citizens, the former being denied the vote. But suffrage has been extended through progressive revisions in the 1945 and 1956 documents. At present all males of 18 years and above may vote, and literate women have the same privilege. Voting is obligatory for all eligible citizens, although illiterate males may vote in public rather than in secret, and this is optional with the individual. The estimated 75 percent illiteracy among adult females suggests the effects of the literacy requirement in limiting the number of female voters.

A revision of the electoral law in the late 1950's called for the application of the D'Hondt system of proportional representation in congressional elections where a coalition of parties had been proclaimed. This led to serious controversy following congressional elections in December of 1961, and the national election board was confronted with a welter of different claims. In early 1962 it ruled that seats would be allotted according to a majority system, using the department as the basis of representation. The provision for proportional representation was held to be imprecisely drafted and not in consonance with the intention of the writers of the constitution.

Public Policy

The absence of competent personnel is a continuing problem for the public service. The situation has been aggravated in recent years, and the solution of problems of importance is often delayed by the lack of trained bureaucrats. The need for personnel has grown rapidly with recent reform efforts, which have led to a proliferation of bureaucratic posts on all levels of government. The addition of programs of social security and agrarian reform, and of an expanding educational and public health service, has left a void to be filled. It was this space into which the Communists stepped in the early postwar years. Policy implementation, especially where a high level of technical competence is required, remains unsure, while the long heritage of graft and the *mordida,* or bribe, has by no means been dissipated.

Domestic Policy

A general consensus is perceivable on the major outlines of domestic policy, with controversy tending to center upon matters of emphasis and implementation. There is general acceptance of the need for such things as financial solvency and the construction of schools, highways, and public works. The parting of the ways comes in discussion of the manner and extent to which the government should intrude. The tendency today is strongly in favor of an expanded role for the state. The number of official bureaus and agencies has multiplied.

Recognition of the individual's right to social security protection in the 1945 constitution led to expansion of a system that now includes protection against old age and disability, hospitalization provisions, and also allotments for widows and orphans. Mobile health units have grown in number over a short period of time, while the construction of new housing received a substantial boost in November of 1959 with the granting of United States aid for the building of low-cost housing projects. Financial, technical, and administrative facilities to improve housing have centered in the Instituto de Fomento de Producción (INFOP), created in 1948. Among the newer organs are the Instituto de Fomento Municipal (INFOM) and the Instituto Nacional de Electrificación (INE), the former an autonomous community development agency and the latter the semi-autonomous government electrical body. An official mortgage bank is also in operation, the Crédito Hipotecario Nacional de Guatemala.

As suggested before, the need for agrarian reform has been recognized for some years. The dispute revolves about its form and substance. The Arbenz reform in 1952 called for the expropriation of uncultivated land and its redistribution among the landless. Compensation, based on far less than the market value of the land, was provided by long-term government bonds; holdings of less than 667 acres were exempted. The major weakness— aside from abortive implementation of the program—was the provision that redistributed land would be leased for twenty-five years. Then, or upon the death of the peasant, land would revert to the state. Furthermore, every aspect of the program was subject to presidential decision against which there was no appeal.

The later Castillo *Estatuto Agrario* was issued in February of 1956 and placed heavy emphasis on the expropriation of unused lands. Large estates being productively worked were in most cases left untouched. Repayment for lands taken was made at existing market prices, and government bonds were eschewed. Relying substantially on North American technical assistance, Castillo pursued a program that focused greatest attention on colonization, resettlement, and the opening of new lands through road construction and further public works. This program, like its predecessor, left something to be desired. The Arbenz plan had enabled the government to retain ultimate control of the land, while compensation was made in virtually worthless certificates. The Castillo program, more soundly conceived but also less extensive in scope, left productive lands untouched and also permitted large landowners to continue many traditional practices of *latifundismo*. The colonization program was only moderately successful, and the cost was high. Later efforts by Ydígoras to enact a new program were blocked in congress while controversy raged unabated.

Foreign Policy

The basis of Guatemalan international policy is the state of relations with the United States. The continuing issues of the postwar period have revolved primarily about the intrusion of the Cold War into hemispheric affairs. In the early 1950's this was reflected by the infiltration of the Communists and the subsequent turbulence. The triumph of Carlos Castillo Armas brought an inevitable official reaction against leftist governments in general, and the same policy guidelines were picked up by Manuel Ydígoras in 1958.

Guatemalan opposition to Fidel Castro's regime in Cuba was stiffened from November of 1960 when a short-lived invasion from the Caribbean was found to include pro-Castroites. Ydígoras, a vocal critic of the Cuban regime, joined with Peru in urging the January 1962 meeting of the Organization of American States to consider the Cuban problem. Continuation of Communist domination of Cuba brings concomitant controversy in Guatemala. Despite the presence of Castro sympathizers, the issue has been less heated than might have been anticipated. Even Juan José Arévalo, discussing his views in 1962, remarked that he regarded the totalitarian nature of the Cuban government as distasteful.

Two other foreign policy issues have loomed large in the past decade, one of them transitory, the other seemingly eternal. In the first case, serious controversy with Mexico brought the neighbors to the brink of hostilities in January of 1959. Controversy over fishing rights in contiguous waters led to a temporary severance of diplomatic relations, and shots were actually exchanged between planes and a fishing fleet. Guatemala's stance was angry; the inflammation was salved only after tempers simmered for several weeks.

Far less susceptible of solution was the historic issue centered on British Honduras—Belice, as it is marked on Guatemalan maps. The area, seized from Spain by the British in colonial times, was claimed by Guatemala until 1859. At that time a treaty ceded the disputed area to Britain, conditional upon the construction by England of a highway to Guatemala City from the Crown territory. Such construction was never undertaken, and the Guatemalans have long entered periodic protests in claiming ownership of the area. The border is sometimes closed down, as it was from 1948 to 1951, and the foreign ministry maintains a Bureau of Belice Affairs which publishes maps and documents supporting the Guatemalan territorial claim. While there is little present likelihood that Britain will tolerate a change in the colony's status, the issue provides a highly convenient means for any beleaguered government in Guatemala City to unite the populace behind it while diverting attention from domestic problems.

There can be no serious doubt but that elemental changes are transpiring in Guatemala to meet the accumulation of problems inherited from previous years. The forms which change will take it is now impossible to foresee.

NOTES FOR CHAPTER II

1. Richard N. Adams, "Social Change in Guatemala and U.S. Policy," in *Social Change in Latin America Today: Its Implications for United States Policy,* Harper & Row, 1960, p. 248.
2. Ronald M. Schneider, *Communism in Guatemala 1944-1954,* Praeger, New York, 1958, p. 9.

SELECTED BIBLIOGRAPHY

Richard N. Adams, "Social Change in Guatemala and U.S. Policy," in *Social Change in Latin America Today: Its Implications for United States Policy,* Harper, New York, 1960, pp. 231-285.

Mary Holleran, *Church and State in Guatemala,* Columbia University Press, New York, 1949.

Daniel James, *Red Design for the Americas: Guatemalan Prelude,* John Day, New York, 1954.

Chester Lloyd Jones, *Guatemala, Past and Present,* University of Minnesota Press, Minneapolis, 1940.

John D. Martz, *Central America: The Crisis and the Challenge,* University of North Carolina Press, Chapel Hill, 1959, pp. 27-80.

Ronald M. Schneider, *Communism in Guatemala 1944-1954,* Praeger, New York, 1958.

Kalman H. Silvert, *A Study in Government: Guatemala,* Middle American Research Institute, Tulane University, New Orleans, 1954.

Nathan L. Whetten, *Guatemala: The Land and the People,* Yale University Press, New Haven, 1961.

EL SALVADOR
San Salvador

EL SALVADOR

THE ARMY AS REFORMER

On the surface, the political culture of El Salvador seems like that of many Latin American nations. There is a marked contrast between the wealth of the few and the poverty of the many. The large estate, producing a single crop for export, continues to be a prominent economic fact of life. The military plays a dominant political role. There is a clear line between urban modernity and rural backwardness. The country has a heritage of political instability, *caudillo* dictatorship, and government by a few elites representing but a small proportion of the population. One is tempted to apply the rules of thumb of Latin American politics to each of these phenomena and let it go at that. But to do so would be to produce a caricature of Salvadorian politics. For the "typical" socio-economic institutions and problems of Latin America take on a peculiar significance in the Salvadorian setting. And the interaction of the classic Latin American power factors has led to the development of a political process which is somewhat unique.

Subtle differences of attitude and value seem to distinguish Salvadorians from their neighbors. Other Central Americans, who delight in giving the visitor thumbnail sketches of the national characteristics of the peoples of the isthmus, sum up the Salvadorians as peculiarly "industrious," "hard-working," and "businesslike." The significance of the selection of this trait to typify a people becomes apparent to the visitor during his first stroll about the capital city of San Salvador. (San Salvador is the city; the nation is El Salvador.) Accustomed to the more leisurely pace of San José or Tegucigalpa, the visitor soon feels pressed by people impatient to pass him by, and quickens his step so as to match that of the city. The experience is not unlike that of a first encounter with the hurried pace of Chicago. The heightened vitality of El Salvador has impressed visitors through the years. In the 1840's, John L. Stephens, in his journal, *Incidents of Travel in Central America, Chiapas and Yucatán*, recorded the following impression of the country.

> From the time of the independence, this state stood foremost in the maintenance of liberal principles; it exhibits throughout an appearance of improvement, a freedom from bigotry and fanaticism, and a development of physical and moral energy not found in any other.

And Alberto de Mestas, ambassador of Spain in El Salvador during the 1940's, notes in his book, *El Salvador, país de lagos y volcanos*, that "the first impression that the traveler gets when he visits El Salvador is that this land is the home of a hard-working and tenacious race."

The greater value placed on "industriousness" is then one of the elements that is said to set El Salvador apart from its neighbors. Other traits might be mentioned that are ascribed to Salvadorians by other Central Americans. They are said to be relatively "apolitical," less interested and intensely involved in the political game that is such a prominent avocation in Latin America, and it is suggested that they take a more reasoned and tolerant approach to social and political problems, despite the fact that they possess one of the more rigid economic class systems in Latin America.

However whimsical such characterizations might seem to be, they may provide us with clues helpful to understanding the vivid distinctiveness of the political culture of El Salvador.

Social and Economic Background

El Salvador is the smallest nation in Latin America. Its area of 34,126 square miles, about the size of the state of Maryland, makes it seem like an archaic survival in this era of the subcontinental nation-state. On this land, studded with volcanoes, tropical forests, and other obstacles to intensive land use, live some 2,320,000 people, about 275 per square mile, the densest concentration of population in Latin America except for Haiti. Some have seen in the conditions of survival in this difficult land an explanation of Salvadorian vitality and hardiness. There is something exceptional, they claim, about a people who plant their crops up to the very rim of active volcanoes.

The land, and its scarcity, is a key economic factor, for this is a predominately agricultural country. El Salvador lives by its exports of coffee, as dependent upon a single product for its economic well-being as any Latin American nation. Coffee regularly accounts for from 70 to 85 percent of the nation's export earnings. Cotton, hemp (primarily for the production of coffee bags), sugar, balsam (for medicine and cosmetics), and indigo (for dyes) are the other major products. Rice, beans, wheat, tobacco, soybeans, and peanuts are grown for domestic consumption.

The basic economic fact of life for El Salvador is the world coffee market. When prices are high, something of a bonanza psychology comes to the nation. The future looks rosy. Coffee production is expanded, new enterprises are started, great plans for the economic development of the nation are proposed with abundant hope for their success. When coffee prices fall, despair comes to El Salvador, the economy contracts, with political and social unrest as a by-product. And coffee prices have fluctuated greatly in the twentieth century, from the lows of the world depression, to the boom of the post-World War II era, to a new decline after 1954.

El Salvador can't live with the coffee market, and can't live without it. Only now developing significant manufacturing industry, virtually every product of the modern world had until recently to come from outside and be paid for in foreign exchange earned through the sale of coffee. Like other Latin American nations, El Salvador seeks to develop her economy, to reduce dependence on the outside world, and to provide a higher standard of living for her people. Yet for El Salvador the alternative means to achieving this goal are strictly limited. The economy rests on agriculture, but there are few new frontiers available, areas of unexploited land that could be opened to increase productivity dramatically. El Salvador is already one of the more efficient agricultural nations of Latin America. Certainly improvements in technique would be fruitful, but cultivation is already intensive and farming on volcanic slopes often precludes the use of some modern mass-production techniques in agriculture. Finally, the market for El Salvador's major products is already glutted, and greater production would seem only to make matters worse. The nation has sought to diversify its agricultural production, but has yet to find a truly viable alternative to coffee. Cotton, which has been enthusiastically promoted in the last fifteen years, is subject to many of the same problems as coffee in the international market.

Many Salvadorians feel that industrialization is the way out for the country, particularly labor-intensive industry, which can build from the strength of the nation's dense and underemployed population. However, industrialization requires capital, and capital must come from the existing agricultural base of the economy. And when Salvadorian policy-makers contemplate available domestic sources of capital, they run head-on into one of the most problematic features of the nation's social and political life.

Throughout most of its modern history, the national life of El Salvador has been dominated by an elite composed of the members of a small number of leading families, whose great wealth is derived from their important position in the coffee industry. In Salvadorian tradition, this elite consists of fourteen families, *los catorce grandes*. However, there is some dispute as to its exact composition. One source indicates that some thirty "clans" control about fifty percent of the national income.

The elite are sophisticated and cosmopolitan. Generally, they give only peripheral attention to the direct management of their extensive properties in El Salvador. Their time is divided between residence in the major cities of the country (usually San Salvador or Santa Ana), participation in the international social set, with frequent visits to North America, Europe, and Mexico, and occasional visits to their estates. The children of these families are usually educated in Europe or North America.

Although they have been increasing their investments in their landholdings and in Salvadorian industry and commerce, they have traditionally preferred to place their money abroad rather than employing it to develop the Salvadorian economy. Given the political and social power of this group, efforts to prevent this flight of capital have posed one of the most difficult problems for Salvadorian policy-makers through the years.

Racially, El Salvador is somewhat more homogeneous than many Latin American nations, and class lines seem to be drawn rather on economic than on racial factors. Discounting the small "white" upper class, and the five percent or so of the population classified as Indian, the great bulk of the population is *mestizo* in origin. The original Salvadorian Indians, living on the fringes of the great Mayan empire to the north, apparently had neither the cultural integrity nor the tractability to survive intact the European conquest, as did their Guatemalan counterparts.

Political History

There is a marked contrast between Salvadorian politics in the nineteenth and twentieth centuries. Until about 1900, San Salvador was turbulent and chaotic, a nation afflicted by chronic instability and bitter civil strife. Since the turn of the century, the nation, while by no means a paragon of democratic virtues, has at least possessed a comparatively stable and orderly political process. The explanation for this transition is not to be found primarily in conditions indigenous to El Salvador, but rather in the nature of the political growing pains that afflicted the entire Central American area in the years immediately following independence.

The political conflicts of Central America in the nineteenth century took place on two different levels. First, with the failure of the early dream of creating a Central American federation, there was the problem of structuring power relations in each of the five separate states. Closely related to this issue was the struggle between Liberals and Conservatives, a conflict that transcended national boundaries. As throughout Latin America, the Liberals were advocates of federalism, separation of Church and State, and in general looked to the ideals of the French and American revolutions for philosophic guidance. The Conservatives favored strong centralized administration, an intimate relation between clerical and secular power, and a greater respect for the political heritage of monarchical Spain.

In the early years of independence, strong Liberal or Conservative *caudillos* who had consolidated power in one nation often saw it to be both an opportunity and a duty to secure the domination of their party in the rest. Frequently they were supported and encouraged by dissident factions in the other countries, who were not loath to call in outside assistance to overthrow an unfavorable regime.

Hence, while the Liberals, who early became dominant in El Salvador, often intervened in the affairs of their neighbors to secure Liberal governments, they too were the victims of incursions from other states. Three times between 1840 and 1870 the great Guatemalan Conservative chieftain Carrera used force to assist Salvadorian Conservatives in overthrowing Liberal regimes, and three times the Liberals displaced these governments through civil strife.

As the great leaders of the independence movement passed away, and as the partisan disputes became less relevant to the concerns of the nations, international conflict became less important in Central America. In the first three decades of the twentieth century, the political processes of the Central American nations became more autonomous, and each developed its distinct characteristics somewhat apart from the international and partisan conflicts of the preceding century. In Nicaragua and Honduras, politics continued to be dominated by clashes, coup and countercoup between Liberal and Conservative forces. Salvadorian political life, however, was developing in a somewhat different manner.

The development of the modern coffee industry, with the growth of its attendant economic elites, was also a product of the decades surrounding the turn of the century. Cognizant of the costs of instability and civil strife, and aware of the economic benefits of modernization through the coffee trade, the new agricultural and commercial leaders sought effective and orderly government. Supported by the most efficient and well-trained army in Central America, government became the province of this elite, surprisingly united on political and economic goals. They were represented through two families, the Meléndez and the Quiñónez, members of which alternated in the presidency consecutively from 1913 to 1927.

The great depression of the 1930's, with its catastrophic effects on the world coffee market, brought an end to this political system. The confidence of the elite in the economic order was shaken. Unrest spread to the countryside, where peasant revolts took place. These uprisings were attributed to the work of foreign Communist organizers. Whether this was true or not, and there is insufficient evidence either to accept or reject the charge, the important fact is that this was believed to be the case. The elite, already uneasy about their economic fate, were further frightened by the prospect of a radical revolution which would endanger their lives and property. The time for the emergence of the "depression dictator," a phenomenon that was to characterize much of Latin America in the 1930's, had come to El Salvador.

The figure who was to emerge to fill this role was one of the most picturesque of modern Latin America. General Maximiliano Hernández Martínez, a professional military officer and minister of war under the government of President Arturo Araujo, staged a military coup and took power in 1931. Ruthlessly, he restored order to the countryside and rid the nation of the "Communist menace." He stabilized the nation's political life and restored financial solvency and faith in the economy.

While quieting the fears and satisfying the aspirations of the elites, he also became a heroic figure to the masses. He carried out a program of public works, building schools, roads, public buildings, and public services in the most grandiose manner. His personal appeal was quite genuine, in part based upon very real eccentricities.

Martínez was a Theosophist and something of a wizard. He made it known that he had occult powers that enabled him to know what individuals were thinking. He would conjure up magic formulas to solve vital national problems. He advised the peasants on mysterious procedures of planting corn, an animistic form of technical assistance. During a smallpox epidemic, he had green lights strung throughout the capital and assured the citizens that these would halt the spread of the disease. He exposed bottles of colored water to sunlight, and recommended them as cures for cancer, heart disease, and appendicitis.

Martínez ruled El Salvador from 1931 to 1944. Either through the use of interim puppet presidents, or through constitutional revisions to permit self-succession, he maintained a façade of legitimacy. But the real bases of his regime were the military, the satisfaction of the elite, who were more concerned with public order and economic well-being than political niceties, and his mass appeal. By the middle 1940's, however, his acceptance was wearing thin.

The manner in which the dictatorship came to an end is somewhat different from the classic pattern of the Central American coup. No conspiratorial movement or activist group can be pinpointed which plotted the revolt. Opposition under the conditions of the Martínez regime was virtually impossible. The instrument used to unseat the strong man was that of the general strike. In the face of an almost total economic paralysis of the capital city, Martínez decided to step down from his long-held place of political leadership. There seems to be little doubt that this strike was a relatively spontaneous undertaking on the part of the middle class of the city of San Salvador. One often quoted description of the events ends as follows.

> In April of that year, a revolution was attempted and failed. The tyrant shot and persecuted the patriots. . . . The people carried out a general shutdown, private and public offices closed, railroads and buses stopped running. Everything stopped. The Government searched for the leaders to capture them and end the revolution. But there were no leaders. The University started it; but, after that, it was all the people spontaneously.[1]

Historically, the general strike of 1944 was the first of two events that mark the transition of El Salvador from the classic *caudillo* pattern of government to its present political system. The civilian president who replaced Martínez, Salvador Castañeda Castro, failed to capture the imagination of the vital political forces of the nation. At the end of his term in 1948, however, he was reluctant to surrender the presidency, and on December 13 the national assembly decreed that the "interests of the nation" required him to continue in office. In response to this threat of *continuismo,* a group of junior officers staged a barracks revolt, removed Castañeda from office, established a military junta, and issued a call for elections and the creation of a new constitution.

The leaders of the "Revolution of 1948" quickly moved to legitimize their rule. By 1950 they had drafted a new constitution, created a political party (the Revolutionary Party of Democratic Unification, or PRUD), and succeeded in duly electing one of their members, Colonel Oscar Osorio, to the presidency.

Osorio's administration, and the presidency of José María Lemus who succeeded him in 1956 and served until 1960, may be considered together as a single period in Salvadorian politics. The intention of these leaders was to carry out what might be described as a controlled revolution, a moderate program of economic and social reform which would satisfy growing agitation for a better standard of living and prevent the outbreak of radical discontent while leaving the existing social and economic structure largely intact. Politically, opposition to the regime would be permitted within carefully defined limits. Political organization and freedom of expression were to be permitted those who did not subscribe to revolutionary political tenets or advocate a thorough overhauling of the nation's social and economic life.

Throughout most of the decade of *prudista* rule, freedom of expression and basic civil liberties were generally respected. However, the role of PRUD as an official party supported by the military, and the government's insistence upon the right to distinguish between "responsible" and "irresponsible" opposition, created great difficulties. The presidential elections of 1956 were the first prominent black mark against the regime. PRUD, in this election, was opposed by a battery of small opposition parties. Shortly before the balloting, the candidates of most of these were disqualified by the PRUD-controlled Council on Elections. The two remaining opposition parties decided to boycott the polls, charging electoral fraud. Thereafter the PRUD candidate, Lemus, won virtually without opposition.

By late 1959, agitation against the regime was becoming acute. Declining coffee prices had slowed down the program of internal development and caused economic uncertainty. Especially among student groups, who had long opposed the regime, the inspiration of the Cuban Revolution gave impetus to agitation against the government. At least maintaining the virtue of consistency, the regime chose to define this as "extremist" opposition, and suppressed the student-led activities with considerable brutality.

On October 26, 1961, the Lemus government was replaced by a military junta. Hardly a revolution, the event represented fundamentally a revision of power alignments within the military in response to civic unrest, in much the same spirit as the "Revolution of 1948." The change did represent a shift to the left in national politics, but again within the context of the "controlled revolution." The military would itself enact necessary reforms, rather than permitting agitation to develop which might cause the situation to slip from its control.

A further revision in intramilitary power relations led to the overthrow of this junta and its replacement by a Civil-Military Directorate, composed of two officers and a civilian, in January 1961. The program of reform of the previous junta was continued.

At the end of 1961, elections were held for a constituent assembly, to revise the Constitution of 1950, and to call elections for the presidency. The Party of National Conciliation (PCN) which was formed by the Civil-Military Directorate, and stood in the same relation to it as PRUD had to the former ruling group, won all fifty-four seats in the constituent assembly. The assembly made minor revisions in the fundamental law, constituted itself the legislature of the nation until 1964, and called for presidential elections for April 29, 1962.

During the months of campaigning that followed, a variety of parties organized, and the classic acrimony of a Salvadorian political campaign filled the newspapers. But the outcome was seldom in doubt. The Party of National Conciliation nominated Julio Adalberto Rivera, an army officer and member of the Civil-Military Directorate, as its candidate for the presidency. An active campaigner, Rivera barnstormed the country with an entourage that included a doctor, a dentist, a lawyer, and an engineer who could be consulted by the citizens. His campaign was based directly on support for the Alliance for Progress and he pledged to carry out in El Salvador the reforms anticipated by the Charter of Punta del Este.

Again, the major opposition parties boycotted the elections, claiming that they were being carried out in an atmosphere that made a democratic outcome impossible. Rivera was elected president, and Francisco Alberto Lima vice-president, without opposition. Of some 800,000 potential voters, Rivera received 134,881 votes, while 13,000 blank ballots and 10,000 invalid votes were cast. The low turnout was attributed to apathy toward the fore-ordained outcome of the election.

A low rate of turnout also characterized the legislative elections of March 1964. Fears that the outcome of the election was rigged were proved unfounded, however, by the victory of a candidate of the opposition Christian Democratic Party for the Mayoralty of San Salvador. The Christian Democrats also won 14 legislative seats, to become the second strongest party after the PCN. Six seats were won by the Partido de Acción Renovadora, or PAR, leaving 32 to the PCN.

A discernible pattern of politics seems to be developing in El Salvador. The events of 1960 and 1962 are more than vaguely reminiscent of political developments in 1948 and 1950. It is easy to dismiss the political record of contemporary El Salvador as "military rule" in the classic Latin American pattern. But the significance of the Salvadorian political process is more complex and subtle than it seems on the surface, and deserves to be examined in greater detail.

Political Processes

Although the key leaders have changed, and the name of the official party is different, it would seem that the political process in El Salvador has remained remarkably consistent during the past fifteen years. The governments that have ruled El Salvador since 1948 may roughly be described as a single regime, based on a subtle coalition of the dominant power factors in the nation. Within this coalition, one finds an effort to reconcile groups which are often in conflict in other societies. To clarify the nature of this strange political equilibrium, one must look more closely at the primary power factors in El Salvador.

The Military

The group of army officers who have controlled Salvadorian politics since 1948 share significant characteristics. Almost all come from the ranks of major and lieutenant colonel, that middle range of the officer corps where promotions come slowly and political activity appears as a promising alternative to the frustrations of immobility in the military hierarchy.

Perhaps even more significantly, these younger officers differ greatly in attitude from the older military caste which they displaced. Many of them claim lower-middle or middle-class origins. By virtue of place of residence, education, social contacts, economic status and aspiration, and social attitudes, they identify more closely with the emergent middle class than with the economic elites. Most have spent some time in military colleges in the United States and have experienced close contact with American military missions.

Finally, as career officers, all have been imbued, since their studies in the national military academy, with the Salvadorian military tradition. The *élan* of the officer corps, a key political factor in many Latin American nations, reaches a high point in El Salvador, which has long possessed one of the more efficient military forces in Latin America, with a real sense of its own professional and elite status. The virtues to be possessed by a Salvadorian officer, his military code of honor, center on patriotism and a selfless, virtually Spartan dedication to duty. Yet the political ramifications of the military value system do not necessarily include rigid self-restraint from political involvement. Rather, the officer has a responsibility to uphold the institutions and honor of the nation. Should self-seeking politicians jeopardize the constitution or the institutions of the nation, it is the duty of the military to intervene. In a sense, the military assumes the responsibilities of judicial review, judging the propriety of political actions.

The sum total of this composite background has been the formation of a group of younger officers dedicated to the orderly and structured economic and social modernization of El Salvador through political action. Through a moderate economic and social transformation, carried out with the order and discipline that the military can provide, free from the unproductive bickerings of politicians, the military can save the nation from the threat of radical revolution and political chaos, and thereby fulfill their duty to protect the nation's institutional integrity. And, thus justified, the military may claim a share of the many attractive perquisites of public office in Latin America.

The Economic Elites

The military has been able to sell its program of economic and social reform largely because of the almost obsessive fears that the Salvadorian upper classes have long held of radical movements and ideas. The "Communist" uprisings of 1932 left a lasting impression on them, an impression reinforced by events in neighboring Guatemala during the administration of Jacobo Arbenz. The Salvadorian military leaders have skillfully played upon these fears by recurrently discovering and crushing "Communist" plots during the period since 1948.

In part, then, the Salvadorian economic elites accepted the military's program as the only viable alternative to a more radical outbreak of mass discontent. In the record and program of the military regimes, and undoubtedly through personal understanding as well, the economic elite found assurance that their privileged position would not be endangered. Although the living standards of the masses were to be bettered, the infrastructure of the nation was to be developed through public works projects, and the economy was to be diversified through industrialization, none of this would come about through the destruction of the great families. The military has constantly elicited the support of the upper classes in the development effort, encouraging them to contribute to the economic development of the nation. When such support has not been forthcoming, and particularly since 1960, the military has sought to compel cooperation with its program. But always such actions are taken in a way that suggests that they are designed to assure the salvation of the upper class, in some ways, in spite of itself.

The Middle Sectors

The emergence of a middle class as a by-product of social change has not been as pronounced a phenomenon in El Salvador as in many nations of Latin America. Furthermore, the characteristic pattern of the formation of this class by mobility from below is somewhat mitigated in this country as members of the upper class choose career patterns and social orientations which are characteristic of the middle group. It is also true that the intense avocational political involvement which characterizes the middle class in many countries is less prevalent in El Salvador. Nevertheless, a substantial number of middle-class political activists do exist in the nation, and it is critical for the success of other power factors that their interests be taken into account.

In its political characteristics, this group is quite comparable to similar elements in other nations. Its members are urban and literate. They identify with their counterparts in the advanced nations and seek to emulate them.

As a social class which has emerged outside the traditional class structure, they are at times unsure of their place in the social order, and they seek a reference group which can take the place of family or community, often through ardent nationalism or identification with a political movement. Their skills are those of the manipulation of the symbols, institutions, and processes of a complex society. Thus, in politics their power rests with their facility in the use of legal and institutional processes and their ability to use the tools of persuasion and organization to achieve support. They are hence champions of the enforcement of democratic processes and legal norms and of development on the model of the advanced nations. Their chosen instrument of political action is the political party.

Political Parties

The military leaders of El Salvador have recognized the desirability of drawing the middle-class political activists into affiliation with the regime and have used the instrument of an official party as the logical means to this end. From 1950 to 1960 the official party was known as the Revolutionary Party of Democratic Unification (PRUD). Since that time it has taken the name of the Party of National Conciliation (PCN). The membership and organization of PRUD was to some extent transferred to the PCN after the coup of 1960, although a small group of followers of the deposed President Lemus did try to reactivate PRUD, with small success, in the campaigns of 1961 and 1962.

Although the official organization dominates the party system, any number of opposition parties are usually active during election periods. Many of these are ephemeral *ad hoc* organizations, which disappear quickly once the purpose for which they were organized has passed, although some are bidding for a measure of permanent identity. The ideological and programmatic spectrum which these opposition groups represent is strictly delimited by the regime's definition of "controlled democracy," that only such opposition would be permitted as would surely operate within the conditions set by the regime and would not propose radical or revolutionary solutions to the nation's problems.

The most prominent opposition group until the 1964 elections was the Party of Renovating Action or PAR. It espouses a program much like that of PRUD or PCN, though militant in its opposition to the official status of these groups and to alleged corruption within the regime, and critical of the regime's failure to provide full electoral democracy. In 1950, this group lost to PRUD by a margin of only 78,868 in the presidential elections, 345,139 to 266,271. In succeeding elections, PAR, although usually active in the campaign, has boycotted the polls, charging electoral malpractice.

The other parties that participated in the elections of 1961 and 1962 may be arrayed as follows. Generally conservative in temper are the Authentic Constitutional Party (PAC) and the National Action Party (PAN). Similar to the PCN or PAR in programmatic outlook are the Social Democrats

(PSD) and the Christian Democrats (PDC), the latter similar to and identified with the Catholic social democratic parties throughout Latin America. Officially outlawed from electoral participation was the Revolutionary Party of April and May (PRAM), considerably to the left and pro-Communist, or at least pro-Castro, in orientation. Two extremely small groups, the Radical Democrats (PRD) and the Democratic Action Party (PAD), also exist.

Elections and Public Opinion

The president and vice-president, legislative representatives, and members of municipal councils, are elected officials in El Salvador. The term of the president was six years until 1962, and will be five years in the future. Legislators and municipal councils are elected for two-year terms. Presidential and legislative elections may not be held at the same time. Campaigning is legally permitted for four months before presidential, two months before legislative, and one month before municipal elections, though the law is not consistently honored.

Throughout the period of the present regime, opposition parties have usually abstained from electoral participation, charging that democratic standards were not upheld and that outcomes were foreordained. This charge requires examination. Clearly the power structure of the present regime made uncertain the efficacy of opposition politics. One wonders what the outcome would have been had an opposition group successfully challenged the official candidates in any one of the elections since 1960. Clearly, substantial malpractice was present in the presidential voting of 1956, particularly with regard to the activities of the Election Council, which disqualified leading opposition candidates on technical grounds. There is also evidence to indicate that the returns from this election were manipulated so as to give PRUD a much higher proportion of the vote in the face of the boycott than many observers feel was possible.

Yet it seems also indicated that the regime enjoyed substantial real popular support, at least until 1957 or 1958. Furthermore, given its political and financial position as an official party, PRUD was a far more effective campaigning vehicle than any of the opposition groups. Hence, there is more than a hint of a strategy familiar to opposition parties throughout Latin America in the electoral boycotts which took place in El Salvador, for frequently such abstentions are used to prevent embarrassment to the party by making the election an inexact test of popular support.

Opposition groups insist that low voter turnouts provide a good representation of voter apathy and opposition to the foreordained nature of Salvadorian elections. If we take as a point of departure the seemingly honest election of 1950, in which about 600,000 votes were cast, we do find some evidence to support this position. Official returns in the 1956 election recorded some 750,000 votes, an increase said to be largely due to the enfranchisement of women during the interelection period. However, most observers feel that these results were falsified, and some unofficial estimates place the number of voters in this election as low as 150,000. In the December 1960 elections for a constituent assembly, generally conceded to have been satisfactorily open and honest, some 383,890 voters went to the polls, about 43.7 percent of those registered. Yet in the May election of 1962, in which the official candidate Rivera was foreordained as winner and opposition groups were not participating, only about 155,000 votes were cast. It would appear then that negative voter attitudes towards the efficacy of electoral participation are reflected in recent Salvadorian elections, a conclusion that seemed confirmed by the failure of over two thirds of the voters to cast ballots in March 1964.

It has often been observed that Salvadorians seem less intensely interested in political affairs than their neighbors in Central America. In the folklore of the region, the Salvadorians are said to be somewhat "apolitical." Perhaps symbolic of this Salvadorian attitude toward politics was a comment by the secretary-general of the PRUD to the author. Commenting on the party's organization, he observed that activity was quite limited between elections, a fact which he noted with some pride, explicitly contrasting his party with other Central American parties, because, "between elections people should get back to work and forget about politicking."

The lower intensity of political interest in El Salvador is also reflected in the nature of the press in this nation. Most newspapers in Central America are committed politically, either actually controlled by a political movement or closely identified with a specific point of view. Much space is devoted to political diatribe and discussion. Yet the leading papers of El Salvador are generally rigorously independent from political involvement. The tone of *La Prensa Gráfica, El Diario de Hoy, Tribuna Libre,* and *Diario Latina,* the leading Salvadorian papers, is much more like that of the North American press, with emphasis on more or less factual reporting in place of the typical Central American pattern of extended space for elaborate political essays and commentary. Of course, this "independent" posture is reflected in the political process as a generally conservative attitude and an acceptance of the existing regime. The primary outlet for opposition comment and re-formist thought has been, throughout the period of the present regime, the irregularly distributed newspaper of the university students' association, *Opinión Estudantil.*

Interest Groups

The nature of associational organization in El Salvador generally reflects the economic and social characteristics of the nation. Such permanent, well-organized groups, with structured access to political decision-makers, as are to be found usually represent the upper economic levels of the nation. Labor unions, peasant leagues, and similar organizations, where they exist at all, are still quite rudimentary and limited in scope. The most potent organizations, not surprisingly, exist in the field of export agriculture. The Coffee

Growers Association, the General Board of Coffee Growers, the Association of Stockmen and Farmers of the Western Zone, are prominent in this group. Some of these organizations possess something like a semi-official status, being linked legally or financially with governmental institutions.

In the industrial and commercial sectors, the Chamber of Commerce and Industry, the Salvadorian Industrial Association, and the Union of Textile Industries are all significant groups. However, their access to decision-makers and their direct involvement in policy formation does not seem as structured or as intertwined with public agencies as that of the dominant groups in the field of export agriculture.

Labor organization is still somewhat incipient although considerable unionization has taken place in the construction and textile industries. Workers in these industries now make up about 40 percent of the membership of the labor union movement. The primary interest organizations in the field of labor are the General Confederation of Syndicates and the new National Workers Association.

Of great importance, because of their demonstrated ability to affect policy and the composition of the regime, are the university student groups. Although many of these are *ad hoc* bodies, some, such as the Law Students Association, have achieved a considerable degree of permanence. In them are often the prominent leaders of opposition to the regime.

The Political Process: An Overview

It is clear that the military leaders of El Salvador have attempted to find a formula for economic and social development that would accommodate the major power factors within the nation. The formal literature of the regime reveals a conscious attempt to find policies that are in the "national interest," that will not endanger the position of any group or interest, but enhance that of each. Yet, given the imperfect articulation and representation of interests in El Salvador, many groups can make their interests precisely known and reinforce them through political processes in only the grossest terms.

At the upper levels, the informal and structured access of the economic elites to decision-makers is well developed. It is here that a political interchange characteristic of open, democratic societies occurs. Here, the ramifications of policy choices are in fact explored, and policy adjustments are made in response to the impact of such policies on well-defined interests. Revisions in the income tax law of 1961 are illustrative. The law was modified after passage to preclude the taxation of legal reserves of corporations or of the undistributed income of financial and insurance companies.

Below this upper level, interest representation is quite imprecise. The regime has few adequate measures of the real nature and intensity of public opinion on various issues. In part, this is due to the lack of significant interest groups among the great bulk of the population. In part, it is because the party system, dominated by an official party and supplemented by fragmented opposition groups which frequently represent no one but their own activist membership, are incapable of requiring that the regime be made accountable to their interests. In part, it is because the lower levels of political involvement in El Salvador give the regime a latitude for decision-making which can be exercised without significant feedback from the groups affected by regime policy. Hence, when opposition to the regime does occur, it frequently takes nonconstitutional forms, which the regime has determined to prevent with the use of armed force.

The regime has itself precluded the establishment of instruments that would enable political leaders to obtain a more accurate reflection of public responses to their policies. Perversion of the electoral test has left the government without the key democratic measure of public attitudes. A legislature constituted entirely of members of the official party is quite dysfunctional as a means of adjusting policy to important interests.

Thus, although the military administrations of El Salvador in the past fifteen years have been generally successful in finding policies which could tie together the gross interests of various sectors of the population, they have done so with small recourse to the tools which would have given them a clearer picture of public opinion, and have hence constantly endangered the stability of the regime through their failure to adequately account for important shifts in attitude among major power factors.

Governmental Institutions

The structure of Salvadorian political institutions today generally follows the pattern established in the Constitution of 1889. This format was revised, once in 1950, primarily to include specific social guarantees, and again in 1960, when the presidential term was reduced from six to five years, and other political reforms were enacted.

The Legislature

In keeping with the dominant Central American pattern, El Salvador has a unicameral legislature, its members elected for two-year terms, which meets in two annual sessions. In addition to normal legislative powers, this body may select the president and vice-president when an election fails to provide any candidate with a majority vote. Although they do not ratify the appointments of cabinet ministers, the legislators have the power to interpellate, i.e., to question a minister and to vote censure if the reply is unsatisfactory.

Under the current regime, the legislature has acted as little more than a rubber stamp for administration policies. Since the mid-1950's, all deputies have been members of the official party. To judge by the author's observation of the deliberations of this body, its debates are on the whole perfunctory. All the votes which he witnessed were unanimous.

This situation seemed likely to change, however, when the legislators elected in 1964 took office, since over a third of them represented opposition parties.

The Presidency

The president of El Salvador must be thirty years of age, not a cleric nor an army officer. (Hence, all recent presidents have formally resigned their military commissions just prior to campaigning for the post.) The president appoints ministers of state, departmental governors, and certain other officials. His actions must be countersigned by the appropriate minister, and these ministers are liable for legislative questioning concering their activities. The president proposes and drafts the national budget. His veto of legislative acts may be overridden by a two-thirds vote, except when questions of constitutionality are involved. He may declare a thirty-day state of siege, suspending basic civil liberties, and may extend it indefinitely, after securing legislative approval when that body is in session.

It is clear that real decision-making authority in contemporary El Salvador is vested in the president and his cabinet. While the president is inevitably a career officer, cabinet membership is predominantly civilian, and is often drawn from the abler members of the professional elites of the nation. Existing ministries include Foreign Affairs, Interior, Education, Public Health and Social Welfare, Defense, Finance, Economy, Public Works, Agriculture, Justice, and Labor and Social Assistance.

The Judiciary

The judiciary is composed of a nine-member supreme court, courts of third, second, and first instance, and at the base, a large number of justices of the peace. The supreme court appoints all justices of the lower courts. All supreme court judges are selected for three-year terms. If reelected twice, they have life tenure until the age of seventy.

Autonomous Institutions

As is true of most Latin American nations, many of the economic functions of government in El Salvador are performed through autonomous institutions or public corporations. These agencies include the Central Reserve Bank, which, nationalized in 1961, was one of the last central banks in Latin America to become a government instrumentality. The Salvadorian Coffee Company, a state trading organization established as a mixed enterprise with joint public and private supervision, was also reorganized in that year, and the appointment of the director of the Central Bank to its board brought it more closely under governmental control than had previously been the case.

Further reorganization in 1961 led to the creation of the Salvadorian Institute of Industrial Development (INSAFI) to replace the Salvadorian Institute of Production Development (INSAFOP) which had been established in the early years of the Osorio government. Also important are the Lempa River Corporation, established on the model of TVA, an Agrarian Credit Bank, the Rural Colonization Institute (ICR), and the Salvadorian Tourist Institute.

Local Government

El Salvador is divided into 14 departments and 39 districts, which are fundamentally administrative units. Departments are presided over by governors appointed by the president, and districts are supervised by local officials of certain dominant communities. Local autonomy does exist at the level of the *municipio*, which is something like the American county, consisting of an urban community and the surrounding rural area which is economically dependent upon it. The town council in each of the 260 *municipios* in El Salvador is elected and consists of an *alcalde* or mayor (the only full-time elected official at this level, who receives a salary consisting of 6½ percent of the taxes collected in the unit); an attorney or *síndico;* and from two to eight *regidores* or aldermen. The *municipios* are subdivided into *cantones* where *comisionados* and *aguaciles* are appointed by the *alcalde* to carry out *municipio* functions in the immediate locality.

Under the national municipal code, each alderman is charged with the supervision of a specific local activity—education, jails, water supply, decorating the town for *fiestas*, etc. In fact, such assignments are usually mere formalities (in one instance an alderman was charged with the public lighting system in a town where there was no public lighting system), and the aldermen generally act corporately as a policy-making board, with specific responsibility for administration vested in the mayor and employees of the community.

In some communities where Indian traditions remain strong a pre-Hispanic form of municipal police force may be found. Here alternating shifts of private citizens, who serve without pay, take turns patrolling the village at night. Where Hispanic influences are prevalent, a paid police force takes over this responsibility. Outside the urban areas, police functions are carried out either by the national army, or by "local commanders" and their staffs, civilians appointed as army officers for set terms who do not wear uniforms, but are charged with rural police functions and the recruitment of young men for the army.

Public Policy

The dominant theme that runs through the moderate and controlled "revolution" that has been under way in El Salvador since 1948, and to which all the specific programs of the regime are in one way or another related, is that of economic development, the effort to increase the nation's productivity, and hence bring about a betterment of the standard of living of its citizens.

Diversification of the Economy

The coffee crisis of the mid-1950's brought a sense of urgency to the persistent Salvadorian desire to free itself from dependence upon the fluctuations of the world coffee market. While consistent efforts have been made to improve and intensify coffee production, and to stabilize world market prices for that crop, the government has sought to find and develop new sources of wealth. Through credit, technical assistance and other measures of encouragement, production of cotton, sugar, corn, and hemp was expanded.

In keeping with the recommendations of a United Nations advisory group, considerable attention was given to industrialization. Legislation favorable to new industry, government credit, and other facilities were provided in this field. The giant hydroelectric power installations of the Lempa River were provided to bring power to the new factories. In many ways, the no-nonsense political policies of the regime were designed to provide stability and guarantee protection for private property so as to encourage wealthy Salvadorians to invest in the industrialization of their nation. The substantial success of this policy may be measured by the fact that value of articles manufactured in El Salvador more than doubled from 1947 to 1957.

Control of Flight Capital

The knottiest problem of Salvadorian development policy has long been that of encouraging the Salvadorian economic elites to invest in the economic progress of the nation. Traditionally, the great families have preferred to place their capital in Europe or the United States. During the Osorio and Lemus administrations, the dominant policy was one of encouraging these potential investors to contribute voluntarily to the development of the nation, with the total policy of the regime structured to reassure them that their property would not be endangered. Since 1960, however, more substantial measures have been taken. Control of foreign exchange received from export sales has been vested in the national bank, and it is available basically only for purchases of foreign products deemed essential to economic development.

The Salvadorian income tax law of 1961 was also designed to assure that the savings of the nation would be put to productive uses. Substantial by Latin American standards, the maximum rates on uninvested capital range from 44 to 76 percent. However, the law provides exemptions to encourage private investment in productive enterprise.

Basic Public Facilities

Throughout the period of the present regime, but particularly during the Osorio administration, attention has been given to the construction of those basic public works which are the responsibility of government the world over. Large-scale highway construction was undertaken, supplementing the already extensive, by Central American standards, network of roads. Public sanitation facilities were extended, and public housing played a major role in the government's program of construction.

Social Reform

Since 1960, increasing attention has been given to the implementation of labor reforms anticipated in the constitutional revision of 1950. The first decade of the present regime was not without its achievements, for it did encourage labor organization, which had been illegal in El Salvador prior to 1945, established a social security system, and to some extent enforced minimum wage and other labor legislation. However, the most controversial reforms have come since the downfall of the Lemus government. Particularly important have been the more effective enforcement of existing laws, and the extension of the labor reform to rural workers, who make up the great bulk of the Salvadorian labor force. Agricultural workers must now be provided with three hot meals a day or a financial equivalent and are guaranteed vacations and maximum working hours, including a paid Sunday holiday. Some large landowners have been vigorous in their opposition to these reforms, threatening migration or cutting back acreage devoted to basic food crops in retaliation, and the government has had difficulty in maintaining its determination to make the reforms effective.

The agrarian labor reforms touch once more upon the ticklish problem of land-ownership patterns in El Salvador. Again, one notes the attempt of the regime to cope with a pressing problem of reform without endangering the position of the dominant elites. Agrarian reform involving the redistribution of existing properties is seldom mentioned in official circles. One evidence of the desire of the regime to avoid involvement in this problem is a recent program to drain a large lake to provide land for resettlement of landless farmers. Given the position of the economic elites in the power structure, the fact that little land is available for colonization, and that the great estates are relatively efficiently exploited and do not contain grotesquely large tracts of unexploited land as in other parts of Latin America, coping with the problem of land ownership and the position of the agricultural worker is indeed a delicate one. Throughout the period since 1948, however, efforts have been made. The Institute of Rural Colonization has established a few "model" communities for rural workers, and efforts have been made to improve standards of living on estates owned by the government. The Rural Credit Bank has attempted to provide the means, on a limited scale, to develop small agricultural properties. Yet the recent labor reforms represent the most dramatic attempt to find a "middle" road between inaction and total reform, and the success or failure of this program is still in the balance.

Central American Integration

Historically, Salvadorians have stood foremost among the champions of Central American unification. El Salvador's economic stake in this program is considerable. Given her overpopulation, it has often seemed that free labor mobility with underpopulated Honduras would be reciprocally advantageous. Furthermore, as the commercial leader of the region, El Salvador is seeking markets for her incipient industries beyond her borders. Already, trade of Salvadorian manufactures with neighboring nations has made up a large part of the increased intra-Central American commerce that has resulted from the newly established common market. San Salvador is also the seat of ODECA, the Organization of Central American States, the political component of the integration efforts, and a Salvadorian was the first secretary-general of this organization.

Conclusions

The recent history of El Salvador provides an interesting case study in the problems of progress in Latin America. In this nation, a program of substantial economic and social reform has been instituted by a government dominated by the military. Here, an effort has been made to formulate an approach to development that would bypass rather than confront head-on the obstacle of a rigid economic and social class system. It is necessary to raise the question of whether the political cost of economic and social achievement has been too high. In all of these respects, it is worthwhile to reflect upon the significance of El Salvador's experience for the problems of the other nations of Latin America. But in drawing such comparisons, one must always bear in mind those features which give a unique distinctiveness to the political life of the smallest of the American republics.

NOTE FOR CHAPTER III

1. Gustavo Magaña Menéndez, *Estudios sociales, políticos y económicos*, Universidad de El Salvador, San Salvador, 1950, p. 102.

SELECTED BIBLIOGRAPHY

Alberto de Mestas, *El Salvador: País de Lagos y Volcanos*, Editorial Cultura Hispánica, Madrid, 1950.
John Martz, *Central America: The Crisis and the Challenge*, University of North Carolina Press, Chapel Hill, 1959.
Dana G. Munro, *The Five Republics of Central America*, Oxford University Press, New York, 1918.
United Nations, Technical Assistance Administration, *Proposals for the Further Economic Development of El Salvador*, United Nations, New York, 1954.
William Vogt, *The Population of El Salvador and Its Natural Resources*, Pan American Union, Washington, 1946.

HONDURAS
Tegucigalpa

HONDURAS

PROBLEMS OF AN APPRENTICE DEMOCRACY

BETWEEN 1948 and 1963, a minor, largely unsung epic of political development and democratic achievement was taking place in the small Central American republic of Honduras. Gradually and fretfully, not without disappointments and difficulties, a series of craftsmanlike politicians were rebuilding the image of a nation whose politics had mostly been reflected in the tales of comic-opera dictatorship contained in O. Henry's *Cabbages and Kings* or the record of the filibusters and banana entrepreneurs of the early part of the twentieth century. A henchman of a dictator, Juan Manuel Gálvez, turned out to be a responsible statesman, and carried out the first honest election in the nation in more than a generation. A military junta took power to resolve an enigmatic constitutional crisis, and quickly restored power to a civilian leader, Ramón Villeda Morales, whom many took to be no more than a radical agitator, but who turned out to be a sound and imaginative administrator and an acutely skillful politician. By the end of Villeda Morales' administration, it appeared to many that Honduras had passed its apprenticeship in democracy, and had established the conditions, however tenuously, for the survival of constitutional process. Those who had followed the process of political transformation in this nation awaited with satisfaction the elections that would replace an elected president with an elected successor for the first time in modern Honduran history. Then, in October 1963, a military coup, carried out only a few weeks before the national elections were to have occurred, interrupted the process of political development that seemed to have been taking place in this land.

It may be that this most recent recurrence of military political intervention makes the accomplishments of fifteen years no more than a wistful tale of what might have been. However, it seems more likely that Honduras' difficulties in maintaining elected civilian government are part of a longer run process of political change, an episode in the rigorous task of overcoming a problematic political heritage. Hence, in discussing the Honduran political system, it is necessary to account both for the factors that led to a measure of democratic practice in this historically tumultuous country and for the setbacks that have marred this pattern of political evolution.

Poverty and underdevelopment are the keynotes of Honduran life. The nation is sometimes described as the Cinderella of Central America, the most impoverished member of the regional family. Ironically, underdevelopment itself may have something to do with the political evolution which the nation seems to be undergoing. Although inequality of income and property is evident, no oligarchy in the accepted sense of the term, grimly determined to maintain its prerogatives in the face of aspirations for social change, may be said to exist. Furthermore, *mestizaje* [racial mixture] is virtually complete in Honduras, and thus racial differences between white and Indian do not reinforce cleavages of class and wealth. Nor has Honduras experienced the growth of industrialization and the dramatic migrations to cities that so many Latin American states have witnessed, resulting in the creation of a dissatisfied and restless urban proletariat, a highly politicized middle class, and a new upper class based on industrial and commercial wealth. Although corruption is a factor which must be considered a part of Honduran political life, the nation's economic structure does not seem to lend itself to the amassment of great fortunes by unscrupulous political leaders. In short, poverty itself, when national in scope and unmixed by grotesque contrast between rich and poor, may in some measure have the effect of softening the political conflicts that are endemic to much of present-day Latin America.

The level of political maturity which the country has achieved must not be overstated. While the deliberations of national leaders in the legislative chamber at Tegucigalpa may be maintained at a certain level of civility, in rural areas the political role of the *cacique* or *pistolero* is still of great importance. Occasional outbursts of irrational hypernationalism and partisan zeal have marred the political record of the past generation, and the major political parties have not entirely renounced the use or threat of violence as a political weapon. Despite evidence of a certain degree of responsibility since World War II, the army remains a factor which must be constantly taken into account by the civilian politician, who endangers military prerogatives at his peril. On the North Coast, as Hondurans refer to their Caribbean lowlands, the three-cornered conflict between foreign agricultural companies, their employees, and the government continues to be an important and occasionally explosive political factor. And, of course, poverty and underdevelopment pose staggering problems and challenges for the performance of government.

Social and Economic Background

The two million Hondurans live scattered among the rugged mountains and valleys of a nation of 43,000 square miles, the most underpopulated of the Central American group, with a density of less than fifty persons per square mile. While all the Central American nations are mountainous, in no other does terrain pose such formidable obstacles to intensive settlement and national integration. The slopes are rocky, comparing unfavorably in their capacity for cultivation with the gentler volcanic mountainsides of other countries. There are fewer and smaller valleys or plateaus which could form the cradle for an integrated community.

Honduras was for many years the banana republic *par excellence*. Yet its national symbol is the pine tree. This simple paradox epitomizes one of the dominant factors in Honduran life—the geographic, cultural, and economic cleavage between the coast and the highlands. The quiet, isolated capital of Tegucigalpa in the mountains seems far away in spirit and interest from the hot, busy city of San Pedro Sula, center of the coastal export agriculture industries. The contrast is in nature and effect not unlike that between Quito and Guayaquil in Ecuador.

Honduras' fame, and her economy, were built on banana cultivation. Throughout much of the twentieth century she was the world's leading producer of that crop, which accounted for the lion's share of her national income. Then, in the early 1950's, Panama and sigatoka diseases joined with the acute storm damage which has been a perpetual cause of loss to the banana industry, and labor unrest, to bring disaster to the industry. The banana companies began to move their operations to more propitious regions.

The decline of banana income was a severe setback to the nation's economy. While work is being done to rehabilitate the industry by changing packing methods and developing disease-resistant strains, efforts have also been made to diversify production. Honduras' second export, coffee, was strengthened, though greatest attention was given to cotton and livestock production. Although bananas remain the principal export, they currently account for no more than about half of export income.

Honduras' economy is and probably long will be primarily agricultural. Some 70 to 80 percent of the population is directly employed in agriculture and about 90 percent of the nation's export income is derived from this source. Such industry as exists is limited to very small-scale consumer's goods factories and operations directly related to export agriculture, such as the manufacture of plastic bags for banana shipment. Except for the smaller operations, most industry is foreign-owned.

Large landholding concentrations do exist in Honduras, many but not all of them representing modern banana, cotton, or livestock operations producing for commercial markets. Nevertheless, Honduras appears to be predominantly a nation of small farming units. According to the agricultural census of 1952, some 78 percent of the properties in the country were under ten hectares in size. It is believed that a large proportion of these small farmers hold no valid title to their lands, living as squatters, planting coffee or subsistence crops on the mountainsides.

Something of the character of the class structure is suggested by the landholding system. Honduras is predominantly a nation of small peasant farmers. Yet this is hardly a Jeffersonian rural yeomanry such as provided the basis for Costa Rica's democratic development. While the Costa Rican smallholder is generally literate, lives in contact with the main stream of his nation's life, and has achieved a moderate standard of living, the average Honduran farmer does not read or write, lives far from adequate transportation and communication facilities, and is condemned to a standard of living not far from total poverty.

The rural smallholder and the employee of the agricultural export company constitute Honduras' working class. The number of industrial laborers is extremely small. The lower and lower-middle classes in the cities are largely dedicated to service occupations and small commerce. The middle class is still rudimentary, composed largely of members of the liberal professions, shopkeepers, and government employees. The landed upper class is by and large wealthy only in Honduran terms, and the fortunes of its members generally do not compare to those of their counterparts in neighboring nations.

A class of new wealth seems to be developing with the expansion of the cotton and livestock industries, however. Politically, the composition of this group is interesting. One sector of it is made up of successful Lebanese and Syrian merchants, who are now investing in agricultural enterprises. For the time being at least, representatives of this group tend to be excluded from political activity, partly by their own choice and partly as a result of the unwelcoming attitudes of the native middle class, from which most political leadership is drawn. A second sector of the new wealthy includes what might be called the political entrepreneurs, persons with political influence who have used their connections to obtain government loans and other services for ventures in commercial agriculture.

Political History

Honduras' tragic political history, dominated by chronic instability and acute civil strife, was in part a result of the nation's central position in the Central American region. Sharing a common border with Guatemala, El Salvador, and Nicaragua, geographic position conspired with political and economic weakness to make Honduras a natural target for the elaboration of the ambitions of political leaders and movements in the rest of Central America.

From the first days of Independence, the battles of Liberal and Conservative chieftains in other nations were often fought out on the soil of Honduras, for the stake of domination of Honduran politics. Imposition of a sympathetic regime in Honduras would be high on the priority list of whichever strong man came to power in Guatemala or Nicaragua during this period.

Although the Washington Conventions of 1907 somewhat reduced international meddling in Honduran politics, the twentieth century has not been free from civil strife, coup and countercoup. None-too-subtle political intervention by foreign business interests and soldiers of fortune complicated the already chaotic internal situation, and contributed to political instability.

In 1923, after a protracted civil war, the Conservatives returned to power, led by Tiburcio Carías. The United States refused to recognize Carías, and a well-qualified civilian, Paz Barahona, assumed formal leadership of the nation. However, the great *caudillo* Carías eventually took over the reins of power definitively in 1932, to begin a regime which lasted sixteen years, prolonged through constitutional manipulation and strong, often dictatorial, suppression of opposition.

In 1948 Carías voluntarily relinquished his position as president of Honduras. His handpicked candidate, Juan Manuel Gálvez, succeeded him. When the quite honest election of 1954 produced no decision with regard to the presidency (the constitution required the victor to have a clear majority) the vice-president, Júlio Lozano Díaz, was empowered to assume that office. In 1957 Lozano was overthrown in a military coup. One year later, the governing junta held elections for a constitutional assembly which elected Liberal Ramón Villeda Morales president for a full constitutional term. The history of this latter period will be dealt with in greater detail in the following section.

The Political Process

The political evolution of Honduras since World War II can only be explained in terms of the total composite performance of the various components of the political system, the competition of parties, the role of the army, the character of interest representation, set against the background of the total economic and social structure of the nation. Of peculiar importance, however, has been the contribution of specific individuals. Much of the character of political change can best be appreciated through an examination of the leadership styles of these statesmen in relation to the institutions and forces which they represented.

The Conservative Contribution: Juan Manuel Gálvez

The National Party today represents the Conservative heritage in Honduras' historic two-party dichotomy. Until 1948 this party was the personalist instrument of "the last *caudillo*," Tiburcio Carías. In an uncontested election, through the party which he controlled, Carías brought to power his minister of war, Juan Manuel Gálvez.

Many were prepared to view Gálvez's administration as a continuation of Carías' rule. However, Gálvez was capable of slackening the tight control which Carías had exercised, while preventing the outbreak of the unrest and revolt that so often followed in the wake of *caudillo* governments in the late 1940's. A genuinely popular leader, he seemed sincerely interested in promoting the growth of democracy within the nation, as well as contributing to Honduras' economic progress.

A self-styled "president in shirt sleeves," the public image Gálvez created was somewhat Lincolnesque. Tall and not handsome, he appeared simple, sincere, and lacking in ostentation. Politically, Gálvez's approach was to govern Honduras as an "honest broker," disinterested and uncommitted. His government contained representatives of all political factions. Although he was the candidate of the National Party, historic descendant of the Conservatives, Gálvez was to say of this alliance: "How can there be Conservatives in a land where practically everything remains to be done? Conservers of what? Of ignorance, of backwardness?" [1] Gálvez claimed that, like all sincere Hondurans, he was a liberal by conviction.

Also revealing was the attitude of the opposition press toward the administration. Without abrogating the right of criticism, the Liberal press, in an unusual gesture (given the virulent style of Honduran journalism) seemed willing to recognize the accomplishments of Gálvez, and concentrated their fire on Carías, who continued to be a strong political force.

> . . . we have said, without slighting the truth, that Gálvez has done more in four and a half years than Carías accomplished in sixteen years of implacable and fierce dictatorship. In politics, you cannot compare the governments of Carías and Gálvez. . . . The former was a dictator in the fullest sense of the term. . . . Gálvez, in contrast, has been tolerant, at least in the past few years; no one is jailed for his party convictions; citizens meet to deliberate political matters and hold party rallies. . . .[2]

In 1954, at the close of his term, Gálvez chose to retire from politics, specifying that his successor be chosen in an open election. Although a substantial faction had developed which sought to persuade Gálvez to succeed himself, bypassing the constitutional prohibition on reelection as Carías had done so many times, Gálvez rejected this opportunity.

The Military Contribution: The *Junta* of 1957

As in many Latin American nations, the army in Honduras plays a prominent political role. Yet, between 1948 and 1963, the Honduran military seemed quite responsible in the exercise of its power. The ability of first Gálvez and later Villeda Morales to maintain themselves in power, to govern within a moderately democratic context, and to deal firmly with threats of irresponsible use of violence was largely due to the support which each received from the military.

The one instance of direct military intervention in the political affairs of the nation during this period was perhaps more a demonstration of this responsibility than its reverse. When Julio Lozano Díaz came to power after the indecisive election of 1954, first reactions to his administration were favorable, if not enthusiastic. However, within a year, his acceptance wore thin. Lozano was taken to task for failing to restore constitutional government. The elections he held in 1956 to select a constituent assembly were blatantly dishonest. Lozano began to deal harshly with opposition leaders. The jails filled with political prisoners and many opposition leaders were forced into exile. Whether through poor counsel or the operation of Lord Acton's dictum, Lozano had become a tyrant. On October 21, 1956, a successful barracks revolt led by a cadre of junior officers forced Lozano from power without a shot being fired. The three-man military junta appointed by the army served for one year as a caretaker government, called free elections for a constitutional convention, and retired from political activity. Although the military remains a potent force in Honduran politics, and politicians tread lightly when dealing with its prerogatives, the political power of the military would seem to have been used, during those fifteen years, primarily to enhance rather than jeopardize the political development of the nation.

The Liberal Contribution: Ramón Villeda Morales

The constitutional convention of 1957 selected the leader of the Liberal Party, a Tegucigalpa obstetrician, as president of Honduras for a full constitutional term. Villeda Morales is a vigorous proponent of the position of the "democratic left" in Latin America. He is a close associate of José Figueres of Costa Rica and Haya de la Torre of Peru. In the style of these leaders, rather than of Gálvez's nonpartisan approach to government, he is an ardent advocate of the modern, well-organized political party as the prime instrument of democratic government. As such, he has worked to reconstruct the Liberal Party, both ideologically and organizationally, into a more potent political force. Preaching the democratic left's ideology of social revolution through institutional transformation rather than violent upheaval, he vigorously prosecuted Honduras' economic and social development through the use of governmental institutions. Yet his speeches were often more radical than his actions, and he was cautious and responsible in many vital areas of public policy, particularly in the always sensitive arena of fiscal and monetary affairs. In the face of threats of insurrection and violence which occurred sporadically throughout his administration, he pursued a rather skillful policy of firm action against the immediate threat without resorting to the suspensions of civil liberties and declarations of states of emergency which are so conventional in Latin America in dealing with challenges of this type.

Interruption of the Process of Maturation: The Coup of 1963

Only a few weeks before the scheduled presidential elections of 1963, a group of military officers, led by Colonel Osvaldo López Arellano, unseated the Villeda Morales government and erased hopes that Honduras would carry out its first fully regular, constitutional presidential succession in modern history. The precise motivation for the coup remains somewhat unclear. The officers themselves justified their action as a response to "Communist plots," and claimed to have discovered substantial quantities of Communist propaganda and plans (some of them, they stated, written in Chinese!). Most observers doubted that the threat of revolutionary activity was as great as claimed, if it existed at all. Other possible motivations for the coup include the heightening of political tension and political activity in the electoral campaign period, much of which would have appeared radical or stability-threatening from the military point of view; conservative uneasiness about the reformist zeal of some leaders of the Villeda Morales government; threats to the perquisites of the military establishment; personal ambition on the part of the officers.

Within two months of taking power, the new military junta convened a constituent assembly and pledged to turn power over to an elected successor to this body in early 1965. Thus, the military leaders sought to present themselves as acting in the tradition of the "caretaker" government of 1957. It may be that the greatest test of the democratic momentum created in Honduras between 1948 and 1963 will be in the capacity of those committed to civilian government to hold the military to this pledge. Yet the essential meaning of the coup of 1963 is clear. Democratic progress in Honduras is contingent on military support, and the military retains the capacity to determine the conditions and uses of political power.

Political Parties

The dominant change in the historic two-party system of Honduras since World War II has been the restructuring of the Liberal Party under Villeda Morales' leadership. Although parties continue to be relatively weak mechanisms in Honduras, the Liberal Party has to a considerable extent become an improved vehicle for modern, democratic campaigning, and its ideological orientation has consciously been redirected toward social welfare principles, in place of its historical advocacy of classical liberalism. Such a reorientation was not carried out without a good deal of internal strain and friction within the party's ranks, which Villeda Morales, proving to be a cannier politican than initially expected, seems largely to have overcome.

Such developments within the Liberal Party seem to have had but a faint response in the Nationalist ranks. The Nationalist Party appeared listless during the Villeda Morales administration, its efforts too often turned toward sporadic and uncoordinated violence, which presented more of a nuisance than an immediate threat to the stability of the Liberal administration.

Although partisan activity in Honduras continues to be based largely on the two-party system, a third faction did develop some degree of importance during the 1950's. This movement was based initially on support for the re-election of Gálvez in 1954. When the personalist hero of the movement refused to ride roughshod over the constitutional provisions prohibiting re-election, the movement found itself with organization and support, but without a candidate. Hastily constituting itself as the Movimiento Nacional Reformista (MNR), and nominating Abraham Williams, vice-president under Carías, as its candidate, it made a respectable showing in the 1954 elections and was represented in the constitutional convention of 1957. Since that time, most of its support has been absorbed by the other parties, and the MNR today maintains only a tenuous existence.

The Electoral System

Democratic evolution in Honduras has taken place in spite of the unsuccessful operation of the machinery for providing peaceful government succession. The election of 1948 was boycotted by the Liberals who were convinced that it would be no more than a sham to legitimate the selection of Carías' hand-picked successor. Gálvez's success overcame these fears, and the elections of 1954 were honest and enthusiastically contested. Unfortunately, the three-cornered race between the Liberals, Nationalists, and MNR produced no absolute majority for any candidate, as required by a constitution based on the premise of a two-party system, and Julio Lozano was empowered to continue an interim government, since the constitution provided no other remedy.

The results of the 1954 Presidential balloting (in round numbers) were:

Liberals, Villeda Morales: 121,000;
Nationalists, Carías: 78,000;
MNR, Williams: 53,000.

The results of the constitutional convention election held by Lozano in 1956 give striking evidence, when compared to 1954 and 1957 returns, that the rule of this president was not wholeheartedly democratic, to say the least. The announced vote for Lozano's "Government Coalition" was 370,318, for the Liberals, 41,724, and for the Nationalists, 2,003!

The eventual selection of a constitutional convention took place under the auspices of the military junta in 1957. The Liberals won 36 seats, the Nationalists 18, and the MNR 4. This convention established itself as an assembly for presidential election and picked Villeda Morales to fill a full constitutional term, arguing that the people had twice shown their preference for this candidate and that a new election would be costly to administer and only serve to stir up national passions.

One must conclude that Honduras has not experienced a governmental transition through actual constitutional processes with the full competition of the active political forces of the nation since before the Carías era. Honduras' period of achievement of a modicum of political stability and civilian control can thus not be attributed to the effective implementation of an established electoral process.

Interest Groups

Organized interest representation in Honduras is extremely weak. While large-scale agriculture and, to a lesser extent, commerce have some limited forms of organized access to decision-makers, the bulk of the population is virtually untouched by such arrangements. Labor unions only exist in any force in the banana areas, where 70 percent of organized labor is concentrated. Although unions have been quite effective in pressing their claims both upon the companies and the government, they represent an infinitesimal part of the labor force, covering under 10,000 employees. Often in the early 1950's, and to some extent up to the present, they have served as vehicles for radical agitation and organization.

The fruit companies themselves have chosen to play a more enlightened political role than in former years, and although their influence is still felt in public affairs, a natural concomitant of their power in the economy, they are in no way the dominant factor that they were in the early part of the twentieth century. Although the fruit companies were vigorously critical of the agrarian reform program of the Villeda Morales government, their influence was diluted by the official policy of the United States during the Kennedy administration, which supported land reform efforts as an essential component of the Alliance for Progress.

University student groups have occasionally acted with impact in the political arena, and they were influential in the overthrow of the Lozano government in 1956. The Catholic Church and its affiliated organizations have yet to play a really aggressive role in contemporary political life.

Middle-Class Politics in a Non-Middle-Class Nation

Government in Honduras during the fifteen years of democratic evolution was largely the preserve of the small, urban middle class. Leaders such as Gálvez and Villeda Morales, reflecting middle-class backgrounds and political styles, reinforced the system through their skills. However, such power as the middle class wielded was always contingent on the support of other power factors, predominantly the military. The troubled course of political change in Honduras reflects the tension between the two. Each can exercise power only within limits set by the other, only by taking the other into account. As civilian governments must not overstep the bounds permitted by the military, so the military in power must assume the role of interim caretaker government, constantly under pressure to restore constitutional procedures.

The Structure of Government

The constitution of 1957 strongly reflects, in its social guarantees, the ideas of the Villeda Morales-led Liberal Party which controlled the convention of that year. However, in the structure of government which it provides, it departs but little from the Honduran tradition. Indeed, the formal structure of government resembles that of other Latin American states in providing for a strong president and a separation of powers.

The president is elected for a six-year term, along with three *designados*, who have no function other than to succeed to the presidency, in the sequence designated, should the office become vacant. The president may not succeed himself or be elected *designado* for the succeeding term, clearly a device to prevent legal *continuismo*. He heads a cabinet of between nine and twelve members.

The members of the single-chamber legislature are likewise elected for a six-year term and prohibited immediate reelection. They are elected in the eighteen departments, which may thus be single-member or multi-member constituencies, depending on their population. Each department has at least one deputy to represent it; deputies must be residents of the departments they represent.

The judicial structure is highly centralized, with most lower judicial and quasi-judicial offices being filled by appointment of the five members of the supreme court themselves. The autonomy of the judiciary is palpably nominal only, however; not only are the supreme court justices elected by the national legislature, but they are given a six-year term which coincides to the day with that of the president.

What these constitutional arrangements boil down to, in effect, is that normally, when a party captures the presidency, the wave of sentiment on which it rode to victory will at the same time bring it control of the legislature, control of the judiciary following in turn. Strong government is thereby virtually guaranteed. Whether or not it will also be responsible government depends on factors not entailed in the formal constitutional structure.

Although control of departmental administration is in the hands of the ministry of the interior, the municipalities elect their own officials locally.

Honduras' principal decentralized institutions are the National Bank and the Development Bank, both established in 1950. The National Bank has come to play a respected role in the nation's economic life, owing in large part to the cautious but skillful policies of its directors. The Development Bank, while serving a number of useful functions, has often been criticized for the extravagance of its expenditures, most conspicuously its skyscraper offices in Comayagüela, and for the political overtones attached to some of its lending activities. In 1961-62 a social security institute began operation, and an autonomous agrarian reform institute was created.

Public Policy

Economic Policy

The very underdevelopment of a country like Honduras delimits its policy alternatives. In Honduras, economic and social advance must begin with such basic projects as the construction of roads and schools. Only when higher levels of development have been achieved may more sophisticated projects be successfully undertaken.

Thus, although the interest in social reform of the Villeda Morales administration was expressed in the consideration and enactment of advanced labor legislation, agrarian reform programs, and other social welfare measures, the impact of such policies was most limited. What government actually did in concrete terms was for the most part ideologically noncontroversial, and progress and reform came in fact to mean largely the more effective provision of the conventional services of the state. Roads and schools were built; public health advanced. The most important project of recent years was the initiation of construction of a large hydroelectric plant on the Río Lindo, financed through a $13,500,000 loan from a French consortium.

However, in countries like Honduras, governments are more apt to be judged by their ideological tone than their policy achievements, and it seems probable that the overthrow of the Villeda Morales government was not unrelated to its reformist aspirations and those of its likely successor, however limited in potential application these may have been.

The factor of foreign support, either through loans or aid, is of greater importance in determining the direction of development policy in relatively small, poor nations like Honduras than in stronger countries. Foreign support is often necessary for projects to be undertaken at all, and it seems clear that most of the development work pursued in recent years was in areas where foreign assistance or financing were available. Thus the Honduran portion of the Pan America Highway was financed totally by United States loans and grants, and World Bank loans account for much of the remainder of Honduran road construction. Such United States-Honduran technical assistance *servicios* as STICA in agriculture, CISP in health, and CIDE in education have accounted for many of the programs undertaken in these fields.

For similar reasons, it seems at present that Honduras will be more influenced by and responsive to the programs of the Alliance for Progress than many other Latin American nations. Already she is well along on her national development plan and has begun to implement an agrarian reform program, as anticipated by the Alliance design. She has submitted project proposals ranging from agrarian colonization, public housing, and port and road construction, to the introduction of a central water supply authority and an educational radio plan.

The land reform law which the congress passed and the president signed in September of 1962 contained many interesting features, among them the provision that the recipients of land distributed under the program (all peasants over sixteen years of age were eligible) would not own the land outright, but rather would receive rights of use, in a form comparable to that of the Mexican *ejido*. Cooperative farming by groups of peasants was encouraged. Landowners (including North American banana growers) complained of the lack of provision for judicial review of expropriations under the law, and of other of its features. President Villeda Morales promised to amend the law to introduce such procedures and also undertook that land expropriated would be compensated for in cash; skeptics commented that this meant that little land would be expropriated, since the treasury never had cash to spare. It remained an open question, therefore, as to how extensive a land reform would actually take place in Honduras.

Foreign Policy

As the central pivot in the Central American chain of nations, Honduras has always been greatly affected by politics in neighboring countries, and has long seemed the key to efforts at regional unification, whether attempted by force or negotiation. In recent years, Honduras has enthusiastically supported Central American economic integration, though with some misgivings about her ability to compete with nations with a greater industrial potential, such as El Salvador and Guatemala. Nonetheless, she looks forward to developing her foodstuff production to supply an expanded Central American market with basic agricultural commodities.

Intra-Central American relations have been much improved by the peaceful acceptance by both Honduras and Nicaragua of the International Court of Justice's recent ruling on a boundary dispute between the two nations. The area in controversy, Gracias a Dios, is a virtually uninhabited tropical rain forest region along the Caribbean coast. For years little valued by either nation, the possibility of petroleum resources awakened interest in its ownership. After years of vehement and at times violent disputation, the two nations agreed to submit the issue to the Hague Court, which eventually ruled in favor of Honduras' claim.

Honduras' relations with the United States have always been complicated by the issue of the banana industry. While nationalistic virulence, historically in many ways justified, has long been a factor no politician could afford to overlook, Honduras has also long been dependent upon the United States for economic survival. All recent presidents have been quite friendly to the United States, and Villeda Morales has been ardent as a champion of inter-American cooperation in such programs as the Alliance for Progress.

We have chosen to characterize Honduras as an "apprentice democracy." Certainly, the period of apprenticeship has been perplexing, painful, and not without reverses. Clearly, the process of political development has not led to the establishment of operative constitutional norms of election, succession, and the lawful competition for power. Rather, Honduras has proceeded by makeshift expedients, from one constituent assembly to the next, interspersed with difficult constitutional crises and military interventions. Yet the Honduras of the present is not the Honduras of 1948. New political expectations have been established. A new generation of civilian leaders has emerged who seek to exercise the skills of democratic politics, and has acquired some experience in the management of a perplexing and frustrating political order. Although the military coup of 1963 may represent a more or less long-lasting setback, it is perhaps unlikely that the aspirations established or the experience gained can be completely erased, or that Honduras need begin again quite from the beginning.

NOTES FOR CHAPTER IV

1. *La Epoca* (Tegucigalpa), Sep. 3, 1951.
2. *El Pueblo* (Tegucigalpa), Nov. 23, 1953.

SELECTED BIBLIOGRAPHY

John D. Martz, *Central America: The Crisis and the Challenge,* University of North Carolina Press, Chapel Hill, 1959.

William S. Stokes, *Honduras: An Area Study in Government,* University of Wisconsin Press, Madison, 1950.

Richard D. Adams, *Cultural Surveys of Panama, Nicaragua, Guatemala, El Salvador, Honduras,* Scientific Publication No. 33, Pan American Sanitary Bureau, Washington, D.C., 1957.

V   *Charles W. Anderson*

NICARAGUA

THE SOMOZA DYNASTY

In 1937 Anastasio "Tacho" Somoza came to power in Nicaragua, For the
next nineteen years he ruled this nation in the classic manner of the Latin
American *caudillo* or strong man. Upon his assassination in 1956, his son
Luis Somoza Debayle succeeded to his place as president. Without rejecting
his father's heritage, Luis Somoza proclaimed his desire to move Nicaragua
toward a more modern and democratic political system. In February 1963
Somoza presided over elections which selected a successor, René Schick
Gutiérrez, not a member of the family, although closely associated with it.
Although Schick has made a few tentative, probing gestures toward reducing the predominance of the Somoza family in the system, there is little
indication that the Somozas are about to withdraw from the politics of the
nation they have dominated for over a quarter of a century. Luis Somoza
continues to be influential in public affairs, and Anastasio Somoza, Jr.,
"Tachito," the second son of the dictator, remains head of the National
Guard.

In studying the Nicaraguan political system, we will be seeking to understand the style and technique of the *caudillo* and thus to gain insight into a
political phenomenon which is very much a part of the political legacy of
Latin America. We will also be concerned with the problem of political
change, with the question of how a bridge can be built between strong-man
rule and a political system more appropriate to the needs of a developing
society. And perhaps most important, we will be searching for the roots
of *caudillo* rule, for the factors in the Nicaraguan political culture that account for the emergence and persistence of this type of personal authority.
For "Tacho" Somoza was among the last of the old-time strong men. He
survived the winds of revolution which brought the downfall of his col-
leagues Ubico in Guatemala, Carías in Honduras, and Hernández in El Salvador and lived to call Nicaragua the Wall of China in Central America—the
last bastion of order and stability in an upset and turbulent region. Nicaragua's political distinctiveness lies in the survival of the archaic political system represented by the Somozas, and it is the basis of this distinctiveness that
we must explore.

Economic and Social Background

Nicaragua is the largest of the Central American republics, a nation about the size of the state of Wisconsin. Of its population of 1,394,000 perhaps 30 percent are literate, and only a small fraction of those who can read and write have had the opportunity to learn to cope with the operation of the modern political and economic institutions of the nation. It is necessary to see Nicaragua's involvement in the twentieth-century world in this perspective. That middle and upper class which edits the newspapers, manages the businesses, conducts the diplomacy, and practices skilled trades and technical professions in Nicaragua is more to the scale of a small American city than of a modern nation-state.

The differences in wealth and status between this thin veneer at the top and the rest of the nation are clear-cut. The as yet small and incipient middle class is much more closely identified with the economic and social elite than with the rural small farmer and the urban lower class. As in many other Latin American nations, wealth in Nicaragua tends to concentrate at the very top of the socio-economic pyramid. While the per capita income of the nation is $150-$200 per year, 1 percent of the population receives about 25 percent of the national income, with the concentration of wealth at the upper end of that 1 percent.

Nicaragua's economic elite bears many resemblances to the landholding upper classes of other Latin American nations. Yet many of the generalizations made about this group do not apply in Nicaragua. It is not a homogeneous oligarchy like the "fourteen families" of El Salvador or the "forty families" of Peru. Factional conflict has long prevented the upper class from acting as a unified force in defense of its interests or as a countervailing force against *caudillo* rule. In background and outlook it is somewhat more diversified than similar groups in other nations. There are, of course, the old families of Spanish extraction, whose names recur in the social and political annals of Nicaraguan history. But in the coffee-growing highlands, the most prominent families have been of English, North American, or German descent. Finally, there is a group that might be called the new rich, whose wealth and influence has derived from their close identification with the Somoza regime. The Somoza family itself has come to occupy the very top place on the economic pyramid, and some would describe Nicaragua as little more than the Somozas' hacienda. To this subject we will return.

The fragmentation of the economic elite is symptomatic of a more general problem of Nicaraguan nationhood. This country has never been able to develop a real sense of national community. Unlike Costa Rica, where a great part of the population settled within the small confines of the *meseta central*, developing over generations of close contact and interaction unique traditions and a sense of their own distinctiveness, Nicaragua established a number of population clusters, separated by geography, economic and social interest, and local tradition, in some instances embellished by fierce enmity toward other communities in the same nation. To use James Busey's well-chosen distinction, Costa Rica developed as an *integrated* nation, Nicaragua as a *disintegrated* one.[1]

Economically, Nicaragua is an underdeveloped nation in the strict meaning of the term, for it does possess substantial natural resources which have not yet been put to use. Probably less than a quarter of the land is used in any way, and the nation's population density of twenty-one persons per square mile is less than that of any other Central American state. The country has a variety of resources and climates. The International Bank, in a survey of the nation's development potential in the early 1950's, reported that "few underdeveloped countries have so great a physical potential for growth and economic development as does Nicaragua."[2]

Yet, historically, Nicaragua has been a nation distinguished for its poverty. Even in the colonial period, when nations such as Peru and Guatemala were centers of wealth and prosperity, Nicaragua was a backwater of the Spanish Empire. Of the economic history of his nation, one Nicaraguan scholar has written:

> By the middle of the sixteenth century, some colonies had agricultural riches; but in Nicaragua, there were but the poor cereals of the Indians and tobacco planted for the account of the Crown. . . . Thus we entered the nineteenth century, we arrived at the dawn of our emancipation, speaking Spanish poorly, our heads filled with metaphysical and theological questions, but for the rest, as poor and backward as when Nicarao received Gil González.[3]

Paradoxically, Nicaragua's historic weakness has been something of a blessing in disguise in terms of her recent economic development. Only peripherally affected by the great commodity booms in coffee and bananas of the late nineteenth and early twentieth century, she presently possesses a greater diversity of production and a smaller degree of dependence on a single export product than any of her neighbors. In recent years, cotton, which became a major Nicaraguan product only after World War II, has been more important than coffee as a source of export earnings. Gold is the third most important product in foreign trade, and the newly developing livestock industry is beginning to search for foreign markets.

Political History

Throughout her century and a half of independent existence, Nicaragua has been afflicted by chronic instability and civil strife, the domestic quarrels of political factions complicated by recurrent foreign intervention, for it was the unfortunate fate of Nicaragua to be located on one of the more promising sites for an interoceanic canal. Her political history may be described as one of virtual chaos punctuated sporadically by harsh dictatorship or by foreign supervision of her domestic affairs.

At the core of the political turmoil which has characterized Nicaragua is the chronic struggle between the Liberal and Conservative parties, which has persisted from the first years of independence up to the present day. While this partisan conflict was manifest in the early political tumult of all of the Central American nations, in Nicaragua the cleavage was accentuated by the addition of local jealousy to factional identification. Throughout Nicaraguan history, the Conservative cause has been championed by the leading families of Granada and the Liberal party has found its center in the upper class of León.

Many commentators insist that the ideological differences between these two camps were insignificant, and that only the rivalry of two groups for supremacy was really in point. The matter is not that easily resolved, for the real differences in attitude and outlook between the two cities have been deep and abiding. The great families of Granada, the Chamorros, Lacayos, Cuadras and the rest, have always considered themselves to be something of a creole aristocracy, steeped in Hispanic culture and respectful of their traditions. The attitude of the elite of León, on the other hand, has historically been more entrepreneurial and commercial in nature. Even the physical appearance of the two towns today betrays significant differences. Granada remains a quiet city of colonial architecture while León is a thriving commercial center. The classic ideological distinctions between the Latin American Conservatives, who supported the traditions of Catholic, monarchical Spain, and the Liberals, more prone to accept the philosophic implications of the French and American revolutions, are not without significance even in present-day Nicaragua.

In the period following independence, the fortunes of the two factions in Nicaragua reflected the course of the larger struggle that was going on throughout Central America. When Francisco Morazán, the great Liberal chieftain, was at the head of the Central American Federation, the Liberals were in the ascendancy in Nicaragua. With his downfall and the collapse of Liberal governments in other republics, the Conservatives came to power in Nicaragua, supported by coreligionists from Honduras and El Salvador.

During this period, the involvement of Nicaragua in the larger international struggle for influence in Central America began. In the colonial period, England had established an outpost of her empire along the Atlantic Coast. In the 1700's, she had devised the "Mosquito Kingdom" as her instrument of government in the eastern lowlands, headed by Indians or Negroes bearing such improbable names as Oldman, George Frederick, and Jeremy, who were completely subservient to the British. Despite repeated protests by the Central American states concerning the British presence, and pleas to the United States for protection under the Monroe Doctrine, the British remained intransigent. This remained the situation until the discovery of gold in California brought United States involvement in the development of transisthmian transportation routes, and hence an interest in the affairs of the region. By the 1840's, British interests in the area were in direct conflict with

Commodore Vanderbilt's newly established Accessory Transit Company, which provided gold seekers with a boat-omnibus route across the lower part of Nicaragua. While the Clayton-Bulwer Treaty pledged the United States and Great Britain to undertake any interoceanic canal as a joint venture, overt conflict between the two powers with the tangential involvement of Nicaragua continued for many years thereafter.

The two themes of foreign intervention and factional strife that have run throughout Nicaragua's history were first fused in the fabulous adventure of William Walker. This American lawyer, doctor, journalist, and vigorous exponent of Manifest Destiny had turned soldier of fortune in the early 1850's, and established a short-lived independent republic in Lower California and Sonora. In 1855 the Nicaraguan Liberals, then on the short end of their perpetual conflict with their rivals in Granada, called upon Walker and his vagabond band to help them turn the tide. The filibuster landed with a force of fifty-seven men soon after, ostensibly to aid the Liberal cause, in reality to take over the country for himself. He seized one of Commodore Vanderbilt's lake steamers, captured Granada, and became first general of the Nicaraguan army and later president of the nation. Many powerful groups in the United States supported Walker's activities; some saw in him a means of redressing the balance of power with the British in the region, and some Southerners hoped that through his activities Nicaragua might be added to the Union as a new slave state. At the same time, a struggle for control of the Accessory Transit Company was under way between Vanderbilt and his agents, Morgan and Garrison. The latter supplied Walker with arms and recruits, in return for which favors, Walker, as president of Nicaragua, revoked Vanderbilt's concession and granted it to them. Vanderbilt, in turn, gave his financial support to the armies of the other Central American states who had risen in arms against the foreign intruder, and with such support and British encouragement, Walker was finally defeated. While most Americans have forgotten the name of William Walker, his defeat can still stir the pride of patriotic Central Americans. It is memorialized in great monuments and frequently serves as a rallying cry in political discourse.

The Walker episode seems to have had a chastening effect on Nicaraguan politics, and for the next thirty years, under a succession of responsible Conservative presidents, the nation achieved a modicum of internal tranquillity and order. However, the respite was short-lived. In 1893 the tyrannical José Santos Zelaya came to power. For sixteen years he ruled the nation through brutality and torture, hounding his Conservative opponents and unscrupulously enriching himself and his friends. Yet during this period internal improvements were made, schools were built, and Nicaragua experienced a period of great economic prosperity.

What followed should be carefully considered by North Americans who would have the United States intervene to end undemocratic governments in Latin America. By 1909 Zelaya was despised at home and abroad. He had sought to foment revolutions in other Central American nations, thus endangering the stability of the region, a factor now of importance to a United States engaged in canal diplomacy. Furthermore, Zelaya brutally assassinated two American soldiers of fortune. An insurrection began in Nicaragua. Secretary of State Knox identified himself with the revolutionaries. Soon Zelaya fled the country, leaving Nicaragua in a state of near-anarchy, deeply in debt to international creditors.

In view of the role of the United States in destroying Zelaya, it became the responsibility of that nation to assist the new Conservative government in getting Nicaragua back on its feet. Furthermore, the clamorings of European investors for action on their defaulted Nicaraguan loans brought with it the implicit threat of intervention, which the United States, its policy based on the concepts of the Monroe Doctrine, was determined to resist.

At the request of the new Nicaraguan government, the United States sent Thomas Dawson, who had just completed a similar mission in the Dominican Republic, to arrange for an agreement between the rival factions and to take over the collection of customs, apportioning the proceeds between the needs of the government and the claims of foreign creditors. Further, the United States government sought to send financial aid to the bankrupt nation. Failing senatorial appropriation of the necessary funds, the United States government *requested* that a group of New York banks provide a loan to the nation, to be secured through the controlled customs receipts as well as by control of the Nicaraguan national bank and railroad. Thus, as a logical part of the sequence of events that followed from the action of the United States in aiding the overthrow of Zelaya, Nicaragua became a ward, for all practical purposes, not only of the American government, but of a group of private banking interests as well.

In 1912, inevitably, the Liberals revolted. Their rallying cry was "Down with American imperialism"—an "imperialism" of course, that was keeping their historic rivals in office. As violence swept the country, the American minister called upon the Conservative government to protect United States lives and property. The government replied that it needed all its forces to put down the rebellion and requested that "the United States guarantee with its forces security for the property of American citizens in Nicaragua and that it extend its protection to all the inhabitants of the Republic." By September, 2,700 United States marines were in Nicaragua, the revolt had been quelled and order restored.

From 1912 until 1933, with the exception of a short period in 1926-27, the "American presence," usually consisting of a legation guard of no more than one hundred marines (under the circumstances a considerable force) maintained order in Nicaragua. Under United States supervision, remarkably honest elections were held in 1928 and 1932, and Liberal presidents were elected. In 1933 Nicaraguans were once more the masters of their own house, and the administration of President Juan B. Sacasa was proving moderately competent. Yet the legacy of American intervention was not yet spent. In 1936 the head of the National Guard took power in a military coup and proclaimed himself president of Nicaragua. That American-appointed commandant of the American-trained police force was none other than Anastasio Somoza.

It is not an easy task to assess the significance of American intervention in Nicaragua. It is so easy to condemn wholeheartedly or to justify righteously. Yet the actions of the United States were complex and its motives many. Dollar diplomacy, connoting investment by powerful economic groups and belief in the manifest destiny of a nation beginning to feel its weight in the world, of course, played a part. Yet throughout the American record in Nicaragua there runs a theme of efforts to bring social and economic progress and democratic government to a troubled land. One wonders whether the spirit of that era was really so different from our own, when the symbol of "development" has mobilized the enthusiasms of so many Americans. And since American intervention in Nicaragua is so often pointed to by critics of the United States around the world, one is led to wonder to what extent the United States was the exploiter and to what extent the victim of a political and social system which we even now only vaguely understand.

In any event, by 1936 Anastasio Somoza was firmly in control of Nicaragua's destiny and continued so until his assassination in 1956. In 1937 he legitimized his rule in an election which was probably no more dishonest than most that have occurred in Nicaraguan history. Through constitutional manipulation, this provided him with a term which lasted until 1946. In that year he turned over power to Leonardo Argüello. Argüello proved surprisingly independent, and after a dispute over the composition of the National Guard, he ordered Somoza to leave the country. Somoza took charge, deposed Argüello, and placed his uncle, Víctor Remón y Reyes, in the presidency. The latter died in 1950; Somoza, selected by the congress, finished out the term, and was then elected for a six-year period. He was assassinated while campaigning for reelection in 1956 at a political rally in León.

His son, Luis, assumed the presidential candidacy of the Liberal Party and was duly elected. During his term in office, he advocated progress toward a more liberal political order and a quickening of the pace of economic and social development, insisting that this is what his father had had in mind all along. He continually reiterated his desire to withdraw his family from political dominance after the elections of 1963.

The Political Process

The Political Culture

To understand the political process of Nicaragua, it is necessary to appreciate the underlying givens or constants which produced in Nicaragua a soil propitious for the emergence of a leader such as Anastasio Somoza and which continue to condition efforts to transform his legacy into a more open and liberal political system.

Fundamental to the political heritage of Nicaragua has been the unending strife between the Liberal and Conservative factions, reinforced by localism and tending toward a perception of politics by the activist in which the interest of the nation as a whole or adherence to mutually recognized rules of the political game must be subordinated to the prospective total dominance of one's own group and the complete degradation of one's rivals. That potential middle sector which has emerged in some nations to champion the cause of constitutionalism and democratic process has in Nicaragua historically been absorbed in partisan strife. That potential civil oligarchy which in some nations found domestic tranquillity to be more in the interest of its favored place in the social order than chronic instability and which served to provide the basis for orderly, albeit not democratic government, has in Nicaragua long given leadership to the rival causes. That potential military elite which in some nations has provided national unity at the price of political suppression has in Nicaragua traditionally served the interests of the warring clans. Hence, when national exhaustion and disintegration has become apparent even to the embattled adversaries, there has seldom been a feasible remedy other than that of a foreign armed force or the strong man who, mobilizing power in the name of his personal authority and legitimizing that authority by his ability to use power to prevent his own downfall, has been capable of restoring peace to the nation. There is in Nicaraguan history virtually no model, no "golden age" to the memory of which an enlightened statesman could appeal as a basis for the reconciliation of the warring factions.

Related to this history of factional strife, as a further facet in the political culture of Nicaragua, is the nation's heritage of guerrilla warfare. The civil wars of Nicaragua have not been the exclusive province of a small political elite, which left the rest of the nation relatively untouched. Insurrection in Nicaragua has not usually been an urban phenomenon. Revolts have more often been staged and fought in the hinterlands than in the streets and barracks of Managua. Thus the country dweller has been brought into the political life of the nation, albeit with a rather unpropitious perspective. In the countryside, as in the written history of the nation, the stories of the guerrilla chieftains have become part of the folklore of the nation. The great "bandit" Sandino, who for many years craftily eluded the marines in the frontier region of Segovia until his assassination by the National Guard, has remained something of a legend for Nicaraguans of all classes and a symbol of opposition to the United States and to Somoza. In many small towns of Nicaragua, one can still find the elderly veteran, wearing his battered khaki campaign hat, who delights in recounting his exploits in the clashes of the twenties and the thirties. This receptivity to political involvement through guerrilla warfare is a factor which must be kept in mind when analyzing Nicaraguan politics, particularly today, in the perspective of the Cuban Revolution.

A further given of Nicaragua's political culture is the role of foreign powers in the nation's internal affairs. Nicaragua's geographic location has long been such that the course of her domestic affairs has affected the interests of the world's great powers. Be it the outpost of the British Empire that once existed on her Atlantic coast, her position close to the Panama Canal, or her sheer geographic proximity to the United States, Nicaraguan policy-makers have always had to take this exogenous factor into account. While the role of foreign capital is not as great as in many Latin American nations, a considerable part of the natural resources of the country are still exploited under concessionary grants to foreigners, and this also has had its impact on Nicaraguan affairs.   *1 0 9 5 4 6*

Finally, in evaluating the setting of the politics of this nation, one must not discount the impact of change. Although her progress has not come as quickly as some would desire, Nicaragua has in the past twenty years moved some distance in the process of economic and social development. In this process of modernization, a new group of leaders has arisen which see the political heritage of Nicaragua not as a legacy to be perpetuated but as a hindrance to be overcome. In part, Nicaragua's past itself accounts for the emergence of this group. The years of occupation by United States marines did much to Americanize Nicaragua and led to a receptivity to United States attitudes, institutions, and customs that is perhaps more marked than in any other Central American nation. Those of her leaders who have spent portions of their lives in exile have been influenced by the cultures of the United States, Mexico, Costa Rica, and other nations in which they have been forced to live and have sought to apply their experiences to the development of Nicaragua upon their return. Finally, the officials and supporters of the Somoza regime itself are to some extent a more nationalized elite than are the older partisans of the rival clans.

The Political Techniques of the Caudillo

Anastasio Somoza was a product of the political culture of Nicaragua, and he shaped its components into the instruments of effective personal authority. It is therefore worthwhile to examine the political technique of the *caudillo*, the manner in which he mobilized and maintained power.

In any *caudillo* regime, the personality of the leader looms large in perceptions of political authority. Loyalty and criticism both attach to the individual rather than to the institutions which he represents. The leadership style of the strong man becomes a fundamental element in the mobilization of power. While probably not fulfilling Max Weber's ideal type of the charismatic leader, the personality of Anastasio Somoza was such as to fascinate and attract the support of large sectors of Nicaragua's population. Fun-loving and extroverted, fond of dancing, practical jokes, and close contact with the people, his style was the direct opposite of that of such dour and severe figures as Jorge Ubico of Guatemala or the middle-class blandness of Manuel Odría of Peru. Portraying himself as the tough he-man, very much the model of direct action rather than abstract thought, his bluntness and crudeness, his grotesque and brutally ironic sense of humor, made him something of a legend in the countryside, while his manner managed to offend many of the intellectuals and the sophisticated members of the upper class. Somoza anecdotes have become part of the folklore of Nicaragua. He would force ministers of state to perform dances at parties. He once personally supervised the raising of one of his boats from the bottom of Lake Nicaragua, dressed in a ludicrous outfit, while the affairs of state ground to a halt in Managua.

In short, Somoza's political style was not attuned to the cultured elite of Nicaragua. He was hardly the poet-president, another archetypal figure in Latin American history. Rather he reflected the fact that a type of political awareness had developed below the level of the elite in Nicaragua, the product of generations of civil strife. His style was that of the guerrilla chieftain. His acts of humiliation of his ministers and of the upper class resembled the crudeness of a campaign in the hinterlands and probably reflected the suppressed desires of his followers in the countryside as well.

Yet Somoza was hardly a revolutionary. Although he claimed to champion the cause of the worker, he had no program for revising the socio-economic structure of the nation. Rather, he offered "peace and progress," a regime of stability in which the well-to-do, if they offered political adulation, or at a minimum, neutrality, could pursue their private ends without hindrance. In a sense, his program often was sufficient to lead the upper class to endure his political style, and his style sufficient to attract mass support without the need for substantive programs of reform.

The control of the National Guard was one of the most consistently used and effective techniques of power which the *caudillo* employed. It lay at the base of the other means which Somoza used to mobilize support and made opposition to the regime a dangerous undertaking, to be soberly considered. Never in his nineteen years of rule did Somoza let control of the army slip from his grasp. His method of insuring that the armed forces would be personally loyal to the *caudillo* was in the classic tradition. The army received the lion's share of the national budget. It possessed the playthings of modern warfare, comfortable salaries, and extensive fringe benefits. Much of the public housing built during the Somoza period was for the benefit of the army. On La Loma de Tiscapa, a hill overlooking Managua and crowned by the presidential palace, a gaudy, tangerine-colored military casino was built. Somoza's tough and buoyant character built a spirit of camaraderie between him and his officers. He was one of the boys in the barracks or the officers' club. He could shoot, ride, and joke with the best of them.

The Somoza strategy of rule, though based on other power factors, did not fail to take account of the middle-class defenders of the form, if not the substance, of democratic procedure, nor the partisans of the historic factions. Through constitutional "revisions" of dubious legality, carefully controlled elections, and skillful manipulation—though seldom ruthless suppression—

of opposition parties, he was able to surround his regime with a façade of constitutionality. His primary instruments to this end were control of the historic Liberal Party and through it of the congress of the nation.

The Liberal Party functioned, in the Somoza scheme of things, to sanction the legitimacy of the regime through identification with a venerable and honorable political cause and to provide a plausible vehicle for carrying out the formalities of democratic processes. It also served to mobilize middle-class and mass support in favor of the regime, provided an agency which could to some extent screen for political purity in matters of patronage and lower-level political recruitment, and gave an outlet for political activists to declare their unswerving adulation for the *caudillo* in the public forum, and thereby seek personal favor.

That last is, to the author, one of the most distasteful aspects of the Somoza regime. Throughout the Somoza period, the party newspaper *Novedades* and party documents and publications provide a consistent record of the most fawning and servile worship of the image of the leader, poems of praise comparing Somoza with the great figures of history and his wife with the purity of the Virgin, and chronicles of the sycophants who were sure to pay their respects or deliver maudlin paeans on every event of significance in the life of the Somoza family. To the author, never has the significance of freedom or the condition of its loss been more clearly evident than in the contemplation of this literature. Whether such activity served a useful purpose for those who engaged in it is also open to conjecture, for Somoza, though not immune to feeling satisfaction at the construction of monuments and stadiums in his honor, did not seem to require the systematic adulation of a Trujillo.

The façade of democracy that Somoza constructed about his regime was apparently intended for publics both domestic and foreign. Somoza consciously sought United States support for his regime and in turn used that support as a means of enhancing his claims to political legitimacy. Somoza's close contact with Franklin D. Roosevelt in 1939 developed into a cult of official veneration for the American President which almost reached the fantastic. The main street of Managua is Franklin D. Roosevelt Avenue. The Somozas' yacht is named for him, and a monument to his memory stands near the presidential palace. While affection for Roosevelt is deep throughout Latin America, the political overtones that it acquires in Nicaragua are unique. Many Somoza apologists indicate that one of the principal justifications for the *caudillo's* long rule was his consistent success in winning economic support from the United States to further the development of Nicaragua.[4] While it is quite untrue that Nicaragua during the Somoza years received unusual benefits from United States foreign aid, it is clear that recent American ambassadors have closely identified themselves with the regime and that the Somozas have used this identification to their own advantage.

The Role of the Opposition

Throughout the long years that Anastasio Somoza was in power in Nicaragua, three forms of opposition to the regime existed. One consisted of the historic Conservative Party, which saw in Somoza more of a continuation of their age-old battle with the Liberals than a new political phenomenon. The second included those forces which emerged specifically to challenge the dictator himself. This sector was quite heterogeneous in character. It included the Independent Liberal Party, which had broken from the parent body over the issue of Somoza's dictatorship and was active throughout the period. It involved the activities of a variety of individuals and groups, often operating in exile, who conspired or publicized sporadically against the regime. The exile groups, geographically dispersed throughout the Caribbean from Miami to San José, lacked the cohesion or leadership to form an effective political force. Also important were a number of young Conservatives, who remained tentatively within the parent party but who challenged that party's failure to make dictatorship the central issue of the faction's political activity. The third source of opposition to Somoza came from outside the country and included such leaders of the Democratic left in Latin America as Figueres of Costa Rica, Betancourt of Venezuela, Muñoz Marín of Puerto Rico, Villeda Morales of Honduras, and Arévalo of Guatemala. These counted as part of their political credo the termination of dictatorship in the Caribbean, and they agitated against the Somoza regime and aided the Nicaraguan exiles. From time to time the enmity between Figueres and Somoza erupted in border clashes between the neighboring countries. On one such occasion, Somoza challenged Figueres to a duel, and the exchange between the heads of state that followed is probably unequaled in the annals of diplomacy between nations. Somoza, in issuing the challenge, is reported to have said to members of the international press: "That little so-and-so. Some day I hope I meet him at the border. I will put a .38 slug through his head. I am the best shot in the Nicaraguan army." To this, Figueres formally replied in kind with the statement, "Somoza is as crazy as a goat in the sun."

Somoza's treatment of domestic opposition can best be described as unpredictable and somewhat whimsical. The regime can hardly be described as totalitarian, and opposition was not systematically reduced. Rather, for long periods the opposition would be permitted to operate freely and openly. Newspapers such as *La Prensa*, the organ of the Conservative Party, and *La Flecha* would publish ringing denunciations of the regime. The Conservative and Independent Liberal parties actively campaigned and propagandized. Then arbitrarily and with little suggestion of thoroughgoing suppression, censorship of the press would be imposed, or specific opposition leaders exiled or imprisoned and exposed to brutal tortures. There was, of course, perhaps more by instinct than design, a method implicit in Somoza's treatment of the opposition. By abjuring the technique of the complete police state and permitting some latitude for opposition activity, he was able to identify and cope with those expressions of dissent that were potentially dangerous to the regime, rather than forcing them to operate clandestinely.

The role of the opposition in Somoza's Nicaragua reflects the nature of the party system during this period. The National Liberal Party (PLN), as the official partisan mechanism, was rich with the perquisites of patronage and the opportunities for adherents to court official favor. The Independent Liberals (PLI), though permitted to attract dissident middle-class support, were carefully prevented from developing a mass appeal. Yet perhaps most significant was the position of the Traditional Conservative Party (PCT) during this period. Despite the agitation of the young Turks within the party, the Conservatives, either because of the outlook of their aged leaders or through a deft instinct for survival, firmly refused to recognize the existence of the twentieth century or of the political realities of their nation. They continued their historic debate with the Liberals over archaic questions of political philosophy. The tracts and manifestoes of the party during this period seem like documents from the nineteenth century. Prominent among their concerns were the age-old questions of the relationship between Church and State and abstract discourses on classical economic theory. They fiercely justified the Bryan-Chammorro Treaty of 1914 and the Conservative role in the intervention of United States marines, all the while largely overlooking the issues of economic development and social reform which had become the central concerns of public opinion throughout Latin America, and the problems of political democracy in Nicaragua.

Since the older Conservative leadership seemed to interpret the Somoza regime as an episode in the rivalry between the historic parties, it was possible for the *caudillo* to incorporate them into his pattern of power by assigning them the role of loyal opposition, thereby enhancing the façade of democracy which was so carefully constructed. Hence, except for their boycott of the polls in 1957, the Conservatives formally contested the elections which brought Somoza to power and maintained the dynasty in control. They were guaranteed a minority role in the congress through a pact between the parties which guaranteed to the second largest one-third of the seats in each house.

The Problem of Political Change

With the death of Anastasio Somoza and the succession of his eldest son Luis to the presidency, Nicaraguan politics entered a new phase. Luis, whose power rested on the same groups that had supported his father, could not totally reject this heritage. He had to cope with a bureaucracy and congress composed largely of the hard-core followers of Anastasio Somoza. The army was in the hands of his brother Anastasio, who apparently inherited much of the hardness and violence which Luis does not seem to possess. Yet, United-States-educated Luis (Louisiana State, the Universities of California and Maryland) seemed to feel that the course of greatest wisdom for him was to loosen the grip in which his father had held Nicaragua, allow greater freedom, soft-pedal the family's role in the nation's economy, and prepare the way for the Somozas to ease their way out of public affairs, thus avoiding the danger of losing everything to a revolutionary movement.

Luis Somoza took pains to delineate a position that would alienate neither the followers of his father nor the elements seeking increased liberalization of Nicaragua's internal affairs. He continually reiterated support for the programs and policies which his father pursued. Soon after taking office, he pledged himself to carry out the "Platform of Government" which was the basis of his father's campaign in 1956. Yet in certain areas Luis distinguished his conception of government from that of the elder Somoza. His approach to problems of economic and social development appeared somewhat more modern than that of the great *caudillo,* and he played down the role of the military in the nation's political life. In 1958, his first full year in office, the military budget was reduced by about one and a half million dollars. Absent from his speeches were the laudatory phrases extolling the virtues of the military that were so apparent in all of Anastasio Somoza's addresses. There is some evidence that Luis sought to de-emphasize the family's economic dominance within the nation.

Throughout his term, Luis sought to give assurances that neither he nor any of his relatives would attempt to succeed to the presidency in the elections of 1963. He proposed that the constitutional and electoral structure of the nation be revised so as to reinstate the prohibition against presidential reelection, and to prevent those within a fourth degree of relation to the president from holding that office. Only on one major issue of political reform was Luis Somoza adamant. The Conservatives have long requested that the Organization of American States supervise the presidential elections, and Luis consistently refused to accept this proposal.

Throughout Luis Somoza's presidential term, public opinion in Nicaragua reacted to these pledges of political reform with a combination of hope mingled with suspicion. There was a subtle tentativeness, something of a wait-and-see attitude about the political process during this period. Not only was Luis' own sincerity in doubt, but many were skeptical of his ability to control his brother, the tough-minded Anastasio or "Tachito," who was commandant of the National Guard. Particularly when Luis suspended civil liberties following a series of allegedly Castro-inspired outbreaks in the early 1960's and dealt harshly with opposition leaders, were many willing to suspect the worst.

The outcome of the 1963 elections initially offered little to encourage those who had hoped that the Somoza influence might be eliminated from national life. The Somocista National Liberals chose as their candidate a long-time officeholder under the Somozas, René Schick Gutiérrez. Although the Traditional Conservative Party seemed at last to have been evolving into a modern and democratic-minded party, its candidate, Fernando Argüero Rocha, refused to stand, in view of the fact that OAS supervision to guarantee the fairness of the poll would not be permitted. The Independent Liberals likewise declined to participate; but the regime was provided with a legitimizing opposition, only too glad to accept its guaranteed third of the legislative seats, by a *pro forma* candidacy sponsored by a more complaisant Conservative faction called the Nicaraguan Conservative Party (PCN).

Schick won easily. The pattern of his administration to date has been disappointing to those who optimistically recalled Gálvez's rejection of Carías in Honduras, and Cárdenas' break with Calles in Mexico. However, it may be that Schick has so far been applying all the pressure that the traffic would bear. There were some indications early in his administration that he hoped to accentuate the role of the Nicaraguan police, perhaps as a counterpoise to the influence of Anastasio, Jr., as head of the National Guard. However, afflicted by ill-health, Schick has in general been less than aggressive as president and has done little more than to maintain the moderate liberalization policies instituted by Luis Somoza.

Governmental Institutions

Of course, discussion of the formal governmental institutions of Nicaragua must be understood within the context of the political process of that nation. Control of party and army gave Anastasio Somoza the power to hand-pick the members of his government; hence executive, legislature, and judiciary usually spoke with one voice. The principle of minority representation, which we will find running throughout the structure of government, was clearly a design of the *caudillo* to incorporate the "loyal opposition" of the historic Conservative Party into his regime. While the façade of democracy which Anastasio Somoza constructed, carefully staffed with sycophants of the regime, was at times more of a factor limiting Luis Somoza's ability to carry out his program than a formal structure to be dependably manipulated, it is still far from the system of checks and balances anticipated by the Nicaraguan constitution.

The Legislature

Nicaragua is the only Central American nation which has a bicameral legislature. Although this structure seems basically to reflect no more than imitation of foreign constitutional models, there are some differences in the powers of the two chambers. All bills are introduced in the lower house. Senatorial objection to a bill passed by the chamber of deputies requires reconsideration by that house. If the deputies do not accept the senate's objections, the bill is passed unless two-thirds of the senators are against it. The chamber of deputies consists of twenty-eight members of the majority party and fourteen members of the leading minority party. The senate is composed of twelve majority and four minority representatives, and also includes living ex-presidents and the defeated presidential candidate. The party which wins the presidential election is thus guaranteed a two-thirds majority in both houses. The term of both houses is six years, coinciding with the presidential term. In effect, presidential victory guarantees legislative control.

The Executive

Although the Somozas greatly accentuated the powers of the office, the Nicaraguan presidency under any circumstances would have been a strong position. In addition to the usual powers granted to a chief executive in a system structured on presidential lines, such as presentation of the budget and appointment and removal of ministers, he may declare a suspension of civil liberties, issue decrees with the force of law, and appoint virtually all local government officials.

The Judiciary

The court system of Nicaragua includes a supreme court, five appellate courts, district courts, and municipal courts. In addition there is a labor court, charged with the adjudication of disputes arising out of the social welfare and labor provisions of the constitution and the labor code. All justices are elected by the legislature for terms varying from one year, in the case of municipal and labor judges, to six years for members of the supreme court. An indication of the political character of the judiciary is the constitutional provision that approximately one-third of the membership of each of the courts in the system should be appointed from the dominant minority party.

Autonomous Institutions

Like other Latin American nations, Nicaragua has made some effort to short-circuit the historic problems of public bureaucracy, and provide a more propitious administrative structure for the new economic tasks of the state through the creation of autonomous institutions.

Two of these agencies were in a sense the products of United States intervention in Nicaragua. The National Bank (which once was a corporation chartered under the laws of the state of Connecticut) and the Pacific Railroad were both largely instruments of United States fiscal management until, with the end of direct American influence, both became organisms of the national government.

Other important autonomous institutions include the National Mortgage Bank, the Institute for National Development (INFONAC), and the Social Security Institute. A new autonomous corporation, the National Institute for Foreign and Domestic Commerce (INCEI), has also been created as something of a state trading agency, designed to regulate overseas sales of Nicaraguan products and to provide marketing services for domestic producers.

The boards of directors of the various autonomous institutions are generally composed of three members, selected by the president and the council of ministers. In keeping with the Somocista pattern, there is a constitutional requirement that one member of each board be selected from the minority party.

Local Government

The nation is divided into 16 departments and 122 *municipios*. The latter are further subdivided into *comarcas* and *cantones*. Departmental administration is supervised by a *jefe político*, a district judge, and a district military commander. At the level of the *municipio*, the principal officials are the mayor or *alcalde*, the local judge, the military commander, an attorney, and a *regidor* or auditor.

All of these officials are appointed by the president of the nation, with the exception of the local judge, who is appointed by his superior in the district. All *municipio* officials are members of the majority party, as determined by elections at the national level, except the auditor, who must come from the minority party. There is no form of local election of officials or of local political autonomy in Nicaragua. On the whole the military commander seems to exercise real authority at the local level, the *alcalde* performing largely ceremonial functions.

In general, local government in Nicaragua seems like a residual appendage of the political system. Its functions have been attenuated to the point where it is primarily charged only with the maintenance of local roads and cemeteries and the supervision of slaughterhouses. Its low efficacy is perhaps indicated by the fact that few *municipios* have government buildings that are adequately maintained, and many are rented out as stores or used as schools. In short, a grass-roots basis for developing democratic political practices is virtually nonexistent in Nicaragua.

Public Policy

Development Policy

Anastasio Somoza insisted that his regime be justified on the basis of its contribution to the progress of the nation. To Somoza, Nicaragua was backward because of its propensity to waste its energy and resources in domestic strife and political agitation. What Nicaragua required he had supplied: internal stability, within which progress and development could take place, and a government actively dedicated to economic and social improvement. The motto Peace and Progress was said to sum up the Somoza Doctrine, a philosophy of government appropriate to the conditions of the nation as he found it. If his regime was not democratic, it was because Nicaragua was not ready for democracy. Economic and social advance must come first.

Yet, was the claim justified? Would Nicaragua have progressed more rapidly without the Somozas, or did their political technique provide conditions for development that could not have taken place except for the presence of the strong man?

In assessing Nicaraguan economic development under the Somozas, one must be aware that there was a fuzzy and overlapping line between private and public economic policy during this period, and it would be somewhat arbitrary to separate the two. Economic policy involved not only the programs of the formal governmental institutions, but also the management of the vast Somoza fortune within Nicaragua and the economic activities of the elite closely associated with the regime.

The Somoza fortune was very much a part of the political economy of the nation. Some have said that, "the Somozas have a large hacienda, and they call it Nicaragua." It has been estimated that the Somoza family owns about 10 percent of the arable land of the republic. In the transportation field, the Somozas own both the Nicaraguan airline, LANICA, and the nation's merchant fleet, the MAMENIC line. The industrial interests of the family include the nation's largest textile factory, its only cement plant, and interests in distilleries, sugar mills, cotton gins, lumber, cattle, soap, and ice-making. Estimates of the fortune of the family vary from $60,000,000 to $150,000,000, much of it held overseas.

In short, much of the industrial development that has taken place in Nicaragua has resulted from Somoza investments. Much of the increased agricultural productivity of the nation is accounted for by Somoza properties. Many of the roads built during the Somoza period led directly to the Somoza estates. Much of the expanded productivity of the nation, its economic diversification, its internal development were, if not directly related to the business activities of the Somozas, accounted for by the entrepreneurship of those closely associated with the regime.

All of this must be borne in mind as it relates to the course of public economic policy in Nicaragua. Clearly, the government was quite successful in expanding agricultural production and in diversifying export products during this period. The development of cotton from an inconsequential crop to the leading export product in ten years was especially dramatic. Advances in livestock production were also considerable. And in both of these areas the Somozas themselves, or groups closely associated with the regime, had substantial holdings. In large part this expansion was induced through credit provided by the three government banking institutions, and in substantial measure such credits went to develop properties of politically prominent families.

In 1950, perhaps sensing the changing tone in world thought on problems of development, and perhaps cognizant of pressure for a more modern approach to public policy, Somoza extended considerably the scope of government involvement in economic activity. A five-year plan was initiated in 1953, based largely on the recommendations of an International Bank for Reconstruction and Development mission. In this latter period, such institutions as INFONAC and the Social Security Institute were established. Commodity stabilization and storage programs for basic agricultural commodities were put into operation. International Bank loans assisted in quite successful programs of road building and electric power development. Steps were taken to implement labor legislation which had first been enacted by Somoza in 1939. Somoza liked to boast that he had constructed over 2,000 schools during his administration—some 550 between 1952 and 1955—and by 1954 he was able to announce that Nicaragua, like Costa Rica, now had more schoolteachers than soldiers.

Under Luis Somoza such programs were expanded and furthered. Although productivity expansion was not as great as the dramatic increases that had been registered earlier, this was a problem common to all countries exporting products similar to those of Nicaragua. In the early 1960's, increasing attention was given to problems of social reform. An extension of the labor code was proposed to provide for agricultural workers, and an agrarian reform program was also formulated.

Although the Somozas cannot be said to have solved any of the great social and economic problems confronting Nicaragua, their performance in attempting to meet these issues is not far different from that of most contemporary regimes in other nations. In certain areas, such as road building and the provision of electric power, they did as well as any Central American nation with the possible exception of El Salvador. Even their minimal efforts in the field of social reform bear comparison with most of the nations in the area.

Foreign Policy

As noted earlier, Nicaragua's geographic position guaranteed that her domestic politics would be very much bound up with Great Power canal diplomacy. Foreign intervention has long been a fact of life for this nation. Like Cuba, the Dominican Republic, Haiti, and Panama, her politics have been closely tied to United States foreign policy.

Contemporary attitudes toward relations with the United States are not uncomplicated. At the official level, the Somoza regime has always been quite responsive to American policy. During World War II, Somoza dealt firmly with enemy aliens, and expropriation of German properties accounted for a substantial portion of the property which came into the possession of those close to the regime. In recent years, Somoza has been ardent in his anti-Communism, although he was willing to cooperate with his small domestic Communist Party during the World War II period of the grand alliance. In turn, the United States has generally supported the Somoza government. American ambassadors have identified closely with the regime and, as noted, Somoza has used American support as part of his political strategy.

Hence it is natural that opposition to the Somoza regime should have a tinge of anti-Americanism about it, accompanied by a more general latent resentment based on the memory of United States intervention. Yet, the feeling toward the United States is always ambivalent, for cultural affinity for the United States also runs deep. Indeed, expressions of anti-Americanism have been quite mild even among opposition groups to date, although the seeds of potential resentment that have been sown could become important in a situation of political tension.

Nicaragua has been officially enthusiastic about plans for the economic integration of Central America and the constitution of the nation explicitly provides for the possibility of Central American union. However, the enmity between the elder Somoza and the governments ideologically opposed to his form of rule was one of the obstacles to increased cooperation within the region. Under Anastasio Somoza, Nicaraguan territory was on several occasions used as a staging area for attacks by exile groups on Costa Rica and Honduras, at times with the involvement of Nicaraguan forces. Luis Somoza tried diligently to improve relations with his neighbors, apparently with some success. Relations between the younger Somoza and the Echandi government in Costa Rica were cordial, at least on the surface, and Nicaragua accepted with surprising graciousness a decision of the International Court at the Hague favoring Honduras in a long-standing boundary dispute between the two nations.

Conclusions

Most assessments of Anastasio Somoza's government have been quite straightforward. He was a "dictator," hence his government was to be contrasted unfavorably with the "democratic" regimes of the hemisphere in the simple dichotomy that has long been used to classify Latin American political systems. Yet the issue is by no means so clear-cut. Anastasio Somoza was the product of a political system quite different from that which gives full validity to such judgments. Seldom in its history has Nicaragua known stability and a regular political process, except that enforced through the indignity of foreign intervention. There was in Nicaragua no standard of political procedure commonly accepted as a test of the propriety of a political regime. Democratic processes were accepted as definitive only by a small sector of the society. For the activists of the countryside, among whom the guerrilla tradition ran strong, the authority of the *caudillo* chieftain was quite as legitimate as that of the elected patrician.

Somoza insisted that his technique of rule was justified insofar as it relieved Nicaragua of its endemic political turmoil and provided a political setting within which the nation could progress. Clearly, political stability was much needed and desired in a nation so long beset by ruinous domestic strife and the chagrin of foreign intervention. Clearly, the economic and social accomplishments of his period are not to be overlooked in assessing the regime, though the question must remain open whether they might have been greater under another type of political system. All of this does not condone brutality, violence, or a cynical perversion of law as techniques of government. Nor does it justify the flagrant self-enrichment of the ruler. To understand a political phenomenon within the context of the political culture from which it emerged does not imply that one must accept that which exists as desirable. But it does mean that the process of evaluating a political event becomes more subtle than is otherwise the case, and must take into account the meaning assigned to that event within the context in which it takes place. It may be that one would want to draw the conclusion that the Somoza regime simply outlived its usefulness—that it set the conditions for Nicaragua to enter a new phase of political development long before the Somozas were willing to relinquish power.

NOTES FOR CHAPTER V

1. "Foundations of Political Contrast: Costa Rica and Nicaragua," *Western Political Quarterly*, XI, Sept. 1958.
2. International Bank for Reconstruction and Finance, *The Economic Development of Nicaragua*, The Johns Hopkins Press, Baltimore, 1953, p. 3.
3. José Gámez, *Historia de Nicaragua*, Escuela de Artes Graficas, Madrid, 1955, pp. 196, 252.
4. José Maria Castellón, *Actuación del Partido Liberal y del Partido Conservador en el Poder*, Editorial Novedades, Managua, 1947, pp. 28-29; *Novedades*, Jan. 10. 1950, April 22, 1950, Feb. 26, 1957.

SELECTED BIBLIOGRAPHY

Isaac Joslin Cox, *Nicaragua and the United States*, World Peace Foundation, Boston, 1927.
José Gámez, *Historia de Nicaragua*, Escuela de Artes Graficas, Madrid, 1955.
International Bank for Reconstruction and Development, *The Economic Development of Nicaragua*, Johns Hopkins Press, Baltimore, 1952.
John Martz, *Central America: The Crisis and the Challenge*, University of North Carolina Press, Chapel Hill, 1959.
Dana G. Munro, *The Five Republics of Central America*, Oxford University Press, New York, 1918.

COSTA RICA

A MEANINGFUL DEMOCRACY

THERE IS NO certainty as to who named Costa Rica, but whoever first called the region the Rich Coast was more influenced by illusions of easy wealth than by any real knowledge of the territory. Costa Rica was not at all rich and except for her fertile soil was substantially without any resources.

Yet, as we shall see, Costa Rica enjoys a standard of living among the highest in Latin America; and, on any definition she is among the most democratic republics of the hemisphere. The experience of Costa Rica (along with Denmark, Iceland, Switzerland, Austria, Uruguay, New Zealand, and a host of other countries) suggests that it is not so much economic resources as patterns of economic and social organization that provide keys to the realization of individual prosperity and freedom. Costa Ricans may well be comparatively free and rather more prosperous than their neighbors precisely because of and not in spite of the shortage of natural resources. Let us see how this phenomenon comes about.

The Environment of Costa Rican Politics

Physical and Human Geography

Costa Rica has an area of only 19,700 square miles. Only tiny El Salvador (8,000 square miles) and Haiti (10,700 square miles) are smaller. The Dominican Republic is roughly the same size as Costa Rica. Except for El Salvador, each of the other republics of Central America (Guatemala, Honduras, and Nicaragua) has over twice the area of Costa Rica.

With a population of about 1,200,000, Costa Rica is slightly ahead of Panama, the least populous country of Latin America. Though there are important *mestizo* elements in the Costa Rican population, European types are more prevalent than in most other Latin American republics, and in culture the country is almost entirely Europeanized. The Indian sector of the population constitutes less than half of one percent of the total and plays no significant role in the social or political life of the republic. Costa Ricans are among the most culturally unified peoples of Latin America.

The central plateau (*meseta central*) is the social, economic, and political heart of the country. The *meseta* has from one to two thousand square miles, depending on the manner of its delineation, and contains over half the population of the republic. San José, the capital (population about 150,000) is at an altitude of about 3800 feet and enjoys a pleasant, semitemperate climate. Except for the ports (Puerto Limón on the Caribbean and Puntarenas and Golfito on the Pacific), all the towns of consequence are located on the *meseta*, within short distances of each other. These include Alajuela, Heredia, Cartago, and many smaller villages. Turrialba is on the slopes of the plateau, in the direction of the Caribbean.

On the *meseta central*, there is a network of roads, many of them paved. The numerous little towns and hamlets are generally clean, with brightly painted or whitewashed houses. San José is more crowded and noisy than are the other settlements, but even in the capital one finds far less of the rich elegance that characterizes other principal cities of Latin America. Churches are not usually ostentatious, there are but few monuments, one sees many fine parks and simple public buildings, and even the finest homes lack the conspicuous display of wealth that is so common elsewhere in Latin America. If extreme wealth is less in evidence, there is also less of the appalling, bestial poverty that one finds in neighboring countries.

With some exceptions, the country between the *meseta central* and the frontiers is sparsely inhabited and enjoys little if any communication with the cultural centers of the republic. Some habitations, including the town of Liberia, are strung along the Pan American highway. The coastal towns of Puerto Limón and Puntarenas are connected to the interior by two efficient railway systems, one diesel and the other electric, and there are some centers of population along those lines of communication.

Two other important regions are the peninsula of Guanacaste, in the northwest, which borders on the western part of the frontier with Nicaragua and juts southward along the Pacific coast; and the region around Golfito, also on the Pacific coast, which is now the center of an important banana-raising industry. The little hamlets in the ranching country of Guanacaste are connected to each other by an indifferent road system.

Costa Rica is not so precipitous as Guatemala or parts of Honduras or Nicaragua. But the country is angular enough, and most of the interior landscape is characterized by steep hills and numerous cultivated valleys. There are mountains, and some of them are volcanic. One can describe much of the landscape as steeply rolling, deeply green, and pastoral. The climate of the interior is temperate, with cool evenings and nights. On the *meseta* there are heavy rains, usually in the afternoons, between May and October, and on the coasts (particularly the Caribbean), the rainfall occurs almost throughout the year.

Though the principal export crops of the country are bananas and coffee, agricultural production for internal consumption is diversified and includes almost everything that is consumed by the population. There are corn, beans, rice, and cane, as well as every sort of tropical fruit. A cattle industry, for both beef and dairy products, is becoming an important feature of the economy.

Proprietorship

An unusual feature of Costa Rican society is the small part played in the economy by the huge hacienda, and the very large role played by small landed proprietors. Though large landed estates (over 1000 hectares or 2500 acres each) occupy almost one-third of the cultivated surface of Costa Rica, they employ less than 6 percent of the entire active agrarian population and account for only about 5 percent of total Costa Rican crop sales. About 79 percent of Costa Rican farmers and 87 percent of total Costa Rican agricultural sales are accounted for by farms of two hundred hectares (five hundred acres) or less. Even more significant, there is much evidence that more than half the total active farmers of Costa Rica are either proprietors or members of proprietor families who work their own farms, or *fincas*. The more usual Latin American quasi-feudal patterns, in which a very tiny minority owns almost all the land, and substantially all of the remainder of the rural population depends for its livelihood upon a few *dons* of the soil, are not characteristic of Costa Rica.[1] Costa Rica is a land of many small farms, and proprietors constitute a notable sector of its population.

The reasons for this unusual state of affairs are not hard to find. When, beginning in 1560, the Spanish first settled the country, they soon found there were no rich minerals. The Indians were not sedentary, as were those of Mexico or Peru, but were more like those of much of the United States and Canada—nomadic and fiercely determined not to be enslaved by the invaders. Thus there was no basis for an exploitative, parasitic, nonproducing ruling class. In fact—and quite in contrast to the more usual situation among the Spanish domains—the settlers found they actually had to work in order not to starve. There are many reliable reports that even the governors of the early province had to plant their own crops and harvest them with their own hands if they were not to perish from hunger. This condition had three effects: (1) by removing the stigma that the feudalistic Spanish ordinarily attached to labor, it taught something about the virtues of production; (2) it forced the creation of many proprietors, for no one could hold or cultivate more than a modest area of land; and (3) because it was not easy to bully or browbeat the farmer-owners, who were dependent upon no one for their existence, there emerged an important tradition of self-reliance, hard work, and independence of spirit. Something of the same sort produced the open societies of the United States and Canada.

Education

Costa Rica is among the most literate countries of Latin America. In a part of the world where it is rare for more than 50 percent of the population to know how to read and write, and where the more usual figure is around 20 percent, the figure for Costa Rica stands at between 75 and 80 percent. Argentina, Chile, and Uruguay are almost entirely literate, and Panama and Cuba (pre-Castro) approach the Costa Rican level. With these exceptions, Costa Rica is something of a phenomenon, and her surprising achievement of literacy is to be attributed to the vigorous efforts of enlightened administrations during the period from 1885 to the present.

Summary

In Costa Rica we find a number of factors in the environment of politics that are exceptional to the Latin American norm. Cultural assimilation is virtually complete. Communications, at least on the *meseta central* and with two principal coastal ports, are good. The economic condition of most of the population is above the usual Latin American standards. Cleavages between an extremely rich feudalistic and parasitic class on the one hand and a destitute mass of brutally poverty-stricken people on the other are not so marked as among her neighbors. Educational standards are relatively high. Proprietors constitute a large segment, perhaps half, of the total population. This latter fact, which arose in part out of the paucity of resources and the ferocity of the Indians, has played a significant part in the formation of the society and politics of the Republic of Costa Rica.

Political History

Costa Rica has had her periods of political violence, but her history is neither so bloody nor so turbulent as is that of almost any other republic of Latin America. Her political history has not been so destructive of her social and economic fabric as have the successive upheavals which many other Latin American republics have suffered.

During most of the period of Spanish rule, Costa Rica was the poorest and most neglected province within the captaincy-general (*capitanía general*) of Guatemala. She was without precious metals, and no one seriously coveted her or cared to improve her communications. Her farmer-settlers isolated themselves on their plots, fought the Indians, and grew for their own subsistence. Except for the maraudings of English pirates and their Indian allies, the epoch was without notable events. Costa Ricans became known as independent and self-willed and for refusing to undertake either their religious or their political obligations. But then, the affairs of Costa Rica were of little concern to Spain, whose interests lay more with the plunder of America than with the problems of an almost unknown, isolated colony whose inhabitants could barely feed themselves, let alone enrich the *conquistadores* or the Crown.

The independence of Costa Rica came in 1821, along with that of the rest of Central America and of Mexico. Between 1823 and 1838 Costa Rica was presumably a part of the fitful and turbulent so-called United Provinces, or federation, of Central America. Since 1838 she has been an independent republic. Out of deference to a Central American federation that had little to commend it, Costa Rica continued for ten years after 1838 to call her executives "chiefs of state" (*jefes de estado*), and it was not until 1848 that she cast aside the last shreds of the federation and used the term *presidente de la república*.

Depending on how one counts certain transitory administrations, Costa Rica has now had some forty-seven different presidents. Of these, only three have been of the military profession. Not more than forty of her one hundred forty years of independence have been under dictatorial regimes, and none of these have been as severe, say, as those of Trujillo of the Dominican Republic, Gómez of Venezuela, Rosas of Argentina, Francia of Paraguay, or Díaz of Mexico. The most rigorous dictators were Lic.[2] Braulio Carrillo (1835-1837 and 1838-1842), Don Juan Rafael Mora (1849-1859), General Tomás Guardia (1870-1882), Don Rafael Yglesias (1894-1902), and Don Federico A. Tinoco (1917-1919).

Of thirty-eight ordinary administrations since 1824 (nine others having been by designation for brief interim periods), nine secured office by force, and the remaining twenty-nine by election. Until recently, elections were often tainted by corruption and strong official persuasion, but at least ten of them have been genuinely competitive and the remainder a sort of reflection of crude community consensus. Of nineteen ordinary administrations since 1889, only two have secured power by force, and the remaining seventeen by election. Eight of these elections have been noncompetitive and nine have been competitive.[3]

Since 1889 Costa Rican administrations have usually followed each other at regular four-year intervals; and even before 1889, political events were not so chaotic as in nearby republics. The last three elections (won in 1953 by Don José Figueres; in 1958 by Lic. Mario Echandi; and in 1962 by Don Francisco J. Orlich) have been particularly notable for the freedom of political competition and honesty with which they were conducted.

The republic has enjoyed the services of some particularly illustrious presidents. Among these, there have been Dr. José María Castro (1847-1849 and 1866-1868); General Próspero Fernández (1882-1885); Lic. Cleto González Víquez (1906-1910 and 1928-1932); and Lic. Ricardo Jiménez (1910-1914, 1924-1928, and 1932-1936). Costa Ricans regard the great educators and democratic presidents, Cleto González Víquez and Ricardo Jiménez, as among their finest political products, and there are many nations, including the United States, that could have benefited from their services. It is also likely that the judgment of history will look favorably upon the figure of José Figueres, who led the revolution for restoration of democracy in 1948 and served as leader of a ruling revolutionary junta during 1948-1949 and as freely elected president during 1953-1958.

Costa Rica has suffered from few wars with her neighbors. During 1856 and 1857, she joined in the general Central American war against the fantastic American filibuster, William Walker, who had seized the presidency of Nicaragua. During 1921 there were some skirmishes with Panama, and in recent years there have been border clashes with Nicaragua, as well as occasional Nicaraguan incursions into Costa Rican territory and even an aerial attack on San José. These conflicts have been of short duration, and have generally been ended under pressure from the Organization of American States (OAS).

Internally, there have been numerous small-scale uprisings, but few of them have been successful. The most notable occurred in 1838, when Braulio Carrillo seized power; in 1842, when the Honduran Central Americanist, Francisco Morazán, utilized opposition to Carrillo to bring about his overthrow; again the same year, when an enraged Costa Rican populace overthrew Morazán; in 1889, when embattled farmers secured respect for the results of an election; in 1917-1919, when the civilian minister of war, Federico A. Tinoco, seized the government and was in turn overthrown; and in 1948, when a revolutionary force led by José Figueres upset a corrupt government that had refused to accede to the electoral victory of Otilio Ulate, an opposition candidate.

In summary, the political history of Costa Rica has been less turbulent than have those of many of her sister republics. She has suffered wars and revolts, but fewer of them than is usual in her part of the world. She has known dictatorships, but they have been less brutal and of shorter duration than is common in Latin America. She has endured fraudulent and meaningless elections, and there have been *golpes de estado*. But on balance, she has experienced more free elections and more civilian government than have most of her Latin American neighbors.

The Processes of Costa Rican Politics

Public Expression

Except for some unusual periods of strong-man rule, free expression has always been a feature of Costa Rican public life. Historical records of the nineteenth century refer to vigorous exchanges of views among public figures, and during almost all of this century freedom of speech and of the press have been regular parts of the Costa Rican political scene.

The several daily newspapers of San José tend to represent set political positions, and most of them can only be described as organs of political parties. Their columns are filled with vigorous editorial comment, and there are times when cabinet ministers and even the president of the republic will defend themselves or expound their views in the columns of the press. Criticism of the president and of his policies is freely expressed, and among opposition newspapers there is none of the slavish reverence for *el presidente de la república* that is encountered in many other Latin American countries.

Freedom of expression is of course guaranteed in the constitution, but this is no mere constitutional platitude. On the contrary, freedom of thought and speech, including expression by the political opposition, is a regular feature of Costa Rican politics.

Political Parties

Costa Rican political competition is vigorous, and not subject to domination or modification by pressures from any official party. While the tendency, as in many other Latin American republics, is toward *personalista* rather than ideological parties, there are predominant points of view that can generally be identified with individual parties. Costa Rican parties also tend to be more durable than are those of several neighboring republics.

There is not usually a multitude of parties in the Costa Rican political field; a common number is three. In recent years, particularly since the turbulent events of 1948, the National Liberation Party (PLN) has been a leading, well-organized, rather permanent political force. While much under the influence of its leader, José Figueres, PLN attempts to provide a body of substantial ideas and to maintain a viable organization regardless of the imminence or results of election campaigns. National Liberation has much in common with several semisocialist, democratic, anti-Communist, western-oriented parties of the Americas—the Democratic Action Party (AD) of Venezuela, the APRA of Peru, and several others.

José Figueres, the dynamic personal force and theorist of PLN, was chief of the provisional junta during 1948-1949, while a new constitution was framed. The party secured election of Figueres as president of the republic for the term 1953-1958, and Francisco J. Orlich for the term 1962-1966. The party publishes numerous pamphlets and books, as well as the daily tabloid *La República,* and is instrumental in the administration of the inter-American International Institute of Political Education. The Institute trains young potential leaders who are nominated by various pro-democratic political parties throughout Latin America.

The National Union Party (PUN) is a more moderate, centrist group. One of its leaders, Otilio Ulate, a prominent journalist, served as president during the period 1949-1953, after the Figueres revolution had assured respect for the results of the election of 1948. In the elections of 1958, PUN supported the candidacy of Mario Echandi, who emerged victorious and served during the period 1958-1962. PUN was officially organized in 1946, but traces its history back to an earlier party, the Democratic, which was founded in 1942 and later disappeared. PUN receives frequent support from the largest daily newspaper of Costa Rica, *La Nación,* as well as from Ulate's daily, *El Diario de Costa Rica.* The party usually elects a substantial number of deputies to the unicameral Legislative Assembly.

A party that has been active in recent years, but whose fortunes are tied very closely to those of its charismatic leader, is the National Republican (PRN). The party is almost exclusively organized around the figure of (medical) Dr. Rafael Calderón Guardia, who served as president during

1940-1944. His rejection by voters in 1948 caused a compliant congress to annul the presidential election results, with the result that forces under José Figueres revolted and overthrew the corrupt government which supported Calderón's candidacy.

Despite the dubious political qualifications of Dr. Calderón, and the inability of his supporters to see any particular virtue in electoral probity, PRN still enjoys a substantial support among voters who have a warm personal attachment for the distinguished physician. Dr. Calderón is a very popular individual. He is said to have continued his medical practice and to have brought many Costa Ricans into the world during his tenure as president. The party has provided a sort of haven for leftist extremists and nationalists who have found shelter in the shadow of the naive Dr. Calderón.

In the eyes of persons who do not understand the basic similarities between left and right extremes, it is curious that PRN, with its motley crew of Communist-oriented extremists, nationalists, and worshipers of the figure of Dr. Calderón Guardia, often makes common cause with wealthy landowners and rightist extremists, as well as with the more moderate PUN.

Political Contests and Elections

Costa Rican law lays down careful rules for the conduct of political campaigns. Parties may propagandize at any time, but they may conduct public demonstrations only within two months of an election. There may be no rallies by two or more different parties in the same town on the same day, and headquarters of different parties may not be within two hundred meters of each other. The law also provides some minutiae for the organizational apparatus of parties, which are to have prescribed types of hierarchical organs at local, regional, and national levels. It is particularly interesting to note that all parties are partly subsidized from the public treasury in amounts that are proportionate to the votes they obtain in national elections.

The Costa Rican constitution and electoral laws go to elaborate lengths to assure that, insofar as human ingenuity can manage it, the electoral process will be free of official influence or corruption. All matters related to elections are under direct supervision of the Supreme Electoral Tribunal (TSE) and of regional electoral councils (*juntas electorales*) which it controls. The three regular and three alternate members of the TSE are chosen by a two-thirds vote of the Supreme Court of Justice, for six-year terms which cannot correspond with those of the legislative, executive, or judicial organs. The unicameral Legislative Assembly must consult the TSE on all electoral matters, may only override the TSE opinion by a two-thirds vote of its membership, and may not override the tribunal's views at all within six months before or four months after an election. Many other details of the law are designed to preserve the integrity of the vote, and, particularly since 1949, Costa Rican elections have been marked by notable electoral rectitude. Members of the TSE are highly respected and are apparently untouched by fraud. Though there are no doubt exceptions to this idyllic pattern, it is clear that honesty of elections and respect for their results are more than mere constitutional formalities.

The campaigns which precede elections are extremely vigorous. Newspapers are full of political advertising, editorials, and expressions of opinion. There are numerous demonstrations and political rallies, with a huge amount of public activity related to the political contests.[4]

Institutions of Costa Rican Government

Regional and Local Government

In territorial organization of authority, Costa Rica adheres to a unitary plan. The country is divided into seven provinces, which are simply administrative subdivisions of the central government, without legislative or other organs of self-government. The provinces are in turn divided into cantons, which are equivalent to municipalities elsewhere in Latin America, and these are governed by elected councils, or *juntas,* each of which includes one member appointed by the president. The smallest units of local governance are the districts, which send voteless delegates to the cantonal councils to work with the elected and voting members, or *regidores.*

The National Executive and Legislature

On the national level, the country elects forty-five deputies and fifteen alternates to a strong, unicameral Legislative Assembly. The president, who is also elected directly, must share power with numerous autonomous and semi-autonomous agencies that are substantially outside of executive control. When the president's party enjoys a clear majority in the legislative assembly, he can be reasonably sure that his program will secure the approval of the deputies. However, it often happens that he is unable to control the legislature, whose members are frequently given to strident criticism of his policies. The president cannot be assured that his annual messages will be received with even a minimum show of respect, and during his presentation of views it has been common for opposition deputies to tolerate and even encourage uproarious hooting and jeering from the galleries.

Though the legislative assembly is only supposed to meet in regular sessions during six months of each year, in split sessions of three months each (May 1-July 31 and September 1-November 30), there is no limit on extraordinary sessions. With payment at a high *per diem* rate, the legislative assembly generally meets during substantially the entire year, so the attention of the country is constantly fixed on the debates and political antics of the deputies. It is clear that in a country as small as Costa Rica, there is little need for the national law-making body to be in continuous session. Daily meetings are likely to be quite short, or else much time is occupied with orations that are as weak in constructive proposal as they are strong in political vituperation. With much time on their hands, there is full opportunity for all the deputies to speak as much as they wish, and the Costa Rican legislators take full advantage of the situation.

Though there is much public criticism of the almost uninterrupted political excitement that the uninhibited deputies engender, there is also great tolerance for their histrionics and a certain enjoyment and appreciation of them. The government has managed to put some excellent legislation into effect, particularly in the realms of housing, banking, and general social reform; and leading sectors of public opinion express themselves as preferring the excesses of liberty to those of tyranny.

The government is very civilian-minded, and even in the present day the president, ministers, and other members of the government are known for their readiness to exchange views and mingle with all elements of the population. One notes a more egalitarian, democratic spirit in such contacts than is common in the paternalistic relations that exist between the *caudillos* and their subjects in several other Latin American republics. The president is not so much a political *patrón* and grantor of favors as he is a companion and equal friend of supporters, and besieged defendant against the lashing attacks of his critics. It is said that the president must spend so much time receiving visits of opponents and friends and writing defensive or explanatory letters to the editors of newspapers that he has little time to conduct the affairs of state. In a weak-presidential, strong-legislative system such as that of Costa Rica, this poses less of a problem than it would in systems more oriented toward the executive branch of government.

As we shall see in our discussion of the Costa Rican constitution, the president is substantially deprived of power to suspend guarantees and is effectively hedged about by constitutional limitations as well as by a traditionally vigorous legislative branch.

The Courts

The Costa Rican judicial system is notably free of external political influence. Lower courts are appointed and supervised by the Supreme Court of Justice, and the executive plays no part in selection of that high tribunal. Only the legislative assembly selects the seventeen high judicial magistrates, and for eight-year terms that bridge two four-year legislative sessions. At the end of each eight-year period, only a two-thirds vote of the legislature may remove judges from office. Complex provisions assure that the legislative assembly will exercise an indirect and minimal influence over the filling of unexpected vacancies in the high court. The supreme court prepares a list of fifty possible alternative judges. From this list, the legislative assembly selects twenty-five names, and during absences of regular justices, the court chooses *by lot* from among the twenty-five.

As is well known, a self-willed despot can usually subvert even the most stringent constitutional guarantees of judicial integrity. In Costa Rica, however, the multiparty system, the weak executive, the traditions of strong legislative participation in government, and a constant surveillance by an alert public opinion have generally combined to assure the preservation of a strong and independent judicial branch.

The Constitution

Before 1871 there were four short-lived Costa Rican constitutional documents, in 1824, 1844, 1847, and 1859. The present Constitution of 1949 is based in large measure on the liberal document of 1871, to which it has added several particularly stringent and ingenious guarantees of free government, as well as provisions for modern social reform.

The charter of 1949 is longer than that of the United States, but is among the shorter Latin American constitutions. It is particularly notable for its precision of expression and is generally not encumbered by the elaborate exceptions, minutiae, and complex disorganization that are features of several other Latin American constitutional documents. Civil rights and protections against abuse of authority, as well as assurances of civilian government, are clearly and succinctly stated, and usually leave little room for evasion or misinterpretation.

The Costa Rican constitution is particularly remarkable for the evidence it contains that very fertile minds were applied to the task of preserving freedom against abuse by the excesses of executive authority. It is evident that its framers placed more confidence in the legislative than in the administrative arm of government, but this is a Costa Rican tradition that can be traced back to the earliest days of the republic.[5]

In article 12, the constitution provides that "the Army as a permanent institution is proscribed," though provision is also made for an adequate police force. There are those who say that the Civil Guard is as well equipped a force of fighting men as any army, but there can be no doubt of its civilian orientation and of its almost complete withdrawal from political affairs.

Suspension of constitutional guarantees is sharply limited in terms of the rights that may be suspended, and the action is almost exclusively a legislative function. During sessions of the legislative assembly, such suspensions may only occur by a two-thirds vote. As we have seen, the deputies are in almost continuous session, and so the executive would have little opportunity to undertake the suspension himself. Even in those rare instances where the president might suspend the guarantees because of adjournment of the legislative assembly, his decree is "equivalent, *ipso facto*" to a convocation of the assembly, "which must meet within the next forty-eight hours" to confirm the action by a "two-thirds vote of its entire membership," or the guarantees are immediately re-established. In a further ingenious provision, it is stated that if the assembly is unable to meet because of lack of a quorum (a frequent Latin American device to assure inaction), then any number of deputies who can meet during the following day shall be authorized to approve or disapprove of the suspension. A two-thirds majority of that number is also necessary for the suspension to continue.

The constitution provides that the president's term shall be for four years, and that he may not be again re-elected until two intervening terms, or eight years, have passed. Since deputies may not be immediately re-elected after their four-year terms, but may again serve after one intervening four-year period, these provisions almost guarantee that an individual can only resume the presidency in an entirely fresh political situation, with completely different legislative personnel.

In another original provision, the constitution states that where two presidential candidates secure the same number of votes, the older one shall be considered victorious. This should effectively prevent any dispute on that score!

Though the president may freely appoint the members of his cabinet, he is not given free rein to issue decrees and to legislate as he pleases. His powers are rather typical of those of a limited executive, and include many ceremonial and nondiscretionary functions.

We have noted the careful provisions against any political tampering with the judicial or electoral functions. The same attention to protection against abuse of authority is to be seen in the financial provisions of the constitution. Though the national treasurer and assistant treasurer are appointed by the executive branch (officially, by the Council of Government, or cabinet) for terms of four years, they may not expend any funds without authority of the office of the Comptroller General of the Republic, which is dependent upon the legislative branch. The comptroller and assistant comptroller are appointed by the legislative assembly, two years after the beginning of a presidential term and for terms of eight years! Thus, the expenditure of public funds is only possible with the sanction of the executive branch (through the national treasurer), and with the approval of the comptroller general, who is appointed by the legislative branch.

While financial malfeasance is not unknown in Costa Rica, it occurs with much less regularity than is common throughout much of the rest of Latin America, and it cannot be doubted that these carefully written constitutional provisions are in large part responsible for this unusual state of affairs.

Patterns of Costa Rican Policy

During this century, with some notable exceptions, Costa Rican administrations have tended to alternate rather regularly between conservatism and reform, but almost always within a framework of democratic moderation. Two exceptional periods were those of Federico A. Tinoco (1917-1919), when the minister of war seized power by violence and attempted a one-man dictatorship; and of Rafael Calderón Guardia (1940-1944) and Teodoro Picado (1944-1948), when extremist elements of both left and right threatened to throw Costa Rica's democracy into disarray. The Calderón-Picado regime, as we have seen, attempted to maintain itself in power despite contrary election returns, and it was only after a revolt led by José Figueres that the elected president, Otilio Ulate of the National Union Party, was able to take office.

Throughout most Costa Rican administrations, and particularly during recent years, certain tendencies have been characteristic of Costa Rican policy.

Emphasis on Education

Since the late nineteenth century, it has been a matter of pride that the educational budget has usually exceeded the military, and that illiteracy has been reduced to a much lower level than is common in Latin America. There is much stress on schools, on teachers and teaching methods, and on getting the maximum possible numbers of children as far in their school work as can be managed. Education is compulsory through the primary levels, and free through the secondary. The very excellent University of Costa Rica, which enjoys its own centralized campus, is supported by public funds and its faculty members devote more of their time to work in the institution than is generally true of professors elsewhere in Latin America. In the rural districts, educational levels have not been so well maintained as in the principal towns, and despite the rules on compulsory education, many farm children receive only a year or two of schooling and have almost no opportunities to obtain books or continue their education.

Stress on Civilian Democracy

Though there is an efficient Civil Guard which is a military force in all but name, there can be no doubt that Costa Rican society is infused with a nonmilitary, civilian spirit. Men in uniform are but rarely seen, and even police officers often do not bother to wear their uniforms when performing their duties. The usual panoply of official cards, stress on title and position, and class consciousness are much less in evidence in Costa Rica than elsewhere in Latin America.

When the traveler arriving at the international airport asks whether he must register with the police (as is done in some Latin American countries), he is likely to be answered with a wink, a smile, and a remark that, "Oh, we don't have any police around here, except only that fellow standing over there." The President of the Republic may often be seen, driving his own car or walking about with friends in downtown San José. On a street adjoining the presidential offices, I once encountered a civil guard, who was talking and joking with an attractive lady. By the time I approached the guard, the lady had gone her way, and the guard said to me, "She's some chicken, isn't she?" I asked who she was, and he replied, "Oh, don't you know? She's the wife of the President of the Republic." Popular and published comment is full of allusions to Costa Rica's easy-going, egalitarian democracy, and this spirit has of course affected many of the features of government that we have described above.

Sense of Social Responsibility

Even before emergence of the influential semisocialist National Liberation Party, Costa Rican governments could usually be counted on to be concerned about the condition of labor, care of the indigent, promotion of education, availability of housing, urban development, maintenance of democratic norms, control of corruption, maintenance of public utilities, and the like. Though none of the problems present in these areas have been fully solved, the trend has generally been to devote much attention to their correction. The "concessionary view of public office," as it is called by Professor R. A. Gomez, is not so evident in Costa Rica as it is in much of the rest of Latin America.[6]

Pro-democratic Foreign Policy

In her foreign policies, Costa Rica stands among the most consistent supporters of Western democracy. Her opposition to despotism, whether of the left or the right, is well known. In World War II she was the first country of this hemisphere to declare war on the Axis. She has unfailingly taken a strong stand in support of Western opposition to the expansion of Soviet influence. During the first few months of the Castro regime in Cuba, Costa Rica was friendly to the revolutionary government, which seemed to be an improvement over the Batista dictatorship. However, relations cooled as soon as the despotic tendencies of *fidelismo* became clear. Political excesses by the *fidelistas*, including particularly the execution of political opponents, repelled the Costa Ricans and caused them to break relations with the Cuban government.

Costa Rica has been no satellite of the United States, and most of her leaders have been dismayed at apparent United States support for tyrannical regimes, such as the Somoza dynasty of Nicaragua. Costa Rica has not always adhered as carefully as she might to the principle of nonintervention, and from time to time her governments—particularly those of National Liberation—have looked the other way while armed civilians have intruded into the internal affairs of Nicaragua and of the dictatorial regimes of the Caribbean. A tendency among Costa Rican public figures has been to support the ideals of United States democracy, but to criticize freely State Department policies where the Costa Ricans have thought them in conflict with United States revolutionary ideals. In the United Nations and the Organization of American States, the republic can always be counted on to support those Western policies which are considered to be clearly in support of the interests of democracy.

Conclusion

It would be quite wrong to contend that Costa Rica is any haven of idyllic perfection or that she has entirely solved any of her pressing social and political problems. She has succeeded better than most Latin American republics in the achievement of popular government, and the conditions of social and political life in the republic are more tolerable than in most of Latin America.

The social and political achievements of Costa Rica have been accomplished in a rural, nonindustrial environment, without assistance from any important mineral resources. In fact, when one contemplates such comparatively successful societies as those of Denmark, Norway, New Zealand, and the like, one is compelled to conclude that in some cases the absence of wealth may prevent emergence of a wealthy, parasitic, nonproducing class, may encourage the multiplication of proprietors, and may actually stimulate the solution of important social problems.[7]

NOTES FOR CHAPTER VI

1. For a much more detailed analysis of these phenomena, and for substantiating sources, see James L. Busey, *Notes on Costa Rican Democracy*, University of Colorado Press, Boulder, 1962, especially Chapter VII and the Epilogue; and "Foundations of Political Contrast: Costa Rica and Nicaragua," *Western Political Quarterly*, IX, Sep. 1958, pp. 627-659.
2. *Licenciado*—the title earned by a law-school graduate in Mexico and some other countries.
3. For more complete data on the character of Costa Rican presidencies, see James L. Busey, "The Presidents of Costa Rica," *The Americas*, XVIII, July 1961, pp. 55-70; also, Cleto González Víquez, *Personal del poder ejecutivo de Costa Rica*. Published by the author, San José, Costa Rica, 1936; reprinted, 1958.
4. A very useful report on a Costa Rican election campaign is to be found in Harry Kantor, *The Costa Rican Election of 1953: A Case Study*, University of Florida Press, Gainesville, 1958.
5. It is said that President José Rafael de Gallegos (1833-1835) could not even visit his ranch at Tres Ríos, a few kilometers from San José, without permission of the congress. Carlos Monge Alfaro, *Historia de Costa Rica*, 9th ed., Imprenta Trejos, S.A., San José, 1959, pp. 156-157.
6. R. A. Gomez, *Government and Politics in Latin America*, Random House, New York, 1960, p. 19.
7. During 1963 and 1964 the volcano Irazú, which overlooks the *meseta central*, has been in almost continuous eruption. A rain of ashes is covering the economic heart of the country, killing vegetation, forcing removal of livestock to other parts, and almost bringing normal life in San José and nearby towns to a standstill. By virtually destroying production where small and medium landed proprietorship has been most marked, the volcano Irazú threatens to destroy the social fabric of the republic.

SELECTED BIBLIOGRAPHY

John and Mavis Biesanz, *Costa Rican Life*, Columbia University Press, New York, 1944.

James L. Busey, "Foundations of Political Contrast: Costa Rica and Nicaragua," *Western Political Quarterly*, XI, Sep. 1958, p. 630.

———, *Latin America: Political Institutions and Processes*, Random House, New York, 1964, Chapter 3, "Costa Rica and Her Neighbors," pp. 50-84.

———, *Notes on Costa Rican Democracy*, University of Colorado Press, Boulder, 1962.

———, "The Presidents of Costa Rica," *The Americas*, XVIII, July 1961, pp. 55-70.

Chester L. Jones, *Costa Rica and Civilization in the Caribbean*, University of Wisconsin Press, Madison, 1935.

Harry Kantor, *The Costa Rican Election of 1953: A Case Study*, University of Florida Press, Gainesville, 1958.

Charles P. Loomis et al., *Turrialba*, Free Press, Glencoe, 1953.

John D. Martz, *Central America, The Crisis and the Challenge*, University of North Carolina Press, Chapel Hill, 1959, Chapter VI.

Sakari Sariola, *Social Class and Social Mobility in a Costa Rican Town*, Inter-American Institute of Agricultural Sciences, Turrialba, Costa Rica, 1954.

Philip L. Wagner, *Nicoya, A Cultural Geography*, University of California Press, Berkeley and Los Angeles, 1958.

VII *Daniel Goldrich*

PANAMA[1]

ALTHOUGH PANAMA is the smallest in population* and one of the weakest of the Latin American countries, its strategic location on the Isthmus has given it a disproportionate prominence in regional and international politics. The canal aside, Panama's power structure, political issues, and problems have many characteristics in common with those of her neighbors.

Because of the overwhelming importance to the whole region of the Cuban Revolution, it seems worthwhile to note a series of characteristics Panama shares with Cuba. Both received national independence (Cuba from Spain, after a transitional period under United States administration, in 1902 and Panama from Colombia in 1903) in part as a result of United States intervention; the United States has also intervened directly in the domestic politics of each, sometimes at their request. The historical importance of United States sugar, mining, and cattle interests to Cuba's economy is paralleled in Panama by the importance of the canal and the interests of the United Fruit Company. Both nations have experienced extensive governmental corruption, widespread poverty and unemployment, and an extreme economic dependence on the United States. In Cuba all this generated the strong nationalism that was further developed and effectively manipulated by Fidel Castro; in Panama also nationalism has increased in intensity. Whether these shared characteristics of history and economy will lead ultimately to similar political outcomes for the two countries remains to be seen.

Socio-Economic Background

Although Panamanians resent the general assumption that the canal is the sum and substance of the country, it is nevertheless a fact that the nation's economy is, in large measure, organized around the great waterway. Outside of the canal and its related enterprises, Panama relies principally on banana and shrimp exports, with the bulk of her population engaged in subsistence agriculture or employed for manual labor on large sugar and cattle haciendas. Between the Canal Zone and the Colombian border lies the Darien half of the country, almost completely undeveloped. The more developed interior between the Zone and Costa Rica contains a very inadequate road network which limits the exploitation of its agricultural resources, and as a result Panama imports a good proportion of its food.

* Just over one million.

131

The consequent economic imbalance between city and rural life is well recognized by economic development experts, and since the 1940's the government has made some effort, with United States technical assistance, to train agricultural technicians, provide rural areas with at least minimum educational facilities, and create a grid of feeder roads to stimulate commercial enterprise among the *campesinos*. However, the gap is still so great that while the city attracts from the country more people than its economy can adequately accommodate, the disparity in financial support and in cultural level discourages educators and technical assistance personnel from completing the needed tasks of development in the rural areas. This is, of course, a problem Panama shares with virtually all the other Latin American countries.

The Panama Canal, the largest economic enterprise in Panama, provides an estimated one-sixth of the national income and seven-tenths of the "export" income. The Panamanians tend to view the canal as their prime natural resource—and the source of greatly increased wealth if they can only convince or otherwise influence the United States government to yield to their demands for a greater share in its management and profits.

The future of the canal is obviously a critical factor in the nation's economy. The necessity for a new canal is acknowledged by the United States—the present canal cannot take the new super-tankers, nor aircraft carriers of the Forrestal class, and is also encountering problems with silting. Should the United States (or conceivably, though improbably, another party) construct an inter-oceanic canal elsewhere, Panama would suffer a severe economic decline. A new canal constructed in Panama would, on the other hand, provide work for Panamanian laborers and technicians and thus give an impressive though temporary lift to the economy.

The position of the United States government has been, on the whole, that the Panamanians have erred in relying too heavily on the canal as the base of their economy. In line with this perspective, the United States technical assistance programs have been directed toward a lessening of this dependence by the development of alternative resources. A major consequence of success in such development would be a dilution of the canal-focused force of Panamanian nationalism.

However, because of the scarcity of domestic entrepreneurial activity in industry, the canal seems likely to retain its position as the most highly visible and important economic enterprise in the country. Panamanians with capital have followed the typical Latin American pattern of investing in real estate or depositing their money in Swiss or other foreign banks. It has not been possible for Panamanian governments to modify this pattern by currency exchange regulations, since the country uses United States dollars as its currency, the national monetary unit having only supplementary use. Pedro Teichert has shown that Panama ranked low in comparison with other Latin American countries in average annual percentage increases in per capita national income and in capital investment during the postwar period, when economic development elsewhere was marked:

While Panama's income is mainly derived from the business of the Canal Zone, it is very unevenly distributed and the nation is completely under-developed by any standard but current per capita income. But, even according to per capita income statistics, between 1945-1955 income has been going down while the average annual increase in the rate of capital invest-ment has been negligible.[2]

In recent years insecurity about local politics, and particularly a fear of radicalism patterned after the Cuban Revolution, have reinforced this tend-ency. The general disinclination to invest in local productive enterprise has contributed to a relatively high level of under- and unemployment and has left the Alliance for Progress at a standstill. This problem was intensified as a result of the anti-United States riots of January 1964. The relative stagna-tion of the economy can be expected to add to the pressure of an increasingly explosive set of political problems, as aspirations both for improved living conditions and social mobility increase with the rapidly increasing popula-tion. A study made public by the United Nations Economic Commission for Latin America has warned that concerted action must be taken in Panama to prevent a decline in the already low level of living.

> In view of the dismal prospects of growth with which the Panamanian economy is faced, a genuine effort should be made to prevent the situation from worsening and to avoid serious economic imbalances. Given the lack of dynamic stimuli for private investment and the demands made by a high investment rate, an increment of almost 90 per cent would be required in government gross investment. This in itself would imply a radical altera-tion in the traditional role of the public sector in Panama.[3]

A prerequisite for vastly increased government investment would be, of course, a reformed tax structure (traditionally and currently a markedly regressive one). A major step in such a reform would be the imposition of taxes on the sectors best able to pay them, perhaps providing tax modifica-tions to encourage industrial entrepreneurship, with implementation by ap-propriate enforcement machinery.

The tax problem is a substantial one for the Panamanian government, in that the country is bisected by the tax-free Canal Zone, with which it has no border controls, so that traditional sales and customs taxes, at least, are dif-ficult to impose and to collect. Because of dependence on United States cur-rency, moreover, it is not possible for the government to expand the money supply in the attempt to promote development. By the same token, of course, Panama has not been faced with the problems of inflation to which such a course may give rise. It would be further necessary to make changes within the government bureaucracy that would permit the acceptance of new norms related to the administration of a program of development. This would amount to a subcultural revolution, since the bureaucracy has traditionally functioned to do hardly more than advance the political and economic ends of its members, with little commitment to the general public benefit.

Dependence on the canal has been a major factor in the limited growth of the economic base. Panama's second city, Colón, the Atlantic terminus of the canal, a few years ago had become virtually an economic ghost town, as Zone employment had decreased since World War II. Its 50,000 inhabitants had little opportunity for other employment, so that the city presented a telling picture of human distress. Thelma King, the national assembly's most rabidly nationalist and social revolutionary member, represents Colón. Although the establishment of a Free Zone at Colón for the warehousing and transshipment of goods has afforded a certain amount of relief, the city's woes are not yet over.

The primacy of the canal in the economy has had important social consequences in Panama as well. The nation's major ethnic problem involves the West Indians who were originally brought to the Isthmus as unskilled labor during the canal construction period. Holding to the English language and to established behavior patterns, their competition for the limited employment opportunities has made them an object of hostility to other Panamanians.

Employment in the Zone, with its superior wages and working conditions for those fortunate enough to find jobs there, has created a mirage of opportunity that continues to lure many from the rural areas. This movement has been given impetus by the limited opportunities for small farmers in the interior, a condition for which neither the canal nor the United States can be blamed. The combined circumstances, however, have added so many to the urban population that a large proportion live in squalor in city tenements or in the slum *barriadas brujas* ("witch quarters") that encircle the city. Much of this population is unemployed or underemployed, and distress is widespread among them.

The underdevelopment of commerce and industry in Panama has also been cited as a critical factor in the relative weakness of the middle class. In the absence of a rapidly expanding economy, the best way of attaining middle class status and income has been through the public bureaucracy.

> With little rational development of industry, professions, or agriculture, the best chance of an individual's getting ahead now lies in the national budget. This is why the economic basis of the Panamanian middle class must lie disproportionately in government jobs.[4]

The political consequences of this dependence on the public bureaucracy will be treated below.

If the nation's economy is underdeveloped, its educational system by comparison with the rest of Latin America is not. Panama ranks high in literacy, teacher-student ratio, and enrollment in primary and secondary schools, as well as in higher education. Unfortunately, it is possible that the process of "modernization" is becoming unbalanced, and Panama may find that its school system is producing more educated young people seeking high levels of success than the primitive economy can accommodate. The political significance of such underemployed and frustrated intellectuals in underdeveloped countries has been widely recognized.

In summary, Panama's economic situation is one of relative stagnation, with the future of the entire economy hinging on decisions about the canal. Though the economic forecast is poor, there are increasing aspirations for a better life, and it thus seems safe to predict that the political system will suffer severe instability if the situation remains unchanged.

Political History

Separatism in Panama developed as a by-product of its low status as a neglected and isolated province of Colombia; it resulted finally in independence in 1903 as the interests of the Panamanian rebels became congruent with those of the United States. Pressure for the construction of an interocean canal had grown strong in the United States, and the Panamanians needed external support to sustain their assertion of independence. So chaotic were the affairs of the new republic that the United States was able to achieve a strongly advantageous canal treaty. During the first decades of independence the United States exerted a dominant political influence in Isthmian affairs that was not only openly acknowledged but sometimes even requested by Panamanian officials. For example, United States intervention was frequently sought to insure orderly elections, an invitation that would be politically impossible today. In connection with the construction and operation of the canal, the United States took over for the major cities of Panama certain usually governmental functions—the provision of water and sewer facilities and the eradication of threats to public health, for example, resulting in great benefits for the urban populace. This dependence on the United States, the labor policies of the Canal Company, plus the superior attitude and the racial prejudice often displayed by United States citizens, engendered a strong and long-lived resentment which created in the Panamanians a psychological state similar to that of colonial peoples elsewhere.

Since the first decades of independence there has been a steady decrease in United States governmental and quasi-governmental activities in Panama, and an equally steady increase in Panamanian demands for a greater control over the canal and a larger share of the wealth it produces.

With this background of Panamanian-United States relations, it is not surprising that Panama's political history has been a history of rising nationalism which seems likely to continue. For one thing, nationalist extremists will not allow the politicians to relax their demands on the United States—public opinion can be powerfully mobilized on any question of nationalism—and any politician lacking overt enthusiasm for nationalism would soon find his public career terminated. In addition, as a result of the sweep of nationalism over Africa, the Middle East, and Asia (and of the Communist-bloc policy of supporting it) Latin American nationalism has gained militant international interest and support. Thus the Egyptians have been active in stimulating Panamanian demands for Canal Zone sovereignty since the nationalization of the Suez Canal. Castro has played on a similar theme, although his communization of Cuba has tended to obscure the nationalist aspect and attraction of his revolution. Nationalist students in Panama have even been drawn to the cause of Lumumba. In short, Panamanian nationalism seems to have become inextricably entwined with the nationalist politics of the new states.

It would be inaccurate, however, to regard the major riots which took place in January 1964 on the Canal Zone–Panama City border as due to foreign influences; local tensions over the always sensitive issue of control over the Canal Zone were clearly responsible. It is thus not possible to dismiss the hundreds of thousands of Panamanians who attended the funeral ceremonies of the "martyred" rioters as *fidelistas* or leftists manipulated by external powers.

Panama's history has displayed less violence and less militarism than most of the Latin American countries, probably because of the political role of the United States during the early decades of independence. United States responsibility for the protection of Panamanian independence was formalized by treaty, and the role of a domestic armed force was thus circumscribed. The larger state's role as arbiter was a substitute for the violent competition employed elsewhere in the region for the making of political decisions. Lately, as the role of the United States has diminished, there has been some tendency in Panama toward an increasing use of violence and military action in political decision-making.

Change in the locus of power and the rules of the political game has been very gradual. No middle-class revolution has yet occurred on the Isthmus, and though more and more people of middle-class background have attained power positions, these have been largely individual rather than group-based achievements. The rise of a proletariat powerful enough to organize politically that characterizes such Latin states as Argentina, Uruguay, Bolivia, and Cuba has had no parallel in Panama. It is difficult to evaluate the extent of democratic practices on the Isthmus, for though there is a trend toward the institutionalizing of a constitutional electoral process, there have been no concomitant social and economic changes that would enable the great mass of citizens to make effective use of democratic political machinery.

The Political Process

If power is defined as effective participation in the making of decisions about what the government does (or does not do), then power in Panama seems to have been clearly concentrated in the hands of a small group of wealthy, prestigious families whose position rests on a combination of land ownership, commerce, and industry. Traditionally, this group has been Panama's oligarchy. The roster of national presidents shows one after another of these families represented, with very few exceptions. The group's power is reflected in basic decisions about the tax structure (heavily regressive), social welfare legislation (implemented only at a low level), and agrarian reform (none). However, concentration of power does not imply a monopoly of power, for members of the middle class and some newly rich have gained important positions. Furthermore, during the past few years a minimum-wage law was enacted which was bitterly opposed by many members of the oligarchy. This attests in part to the sporadic power of the working class, but also to the realization of the wealthy that they must make gestures to the working class if they are to check the development of a social revolutionary tide. Because of the poor economic or political organization of the urban working class, the absolute lack of organization of the *campesinos*, and the scarcity of employment opportunities, it is questionable whether such laws as that setting minimum wages are actually implemented. Unfortunately, there has been no study of the administration of law in Panama, let alone any treatment indicating the extent to which sanctions are used to discourage the disadvantaged from attempting to invoke a formally protective law.

The Military

Although it gets no conspicuous attention in the international press, the Panamanian Guardia Nacional (the only armed force in the country) plays an important role in national politics. Since early in the thirties, when it became apparent that the United States no longer wanted to play the role of arbiter in Panamanian internal affairs, the power of the Guardia has grown. Its main function has been to maintain or attain order when electoral competition degenerated into physical violence. Since the elements most anxious for social reform have never been able to articulate their wants effectively, nor to organize in support of their inchoate demands, the Guardia has been spared the necessity of defining its position on this troubling question.

Its identity as an autonomous power center emerged most clearly during the Remón period. José Remón, a man of modest social background, had made his career in the Guardia, and rose to its top post in the mid-1940's. He was able to secure greatly increased funds, which he used to modernize training methods and equipment, and to improve salaries and fringe benefits (for example, the provision of low-cost housing) for officers and enlisted men. This resulted in a rise in morale which Remón converted to strong support for his political aims. After for some time being a power-not-too-far-behind-the-throne, he ran for the presidency in 1952. Although the Guardia was presumed to be an important base for his candidacy, it is difficult to specify exactly how it exercised influence. It is conceivable that its reputation was sufficient to discourage some opposition, but there were also complaints about specific Guard actions during the election.

During Remón's presidency the Guardia for the first time found itself supporting an administration actively committed to social reform, political honesty, and economic development. Under Remón the tax system was modified and, more important, the imposition of taxes was followed by enforced collection (a thoroughgoing break with Panamanian precedent). Negro Panamanians, mostly lower class, were accorded higher status, and the government took a strong stand against ethnic discrimination in Canal Zone employment policies that culminated in a more favorable treaty revision. Initial steps were taken toward the development of industry and agriculture, and the public bureaucracy was shaken to learn that the president expected work to be done toward these ends. There was considerable oligarchic opposition to these policies, but Remón's standing with the Guardia prevented any direct assault on his program. With his assassination in 1955, in a crime whose origin remains unclear, the reform period ended. Since then, the Guardia has supported the re-establishment of a power structure operating to preserve the status quo and has not appeared to have a definable, independent political position except for its permanent, unspoken demand for the continuation of its perquisites.

The Guardia's current support of the political system may be a function of the ideological position of its officers, or it may be a simple contentment with the relatively good life the system provides it. It is frequently hypothesized that the Latin American military in general is shifting toward an increasingly liberal sociopolitical orientation as its leadership becomes increasingly middle class and proletarian. However, an alternative hypothesis as yet untestable is that the recruit or officer of poor or modest background considers himself lucky to achieve the rewards of military life and tends to give strong support to the system that provides them, regardless of the disadvantages of that system for his less fortunate fellows. The personalistic orientation of Latin Americans so widely noted by observers would suggest that the second hypothesis has greater applicability. The recent activities of the Guardia Nacional, at any rate, suggest that its officers are committed to "order," and that extremists, particularly on the left, will not be tolerated. Its harassment of local *fidelistas* and apparent Communist sympathizers, its general hostility toward students because of their affinity with the left and their disrespect for formal authority is evidence in this direction. Whether the Guardia would try to take independent action against nontotalitarian, less radical leftists if they should become politically organized remains to be seen.

It is equally possible that the Guardia is simply becoming more committed to civilian supremacy in politics, and that its anti-extremist activity reflects only the policy position of the administration of the present president, Roberto F. Chiari, which is firmly opposed to the Cuban regime and to Communism. Chiari's frequent public statements praising the Guardia and encouraging it to follow the constitutional path, although seeming to reflect its growing acceptance of civil authority, may equally well indicate his own recognition of its essential autonomy.

In either case, it is undeniable that the Guardia is becoming increasingly professional in its knowledge and use of modern techniques of defense and internal security. For example, it is now training its members in antiguerrilla warfare. All of this makes the task of the revolutionary increasingly difficult and augments the potential power of the military in politics.

Party Competition

Panamanian politics illustrates the danger of assuming that political competition per se reflects a healthily democratic system. There has been much competition, but it has occurred between politicians dedicated essentially to the status quo, who contest against one another on a personal, absolutely unprogrammatic basis. There have been myriads of parties and a host of partisan coalitions, but hardly any have represented ideological positions. Only rarely can a party be identified with a program for what the government should do, except for rewarding the followers of the victor.

In recent history there have been three exceptions. The first and most important has been the *panameñista* movement, organized about Arnulfo Arias, who was president in 1941 and in 1951 and ran a very close second (if the ballots were counted correctly, a premise which has been widely challenged) in the presidential elections of May 1964. *Panameñismo* has been primarily nationalist, tapping the most widespread and multiform ideological current in the country. Arias had no program but hostility to foreigners, in which he included the United States, the Canal Zone residents, and the West Indian and Chinese minorities. He was in practice authoritarian, being the only president in recent times who systematically suspended constitutional liberties and prevented the expression of opposition. Despite his capacity for antagonizing those who value order and constitutional democracy, Arias seems to be the most charismatic political leader in the country, and by adding the invocation of radical nationalism to his charisma he has created a mass following.

Arias' *panameñismo* has not so far resulted in any major change in the power structure or the regime. But with the injection of social revolution into nationalism in Latin America and the economically underdeveloped world in general, a new tide of *panameñismo* may lead to such changes, as ideologues within the ranks of the diffuse nationalist movement, seeking a variety of political, economic, and social innovations, attain positions of power. Curiously enough, Arias himself had become much less anti-American by the time of his presidential candidacy of 1964; this moderation may have been partly responsible for his defeat, in view of the strong anti-American feelings prevalent after the January riots.

Control of the symbolism of nationalism is passing from the hands of the traditional elite, whose long habit of focusing public attention on alleged United States transgressions was generally successful in diverting that attention from the results of their own exploitation. The attempted invasion of the Canal Zone on Panamanian Independence Day, 1959, led by nationalist politicians and encouraged by a variety of extremists, had to be repelled by United States troops with fixed bayonets after much rock-throwing, use of tear gas, and widespread personal injury and damage to property. The intensity and hysterical uncontrollability of the affair was shocking to Panamanians and United States leaders as well, and marked the emergence of a new trend toward a "social" nationalism, reflected unmistakably in the affinity between Panamanian *fidelistas* and nationalists right after the Cuban Revolution. As Eric Hoffer's analyses in *The True Believer* indicate, there is a danger inherent in trying to check one mass movement by substituting another for it. The Panamanian oligarchy manipulated nationalist sentiment to check a locally oriented reform movement, and then found their success inspiring others to manipulate the same symbols in an attempt to destroy the traditional system they have so long controlled. That they probably recognize this danger is suggested by the alliance which was formed by leading politicians against the 1964 presidential candidacy of Arnulfo Arias. This situation in Panama is comparable to similar ones in the history of the more industrialized countries of Latin America. According to John J. Johnson, while "middle sector" politicians used nationalism in the early twentieth century against the coalition of local mining and agricultural interests and foreign businessmen, today politicians representing working-class interests have seized the issue and are using it in a manner to jeopardize the now considerable power of the middle sectors.[5] The situation in Panama is similar generally though not in detail, since the middle sectors there have not yet attained a high degree of power.

The radical youth movement is another exception to the generalization that political competition in Panama is not programmatic. It includes a congeries of dramatically styled "revolutionary" student groups that are associated, at least in ideology, with the Cuban Revolution. Though the movement gained considerable national attention by a 1959 uprising, by attempts to bomb opponents, and by the police discovery of a collection of propaganda and uniforms, it has apparently failed to establish a continuing mass organization. Mainly responsible for its failure was the systematic opposition of the Chiari administration to *fidelismo*. Another factor militating against the organization of this sort of movement was the apparently sharp decline in public sympathy for the Cuban Revolution since late in 1960.

The third exception to the generalization is the recently organized Christian Democratic Party, which represents a moderate reformist and democratic position. Led by respected professional men and university students, it has implored the Establishment to support reform before a wave of totalitarian social revolution engulfs the country. It is shunned by the wealthy and by the professional politicians, and at the time of writing had not yet become effectively organized for electoral competition. Though the party's leadership seems to stand for much of President Chiari's stated program, there has been no coalition between the two elements.

Panama's relative lack of political competition on other than a personal basis reflects the lack of organization of several interests that are prominently represented in the politics of other Latin American countries. The sparsity of industry reduces the basis for labor unions, and though urban unions exist, they are not very assertive. The only notable agricultural union, which serves the United Fruit Company dominated banana industry, is perhaps tolerated only because the company is a foreign one. Contributing also to the political weakness of the working class is its ethnic division between Spanish-speaking stock and English speakers of West Indian origin; hostility between groups of similar socio-economic level may overwhelm any tendency they might otherwise have toward uniting in an urban working-class political or economic movement. This could be a continuing problem so long as nationalism remains the primary issue in Panama, because antagonism toward the West Indians has been a recurrent and prominent component of nationalist upsurges.

The concentration of such a large proportion of middle-class positions in the government bureaucracy may account for the lack of an independent middle class with real political significance. Employment in the civil service necessarily depends on the good will of the politicians, who represent either personal or upper-class interests; this in itself tends to stifle the articulation of new demands, and in addition alternative middle-status employment is very scarce in Panama. Frustration on the domestic political level may account for the often reported vigorous nationalism that seems to characterize many of these middle-class people. Unable to organize in behalf of their interests in domestic affairs, they project their hostility onto the United States; the canal, highly visible and bristling with attractive middle-status positions that would be available to Panamanians if the waterway were nationalized, stands as a constant source of envy. Whether or not the middle class has any recognition of the potentially radical course a nationalist movement might take cannot as yet be determined. It does seem likely, however, that the recent political experiences of the Cuban middle class under a regime originally identified with nationalist reform may moderate the nationalist sentiments of the middle-class Panamanians.

The present writer's studies of the political orientations of Panamanian young people point up another ambivalence in Panamanian nationalism. At one predominantly middle-class secondary school, the students were about evenly divided on the question of whether Panama could operate the canal without the assistance of the United States, and less than a fourth strongly believed it could. It seems likely that middle-class nationalism in Panama is still emerging from a state of defensive lack of self-confidence into one of assertiveness and conviction of efficacy, the latter orientation seeming pronounced among another sample of students, at the university's law school.

Student Political Activity

Since there are almost no well-integrated and articulate organizations to advance middle-class and proletarian interests, the students—university and secondary—tend to monopolize the expression of dissatisfaction and demands for reform; they perform this function almost continuously. They have a traditional role as spokesmen for the people, are well-organized, and extremely sensitive to the activities of the politicians.

There are two major centers of student politics, the National University and the National Institute (a secondary school), whose student bodies frequently join forces in political action, engaging periodically in the demonstrations considered typical of Latin American students. In some of these latter the National Institute students (characterized as "the brains") have mobilized the students from other schools as "shock troops." Because the students have considerable political status among the people, the government has dealt very carefully with their demands. Often the formal negotiations between government and students have assumed a curious resemblance to dealings between independent states. The students' habitual recourse to the public streets for the making of their demands or protests has resulted in very hostile relations with the Guardia Nacional. In 1958 several National Institute students lost their lives in an encounter with the Guardia, and while it is very difficult in such a melee to reconstruct events and fix the responsibility for bloodshed, it is a reflection of the students' standing in the society that the government against which they were rioting has chosen to indemnify the families of the slain.

At the University the activists tend to fall into two groups: the extremists like the supporters of the current Cuban regime and a coalition of moderate social democrats and Christian Democrats. Few if any of the students uphold the status quo or have right-wing orientations. (The Panamanian students who do probably attend foreign universities.) Recently students from Catholic secondary schools have for the first time become politically active also, rallying to the cause of anti-Communism and opposition to Fidel Castro.

The writer's studies of student political orientations show little support for the prevailing political system among any group of students, but indicate that the great bulk are not in absolute opposition to the country's ruling group. Rather, there is an extreme degree of ambivalence, the negative part of which is a reaction against endemic corruption and against officials unresponsive to the needs of the poor. The positive part embodies a high valuation of democracy, even though democratic forms and symbols have been manipulated for so long without effecting any amelioration of the lot of most citizens. No matter how strongly they may favor political, social, or economic change, there seem to be very few students who endorse the use of systematic violence and coercion. However, these orientations are not necessarily permanent. There is an extremely strong aspiration for success among the students regardless of class background, and they have almost as high an expectation of achievement. Should they be disappointed in these desires, should the society fail to provide sufficient positions of the desired income and status, the frustrated might well find their political values changing in favor of more extreme methods and institutions.

The 1960 Election and Its Aftermath

Latin America currently faces renewed pressures toward dictatorship and militarism in a heightening of the struggle between the forces of reaction, reform, and revolution. Yet in Panama, the presidential election of 1960 was at least a partial triumph for democracy, and the new government represented a moderate, consensual approach toward economic development and social justice. Was this a real deviation from the general regional norm, or only the same old political pattern under a new disguise?

In May 1960 it was generally assumed that the "official" candidate would gain the usual victory. However, he lost to one of the two opposition candidates in an election in which there were none of the usual complaints that the Guardia had intervened illegally nor that the National Elections Board had manipulated ballot tabulations. Roberto Chiari was declared winner straightforwardly and took office in October without there having been any threat that his predecessor might attempt to stay on in power. Up to that point there was no more apparent significance to the election than that the forms of political democracy has been unprecedentedly observed.

After the inauguration, however, Chiari presented himself to the public as a forceful advocate of social reform and economic development, an antagonist of Castro and the Communists, and a moderate nationalist who through constructive, rational argument aimed to persuade the United States to make major concessions about the canal. He told his fellow oligarchs that he might well be the last president to be elected from their narrow circle; he warned them that change was bound to come soon, and that they had it within their power to accommodate it peacefully and constructively by supporting reform or, if they stubbornly refused to acknowledge the imperatives of the changing society, to abandon the field to the totalitarians, citing the case of Cuba as an example. His forcefully articulated position and the fact of his democratic election appeared to raise the morale and hopes of the advocates of reform and constitutional democracy to a point of euphoria. His widespread popularity helped him a great deal in his subsequent campaign to suppress extremist and *fidelista* activity and to accomplish an ultimately complete severance of diplomatic relations with Cuba; he was able to establish a principle of "we will do it our way." He entered into negotiations with the able United States ambassador and other officials to improve relations between Panama and the occupants of the Zone and to gain substantial United States assistance in economic development. An early product of these efforts was the launching of low-cost public housing projects in the worst-housed areas of Panama City and of a model self-help home-construction project in one of the *barriadas brujas;* for these projects the United States contributed funds, materials, and technical assistance.

Since then, the United States has provided assistance on a wide range of development projects; relations between the two countries were much improved after the near-disaster of 1959, and the local *fidelista* threat diminished considerably. The only thing that did not change substantially was public policy. The national assembly elected at the same time as Chiari was dominated by opposition parties; but the cause of the policy deadlock was not, apparently, partisan intransigence but rather the traditional orientations of the deputies. Reform is not an acknowledged value among them, let alone perceived as an immediate necessity. Jockeying for personal advantage within the political structure continued to occupy them, and while there was no overt opposition to Chiari's program, it was for the most part simply ignored. There has been some minor tax revision, but nothing has been done to harness local capital for the purposes of development. An agrarian reform law was passed, but its implementation was problematical.

As the Chiari presidency moved into its final year, it became clear that despite some economic growth, the reform program had been blocked or never given impetus at all. Alliance for Progress projects aimed at strengthening the social and economic bases for development through schools, roads, and agricultural facilities generally had similar histories. Another electoral campaign developed among the same personalist parties and politicians of the past, reflecting the continuity of the traditional political process and the reformists' failure to create any political mechanism through which changes might be accomplished. A resurvey of students in an upper- and upper-middle-class private high school in late 1963 indicated that a wave of cynicism had developed within even this privileged sector, as a consequence of the high expectations of 1960 and their subsequent frustration.

It remains to be seen how the Panamanians who benefit from the *status quo* will react to the attempt to develop a strong organization dedicated to social reform. While civil liberties have been more successfully institutionalized in Panama than in many other countries in the region, there have been no concerted attempts to organize in opposition to the *status quo;* so the actual commitment to civil liberties has not been really tested. It must also be kept in mind that one cannot assume a commitment to civil liberties on the part of Panamanian reformists. Students' zeal has sometimes led them to use political methods far outside these limits.

The reopening of negotiations with the United States for a revision of the Canal Treaty created within Panama a political climate with a high potential for a resurgence of radical nationalism. Chiari had staked the political prestige of his administration on gaining major concessions from the United States; although United States officials have no doubt been aware of Chiari's needs, they also operate within a political climate, one that they have so far assessed as unfavorable to any negotiated reduction of United States authority in the Canal Zone. The January 1964 riots have raised nationalist demands and expectations of the government to new heights, and probably have reduced the salience of development programs and the Alliance for Progress. Although Arnulfo Arias was defeated for the presidency by Marco A. Robles, who was backed by President Chiari, this did not signify a defeat for extreme nationalism; in fact, Arias may have lost because he had greatly modified his former anti-United States position and talked of the need to work together with the United States. It seems certain that the Panamanian administration coming to office in October 1964 will find its capacity to maneuver quite limited by an aroused nationalist populace.

Governmental Institutions

By Panama's constitution, governmental powers are distributed among the three traditional branches, but by tradition neither the legislature nor the courts have demonstrated much independence of the president. Perhaps as a result, there has been little academic interest in the selection and behavior of deputies or judges. However, very recent experience suggests that as demands for major policy change make themselves felt in the formal governmental process, the formal distribution of power between the executive and the legislature becomes quite important. As was noted in the preceding section, President Chiari's program of government-guided economic development and social reform has had little implementation from the single-chamber legislature. Choosing to operate constitutionally, he has attempted to persuade rather than coerce the deputies to support his program, but persuasion, particularly when there is no supportive political organization such as a mass-based party, has not been adequate to the task. The formal distribution of power has therefore become an important factor in Panamanian government. The fact that legislative deputies are elected by proportional representation has contributed to the difficulties involved in creating a majority party. The deputies are elected for a four-year term which coincides with that of the president; the five justices of the supreme court are appointed by the president, and confirmed by the assembly, for ten-year terms.

Another current brake on the forces of political change is the constitutional prohibition against re-election of an individual to the presidency until the next two terms have elapsed. Without strongly organized programmatic parties, this is very likely to result in little continuity in support for a body of policies, especially given the short four-year term. The strongly personalist traditions militate against the likelihood of two successive presidents having the same political interests or commitments and, again, in the absence of programmatic parties, power gravitates toward the maintenance of the status quo. Such constitutional provisions have been deliberately adopted in Latin America to discourage *continuismo* and other dictatorial tendencies of political leaders. However, if the leader should happen, like Chiari, to have any commitment to constitutionalism, this kind of provision operates toward the retardation of reform.

The same situation obtains in the public bureaucracy. The lack of a merit system of employment has meant a virtually complete turnover of personnel with each new president as he rewards his supporters. This patronage practice has inflated the bureaucracy with myriads of *botellas* (non-essential positions) as well. All this has tended to encourage short-term, individualistic perspectives as guides in administrative behavior to the detriment of any program, particularly any program involving economic development, which requires coordination over time. Without a merit system, the only bases of administrative efficiency in program effectuation would seem to be a highly organized and continuing executive leadership or revolutionary euphoria, neither of which obtains in contemporary Panama. In the absence of a dynamically expanding economy, however, the large bureaucracy has at least made it possible for many Panamanians to acquire white-collar positions that yield moderately high income and middle-class status, and has thereby satisfied some of the increasing demands for social mobility.

Public Policy

Since the nature of public policy has been treated throughout this chapter, the following is intended as a brief summary of the policy situation.

The scope of government is rather restricted in Panama in comparison with many other Latin American countries. A program of economic development, though limited in scope and gradual in rate, is discernible, but specific evaluations compared to other programs within the region are difficult even to speculate about, so limited are the available data. Clearly, however, the Panamanian government has been unable to tap available local capital directly for development purposes. Nor has it been able to create a sufficiently attractive economic climate to overcome the traditional disinclination to invest in productive enterprise. Though it is not current policy, the idea of nationalizing the canal may have an increasing appeal for the growing proportion of citizens who are ambitious for socio-economic advancement within an economy held to a virtual standstill.

Prevailing policy in the main supports the present distribution of wealth and status. Though there has been an increase in demands for tax, land, and housing reforms, for example, there has been little policy change as yet. It is still an open question whether gradual reform can be instituted soon enough to stave off a more radical, revolutionary approach, but even if the evolutionary approach should fail, recourse to extreme measures may still be a long way in the future.

Current foreign policy reflects a commitment along with the United States in an anti-Castro, anti-Communist stance. Panama relies heavily on the United States for economic development funds and is at the same time maneuvering for major concessions in the Canal Treaty, concessions which public opinion in the United States is probably little prepared to entertain.

NOTES FOR CHAPTER VII

1. The research upon which much of this chapter is based was supported by the Bureau of Social and Political Research and the Office of International Programs at Michigan State University and the Institute for Community Studies and the Office of Scientific and Scholarly Research at the University of Oregon.

2. Pedro C. M. Teichert, *Economic Policy Revolution and Industrialization in Latin America*, Bureau of Business Research, University of Mississippi, Oxford, 1959, p. 31.
3. "The Economic Development of Panama," *Economic Bulletin for Latin America*, IV, Oct. 1959, pp. 56-7.
4. John Biesanz and Luke M. Smith, "Panamanian Politics," *Journal of Politics*, XIV, Aug. 1952, p. 388.
5. John J. Johnson, *Political Change in Latin America: The Emergence of the Middle Sectors*, Stanford University Press, Stanford, 1958, pp. 188-91.

SELECTED BIBLIOGRAPHY

Richard N. Adams, *Culture Surveys of Panama, Nicaragua, Guatemala, El Salvador, Honduras*, Pan American Sanitary Bureau, World Health Organization, Washington, 1957.

John and Mavis Biesanz, *The People of Panama*, Columbia University Press, New York, 1955.

John Biesanz and Luke M. Smith, "Panamanian Politics," *Journal of Politics*, XIV, Aug. 1952, pp. 386-402.

Theo R. Crevenna, (Ed.), *Materiales para el Estudio de la Clase Media en la America Latina—IV: La Clase Media en Panama, El Salvador, Honduras, y Nicaragua*, Pan American Union, Washington, 1950.

"The Economic Development of Panama," *Economic Bulletin for Latin America*, IV, Oct. 1959, pp. 48-59.

Daniel Goldrich and Edward W. Scott, "Developing Political Orientations of Panamanian Students," *Journal of Politics*, XXIII, Feb. 1961, pp. 84-107.

———, "Toward an Estimate of Social Revolutions in Latin America; Some Orienting Concepts and Case Study," *Centennial Review*, VI, Summer 1962, pp. 394-408.

———, *Radical Nationalism: the Political Orientations of Panamanian Law Students*, Bureau of Social and Political Research, Michigan State University, East Lansing, 1962.

John D. Martz, *Central America: The Crisis and the Challenge*, University of North Carolina Press, Chapel Hill, 1959.

Martin B. Travis and James T. Watkins, "Control of the Panama Canal: An Obsolete Shibboleth?" *Foreign Affairs*, XXXVII, April 1959, pp. 406-418.

Subcommittee on Inter-American Affairs, Committee on Foreign Affairs, U.S. House of Representatives, 86th Congress, "Report on United States Relations with Panama," U.S. Government Printing Office, Washington, 1960.

VIII *Rayford W. Logan and Martin C. Needler*

HAITI

Social and Economic Background

Haiti stands out from the other Latin American countries in many ways. The first state to become an independent republic, it may be the last to become a functioning constitutional democracy.

Haiti occupies the mountainous Western third of the island of Hispaniola in the Caribbean. This portion of the island was ceded to France by Spain in 1697; the Spanish had been masters of the island since Columbus set foot on it, in November of 1492. The remainder of Hispaniola is occupied today by the Dominican Republic. Although the predominant coffee culture gives the Haitian economy some features in common with the economies of other Latin American states, Haitian society exhibits radically different patterns.

Haiti is the only predominantly Negro nation in Latin America; it is the only independent nation in Latin America whose European culture is French; and it has, with the possible exception of Bolivia, the lowest per capita income. The low level of this per capita income of about $72 a year is due more to the country's population density, the greatest of the Latin American nations, to the rudimentary state of agricultural technology, and to its lack of arable land and of natural resources than to its ethnic composition or its French culture.

The people of Haiti are about 99 percent Negro and colored, with "blacks" accounting for more than 90 percent. "Black" is an imprecise term; it may mean black or any shade of brown. Status sometimes determines "color": a folk expression says mockingly that "a poor white man is a mulatto, a poor mulatto is a Negro; a rich Negro is a mulatto, a rich mulatto is a white man."

While race in a biological sense has no explanatory relevance, the slave origin of most of the population is central in understanding Haiti's poverty. Saint-Domingue (the French colonial name for Haiti) had about 500,000 slaves, nearly all of whom were Negroes, and only about 35,000 whites and 35,000 mulattoes. These slaves came from many different parts of Africa and spoke languages often unintelligible to each other. Practically all of them were illiterate in any language when Haiti became independent on January 1, 1804.

By way of contrast mulattoes, who owned about one-third of the slaves and of the plantations, took inordinate pride in their French culture, although

149

white Frenchmen scorned the efforts of the mulattoes to emulate them. One of the worst aspects of this emulation was contempt for the slaves.

It is thus understandable that Haiti has failed to achieve a symbiosis of the French-acculturated mulattoes and of the Negroes, whose African origins survive in the majority of the people. This divisive effect, rooted in the colonial period, has been the central theme in Haitian history, especially since French-acculturated Negroes are as contemptuous of the African masses as are the mulattoes.

Independence and the Caste System

The War for Emancipation and Independence accentuated this division of the population. White Frenchmen in Saint-Domingue wanted liberty, equality, and fraternity, as did the French revolutionists of 1789, but were not willing to grant it to mulattoes. Mulattoes wanted liberty, equality, and fraternity, but were unwilling to accord it to slaves. If the slaves wanted to enjoy the blessings of liberty, they would have to fight for it themselves; and in 1791 they began a revolt to gain emancipation.

The revolt became a miniature international war after the outbreak of war in Europe in 1793. France decreed the emancipation of the slaves in 1794, partly in order to insure their support against Britain and Spain. French forces in Saint-Domingue, fighting alongside the slaves, led principally by the black generals Toussaint L'Ouverture, Jean-Jacques Dessalines, and Henri Christophe, quickly defeated the Spaniards and in 1798 drove British troops out of Saint-Domingue. In that year France named Toussaint L'Ouverture commander-in-chief of all the French forces in the territory. In the same year the United States began the undeclared Naval War with France, which seemed at the time to be a greater enemy to the young republic than Britain. Since Toussaint supported the United States, American warships aided him in the so-called War of the Castes (1800).

In the years that followed, the changes on the French political scene, as the Republic was succeeded by the Empire, together with uncertainty about French intentions and the intervention of other states' forces against France, added to the confusion of Haitian politics. The war between blacks and mulattoes—won by the blacks under Toussaint—was followed, after a period, by their cooperation against the French, after Toussaint was seized by treachery and deported to Europe to pave the way for the restoration of slavery which Napoleon had ordered. With British naval assistance and American supplies, the anti-French forces were victorious.

But the united front of Negroes and mulattoes, forged by the war against white Frenchmen, did not long endure. On January 1, 1804, Dessalines proclaimed the independence of the first Latin American nation. From that time to the present day, the clash of color and class rooted in the colonial period and in the hostilities of the War of Independence has inhibited the integration of French and African cultures. This clash is not uncommon in the other Latin American nations, for most of them have similar problems with respect to their white, *mestizo*, Indian, colored, and Negro peoples. But no other Latin American nation, not even the Dominican Republic or Cuba, has as high a percentage of Negroes as does Haiti.

No other Latin American nation has repudiated its European culture as much as has Haiti. There, hatred of Frenchmen—a legacy of the colonial period and of the War of Independence—excluded practically all whites from participation in the development of the country for more than a century after independence. It is true that Christophe (King Henry I) admitted a few English teachers in the northern part of the island during the second decade of the nineteenth century, and in the latter part of that century a few Syrians, Germans, and Chinese established themselves as merchants and traders, and a small number of Americans as missionaries. Nevertheless—although the Haitian elite resented the term—Haiti, because of its fear that a white man meant a slaveholder, became in large measure the Black Republic.

The Haitian elite, most of whom until recently were mulattoes, took great pride in their French language and culture, including Catholicism. These were symbols of status which set them apart from the black masses, who spoke Creole, an amalgam of a simplified eighteenth-century French with African dialects, and who practiced Vodun (Voodoo), a folk religion compounded of African rites and beliefs and Catholicism. Most members of the elite, however, speak and understand Creole as a means of communication with servants and, for political reasons, of identification with the masses. Similarly, many of the elite are not averse to practicing Vodun; President François Duvalier's support by the masses stems in part from the popular belief that he is a high priest of Vodun. After the American occupation, which lasted from 1915 to 1934, and subsequent American financial dominance lasting until about 1961, knowledge of the English language and American manners and customs became an additional status symbol among the elite. The masses were affected very little by this change, however.

Economic and Social Problems

The War of Independence bequeathed to Haiti not only hatred of whites and an increased hostility between mulattoes and blacks; the war also left a legacy of poverty. Saint-Domingue had been the most productive of the French colonies; Haiti soon became one of the poorest of the Latin American nations, for the war resulted in the destruction of most of the machinery used in the production of sugar and indigo, the two principal crops.

Haiti has remained primarily an agricultural country, with an area of 10,711 square miles, about the size of Maryland. Arable land constitutes about 13 percent of the total surface; permanent meadows and pastures, 12 percent. This arable land is so small that it provides only a subsistence livelihood for a population estimated in 1960 as 3,500,000, nearly nine-tenths of whom live in small townships of fewer than 500 persons. Coffee is grown on the slopes of the mountains which constitute about 75 percent of the total area. In order to cultivate this crop peasants cut down the trees and thus increase the erosion caused by heavy rains. In terms of arable and productive land, Haiti has a higher population density, about 925 per square mile, than does any other Latin American country. Neither the American occupation nor subsequent American financial aid and technical assistance have measurably ameliorated Haiti's basic plight of too little land and too many people. Irrigation of the Artibonite River Valley, which might have added substantially to the amount of arable land, had been abandoned before the United States withdrew practically all economic aid in 1963 because of the increasingly dictatorial and anti-American orientation of Duvalier's regime.

Despite promises made by the United States in treaties of 1916 and 1917 to aid in the commercial development of Haiti, Haiti is as dependent upon coffee as its principal export as it was prior to the American occupation. During the fiscal year October 1, 1958, to September 30, 1959, when exports amounted to a little more than $20,000,000, coffee accounted for about 65 percent. Sisal, which became important during World War II, when supplies of hemp were almost shut off from other parts of the world, accounted for about 25 percent. The one known relatively important mineral resource, bauxite, amounted in 1959 to only 448,000 short tons. Local industries consisted primarily of small factories for bread, ice, cotton textiles, cement, and soap, electric power stations, and automobile service stations. There were only about 200 miles of operating railways, the shortest mileage in any Latin American nation, poorly equipped freight trains, and about 2,000 miles of road network, the shortest in the area except for Honduras. Haiti had the smallest number of telephones, about one per thousand population, and the smallest number of radio receivers, about six per thousand.

In the early 1960's one of Haiti's principal imports was wheat flour, for upper-class Haitians insisted upon their *baguette* as much as did Frenchmen in France. Automobiles, spare parts, and cloth fabrics were also important imports.

The rate of illiteracy in Haiti is the highest in Latin America, close to 90 percent. Since the national budget, approximately $35 million annually over the past few years, equals only about $10 per capita and since much of this is spent on defense, representation abroad, the upkeep of the presidency, and administration, not much is left for education, public works, public health, and other socially desirable purposes. During 1962 and 1963 President Duvalier spent increasingly large sums for military purposes, and probably for a substantial bank account abroad in the event that he deemed escape necessary and feasible.

Another important social ill is the slow rate of emancipation of women from practices rooted in their African origins and in the colonial period. Formal marriage was not a common practice; women did much of the work in the fields; they were generally denied the few opportunities for education enjoyed by a small minority of men. After independence, when fear of renewed invasions required substantially large bodies of soldiers, women continued to labor in the fields and to bring fruits and vegetables for sale in market places. Later, during struggles for power among Haitian leaders, large numbers of men engaged in fighting and women had to do much of the same kind of work.

Until recently upper-class women disdained gainful employment. Since the American occupation, however, an increasing number have become teachers, stenographers, and clerks; and a few have entered the professions. Not until the constitution of November 25, 1950, however, were women given the right to vote in municipal elections; three years later they could vote in national elections. The 1950 Constitution recognized the right of women to fill any government post. Since most elections since then have been rigged and since few women had the training or the experience for the higher government posts, these constitutional rights have not noticeably ameliorated the plight of women.

With an expanding population which was barred by law from migrating to most Latin American countries, with little hope for a significant increase in the amount of arable land, with its principal export crop, coffee, suffering from overproduction in the world market, with little likelihood of substantial industrialization, and under the constant threat of invasion and internal revolt against a ruthless dictator, Haiti faced in 1964 a bleak future.

Political History

From 1804 to 1915 Haiti maintained a precarious independence. Strong military figures, like the *caudillos* who flourished in Spanish America, predominated among the country's rulers. With the exception of Emperor Dessalines, 1804-1806, King Henri Christophe, 1811-1820, and Emperor Faustin I, 1849-1859, these rulers bore the title of President. Between 1804, and the beginning of the American occupation on July 28, 1915, Haiti had twenty-six different rulers. The average of a little more than four years per ruler gives a false picture of what appears to be relative stability. Christophe ruled for more than thirteen years; Alexander Pétion, for eleven; Jean-Pierre Boyer, for twenty-five; Faustin Soulouque, for almost twelve; Fabre Geffard for eight; Etienne Félicité Solomon, for almost nine. As in many countries, a period of long rule was sometimes followed by a series of revolutions; for example, after the overthrow of Boyer in 1843, four presidents served short terms of office until the advent of Soulouque to power in 1847. After twenty years of rule by Faustin Soulouque and Geffard, 1847-1867, four presidents served briefly between 1867 and 1879. The worst period of instability, which lasted from August 1911 to July 28, 1915, witnessed the rapid succession of six presidents, none of whom served a full year and all of whom died by violence. Thus the periods of greatest stability came soon after independence and during the middle period of Haitian history.

Haiti's domestic problems were aggravated until the last quarter of the nineteenth century by the periodic attempts of her leaders to gain control of the entire island. Toussaint L'Ouverture launched an army in 1800 or 1801 which took possession of Santo Domingo. Dessalines failed in his effort to drive out French troops who had been called to the rescue of Santo Domingo following the capture of Toussaint. After the death of Pétion in 1818 and of Christophe in 1820, President Boyer gained control of Haiti and in 1822 of the eastern part of the island. This occupation, which many Dominican writers call the Period of Ethiopianization or of Africanization, ended in 1843 when Boyer was forced to resign by revolutionists. Faustin renewed the attempts to gain control of the Dominican Republic but was finally defeated. After a period of disorder and great bloodshed, climaxed in 1915 by the assassination of President Vilbrun Guillaume Sam, United States forces intervened and occupied the country.

The American Occupation

The motives which prompted United States intervention were complex. Dismay at the violence and bloodshed of Haitian politics, and simple impatience with the disorder and chaos which existed, helped create an interventionist mood. The desire to protect American investments in Haiti seems to have been a consideration in some quarters, although the amounts involved were not great. Strategic considerations played a large role, it is clear; war had begun in Europe, and Germany had actually sent a battleship and troops to Port-au-Prince in 1914, shortly before the outbreak of war, to enforce collection of debts owed to German investors. The Germans had withdrawn, however, and the commitment of German forces elsewhere ruled out their return.

It seems likely that, in the official thinking of the time, no explicit attempt was made to weigh considerations of security against those of humanitarianism, of constitutional procedures, and of financial responsibility. There was no need, since policies urged on the basis of all these considerations tended to the same result: that the marines should be sent to Haiti to restore order and prudent fiscal management. However, the basic long-run factor at work was probably concern for the meeting of financial obligations. United States authorities had suggested to a previous Haitian government the establishment of American administration of the country's finances; the catalyst of intervention seems to have been the disorder and loss of life of the short-lived Sam administration.

The United States occupation operated as a benevolent despotism. The marines brought order. They built bridges and roads, schools and hospitals. Fiscal administration was honest and debts were paid. On the other hand, manifestations of the natural resentment of the people at being ruled by foreigners were dealt with harshly. Especial brutality was shown by the marines in the so-called Cacos War of 1919-1922. The *cacos* were bandits who had long infested the hills of Haiti; when the marines came they fought in guerrilla fashion against the attempt to pacify the country. The experience of American rule in Haiti over a recalcitrant population demonstrated a truth which colonial rulers were to become unpleasantly conscious of in other parts of the globe in years to come: a foreign administration, regardless of the good it may incidentally do, remains resented because it is foreign.

The United States finally faced the realization that rule by marines could not continue indefinitely when late in 1929 marines fired into a mob of civilian rioters, killing and wounding several score Haitians, including women and children. Troops were eventually withdrawn in 1934.

The occupation operated behind a flimsy façade of constitutional civilian rule. The American authorities worked by preference with the educated elite, and the two more-or-less puppet presidents of the occupation period were mulattoes, Philip Sudre Dartiguenave and Louis Borno.

The Years Since the Withdrawal of the Marines

There seems little point in examining in detail the personalities or the policies of the Haitian presidents who have held office since the withdrawal of the United States marines. Haitian history reveals patterns not of progress but of stagnation; the cycle of political events leaves the land and the people much as before.

The last president to take office during the period of the American occupation of the country, Sténio Vincent, is worthy of note in the perspective of Haitian history principally as the only president in the twentieth century to have finished his term peacefully and handed power over to his elected successor. To be sure, Vincent completed a total of over ten years in office by virtue of serving the first term under the provisions of a new constitution which signalized the end of the American occupation, after already having served several years under American rule. He had also hand-picked his successor, Lescot, and installed him by virtue of elections which were less than free.

Lescot was overthrown in 1946 and succeeded in due course by President Dumarsais Estimé, a former schoolteacher and a black. Estimé probably deserves recognition as the most progressive of Haiti's twentieth-century presidents, a progressive income tax and a program of labor and social security legislation being enacted during his term. It was also during the four years of Estimé's period of office that the beginnings of political party and labor union organization appeared.

Estimé was overthrown in his turn by Paul Magloire, a Negro general of markedly more conservative orientation, who ruled in a more dictatorial fashion than Estimé, although he did continue some of his predecessor's social programs. Magloire was himself overthrown at the end of 1956 when attempting to extend his term of office, and after a confused interregnum Dr. François Duvalier was chosen president in a rigged election less than a year later.

The Political Process

Groups in the Political Process

One can say that for practical purposes political parties do not exist in Haiti, although the movements which form around individual leaders in the period when political activity is free may dignify themselves with the name of party. It makes more sense to look at the group structure of Haitian politics in terms of the various economic and social forces which have been the significant political actors, beginning with the basic split in Haitian society between the elite and the masses.

In Haiti "the elite" is not simply a term used for the convenience of the sociologist. As pointed out above, a self-conscious class which refers to itself as the elite exists. One should note that the characteristics of this group differ in important respects from the elements usually referred to in the Hispanic American countries as "the oligarchy." Members of the elite can be distinguished from the masses in various respects. They are of French culture, using the French language by preference, whereas the masses speak Creole. The elite is Catholic or agnostic; the operating faith of the masses, coexisting uneasily with a nominal Catholicism, is Vodun. The elite is educated; the masses are illiterate. The elite does not engage in manual work, but lives on the proceeds of rent or on professional incomes; the masses are small farmers. Yet in Haiti the elite is not a land-owning aristocracy; its members do not own the large estates typical of the Hispanic "oligarchies." Moreover, except for the period of American occupation and the years immediately following, the elite is not normally entrenched in political power in Haiti; that is typically wielded by leaders who base their political position on mass support. Members of the elite are likely in Port-au-Prince to be lighter in complexion; this applies less frequently outside the capital.

The peasant masses and the lower classes in the cities, among whom anti-elite feelings can be and have been mobilized by political leaders, live at very low levels as measured by any social and economic criteria. The peasants farm minuscule plots of land in very primitive fashion; the growing of coffee berries, the leading cash crop, is so haphazard as to constitute almost a gathering rather than an agricultural economy properly speaking. A key problem of the peasants' livelihood is the scarcity of land, population on Haiti being extremely dense (three hundred to the square mile) for an agricultural system.

A group of key importance in Haiti's political processes is normally the Garde d'Haïti. The Garde is Haiti's army, a small but well-trained and well-disciplined force originally organized at the end of the United States occupation and trained by the marines as a nonpolitical constabulary force to keep order in the country after the Americans withdrew. Needless to say, a force of this kind could not long remain nonpolitical, and in the years following the American occupation the Garde acted as the balance-wheel of Haitian politics, overthrowing presidents who seemed to be exceeding their proper role, supervising elections, and frequently providing the president from among the Garde's own ranks. Thus this small force, which numbered 2500 when first formed and which stood at a strength of 5000 at the end of President Magloire's term of office, acted to all intents and purposes in the role of a Praetorian Guard.

Given the low level of economic development in the country, together with the strictness with which it has been ruled by dictators, organizations representing economic interest groups have been of less significance in Haiti than in any other country in the hemisphere. The importance which labor unions were beginning to acquire during the late 1940's and early 1950's has since disappeared. The peasants are unorganized. The only economically defined group which has been able to translate economic function into political power in recent years is the merchants of the capital, Port-au-Prince; their stoppage of business as a protest against Magloire's attempt to perpetuate himself in power was instrumental in bringing about his resignation.

The Political Cycle

The pattern of politics in Haiti before Duvalier exhibited a cyclical quality. A president would be elected who might devote himself more or less to small-scale programs of economic and social betterment, but who would be concerned principally with keeping himself in power and controlling the opposition; he would attempt to extend his term of office beyond the constitutional limit of one term, or would begin maneuvers preparatory to doing so, such as initiating the process of constitutional revision; this would catalyze a movement to overthrow him, either by the population of Port-au-Prince, led by rivals themselves desirous of coming to power, or by the leadership of the Garde d'Haïti; a period of chaos would ensue, which would terminate in the election and inauguration of a new president whose election and assumption of power was guaranteed by his being the choice of the commanders of the Garde. And the cycle would resume.

Politics under Duvalier

President Duvalier managed to break this pattern and was able to establish himself as a ruler as tyrannical and bizarre as the classic figures of Haitian history. One would have been hard put to it to predict accurately the character of Duvalier's presidency on the basis of his record before he came to office. A physician who had attended the School of Public Health at the University of Michigan, Dr. Duvalier was highly regarded for his work to improve public health standards among the Haitian peasantry and was also well known for his books on the ethnology of the Haitian people. One might have felt justified in predicting an administration dedicated to social amelioration and economic reconstruction, and indeed, the first days of the new regime were filled with talk of bold new programs.

Duvalier rapidly fell into the normal pattern of Haitian presidents, however, devoting himself to the persecution of his enemies and the consolidation of his power, using anti-elite demagoguery in the attempt to maintain the support of the masses. Nor has Duvalier been above making payoffs to the *hagouns*, the priests of Vodun, to build him up, in the popular consciousness, into a supernatural figure with magical powers.

Duvalier has shown himself aware of the traditional stumbling blocks of the Haitian dictator—the power of the Garde d'Haïti and the crystallization of hostile opinions that rapidly takes place in response to an attempt to extend the president's term. The Garde d'Haïti has been eliminated and replaced by a "militia" to which the actual function of "maintaining order" has been entrusted. In addition to this militia, Duvalier's apparatus of force includes a small presidential bodyguard which also has custody of the arsenal of weapons stored in the basement of the Presidential Palace, and a network of secret police known by its nickname of Ton-Tons Macoutes, the Creole term for bogeymen. This body of political gangsters is entrusted with ferreting out opposition to the regime, and its members are given a free hand to ignore the elementary rules of law and order and indeed of human decency in the pursuit of their mission; the toughs whom Duvalier found to do this work have a long list of atrocities credited to their names.

Duvalier managed to surmount the reelection crisis, although by the slimmest of margins, by resort to an ingenious stratagem. In 1961, after he had served four years of his six-year term, congressional elections were held. On the ballot, preceding the list of—uncontested—legislative candidates, there stood the legend "Dr. François Duvalier, President." After the election, which not unexpectedly resulted in a victory for the only candidates in the field, that is, Duvalier's supporters, the president announced that at the same time the voters had pleased to elect him to a new term of office. The point of this bizarre procedure was that it avoided the heightening of tension and the crystallization of opposition which would have ensued had Duvalier mounted a campaign to change the constitution and to reelect himself at the normal election time. The United States ambassador, alone among ambassadors of the Western Hemisphere countries, absented himself from Duvalier's second inaugural ceremonies, an interesting comment on the standard Latin American charges that the United States encourages dictatorships. The date that marked the end of Duvalier's legal period of office in 1963 was accompanied by scattered terrorist attempts on his life, and shortly thereafter a small-scale invasion, probably originating on Dominican territory, was initiated by General Léon Cantave, who had been associated with President Magloire. However, the dictator was well prepared for attempts to overthrow him, and he managed to maintain his grip on power. The Presidential Palace had been converted into a fortress from which Duvalier emerged only on rare occasions, protected by a miniature army.

Haiti under Duvalier thus became, after Duvalier's first years in office, as much of a totalitarian state as the undeveloped technology at his disposal made possible. The militia formed his storm troopers, and the Ton-Tons Macoutes his secret police; the press, the radio, and to some extent the network of Vodun priests became elements of his propaganda apparatus.

That other leading feature of a totalitarian system which Prime Minister Khrushchev has taught us to call "the cult of personality" was much in evidence. Duvalier's puppet legislature busied itself with heaping extravagant flattery on the dictator's head and in voting him grandiloquent new titles. Neon signs in the capital proclaimed him to be the savior of the nation. In fact, the only genuine program the regime seemed to have was the construction of a housing development named Duvalierville in the president's honor.

Just as the apparatus of dictatorship followed the form which has become all too familiar in the twentieth century, so did Duvalier's character degenerate, in the classic fashion of tyrants. Duvalier's own speeches showed more and more of the megalomania which afflicted him; the dictator became dominated by fear of his enemies—as well he might—and even the closest of his early associates deserted him before they should meet the fate of those suspected of disloyalty; rumors spread that Duvalier had actually come to believe in the superstitions of Vodun and was attempting to cast spells on his enemies.

Like others of his kind, Duvalier clashed with the Church, principally over his protection of the Vodun cult (which he referred to as part of the nation's rich cultural heritage) against the Church's attempts to eliminate cult practices. The dictator also resented the clergy's retention of an independent voice and an influence which could not be controlled by the regime; he was especially suspicious of the Church's contacts with students, who constituted in the early years one of the major sources of opposition to the regime. In prosecuting his conflict with the Church, Duvalier could make use of chauvinistic appeals, since the priests in Haiti were mostly of French and French Canadian derivation despite a continuing attempt to draw more Haitians into the priesthood. Duvalier has not scrupled to have the Church's bishops deported from the country, even going so far as to allege as a ground for the deportation of Archbishop François Poirier in November of 1960 that the archbishop had been financing Communist activities, a charge which grew out of his contacts with the university students. This action earned Duvalier excommunication.

Finally, in mid-1964, "in response to popular demand," Duvalier declared himself president for life, with the power to name his successor. He thus became the twentieth-century equivalent to the self-appointed kings and emperors of early Haitian history.

Regardless of how well entrenched Duvalier seemed to be when his opponents tried to overthrow him at the conclusion of his first six years in office, nothing could be surer than that, in the classic pattern of Haitian presidents, he too would be overthrown and he would be lucky to escape with his life.

It did seem, to be sure, that "Papa Doc," as he was known to his supporters among the masses, had wrought changes in Haitian politics—the eclipse in the power of the Garde d'Haïti, the crushing of the student movement, the dispersal abroad of many of the elite leadership—but since he had put nothing in their place but a purely personal apparatus of power which would be swept away along with him, it seemed likely that after Duvalier Haitian politics would again revert to their normal pattern.

Governmental Structure and Public Policy

Given the pattern of politics described above, it is clear that the formal institutions of government described in the constitution and the organic laws are of less significance in the fluid Haitian situation than they would be even elsewhere in Latin America. Nevertheless several features stand out.

The constitution is noteworthy on two accounts. One is that in the tradition of Continental European constitutional law, the constitution is not intended as a severe restricter of the scope of governmental activity in the style of the United States Constitution. The sections on individual liberties make clear that these are not to be taken as absolute, but are contingent on the necessities of effective government; little opportunity is afforded for the judiciary to overrule legislative or executive acts on constitutional grounds.

President and Legislature

The other central feature of the formal institutional structure is the power legally assigned to the president. This is reflected, for example, in the president's appointive powers, which extend to all nonelective offices, including judges and local administrators as well as national officers. It is worthy of note that presidential appointments do not require confirmation by the legislature, and the president may remove any official except a judge at his discretion.

The president's role as chief legislator is also explicitly acknowledged; he may introduce bills into the national assembly, and the legislature's powers of amending his budget are limited.

Election of the president was by the legislature until 1950. Since then the president has been chosen by the electorate at large, which incidentally includes illiterates, as it would have to in Haiti in order to approach any sort of representative character. The president's term is six years and he may not, legally, be immediately reelected.

The legislature follows the typical Latin American pattern. There are two houses, a senate and a chamber of deputies, members of which are elected by a district system. In form the legislature passes laws and must approve treaties and the declaration of war. The term of senators is six years, coinciding with the president's term; but the deputies' four-year term means (if one assumes that these matters are being arranged as the constitution says they should be) that only one out of three elections to the chamber would take place simultaneously with a presidential election. Needless to say, elections in Haiti have not followed the constitutional schedule for very long periods of time.

In April 1961 Duvalier decreed the election of a single-chamber legislature —the body which serves at the time of writing—of 58 members, in plain violation of the constitutional prescription.

Public Policy

There is little of a tradition to Haitian public policy. Normally the projects of one administration are forgotten by the next, except for those which are given continuity because they are being prosecuted in conjunction with an international organization. Programs of this type are actually frequent in Haiti: the Pan American Health Organization has long been active in campaigns in the rural areas against transmittable diseases such as yaws, and the United Nations technical agencies sponsor various projects. The United States too has given assistance to Haitian development projects over the years. The most important of these in recent years was the large irrigation dam in the Artibonite Valley. But construction on the dam was halted and American aid funds, then running at a total rate, for both budgetary support and special projects, of 13.5 million dollars annually, were first partially and then completely discontinued when President Duvalier insisted, against American objections, on dismissing able engineering personnel and replacing them with political appointees whom the United States regarded as unqualified. United States aid to build a jet airport outside Port-au-Prince was pledged after the break-off of aid, however. Skeptics pointed out that the negotiation of the agreement coincided with a meeting of the Organization of American States in which the vote of Haiti was crucial to a two-thirds majority necessary to pass a motion censuring Castro's Cuba. The story had it that Dean Rusk's expense account for the day read "Breakfast, two dollars. Lunch with Haitian delegate, 2.8 million dollars"; but this grant too was withheld as relations between the two countries deteriorated during 1962 and 1963.

Although an income tax had been introduced during the presidency of Estimé, the Haitian budget before the withdrawal of American aid was based principally on uneconomic export duties, with about another one-sixth (some six million dollars) coming from United States aid, and supplemented by an occasional arbitrary "forced loan" levied against members of the business community. The extraordinary corruption of the Duvalier regime, together with the cost of maintaining the apparatus of dictatorial terror, not only left no funds available for development projects but even made it impossible to carry on the minimal functions discharged by governments elsewhere. Outside the capital law and order were not even maintained; teachers trained with the help of United States funds were not employed because no money was available to pay their salaries, and the schools stood vacant; roads outside the capital became overgrown with vegetation. In other words, the entire budget, or that portion of it which did not disappear unaccountably, was devoted to paying salaries—the salaries, that is, not of those whose services were necessary to the public welfare, but of the supporters of Duvalier for whom a place on the public payroll had been found. Meanwhile, about 150 professional and technical people from Haiti were working for United Nations' technical assistance projects, mainly in Africa—more than from any other Latin American state. Haitian judges were staffing the Congolese judicial system, for judges were not needed in a land without justice.

Conclusion

A fatalist might look at Haiti and conclude that the country was sinking ever deeper in a vicious descending spiral of misery and dictatorship punctuated by periods of anarchy; and he might be right. He would be on an unsound footing, however, if he were to argue that because the Haitian masses are illiterate and superstitious no basis for social or political development exists.

For the outside observer it seems clear at what point the vicious circle should be broken. Judging by the experience of other countries, the point to attack is not illiteracy or economic underdevelopment; attempts to remedy these must be long-range and sustained. What Haiti needs first of all, what provides a basis for any possible progress in the social and economic spheres, is the establishment of the political continuity which would make any kind of long-run program possible. In other words, what Haiti lacked most of all was a political party structure which could provide continuity below the level of the comings and goings of individual personalities; which could provide continuity to policy and make possible procedures for the orderly transfer of power. In the fall of 1964, however, the prerequisite for any future at all for the Haitian nation was its emergence from the dark night of its most recent despotism.

SELECTED BIBLIOGRAPHY

Maurice DeYoung, "Class Parameters in Haitian Society," *Journal of Inter-American Studies*, July 1959.
James G. Leyburn, *The Haitian People*, Yale University Press, New Haven, 1941.
Rayford W. Logan, *The Diplomatic Relations of the United States with Haiti*, University of North Carolina Press, Chapel Hill, 1941.
Arthur C. Millspaugh, *Haiti Under American Control*, World Peace Foundation, Boston, 1931.
Selden Rodman, *Haiti: The Black Republic*, Devin-Adair, New York, 1954.

DOMINICAN
REPUBLIC

Santo
Domingo

A. Terry Rambo

THE DOMINICAN
REPUBLIC

THE LAND that today is called the Dominican Republic and was known in former times by the name of its capital, Santo Domingo, occupies the eastern two-thirds of the island of Hispaniola, which it shares with Haiti. Columbus set foot on the island in 1492 and was overjoyed to find it fertile, well-watered, and of temperate climate. The land offered all that could make it a paradise on earth. Yet its modern history begins with rapine, slavery, and genocide and ends, a few short years ago, with tyranny, robbery, and sadistic torture.

The peaceful Arawak Indians of the island were killed or worked to death by the Spaniards or committed suicide in such numbers that almost all were gone within fifty years of Columbus's landing. Even within twenty years, so few were left that the first load of slaves from Africa were brought in to do the Spaniards' work.

Overshadowing the twentieth-century history of Santo Domingo stands the grim figure of the most oppressive Latin American dictator of the century, the vain, greedy, astute, brutal Rafael Leonidas Trujillo Molina. The assassination of Trujillo on May 30, 1961, marked the end of a long night of tyranny, but not yet the dawn of an era of civil peace and liberty for the Dominicans. The Generalissimo cast a long shadow; it would prove difficult to replace the conditioned social reflexes of despotism with the responsibly autonomous behavior of free men.

Social and Economic Background

The Dominican Republic is divided into a series of isolated valleys and basins by the sparsely settled Cordillera Central, a high forested mountain range running from east to west through the middle of the island. On the northern side of the range lies the Cibao, a rich agricultural region where most of the country's three million inhabitants are concentrated. Across the mountains the southeastern coastal plain spreads eastward from the national capital of Santo Domingo to the end of the island. Population density is low near the Haitian border, but the government has settled agricultural colonies in the area in an attempt to populate this isolated region.

Communication between the various regions of the Republic was difficult prior to the construction of roads by the American occupation forces in the 1920's. The Trujillo government continued this program; there is now a road network of 4500 miles and any place in the country is within eight hours' drive of the capital. The political implications are obvious when it is considered that formerly to travel the 90 miles from Santo Domingo to Santiago in the Cibao involved several days on horseback.

Racially the Dominican population has been classified as 15 percent white, 15 percent Negro, and 70 percent mulatto. The lighter-skinned elements are concentrated in the urban upper social strata while the Negroes are located especially in the provinces with large sugar-cane plantations. The Trujillo regime followed what was virtually a policy of white supremacy and encouraged European immigration in the hope of "lightening" the population. Negro immigration was prohibited, although Haitians and British West Indians were brought in on a seasonal basis as agricultural laborers.

Today the population of the Dominican Republic is about 3½ million, with an annual increase rate of over 3½ percent, in spite of one of the highest rates of infant mortality in Latin America and of the generally low standards of health and the poor diet prevailing in the rural areas. The low median age of eighteen reflects the fact that the population doubles within twenty-five years at the present rate of growth; one out of four Dominicans is under seven years of age. Thus the Dominican Republic must face in an acute form a problem common to all of the Latin American nations: the relatively small population of working age must support a large nonproductive group of children, while the economy is distorted to provide the basic facilities of education, health, and welfare for the ever-increasing number of people.

Although the Dominican Republic remains predominantly rural, there has in recent years been a considerable internal migration from the more densely populated agricultural regions to the cities. Santo Domingo, in consequence, has doubled in population in the last ten years, to over 300,000. Santiago is the second largest city with 80,000, while there are fourteen other urban centers with more than 10,000 population.

Figures on literacy, as is the case with all statistics of direct political significance released during the era of Trujillo, are of dubious validity. Sixty percent of the population was considered literate in 1956. Literacy is much greater in the cities than in the rural areas, of course; there illiterates constitute about 70 percent of the population. The government devotes about 10 percent of the national budget to education and operates more than 4,000 primary schools. Less than half of the school age population attend, however, while secondary education is available to less than 2 percent of Dominicans.

Dominican society was long a two-class system of the standard Latin American pattern. But some recent political and economic developments have allowed new urban social groupings to emerge which have blurred the old dichotomy between urban aristocracy and rural peasantry. At the same time the white aristocracy with roots in the colonial period, its wealth derived from land ownership, has been augmented and to some degree supplanted by a new elite of military officers, politicians, and businessmen (often one individual is all three) who attained wealth and position under the Trujillo regime. The Benefactor himself was born into a family of low social position and was never accepted as a social equal by the old aristocracy, although by and large they supported his regime.

In addition, a fairly large group of lower-level white-collar government and commercial employees has developed since the rapid expansion of the Dominican bureaucracy in the 1930's. While educated and aspiring to higher economic and social status, these individuals do not form a self-conscious and economically independent class capable of unified political action.

As a result of Trujillo's much publicized industrialization program, a number of secondary and tertiary industries were established in Santo Domingo and in other urban centers, and a class of wage laborers emerged. Low wages and bad working conditions in industry led to considerable unrest after World War II, and Communist labor leaders—who had earlier been allowed by Trujillo to infiltrate the government-controlled labor unions—led several strikes. This was going too far, however, and Trujillo crushed the strikes with great brutality, imprisoning or exiling the leadership. Thus ended at least the overt display of dissatisfaction by the workers. The government also began to construct low-income housing, but the program was not adequate to the need and many workers still live in the slums surrounding Santo Domingo.

What might be called a rural proletariat of wage laborers has also formed as in many areas the plantations have absorbed the land of the independent peasantry. These laborers are employed primarily on the sugar plantations, where they must compete with the cheaper Haitian migrant labor.

The peasants, the traditional lower class, are still the largest social element, but they are declining in relative numbers as the economy develops. Generally illiterate and tending to be darker-skinned than the upper classes, the peasants form almost a separate caste, speaking a distinctive dialect of Spanish and practicing a folk variety of Catholicism. Trujillo's government actively promoted the cult of personality with such success that many peasants seemingly rearranged the order of precedence to believe in Trujillo and God rather than in the "Dios y Trujillo" of the official slogan. They loyally supported the government during the abortive Cuban-backed exile invasion in 1959, and are evidently politically apathetic since the fall of Trujillo.

While not strictly speaking a monocultural economy, the Dominican Republic faces the problems of excessive susceptibility to outside influences of such an economy, as most of its foreign exchange is derived from three crops: sugar, coffee, and cacao. The world market for these (especially for sugar, which constitutes 45 percent of the country's exports) is highly competitive and was until recently suffering from a long-term downward price trend. The country's trade position was strong, however, until 1959, when large-scale arms purchases led to an unfavorable balance of trade and necessitated the floating of a foreign loan. After Trujillo was assassinated, the United States extended considerable economic aid to the civilian successor governments; this was halted temporarily after the military *coup d'état* of September 1963.

The average Dominican annual per capita income at the end of the Trujillo era was calculated as $243, but the maldistribution of wealth in the country made this a meaningless figure. In reality, the income of the urban worker is closer to $100 per capita, with that of the peasant about one-third as great.

About 80 percent of the labor force is employed in agricultural activities, but only three-quarters of the farmers work their own land, and over half of the farms are *minifundia* of less than five acres. Plots of this nature are often located on the poorer lands of the hillsides and are farmed by primitive methods, barely providing subsistence to their owners. The plantations are located on the better soils of the plains and are often mechanized and irrigated, with resultant high productivity; frequently, however, the absentee landlords pay little attention to their possessions, productivity is low, and the land is misused. At the time of Trujillo's death, the largest 61 *latifundias* contained 16 percent of all the arable land in the country; as the population increases land reform will become a more pressing political problem. At present, colonization of the frontier zone can still absorb many of the landless.

Industry is largely devoted to the processing of agricultural produce, sugar mills alone accounting for two-thirds of the total industrial capitalization. Considerable foreign capital was at one time invested in sugar and banana plantations and in mining, but the government purchased all but one of the sugar mills and the later deterioration of political conditions led to a cessation of new investment and withdrawal of much capital. As part of its campaign of economic diversification, the government promoted light industry through the granting of tax benefits and the establishment of high tariffs. Needless to say, preferential treatment of this kind, together with generous government financing, was provided most particularly to those industries established by the Trujillo family and the dictator's numerous cronies.

The tax system was regressive and largely based on indirect taxes. A type of income tax existed and there was also a progressive tax on business income; all members of Trujillo's family and all military officers were tax-exempt, however, leaving a rather narrow base when one considers that the Trujillo clique actually received over 30 percent of the national income!

Economic prospects have not been encouraging. The possibility of considerable agricultural development exists, as only 50 percent of the potentially arable land is currently in use, but much of this new land is of low quality and will require large capital investment in irrigation works before it will be productive. Moreover, further industrialization will not come easily in view of the small internal market and of the high cost of Dominican-made goods, which results from the low productivity of the workers.

Early History

The island of Hispaniola was discovered by Columbus on his first voyage and rapidly developed into the focal point for Spanish colonization efforts in the New World. By 1517 Santo Domingo had a population of 60,000, with large numbers of Negro slaves replacing the rapidly disappearing Indians as laborers on the sugar plantations and cattle ranches. The discovery of Mexico and Peru diverted Spanish interest to the mainland, however, and by the mid-sixteenth century the population of Santo Domingo had decreased to half what it had been fifty years before, and the economy had stagnated.

The colonial government in the capital city exercised little control over the interior. There the plantations operated as autonomous feudal entities. Although slavery persisted, it was in a form less harsh than in neighboring Haiti, where the French had built a prosperous colony.

The unrest which was generated on the island by the French Revolution was manifested in slave uprisings by the Haitians, and these were supported by the Dominicans as part of Spain's war effort against France. When a European peace treaty was signed, however, Santo Domingo was surrendered by the Spanish to the French, and in 1798 Franco-Haitian troops led by Toussaint L'Overture invaded the eastern end of the island. After the Haitian proclamation of independence in 1802, Napoleon sent an army to recover the former colony and succeeded in driving the Negro forces from Santo Domingo; but the French troops were decimated by yellow fever, and the Haitians regained their independence under the dictator Dessalines. Bloody seesaw fighting then commenced between the remnants of the French army and the Haitians for control of Santo Domingo, which culminated in the total defeat of the forces of Dessalines. Rather than showing gratitude to the French for their liberation, however, the Dominicans soon rebelled and proclaimed their loyalty to Spain and to the anti-Napoleon junta in the motherland.

The restoration of Ferdinand to the Spanish throne brought the readoption of reactionary colonial policies, and in 1821, after years of guerrilla warfare, the disgusted Dominican colonists ousted the Spanish and sought to join Bolívar's Colombia. Before they could be admitted, the Haitians seized control again, this time without meeting any resistance.

For twenty-two years Santo Domingo was occupied, and it is not too much to say that its economy and culture were utterly destroyed. White Dominicans were subjected to every conceivable humiliation by their captors; their only response for a long time was humble submission, but in 1838 Juan Duarte founded La Trinitaria, a secret revolutionary society, and discontented elements coalesced around it, finally driving the Haitians out in 1844.

The revolutionary forces were soon divided, however, between the followers of Duarte, who sought an independent republic, and the followers of Buenaventura Báez and General Santana, who sought to convert the country into the protectorate of a European power. Neither Báez nor Santana held what could be called a clear ideological position, although the former tended to favor the French and the latter supported the Spanish. Such mass support as each had, despite the nominal existence of political parties, was arranged by bribing the local *caciques* who controlled the provinces of the interior. Although Santana succeeded in exiling Duarte and his followers, the Dominican Republic was forced to endure a long series of revolutions and counter-revolutions as Santana and Báez struggled for supremacy. Finally, in 1861 Santana arranged for Spain to annex the former colony, seeing this as a way of maintaining himself in power.

The ineptitude and corruption of the colonial administration and the replacement of Dominicans by Spanish officials soon provoked several revolts in the Cibao, and in 1865 the Spanish, after their army, like that of the French sixty years before, was destroyed by yellow fever, evacuated the island. The provisional revolutionary government which then succeeded to power was soon rendered ineffective by internal dissension, and Báez again took power. In an attempt to secure funds to stabilize his government he sought a European loan and even tried to sell or lease Samana Bay to the United States. But popular revulsion at this attempted "betrayal of the fatherland" led to a successful revolution and the ouster in 1873 of Báez. The followers of Báez overthrew the reform government which eventually replaced him and took power for a few years, but the Cibao again rebelled and the reformers were returned to power in 1880. Aided by an honest administration the economy revived, and in 1882 fair elections were held for the second time in the republic's history. But the hopes that anyone had for a peaceful and constitutional order to evolve were disappointed, for General Ulises Heureaux was elected, beginning a dictatorship of seventeen years' duration.

A brave but vain military leader who commanded the absolute loyalty of his troops, Heureaux relied on terror and corruption to maintain his regime. He employed a large corps of spies both in the Dominican Republic and abroad and was always well informed on impending plots against his rule. Suspicious of his supporters as well as of his opponents, Heureaux jailed or murdered any that showed signs of independence. He maintained the fiction of constitutional government, however, and held periodic elections which were used, in effect, as a means of dividing the opposition forces.

Heureaux used the imaginary threat of invasion from Haiti to mobilize popular support for his rule and attempted to play the Great Powers off against each other. To maintain his government the dictator was forced to obtain large foreign loans by mortgaging the receipts of the Dominican customs houses, but he soon exhausted these new resources in attempting to suppress the constant revolutionary activity in the Cibao.

Heureaux was assassinated in 1899, but the populace remained a passive onlooker as the rebel forces were severely battered by forces loyal to Heureaux's vice-president. At last the revolutionaries were temporarily victorious and set up a reform government under General Horacio Vásquez, but its following was fragmented by personal feuds, and former military supporters of Heureaux, charging that the government was unable to maintain order, staged a successful revolt and exiled Vásquez. Again the country was in chaos. Rapidly changing central governments were unable to control the rural areas, and the provincial governors became virtual warlords, controlling private armies and ignoring orders fom the capital.

An able dictator, Ramón Cáceres, restored some degree of order, but could never control the activities of the *gavilleros*, or bandits, who terrorized the peasants and brought agricultural activity to a standstill. Even the huge American-owned sugar plantations were forced to make protection payments in order to stay in operation.

When the government could no longer meet interest payments on the foreign debt, various European powers began to threaten punitive action; to forestall this and to protect the interests of a large American creditor firm— The San Domingo Improvement Corporation—the United States Government took over collection of the customs duties under an agreement with Cáceres in 1904. With the assassination of the dictator in 1911 the last vestiges of order disappeared, and the United States became increasingly involved in the affairs of the republic in the attempt to stabilize the situation. In 1916 the United States refused to turn over the customs revenues to the newly elected president, Dr. Francisco Henríquez y Carvajal, unless he accepted an American financial advisor and an American-officered constabulary. When this affront to their sovereignty was rejected by the Dominicans, President Wilson ordered American marines to occupy the island.

President Henríquez refused to act as a puppet ruler, and the Dominican congress was dissolved. This forced the United States to set up a direct military government, ruling by decree. Needless to say, their new regime was greatly resented by the Dominicans; the marines resorted to much unnecessary brutality in suppressing their resistance. All civilians were disarmed, and the forces of the provincial governors were broken up, while a nonpartisan Dominican constabulary was organized and trained by the marines as the country's sole armed force. Since the upper classes refused to collaborate with the occupation government, this constabulary succeeded in recruiting only the worst elements of Dominican society, who were now to become the most important force in local politics. The occupation government also developed a road system linking the Cibao to Santo Domingo, thus reducing the isolation of the country's rural regions.

As part of the process of liquidating their inherited overseas commitments carried out by the Republican administrations which followed Wilson, the United States occupation forces were in 1924 evacuated from the Dominican Republic, after they had overseen the election of Horacio Vásquez to the presidency. Vásquez proved an inept president, and in 1930, when he tried to extend his term, he was overthrown by Rafael Estrella Ureña, who had seized the *cuartel* (barracks) in Santiago and marched on the capital. Ureña was materially aided in his bid for power by the act of the commander of the erstwhile constabulary (which had been renamed the National Army), Rafael L. Trujillo, in ordering his troops not to fire on the rebels. Trujillo had enlisted in the constabulary soon after it was formed and had quickly risen to be its commander. As head of the army he was able to control promotions and build a loyal personal following. In the elections which ensued, Trujillo was chosen president, after he had intimidated the opposition with a series of murders carried out by his followers in the army.

The Era of Trujillo

A twentieth-century Latin American president who shall be nameless is reported to have said, in excuse for the corruption of his regime, "I steal but I build." Similar claims have frequently been advanced on Trujillo's behalf by his apologists, Dominican and North American, but with far less justification for their views. In reality Trujillo seems to have built so that he might steal, since he received an automatic 10 percent kickback on every government contract, and since a large percentage of all investment was channeled into companies owned by his family and supporters. Estimates of the personal wealth of the dictator at his death reach staggering levels, with a minimum figure of $500 million generally accepted as reliable.

Soon after taking office Trujillo was given the opportunity to demonstrate his administrative ability, incidentally enriching himself from the relief funds at his disposal, by rebuilding the hurricane-leveled capital city. His administration continued to advocate development projects, particularly the construction of an extensive road network and the diversification of agriculture. Meanwhile, the army increased in size and efficiency as the percentage of the national budget devoted to "defense" steadily grew.

The price of the regime's economic development activities was paid in blood, however, as suspected opponents of the regime were imprisoned or killed, usually in "accidents," and their property confiscated for the Trujillo family's benefit. Even Dominicans living in exile were not safe from the dictator's efficient secret police. The kidnaping of Jesús María de Galíndez from the streets of New York in 1956, to be tortured to death in the Dominican Republic, was merely one episode in the saga of terror and sudden death written by the tyrant's agents abroad.

Trujillo deliberately set out to humiliate the aristocracy which had refused him social acceptance. Fear of destructive taxation of their properties if they resisted the regime was mixed with the temptation of the lucrative opportunities open to those who cooperated, and most of the social elite eventually joined with the rest of the nation in mouthing the flattery which Trujillo demanded as proof of loyalty. In addition, many scions of aristocratic families were conscripted into the officer corps of the army and were thus implicated in the excesses of the regime.

In 1931 the Partido Dominicano was founded by Trujillo; within a year it had a membership equaling 80 percent of the electorate. No opposition parties were allowed until 1947, when two short-lived parties were organized by the government as part of a "democratization" propaganda campaign. After his unopposed re-election in 1934, the dictator was securely entrenched domestically; but world-wide revulsion at the massacre of 20,000 Haitian squatters in the border provinces carried out by the Dominican army in 1937 induced Trujillo to make his much-publicized offer to accept the settlement of 100,000 European refugees in the Dominican Republic. In reality, fewer than eight hundred Jewish immigrants ever arrived, although a larger number of Spanish Republican exiles were admitted—among them the Galíndez Suárez who was to be kidnaped twenty years later in New York.

In 1938 Trujillo demonstrated his devotion to constitutional procedures by supervising the election to the presidency of Jacinto Peynado, a man qualified for the position by virtue of being the dictator's dentist; Trujillo contented himself with the command of the army. The Dominican Republic was quick to declare war on the Axis after the attack on Pearl Harbor, and received the benefits of being an ally of the United States in spite of Trujillo's previous fascist sympathies and the negligible contribution his forces made to the common defense effort. The Generalissimo returned to the presidency in 1942 and was continuously re-elected thereafter until 1952, when he allowed his brother Hector to assume the title; again he remained as commander of the armed forces.

The end of the war brought a democratic upsurge in Latin America, and Trujillo felt under obligation to demonstrate that the Dominican government was in step with the times. Several opposition parties were briefly allowed to exist, and Communists were allowed to take office in the government-dominated labor unions, but all opposition was soon suppressed when it appeared to be getting out of control. A group of exiles attempted to launch an invasion from Cuba at this time (the Cayo Confites affair, in which Fidel Castro participated) but the United States, together with the Cuban government, intervened, and the force was disbanded.

Fidel Castro's rise to power marked the turning point in the fortunes of the Trujillo government. Another exile invasion was put down with little difficulty in 1959, but the subsequent discovery of a large internal revolutionary movement shook the dictator's confidence. The brutal suppression of this movement led even the Dominican bishops, who had formerly been among Trujillo's firmest allies, to protest in 1960 the excesses of the government in a pastoral letter. The beginning of the end came for Trujillo when his agents tried—and narrowly failed—to assassinate President Rómulo Betancourt of Venezuela, a leading liberal and long a foe of Trujillo. On Venezuelan insistence, the Organization of American States recommended that its members break diplomatic relations with the dictatorship and impose a limited economic embargo on trade with the island republic. The United States complied with the recommendation, although the Dominican sugar quota, which is set by Congress, was not affected.

Trujillo responded to the increasing pressure from the democratic governments of the hemisphere by attempting to veer to the left, presumably hoping to intimidate the United States into a change of policy. An opposition party of Castroite orientation was allowed to form and secret negotiations were begun with Cuba and the Soviet bloc.

This line of policy seemed without result, however, and the dictator wheeled out the old "democratization" routine once more. Greater freedom for opposition activity was promised, and Hector Trujillo, again in temporary possession of the presidency, resigned and was succeeded by the vice-president, a nondescript long-time servant of the regime named Joaquín Balaguer.

This was the situation when, on May 30, 1961, Trujillo was ambushed and machine-gunned to death as he was being driven to visit his mistress, on the road to San Cristóbal, his birthplace. He was nearly seventy, and had held power a little over thirty years.

The Political Process under Trujillo

Trujillo's genius lay in his ability to channel the forces of the time, internal and external, to serve his own ends. Basically a pragmatist, Trujillo never restricted his political flexibility with a rigid ideology and was always able to adapt the façade of his regime to the dominant external configurations of power. When there was advantage in being antifascist, Trujillo was antifascist, and when the Cold War developed, Trujillo had himself proclaimed "The First Anti-Communist of the Hemisphere." The official ideology of the moment never altered the basic character of the regime—a successful fusion of traditional Hispanic *caudillismo* with the technical apparatus of modern European totalitarianism: the man on horseback had learned to drive a tank.

The armed forces were the basis of the power structure, and Trujillo always maintained direct personal control over them. With the civilian population disarmed, no revolution could hope to succeed without military support, and Trujillo took every precaution against the alienation of the army's loyalty. The military budget was always large and the personnel were well-paid and well-treated. Promotion was rapid, and men of lower class could improve their social and economic position in a manner that was denied them in civilian life. The officer corps formed an arrogant caste, immune to the laws and regulations governing civilian conduct. Officers were tax-exempt and often enjoyed opportunities to enrich themselves through corruption besides. Such privileges were granted only to those who demonstrated absolute loyalty to the dictator, however. In addition, the command structure was frequently overhauled to forestall the development of close bonds between officers and the troops they commanded; and the ammunition supply in the provincial garrisons was always held to a strict minimum. The air force maintained separate infantry units from those of the army, so that the services counterbalanced each other.

The secret police were with similar intent divided into a number of autonomous agencies. These maintained an extensive network of paid informers, which made Dominicans distrust each other, and increased tremendously the problems of organizing a revolutionary movement. That no mass opposition organizations were ever able to avoid discovery indicates the efficiency of the government spy system. An understanding of the magnitude of official terrorism under Trujillo is necessary to the understanding of the political apathy exhibited by most Dominicans. For thirty years the slightest expression of antigovernment sentiment was impossible. Thousands of suspected dissidents were murdered and thousands more imprisoned and tortured. As the kidnaping of Jesús Galíndez from New York City demonstrated, even exile brought no security to known opponents of Trujillo.

Overt political activity occurred only in the context of the Partido Dominicano—the government mass party. Membership was compulsory for government employees and essential for business and professional people. A party card was necessary to participate in many activities, and the threat of expulsion from membership was a powerful sanction over the behavior of members. The PD was financed by an automatic 10 percent deduction from the salary of government personnel, augmented by the income from numerous party-owned businesses. Funds were devoted to financing public welfare activities designed to promote the popularity of Trujillo with the masses. Free milk and shoes were distributed to the poor, and medical aid was supplied to the elderly. The party's financial burden was hardly excessive, though, since many of these functions were actually paid for by the government.

Roman Catholicism became the official religion of the Dominican Republic after a concordat was concluded with the Vatican in 1955, and the clergy gave strong support to Trujillo. The government reciprocated by suppressing the Jehovah's Witnesses and by requiring all its employees to belong to Catholic associations. In 1960 police brutality in the suppression of a revolutionary plot was denounced by the Dominican bishops, however, and Church-State relations grew strained. Yet the post-Trujillo political stance adopted by the Church indicates that no basic commitment to democracy or social reform had led to the break.

Trujillo was generally successful in maintaining United States government support of his regime or at least tolerance for it until shortly before the end came. The Dominican government ran a well-financed publicity campaign proclaiming the anti-Communist virtues of Trujillo, and its claims were accepted at face value by many American Congressmen.

There seems little doubt that the cynical dictator believed he could purchase the favor of highly placed Americans, as he had that of many Dominicans. Lucrative business arrangements of various kinds were made with members of prominent American families—a relative by marriage of President Eisenhower, one of the sons of President Roosevelt, the brother of the designer of Jacqueline Kennedy's gowns—who often unwittingly contributed to making the Dominican tyranny seem respectable in the eyes of those who knew nothing of the sordid reality behind the glitter.

Trujillo's relations with other Latin American governments were of an opportunistic nature, although he seems to have developed a personal enmity for Rómulo Betancourt of Venezuela. This led him to commit one of his few diplomatic blunders, one which contributed to his downfall. None of the governments of the hemisphere had any use for Trujillo, not even the dictatorships. Anastasio Somoza was always careful to point out the differences between his rule and that of Trujillo, for example. The feeling was reciprocated, and the story of how Trujillo relieved Fulgencio Batista of most of the money which accompanied him on his last flight from Cuba by charging him fantastically for rent has become classic.

A feature of the regime which exceeded any merely functional requirement for the maintenance of the dictatorship was its crass deification of Trujillo. The chief function of the press seemed to be to sing his praises, and no issue of a newspaper dared appear without his picture. Members of the puppet legislature vied with each other in flattering him and inventing extravagant new titles for him. His name was given to streets, squares, schools, even a mountain, and ancient Santo Domingo, the capital, was even named Ciudad Trujillo in his honor. (The former name is now restored.) The public education system was a major tool of the personality cult. Discouragingly enough, the indoctrination took hold among the poorer classes, in the rural areas as well as the city, and thousands wept at Trujillo's obsequies. Opposition to the dictator was strongest among the bourgeois elements of the population.

The dictator's control was absolute not only in the armed forces, the communications media, education, and the bureaucracy but also in the economy. The Trujillo family owned most of the sugar mills and much of the land, and Trujillo himself was a partner in a fantastic range of enterprises. After the fall of the dictator, it was calculated that 45 percent of the total labor force had been *directly* employed by Trujillo concerns, apart from the 35 percent employed by the government. This adds another dimension to the scope of the tyrant's control of the hapless Dominican population.

Politics and Government Since Trujillo

The six months which succeeded the assassination of the dictator were confused. The struggle for power among Trujillo's heirs was fought out under the complementary pressures of popular demonstrations in favor of democratization, led especially by the Unión Cívica Nacional, a movement of business and professional leaders, and similar demands of the Organization of

American States, given point by the partial economic embargo and supported by the United States.

Under these circumstances President Balaguer tried to give some substance to the now suddenly meaningful democratization program. To what extent his moves were designed solely to induce the lifting of the economic sanctions and how far the process would have been permitted to go, are questions about which one may justifiably remain skeptical. Or rather, Balaguer was the agent through whom this policy was dictated, first by the dead dictator's son Rafael Trujillo (Ramfis) and then by Pedro Rafael Rodríguez Echevarría, his successor as minister of the armed forces.

Party activity was allowed, and dozens of groups were formed, although it took some time to make clear to the police what the appropriate line of conduct for them was under the new circumstances. In its initial stages the struggle for power was staged within the Trujillo family. "Ramfis," on the one hand, was willing that there should be at least some gestures in the direction of democratization. On the other hand, the two most politically active of Trujillo's many brothers, Hector and José Arismendi, wished to maintain the late dictator's system. Although the brothers left the island on October 22, 1961, they returned suddenly on November 15 and attempted to seize power. Now it was Ramfis's turn to leave the country. Before the counter-revolution could be definitively imposed, Uncle Sam took a hand. On November 18, ships of the United States Second Fleet appeared just outside the three-mile limit defining Dominican territorial waters; contingents of marines ready to land were reported to be on board, and American jet fighters flew by overhead. In the face of clearly stated American support for democratization and the implied threat of intervention, the Trujillo brothers gave up the struggle and left the island for the last time, while the United States enjoyed the all too infrequent acclaim of popular demonstrations. The new strong man of the Balaguer government, General Rodríguez Echavarría of the Air Force, gave his support to the democratization movement, at least temporarily and in part.

The political crisis was resolved by the installation of a Council of State, which assumed control on January 1, 1962. The council was made up of representatives of opposition groups, led by Rafael Bonnelly of the UCN, together with the only two members of the group which had assassinated Trujillo to escape Ramfis's vengeance, Generals Antonio Imbert Barrera and Luis Amiama Tió. An attempt by Rodríguez Echavarría to change the membership of the council was headed off, and he was replaced as head of the armed forces by General Elvy Viñas Román.

The head of the UCN, Viriato Fiallo, did not participate in the council, holding himself in reserve for the presidential elections which the council scheduled for later in the year. Besides administering the country, the council of state introduced a new constitution, which provided for a four-year presidential term and no re-election.

Nineteen sixty-two was an uneasy year politically as the country prepared itself for democracy. Political parties sprouted like mushrooms, split, and re-formed. The leading groups were the UCN and the Partido Dominicano Revolucionario or PRD, headed by Juan Bosch. The PRD considered itself a party of the democratic left and Bosch himself was close, personally as well as politically, to President Rómulo Betancourt of Venezuela and Governor Luis Muñoz Marín of Puerto Rico. Among the welter of other political parties was the Fourteenth of July Movement, which tended to be pro-Castro; the Communist Party itself, which went by the name of the Dominican Popular Socialist Party, was outlawed, as was the extreme left-wing MPD, the Popular Dominican Movement, which had been permitted to organize by Trujillo in the last period of his reign as part of his attempt to forge ties with Cuba and the Soviet Union in the hope of intimidating the United States into withdrawing its condemnation of his regime.

The interim government survived the political turmoil, which reportedly included an attempt by General Imbert to extend his power in preparation for a *coup d'état*, and the promised elections were finally held in December.

The leading candidates for the presidency were Fiallo and Bosch, with Fiallo and the UCN coming to be regarded as a conservative party standing for business, the Church, and the upper classes, and Bosch making his strongest appeal to the lower classes and to the peasants. In a model election, marked by an absence of public disturbance and the turnout of over 90 percent of the voters, Bosch scored a landslide victory with about 64 percent of the vote to Fiallo's 32 percent. In addition, the PRD captured over two-thirds of the seats in each house of congress. Bosch ran strongly in the rural areas, except for the Cibao, presumably as a result of his strong pledge to undertake a land-reform program. Other elements in Bosch's platform had been economic development and diversification, and a promise to forget the past and not to take harsh reprisals against those who had supported Trujillo.

As president, Bosch attempted to live up to his program and began the distribution of land, much land having come into possession of the state as Trujillo's heir. The new constitution, adopted in May by the PRD-dominated legislature, prohibited the mortgaging of small farms in the attempt to prevent the reconcentration of land ownership.

This constitution provoked much dismay on the part of the clergy, since it provided for the separation of Church and State and the relinquishment by the Church of the privileged position it had long enjoyed in the Dominican Republic. Included in it were provisions for divorce and for state inspection of religious schools.

While the Church was unhappy over the new constitution, and landowners were displeased by the prospect of land reform, other groups, too, had cause to regret the election of Juan Bosch. The armed forces became suspicious that Bosch was establishing a rival force in his organization of a militia "to guard the cane fields." Conservative Dominicans generally were unhappy

over Bosch's scrupulous respect for civil liberties, which included the allowing of free speech to people they regarded as Communists. Of course, in the
terms in which they had been taught by Trujillo, anyone who sponsored
land reform and tried to limit the authority of the Church looked rather like
a Communist himself, and almost from the beginning of Bosch's term, opposition elements kept up a perpetual attack on the new government and those
who staffed it, alleging them to be Communists—and many of these charges
were repeated in the United States press.

For his part, Bosch did little to attempt to conciliate the opposition. His
long years of exile had left the writer and academician stern and uncompromising, and there was much that critics of his administration could find to
criticize, especially given the inexperience of the leaders of the new government.

Finally, in September of 1963 the long prepared *coup d'état* came, managed by Minister of the Armed Forces Elvy Viñas Román and a fanatically
anti-Communist general named Elias Wessin y Wessin. Bosch returned to
exile, and a provisional civilian junta was placed in office.

Although considerable domestic opposition to the coup was manifested,
especially by PRD legislators and by students, and although the United
States withheld recognition of the new government and made clear its dis-
approval, resistance gradually petered out.

Most of the opposition groups, the UCN among them, collaborated with
the new regime, which was thus supported by a coalition of the classic reactionary forces of Latin America: business, the military, the Church, the
landowners. If the PRD maintained the loyalty of those who had helped it
elect Bosch, it seemed clear that the Dominican Republic was headed for the
type of political dilemma that had long dominated the political situation in
Peru: despite their constitutional professions the ruling civilian and military
groups would be impelled to continue to tread the path of dictatorship because they feared the response which they knew an appeal to the people
would bring.

SELECTED BIBLIOGRAPHY

Gerald Clark, *The Coming Explosion in Latin America*, David MacKay, New
York, 1963, Chapter 10.
R. E. Crist, "Cultural Dichotomy in the Island of Hispaniola," *Economic
Geography*, Vol. 28, 1952.
D. R. Dyer, "Distribution of Population on Hispaniola," *Economic Geography*,
Vol. 30, 1954.
Jesús de Galíndez Suárez, *La Era de Trujillo*, Editorial del Pacífico, Santiago de
Chile, 1956.
Marvin Goldwert, "The Constabulary in the Dominican Republic and Nicaragua,"
Latin American Monographs, No. 17, University of Florida Press, Gainesville,
1962.

Carl Kelsey, "The American Intervention in Haiti and the Dominican Republic," *The Annals of the American Academy of Political and Social Science*, Vol. 100, 1922.

Germán E. Ornes, *Trujillo: Little Caesar of the Caribbean*, Thomas Nelson and Sons, New York, 1958.

Sumner Welles, *Naboth's Vineyard*, 2 vols., Payson and Clarke, New York, 1928.

X   *C. A. M. Hennessy*

CUBA

THE POLITICS OF FRUSTRATED
NATIONALISM

CUBA's geographical position and potential wealth have long drawn the island into economic, diplomatic, and political conflicts with the outside world. Unable to vegetate in a backwater, but exposed to the blast of foreign influences, the search for national identity has been more prolonged and painful than elsewhere in Latin America. Because Cuban nationalism can draw no sustenance from pre-Spanish roots, unlike that, for example, of Mexico, nationalists have been obsessed with the epic struggles for independence between 1868 and 1898.

In these struggles Martí, the Cuban Mazzini, occupies a crucial position, devoting his life and sacrificing his happiness to the cause of independence. After his death in action in 1895 at the onset of the final phase of the struggle against Spain, he became the symbol of a democratic, racially harmonious, economically and politically independent Cuba. Castro's inspiration in prison was Martí, not Marx, and the heroes of the 1950's are coupled in popular imagination with those of the 1890's in a link which emphasizes the concept of continuous revolution.

Many of the strains and stresses within Cuban society were exposed only after Independence. Although most of these were the legacy of colonial rule or the result of internal conflict, the United States provided a convenient scapegoat. Political control from Spain seemed to have been replaced by economic control from the United States. Hence the growth of the myth that the revolution of 1895-8 had been frustrated by outside intervention and that the unity of the nation in arms had been sacrificed to the needs of economic imperialism. The threat to the new nation's identity from United States influence, combined with the legacies of Spanish rule, conditioned the growth of an unstable Cuban nationalism which could only be sustained by outbursts of violent anti-Americanism. It is against this background that Cuban politics must always be viewed.

Social and Economic Background

The Colonial Economy

The early Spaniards lost interest in Cuba once they realized that it had no gold and that the indigenous population was dying out through disease and exploitation. Although small-scale production of sugar and tobacco began in the sixteenth century, stock raising continued as the main source of livelihood, supplying the *flotas* which called at Havana on their way to Seville from Veracruz.

The strategic significance of the island was not fully appreciated until its capture by the English in 1762. Although they left within ten months, following the Treaty of Paris, the English occupation marked a decisive phase in Cuban development as it opened her ports to North American trade, gave an impetus to the sugar plantation economy through large importations of African slaves and, by emphasizing to the Spaniards the strategic importance of Havana, led to its expansion into the most formidable garrison town in the Caribbean.

The decline of British West Indian sugar and the destruction of Haiti as the world's leading sugar producer set the seal on Cuba's future economic development. High prices and increased demand in Europe stimulated the sugar revolution which, by mid-nineteenth century, made Cuba the richest colony for its size possessed by any European power.

The Independence struggles of continental Latin America had left Cuba almost unruffled. A boom economy, the fear of a slave rising after the Haitian pattern, and favorable land legislation which opened up uncultivated and Crown estates prevented creole discontent. It was clear, too, that the future of Cuba would be decided by power politics. Each of the Great Powers preferred to see a weakened Spain in control rather than a vacuum which might invite intervention by a foreign rival.

Deprived of her continental possessions, Spain finally recognized the enormous potential wealth in the neglected colony. Cuba became the center of a new network of commercial relationships by which the colony's protected market subsidized the peninsular interests of Santander shipping, Castilian wheat and, later, Catalan industry. The great Spanish commercial houses dominated economic life, and in the absence of banks acted as creditors to debt-ridden creole planters. The island also became an El Dorado for poor Galicians and Canary Islanders forced abroad by population pressure. It was this poor-white element which threw up the pro-Spanish urban mobs during the later Independence struggles. In addition, the Cuban administration provided a haven for a job-hungry bureaucratic class whose needs even the swollen peninsular bureaucracy was unable to meet.

The prejudices implicit in a slave plantation economy made it difficult for white immigrants to accept work on the land except in the tobacco *vegas* of Pinar del Río. Very few, therefore, of the Spanish immigrants became Cubanized; they tended to remain in tight urban groups, often nullifying the liberal policies of the metropolitan government by intimidating the local administration.

The Evolution of a Single-Crop Economy

By the 1880's the second stage of the sugar revolution was accelerating, impelled by the abolition of slavery and increased United States investment, which led to the cultivation of cane being separated from the industrial process of grinding. A *colono* class of small cane producers replaced the plantation slaves. A relentless process of centralization perpetuated and extended the *latifundia*. The *colonos* were reduced to complete dependence on the mills, the output of which fluctuated according to the demands of the United States market. The lending role of Spanish merchant houses was taken over by United States banks, which now acquired a dominant interest in the sugar industry, especially after the disastrous crash of 1920-21. Slavery was not replaced by a smallholding peasantry in a diversified economy, the ideal of some mid-century Cuban reformers, but by a new form of market relationships over which Cubans had little control and which further inhibited the development of a rural middle class.

United States trade and investments in the island increased rapidly after 1899. Exports to Cuba rose ninefold between 1897 and 1914, by which date Cuba had become the United States' sixth largest customer. Between 1913 and 1928, United States investments increased 536 percent and constituted 17.7 percent of all United States investments in Latin America. By 1928 as much as 75 percent of the sugar crop was under United States control. By the 1950's sugar made up 80 percent of Cuba's exports, and 40 percent of the profits of this went to United States-owned companies. In addition, United States companies owned public utilities and in the 1950's provided between 70 and 80 percent of all Cuban imports.[1] United States capital investment was mainly responsible for making Cuban industry the most highly capitalized in Latin America relative to population.

Dependence on the single export crop of sugar condemned the landless agricultural laborer to unemployment for half of every year in the dead season, while importation of Haitian and Jamaican labor lowered wages during the cutting months. Poor rural conditions encouraged endemic banditry and a drift to the towns until by the 1960's nearly 60 percent of the island's 6¾ million inhabitants were loosely classified as urban, and 21 percent were crammed into Greater Havana. Living conditions were worst in Oriente, the largest and most rural of the six provinces, which had over half the island's colored population, together with the highest illiteracy rate. Economically backward, Oriente is the cradle of Cuban revolutions: apart from that of 1933 every significant revolutionary movement has originated there.

Social Structure

The economic exhaustion of the Independence war and the legacies of colonial misrule distorted the new republic's social structure. Collapse of Spanish rule was not followed by a wholesale exodus of Spaniards; commerce and the retail trade remained largely in their hands, and the Catholic Church was their preserve. They continued to enjoy social and economic power and the privileges of mutual benefit societies with their lavish club premises. North Americans, too, occupied a privileged economic position. New sugar *centrales* were administered by United States personnel. Because of the island's low educational standards few Cubans qualified for technical posts; hence the significance of the Cubanization laws of 1933 under which employers had to employ 50 percent Cubans.

In this neocolonial society the openings for the small middle sector were limited. To own land was the hallmark of social success, while manual work was scorned through its association with slavery. Although it is possible to talk of a Cuban middle class in economic or even political terms, sociologists have suggested that the real dichotomy in Cuban society is between an upper class and a lower class, each based on sociopsychological factors rather than on income or wealth. The middle sector lacks homogeneity and a sense of self-identification, living beyond its means trying to achieve upper-class status. Hence the hopes its members have often placed on revolution as a means of overthrowing the political order and hastening their admission to the upper class.

Martí's new Cuba was to be free from racial prejudice; but although there was no legal discrimination, colored people found it difficult to rise in the social scale. In the mid-1950's roughly 75 percent of the population were classified as white, 12 percent as Negro, 12 percent as mixed, and 1 percent Oriental, descendants of Chinese indentured laborers. In prestigious occupations colored people were underrepresented, but many were skilled workers and taught in public schools. If a low educational rating was one reason why they did not rise socially, the blame must rest partly with the notoriously neglected public education system in which most of their children were educated. Politically, colored people have been most active in labor organizations and it is now deliberate policy to advance their status and to eradicate the stigma of their sugar-plantation ancestry.

Sugar has ruled in Cuba as ruthlessly as King Cotton in the Southern states of the United States. The social structure, the pattern of trade, political alignments, the distribution of wealth, and the social attitudes of its people have been irrevocably linked to a single crop. The legacy of colonial rule has been a racially divided society, a distorted economy, an impoverished rural population, a corrupted administration, a devastated countryside, and a harvest of martyrs. Political independence, however, did not solve the problems bequeathed by colonialism; it exacerbated them.

Political History

The Era of United States Interventions

Cubans had little experience of political responsibility during the colonial period. Apart from the Cadiz Cortes of 1810-14, and between 1820 and 1823, the principle of colonial representation was strongly resisted by Spain until the 1880's, when a party system began to develop. Meanwhile, in exile, Martí was building up the Revolutionary Cuban Party (PRC), the hard spine of the independence movement, which was responsible for reopening hostilities in 1895. But his death in 1895, three years before the United States intervened, removed the one person who might have given direction to Cuban politics.

From 1898 until 1902, as an outcome of the defeat of Spain in the Spanish-American War, Cuba was under United States military government. After the Spanish withdrawal the Cuban army did not play the dominant role, as might have been expected from Latin American precedent, largely because General Máximo Gómez refused to play at politics and the United States offered a loan to pay off and demobilize soldiers. The American military governor, assisted by Cuban secretaries, was the supreme authority.

Relations between the two nations were not easy. United States administration, although enlightened and efficient, was resented as paternalistic by all except the most conservative, and the continued presence of United States forces irritated Cubans who felt that the long arduous years of irregular warfare, rather than the short sharp intervention of the United States army, had been the main factor in Spain's defeat. Differing interpretations of the course of the 1895-8 war (reflected in textbook histories) were to remain a constant source of misunderstanding in later years.

Elections for the Constituent Assembly were held in September 1900, two months after the municipal elections had shown that political forces were divided between the Nationalists of Havana, the Republicans of Santa Clara, and the Democratic Union, a rump of the old Autonomist Party which had favored qualified independence. By February 1901 the thirty-one delegates completed a draft constitution in which the democratic, secular ideas of Martí were enshrined. A bitter struggle then ensued over the clauses regulating future United States-Cuban relations. Opinion in both countries was divided over the outcome: a definition of the island's sovereignty in foreign affairs which allowed the United States to intervene "for the preservation of Cuban independence, the maintenance of a government adequate for the protection of life, property and individual liberty. . . ." This "Platt Amendment" was the inhibiting factor in Cuba's independence, instilling a sense of inadequacy, frustration, and pessimism in the island, and becoming a standing invitation to nationalist incitement until it was finally abrogated in 1934 as part of Roosevelt's Good Neighbor policy.

The first presidential elections, in December 1901, were won by Estrada Palma, the honest and austere Cuban delegate in the United States during the war. His election owed much to the support of the great war hero Máximo Gómez who, by refusing to stand himself, ensured a civilian gloss to the first Cuban government. The United States forces then withdrew, having repaired the ravages of war but little able to offset the numbing influence of colonial rule.

The policy of economy, antimilitarism, educational expansion, public works, and comparatively honest administration give some justification to the description of Estrada Palma's government as the best years of the Republic. But the test of the political system came with the first congressional elections in February 1904, when the Moderates (ex-Nationalists) replaced the Liberals (ex-Republicans). The Liberals, asserting fraud, resorted to the *retraimiento*, withdrawing from congress and from the presidential elections of 1905. Estrada Palma's re-election sparked off the Liberal Revolution of August 1906, which led the Moderates to appeal for United States intervention in order to stave off civil war.

The second United States intervention lasted from September 1906 until January 1909. As Secretary of War (later President) Taft had recognized the fraudulence of the 1905 elections, the Cuban congress was dissolved and Governor Magoon took over responsibility for legislation. In 1909 the Liberals won at the polls and Miguel Gómez (Máximo had died in 1905) became president. Unable to exploit the Oriente Race War of 1912 politically and with his party split, Gómez failed to secure renomination and in the 1913 congressional and presidential elections the Conservatives (who replaced the Moderates in 1907), led by Mario García Menocal were returned. This ushered in a twelve-year period of Conservative ascendancy.

Division among the Liberals may have been the reason for Menocal's decision to stand again for the Conservatives in 1916, but their unexpected strength led to the government's falsification of voting returns. This was followed by Liberal attempts to blackmail Menocal with the threat of United States intervention; but the United States was reluctant to become involved in Cuban affairs with war threatening in Europe, and the Liberals' revolution collapsed when the United States supported Menocal. Menocal's second term was a "classic and vulgar dictatorship" in Mendieta's phrase, for the war boom brought the "dance of the millions" in which a garish *nouveau riche* class of sugar profiteers entered public life.

Another Conservative walkover gave Alfredo Zayas the presidency and again the Liberals' hope for United States supervision of free elections was dashed. General Enoch Crowder was sent to act in an advisory capacity and to mediate between rival factions, but not even his persuasive skill or the threat of intervention could force Zayas to reform. Patient but timid, Zayas was no person to regenerate Cuban public life, and it was during his office that new and younger opposition elements became vocal.

Gerardo Machado succeeded Zayas in the elections of 1925, after the latter withdrew from the candidacy. For the first time since Gómez's election in 1909 the Liberals were in power, but with the opportunity to fatten on the pastures of patronage, they were in no mood to listen to ever-louder voices of discontent. When in 1928 Machado altered the constitution and extended his term of office, resistance snowballed. A strengthened army, closer alliance with United States business interests, and ruthless suppression postponed the crisis until the effects of the Depression united opposition forces in the Revolution of 1933. A general strike in August and withdrawal of army support forced Machado to flee the country.

Batista and the Auténticos

The 1933 Revolution introduced three new forces into Cuban politics— the army, the Student Directorate of Havana University, and organized labor. The first government (under Céspedes, the insignificant son of a famous father, and the candidate of Sumner Welles, the United States ambassador) was overthrown by the radical nationalist Grau San Martín, supported by the Student Directorate. The new government, beset by rising lawlessness, attacked by the Communists, and snubbed by the United States, was unable to placate the army on which its power ultimately rested. Fulgencio Batista, an affable and astute *mestizo* sergeant, son of a poor Oriente can-cutter, had purged the army of *machadista* officers and now, as self-promoted Army Chief, forced Grau's resignation in January 1934, replacing him by the first of a series of presidents destined to be both pliable in his hands and more amenable to United States business interests.

For the next six years Batista was the manipulator of six puppet presidents. The new regime rested on the traditional use of political patronage, a tame labor movement, and a pampered army. Up to 1937 Batistsa ruled with a heavy hand: a general strike in 1935 was ruthlessly crushed and he began to acquire a reputation as bad as Machado's. In 1937, however, his policy changed; exactly why has never been satisfactorily explained. A three-year plan for social and economic development was drawn up, the regime was outwardly liberalized, and the Communists were legalized and permitted to organize a front-type party, the Partido Unión Revolucionaria, under Juan Marinello. Those Communists who have since distinguished between the "good" Batista and the "bad" Batista claim that it was their influence which persuaded him to convoke a constituent assembly in 1939 to draw up a new constitution.

Certainly left-wing influence was strongly reflected in the 1940 constitution, which incorporated safeguards for labor and included a promise of agrarian reform. By exploiting the popularity of this constitution Batista was elected president by an overwhelming majority in the same year. By the time of the next presidential elections in 1944, however, the Auténticos, which Grau had founded ten years earlier, had built up a party machine which enabled Grau to win a sweeping victory over Saladrigas, Batista's candidate. Batista accepted the result and left office at the conclusion of his term.

Until 1952 the president was an Auténtico, Prío Socarras succeeding Grau in 1948. But the party did not live up to its high promise. The constitution was one obstacle which made the program's implementation difficult; by encouraging a multiparty system it favored electoral and working alliances which watered down the party's revolutionary aims. Grau's aggressive personality, an asset in opposition, was also a liability in power. The party's failure to break the pattern of corruption led to the hiving off in 1946 of a group under Eduardo Chibas, the incorruptible firebrand of Cuban politics, who founded the Cuban People's Party (Ortodoxos). In spite of this split Grau felt strong enough in 1947 to break his tenuous links with the Communists and to attack their entrenched position in the CTC (the dominant labor federation) by setting up an Auténtico-dominated Confederation.

Though Grau's term had put the Communists on the defensive, the presidential elections of 1948 were still no cause for self-congratulation. The Auténticos had fought in alliance with the right-wing Republicans, and although they polled 46 percent of the votes the new Ortodoxos, with a surprisingly large 16 percent, could claim to represent the purity of the Auténtico revolutionary ideal. Chibás's dramatic suicide at the end of one of his famous radio programs in 1951 deprived the party of its leader at a time when it looked as if the Ortodoxos might win the 1952 elections. These, however, never took place. On March 10, 1952, Batista, accusing Prío of plotting a pre-election coup, staged his own coup with the support of junior army officers. Resistance was almost nonexistent. Prío refused to give arms to the students, and the Auténtico unions refused to follow the CTC secretary-general Mujal's call for a general strike. Mujal, himself an ex-Communist, later came to terms with Batista. Such was the inglorious end of the Auténticos' domination of the CTC.

Both Auténticos and Ortodoxos were divided over the appropriate attitude to take toward Batista—some, like Prío Socarras, went into exile. Others, including Grau, accepted Batista's challenge of elections for 1954. But even Grau eventually withdrew, accusing Batista of rigging them. In fact, the government coalition was returned unopposed, and Batista was elected president with an estimated 50 percent poll. Prío returned in 1955 to organize an anti-Batista front, only to be exiled in April 1956. It was after this that Prío began negotiating with various revolutionary groups in exile who were plotting armed insurrection.

The Rise of Fidel Castro

Three years earlier, on July 26, 1953, a symbolic gesture of defiance had been made by a group of 165 youths who assaulted the Moncada Barracks in Santiago. The few who were not killed were imprisoned. Neither the government nor the country thought this different in kind from the many other insurrectionary outbursts which had become the stock-in-trade of Cuban revolutionary politics. In retrospect, the most remarkable feature of the affair was the famous "history will absolve me" speech made at his trial by the expedition's leader, Fidel Castro, the twenty-seven-year-old son of an Oriente landowner and then a Havana lawyer, whose political apprenticeship had been served in student politics and who had been a great admirer of Chibás. The aims which he outlined in his speech bore an Ortodoxo imprint and included the restoration of the 1940 constitution, agrarian reform, profit-sharing in industry, protection for cane planters, administrative and educational reform, rent reform, and the nationalization of public utilities.

In May 1955, after release from prison in an amnesty, Castro continued his plotting from Mexico, and in December 1956 he launched an expedition to the south coast of Oriente. The twelve of the original eighty-six who survived the landing took to the Sierra Maestra and organized guerrilla resistance which soon compelled Batista to mount a full-scale military campaign. Resistance elsewhere was at first confined to Havana, where the Revolutionary Directorate of the University began urban terrorism. Other opposition groups were linked together in the Civic Resistance Movement. Early in 1958 a second guerrilla front was opened in the Escambray Mountains. But organized labor held aloof. In April 1958 Castro's strike call went unheeded by both Mujal's CTC, which had come to a working agreement with the dictator, and by the Communists, who, although outlawed in 1953, looked askance at Castro's rebellion as a movement of *petit-bourgeois* romantics.

By mid-1958 resistance had become so stiff that Batista made a bid to salvage support by new elections in November. In these purely nominal elections, with possibly a 30 percent poll, Batista's candidate was returned. However, urban terrorism and guerrilla activity had demoralized the army. Reports that it was disintegrating finally decided Batista to flee the island on January 1st, 1959.

The first revolutionary government was a coalition of the Civic Resistance Movement and Castro's Twenty-sixth of July Movement, but Castro's popularity was so overwhelming that he was able to ignore the rumps of the pre-revolutionary parties whose representatives wanted legal recognition, free elections, and the restoration of the 1940 constitution. But even social radicals within the Twenty-sixth of July Movement were alienated by favors shown to the PSP (Partido Socialista Popular, the name adopted by the Communists in 1940), now the only legal party, and by the steady infiltration of Communists into the army and administration. From late 1959 on, the *batistianos* in exile were joined by a growing stream of middle-class Cubans disheartened by extensive socialization measures. The United States government, sensitive to pressures from commercial concerns which had been nationalized, as well as from the growing exile community, drastically reduced the sugar quota[2] in mid-1960. During 1960, as the Cuban economy, in search of new markets, became increasingly linked to Russia and Eastern Europe, ideological and political ties with the Communist countries were strengthened.

Economic sanctions by the United States, as well as the activities of Cuban exiles, culminated in the disastrous Playa Giron invasion of April 1961, in which an exile force organized and equipped by the United States government, acting through the Central Intelligence Agency, was defeated. The result was a heightened siege mentality, enabling the government to justify further arbitrary measures. In mid-1961 Castro announced the projected formation of a revolutionary party in which the PSP would form the hard core and which would take the place of the amorphous and by now weakened Twenty-sixth of July Movement.

Political Processes

Until the early 1930's politics rotated around the struggle between two main parties. The distinction between the two earliest, the Nationalists of Havana and the Republicans of Santa Clara, was one between centralization and states' rights; but this was soon blurred by the demands of the spoils system. In the context of conflict for government office, presidential re-election became the vital issue and the big crises of 1905-6, 1916-17, and 1928 may be largely attributed to a rotation system which failed to rotate. But whereas in nineteenth-century Spain, and in parts of Latin America, the army often intervened as the moderator, in Cuba the United States found itself playing this unenviable role. The Platt Amendment was a standing invitation to a defeated party to court United States intervention as a means of reversing the decision of a rigged election. A discredited party in power might even goad the United States to intervene in order to rally nationalist feeling. Not the least of the criticisms against the Amendment was its cramping effect on the development of a sense of responsibility among Cuban politicians.

Attempts to modify the two-party system were sidetracked as in the 1910 Morúa Law forbidding racialist parties, and as in 1925 when the government reacted to the emergence of new vocal opposition groups by restricting the organization of new parties or the reorganization of existing ones. One of the strongest opposition elements was the Veterans' Association, which the economic crisis of the early 1920's had turned from being an interest group concerned primarily with pensions into a "moralization group" claiming to put patriotic interests above those of party. Soon this moral regeneration role was taken over by others representing a younger generation reacting violently against the old discredited system, for whom elderly war heroes had lost their allure.

Havana University was the focal point of this new activity and from 1923 the students became one of the most important forces in Cuban politics. The initial impetus came from the continental University Reform movement and led to the founding in 1923 of the José Martí Popular University for extension work among the poor. Later in the year students purged the university of its professors and forced the government to recognize the principle of co-government, with student representation on Faculty Boards and the autonomy of the university precincts. In 1927 the Student Federation (FEU) was founded by Mella—a founder member of the Cuban Communist Party —but his assassination in Mexico two years later weakened Communist influence. *Aprismo*[3] rather than Communism was the ideology of the Student Directorate which organized revolutionary activity in the early 1930's and which was the main support of Grau San Martín, himself a university professor, during his brief term as president between September 1933 and January 1934.

Again in the 1950's, students spearheaded the attack against dictatorship. A tradition of opposition to tyranny, with a growing list of martyrs stretching back to the eight medical students shot in 1871, gave the students a hallowed place in Cuban politics which enabled them to assume the moral leadership of the urban resistance of the mid-1950's. Mostly the *déraciné* sons of middle-sector parents, students faced a bleak future as underemployed intellectuals or professional men in a society which denied spiritual values. To many the choice was a stark one between revolution or acceptance of the corrupting norms of political behavior. The novelty in 1959 was that for the first time a group of young revolutionaries after seizing power did not reward themselves with the "ownership of government" but began a full-scale social revolution. The common phenomenon in Latin America of students acting as a self-conscious elite finds its most acute expression in Cuba.

During the thirties Machado's and later Batista's refusal to allow a viable constitutional system to develop had forced opposition underground and led to a multiplicity of terrorist groups. Some, like the Student Directorate or the ABC, had political and social aims; others, like Guiteras's Jóven Cuba, were born in the disillusion of Grau's defeat in 1934; and yet others, like the UIR of the late 1930's or Rolando Masferrer's anti-Castro MSR, were mere political gangsterism. Terrorism can be a two-edged sword and a self-defeating political weapon, purity of aim becoming corrupted by the ruthlessness of method, especially when it lacks the utopian vision of, say, Spanish anarchism. What is so striking about Cuban terrorism is the ease with which it swept up the rootless younger generation and nationalist middle-class groups, who resorted to it rather than try to widen the social basis of their opposition by mass organization. Grau alone drew the lesson from the failures of 1933 and founded the Auténticos in the next year, a nationalist, anti-imperialist party with a wide program of political democracy, agrarian reform, economic planning, gradual socialization of industry, and social security. For the first time a parliamentary party appealed to the working class.

The tobacco workers were traditionally the most highly organized group in Cuban labor, and it was among them that the issue between socialism and anarchism had been fought out at the end of the colonial period. Militant though they might be, as in the 1902 general strike, their political role was unimportant; efforts to found a Cuban socialist party met with little response nor did the anarchosyndicalists widen their appeal. The absence of a strong non-Communist left is an important factor in accounting for the quick build-up of Communist influence in the early 1930's. The Cuban Communist Party, founded in 1925 (illegal to 1938 and again between 1953 and 1959), was the first party since Martí's PRC to appeal to any but the middle sector. Linked with bourgeois elements through the Anti-Imperialist League, and with the support of intellectuals like Marinello and Guillén, the Communists' main strength in the 1930's came to lie in their domination of the Cuban Labor Confederation (CNOC). The political effectiveness of the general strike of 1933 first revealed the potentialities of organized labor. Communist support had become vital for the success of the 1933 strike which overthrew Machado, just as their holding aloof in 1952 and 1958 or committing themselves too late, as in 1935, was an important factor in the failure of these strikes. Although the Communists were active among sugar workers in the early 1930's, and in spite of the brief establishment of soviets in some *centrales* in 1933, their interest in the rural population declined as they developed their urban strength by gaining control of key labor unions such as the Havana transport workers. Past neglect of the rural sector may still cause the party embarrassment in its conflicts with Castro.

Difficult communications and illiteracy reduced the effectiveness of mass appeal. The plums of office were to be picked in Havana, and this was where the main effort was directed. The Cuban press was almost entirely Havana-based. In 1917, for example, there were thirty-seven daily papers—twice as many as in New York—and in 1956 Havana had only two fewer dailies than London. Illegal government subsidies helped to finance them and indirectly to employ a substantial group of the middle sector. However, Cuban politics and *personalismo* have always placed a premium on oratory: Batista was a master of the old-style Spanish military harangue. Radio and television therefore had a greater impact than in more literate countries. It is hard to imagine the Ortodoxos without Chibás's weekly radio talk, or Castro without his mammoth television appearances. With Havana's many channels and the world's eighth highest per capita ownership of receivers, Cuba was the setting for the first television revolution by which charismatic leadership was impressed upon the masses.

In Cuban politics personalities have always been more important than programs. People have been *zayistas*, *machadistas*, *batistianos* or *fidelistas* before they have been Conservatives, Liberals, etc. The easy acceptance of corruption might be related to this personalist approach, but although in primitive societies corruption may perhaps fulfill a useful social function, where extended family and kinship relationships exact a firmer loyalty than the impersonal State, the dependence of Cuba on international markets postulated an uncorrupt bureaucracy if the interests of the mass of the people were to be safeguarded. However, the *patrón* relationship, firmly rooted in society, is extended into the political sphere, where a sense of kinship is deliberately fostered to bind followers to their leader. Greater emphasis is placed on this personal bond than on impersonal government institutions. Law still emanates from the *líder máximo* and some of Castro's success may be attributed to his brilliant exploitation of this relationship. How far he will be able to use it to purify government on a lasting basis is one of the open questions of the Revolution.

If *personalismo* rather than principle has dominated politics, *caudillismo* based on the army was not an evil of Cuban government until after 1933. During the late 1920's, the gradual absorption of senior officers into the graft system alienated professional-minded younger officers. Machado's under-mining of their authority with the ranks emasculated them as a revolutionary force, however, and prepared the way for the sergeants' takeover in 1933. The new officer corps's loyalty was ensured by lavish benefits, but as soon as the army had to fulfill a police function after 1953, it disintegrated. The old Cuban army fulfilled no useful political function; it was never a moder-ating force, but the inefficient instrument of a repressive dictatorship.

Similarly, in religion Cuban experience has been distinctive. Martí's ideal of a secular state was realized in the 1901 Constitution, which separated Church and State. The Catholic Church has never exercised a strong political influence. It had been discredited during the Wars of Independence through its attitude towards Spain. It had not seriously tried to proselytize the slaves; many Africanist cults like the Abakuá retained a hold among Negroes. It was an urban church, little interested in the rural population, and in the 1950's most of the 700 priests were Spaniards. Anti-Catholicism is thus an-other expression of nationalism. Catholicism also had to face a strong chal-lenge from many United States Protestant sects which were established after Independence.

A Church divorced from politics meant that anticlericalism could not become the dynamic of a radical middle-class party as in Chile or Argentina. Nor was there any other issue except an ill-defined anti-United States nation-alism to give the middle sector cohesion. Spanish colonial practice had be-queathed the notion of public service as a source of private profit, so the bureaucracy, with its accompanying perquisites, became the most over-subscribed middle-sector career, especially after 1933, when new social and economic responsibilities made the government the largest employer for the middle sector: some 80 percent of the budget of 1949-50 went for salary payments. *Botelleros*—officeholders who did no work—were the earliest casualties of the administrative purges of 1959.

Revolutionary politics had an irresistible attraction for lawyers, journal-ists, doctors, and university professors whose incomes did not match their social aspirations. But "revolution" did not mean a radical transformation of society so much as a means of gaining admission into the coveted upper class. That revolution could mean something more than this was the shock they had to assimilate after 1959.

Governmental Institutions

Cuba's Constitutions

The key documents in Cuban constitutional development have been the Constitution of 1901 with its amendments in 1929, 1933, and 1934, the Constitution of 1940, and the Fundamental Law of February 7, 1959 (which the pragmatic development of the Revolution has modified in numberless ways).

The Constitution of 1901 provided for a separation of powers in which strong personal authority was vested in the president, and a legislature which, because of lack of sufficient checks or controls over the president, became a factious and ineffectual body. Its inefficacy as an instrument of radical change and even as a reflection of public opinion meant that the presidential system became discredited and political life divorced from the real life of the nation. The Revolution of 1933, although it seemed to presage a complete social as well as political change, did not fundamentally alter the pattern of government.

Not until 1940 did the aims of the Revolution of 1933 find any reflection in constitutional form. The Constitution of 1940 was a remarkable and influential document, representing the ideas of veteran reformer José Cortina, but many of its clauses were to remain an aspiration rather than an actuality. It departed from the doctrine of the separation of powers by establishing a bicameral and semiparliamentary system designed to curb the abuse of the presidential office. The president was to be elected by universal suffrage for a four-year period and could only serve a second period after eight years had elapsed. The cabinet chosen by the president was responsible to congress, which consisted of two chambers, the powers of which were similar to those in the Constitution of 1901 except for greater control over the executive. However, this was limited by a clause forbidding votes of confidence during the first and last six months of a president's term of office.

The judiciary was declared independent. Appointment to the supreme court was by the president with the senate's approval from a list presented by an electoral college. Three autonomous bodies, a Superior Electoral Court, a Board of Public Office, and a Tribunal of Accounts, were written into the constitution and regulated those most common areas of abuse, elections, public appointments, and government accounting.

The constitution could be amended either by petition from 100,000 literate voters, to be followed by a referendum, or by a two-thirds majority of congress. Sixty-one of the two hundred and eighty-six articles dealt with social and economic matters which would require further elaboration by legislative action. Most of the section on labor incorporated legislation passed since 1933, which theoretically made the Cuban constitution one of the most advanced in the world.

Many of its provisions, however, were not implemented and the war distorted constitutional development by enabling Batista to get extra powers making him less dependent on congress. Neither were his successors, Grau San Martín nor Prío Socarrás, amenable to parliamentary control.

The Institutions of the Revolution

The Revolution of 1959 was characterized by a pragmatic approach to institutional problems. Few plans had been made for organizational reform, but in spite of earlier commitments Castro refused to restore an unmodified 1940 constitution. By the Fundamental Law of February 7, 1959, the council of ministers assumed the functions of congress and the power to amend laws by a two-thirds vote. Four new ministries were created—Social Welfare, Economy, Misappropriated Property, and the Study of Revolutionary Laws. As all elective posts were abolished, officers of the Rebel Army, acting as government commissioners, took over provincial and municipal administration. Apart from these changes, early measures involving purges of the administration and of Batista supporters did not require radical structural alterations, except a suspension of the independent judiciary's function as legal procedures were subordinated to political control.

Revolutionary tribunals tried war criminals in summary trials in which popular clamor often predetermined judgment. These furnished revolutionary legitimation for a revenge which after earlier revolutions had been expressed in more spontaneous but even more horrifying manner. Dissolved in May 1959, the revolutionary tribunals were reinstituted in October to deal with suspected counterrevolutionaries. New laws sanctioned the arbitrary powers of the reorganized police units while the wholesale emigration of lawyers left justice in the hands of committed revolutionaries.

Until midsummer 1959 the conflict between moderates of the Civilian Revolutionary Front and radicals was fought out in the cabinet, but with the resignation of five members over the Agrarian Reform Law, and of President Urrutia in protest against Communist infiltration, the cabinet became a homogeneous radical body whose function was to give the force of law to decisions reached by the small inner junta of the Central Planning Council. This junta was formed in February 1960 and included Castro, his brother Raúl, minister of the armed forces, "Che" Guevara, president of the national bank, Finance Minister Aztaraín, and Nuñez Jiménez, director of INRA, the National Agrarian Reform Institute.

The president's role is difficult to assess. The uneasy tension between Urrutia, the first president, and Castro, who succeeded Miró Cardona as prime minister in February of 1960, came to a climax when Castro forced Urrutia to resign, accusing him of counterrevolutionary tendencies because of his public criticisms of the Communists. Osvaldo Dorticós, more acceptable to the PSP, who then became president, has since worked in outward harmony with Castro.

The hard core of the new revolutionary administration, mainly staffed by young officers of the Rebel Army, and the institution most closely connected with the Twenty-sixth of July Movement, was INRA (National Institute of Agrarian Reform), the function of which was much wider than its name suggests. In addition to its agrarian concerns, it also had responsibility for reorganizing the national economy under government control and administering nationalized foreign and Cuban enterprises. With control of nearly 60 percent of all land, INRA was the most powerful of the governmental agencies. A Department of Industrialization, set up in mid-1959 under Guevara's control, directed economic planning and supervised the Petroleum and Mining Institutes.

The exigencies of an increasingly planned economy cut INRA down to size, however. In early 1961 industrial administration was transferred to the new Ministry of Industry, again headed by Guevara, while the control of the wholesale and retail trade, along with the mechanics of price control, were transferred to the Ministry of Internal Trade which, together with the Ministry of Foreign Trade, replaced the old Ministry of Commerce. With the Ministry of Labor's new control of employment, INRA's power was further reduced. These changes were a process of rationalization and centralization. But the fact that PSP veteran Carlos Rafael Rodríguez, ex-editor of *Hoy*, the Communist daily, was appointed director of INRA in February 1962 was symptomatic of growing Communist predominance.

Other leading government agencies outside the ministries include the Institute of Savings and Housing (INAV), the Institute for Friendship among Peoples (ICAP), the Institute for Sports and Recreation (INDER), and the National Institute for Tourism (INIT).

To meet planning needs at the local level, regional, provincial, and municipal JUCEI (Juntas Unificadas de Coordinación, Ejecución y Inspección) were established first by Raúl Castro in March 1961 in Oriente and then in other provinces. In these integrating juntas, representatives of the various local revolutionary organizations decided priorities, ways of avoiding duplication, and mutual aid schemes. This was the first preliminary step in making a planned national economy a reality.

Political Leadership and Control

The dominant part played by the Rebel Army officers in INRA showed the original role the army was to play in the new society. Deliberately flouting traditional functions and flaunting unkempt beards, army officers were the backbone of the radicalization of the revolution. But the Hubert Matos affair in late 1959, when this popular senior officer was tried and imprisoned for criticizing Communist influence, was a straw in the wind.

Guarding against unreliability in other officers and the possibility of their following traditional Latin American militarist patterns, Castro downgraded the army's political role by forming the civilian militia in late 1959. The threat of invasion in 1960 too emphasized the need for a "military" rather than a "political" army. The militia, reputedly numbering a quarter of a million, increased participation by the masses and gave revolutionary purpose to the lives of men and women of all ages who previously had no stake in politics, at the same time as it provided indoctrination centers and a counterweight to the army. The disruption of production involved in the absence of people from their jobs to participate in militia activities, perhaps together with doubts over the political reliability of the militia, led in late 1963 to the creation of a new army based on conscription, which was gradually to replace the militia.

To deal with counterrevolutionary activity, the CDR (Comités de Defensa de la Revolución) were formed. These vigilance committees are to be found in every street or block and exercise a petty inquisition over citizens' activities.

Divisions within the Twenty-sixth of July Movement and the evaporation of much early middle-class support led Castro to rely increasingly on the PSP, the only political party tolerated in the new regime. In return for key posts which were being vacated by Castro's erstwhile supporters, the PSP was prepared to accept the willful personal leadership of Castro, who in turn was willing to give the Revolution an ideology, which up till then it had lacked, by grafting Marxist-Leninist dogmas on to Martí's ideas.

In the CTC, where non-Communist Twenty-sixth of July supporters were entrenched, Castro's influence was used to increase PSP power and to oust the non-Communist David Salvador from its leadership in November 1959. Together with the militia, the CTC, or CTC(R) as it is now called, with nearly a million and a quarter members under its PSP secretary Jesús Soto, became a pillar of Communist support for Castro.

The disintegration of the Twenty-sixth of July Movement in late 1959 and 1960 posed the problem of party organization. Revolutionary euphoria had produced a bewildering number of groups imprecisely related to each other and, useful though a "movement" concept may have been in uniting a wide range of opinion against Batista, the effects of the United States embargo and the vast increase in governmental planning demanded a more formal political structure.

The first official pronouncement of the formation of a revolutionary party was made by Castro at the Twenty-sixth of July rally in 1961, three months after the designation of the Revolution as "socialist." The first stage was the setting up of a preparatory organization, the ORI (Organizaciones Revolucionarias Integradas). Its function was to select and train the cadres of the new party, to be called the PURS (Partido Unido de la Revolución Socialista) in which would be fused the Twenty-sixth of July Movement, the PSP, and the student Directorio Revolucionario. The leadership included prominent PSP old-time militants like Blas Roca, the Escalante brothers, and Joaquín Ordoqui. The orientation was Marxist-Leninist, to which views Castro first publicly subscribed in a speech on December 1, 1961.

The lengthening time lag between the announcement of the ORI and the nonappearance of the PURS seems to have been caused by acute political conflict within the new nuclei, which was openly revealed by Castro's dismissal of Aníbal Escalante, the national ORI's secretary-general. In a speech in March 1962, Castro accused Escalante of packing the new nuclei with old-time PSP members, of giving orders without reference to the Council of Ministers, and of the cardinal sin of sectarianism and personalism.

Since Escalante's dismissal and subsequent purges within the ORI, the party has been slowly built up in factories where workers' assemblies select "exemplary workers" for party membership. Selection committees of government nominees then choose the new members after scrutinizing the candidates' antecedents. In addition to full members there are also probationary members (*aspirantes*), as in the Soviet Union, who serve a period of apprenticeship before being admitted. Up to mid-1964 party membership stood at 32,000, of whom the majority are state employees and factory workers. Although the PURS is a "workers-peasants" party, peasants are poorly represented—by mid-1964 they constituted only 4 percent of the total. It is a selective and not a mass party. The twenty-five man National Directorate is carefully balanced between fourteen 'new Communists' (ex-Twenty-sixth of July members), ten ex-PSP members and one ex-Revolutionary Directorate. The most obvious difference between these old and new Communists is one of age. Eight of the ex-PSP members are over fifty years of age while the ex-Twenty-sixth of July members are in their thirties.

A host of supporting organizations, closely associated with the government but reputedly of popular origin, share the task of activating students, workers, and peasants. Everyone between fourteen and twenty-five is eligible to join the Unión de Juventud Comunista or UJC (before 1962 the Asociación de Jóvenes Rebeldes, or AJR) with its preparatory organization, the Rebel Pioneers, for children between seven and fourteen. An important role is assigned to the FMC (Federación de Mujeres Cubanas) to heighten the revolutionary consciousness of the previously apolitical sex. The old *colegios* or professional associations were purged and reorganized to ensure their loyalty to the revolution. In the reformed University (of which Marinello, the veteran PSP leader, was the first rector appointed after the Revolution), a purged FEU, the student union, holds a watching brief over professors' opinions to ensure that loyalty to their professional ethic does not prevail over loyalty to the Revolution. A network of EIR's (Escuelas de Instrucción Revolucionaria) act as indoctrination centers for party militants.

Public Policy

Agrarian Policy

Only four months after Batista's fall the Agrarian Reform Law was passed by presidential decree on May 17, 1959. "Economic independence"—the cry of every Cuban nationalist, whether a Zayas, a Grau or a Castro—could not be achieved so long as the Cuban economy was dependent on a single export crop. The idea was not new. Martí had preached the impossibility of political liberty without economic freedom, the historian Guerra Sánchez had waged a long campaign to expose the evils of latifundia, Grau had been committed to agrarian reform, the Constitution of 1940 provided for it in clause 90, a World Bank Report in 1950 recommended it; but it was not until 1959 an attempt was made to translate words into deeds.

Agrarian Reform had three main aims: to Cubanize and socialize the sugar industry and sugar estates, to distribute land to the landless, and to diversify agricultural production. The assumption that the dynamic forces released by the Revolution would prevent any drop in production was partly justified by the record harvest of 1961; but the sharp drops after 1962 partially bear out the criticism that economic factors had been subordinated to political ends.

The Reform allowed for three distinct types of holdings—*granjas del pueblo*, state farms on the *sovkhoz* model (mainly huge cattle ranches); sugar cooperatives under the close control of INRA now scheduled to be turned into state enterprises also; and small peasant proprietors. To assuage the land hunger of a landless proletariat, large estates were parceled out to be enjoyed in usufruct; that is, titles of land ownership were not given out with the land. These new peasant owners, together with those already existing, were organized in May 1961 in a national body, ANAP (Asociación Nacional de Agricultores Pequeños). Distributive co-operatives were set up to provide tractors, seeds, technical advice, etc., and although this organization was envisioned as a transitory phase between peasant ownership and collectivization, there was at first little pressure to collectivize, and the initiative to form cooperatives was left to individual groups. Only those with less than 67 hectares could become members of ANAP, which left in the private sector those who held land up to the 670 hectares allowed by the Agrarian Reform Law. These, owning perhaps as much as 44 per cent of agricultural land, were the Cuban *kulaks*. They have since been dispossessed for "sabotaging production" and for "counterrevolutionary activities" by the Second Agrarian Reform of October 1963. Now 70 percent of the land is state-owned and those small peasants (with a maximum of 165 acres) who remain are closely supervised by ANAP.

The first agrarian reform bound the mass of the rural population to Castro without alienating any significant number of the middle sector apart from the "sugar bourgeoisie" (62 percent of sugar output in 1958 came from Cuban-owned mills). More significant in accounting for their alienation was the government's refusal to restore the Constitution of 1940 and to hold free elections, the threat to the freedom of education, the attack on the private school system and on religious freedom, and the more tangible cause of an increasingly directed economy.

Economic and Social Policy

The Urban Reform Law of October 1960, limiting income derived from rents to $600 a month, struck at the favorite middle-sector investment in real estate. By the decrees of July and October 1960, all big foreign and Cuban businesses were nationalized. The government's attitude towards small businesses, alternating between threats, assurances, and cajolery, led to uncertainty and to many closures as owners went into exile. The rapid alienation of the middle sector led to acute shortages of managerial and technical staff which impelled the government to draw closer to the Eastern bloc and to initiate crash programs to train administrative cadres to manage the new state concerns. The deliberate repudiation of middle and lower middle groups presupposed that Russia would underwrite the Cuban economy and provide massive technical aid.

In 1961, *El Año de la Educación*, priority was given to the campaign against illiteracy. Between the early thirties and mid-forties literacy had not increased, and by the early fifties it was said to have declined. The alphabetization campaign was an imaginative idea to grapple with adult illiteracy in rural areas, where the problem was most acute. Youngsters, released from school for the purpose and organized into teaching brigades, were sent into isolated areas. An uneven follow-up campaign makes the claim to have eradicated illiteracy suspect, but Cuban youth had been given a vivid interest in the Revolution, urban-rural barriers had been broken down, and the Revolution had been brought to the poorest homes, opening them up to government propaganda. The overwhelming support for the Revolution among Cuban youth is one of its most disarming features. The energies of the younger generation, which in the late 1920's and early 1930's went into fruitless terroristic activities, have been canalized and exploited in a way which must have few equals in modern history. The price at which this has been achieved has been the complete and unquestioning acceptance of Marxist-Leninist dogmas, amply reflected, for example, in *Mella*, the organ of the UJC.

The new regime also gave high priority to reforming the public education system. In July 1961 a law nationalizing teaching was passed; private schools, officially regarded as counterrevolutionary centers, virtually disappeared. PSP leader Marinello's appointment as rector of Havana University put the seal on the university reform movement, which shifted the emphasis from a literary, formal, and legalistic education to one dominated by science and technology.

In 1962 followed the first Year of Planning (*El Año de la Planificación*)— a directed effort to increase production and to expand industry. With the help of Communist Eastern-bloc technicians, mines were to be developed to provide raw materials for new Cuban industries at the same time as industrial plants for sugar by-products were to be set up. Shortage of technicians, managers, and even of labor (as nonmechanized cane cutting tied workers to the land), service in the militia, and indoctrination courses led to a self-confessed drop in production and to a change from the early promises to warnings of inevitable shortages and the postponing of improved living conditions. Over-ambitious plans such as those in road building and housing have had to be shelved.

After Castro's visit to Moscow in May 1963 the Cuban government accepted the principle of the international socialist division of labor, which led to a reversal of the Revolution's original emphasis on agricultural diversification and industrialization. Priority is now given, as before 1959, to sugar as the main export crop, with the Soviet Union guaranteeing a market until 1970. The introduction of compulsory military service for a three-year period in November 1963 must be seen as an integral part of this new agricultural policy as it will both provide a cheap and mobile labor force and help to make easier the political indoctrination of the rural population.

Hardships and changes of economic policy tend to be attributed to "imperialism" and the economic blockade. The David-Goliath image has a powerful imaginative appeal while the tight control of publishing by the National Printing Office and the habitual use by the press of the government-owned Prensa Latina News Agency have insulated Cubans from all but the official line.

General Significance of the Cuban Revolution

The change from the Cuban-oriented "humanism" of 1959, rooted in Martí, to the explicit acceptance of Marxist-Leninism and to Cuba's incorporation in a non-American bloc, has perhaps weakened rather than strengthened Castro's influence in Latin America. Castro has always scorned the OAS as a United States puppet and, pointing to the cautious nonalignment policies of Mexico and Brazil, asserts that the 70 percent of Latin America's population in these two countries supports his stand against the United States. But by introducing the Cold War into the Western Hemisphere and thus clarifying the distinction between anti-American nationalism and pro-Russian Communism, the Cuban rocket crisis of November 1962 would seem to have made this assumption less tenable. However, his image remains undimmed among the younger generation and is a constant inspiration to the pro-Chinese groups in the Latin American Communist parties, who accept Che Guevara's thesis that only violent revolution by guerrilla warfare will bring the drastic social change which the continent needs.

The Cuban government lives in the perpetual hope and expectation that similar revolutions will break out elsewhere in Latin America. Until Quadros's fall in August 1961, at the moment when a commercial and cultural agreement was about to be signed between the two powers, Brazil was regarded as the most likely country to initiate the continental revolution. Now, with Venezuela, Colombia, and Peru seen as the most likely targets for Cuban propaganda, vitriolic attacks are launched on left-wing democratic parties and leaders there who might provide an alternative course of revolutionary change.

Although the Cuban Revolution provides an inspiration to Latin American radicals, it is not so clear that it provides a model. Cuba's revolution, like her history, seems to be *sui generis*. The island has no Indian problem, no linguistic complications, no climatic or geographical obstacles. The land is immensely fertile; few countries could have so high a national income to be redistributed in the first phase of a social revolution. Cuba was among the most highly developed of Latin American countries, one of the most highly urbanized, fourth in the number of literates, third in the number of people receiving higher education. At the time of Castro's coming to power, per capita income in Cuba was third highest in Latin America. The proximity of the United States has provided an irritant and a spur to violent nationalism which in more geographically removed countries would need even more artificial stimulation. Whether the rest of Latin America will succumb to Cuban propaganda or accept the possible benefits offered by the Alliance for Progress could be decided, in the last analysis, by the irrational force of such nationalism rather than by more rational calculation.

NOTES FOR CHAPTER X

1. Robert F. Smith, *The United States and Cuba*, pp. 29, 166, 175.
2. For some time the amount of sugar bought by the United States from abroad has been set as an annual quota from each country by Act of Congress.
3. For a discussion of this ideology, see Chapter 14 on Peru.

SELECTED BIBLIOGRAPHY

R. J. Alexander, *Communism in Latin America*, New Brunswick, N.J., 1957.
Fidel Castro, *History Will Absolve Me*, New York, 1959.
C. E. Chapman, *A History of the Cuban Republic*, New York, 1927.
H. E. Davis, *Government and Politics in Latin America*, New York, 1958.
T. Draper, *Castro's Revolution*, London, 1962.
Foreign Policy Association, Commission on Cuban Affairs, *Problems of the New Cuba*, New York, 1935.
R. B. Gray, *José Martí: Cuban Patriot*, Gainesville, 1962.
L. Jenks, *Our Cuban Colony*, New York, 1928.
Wyatt MacGaffey and Clifford R. Barnett. *Cuba: Its People, Its Society, Its Culture*, New Haven, 1962.
J. Mañach, *Martí: Apostle of Freedom*, New York, 1950.

Lowry Nelson, *Rural Cuba*, Minneapolis, 1950.

F. Ortiz, *Cuban Counterpoint: Tobacco and Sugar*, New York, 1947.

R. Hart Phillips, *Cuba: Island of Paradox*, New York, 1959.

Dudley Seers and others, *Cuba: the Economic and Social Revolution*, Chapel Hill, 1964.

R. F. Smith, *The United States and Cuba: Business and Diplomacy, 1917-1960*, New York, 1960.

William S. Stokes, "The Cuban Parliamentary System in Action, 1940-1947," *Journal of Politics*, II (May, 1949), 335-364.

———, "The Cuban Revolution and the Presidential Elections," *Hispanic American Historical Review*, XXXI, No. 1, Feb. 1951, pp. 609-626.

XI   *John D. Martz*

COLOMBIA

QUALIFIED DEMOCRACY

LYING at the extreme northwestern corner of the continental land mass, the "gateway of South America" stands apart from its neighbors geographically. A land of rugged contrasts, Colombia is the most Andean of the mountain republics. Its most significant form of distinction is political rather than topographical, however. Over a long span of time, governmental institutions have been similar to those of surrounding republics. Yet the mainstream of Colombian history has carved out a political culture that is unique in all of Latin America.

For a nation that has long prided herself on political maturity and a firm commitment to democratic ways, Colombia has yet to achieve a fundamental understanding of the spirit of compromise and tolerance that is basic to a fully viable democratic system. The contemporary institutional arrangement, which will be detailed below, has been referred to as a "controlled democracy." In a more basic sense, however, Colombian politics must be described as the politics of qualified democracy.

It seems paradoxical to posit reservations in the face of the general Colombian reputation as strongly democratic. This reputation exploded, for reasons that seemed inexplicable, just after World War II. The occurrences of recent years, however, have brought the realities of the Colombian political culture into sharper focus. The unwillingness of the upper class to share in the political process with the masses led to social and political dislocations that continue to agitate the system today.

Practical operation of this system has been dependent upon a small oligarchy far from representative of any broad national consensus. Although this condition is currently in a state of flux, there seems little present reason to expect any great change. In fact, recent changes in the Constitution produce the form of qualified democracy quite explicitly. The complete parity of Liberal and Conservative representation at all levels of government introduced in 1958 blocks intervention of other parties and at the same time distorts the electoral picture of the national will. The result is in effect an unparalleled experiment in controlled democracy.

The style of Colombian politics has fallen far short of the democratic ideal. Party rivalry, although largely restricted to competing segments of the social elite, has carried political intolerance and inflexibility to extremes. Bitterness and unbending dogmatism of political interplay have violated the sense of moderation and responsibility entailed in true democracy. An exaggerated influence of personalities remains, although charisma is admittedly weaker and less pervasive than it is in many other Latin American countries.

The turbulence of recent years is not, as some have suggested, a regression from earlier standards, but rather an indication that the Colombian democratic ideal has long contained basic shortcomings. Perhaps the very core of the present institutional experiment is the need to create an understanding of and a commitment to democracy that will shed the tacit qualifications of the past. To be effective, this means acceptance by the upper class of the social and economic necessities of the masses, leading to a democratization of national politics.

There must be an end to the blind intransigence and self-serving partisanship of the party system. Until this may in some degree be accomplished, the Colombian political culture will continue to be that of qualified democracy. Yet this circumstance must eventually be corrected if the nation is to overcome the divisive struggles of recent years that have been such impediments to necessary progress.

Social and Economic Background

Nature of Contemporary Society

Ethnically the Colombians are not an Indian people. With the exception of the Chibcha tribe to the east, the land was populated by migratory hunters and fishermen when the colonizers arrived. Intermarriage of Spaniard and Indian led in time to today's *mestizo* complex, although pure whites, estimated at some 20 percent, have retained a dominant social and political position. Since upper-class whites tend to marry within their own group, the aristocracy has retained much "purity of blood."

Historically a rural people, the Colombians even today have over half their population living and working on the land. But currents of urbanization are running strong. The impact of industrialization turns people toward the city. An urban mental outlook has been reinforced by a spreading awareness of the benefits of modern life that further attracts a flow of workers to the city.

Swollen beyond capacity, the urban proletariat is amorphous and disorganized. Social and economic conditions have lowered its boiling point. Resentment has become a powerful and a dangerous force. Added to low wages, chronic unemployment, inadequate housing, and social inequality, the consequences have been unfortunate. The historic gulf between an educated minority and the poverty-stricken masses is sizable and growing.

With the labor movement maturing under the wing of official acceptance, new and vigorous demands are being pressed by the industrial proletariat. As its ranks are being enlarged, a politically ambitious middle class is searching for self-expression. While development is slower than in such nations as

Argentina and Chile, progress is perceptible, especially in the large cities. Local variations on this basic theme, reflecting the introduction of extensive manufacturing, are most notable in Bogotá, Medellín, and Cali.

The potential demand for social revolution in the cities is great, but the rural problem is scarcely less serious. *Latifundismo* has not been pronounced, for Colombia is a nation of small farms, notwithstanding exceptions in the Cauca coffee plantations and the Caribbean banana complex. But tenancy on a fixed-rent basis is common. The tenant-laborer often receives the use of a plot in exchange for a given amount of work for the owner. Moreover, there are at least 700,000 units of no more than five acres. Agricultural production is inevitably low, and land utilization characteristically inefficient.

The unproductive nature of the five-acre *minifundio* is aggravated by the problem of *colonos* or squatters, who simply occupy unused land without having legal title. The exploitative mentality of many large landowners further contributes to retarded conditions. Since some 80 percent of national income is earned through the sale of coffee—which is dependent upon price fluctuations of the international market—the economy has not yet freed itself from excessive reliance upon a single crop. All the evils and uncertainties of a monocultural export economy continue to confront the nation.

The present deformities of Colombian society and economy are by no means unique, although some of the circumstances differ from those of neighboring countries. If current needs are ignored indefinitely, explosive protest will be the unavoidable consequence. Two occurrences have already provided grim testimony to this fact: the notorious *bogotazo* of 1948 and the continual draining of Colombia's lifeblood through fifteen years of rural violence and banditry. Both stand out in contemporary Latin America as stark warnings of the incendiary violence that can flare up uncontrollably.

The *bogotazo*, triggered by the shooting of Jorge Eliécer Gaitán on April 9, 1948 (Black Friday), led to an outburst unequaled in recent years. By evening the destruction of the burning capital led foreign correspondents to compare Bogotá with London at the height of the blitz. Although Communist opportunism fanned the flames of protest, basically the rioting was a spontaneous manifestation of the deteriorating fabric of Colombian urban life.

The rural counterpart is the mixture of partisanship and outright criminality that has ravaged the countryside since 1947. Initiated by outbursts of political guerrilla forces, with the different guerrilla bands identifying themselves as either Conservatives or Liberals and limiting their attacks to partisans of the opposite faith, the involvement of parties was finally eliminated, leaving a residue that continues in outright banditry. Pillaging and rapine have not ended, and fifteen years after the start of the violence, moderate estimates place the total death toll at no fewer than 300,000.

During the early years of bloodshed the impact of religious issues was strongly felt; the inordinate strength of the Roman Catholic Church, only slightly weakened in the last few years, remains a feature of contemporary society. Religion has long been in the forefront of national politics and has played a fundamental role in the rivalry of Liberals and Conservatives. The Constitution of 1886 reflected the clerical position by officially establishing the Church. The Concordat of 1887-88 then guaranteed official protection to the Church while allotting to the public authorities formal control of education. Later revisions from the Concordat of 1942 only nominally loosened the preeminence of the Church. In a political sense the Church's position changed but little. The government has exercised but weakly its educational prerogatives.

In the early 1950's, under Conservative Laureano Gómez, the controversial "persecution of the Protestants" became a part of civil disorder. Attacks by government forces on Liberal guerrillas sometimes involved Protestant missionaries, thus increasing tensions. Foreign as well as Colombian observers differed on the extent of religious conflict, however. Neither the Catholic hierarchy nor the Protestant evangelical movement acted with a high degree of responsibility. In any case, the more recent restoration of constructive government has included a softening of religious antagonisms. Colombia remains among the most Catholic nations of the hemisphere.

Regional Variations

The spirit of localism is a reality of Colombian life. Geographic factors made this inevitable, and regional loyalties have existed since the colonial era. For a summary view, four areas stand out. The early settler in the highlands of Cundinamarca and Boyacá was of Castilian or Andalusian origin, and today's resident of Bogotá has evolved as an individual of reserve occasionally bordering on indifference. Passionately interested in politics, frequently mindful of the arts, he gives appreciative attention to the refinements of life.

Standing in sharp contrast is the region of Antioquia and Caldas, with the city of Medellín the industrial heart of the nation. Many early colonists here were Basque, and the energetic settlers soon assumed the economic leadership they have retained to the present. The *antioqueño* is ambitious, hardworking, and strongly Conservative in political outlook. Medellín, now a city of more than half a million, has become a focus of rivalry with Bogotá.

A third major region is the Cauca Valley lying to the south and west. First colonized by Castilians and Estremadurans, a rapid intermingling with the Indians brought a mixing of races. Thriving Cali, Colombia's third city, is the hub of the valley's activity, and the *caucano* gives further impetus to national progress. Farther to the south lie the cities of Popayán and Pasto, former centers of royalist loyalty and populated largely by whites of unmixed ancestry. Citizens here are noted for traditionalism and religious zeal.

Finally our attention turns to the *costeño*—the citizen of one of the three rival Caribbean ports. Here the Spanish element was largely Catalan. The sizable presence of Negroes has produced a substantial number of mulattoes. The *costeño* tends to be expansive and vehement in self-expression and enjoys a breadth and toleration born of the unbounded sea that confronts him.

Each of the ports—Cartagena, Barranquilla, and Santa Marta—has enjoyed periods of dominance. The latter is currently reasserting primacy as the result of the recent completion of a railway from Bogotá, the first such land connection between the highlands and the coast.

Despite inevitable superficialities in this brief treatment, suffice it to reiterate the varying development of Colombians in the several major regions. Geography and demography have contributed to the regional particularism that finds expression in social and political characteristics. The onrush of modern life has by no means broken down such regional distinctions, notwithstanding unmistakable signs of the steady restructuring of Colombian society.

Political History

Evolution of a Stable Order

The historic clash of ideas over clericalism and over federalism versus centralism was responsible for great political turbulence in the nineteenth century. Doctrinal differences between Liberals and Conservatives are presented in greater detail below. For more than a century, indeed, the basic outline of events followed the shifting tides in the fortunes of the two parties. The storied clash of personality and philosophy between Simón Bolívar and Francisco de Paula Santander carried through the years, embodied in the rivalry between Conservatives and Liberals.

Changes in regime between centralizing Conservatives and federalist Liberals came rapidly in the early years of independence, but by the close of the 1850's the disintegrative tendencies of the federalist Granadine Confederation, as the Colombian polity was then named, led to a rise in centralist sympathies. The Liberals managed to maintain themselves in power through the two decades beginning in 1860, but the induction of Rafael Núñez as president in 1880 marked the start of a fifty-year period of Conservative domination. Serving from 1880-82 and 1884-94, Núñez set the tone for the next half-century by his sponsorship of the Constitution of 1886. This is described more fully below.

Núñez' emergent dictatorship saw the canonization of strong centralized government under conditions of press censorship and political repression. The concordat with the Vatican restored Catholicism as the national religion while revoking earlier anticlerical legislation. Núñez is still a controversial figure, attacked by some while hailed by others as the national Regenerator. With his death, there came a revival of civil war. But the Thousand Days' War at the turn of the century failed to break Conservative hegemony, nor did the traumatic shock of the loss of Panama in 1903.

The remainder of the Conservative period saw slow progress toward free elections, party coexistence of a sort, and free discussion of political issues in the press. Long years in office brought the inevitable petrifaction of the Conservatives, and the disastrous international depression paved the way for a Liberal victory in 1930. By 1934 the nation had risen from the depths of the economic trough, the labor force was beginning to recognize its own existence, and the masses were on the verge of awakening to the realities of the twentieth century. At this juncture a reformist wave brought to the presidency Alfonso López, a social-minded patrician fully cognizant of the changing order of national life.

Dawning of a New Era

A masterly politician as well as an intelligent reformer, López was a pragmatist compared by his admirers with the Roosevelt of the early New Deal. His policy of the *revolución en marcha* brought tax revisions, land laws, labor reforms, and measures of social welfare. His abiding belief in the role of the state was reflected in constitutional modifications that were adopted in 1936 despite a tempest of embittered opposition. Opposed by the right wing of his own party, López was obliged to devote much of his term to the propagandizing of his views, and many reforms were not fully implemented. Thus, unable to succeed himself, the president fought the candidacy of Eduardo Santos, spokesman of the right-wing Liberals.

Although scarcely the unenlightened oligarch López made him out to be, Santos as president was a gradualist, believing that López had gone too far too fast. Rejecting the thesis of extensive state intervention, Santos brought to a halt large portions of his predecessor's program. His major contribution was a restoration of balance and stability to the operation of national government. The verve and zest of the days from 1934 to 1938 were gone, but the bitterness of controversy was also moderated. By the close of Santos' term, Alfonso López determined to regain power. Despite a struggle as heated as that of 1938, the aspirant again overcame the wishes of the incumbent.

López' second term was an unhappy one. The man who had so aroused the popular imagination found himself frustrated at every turn. His new administration was characterized as "the reform of the reformer." Congressional obstructionism was significant, for the reviving Conservatives united with moderate Liberals to dilute López' policies. The prevalent strain in these years was that of deteriorating public morality and responsibility. Controversy was raised to new peaks by the skillful prodding of Conservative leader Laureano Gómez, the rebuilder of his party. Minor scandals were inflated beyond their true proportions, and circumstantial accusations were directed at the presidential family. In July of 1945, an exhausted López resigned office.

The final year of his term was served out by Alberto Lleras Camargo, a political *wunderkind* of thirty-nine whose diplomatic duties had removed him from the worst of the political wars. Lleras organized a bipartisan government as a holding operation, taking three Conservatives into the cabinet. Successful in keeping down the lid on partisan excesses, he conducted national elections from which a minority candidate emerged victorious. With the opening of the postwar period in Colombia, however, the progressive irresponsibility of the parties led to a further deterioration of democratic traditions.

Decline of Political Responsibility

The Liberal split proved instrumental in the Conservatives' return to power after a sixteen-year hiatus. With the retirement of López the left-wing Liberals fell under the spell of Jorge Eliécer Gaitán. Political agitator, social nonconformist, charismatic personality and champion of the poor, Gaitán built his popularity as a critic of oligarchical privilege. His unacceptability to the Liberal right wing resulted in the nomination of a second Liberal candidate, the Liberals allowing themselves to indulge in the luxury of an open split in the belief that the Conservatives would not field a candidate. Barely six weeks before the election Gómez seized on the division by securing the nomination of moderate Conservative Mariano Ospina Pérez, who won the election although receiving but 42 percent of the vote.

Ospina's task was not an easy one. His minority position was further weakened by Gómez' continued direction of the Conservative party, while Gaitán's capture of Liberal party machinery put a vocal and vibrant critic at the head of the opposition. Ospina organized a National Union coalition which included six Liberal cabinet ministers and several departmental governorships. Abrasive relations with Gaitán led to the eventual resignation of the Liberal ministers, however, and the administration became increasingly fragile.

The government was further plagued by social and economic problems inherited from the war years. The plight of the masses was aggravated while outbreaks of violence were reported in the hinterland. Banditry increased as partisan tempers simmered. The inevitable explosion came with the calamitous *bogotazo*. The assassination of Gaitán in the heart of Bogotá at midday sparked a visitation of fury that Colombian leadership had brought on itself by its adamant refusal to adjust to changes in national life. The two-day outburst left the center of the capital in flames, with store windows smashed and merchandise looted. The extension of violence to outlying areas brought loss of life, desecration of churches, and the violation of young schoolgirls. It was a brutal but inevitable demand by the people for social revolution.

President Ospina held firm through the riots and reconstituted the previous coalition. The remaining months of his administration saw eventual Liberal withdrawal from the government, further rural violence, and interparty hostility that led to Liberal abstention from politics in protest against electoral coercion and intimidation. Laureano Gómez thus won the uncontested presidential elections. Dedicated adherent of the extreme right, a brilliant party organizer and implacable oratorical performer, Gómez' political direction of the resurgent Conservative hegemony was remarkable. With his inauguration in 1950 a lengthy period of dictatorship—both civilian and military—was introduced to Colombia.

Waves of Repression

Civil war increased in magnitude under Gómez while party activity diminished. Liberal leaders either withdrew from politics or went into voluntary exile. Only the major population centers were untouched by violence. The economy boomed, to the advantage of the upper classes but the unrelieved misery of the masses. Moderate Conservatives turned from the regime but Gómez was undaunted by the erosion of support and directed the drafting of a new constitution based on corporative, fascistic principles. Its adoption was averted in June of 1953 when the armed forces unwillingly ousted Gómez in a bloodless coup that was cheered by a weary nation.

Civilian irresponsibility forced the reluctant General Gustavo Rojas Pinilla to assume power. This temporarily reduced the magnitude of civil war, but as time passed peace proved as elusive as ever. The regime degenerated into brutal, unthinking caesarism. Civil liberties were violated, press censorship was clamped down, and the administration dipped its hands into the treasury while the economy foundered. The result was perhaps the most inept military dictatorship in the annals of contemporary Latin American despotism. Rojas' attempt to organize a *peronista*-type amalgam of workers and peasants was ludicrous, and efforts in 1957 to extend his presidency without elections brought on a wave of indignation which carried him into exile.

The trappings of repression were dismantled by a transitional five-man military junta. It remained for civilian leaders to reach fundamental agreement permitting representative government to be restored; two meetings spaced a year apart between Liberal Alberto Lleras Camargo and Conservative Laureano Gómez in Spain sketched the form to be adopted. Their first meeting in July of 1956 led to the Pact of Benidorm pledging party cooperation in opposition to the dictatorship. Joint action was designed to reestablish freedom and constitutional guarantees. The following July Lleras and Gómez again conferred in Spain at a small town near Barcelona. The two party leaders drew up the Declaration of Sitges, the essence of which was the extraordinary form of bipartisanship that was effected in 1958.

The Bipartisan Experiment

The Sitges agreement sought the road to national unity and responsible government through adherence to a Frente Nacional. Its two basic principles were known as *paridad* and *alternación*, each of which required implementation in the form of constitutional amendment. *Paridad* provided for complete equality of Conservative and Liberal representation in all national, departmental, and municipal offices. This would extend to legislative, executive, and judicial posts. *Alternación* dictated the alternation of Conservatives and Liberals in the presidency for a twelve-year period. Lleras and Gómez agreed that the first such executive would be a Conservative, with a Liberal following in 1962.

Implementation of the Declaration of Sitges proved difficult. Months of further negotiation were followed with the historic plebiscite on December 1, 1957. In a total vote of 4,397,090 there were 4,169,294 that approved the reform. A significant variation from the original plan was its extension from twelve to sixteen years, thus carrying until 1974. The delicately wrought experiment was almost shattered by selection of a candidate for the first presidential term under the agreement. The apparent Conservative choice, Guillermo León Valencia, was a moderate politician unacceptable to Gómez. But the temporary impasse was removed with the inducement of an unwilling Lleras to accept the nomination. He was elected overwhelmingly in May and took office on August 7, 1958.

Alberto Lleras Camargo had himself declared that the first president under the agreement would necessarily be "a magician, prophet, redeemer, savior, and pacifier who can transform a ruined republic into a prosperous one." His miracle-working depended upon party responsibility, for basic to the agreement was the desire to create a period of convalescence during which a reorientation away from narrow, selfish partisanship might be effected. Neither Liberals nor Conservatives acted appropriately, however, falling instead into their customary internecine feuding in apparent indifference to the fate of the president's program.

A new Liberal faction developed about Alfonso López Michelsen, son of the former president. Claiming to be heirs to the reformist mantle of Gaitán, the group adopted the slogan of "health, education, and housing," calling for termination of the Frente Nacional in 1962. Conservative fragmentation was more severe, the party dividing between the followers of Gómez, who supported the coalition, and those of Ospina, who opposed it. Small personalist factions led by three other Conservatives further complicated the situation.

The opportunism of party politics was further suggested by the March 1960 congressional elections. *Ospinista* Conservatives defeated the followers of Gómez, leading to a complete reversal of positions. The *ospinistas* then ended their opposition to the coalition, requesting their share of cabinet seats. The *laureanistas*, on the other hand, followed their aging leader into criticism of the Frente. On the Liberal side, the unexpected strength of the López Michelsen faction was formalized as the Movimiento Revolucionario Liberal (MRL). Disappointment among "regular" Liberals led to the resignation of the party's leadership.

The 1960 elections merely clouded the picture. Liberals retained their popular majority, but far more striking was the widespread incidence of *retraimiento*, or abstention. Popular feeling feared a return to customary party irresponsibility and thus turned away from traditional leadership. Abstention was more a sign of the desire for responsible politics than of apathy. As the Lleras administration headed toward national elections in 1962, its efforts were increasingly obstructed by the furious interplay of partisanship, especially in the congress.

Laboring tenaciously to bring some semblance of order from party anarchy, the president enacted his program largely through executive decree or administrative initiative. Matters of public policy all too often were ignored by the legislature. Pacification was achieved in part, but banditry remained in some areas. Economic growth depended almost entirely upon executive action in the absence of adequate legislation. Only through the efforts of Lleras and his technicians was Colombia able to submit a prompt and detailed development plan to North American officials of the Alliance for Progress.

Extension of the National Front

With his term drawing to a close, Lleras had restored some degree of calm and economic well-being following the disastrous years of military dictatorship. Although he had brilliantly won a breathing spell for Colombian democracy, the president watched apprehensively for the critical elections of 1962, with the future of bipartisan experiment clearly jeopardized. The absence of new faces on the horizon was a harbinger of possible difficulties, for men like the septuagenarians Gómez and Ospina remained dominant on the political scene. Their separate stances raised the problem of selecting a Conservative presidential candidate acceptable to all.

Congressional elections in March of 1962 returned a majority of Liberal and Conservative legislators favorable to continuation of the Frente. A substantial showing by the MRL failed to overcome the dominant Liberals, while the *ospinista* Conservatives won a surprisingly convincing victory over the Gómez adherents. Once more the Liberals proved their position as the majority party, although winning only 52 percent of the vote as compared with 58 percent in 1960. Thus the moderate Conservatives under Mariano Ospina Pérez were in a position to select the party's nominee for president. After brief hesitation the choice of Guillermo León Valencia was announced; Liberal agreement was prompt, and Valencia won election as second president of the Frente Nacional on May 6, 1962.

The most striking feature was again the high rate of abstention. Official figures showed that some 5,877,000 voters held their *cédulas* and were eligible to vote. An additional 2 million were believed to be eligible for registration. The recorded abstention was 55 percent, with only 2,608,672 going to the polls. Final figures gave Valencia 1,628,018 votes, roughly 62 percent of the total. Frente critic López Michelsen received 611,632, with two minor candidates far to the rear. With Valencia's inauguration in August of 1962 the second bipartisan government took office. This was a feat in itself, for the chances of the Frente's continuing beyond Lleras' term had often appeared slight. It still seemed highly unlikely to many observers that the agreement could possibly survive until 1974.

The continuing drift of events was further reflected in the March 1964 congressional elections. Although pro-Frente Liberals and Conservatives won 68 percent of the vote, dissident factions made striking inroads. The degree of public dissatisfaction was recorded in the vote for Rojas Pinilla's Conservative faction, whose 1962 total of 3 percent rose to a remarkable 18 percent. An equally telling condemnation of the existing system was reflected in an abstention of 70 percent of the eligible voters, as slightly fewer than 2 million Colombians took the trouble to vote.

So long as the Frente does last, the nature of Colombian politics will be essentially artificial. This was the price that Lleras and Gómez agreed to pay in order to permit a renaissance of democratic life. The two-party system itself benefited from the system that tended to block formal emergence of third parties of major proportions. Still, the rise of new forces, competing with older groups despite the provisions of the National Front agreement, increasingly puts the traditional parties on their mettle. Whatever the duration of the Frente, however, the prerequisite for a progressive political future remains both the awareness and concomitant willingness to meet the crying, long unanswered social and economic needs.

Political Processes

Political Parties

The operation of the party system is of primordial importance to the Colombian political milieu. In a region where multiparty systems are more often the rule, Colombia has retained a basic party dualism throughout its history. This began in the last century with the usual divisions of Liberal and Conservative over the historic controversies common to all the newly independent republics. "The two great issues which determined party alignment during the first half of the century of independence were the separation of Church and state and centralization." [1]

In Colombia, however, the passage of time did not lead to a fragmentation of Liberal and Conservative collectivities. Both parties drew upon members of the small ruling oligarchy to perpetuate their control. Political struggle remained a sport for the aristocracy; only those from the social elite could gain admittance. With the interests of but one class represented, it was possible to pursue the futile struggle over the clerical question, and polemical controversy over centralism and federalism continued. National leaders of both parties were almost always recruited from the same tiny minority.

The party struggle was in a large measure far less than national in scope. With the masses effectively excluded from politics, party dualism continued through long periods of dominance by first one group, then the other. Strong local allegiances added to the inevitable sense of geographic isolation that even today remains in some areas. Since the parties were difficult to penetrate from below the oligarchy, political awareness on the part of the masses was minimized.

The impact of modern technology began to be felt after World War I, and the collectivities grudgingly began to give ground where necessary. Yet there was little willingness to do more than accommodate the strongest pressures. Even today the Liberals and Conservatives are reluctant to accept the rise of an incipient middle class that intrudes substantial dynamism into national politics. Narrow class interests predominate over the need for basic adjustment to contemporary socio-economic realities.

The Liberal and Conservative party organizations are similar and have changed little over the past generation. Controlled at the national level by periodic conventions and a continuing directorate, they each extend the chain of command to departmental and local assemblies. At the lowest level the municipal directorate is dominant. Russell Fitzgibbon has observed that party mechanisms in Colombia come "almost as close as any [in Latin America] in carrying their organization down to the grass roots." [2] Organizational efficiency has become increasingly important in recent years with the introduction of mass communications media. The present sharing of responsibility for local government under the bipartisan agreement has tended to broaden the capacity of local party figures. Yet national leaders still make periodic trips into all corners of the nation to test opinion, confer with local leaders, and pass along the thinking of the national organization.

Party ideology has undergone slow changes. Despite inevitable consensus on some matters, differences have been basic. The Liberals, historically the champions of anticlericalism, decentralized government, and free trade, have modified their doctrine somewhat more than the Conservatives. While urging religious toleration, they have backed away from the frontal attacks on the Church that were once common. Willing to recognize the role of Catholicism in national life, their only insistence is on the effective separation of Church and State.

Liberal commitment to decentralized government through federalism has also weakened, for the party has come to accept state intervention and the concomitant strong central government. Party doctrine advocates political centralization and administrative decentralization, but this has merely compounded confusion on the question. Federalism is supported more in theory than in practice, while the heritage of free trade and economic *laissez faire* has been abandoned. Since the advent of Alfonso López in 1934 the party has reaffirmed the necessity of promoting economic development through public means. Today there is a firm commitment to governmental responsibility for providing for the needs of the ordinary citizen.

Perhaps above all else the party has sought recognition as unique bearer of progressive reformism. Characteristic was the statement of a party leader that "Liberalism is fundamentally dynamic; it is identified with the propelling and impelling forces of society." The impetus of social reformism has been strong since the 1930's, although intraparty controversy still arises occasionally. At its harshest, the division led to bitter competition between the López and Santos wings, reaching its pinnacle with the nomination of two Liberal presidential candidates in 1946. Loss of power to a minority Conservative candidate impressed party leaders with the folly of such a division, and today the dispute is less heated. Even so, the disagreement has been recorded in certain criticisms of the gradualist course of the Lleras administration. The organization of López Michelsen's faction was in part a reflection of this divergence in outlook.

The Conservative party advocates close cooperation with the Church, limited suffrage, often defined in terms of heads of family, the maintenance of class privileges, and highly centralized government which holds local officials subservient to directives from the authorities in Bogotá. Order is emphasized as a prerequisite for progress. A degree of paternalism remains in Conservative thought, with a lingering inclination to encourage individual conformity to the behavior appropriate to one's station. As a Conservative intellectual has put it, "Conservatism establishes the social necessity of a hierarchy, imposed by the prestige of merit. . . ." Reliance upon the family was mirrored in 1953 by the Conservative draft of a proposed constitution using the family as the basis for voting rights and local representation.

Allegiance to the Roman Catholic Church is unconditional. Party support has been instrumental in the inordinate strength of Catholicism. Mutual support of Church and State is regarded as indispensable. Although Liberal anticlericalism has moderated in recent times, Conservatives continue to paint their opponents as godless and atheistic. Thus one even finds occasional references to Liberal advocacy of divorce, a subject the latter have generally avoided. A striking Conservative trait is the extraordinary militancy of its spokesmen and an aggressive pugnacity that often turns inward upon itself. The extreme right wing of the party has shown a notable propensity to leap for the opponent's jugular, waging bitter war with quarter neither asked nor given.

Neither party has preserved its doctrinal purity, and with opportunism running high, deviations on the grounds of political expediency are not uncommon. However, oligarchic leadership within both parties has willingly withdrawn where necessary for the protection of class interests. Nor have the Conservatives maintained a monopoly on political ferocity. Party warfare is constant and unremitting. It takes place with a primitive force; concession is reckoned as weakness and strength calls for even greater strength.

In view of the recent growth in popular political participation, it is surprising that the national party system has not seen a proliferation of splinter parties to complicate the picture. The force of tradition militates against them, however. In the past quarter-century there have been a number of minor parties, but none have broken the Liberal-Conservative virtual monopoly. Indeed, no third party has survived more than a few years, with the sole exception of the Communists, and even they have reorganized and revised their party drastically from time to time.

Transient political groups have been more in the nature of factions than full-blown parties. Successes have been fleeting, whether the parties were essentially ideological or personalistic. The former category has included Communists and Socialists. The Communist party has long been weak and divided. An ideological split in 1947 caused its separation into two rival groups, and the later re-establishment of a single party has failed to strengthen the movement substantially. Colombian Socialists have been even more on the periphery of national politics. The present Partido Popular Socialista Colombiano (PPSC) has never won widespread support. Jorge Eliécer Gaitán once scoffed that the Socialists lacked political sex appeal. This has not changed.

In the context of the 1960's the magnetism of Fidel Castro has lent greater appeal to parties of the extreme left, but the ideological party in Colombia has progressed little. What third-party strength has been observed comes from the personalist groups. In the 1930's several such factions cropped up, led by ambitious young politicians impatient for advancement within the traditional parties. A notable example was that of Gaitán himself, who later found the course of political strength running in the Liberal Party. Since adoption of the Frente Nacional in 1958, López Michelsen's MRL has served as the vehicle for his personal ambitions. The abortive third-party efforts of Gustavo Rojas Pinilla during his dictatorship and again during the 1962 presidential elections were also personalistic in nature.

While such factional groups come and go, the traditional parties perpetuate themselves, notwithstanding the negativism of their inflexibility and their reluctance to yield concessions to emergent social forces. The relative abdication of responsibility by Liberals and Conservatives in the postwar years has been alluded to earlier. Instead of permitting the rise of a third effective national party, this led in time to the experimental form of controlled democracy initiated in 1958. One of the criteria upon which a lasting evaluation of the bipartisan arrangement must eventually be based will be the degree to which the two major parties learn to coexist and compete within the same political sphere. The Colombian tradition has long been one of extremes, where "the dark is midnight black, the light as blinding as a snow-blanketed plain. Between, there is precious little grey." [3]

Interest Groups

The ruling elite has long delayed the development of organized groups. The political system is nonetheless becoming increasingly seasoned with the ingredients of group activity. Labor and business have organized and exert substantial influence. The dynamism of contemporary social forces and an awakening industrial proletariat make both crucial in the formation of public policy.

Slowly at first, industrialism has given a mounting impetus to the labor movement. Despite long hostility on the part of both government and management, trade unions were created and built up during the interval between the world wars. The Confederación de Trabajadores de Colombia (CTC) was organized in 1936, gaining recognition and approval from the López administration. Essentially Liberal in orientation, the CTC divided in 1940 following a Communist attempt to seize control. Although the CTC survived this threat, its primacy was seriously challenged in 1946 by the rival Unión de Trabajadores Colombianos (UTC).

Winning substantial encouragement from the Conservative government of the day, the UTC made inroads into the CTC, aided by a general reaction against the Liberals. Gifted with energetic leadership, the UTC expanded rapidly and soon outstripped the older organization in power and influence. Membership in hemispheric Organización Regional Inter-Americana de Trabajadores (ORIT) unquestionably enhanced its prestige. Both the UTC and CTC lost their freedom of action during the *rojista* dictatorship, however. The general attempted to form his own labor movement with a reorganized version of the Confederación Nacional de Trabajo (CNT), formerly a *peronista*-inspired group. But success was minimal, and the CNT collapsed with the ouster of the dictator.

Since 1957 trade unionism has flourished, with the UTC firmly established as the preponderant force of the labor movement. Freedom of action and the pro-labor stance of the government have led to some irresponsibility on the part of certain local affiliates. This is not startling in view of the relative inexperience with union democracy in the usual sense. National labor leaders have shown themselves generally aware of their overall responsibility, however, as well as their role in the political system.

Businessmen and industrialists have also formed interest groups, among the first of which was the Asociación Patronal Económica Nacional (APEN) in the 1930's. By the end of the decade a series of vertical class organizations emerged as means of protecting commercial interests against the rise of labor. Of particular note were the merchants' Federación Nacional de Comerciantes (FENALCO) and the industrialists' Asociación Nacional de Industriales (ANDI). Both resisted the granting of concessions to labor. Class and economic interests naturally continue to dictate their policies, although the early tinge of reaction has gradually been dissipating. Their influence is most commonly exerted within the channels of bureaucracy, rather than in public view.

A variety of other organizations represent occupational sectors of national life. Cattle, cotton, banking, and agrarian interests are among those which have established formal bodies. The total effect of such diffuse interest groups has been slow but steady progress in moving against long-dominant oligarchic interests. The most influential and progressive-minded of the organized business groups has been the national coffee-growers' federation. Established in 1927, the Federacion Nacional de Cafeteros Colombianos (FNCC) has held itself independent from the government while consistently advocating constructive fiscal and credit policies.

There are many more professional and occupational interest groups, with the student movement possessing its characteristic Latin American strength. The national student union has been militantly active for years. Well-organized but for a temporary splintering caused by a pro-Rojas faction, the federation has played a strong if occasionally disruptive role. Its democratizing influence should not be underestimated, however. Students were in the vanguard of the civil uprising against Gustavo Rojas Pinilla in 1957. More recently the responsible student leadership has stood up against the disturbing influence of revolutionary Cuba. The university students' Consejo Superior Estudiantil has exerted a positive influence on higher education, occasionally buttressed, as during the 1961 dispute at the University of Medellín, by direct presidential intervention.

The Military

The role of the military, although not formally constituting an interest group as such, must necessarily be included in the consideration of Colombian political processes. The armed forces are in the nature of an institutional pressure group, for direct political intervention has been, by Latin American standards, remarkably infrequent. With the sole exception of a brief protest by the garrison at Pasto in 1944, the military stood aloof from politics for more than half a century until its assumption of power in June of 1953.

Although the seizure of power by Rojas was unavoidable at the time, the subsequent degeneration of his provisional regime into a permanent dictatorship cast a pall upon the military tradition of nonpartisanship that has not yet entirely lifted. A partial cleansing came through the enlightened behavior of the provisional junta that conducted national elections and delivered power into the hands of civilians. Yet the feeling that military *dignidad* had been sullied has not wholly disappeared.

The political neutrality of the armed forces has been secured at a price, to be sure. The military share of the budget remains large and virtually constant through all political vicissitudes, with the officer corps constituting a largely autonomous military elite. The Ministry of War is traditionally awarded to a military man. Pampering has been carried to the extent of permitting an officer to retire with fifteen years' service on a pension equal to half his salary at the time of retirement. The effort to divorce the armed forces from politics includes the proscription of officers on active duty from candidacy for office as well as a denial of suffrage to enlisted men.

The Press

The Colombian press has been among the most politically influential in the hemisphere, boasting a number of widely noted journals. Freedom is assured through article 36 of the Constitution, the only reservation being that of remaining respectful of individuals, the social order, and public tranquillity. Despite the incidence of censorship under both Gómez and Rojas, the record has generally been excellent. International news is covered in some detail, although domestic politics provide the central focus of interest. While the degree of partisan affiliation varies, none of the major dailies can be said to be wholly free from party orientation.

El Liberal served in the 1930's and early 1940's as the organ for Alfonso López and thus was often at odds with *El Tiempo*, which inclined toward the moderate wing of the Liberals. The latter, founded in 1911 by Eduardo Santos, enjoys high repute throughout the hemisphere. Its coverage of Colombian politics has become less partisan with the retirement of Santos from political life. *El Siglo*, established by Laureano Gómez in 1935, remains the major Conservative newspaper. Staunchly partisan throughout its existence, it has bitterly opposed the Liberal journals and since the time of founding has been the major mouthpiece of current *laureanista* views. The oldest Bogotá daily, *El Espectador*, has long been directed by the Cano family and has pursued a generally Liberal line.

The years of press censorship already alluded to were not sufficient to tear down the strongly ingrained tradition of freedom. To be sure, the Rojas censorship in particular was both quixotic and repressive, while the turbulence of the early 1950's led to the burning of the offices and plants of both *El Tiempo* and *El Espectador* in 1952. While the general tone of the press has often tended to exacerbate already overheated political passions, the experience of the 1950's has led to greater political sophistication and a lessening of unremitting partisanship. Thus the press remains a constructive force for democracy in Colombian political culture.

Governmental Institutions

The Constitution

Evolution of the basic Colombian document has been reasonably orderly, although the present constitution is at least the tenth since the proclamation of independence. Constitutional revision has long reflected differences over the question of centralism and federalism as an extension of temporary domination by either Liberals or Conservatives. The document drawn up by the Congress of Angostura in 1819 was centralist, but by the 1850's federalism had been adopted. The Granadine Confederation, as the nation was then called, disintegrated into little more than a collection of semi-independent states, and vacillation between central government and local autonomy was further mirrored in the constitutions of 1858 and 1863.

The lack of national cohesion, difficulties of transportation and communication, and old traditions of municipal autonomy had strengthened regional particularism, and the realization slowly grew that a strong central government was required; the resurgence of the Conservatives contributed to a change of orientation. So it was that in 1886 a national conference met in Bogotá under the aegis of the dictator Rafael Núñez to draw up a new charter.

Colombia was defined as a unitary republic and, despite concessions to localism, centralist principles were largely upheld. Sovereignty was entrusted to the nation itself, from which emanated the responsibility for protection of life and property. The document promised the fulfillment of "social duties for both state and individual." The exclusive determination of policy was placed in the hands of the central government. Departmental and municipal powers were largely restricted to the local execution of national laws according to directives from the capital. In practice the central government became almost omnipotent.

The Constitution of 1886 has remained in effect since its drafting, although amendments have been added during the intervening years. A 1936 codification dealt in large part with social matters. President López attempted to incorporate measures recognizing the growing need for labor and social reform. Work was defined as a social obligation deserving official protection. With the exception of government employees, workers were guaranteed the right to strike. The 1936 codification also embraced political reforms which included the popular election of senators by departments, reduction of the presidential term to four years, and a modification of the judicial system which strengthened the powers of the Supreme Court.

Further codification came in 1945 with formal recognition that property was a social function with implications of obligation. The state was granted the right of intervention in both public and private activities "for the purpose of regionalizing production, distribution, and consumption of goods, or to give labor just protection to which it has a right." More drastic modifications were under discussion in 1953, embracing the corporative ideas of Laureano Gómez, when his ouster prevented their adoption. The most recent changes in the constitution have come with the bipartisan agreement following the restoration of free government. This round of modifications rested on the twin pillars of *paridad* and *alternación* discussed above.

The bill of rights follows traditional lines, setting forth individual freedom, protection against arbitrary arrest, the right of assembly, and the social guarantees included in 1936 and 1945. A series of reservations permit official limitation of public liberties in certain circumstances, however. The government may dissolve any meeting that creates a disturbance or blocks public roadways, the decision being reached unilaterally within the executive branch. Article 42 provides for the suspension of guarantees in time of emergency through the declaration of a state of siege. The judgment is presidential, issued with the approval of his cabinet.

The imposition of a state of siege by Mariano Ospina Pérez in 1949 extended for a record length of eight years under Gómez and Rojas, and led to demands for modification. In December of 1960 congress passed into law a measure limiting presidential powers during a state of siege. Following such an emergency declaration the president is required to convene the legislature immediately. Failing this, the congress can call itself into special session and raise the question of the constitutionality of executive decrees before the supreme court. If the court fails to take action within six days, the contested decree is automatically revoked.

The Executive

Elected to a four-year term by direct vote, the president is eligible for a second term only after at least one full term out of office. He is not permitted to leave national soil during his first year out of office. Cabinet ministers and most civilians in public service are named by presidential appointment. The president may also direct the armed forces personally, although he is required to renounce other executive powers temporarily if he intends to leave Bogotá.

He is responsible for opening and closing congressional sessions and may call the legislature into emergency meeting at his own discretion. The cabinet may initiate bills, and the presidential veto is overridden only by a two-thirds vote of the assembled bicameral congress. However, if a bill is vetoed on a question of alleged unconstitutionality, the final decision is taken by the supreme court, with congress having no power of reversal.

In modern times the cabinet has generally been composed of thirteen ministries: government (interior), foreign relations, war, finance, education, labor, agriculture, justice, economy, public works, mines and petroleum, health, and communications. Customarily the post of foreign minister is the most prestigious, although the minister of government wields more power. The latter is responsible for the administration of local affairs, directs the national police force, and supervises departmental governors. If the military exerts an overt influence, the minister of war grows in public significance.

Presidential succession in the Constitution has been controversial. Original provisions for a vice-president were discarded, and current practice calls for congressional election of a *designado* at the beginning of the session. Recent history suggests the lack of any established custom, however. López' resignation in 1945 led to the succession of Lleras. Later, the stricken Laureano Gómez in 1951 personally selected his minister of war as acting president, retaining for himself the "titular presidency." Election of a *designado* has been entwined with congressional political interplay, and no completely satisfactory means for accomplishing it has yet been accepted.

The Legislature

Colombia's bicameral body consists of the Senate and the Chamber of Representatives. The upper house is elected by popular vote every four years, senators being chosen by each department at a ratio of one senator for every 190,000 inhabitants and one for each fraction over 95,000. The effects of population disparity are modified by the limitation that there be no more than nine and no fewer than three senators per department. The chamber of representatives is elected on the basis of one deputy for every 90,000 persons and one for every remaining fraction over 45,000, for a two-year term. Opening on July 20, national Independence Day, the Congress meets annually for 150-day sessions. There is no provision for the extension of meetings. If recalled by the president, the Congress can discuss only the matters laid before it; there is no legislative discretion involved.

Both houses elect their presiding officers individually, with the usual *mesa directiva* guiding the course of legislation. Bills receive three readings before final approval. The first reading consists of a discussion of general principles, and the second of the detailed provisions, while the third is normally a formality. Cabinet ministers share the legislative power to introduce bills, thus providing the president with the effective exercise of the right of legislative initiative. Most legislation may originate in either house, although revenue bills must come from the chamber, which is further empowered to conduct the annual audit of public accounts. In impeachment proceedings, charges are brought before the Chamber, with the Senate later sitting as a ruling tribunal. Conviction requires a two-thirds vote.

The Judiciary

At the apex of the judicial pyramid is the Corte Suprema de Justicia (CSJ). In practice it is subdivided in terms of its four constitutional functions: civil cases, criminal appeals from lower courts, cases involving high public officials, and miscellaneous general matters. The 1936 codification grants to the court the power to judge the constitutionality of legislation. Although meeting regularly, the court may be convened whenever its president chooses. Judges are elected for five-year terms, half by the senate and half by the chamber. When a vacancy occurs, the Colombian president sends a list of three names from which the legislature picks one. The court itself elects its presiding judge from among the membership.

Beneath the supreme court each department has its own superior court, members of which are appointed by the supreme court from lists presented by departmental assemblies. Further down the pyramid are circuit judges and justices of the peace. The Colombian judiciary has also a series of administrative courts to deal with civil suits brought against the government. Following the Continental legal system, this is headed by a Consejo de Estado or Council of State. Local administrative courts operate under the aegis and jurisdictional direction of the Council.

A hybrid creature both judicial and executive in nature, the Council of State was long inoperative following its establishment in 1831. Although active in this century, it possesses little inherent political power. In matters of administration it is the supreme consultative body. The president is not required to rely on it ordinarily, requiring its consent only when preparing to call an extraordinary congressional session. The Council also prepares projected legislation to be sent before the congress. Three Council members are chosen by each house of congress; the seventh is named by the president and serves as chairman. The six congressional appointees serve four-year terms, half of which are renewed every two years.

Local Government

The republic is divided internally into seventeen departments, the most recent addition being Meta. There are also intendencies and *comisarías* which may attain departmental status after becoming populous enough and attaining a sufficient degree of economic development. In the centralized Colombian apparatus, departmental governors are appointed by the president and are responsible to him through the minister of government. The practice until recently has been to name the governors from military ranks, although the Lleras administration departed from this practice somewhat. Civilian appointees are traditionally selected on the basis of party affiliation, thus extending from Bogotá the dominance of the party currently in office.

The governor appoints his own assistants and exercises personal supervision over departmental affairs. Departmental popular assemblies exist, of two years' duration, their size varying according to departmental population, their political power according to the governor's inclinations. The assembly normally has little real authority, for its legislation must not be contradictory to that of the national congress, while the governor exercises the right of absolute veto. The municipality has perhaps a higher degree of authority. The mayor is still appointed by the governor, however, and may be removed without notice. While the local voter does choose his municipal council of a dozen or more, it has little authority in the setting of policy. This has changed somewhat with the introduction of bipartisan government, and the trend is toward greater local rule.

The Electoral System

Suffrage is limited to literate citizens of at least twenty-one years. Women won the right to vote in 1954, rather ironically as the result of legislation by the hand-picked Constituent Assembly convened by Rojas. Female suffrage has since been retained. On election day the voter receives ballots from each of the competing parties, which have printed the ballots themselves. In the voting booth he places the ballot of his choice into an official envelope while discarding the other. Thus he is encouraged for the sake of convenience to vote a straight party ticket, although it is possible to split one's vote. The voter has a finger daubed in indelible ink to avoid multiple voting. In times of an abstentionist protest, the Colombian will show his uninked hand with pride. The reverse may also happen.

A modified version of proportional representation has been the usual practice, but this has been complicated greatly by the constitutional revisions of 1958. Party preferences are still indicated by the voter, of course, so the appeal of the rival parties is reflected in the election returns; but at the same time, the requirement for absolute parity of representation at all levels makes the selection of individual candidates devolve in large part upon the Liberal and Conservative party organizations. The artificiality of the temporary arrangement is thus particularly noticeable in the electoral system, and the termination of *paridad* will bring a substantial alteration.

Public Policy

Role of the State

Fundamental to the formation of public policy is the broad commitment to the principle of state intervention. The constitutional basis for this was cited in reference to the 1936 codification. The impetus given by the first López administration continued long after the days of the *revolución en marcha*. Colombians have come to accept the belief that extensive intervention is necessary to provide for social necessities and organize effectively the direction of the national economy.

The plethora of national agencies need not be listed exhaustively. A typical example is the Instituto de Fomento Industrial, formed in 1940 for the planning of industrial enterprise where private business was inadequate. Its projects have met with varied success, including such enterprises as a rubber-tire company, an edible-oil plant, a tanning-extract factory, and a naval construction yard. The Instituto has withdrawn from sugar processing, fats, yeast, and zinc production. Its role has been exerted in the mechanization of coal mining in Valle and in the construction of the Paz del Río steel mill.

Nineteen-forty also saw the creation of the Instituto de Fomento Municipal, while the Instituto de Crédito Territorial took upon itself the task of providing rural credit and loans. Broader financial control is exercised through the Caja Colombiana de Ahorros, which holds some 80 percent of all savings deposits. Among the responsibilities of the Banco de la República has been Colombia's emerald and salt mines. Development and exploitation of petroleum is largely in the hands of the Empress Colombiana de Petróleos (ECOPETROL), which established a virtual monopoly by taking over the fields and refinery of Tropical Oil in the early 1950's. The field of transport is dominated by the nationalization of the railroads, which began in 1912, and the purchase of what is now the national airline in 1956.

Efforts to increase the official role in the development of agriculture rests on several organs. In addition to the Instituto de Crédito Territorial, the Caja de Crédito Agraria, Industrial y Minero (Agricultural Bank) provides loans to small farmers while the Banco Central Hipotecario eases mortgage difficulties. Price controls are administered through the Instituto Nacional de Abastecimientos. Comparable cabinet responsibilities have been divided since the 1947 reorganization of the ministry of national economy into a ministry of agriculture and a ministry of economy. To those who protest the extent of the state role, the general Colombian view is well expressed in the words of Ricardo Silva, observing that "modern and social justice . . . requires that the State be reinvested with all the powers necessary to intervene, direct, plan and organize the economy, subordinated to the common well-being." [4]

Domestic Policy

The basic problem of economic expansion has been sharpened in recent years. Bipartisan support exists for the outlines of the program for economic progress proclaimed by Alberto Lleras Camargo early in 1960. Beyond price stabilization, this envisioned an annual production increase of 5 percent, which over a 25-year period would double per capita income. Productive investment was viewed as fundamental to economic progress, and the pro-portion of national income devoted to investment would be raised from 16 to at least 20 percent. The gap between imports and exports—an inevitable fact of life in contemporary Colombia—requires an extended program call-ing for the reduction of imports and the diversification of exports. In the context of the latter goal, a program of agrarian reform has been adopted.

Agricultural diversification has long been called for by knowledgeable Colombians. Over a long period of time, however, remarkably little was accomplished. By 1960 data revealed that although industrial production had risen 66 percent in the previous thirty years, the increase of agricultural output over the same span was merely 14 percent. Action was finally taken in 1960 under the prodding of President Lleras. While the legislature haggled over patronage and political prestige, Lleras increased government invest-ment substantially through the Agrarian Bank in conjunction with a newly drafted plan for the distribution of unoccupied public lands for colonization.

In the meantime an agrarian reform bill has been adopted. The pro-posed legislation called for 90 percent expropriation of land between 700 and 800 hectares in extent, with 100 percent expropriation of plots of land above 800 hectares. Such provisions were not wholly realistic, since the Colombian land problem is less that of too few small farms than that of the unpro-ductive utilization of land. Certain provisions, however, besides the formal-ization of generous credit and mortgage policies from the government, opened the way for official encouragement of diversification and added public instruction in more advanced agricultural techniques. Concerted ef-forts by national party leaders finally obtained final passage of the agrarian reform in late 1961, and Law 135 took effect with its signing by Lleras Camargo on December 13. Pressures from rural unrest combined with in-flationary and fiscal problems to persuade the political elite of the necessity of the program. Despite the apparent necessity of rapid implementation, however, the reform soon bogged down in the general inactivity of the subsequent Valencia administration.

Earlier references to the evolution of the trade-union movement have indicated the existence of a longstanding issue over labor policy. Neverthe-less, the eventual outcome has been the inevitable triumph of labor organiza-tion in winning a place for itself in national life. The nature of its acceptance is as yet uneven, though. Inauguration of the Valencia administration led to speculation that the new government might prove less pro-labor than its predecessor. The basic decision on this point was made in pre-World War II years, however. Despite the mistreatment that the labor movement suffered under the Gómez and Rojas regimes, its validity in national economic life is no longer seriously in question.

A continuing problem of domestic policy is that of pacification of the countryside. Every government since the late 1940's has grappled with the problem, to little effect. The genesis and growth of rural violence have been described above. Suffice it to repeat here that the political overtones of the phenomenon have long since been dissipated. What remains is a problem of banditry and lawlessness. Despite repeated government declarations through the years that all such difficulties were at an end, the problem continues today. Indeed, there is little likelihood that it can be extinguished entirely without a concentrated effort and expenditure beyond the present capacity of the government. Depredations are less deleterious to Colombian agriculture than they once were, but the loss of life and defiance of public authority continue as a virtual constant before the makers of public policy.

Foreign Policy

Traditionally the focus of Colombian policy-makers has been away from foreign affairs, except for occasional episodic events. Today, however, considerations of hemispheric affairs in particular are receiving serious attention. A definite shift in emphasis has come about in the last few years. The long interest of President Lleras in the inter-American system partially supplies one basis for this, for his diplomatic experience includes service as first secretary-general of the Organization of American States. This is not the whole answer, however. The intrusion of the Cold War and the growing understanding of economic interdependence has led to a general shift in attitudes.

Under the leadership of Lleras the Colombians became a stabilizing influence within the OAS. Sharp divisions over the proper approach to *fidelista* Cuba were smoothed over by the Colombians on several occasions. Public opinion generally has supported a stance critical of the Castro regime, but the government has been more than a little successful in calming the atmosphere in which the controversial question was discussed. Colombia has in fact developed as one of the most responsible pillars of the inter-American system. The first nation to deliver a detailed development plan to United States officials of the Alliance for Progress, the government and people were warm in their greeting to President Kennedy and his wife on their ceremonial visit in December of 1961.

The leading role taken by Colombian diplomacy in this respect has been paralleled by a growing responsibility assumed on another level. With the benefits of regional cooperation becoming clearer, Colombian foreign minister Julio César Turbay Ayala became a prime mover in tying together a series of binational study commissions and trade organizations. Colombia has collaborated separately with Venezuela, Panama, Peru, and Ecuador in this activity. Regional transportation has been encouraged with a revival of the long-moribund Flota Gran Colombiana, a joint shipping fleet of Colombia, Ecuador, and Venezuela. Comparable discussions have been held to consider a possible Flota Aérea Gran Colombiana to include Panama, Venezuela, and Colombia.

A significant signpost to the road of future economic development and political maturity has come with Colombian membership in the Latin American Free Trade Area. This has opened a whole new set of policy questions that will demand attention for years to come. Becoming the eighth member of LAFTA in December of 1961, Colombia has thus moved toward a degree of regional economic integration, with the accompanying lowering of tariff walls and the inauguration of a program of multinational cooperation for the encouragement and development of industry. General economic development has become the major goal looming on the horizon.

By so committing herself to regional cooperation on a significant scale, Colombia has associated herself with a movement holding some promise of greater economic and political fulfillment. Among the likely results is a fundamental reorientation of thinking and attitudes across the entire spectrum of policy. Whether long-abiding political attitudes will change is p oblematical. Yet in any event Colombia's qualified democracy has necessarily to be temporary; otherwise the subsequent upheaval will be drastic. The winds of social change are blowing strong, and the national political style must bend with them. In the absence of substantial political reorientation of both attitudes and procedures, turbulence may follow that will inevitably cause a fundamental revision of the present political system.

NOTES FOR CHAPTER XI

1. W. Whatley Pierson and Federico G. Gil, *Governments of Latin America*, McGraw-Hill, New York, 1957, p. 317.
2. Russell H. Fitzgibbon, "The Party Potpourri in Latin America," *Western Political Quarterly*, X, No. 1, March 1957, p. 17.
3. John D. Martz, *Colombia: A Contemporary Political Study*, University of North Carolina Press, Chapel Hill, 1962, p. 19.
4. Ricardo Silva, *Los Trabajadores ante los Partidos*, Editorial Antares, Bogotá, 1955, pp. 38-39.

SELECTED BIBLIOGRAPHY

Lauchlin Currie, *The Basis of a Development Program for Colombia: The Currie Mission Report*, The Johns Hopkins Press, Baltimore, 1950.
Orlando Fals-Borda, *Peasant Society in the Colombian Andes: A Social Study of Saucio*, University of Florida Press, Gainesville, 1957.
Vernon L. Fluharty, *Dance of the Millions: Military Rule and the Social Revolution in Colombia, 1930-1956*, University of Pittsburgh Press, Pittsburgh, 1957.
W. O. Galbraith, *Colombia: A General Survey*, Royal Institute of International Affairs, London, 1953.
Jesús María Henao and Gerardo Arrubla, *History of Colombia*, translated by J. Fred Rippy, University of North Carolina Press, Chapel Hill, 1938.
Albert O. Hirschman, "Land Uses and Land Reform in Colombia," *Journeys Toward Progress: Studies of Economic Policy-Making in Latin America*, Twentieth Century Fund, New York, 1963, pp. 93-159.
John D. Martz, *Colombia: A Contemporary Political Study*, University of North Carolina Press, Chapel Hill, 1962.
John D. Martz, "Political Parties in Colombia and Venezuela: Contrasts in Substance and Style," *Western Political Quarterly*, XVII, No. 4, Dec. 1964.
Kathleen Romoli, *Colombia: Gateway to South America*, Doubleday, New York, 1941.

VENEZUELA

VENEZUELA is one of the wealthiest countries in Latin America, with an average per capita income of about $700. Its wealth is derived principally from the riches of its oil and iron resources. In spite of the country's wealth, the majority of its people live on incomes far below the average, in great poverty and misery. It is a country which has been marred by wars and revolutions brought on by the ambitions of would-be dictators. It has seen a succession of generals seize the powers of government proclaiming national redemption and democracy, only to rule as despots and economic overlords. Not until after the death of the dictator Juan Vicente Gómez in 1935 did the people of Venezuela experience even a shred of democracy.

Today the situation is changing. Venezuela is in the throes of a tremendous social ferment in which a frontal assault is being made on the entrenched privileged forces of society. Determined efforts are now being made by a reform-minded administration to reduce the discrepancy between an under-developed people and advanced social laws. New emphasis is being placed on universal education, agrarian reform, and political democracy. The great wealth of Venezuela is being used to promote programs which, if carried out, will bring about significant changes in the power structure, in the economy, and in society.

The task of modernizing Venezuela's archaic economic and political system is not an easy one, for it must combat antagonistic concepts and practices which are deeply embedded in the political culture and ethic of the country. It is to these forces we now direct our attention.

Physical, Economic and Social Factors

Physical Bases

Venezuela's 352,153 square miles (about the size of Texas and Oklahoma combined) may be divided into four well-defined regions. Ten percent of the national territory consists of a narrow, partly arid belt of lowlands lying between the steeply rising coastal mountains and the Caribbean Sea. It supports 8 percent of the population. At the western tip of the lowlands is the Maracaibo region, which for many years was one of the poorest sections

of the country. The discovery of oil in and near Lake Maracaibo transformed the region, and today the city of Maracaibo is a modern metropolis
and the second largest industrial city in Venezuela. Only seventy miles from
this civilized center live the savage, completely untamed Motilón Indians,
who have until recently resisted all efforts to integrate them into the national life.

The mountains constitute the second major geographical region of Venezuela. Here, in 12 percent of the national domain, live 65 percent of the
people. In the central mountain area of the northern spur of the Andes
are found the capital city of Caracas, large coffee holdings, sugar haciendas,
and the rich farmlands surrounding Lake Valencia. Because of its agricultural
importance this has become a region dominated by an agricultural oligarchy
and large estates maintained by cheap peon labor. In the western spur of the
Andes lies the Sierra Nevada de Mérida, whose early inaccessibility dis-
couraged latifundia; hence it is characterized by smaller landholdings and is
populated by small clusters of people, mainly mestizos and Indians. The rise
of coffee as a commercial crop was instrumental in ending the commercial
isolation of the Andean section of Venezuela.

Lying between the southernmost part of Venezuela and the coastal mountains are the great grassland prairies, the *llanos*, which occupy 33 percent of
the national territory and support 25 percent of its population. For six
months of the year this vast, featureless plain, 600 miles long and 200 miles
wide, is subject to rainfall so heavy that much of it lies under water and
animal life must take refuge in the scarce elevated areas. As the six months'
dry season progresses, mud turns to deep layers of dust, vegetation shrivels,
the heat becomes intense, and the streams dry up. Even the aboriginal Indians
avoided this harsh area, and it remained for the hardier European and
mestizo strains to settle and colonize it. Although the country is far from
ideal for cattle raising, a type of culture based on that industry has grown
up, managed by a rough and for many years lawless breed of man to whom
cattle-raising was a way of life. Forced by his environment to become a
tough, self-reliant individual, the *llanero* played an important part in the
War of Independence and later uprisings. Now the discovery of oil in parts
of the *llanos* is gradually transforming the economy of the region.

The fourth great area of Venezuela is the Guiana Highland which stretches
from the *llanos* south to Brazil and west to Colombia. It composes 45 percent
of the total area and is very sparsely populated, largely inaccessible, and
undeveloped. At its northeastern tip, however, near the river port of San
Felix on the Orinoco River, a vast new industrial steel complex is being
constructed by the government to take advantage of nearby rich deposits
of iron, manganese, and limestone, low-cost power, and cheap transportation via the Orinoco. The plant has been producing pig iron since 1961 and
began the production of steel in July 1962.

These diverse geographical divisions of Venezuela have provided a strong
regional orientation to its politics, as we shall see below.

Economic Bases

Venezuela's great dependence on the oil and iron industries has brought about a lopsidedness in the economy which the government is striving to remedy. These two industries, while employing only 2 percent of the labor force, account for 25 percent of the gross national product. They also provide 92 percent of the country's foreign exchange requirements and supply the government with two-thirds of its total revenues (in the form of 50 percent of their gross profits and considerable amounts in taxes). The employees of the seventeen foreign oil companies also enjoy material benefits in health care, training, and housing. Since most of its oil is earmarked for export, Venezuela is remarkably sensitive to fluctuations in the world price of oil, a condition over which it has little control.

Agriculture, on the other hand, contributes only 6 percent to the gross domestic product, but employs 33 percent of the economically active population. Many of the farmers exist on a subsistence pattern and hence contribute little to the economy. The chief agricultural products are coffee and cacao, both of which are exported in large quantities. The principal farm product in terms of land use and value is beef.

Venezuela has a modest manufacturing base in foods and related products, textiles, pharmaceuticals, and cigarettes. In 1961, over $218 million was invested in new manufacturing ventures. Foreign investment in Venezuela in all industries in 1959 amounted to $6 billion, 67.5 percent of which came from the United States.

Social Bases

Venezuela is experiencing one of the most rapid rates of population growth in the world. Increasing at an annual rate of 3.6 percent the estimated population in 1963 was 8,255,500 persons. This startling population explosion is due primarily to natural increase. Not until after World War II, when Venezuela opened its doors to European refugees, did immigration contribute significantly to it. Whereas in 1946 there were fewer than 70,000 foreigners living in Venezuela, by the end of 1961 they numbered more than 700,000. Most of the immigrants (69 percent) are easily assimilated into Venezuelan life, having come from the similar and related cultures of Spain, Italy, Portugal, Colombia, and Cuba. About 52,000 United States citizens are employed in Venezuela in the oil and iron industries. In all, some sixty-one nationalities are represented in the country. In 1961 some 12,000 aliens became Venezuelan citizens.

Many of the immigrants, originally destined for agricultural pursuits, become disenchanted with the harsh and primitive conditions which prevail in many of the rural areas and return to the already overcrowded cities seeking employment. Alien doctors, lawyers, and other professional men are not permitted to practice their professions in the cities in competition with native Venezuelans. Rather than go to the small rural centers where their skills are desperately needed, these people accept other types of employment in the several large cities.

This fact, together with the increasing tendency of the rural population to migrate to urban centers in search of work, helps to explain the growing urbanization of the population. In 1962 some 68 percent of the people were classified as urban (that is, living in or near a town with 1,000 or more inhabitants). The largest city in the republic is the capital, Caracas, which in 1963 had a metropolitan population of 1,372,435. The second major city of Venezuela, Maracaibo, had 440,000 and was followed by Barquisimeto with 204,000 and Valencia with 165,000.

Racially, 65 percent of the Venezuelan people may trace their origins to the intermarriage of Indians, Negroes, and whites. The *mestizos*, as they are called, are found at all levels of society and throughout the populated areas of Venezuela. Whites account for 20 percent of the total population and are concentrated mainly in the larger urban areas. The Negro component (about 8 percent) dwells in the lowlands along the coast, while the Indian element (variously estimated from 2 to 7 percent of the population) lives in the remote jungle and forest regions. Never an important political or social force, the Indians are gradually losing their separate identity.

The rapidity with which the population is expanding has posed grave problems for the government. It must, for example, find ways and means of providing a minimum of 500,000 new jobs and 700,000 new living units by 1965 if the population increase is to be accommodated. The predominantly youthful complexion of the people (50 percent are twenty-one years of age or under) will make this search a long-continuing one. The population is increasing faster than the economic growth of the country. In 1961, in spite of an increase of 1.4 percent in the gross domestic product, the average per capita income decreased by 1.2 percent as a result of the population expansion.

Social Organization

As Venezuela proceeds with her plans of industrialization, diversification of her economy, land distribution, and educational reform, the social and economic bases of society will inevitably change. Over the past thirteen years, for example, the middle class has grown by 7 percent until it now includes 15 percent of the economically productive population. The increase may be attributed to immigration, to the growing numbers of salaried individuals, professional people (including military men), and commercial and industrial personnel, and to an expanding government bureaucracy. As these people amass material possessions they tend to become more conservative in their political views and begin to identify themselves with the upper class and its values.

The upper class in Venezuelan society consists of the rural agricultural oligarchy (1 percent of the population owns more than 50 percent of the land in many areas of Venezuela), the proud, old aristocratic families, the

new industrial tycoons, wealthy merchants, and large urban property owners. Their political power comes from their monopoly of the educational
system and the prestige of their names and their family connections, as well
as from their great wealth. About 5 percent of the Venezuelan people may
be classified as upper class.

A tremendous gulf exists between the upper and lower classes except in the
cities, where the small middle sectors serve to obscure the differences. Over
80 percent of the rural population are landless, poverty-stricken, illiterate,
and diseased. They are either unemployed and migratory, or economically
tied to one of the great estates. Their urban counterparts are squatters who
may be found living in squalid and unsanitary *ranchitos* in the ravines, hills,
and outskirts of the cities.

Upward social mobility is possible between the classes, provided the
aspirant can somehow acquire the necessary cultural and economic prerequisites such as education, proper speech and clothing, and suitable employment. Race, as a determinant of class, is much less influential in Venezuela than it is in Anglo-Saxon countries.

Political History

The Colonial Period

Throughout most of the colonial period Venezuela was a poor and
neglected possession of Spain. Its lack of mineral wealth, its belligerent
Indians (made even more hostile by the depredations of slave traders), and
its remoteness from the centers of Spanish power in Mexico and Santo
Domingo, caused Spain to lose interest in it. Charles V held the territory in
so little regard that he granted to the German banking house of Welser the
exclusive rights to explore, conquer, and colonize the region. The venture
did not prove remunerative for either party and in 1650 Spain rescinded the
grant and undertook the difficult task of occupying and settling the land
herself.

The seven provinces which eventually came to make up Venezuela were
shifted from one administrative jurisdiction to another until the year 1777,
when they became an autonomous captaincy-general within the Spanish
Empire. Long accustomed to economic and political isolation from each
other, the provinces failed to develop any sense of cohesion or identity during their thirty-six years as a captaincy-general. Indeed, regional differences,
economic rivalries, and cultural jealousies were so pronounced during both
the struggle for independence and the later efforts to create a national state
that Simón Bolívar, the revered Liberator, almost despaired of them. "Each
province," he wrote, "governed itself independently . . . and each city
pretended to the same prerogatives, citing . . . the theory that all men and
all people enjoy the right of instituting at their own pleasure the government
which seems most suitable to them." [1] It was not surprising, therefore, that

the provinces should have embraced the federal system in their first constitution, or that their attachment to it should have continued to the present
day.

With the declaration of independence from Spain in 1811, following the
conquest of the latter by Napoleon, Venezuela began a ten-year struggle
to break its ties with the mother country. Its efforts to do so were greatly
hindered by internecine warfare between patriots and royalist sympathizers
in Venezuelan society, a disastrous earthquake, regional differences, and the
antagonistic attitude of the Church toward the rebels.

In 1821 the power of Spain was finally broken at a cost to Venezuela of
one-fourth of its population and great property damage. Later in the same
year Venezuela entered into a political union with Colombia and Ecuador.
The truly independent history of Venezuela began in 1830 when the sepa-
ratist sentiments of its conservative oligarchy caused Venezuela to withdraw
from the union.

Venezuelan history has so consistently been molded by the events and
fortunes engendered by the struggles of its leaders for personal power that
it is convenient to divide the national period into eras dominated by each
of them.

General Antonio Páez (1830-1848)

The first great political figure to control the destinies of the nation was
one of its military heroes of independence, General Páez. For eighteen years
he governed Venezuela, either from the presidential palace (where he served
two nonconsecutive terms) or from his private residence. Aided by the
Constitution of 1830, which struck at the privileged powers of the Church
and the army and protected the preferred position of the old colonial elite,
the landowners, professional men, and wealthy merchants, he withstood five
major rebellions and succeeded in bringing a considerable degree of political
stability to the country. Páez encouraged agriculture and began to rebuild
the devastated economy. Greater responsibility in fiscal matters on the part
of the Venezuelan government under his guidance inspired confidence in its
credit abroad.[2]

General Páez and the Conservative oligarchy which he represented had
their opponents, of course. Dissatisfaction with Páez's conservative approach
to politics and his failure to implement some of the liberal provisions of the
constitution coalesced around Antonio Leocadio Guzmán, the leader of
the Liberal Party which had been organized in 1840. The new party drew
its strength from debt-ridden farmers, small businessmen, and many of the
reform-minded intellectuals. It included in its platform demands for wider
suffrage, emancipation of the slaves, and abolition of capital punishment.
The Liberals found it impossible to dislodge the oligarchy from government,
however, because of the latter's fraudulent manipulation of the electoral
process.

General José Tadeo Monagas (1848-1858)

General Monagas was elected to the presidency with conservative support in 1846. Only 60,000 persons in a total population of 1,275,000 voted in the election. When Monagas' Liberal sympathies lost him the support of the Conservatives in 1848 he declared a dictatorship and exiled General Páez. Although he dismissed Conservatives from his cabinet and appointed Liberals, he soon demonstrated that he was more interested in building a personal base of power than he was in furthering the interests or programs of either party.

In 1854 during the administration of Monagas' brother, whose election he had arranged, one plank of the Liberal program was achieved: the abolition of slavery.

The efforts of Monagas to establish a rotating presidency within his own family and his tampering with the 1830 Constitution contributed to his downfall. Liberals and Conservatives combined forces to unseat him in 1858.

The Federal War (1858-1863)

The inability of the two parties to agree on a form of government subsequent to the overthrow of Monagas plunged Venezuela into a prolonged period of civil war. The Conservatives called for a strong, centralized system while the Liberals advocated federalism. If we are to believe the words of Antonio Guzmán Blanco, the Liberal attachment to federalism was something less than genuine. He declared, "If our opponents had said 'federalism,' we should have cried 'centralism.'" However superficial his original attachment to federalism was, Guzmán Blanco succeeded in instilling in his followers a belief that as a divinely inspired principle, federalism would harmonize all the diverse tendencies, interests, and forces of man. Thousands of men died in the Federal War, however, without ever understanding the cause for which they were fighting.[3]

The forces supporting federalism were finally victorious in 1863 and a constitution establishing a federal system was adopted by the twenty states in 1864. Real peace did not come to the country until 1870, when Antonio Guzmán Blanco, son of the Liberal leader, succeeded in driving a Conservative administration from power.

Antonio Guzmán Blanco (1870-1888)

Professing liberal ideas, but in fact governing the country in a tyrannical fashion, the vain Guzmán Blanco initiated a thoroughgoing dictatorship which lasted until 1888. During these years he broke the power of the Church by confiscating a good deal of its property (particularly that of the monasteries), exiling the bishop of Caracas, secularizing the control of marriage and the registration of vital statistics, and encouraging Protestant sects to send missionaries to Venezuela. The Church ceased to be a political force for years as a result of his measures.

Guzmán Blanco's economic policies included the encouragement of foreign investments, grants of valuable concessions to foreign concerns, and the construction of railroads and roads. Some advances in education were achieved, such as the building of primary and secondary schools and several professional institutions. He improved the fiscal and financial machinery of the government and insisted on honesty for all but himself. Little was done, however, to improve the lot of the masses or to change the inequities existing in the agricultural sector.

General Joaquín Crespo (1892-1899)

Guzmán Blanco was overthrown in 1888 and his downfall ushered in a period of political confusion which ended in 1892 with the accession to power of another dictator-general, Joaquín Crespo, whose battle cry was *"Legalismo!"* During the corrupt and inefficient administration of Crespo, a long-standing dispute between Great Britain and Venezuela over the boundary line between British Guiana and Venezuela was mediated by an arbitration commission which awarded the bulk of the disputed territory to Great Britain.

General Cipriano Castro (1899-1908)

When Cipriano Castro, the "Lion of the Andes" seized the presidency in 1899 he inaugurated a 58-year period of almost unbroken Andean control of the political destinies of Venezuela.

Uneducated, immoral, reckless, and disorderly, Castro gave Venezuela one of the worst administrations it has ever had. His mismanagement of national affairs brought demands from foreign governments for compensation for damages suffered by their nationals during the frequent revolts which occurred during his regime. Upon Castro's refusal to pay, the governments of Great Britain, Germany, and Italy in 1902 precipitated a hemispheric crisis by blockading the ports of Venezuela. The issue was settled (with United States participation) by a mixed arbitration tribunal which reduced the exaggerated claims of the foreign powers.

For nine years Venezuela endured the stupidities and tyrannies of Castro. In 1908, while he was abroad undergoing medical treatment, his vice-president, Juan Vicente Gómez, usurped the presidency and invited Castro to remain permanently in Europe.

Juan Vicente Gómez (1908-1935)

For the next twenty-seven years Venezuela was in the grip of the most heavy-handed and ruthless dictatorship in its history. A self-educated, illegitimate half-breed from the Andes, Gómez demonstrated in his climb to power that he was both an astute judge of men and a calculating opportunist.

Gómez' greed, cruelty, and insensitivity to suffering were amply demonstrated during his long rule. He managed Venezuela as a private estate, appropriating the choicest estates and properties to himself and his numerous natural progeny. His was a disciplined police state with an elaborate spy system, a well-equipped and well-trained army, and numerous political prisons for those who had the temerity to criticize him. Civil liberties were nonexistent during his long rule.

Since no political competition was permitted, political parties disappeared and elections became meaningless. Gómez completely controlled both the national congress and the state legislatures, whose members were personally selected by him or his agents. The rubber-stamp legislative bodies obediently approved seven constitutional changes to accommodate his whims. Nothing but fulsome praise was reported of him. Typical was a eulogy delivered by a member of the 1935 congress which described Gómez as a superior man "with a soul as lofty as the clouds of his native Andes," a Moses who came to "illumine the path to the promised land."

Gómez, the "Well Deserving," did confer the boon of domestic peace and order on his country. The most significant economic development of his regime, however, was the sudden and fantastic expansion of the oil industry. Rich deposits had been discovered as early as 1914. The liberal oil law of 1920 encouraged foreign companies to exploit the oil resources by granting them low export taxes and guaranteeing their property rights. In the space of ten years Venezuela became the second largest oil-producing country in the world. The development of oil brought such wealth to Venezuela that it was able not only to survive the depression of 1929 but also to reduce its national debt significantly. Much of the wealth, however, was siphoned off by Gómez and his family and supporters. The common people derived little benefit from it.

The Period Between 1936 and 1948

Gómez died a natural death in December 1935. His place was taken by his minister of war, General Eleázar López Contreras, who restored after a time the liberties of speech and press and dismissed many of the followers of Gómez from the government. A new constitution was written, as well as a new labor code recognizing the rights of labor to organize and bargain collectively. López Contreras also initiated a three-year program of domestic improvement which included construction of schools, port facilities, new roads, and needed public works.

Under the Constitution of 1936, which prescribed election of the president by the congress, López Contreras was able through his control of the legislature to choose his successor, and he delivered his office to General Medina Angarita in 1941.

Medina Angarita's administration was distinguished by a revision of the basic oil law in such a way as to bring the government a greater share of the oil companies' profits. He was removed from office late in 1945 in a revolution led by a group of dissatisfied military officers and supported by the left-of-center political party Acción Democrática (AD). The leaders of AD saw little opportunity of coming to power by means other than violence, for the presidentially dominated congress was expected to elect Medina Angarita's choice.

AD supplied four members of the seven-man junta which was set up to govern Venezuela until a new constitutional order could be legalized; the president of the junta was Rómulo Betancourt, a leading figure in AD. In 1948 the junta turned over its power to a civilian president elected under the terms of a new constitution which had been adopted in 1947.

In the election of 1947, the first free and fair one in Venezuelan history, AD scored a victory in both houses of congress and elected its candidate, the novelist Rómulo Gallegos, to the presidency. The military forces, however, were not prepared to accept a subordinate role or a curtailment of their privileges under Gallegos and in November 1948 when he refused to give them the extra cabinet seats they demanded, they removed him.

A new provisional government, this time made up entirely of military men, took over control of the country. The assassination of its young leader Lieutenant Colonel Carlos Delgado Chalbaud in 1950 shocked the Venezuelan people. Despite the turbulent nature of their politics, they had never had a chief of state killed in office. Delgado Chalbaud's death provided Marcos Pérez Jiménez, another member of the junta, with his chance to seize control. Pérez Jiménez governed Venezuela from 1950 to 1958, first as the real power in the reconstituted junta, then as provisional president, and finally as constitutional president under a constitution written expressly for him by a controlled constitutional assembly.[4]

Marcos Pérez Jiménez

We need not concern ourselves here with the unsavory accounts of the new dictator's personal life and associates. According to reliable sources, however, corruption was rife and government expenditures were colossal, particularly in the area of public works. Pérez Jiménez is reported to have amassed a personal fortune in excess of $250 million.

Throughout his dictatorship both AD and the Communist Party were outlawed and the activities of groups other than those who vociferously supported him were severely curtailed. Indeed, the president is alleged to have told the president-elect of Peru in 1955 that Venezuelans were "not inclined to political parties." [5] Certainly during his administration it was the better part of valor not to be so inclined, for his oppressive government made systematic efforts to harass and eradicate the opposition political parties.

We may catch a little of the flavor of the political philosophy of Pérez Jiménez in a statement attributed to him by *Time* magazine: "I make every effort to give Venezuelans the kind of government adapted to them. . . . We are still in our infant years and we still need halters. . . . There must be a leader who shows the way without being perturbed by the necessity of winning demagogic popularity." [6]

The Venezuelan people apparently thought otherwise. Not long after they had voted in a rigged, controlled, and unconstitutional "plebiscite" on December 15, 1957, to continue the dictator in office for another five years, they expressed their resentment at such a flagrant disregard of legality by participating in a general strike, on January 21, 1958. The strike matured into a full-scale uprising the next day. Pérez Jiménez tearfully capitulated, when it appeared that nothing short of capitulation would satisfy the aroused population, and fled to the Dominican Republic on January 23. His overthrow was accomplished through mass discontent of the people, focused and directed by a "Patriotic Junta" and through the defection of segments of the army and the navy.

Since Pérez Jiménez

Following the traditional pattern in Latin American politics, a provisional junta, under the leadership of Admiral Wolfgang Larrazábal, was installed to govern until elections could be arranged. After a period of planning and consolidation, the provisional government announced elections for December 7, 1958. When initial attempts to agree on a common presidential candidate failed, each of the three major parties put forth its own candidate. The victor was Rómulo Betancourt, candidate of AD, who was elected by 47 percent of the popular vote for a five-year term of office beginning February 13, 1959. Acción Democrática also captured control of both houses of the congress in Venezuela's second free and fair election.

AD maintained its control of the Presidency with the victory of Raúl Leoni in the elections of 1963. It also remained the leading party in the congress, although with a reduced number of seats. The policies followed by the AD administrations are discussed below.

Political Culture[7]

Contemporary political institutions in Venezuela cannot be adequately understood without an acquaintance with persistent conditioning factors of national political life such as regionalism, personalism, and militarism.

Regionalism

A powerful force which shaped the lines of Venezuelan political development is regionalism. Although it no longer plays the role that it did prior to the Gómez regime, nevertheless elements of it linger on. For one thing, in the last half-century, with only a brief interlude in 1945-48, the military barracks of the Andean state of Táchira have furnished all the presidents of Venezuela: Generals Gómez, López Contreras, Medina Angarita, and Pérez Jiménez. The pre-eminence of Táchira in national politics has naturally given rise to bitter jealousy in the people of other regions and states, but so strong has been the military power of the men of Táchira that little progress has been made in breaking their hold over the government.

Regionalism also manifests itself in cultural and economic ways. For many years there was considerable cultural rivalry between the aristocratic families of Caracas and those of Cumaná. A similar rivalry persists to this day between Caracas and the Andean city of Mérida, which considers itself the intellectual and cultural superior of the capital city, being the seat of a great university and the home of many distinguished families. There are few common interests between the proud families of the Andes and the rough *llaneros* of the great plains. Their economic interests, coffee for the former and cattle and oil for the latter, help to accentuate the differences.

Strong attachments and pride in localities, the isolation of the regions one from another, and the difficulty of communication between them all combined to produce in the people of Venezuela during its formative years a strong demand for self-government and account in part for the later adoption of the federal system of government.

Caudillismo and Personalismo

The periods of dictatorship to which the Venezuelan people have been subjected during the course of their political evolution have conditioned them to the principle of authoritarianism in the organization and application of political power. It may be argued, as Venezuelan students of government argue, that the people themselves have encouraged and cultivated the development of *ejecutivismo* in government; the struggle for power has been aggravated by a strong tendency on their part to associate themselves with powerful personalities rather than with programs and issues. This tendency we may label *personalismo*. A politically ambitious *caudillo* (local boss), having once demonstrated his leadership abilities in the local arena, has not found it difficult to acquire a following that is willing to support him in almost any enterprise.

Strong contending regional rivals virtually disappeared under Gómez, who bought their loyalty by liberal subsidies. The absence of strong local leaders does not mean, however, that *caudillismo* is dead; far from it. Their place has been taken by men who achieve power in national politics through their ability to placate and manipulate the various power groups within the armed forces. Thus the struggle for power in the period from 1945 to 1958 was not between contending regional rivals, but between powerful leaders within the military.

Militarism

The followers of General Páez were political realists when they said to him in 1830, "General, you are the fatherland." The influence of the military forces was decisive in the struggle for independence and has been a dominant force in Venezuelan politics ever since.

In 1945 the Venezuelan constitutionalist Ernesto Wolff observed that the title of "general" had come to be a necessity for the discharge of the duties not only of the presidency but also of most other high offices.[8] Certainly the roster of Venezuelan executives is notably lacking in men of nonmilitary status. Two civilians, it is true, occupied the presidency during the twenty-seven-year rule of Gómez, but they were puppets. Since 1894 only two civilian presidents, Rómulo Gallegos and Rómulo Betancourt, have possessed real power in their own right. Gallegos was removed after nine months in office by a military clique which announced that its great desire was to demonstrate that it knew how to rule and prepare the people for democracy.

Although the military was not overtly in office at the end of 1963, they were still the most important power factor in Venezuelan politics. President Betancourt was astute enough to realize that he could not tamper with the military machine with impunity. He survived numerous attempts to depose him only because enough of the armed forces continued to support him and his program. President Raúl Leoni will have to operate within much the same context.

Cesarismo Democrático

An important element in the Venezuelan conception of authority may be found in the philosophy of the "democratic caesar." It was first conceptualized by Pedro Vallanilla Lanz during the regime of Gómez, but it had been an operative principle of government from the time of General Páez. In that era of "sonnets and sociology," Vallanilla Lanz's effort was only one of many that sought to justify and rationalize the harsh rule of Gómez. The philosophy revolves around the premise that for Latin America dictatorship is not a necessary evil but the ideal and appropriate form of government. The nature of the Venezuelan people, so the argument ran, excluded every system of government that was not a presidential dictatorship. Vallanilla Lanz asserted that the authority of the *caudillo*-president was founded upon the unconscious suggestion of the majority. He viewed Venezuelan society as one made up of individuals who turned instinctively to wise, strong, and valiant men. The democratic caesar, always representing the popular sovereign, was democracy personified, the nation made man. The antagonistic concepts of democracy and autocracy were somehow mystically resolved and harmonized in him, producing a political environment in which all men were equal under a common chief.

Venezuela's paper constitutions were the targets for the followers of Vallanilla Lanz, who, for the most part, were contemptuous of the republican and democratic principles contained in them. Vallanilla Lanz argued, as Bolívar had argued many years earlier, that Venezuelan society lacked the elements necessary for the success of democracy. Another disciple of the school called democracy a "mystic doctrine" which was giving way to a national desire to make the country great by "utilizing all its forces, organized to function harmoniously through the control which can be exercised only by a Supreme Director." [9]

The Constitution in Venezuelan Political Culture

Venezuelans have come to regard their constitutional fabric with a good deal of cynicism. A contributing factor to this attitude has been the inclination of their constitutional assemblies to pattern the basic law on foreign constitutions and principles not readily transferable from their native environment. The Venezuelan constitutions have thus been more the product of reason than of experience; the Constitution of 1961 is not a cumulative expression of a long period of political evolution. Perhaps the most far-fetched borrowing appeared in the Constitution of 1881 in which Guzmán Blanco instituted a modified form of the Swiss collegial executive (without having the slightest intention of sharing power with anyone). Venezuelans themselves criticize this tendency to emulate others, but the practice continues.

Venezuela has had twenty-six constitutions since 1811. It is fair to point out that many of them have differed only slightly from each other, responding to the demands of the ruling dictator. Three of the seven constitutions of Gómez, for example, did little more than create and abolish the vice-presidency to accommodate members of his family. The prevalence of such personal manipulations of the constitution is another reason why the people have lost respect for it.

Constitutionalism, that is, the ideal of limited government, flourishes only in societies in which a concern for the rule of law is a basic and valued part of the political ethic and in which there is a reasonable connection between constitutional theory and practice. Neither can be legislated. Because the political, social, and economic institutions of Venezuela have rested upon authoritarian and undemocratic concepts, limited democratic government has not been achieved. The constitution and its guarantees have so often been caught up in the interplay of political passions and selfish forces and so often has it been disregarded by those in power that Venezuelans think of it as a "little yellow book that is written every year and broken every day." The power and influence of the executive in Venezuelan politics has been so extensive that the basic law has been only what he has chosen to recognize as such. The constitution therefore cannot be considered an instrument of restraint.

Is it an instrument of power? The constitution, of course, does confer legality, authority, and power on the president and other government officials. At the same time, much of the power of the president rests upon extraconstitutional foundations: army, family, business connections. An impressive list of powers is meaningless unless they can be exercised. The president cannot do so effectively merely because he is president; army support is absolutely necessary. President Betancourt was a relatively weak president because he had no such extraconstitutional basis of power other than his party.

The Venezuelan constitution, despite these drawbacks, performs certain functions: It clears the air when a new regime comes to power; it invests a revolutionary government with treasured legality; it is a vehicle for advanced economic and social doctrines, and it keeps before the people the ideals of democracy.

The Acquisition of Political Power

Political Deference and Violence

The political process in Venezuela since Independence has been characterized by two contradictory tendencies: a pronounced habit of servility, deference, and apathy on the part of the people towards those in power (and of the lower classes toward the upper), and the disposition to resort to violence to achieve political objectives.

In such titles as "The Illustrious American," "The Well Deserving," "The Regenerator," and "Hero of Duty," one can see the overt expression of political subservience. Documentary literature is full of the most adulatory references to the president while he is in office. Until the administration of President Betancourt (who was greatly beset by opposition forces) praise of the president was an indispensable duty for party, press, and politician. In the face of such tyrannies as they have endured, perhaps apathy and acquiescence was the only posture the people could adopt. Their true feelings can best be judged by the explosions which accompany and follow the downfall of their dictators.

There have been many minor uprisings and several bloody revolts in the course of Venezuelan history which seem to give the lie to the charge of apathy. Most of the revolts, however, have been motivated by personal considerations and have involved only small numbers of people who thought the rewards of obtaining political power worth great risks. Nevertheless, Venezuelans in general have always been ready and still are ready to use force and violence to achieve their ends.[10] The numerous disturbances and uprisings against the government of President Betancourt gave evidence that this tendency is still very much alive.

Powerful overthrows of the government took place in 1945, 1948, and 1958. Only that of 1958 involved widespread participation by the people, which was perhaps its most significant feature. Long quiescent and apathetic, the population demonstrated vigorously and effectively against the dictatorship at the risk of great danger to themselves.

For the volatile Venezuelan, revolt has proved to be a quicker and more effective method of acquiring political power than have elections.

Elections in the Political Process[11]

Venezuelans have little reason to regard the electoral process of achieving power with anything but cynicism. During most of their history free and fair elections have simply been unknown. Perhaps the greatest electoral farce of all was Guzmán Blanco's 1874 constitutional provision requiring voters to *sign* and deposit their ballots in the presence of the electoral judges! Only one person had the temerity to vote against him.

Let us consider as a case study the elections of November 30, 1952, in which members of a constitutional convention were chosen. The regime, overconfident that it would be continued in power through massive popular support, took ample precautions to insure an orderly, fair, and secret election. The authorities placed a ban on travel and on the sale of alcohol for the day. Witnesses representing each of the parties were entitled to be present when the empty ballot box was sealed, and to remain through the voting and the tabulation. Double voting was eliminated by the simple device of requiring the voter to dip a finger in a bottle of indelible ink before leaving the polls. Upon identifying himself to the election officials, the voter was given five colored ballots (adopted for the convenience of illiterates). His instructions were to discard the unused four ballots in a special receptacle in the voting booth and deposit his choice, sealed in an envelope, in the ballot box in the presence of the judges. Observers of the election are agreed that the voters were able to cast their ballots in complete secrecy.

The election was orderly and without incident. The Supreme Electoral Council issued its first bulletin on the evening of election day when only a few scattered returns were in. Trouble began with the publication on December 1 of returns which clearly indicated an unfavorable trend for the government. The Democratic Republican Union (URD) was leading the Independent Electoral Front (FEI), a coalition of groups supporting Marcos Pérez Jiménez, by 147,965 votes. In the light of this development, the government suddenly placed tight restrictions on the news.

With the resumption of news after an interval of several days (during which the provisional junta had resigned in favor of a provisional presidency under Marcos Pérez Jiménez) a decidedly different trend was apparent. Now the FEI and its affiliates led the opposition parties by 98,000 votes. URD had been confident of victory on the basis of the earlier returns, and the dissatisfaction of its leaders grew to such ominous proportions that the new minister of the interior ordered them to take an extended vacation abroad.

Final election figures were made public on December 13. According to the figures, FEI groups had captured 788,086 votes; the URD, 638,336; and the Christian Socialist Party (COPEI), 300,309. Two other minor parties polled a combined 41,259 votes.

A study of the final bulletin reveals some interesting details which support the opposition charges of irregularities in the election. The state of Nueva Esparta split a total vote of 26,933 almost evenly between URD and the Electoral Front (a state affiliate of FEI). The state was entitled to two delegates on a proportional basis. The Electoral Front was given both seats in spite of the fact that URD had polled only 106 fewer votes. Under the electoral quotient system URD was entitled to one of the two seats, as it was also in the states of Barinas, Bolívar, and Cojedes. Government supporters were awarded both seats in each case. If the same procedure for allotting seats had been followed elsewhere, however, the government parties would not have elected delegates in the states of Monagas, Yaracuy, and Trujillo. As it was, they elected delegates in every state in the union.

This bald manipulation of the electoral returns was a gross violation of the government's promise to adhere strictly to the wishes of the people, a violation made even more repugnant because voting was compulsory. Numerous Venezuelan men wore black arm bands in mourning over the fiasco. The farcical illegal plebiscite staged to re-elect Pérez Jiménez in 1957 added insult to injury.

The fairness and freedom of the elections of 1958 and 1963, however, have mitigated to some degree the bitterness and cynicism engendered by the debacles of 1952 and 1957. The fact that President Betancourt was able to survive many terrorist attempts to overthrow him, to carry out an election in the face of powerful Communist intimidation, and to turn over his power to an elected successor in March 1964, has endowed the electoral method with much greater respectability. But before it can be said to be reasonably secure in the political culture of Venezuela, several more free elections without dictatorial interference or interlude will have to take place. Venezuelans have more reason to be optimistic about such a prospect now than ever before in their history.

Political Parties

Until the advent of Acción Democrática in 1941, political parties rarely offered to Venezuelans any genuine policy or program alternatives. Cristóbal Benítez' definition in 1930 of a party as a group of men who profess the same political ideas and who try to obtain power to put them into effect would certainly apply to most of the parties prior to that time. The struggle was not over doctrine or economic ideas but for power and for the financial rewards which, directly or indirectly, stemmed from the possession of power.

It is true that there were Conservative and Liberal parties during most of the nineteenth century. The Conservatives, oligarchic and traditionalist in their views, supported the privileged official position of the Church in society and centralized strong government. The Liberals, on the other hand, professing egalitarian notions, were against privilege in general, favored a decentralized government and democracy, and pitted their progressivism against the traditionalism of the Conservatives. The differences between the two forces were largely academic, for, said José Gil Fortuol, each of them forgot, in power, "the contradictions which had separated them in opposition." [13]

From time to time, minor political factions arose in response to local conditions and personalistic considerations, but they were short-lived.

Political parties played no role at all in the political life of Venezuela during the twenty-seven-year rule of Gómez (and not much during the eight-year rule of Marcos Pérez Jiménez). A fairly large number of parties did blossom forth in the liberalized atmosphere which prevailed after the death of Gómez in 1936, however. It was during this period that Acción Democrática and COPEI (now called the Christian Socialist Party) were legalized. Most of the narrowly based parties disappeared after one election; in the constitutional assembly elections in 1946, for example, of the fourteen parties which ran candidates, only three survived to participate in the presidential and congressional elections a year later. They were AD, COPEI, and the Communist Party. The Democratic Republican Union (URD) appeared in 1948.

Acción Democrática

Of all the parties which have appeared since 1941, the reformist, left-of-center Acción Democrática has been the largest and longest-lived. It has been the majority party since 1945, when it helped the military unseat President Medina Angarita. It furnished the president of the junta which governed until another member of its party, Rómulo Gallegos, took over as president in 1948. It controlled both houses of congress until the revolution of 1948 drove it from power. From 1948 to 1958 it was outlawed, but came back to power in the elections of 1958, capturing the presidency and both houses of congress. In the interests of national unity, however, President Betancourt formed a coalition government which included members of both COPEI and URD, the leading opposition party. In 1960, URD withdrew from the coalition, and it has since been an extremely vigorous and vocal opponent of the government.

In the same year, AD was rent by the first of two splits when a group of Marxist, pro-Castro dissidents bolted the party to become the Movement of the Revolutionary Left (MIR). In 1962 another group of members, dissatisfied with the growing centrist orientation of President Betancourt, and demanding more agrarian reform, left the party. This group was known as AD-ARS, while the parent body is called the Old Guard. We shall look at the social and economic philosophy of the Old Guard in the next section, which deals with public policy. The dissidents of 1962 have dwindled into insignificance as a result of their poor showing in the 1963 elections.

COPEI

The junior partner of AD in the coalition government of Venezuela at the end of 1963, the Christian Democratic Party, is also moderately leftist and reflects the social doctrines of the Catholic Church. According to its program, the party stands for greater protection of private education, honest administration in government, public improvement of the country as a whole, an open and autonomous university, respect for human dignity, freedom of labor to organize, effective improvement of the working class, aid to private groups to stimulate the national economy, and, finally, "disinterested" religious freedom. As a result of the 1963 elections, COPEI became the second largest party in popular support.

URD

The Democratic Republican Union was the leading opposition party up to that time. It emphasized equal guarantees for all, effective popular suffrage, honest administration, improvement in the lot of the average man, restricted immigration, and nonmilitary institutions.

All three of the principal parties expressed their interest in land reform, better housing, and more participation by Venezuela in the oil industry.

The Communist Party

The Communist Party was legalized after the downfall of Marcos Pérez Jiménez, and in the elections of 1958 it managed to capture two senate and seven deputy seats. As might be expected, it was an extremely vigorous, outspoken, and obstructive minority in the congress. One of the Communist deputies went so far as to participate in a marine-led revolt against the government in May 1962, for which he was detained by the police. For activities of this sort the party, along with the MIR, was suspended and subject to restrictions on its public meetings. Neither party was permitted to participate in the elections of December 1963.

Newer Parties

Two other groups received sizable numbers of votes in 1963. Although both were clearly *ad hoc* groupings organized to support the presidential candidacies of specific individuals, the possibility existed that each would be organized on a more permanent basis. One of these movements was of a moderately leftist coloration and supported the candidacy of Admiral Larrazábal; the other, somewhat more conservative, campaigned for the distinguished writer Arturo Uslar Pietri.

Pressure Groups

The Armed Forces

Possessing institutional bases of power which render them a state within a state, the armed forces are perhaps the most formidable pressure group in Venezuela. No administration, least of all an elected civilian one, could remain in office a day without the acquiescence of the armed forces, nor could it tamper with their privileged status with impunity. Governments which do not heed their demands do not last long, as President Gallegos found out in 1948.

The armed forces are no longer unified in philosophy or in outlook, however. The demands of the social and economic revolution which is sweeping over Latin America have found sympathizers within the military machine in Venezuela and enough officers lent their support to the aims and objectives of the Betancourt administration to enable it to survive numerous attempts to overthrow it. There is no assurance, however, that the more traditionalist, interventionist-minded officers, imbued with a sense of their obligation to direct the destinies of the nation, will not reassert themselves.

Labor

The present membership of the Venezuelan Confederation of Labor is over 1,300,000, or about a sixth of the total population. Permitted to organize, bargain, and strike under a paternalistic labor law, the unions have been increasingly able to make their weight felt in politics. Increasingly, however, the labor movement has become involved in and affected by political party disputes. Each wing of the badly split Acción Democrática party and its supporters has tried to gain control of the peasant leagues, the oil workers' union, and the Confederation itself. Many unions now have two sets of officers, each claiming to be the official organization. The division within the labor force brought on by this dispute can only weaken its effectiveness as an organized pressure group.

The Church

The political power and influence of the Church has never been particularly strong in Venezuela. Anticlerical sentiment, springing from the Church's support of the Crown in the struggle for independence and its identification with the oligarchic forces of society, manifested itself in political ways after 1850. Under the restrictive decrees of Guzmán Blanco the Church was dealt a near-mortal blow.

The Church broke out of its long habit of quiescence in the latter half of 1957 by publicly condemning the corruption in government and the unequal distribution of wealth in the country. The publicity given by the Church to the vices of the government helped to bring to a head the discontent which finally unseated Pérez Jiménez in 1958.

The influence of the Church today is felt principally in the field of education (25 percent of the school children are in its private schools) and social action. The political vehicle of its social concerns is the Christian Socialist Party.

Students

The students and faculty members of the Venezuelan universities have always been an active and articulate political force. Not only do students strike within the university community for desired reforms and against too much political interference in their autonomous institution, but they also express their political concerns in vigorous protests and public demonstrations against governments of which they disapprove. More than one major revolt has originated in the academic halls. The universities have been fruitful sources of dissension and unrest, and in recognition of this fact dictators in the past have either curtailed their activities or closed the university system entirely for long periods. Many and perhaps most of the terrorists of MIR and Communist orientation responsible for the acts of sabotage frequent during the latter years of the Betancourt administration appear to have been students.

Landowners

The land-distribution program being carried out under the Agrarian Reform Law is gradually reducing both the number and power of the staunchly traditional and conservative landed oligarchy. This tiny group is due for extinction if and when the land-reform program is completed. The landowners are naturally bitter and obstructive enemies of the reformist administration in Venezuela.

Public Opinion

The basic prerequisites for an informed public capable of making discerning judgments about its political officers and their policies would appear to be a literate population and a free press. Neither has existed in any significant degree in Venezuela. Until the Betancourt government began its massive assault on illiteracy, over one-half the people could neither read nor write; 28 percent still cannot do so.

The acceptance of political situations which diverge widely from the constitution can be explained in part by the lack of an informed public opinion. A government which claimed to be supported by such an opinion would be, in the words of one Venezuelan author, "delirious." [14] The people simply have not had access to information. During most of its history the country has lacked a free press. For years the only public inkling that Venezuelans had that their governments were less than perfect were the voluminous charges made by a new administration to justify the overthrow of its predecessor.

In the five years of the Betancourt administration, censorship of the press ranged from moderate to extreme. The Caracas press often carried vitriolic attacks on the government, and the government retaliated by temporarily suspending publication of the offending journals and detaining their editors. Official censorship was in effect during much of 1962 and 1963.

The Federal System

Venezuela's twenty-sixth constitution, adopted on January 23, 1961, describes the form of government as democratic, responsible, elective, representative, and federal.

A federal system of government is one in which the powers of the nation are divided between two jurisdictions, national and state, in such a way that each has powers it may exercise independently of the other. Each is supreme within the sphere assigned to it by the constitution. Let us examine Venezuelan federalism with this definition in mind.

The federal union of Venezuela consists of twenty states, a Federal District, two Federal Territories, and seventy-two island dependencies. The states have always occupied a weak position in the basic governmental structure, a fact amply demonstrated by the number of territorial changes they have sustained since the adoption of the federal system in 1864.[15] State sovereignty was respected in none of the changes, the initiative coming in each case from the national Congress, acting on orders from the president. Yet the states have unanimously ratified the territorial changes required of them. The record of state territorial instability in Venezuela is in striking contrast to the territorial stability of the state in the American system and indicates a position of marked subordination to the national government.

Division of Power

The operation of the federal system since 1864 has been marked by a decided trend toward concentration of power in the national government and in particular, in the national executive. Whereas in 1864 the states had important powers of their own and, in theory, at least, possessed all powers not granted to the national government, by 1953 they had lost all but those permitting them to write their constitutions, change their names, and administer the revenue they received from the national treasury. The Constitution of 1961 continues these powers and restores to the states the right to determine the organization of their public powers, municipalities, and police forces. It also restores the reserve powers clause, but this means little in the face of such extensive grants to the national government. All state power, moreover, must be exercised in conformity to standards laid down in the national constitution and national laws.

Fiscal Relations

The states of the Venezuelan union have lost most of their power to tax. Not only are they excluded from all fields taxed by the national government, but they are also forbidden to levy taxes in areas granted to the towns and cities, which derive their income from taxes on public entertainment, commerce and industry, certain types of licenses, urban real estate, and municipal services. The control of a dependable source of income, a necessary condition for autonomy, is thus denied to the states, being divided between the national government, which takes the lion's share, and the municipalities.

To offset the loss to the states of their revenue, the national government, since 1925, has granted to them a share of its annual estimated ordinary revenue. The Constitution of 1961 provides that the government shall distribute to the states at least 12.5 percent of such revenue and that this minimum figure shall be increased at the rate of ½ percent each year beginning in 1962 until it reaches a minimum of 15 percent. Allocation of the funds is made to the states on the basis of 30 percent in equal amounts and 70 percent according to their populations. The states, which must distribute 20 percent of the money to their towns and cities on a proportional basis, derive 90 percent of their income from the allotment. The rest of their revenue comes from such things as drivers' licenses, license plates, rents from state properties, and market fees.

The states must coordinate their budgets and expenditures with directives issued by the national government, which suggests appropriate ways to utilize the funds to fit in with national plans of development.

The Township in the Federal System

In Venezuela the municipality is declared to be independent of the state in economic and administrative matters, subject only to national laws and regulations. The meager traces of federalism that remain in the constitutional system seem to point more to a division of power between national and municipal governments than to a division between state and national governments.

The Judiciary in the Federal System

In 1945 the states surrendered their last major power when they ratified a constitutional amendment which conferred upon the national government exclusive control of the judicial system. The actual transfer of power from the states to the national government did not occur until November 1948, when a nationalizing decree abrogated all the state judicial codes and statutes and promulgated the national one in their stead. A ministry of justice was created in 1950 to supervise not only the unified judicial structure, but also all penitentiaries and other correctional institutions.

State Governors

From 1864 to 1953 the people of the several states had the theoretical right to elect their chief executives. Because of the powerful position of the president, however, state governors have always been chosen or at least tolerated by him. Juan Vicente Gómez established the constitutional basis for the previously informal practice of presidential appointment of state executives by having the states amend the constitution in 1925 in such a way as to confer upon him the authority to exercise any power they might choose to delegate to him. All of them immediately amended their own constitutions to empower him to appoint their governors. The states have recovered the right in the 1961 constitution, but President Betancourt continued to appoint all of the state governors.

The state governor is in an ambiguous position. The national constitution declares him to be an agent of the national government charged with executing faithfully all the national laws, while at the same time he is charged by the state constitution with the task of preserving the autonomy of the state against all encroachments. This latter provision is meaningless, for there is virtually no autonomy to preserve.

Governors have always been chosen more for their political reliability than for their administrative ability. The average tenure in office for a governor during the period 1935-1953 was 15.9 months. Since then they have enjoyed a somewhat longer average tenure.

Although no adequate study has been made of the power and influence of the governor vis-à-vis the unicameral state legislatures, what evidence is available points to the conclusion that the legislatures have been almost completely at the command of the governor. The amazing uniformity of state laws and state organization suggests that the legislatures are subject to a high degree of direction from the central government. If Marcos Pérez Jiménez had not been overthrown in 1958 this degree of direction would undoubtedly have increased, for in a special session called in December 1957, after his plebiscite, his subservient congress violated the constitution by electing the members of the twenty state legislatures and all of the municipal councils throughout Venezuela!

On the basis of the foregoing evidence, it would appear that federalism is a fiction in Venezuela. What has always existed in fact is a centralized, unitary form of government and the Venezuelans are perfectly aware of it. It may be that their devotion to federalism is to the principle and not to practical application, and that in the final analysis it remains in existence only as a response to the emotional idealism of the Venezuelan people who see in it the unattainable goal of local self-government.

The National Executive

Method of Election

The presidents of Venezuela have been elected by a variety of methods in the past, but the Constitution of 1961 calls for the president's election for a five-year term by simple majority of the popular vote. Suffrage is universal for all persons over the age of eighteen years and is obligatory. The president is ineligible for another term until ten years have elapsed from the last day of his incumbency. He must be at least thirty years old and a native-born Venezuelan. In the event of the death of the president in office, the congress is empowered to appoint a successor for the remainder of the term. There is no vice-president.

Extent of Executive Powers

Presidential powers are extensive and may be divided into three categories: those which he exercises through the medium of his council of ministers; those exercised by him through his individual ministers; and those which belong exclusively to him. In the past this has been a purely formal division with little practical meaning, for the president has had complete control over his ministers. When the president depends upon the support of another party in order to govern and therefore enters into a coalition with it, he must of necessity be less than dictatorial. Venezuela was governed by such a coalition between Acción Democrática and COPEI throughout President Betancourt's administration. Coalition government is a new phenomenon in Venezuela, long accustomed to the dominance of a single party.

Without classifying his powers according to the above categories we may note the following grants of authority to the president: he may call special sessions of congress; issue and revise administrative regulations; create, suppress, or modify public services; conclude treaties, contracts, or agreements with foreign states; decree additional credits to the budget; initiate action against state officials; direct foreign relations; nominate and remove state governors and all other national officials whose appointment is not lodged elsewhere; administer the national territories and dependencies, establish standards for the utilization of income of the states and the coordination of state budgets with that of the national government, and negotiate loans and contracts. Furthermore, he may name and remove the ministers of his cabinet; reserve any portfolio in it for himself; attach to his executive office any public service he deems convenient; declare war and negotiate peace when the congress so decrees; exercise state powers delegated to him by the states; fix the size of the armed forces and act as their commander-in-chief, administer the public finances, and suspend the constitutional guarantees either totally or in part in times of national or international emergency.

These powers, taken in the aggregate, cloak the president with enormous authority and completely overshadow the paltry grants to the congress. If there is any one section of the constitution which can be said to reflect the nature of political power in modern Venezuela, it is that which deals with the executive power.

The Exercise of Executive Powers

In view of the fact that the government has always been strongly *ejecutevista* in orientation, it is appropriate to examine the practical application of the president's power. Although the main body of law rests upon legislation duly passed by the congress, the president and his staff have been the authors of most of it. He can, however, bypass the congress and effect far-reaching and major governmental changes without consulting that body. His power to do so comes from such constitutional provisions as those giving him the right to create and suppress public services. He has had a free hand in such important matters as the creation of new executive departments. The ministries of agriculture and livestock, health and social welfare, justice, and mines and hydrocarbons have all been created by executive decree since 1936.

Another common use of the presidential decree power extends to the creation of "autonomous institutes." These quasi-governmental bodies possess definite legal personalities, their own property, and considerable independent authority. All are endowed initially with large sums of public monies. Examples of such concerns are the Venezuela Development Corporation, the Venezuelan Airmail Line, the National Agrarian Institute, and University City. The most recent use of this power was the decree by President Betancourt on December 30, 1960, setting up the Venezuelan Corporation of Guayana with full power to develop a gigantic industrial complex in the Guayanan area of Venezuela.

Apart from the more common use of the decree as a regulatory device, the power is frequently used by the president to provide additional credits to various departments outside of those authorized in the national budget.[16] Because the government adheres steadfastly to the principle of a balanced budget and because it always spends more than it plans, recourse to the additional credit power has been necessary. In practice, the discretionary power which the president enjoys with respect to the expenditure of public funds depends solely on whether the revenues received during the year are larger than those anticipated in the budget. Almost invariably large cash surpluses accumulate in the treasury as a result of the consistent underestimation of the national revenue. Since 1944 the president, acting through the minister of finance, has had the power to transfer this surplus each month into a Special Reserve Fund from which he may decree expenditures not authorized in the budget. It is not unusual at all for the executive to authorize additional expenses totaling 40 percent of the original budget for the fiscal year.

So greatly was this power abused by Gómez and others, and so greatly did it contribute to the enrichment and power of the president, that the Constitution of 1961 attempts to place some restrictions upon it. Today the president must have the prior authorization of the two chambers of congress in joint session (or that of the delegated committee of congress if it is not in session) to decree extra expenditures.

One further use of the decree power should be noted. Like many other Latin American executives the president of Venezuela may suspend constitutional guarantees, either totally or in part, when in his opinion and that of his council of ministers, situations arise which could create national or international emergencies. The power to suspend parts of the constitution has been an effective weapon in the hands of presidents who have used it to harass their political enemies. Limited suspensions in times of unrest and revolt or total suspensions of the constitution following violent changes of power have had a paralyzing effect on the political life of the nation. Curtailment of liberties usually extends to such things as inviolability of mail, residence, and records, liberty of travel, speech, press and assembly, freedom from arbitrary arrest, and the right not to be held *incomunicado*.

In order to deal effectively with the terrorist activities inspired by Castro supporters and Communists, which had plagued his regime since it took office in 1958, President Betancourt found it necessary to suspend certain rights guaranteed by the constitution. The restrictions were decreed in November 1960; except for brief periods they were in suspension until the end of his term.

The National Congress

The national congress of Venezuela is bicameral. Under a law which took effect in 1964, congress is elected by direct vote in the proportion of two senators from each state and the Federal District, and one deputy for every 50,000 persons, plus one for every fraction over 25,000 in each state. Every state, regardless of population, is entitled to two deputies.

The Constitution of 1961 specifically forbids any appointed public official from seeking election to the congress until three months after he has ceased to hold such an office. The provision is in recognition of the fact that past congresses were composed largely of public officials of all categories, who, as appointees of the president or his agent the state governor, were less than independent of the executive branch of the government.

In its initial session congress elects its president and vice-president as well as presiding officers for both chambers. Permanent subject-matter committees are set up by both legislative bodies to study in advance the matters to be considered by them. When congress is in recess, a delegated committee consisting of the president and vice-president of congress and twenty-one additional members drawn from both houses is empowered to appoint special commissions, authorize the national president to act on matters of public interest, approve or disapprove extraordinary budget appropriations, and exercise the investigative power of the congress; in short, to provide the executive with the legislative authority he needs for certain acts.

Bills may be introduced by any three senators or deputies, by the national executive, the delegated committee, the permanent committees, and, on judicial matters, by the supreme court of justice.

Congress may legislate on all matters within the competence of the national government, except in those areas reserved to the executive. All laws passed by it must be promulgated by the president within ten days, unless he asks congress to reconsider parts or all of the bill. The congress may override the president's objections by a two-thirds majority of the members present, in which case he must promulgate the law within five days. If the president feels the proposed law is unconstitutional he may ask the advice of the supreme court of justice, which must render an opinion within ten days.

Executive-Legislative Relations

Venezuelan presidents have demonstrated considerable reluctance to observe the functional separation of powers decreed by the various constitutions. As a result, the initiative of congress (an "assembly of employees") was for decades limited to erecting statues of or conferring honors and titles on the omnipotent executive. Venezuelan students are generally agreed that the principal role of past legislatures has been to enact into law, speedily and without modification, all proposals that came to it from the president. "Everyone knows," said a Gómez congressman, "that orders accompanied every bill not to change so much as a comma." Such important measures as the budget were passed year after year with very insignificant changes or none at all. Indeed, the Constitution of 1953 specified that the budget would go into effect on July 1, with or without the approval of congress. Such a provision, of course, made a mockery of congress's supposed power of the purse.

Because of the executive orientation of Venezuelan government and politics, congressmen have rarely made use of their prerogative to initiate legislation on their own, for without prior executive approval it would come to nought. On the other hand, recommendation by the president ensured the enactment of any legislation.

This situation has changed somewhat since the inauguration of President Betancourt in 1958. The subservience of congress to the president has not prevailed to such a degree since then. In 1962 President Betancourt found himself in a situation unique for a Venezuelan president: he was faced with a divided congress. One wing of his badly split Acción Democrática, in coalition with COPEI, had a majority of seats in the senate, but the chamber of deputies was in the hands of defecting members of his party and other groups openly hostile to him.

Relations between the congress and President Betancourt were unsatisfactory, and so were the relations between the two houses of congress. The opposition-controlled chamber of deputies even had the temerity to censure a minister for an executive act, a course of action almost unheard of in a Venezuela accustomed to no nonsense from congress. The chamber, in 1962, continued to show an independent spirit by undertaking to investigate the detention of state legislators and a national deputy by the national government for subversive activities, the alleged shooting and torturing of prisoners, and the minister of education's two-year suspension of teachers from their posts for participating in demonstrations. In another independent act the congress as a whole, on April 6, 1962, voted to restore constitutional liberties.

The Judiciary

Although Venezuela is technically a federal state, the judicial system is entirely controlled by the national government; hence there are no state courts. Jurisdiction in Venezuela embraces civil, mercantile, penal, labor, fiscal, and military cases. The first three categories are exercised by ordinary courts, the latter by special courts. Some of the ordinary courts have competence in all three categories; others may be assigned only one area, or two.

The Supreme Court of Justice

At the apex of the ordinary judiciary is the Supreme Court of Justice, which functions through three chambers, each of which deals with distinct types of cases. The jurisdiction of the court extends to conflicts in which one party is the Republic, a state, or a municipality; to the determination of the constitutionality of executive and legislative acts on both state and national levels; to jurisdictional disputes between courts; and to cases rising on appeal from the lower courts. It is made up of nine judges, appointed by congress for staggered terms of nine years.

The Superior Courts

Beneath the supreme court are the Superior Courts of which there is at least one in each of the seventeen judicial districts into which Venezuela is divided. Superior courts have original jurisdiction in cases involving complaints about the administration of justice within their districts and they hear cases rising on appeal. They also admit lawyers to the bar.

The Inferior Courts

The inferior courts consist of Courts of Instruction which draw up indictments; Municipal Courts in every town with original jurisdiction in cases involving minor sums and in civil registry matters; District Courts with both original and appellate jurisdiction in cases involving sums fixed by law; and Courts of First Instance, which resemble our own federal district courts.

Public Policy

The Platform of Acción Democrática

Since AD is the party whose policies are being translated into realities at the time of writing, it might be useful to note a number of the points outlined in the party program. AD advocates a program of land distribution, development of Venezuela's natural resources in ways more beneficial to Venezuelans, steady improvement in the welfare of the underprivileged classes, encouragement of industrialization and diversification of both industry and agriculture, the attraction of immigrants, expansion of educational facilities and opportunities, closer cooperation with other democratic regimes in Latin America, the repudiation of despotic governments, effective participation in the United Nations, and a strengthening of the Organization of American States as a dynamic agency of hemispheric cooperation.

The principal challenge to the Betancourt regime was that of making life more tolerable for the ordinary Venezuelan, particularly for the mass of propertyless peasants.

AD entered its sixth consecutive year of power in 1964. In spite of numerous civil disturbances and efforts to overthrow it, it has been able to implement those policies in significant ways. Since the Leoni administration which took power in 1964 is committed to the pursuit of the same goals as the government of President Betancourt which it succeeded, no distinction between the policies of the two will be made below.

Agrarian Reform

The Law of Agrarian Reform was promulgated on March 5, 1960. The statute provides for the expropriation, with due compensation, of unused or inefficiently used land. A National Agrarian Institute is authorized to use nationally owned land and to purchase other property from private individuals and from state and local governments. It pays 30 percent in cash for the land and the rest in long-term bonds. The Institute then resells the land on a long-term repayment basis to peasants who have made proper application for it.

The government varies its methods of agrarian reform. In some areas it attempts to persuade farmers to organize cooperatives, and in others individual ownership is the basis of reform. In the words of President Betancourt, these variations depend "on the different circumstances offered by a country with a million square kilometers of area, with valleys, mountains, plains, with a geography that is so complex and with regional situations which vary sharply from one zone to another." [17]

The Betancourt government purchased and redistributed over 3 million acres of land to more than 56,700 farming families. It hoped to settle at least 100,000 more families on their own land before the expiration of its term of office in 1964. However, fewer than 90,000 applications for the land were received and 35,000 of these were for land unsuited for agriculture. Difficulties have arisen over titles and ownership, for some of the peasants have received land that had not yet been surveyed. Nevertheless, the government made substantial progress in this area of its program.

Agricultural Policy

The government of President Leoni now seeks to make Venezuela self-sufficient in a number of food products, thereby lessening its dependence on the import market. It hopes to do away with the seasonal market glut by long-range planning and controlled distribution. In addition to careful planning, the government has tried to stimulate the raising of poultry and the production of new crops: corn, potatoes, and fruit trees, among others. During the first three years of AD administration over 47,000 acres of irrigated land was added to the agricultural sector, and 3,726 miles of vital farm-to-market roads were either built or repaired. Several national banks provide funds for the assistance of farmers and cattlemen.

Labor Policy

Relations between management and labor are regulated in detail by the Law of 1947, enacted when AD was in power the first time. It specifies an eight-hour day and a forty-eight-hour week, with adequate overtime compensation. The national executive may, through an appointed labor-management commission, decree minimum wages in specific industries. Detailed provisions spell out responsibilities and compensation for accident and occupational diseases. All enterprises are required to distribute 10 percent of their annual net profits to their employees at the end of the fiscal year. Liberal severance allowances are mandatory. At least 75 percent of all employees in a business concern must be Venezuelans. Labor has the right to bargain collectively and to organize, but no one may be compelled to join a union. The right to strike is guaranteed under conditions set forth in the law, but strikes may not be initiated until labor has exhausted the conciliation procedures established by law.

The principal concern of the government in the area of labor policy is the large number of unemployed persons in the labor force. Over 280,000 persons, or 12 percent of Venezuelan workers, are unemployed. The government has called for the creation of 100,000 new jobs per year for the next five years in order to keep up with the expanding labor force.

Housing

At the end of 1963 some 40 percent of the people of Venezuela lived in substandard dwellings, and over 300,000 persons in Caracas were ill-housed or not housed at all. The national housing shortage was estimated at 700,000 living units. To relieve this situation the government has initiated a large-scale construction program and since 1959 has built 18,400 low-cost units. At least 65,000 living units a year will be needed for the next twenty years, however, to keep abreast of the requirements of the burgeoning population.

Education

Excellent progress is being made in the field of education, primarily in the area of reducing illiteracy. According to the government, 3.7 percent of the Gross National Product is spent on education. An adult education program and free distribution of books to rural centers has contributed to a reduction in illiteracy from over 50 percent of the population to 21 percent according to official figures. Despite an extensive school construction program (enough classrooms to accommodate 200,000 students in three years) there still remains a 50 percent deficiency in classrooms. Today, 75 percent of all children of school age are in school, however, as compared with 31 percent in 1945.

Oil and Mining

The Leoni administration hopes to reduce Venezuela's excessive dependence on oil by a more adequate exploitation and development of its nickel and iron deposits. Although it does not contemplate nationalization of the oil industry, the policy of the government may be described as one of "Venezuelization." The policy calls for greater oil production and greater use of Venezuelan laborers, technicians, and materials. The government announced in 1962 that it would no longer grant concessions to foreign companies and asked them to develop the extensive holdings they now possess. An autonomous institute, the Venezuelan Oil Corporation, has been set up to supervise Venezuela's own efforts in the oil industry. Foreign companies must now deal with this corporation, which had four wells of its own in operation at the end of 1962. Venezuela is a member of the Organization of Petroleum-Exporting Countries, which is searching for ways to protect the interests of the member states in the world market.

Industrial Policy

In the field of industry the Venezuelan government endeavors to stimulate diversification, and in 1961 it registered 6,921 new industrial establishments. The government plays a major role in planning for the industrial development of Venezuela and is implementing a plan which seeks to avoid a profusion of competing industries which, in the opinion of its experts, would result in an inefficient use of investment capital. Foreign investment is welcome, not only in industry, but also in mining and agricultural ventures—in short, in any undertaking which will create wealth. Investment is attracted through such devices as liberal exemptions from import duties on essential materiel requirements.

Immigration

The present administration of Venezuela is following a policy of encouraging immigrants with skills in agriculture, stockbreeding, industry, and mechanics. It will not admit persons who are not of the white race, however, nor those who have mental, moral, or physical disabilities. Those who are accepted are entitled to maintenance by the government for a limited time, free transportation within the country to their destination, duty-free entry of their personal belongings and, at the discretion of the National Executive, free plots of land on the same basis as Venezuelans.

Foreign Policy

In its relations with other Latin American countries, Venezuela under President Betancourt followed a policy of seeking hemispheric unity and the consolidation of democratic regimes. It consistently took a dim view of dictatorial governments. In an outburst of enthusiasm over the downfall of Batista, the Venezuelan government congratulated the new Cuban regime, but relations between the two countries progressively deteriorated and Venezuela supported a 1960 resolution of the Organization of American States which implicitly condemned the Castro regime. It broke diplomatic relations with Cuba in 1961 and voted with thirteen other countries to exclude Cuba from the inter-American system.

Venezuela also severed diplomatic relations with Rafael Trujillo's Dominican Republic and in the 1960 meeting of the OAS charged that country with genocide and unsuccessfully petitioned that it, too, be excluded from the organization. In 1962 the Venezuelan government announced that it would no longer recognize any regime which came to power through illegal means and asked the OAS, again unsuccessfully, to investigate the military seizure of power in Peru. Similarly, it withdrew its ambassador from other states in which military seizures of power took place.

In 1962 Venezuela reopened the issue of the British Guiana boundary by placing before the United Nations its nineteenth-century claim to two-thirds of the territory of British Guiana, which it claimed was improperly awarded to Great Britain by the arbitration tribunal of 1899.

Many of the socio-economic reforms being carried out or planned by the Betancourt administration are consonant with the general aims of the Alliance for Progress, and therefore Venezuela has shared extensively in the financial benefits of the program. By the end of 1961 it had negotiated over $150 million in loans from the United States and international lending agencies to help further its internal improvements.

NOTES FOR CHAPTER XII

1. Victor A. Belaúnde, *Bolívar and the Political Thought of the Spanish American Revolution* (1938), p. 132.
2. Edwin Lieuwen, *Venezuela* (1961), p. 35.
3. Carlos Siso, *La Formación del Pueblo Venezolano* (1959), II, p. 280. A dying soldier described federalism as a "thing so great that it ranks after God." *Idem.*
4. For a detailed study of the constitutional assembly see my article, "The 1952 Venezuelan Elections: A Lesson for 1957," *Western Political Quarterly*, Sep. 1957, pp. 451-558.
5. *New York Times*, June 12, 1955, p. 11.
6. *Time*, Feb. 28, 1955, p. 29.
7. The material in this section and in the section dealing with the national executive has appeared in substantially the same form in my article, "Executive Power in Venezuela," in the *American Political Science Review* (June, 1956) and is reprinted and paraphrased here with the permission of the editor.
8. *Tratado de Derecho Constitucional Venezolano* (1945), II, p. 401. Military control of the government was of course the dominant feature of the government from 1948 to 1958. At an earlier time in Venezuelan history military men made up most of the membership of Congress. In 1873, for example, 19 of the 30 senators and 50 of the 70 deputies were generals!
9. Pedro Manuel Arcaya, *The Gómez Regime in Venezuela* (1936), p. 59.
10. David León Ramón, *Hombres y Sucesos de Venezuela* (1952), p. 15.
11. The material in this section has appeared in substantially the same form in the reference cited in Note 4 and is reprinted and paraphrased here with the permission of the editors.
12. *Hispanic American Report*, Nov. 1962, Vol. 15, No. 9, p. 821.
13. *Historia Constitucional de Venezuela* (1907), I, pp. 84-85.
14. Juan Penzini Hernández, *Democracia habemos* (1939), p. 265.
15. The congress of 1856 created a territorial division embracing 21 states. In 1864 the number was 20; 1881, 9; 1899, 20; 1904, 13; 1909, 20.
16. From 1914 to 1942 a total of $362 million was added to the original budgets in 1,714 separate decrees.
17. *The Christian Science Monitor*, April 12, 1962, p. 13c.

SELECTED BIBLIOGRAPHY

Pedro Manuel Arcaya, *The Gómez Regime in Venezuela*, Sun Printing Press, Washington, D.C., 1936.

Olga Briceño, *Cocks and Bulls in Caracas*, Houghton Mifflin, Boston, 1945.

Clinton J. Daniel, *Gómez, Tyrant of the Andes*, Morrow, New York, 1936.

Alfred P. Jankus, *Venezuela, Land of Opportunity*, Pageant, New York, 1956.

Edwin Lieuwen, *Venezuela*, Oxford University Press, New York, 1961.

William D. Marland, *Venezuela through Its History*, Crowell, New York, 1954.

Pan American Union, *A Statement of the Laws of Venezuela*, Washington, D.C., 1962.

Royal Institute of International Affairs, *Venezuela: A Brief Political and Economic Survey*, London, 1958.

Mary Watters, *A History of the Church in Venezuela, 1810-1930*, University of North Carolina Press, Chapel Hill, 1933.

George S. Wise, *Caudillo: A Portrait of Antonio Guzmán Blanco*, Columbia University Press, New York, 1951.

Raymond A. Wohlrabe, *The Land and People of Venezuela*, Lippincott, Philadelphia, 1959.

XIII

George I. Blanksten

ECUADOR

THE POLITICS OF INSTABILITY

"Ecuador," one of the country's recent presidents used to say with some justification, "is a very difficult country to govern." [1] Although it is one of the smallest of the Latin-American countries—the national population is estimated at only 4,300,000—Ecuador has been endowed with more political problems than have most countries many times its size. Prominent among these problems is a marked lack of political integration. The people of Ecuador are divided among themselves in a number of ways. These divisions are deep enough to separate the people in groupings which are often isolated from each other. Three dimensions of this lack of national integration set the social and economic backgrounds against which the political patterns of Ecuador have developed. These dimensions are, first, the vertical, characterized by a rigid class system; next, the horizontal, expressed through a vigorous political regionalism; and finally, the rural-urban cleavage, sharply distinguishing life in the cities of Ecuador from the customs and usages of the rural areas.

The Society and Culture of Ecuador

The Class System

The vertical dimension of Ecuador's lack of political integration is expressed through the rigid three-level class system. The three groups in the system are the so-called "whites," about 15 percent of the population; the *cholos* or *mestizos*, approximately 25 percent; and the Indians, a little more than half of the population. For the popular mind these designations often bear a racial connotation. But the bases of differentiation among these groups are social rather than biological. An individual's way of life rather than the physical characteristics of his body determines the class with which he is identified. In countries like Ecuador the question of race is not a problem in the European sense of the word.

The so-called whites constitute a ruling class. This Spanish-speaking group dress much like business and professional people in the United States. Ecuador's large individual landholders are whites, as are the bulk of the political leaders, government officials, and even most of the voters. Considerable prestige attaches to the white, who is, to his face at least, treated with great respect and deference by the *cholos* and, more especially, by the Indians. Most of the country's formally educated people are whites, who enjoy a virtual monopoly on the liberal professions and the higher ranks in the army.

The *cholo* or *mestizo* class represents a fusion or joining together of white and Indian ways of life. The population dynamics of Ecuador, characterized by continued fusion of the groups in the country, suggest that this group is an expanding force in the country's national life. As such, the *cholo*—sometimes called the Ecuadoran of tomorrow—may well come to preside over an eventual synthesizing of the cultural elements today still rigidly separated from each other by the class system.

At the bottom of the social scale are the Indians, about half the population. The whites regard the Indians as a subject and abject race; and it is in the separation of the Indian from what is called the national life that the rigidity of the class system of Ecuador finds its sharpest expression. A complete social separation between the Indian and the white is one of the most marked cultural characteristics of the nation. Different customs, dress, and values all tend to isolate them from each other unless brought together for the transaction of some business in which one finds the other indispensable. Friendless and hopeless in a basically hostile social environment, the Ecuadoran Indian frequently impresses the foreign observer as being a maladjusted and suppressed person.

Regionalism

The lack of political integration in Ecuador expresses itself horizontally through political regionalism. The Andes Mountains, running roughly from north to south through Ecuador in two more or less parallel ranges, divide the continental territory of the republic into three regions—the Coast, bounded on the west by the Pacific Ocean and on the east by the western cordillera of the Andes; the Sierra, the highlands nestled in between the eastern and the western ranges; and the Oriente, Ecuador's share of the Amazon jungle, lying east of the mountains. Ecuadoran politics often reflects a regional struggle for power between the Coast and the Sierra. The Oriente plays virtually no role in this; neither do the Galápagos Islands, a fourth part of Ecuador lying between five and seven hundred miles off the country's Pacific coast.

The region known as the Coast contains about one-third of the national population. Social and political liberalism, as manifested in Ecuador, has for the most part been centered in this region. "The Coast is open toward the outside, toward novelty, toward foreign ways," one observer has pointed out. "Its cities are modern cities. . . . Perennial unrest agitates it, the perennial change of ideas and fervors. It is the open eye of Ecuador, always in search of what other peoples have to make them stronger, richer, and happier. From the Coast comes liberalism as action and as government." [2]

Guayaquil, Ecuador's largest city and major seaport, is located in this region.

The Sierra, the high valley cradled between the eastern and western ranges of the Andes, is larger than the Coast and contains about 60 percent of the people of Ecuador. Traditionally, the Sierra has been the country's stronghold of social and political conservatism. Hoary traditions and social usages, exaggerated formality in speech and conduct, and colonial customs and practices remain very much alive in the region. It has been said that it "lives an intimate, silent, and solemn life: its cities are syntheses of Ecuadoran history, as are its customs and its mores; the colonial spirit still vibrates in its temples. . . . In the inter-Andean peoples tradition remains intact, with all its beauty and pomp, with its hates and its beliefs, its fears and its enthusiasms." [3] Quito, the national capital, is in the Sierra.

Although the other two sections of Ecuador—the Oriente and the Galápagos Islands—are interesting in many ways, they do not play an active part in political regionalism; both are largely undeveloped and underpopulated. A group of Oriente Indians, the *jívaros*, have gained some fame because of their fascinating custom of severing and shrinking human heads. The Galápagos, for their part, boast a remarkable history of visitors—Charles Darwin, Herman Melville, the celebrated pirate William Dampier, and Alexander Selkirk, who was the prototype of Robinson Crusoe, to speak of no others. Despite these distinctions, the jungle and the islands play negligible roles in Ecuadoran national life. Sparsely populated, the Oriente contains only about 5 percent of the country's people, and the picturesque Galápagos account for less than 1 percent.

As a result of a military campaign by Peru in 1940, Ecuador was forced to see the victorious Peruvians take control of disputed territory on the Amazon, approximately equal in area to all the remaining national territory of Ecuador, claims and counterclaims over which dated back to Colonial times. Bitterness over the defeat contributed to the subsequent overthrow of Dr. Carlos Alberto Arroyo del Río, who was president at the time of the inauguration of hostilities. The establishment of Peruvian control over the disputed territory is still actively resented, and relations with Peru remain poor; there are also periodic outbreaks of hostility towards Argentina, Brazil, Chile, and the United States, the states which signed the Rio Protocol guaranteeing control by Peru of the disputed area.

Rural-Urban Differences

The sharp cleavage between life in the larger Ecuadoran cities, on the one hand, and on the other, the customs and usages of the rural areas constitutes a third dimension of the lack of political integration of the country. In general, the cities are European-like and modern while the rural areas, especially in the Sierra, live a more traditional, slowly changing, somewhat feudal and backward life.

Rural life is essentially traditional and indigenous. Changing slowly, it is —particularly in the Sierra—the chief remaining stronghold of Indian culture. The Indian is predominantly an agricultural worker. He either lives on a large landed estate, an hacienda owned by a white; owns his own small parcel of land; or is a member of a community which collectively owns and farms its land. The soil is the foundation of the Indian economy: an Indian separated from the land is like a disembodied spirit. Though the earth is the center of his universe, the Indian has little interest in such things as "having title" to the land. The structure of rural landownership—vast haciendas held by a small white landowning aristocracy—underlies the essentially feudal nature of the rural economy, with the Indian frequently occupying a position strongly reminiscent of the serf of medieval Europe. "The servitude which the landowner has established is horrible," the author of a major study of the Ecuadoran Indian has concluded. "All the literature concerned with the social problems of Ecuador and the reform of prevailing conditions is a story of the hardships suffered by the agricultural worker at the hands of the *patrón* and a protest. . . . The hacienda has established a true slavery." [4]

Life in the major cities, on the other hand, is more Europeanized and modern. For most foreign visitors, it should be pointed out, the story of Ecuador is a tale of two cities, Quito and Guayaquil. The national capital, sometimes called the City of Light or the City of Eternal Spring, has historically been the political nerve center of the Sierra. Guayaquil—the Pearl of the Pacific—has performed a similar function on the Coast. Political regionalism, in large measure based on these municipalities, has meant the distribution of national political influence between them. The municipal council at Quito often provides the political leadership of the Sierra, with the Guayaquil council frequently doing the same for the Coast. The autonomy of Quito and Guayaquil is especially obvious and is not enjoyed on a comparable scale by the other municipalities of the republic. A few of the older cities—Cuenca, Ambato, Riobamba, and Latacunga—enjoy something of political autonomy, but to a lesser degree than do Quito and Guayaquil. In more recent times, economic development has tended to take hold in the cities more readily than in the rural areas, thus intensifying the gulf between rural and urban life. Accordingly, serious economic as well as cultural and political differences underscore this third dimension of the lack of integration of Ecuadoran national life.

Political History

Ecuador's political history has been both colorful and dramatic; unfortunately, only its highlights can be touched upon here. What is now Ecuador was a part of the Inca Empire when the Spanish *conquistadores*, under the initial leadership of Francisco Pizarro, arrived early in the 1530's. After a number of tragic struggles with the Indians, Spanish colonial power was established at Quito in 1534. "The founding of our city of Quito took place, then, forty-two years after the discovery of America," Ecuador's leading historian has recorded. "Charles V and his insane mother Doña Juana ruled Spain, Pope Clement VII governed the Church, and Henry VIII had begun in England his persecution of the Catholics." [5]

During the Spanish colonial period, Ecuador's political orientation alternated like a pendulum, between Peru to the south and Colombia to the north. Initially, Ecuador was considered a part of the Viceroyalty of New Castile, which was created, with its capital at Lima, in 1543. In the eighteenth century, however, the Emperor Philip V embarked upon a program of administrative reform for the overseas colonies. During the course of this program he established in 1717 the Viceroyalty of New Granada, carved out of the northern part of New Castile, with the capital of the new viceroyalty established at Bogotá. Ecuador was considered to be a part of New Granada, and New Castile was abolished in 1724. However, it was re-established, with a new name—the Viceroyalty of Peru—in 1739. Since then, Ecuador's political orientation has vacillated between north and south, and its boundary with Peru has been uncertain and disputed.

In any case, Ecuador's fate was linked with that of New Granada when the Latin American Wars for Independence against Spain began early in the nineteenth century. What is now Ecuador was known as the Department of the South within Gran Colombia, which dated its independence from 1819, although Spanish military power was not really broken in the area until the decisive Battle of Pichincha in 1824. General Simón Bolívar's Gran Colombia lived a politically tortured existence, centers of disaffection and secessionism being especially strong at Caracas and Quito. In 1830, the year of Bolívar's death, Gran Colombia came to an end when Generals José Antonio Páez and Juan José Flores, placing themselves at the head of secessionist movements at Caracas and Quito, respectively, established the republics of Venezuela and Ecuador.

Since 1830, then, Ecuador has been an independent state. Its political history during that time may be divided roughly into six periods—the era of General Flores, 1830-1845; the beginnings of Ecuadoran nationalism, 1845-1859; the García Moreno period, 1859-1875; a twenty-year period of marked political instability, until 1895; the Radical-Liberal era, 1895-1944; and the post-Radical-Liberal period, since 1944.

The Flores Era

General Juan José Flores, who led the secession from Gran Colombia, became Ecuador's first president in 1830 and remained in power for fifteen years. He was thirty years of age and almost illiterate when he became president. Having an essentially police concept of government, he ruled the country largely by violence. Opposition to President Flores began to form as early as 1833, centered on a strongly nationalist group at Quito which published a periodical called *El Quiteño Libre*. This group formed the nucleus of the revolution which, on March 6, 1845, overthrew the government of General Juan José Flores and drove him into exile.

Nationalist Beginnings

The revolutionists of 1845 endeavored to establish the principle of nationalism. "In Ecuador there are three commanding generals," they had protested during their struggle against Flores. "The commander at Cuenca is a Venezuelan general, at Guayas an Irish general, and at Pichincha an English general. The Inspector General of the Army is a Frenchman. . . . All of the principal officers are foreigners." [6] It was of major significance that Colombians and Venezuelans were for the first time spoken of as foreigners. Ecuadoran nationalism was beginning to be a reality.

The García Moreno Period

The overthrow of the government of President Francisco Robles in 1859 ushered in the most bizarre epoch in Ecuadoran national history. The country was dominated during the ensuing sixteen years by the fabulous Gabriel García Moreno, who remains the most controversial figure in Ecuadoran national life. He is generally regarded as one of the two greatest presidents in the history of the republic. "Every Conservative will tell you that García Moreno was the greatest president and grudgingly admit that Eloy Alfaro was the next greatest," one observer has noted. "Most [Radical] Liberals will say that Eloy Alfaro was the greatest President of Ecuador, but, if they do, will unfailingly admit that García Moreno was second only to him." [7] Between 1859 and 1875, Ecuadoran politics had meaning only as it related to García Moreno. Early in the 1860's he undertook the reformation of the Church in the country. His intense Catholicism led him to seek an extension of rigid hierarchy to the social order, and his concept of the state was essentially authoritarian. For him such concepts as liberty and equality were synonyms for anarchy, and were evils to be eschewed at virtually any cost. During his time religious intolerance became law in Ecuador, Church and State were reunited, and only practicing Roman Catholics were permitted to be citizens. His conservative dictatorship marked the apogee of the political power of the Church in the history of the country.

Political Instability

In 1875 Gabriel García Moreno was struck down by the assassin Faustino Lemus Rayo. The ensuing twenty years were marked by excessive political instability and frequent dictatorship. During this period Ecuador had two constitutions, one written in 1878, the other in 1883. These relaxed the theocratic authoritarianism of the preceding era, although the Church remained the dominant political force in national life.

The Radical-Liberal Era

A new epoch came into being with the significant Radical-Liberal revolution of 1895, led by the remarkable General Eloy Alfaro. During the Radical-Liberal period, which endured until 1944, steps were taken to reduce the political power of the Church. Religious orders were banned in the country, and religious qualifications for the exercise of political and civil rights were terminated. Although Roman Catholicism remained the sole permitted religion, only native-born clergy were allowed to operate in the republic. During the Radical-Liberal era, so-called "revolutions" occurred with decreasing frequency, but the closing years of the period were marked by a sharp deterioration in the integrity of the electoral process.

The Contemporary Period

The remainder of this chapter deals primarily with Ecuadoran politics since the overthrow in 1944 of the government of Dr. Carlos Alberto Arroyo del Río, the last of the Radical-Liberal presidents. As is noted in later pages, the influence of the traditional political parties has declined since 1944, and the Church has regained a portion of its former power.

The Political Process

The operation of Ecuadoran political processes reflects, in large part, the state of the political integration of the society. Political parties, the press, and the interest groups tend to function in ways expressing the class system, the political regionalism, and the rural-urban divisions which are fundamentally representative of Ecuadoran national life.

The system of political parties does not conform to the familiar dichotomy of biparty and multiparty systems. Two major parties—the Conservatives and the Radical-Liberals—exist, to be sure; but neither of these has been in sustained power on a national basis since the Revolution of 1944. Third parties and *ad hoc* parties have played roles of increasing importance in recent decades (see below).

The Conservative Party

This is the oldest party now functioning in Ecuador. Custom and tradition have grown increasingly significant in the operation of the machinery of this organization, one of the country's two major parties. Although rank-and-file members have a greater voice in the decisions of the Conservative than of any other Ecuadoran party, the strength of custom and tradition in general causes the Conservatives to pay great deference to the views and wishes of their old guard leaders. Accordingly, this old guard—persons who have been active as party regulars for a great number of years, and who have been Conservative in terms of their family and regional heritages—plays a dominant part in the life of the organization.

Its strength concentrated in the Sierra, the Conservative Party has long been the political spokesman of the Church, and has claimed Gabriel García Moreno as the party's greatest hero. "Man is essentially a religious being and religion, consequently, is a natural phenomenon," a statement of the political doctrine of the Conservative Party has declared. "The end of man is God, whom he should serve and adore in order to enjoy after death the beatified possession of divinity. . . . The purpose of the state is to facilitate religious action so that its subjects will not lack the necessities of the spirit and will be able to obtain in the next life the happiness which can never be achieved in this." [8] The Conservatives hold that there is an innate right to private property, and that man is civilized insofar as he possesses tradition.

As we have seen, the Conservatives were in power nationally during much of the latter part of the nineteenth century, that is, until the Radical-Liberal Revolution of 1895. Thereafter, and until 1944, the Conservatives were essentially an opposition party. Their strength has been increasing in recent years; indeed, a Conservative president, the first since the 1890's, was elected to office in 1956. President Camilo Ponce Enríquez served out the four-year presidential term which ended in 1960.

The Radical Liberals

The other major party, the Radical Liberals, was in power almost uninterruptedly from 1895 until 1944, but has been substantially weakened since the latter date. Principles formally endorsed by the Radical-Liberal Party include the right to life, liberty of conscience, free expression of thought, liberty of labor, and the right of association. The party has also defended the principle of private ownership of land and other forms of property.

The major doctrinal difference between the Radical Liberals and the Conservatives has revolved around the question of the Church, the Radical Liberals championing the separation of Church and State. The principal difference between the two major parties in terms of regionalism is reflected in the fact that the Conservatives are based in the Sierra while the Radical Liberals are largely the party of the Coast. From the standpoint of the national economy, both parties rest on the institution of land ownership, although the Conservatives do so more exclusively than the Radical Liberals, who have been more interested in the development of trade and industry in Ecuador and the attraction of foreign capital to the country.

It was a Radical-Liberal government, headed by President Carlos Alberto Arroyo del Río, that was overthrown in the Revolution of 1944. Radical-Liberal strength has persistently weakened since then, and many politicians have deserted the party. With the decline in recent years of the two major parties, "third" and "ad hoc" parties have become increasingly important in the national political life of Ecuador.

Third Parties and Ad Hoc Parties

The two chief third parties are the Socialists and the Communists. Founded in 1925, the Socialist Party of Ecuador has been an opposition organization during most of its history. The Socialists are the only party in the country whose formal tables of organization provide for representation of the Indians in the determination of the affairs of the party. Provision is made for "functional representatives" of the Indians in the structure of the Socialist Party. These representatives are not themselves Indians, but many of Ecuador's *indigenistas*—i.e., scholars and other persons interested in the problems of the Indian—have become affiliated with the Socialists on the ground that this is the only national party indicating a concern with the problem of the Indian.

The Communist Party of Ecuador is small and generally weak, although it has become increasingly active since the Castro Revolution in Cuba. In domestic Ecuadoran politics, the Communists have sometimes cooperated with the Socialists, but in matters of foreign affairs the Communists have consistently urged Ecuadoran collaboration with the Soviet Union and with Castro's Cuba.

Ad hoc parties—even more than the third parties—have been of growing importance in Ecuadoran politics in recent decades. It is these, rather than the major parties or even the Socialists and Communists, which have exercised power nationally on an increasing scale since the revolution of 1944. *Ad hoc* parties are extremely fluid and unstable organizations which are created for the purpose of achieving short-range political objectives and which disappear when those ends have been accomplished or defeated. Such parties exist in varying numbers at different times. It is normally impossible—and unrewarding—to determine the exact number of these organizations operating at any given moment. Entities such as these prompted the inspired observation that "nothing is simpler than to found a political party. To form a political party only three people and one object are necessary: a president, a vice-president, a secretary, and a rubber stamp. The party can get along even without the vice-president and the secretary. . . . There have been cases in which the existence of only the rubber stamp has been sufficient."[9] These organizations may be of the extreme right or the extreme left, and are occasionally located near the center of the political spectrum. Rightist "ad hoc" organizations have been typified by the Ecuadoran National Revolutionary Union (U.N.R.E.) and the Ecuadoran Nationalist Revolutionary Association (A.R.N.E.); leftist groups have been the Socialist Revolutionary Vanguard and the Popular Union; and the National Civic Democratic Movement (M.C.D.N.) was a recent example of a transitory party standing closer to the political center. Organizations such as these have played important parts in many of the post-1944 governments of Ecuador.

The Press

The Ecuadoran press is largely urban; most of the country's major newspapers are published in Quito and Guayaquil. The chief papers published at Quito are *El Comercio* (founded in 1905), often representing governmental and commercial interests; *El Día* (1913); *El Debate* (1937); *Últimas Notícias* (1938); *La Patria* (1942), a pro-clerical paper; and *La Tierra* (1945), the Socialist organ. The major dailies published at Guayaquil are *El Telégrafo* (1884), *El Universo* (1921), and *La Prensa* (1923). While all three are considered to be Radical-Liberal journals, *El Telégrafo* is, in general, the most authoritative and the most commercially oriented of the Radical-Liberal papers of the port city.

Interest Groups

In general, three broad types of interest groups function in Ecuadoran politics. These are institutional, associational, and nonassociational groups.[10] Institutional groups are formally constituted agencies, or segments of them, with established roles in the political system, roles usually recognized and generally accepted. Three such institutional interest groups are significant in the Ecuadoran political pattern. The first of these is the Roman Catholic Church. Its relationship to the Conservative Party has already been noted. It need only be added that, in contemporary times, there is no Latin American country in which the Church is more active politically than it is in Ecuador.

A second institutional interest group of importance in Ecuador is the army. Textbooks used in the country's military schools teach that "the last step in a military career is the presidency of the republic," [11] and over 30 percent of the presidents of Ecuador have been army officers. An emphasis on militarism is evident almost everywhere in the Sierra and the Coast. Military parades, complete with fixed bayonets and blaring bands playing in the plaintive five-tone minor scale of most Ecuadoran music, are held at virtually the slightest provocation, whether the occasion be one of the republic's numerous national holidays or the presentation of the credentials of a newly arrived diplomat. Although a recent study indicates that the armed forces of Ecuador are becoming somewhat less political than formerly, they still operate as a major interest group in the country's politics.[12]

There is some evidence that government workers also constitute an institutional interest group in Ecuador. However, little is concretely known about this, as studies of bureaucracy and the process of bureaucratization are only being begun in Latin America at this time. Ecuador does not have a nonpolitical civil service, and government employees are a politically active interest group. Systematic study of this phenomenon remains to be undertaken in the country.[13]

Associational interest groups may be defined as consciously organized associations which lie outside the formal structure of government and which nevertheless include the performance of political functions among their objectives. A number of groups of this type play major roles in the politics of Ecuador. Associations of landowners provide significant illustrations; these groups, of course, wield political as well as economic power. Organized labor also functions as an associational interest group. This group is still relatively small in Ecuador, but it seems likely that it will grow in size and influence as the economic development of the country progresses. Student, professional, and veterans' associations provide additional examples of such groups active in national politics.

Finally, there are the nonassociational interest groups. These are not formally or consciously organized. Indeed, they may be regarded more as latent or potential than as currently functioning political groups. In Ecuador nonassociational interests tend to coalesce around such symbols as class, status, ethnic group, and region. Classes, of course, are not formally or consciously organized groups; yet significant political interests arise from them. Political interests similarly coalesce around such unorganized groups as the Indians and the *cholos*, the *costeños* and the *serranos*.

Ecuadoran "Revolutions"

Ecuadoran politics are generally regarded as being among the most unstable in Latin America. So-called revolutions are fairly frequent in the country. Governments are frequently changed by other than constitutional means, but these revolutions are usually not accompanied by fundamental changes in the social or political order. In the typical Ecuadoran revolution, the changes are restricted to the replacement of the president and his immediate aides, the basic political system remaining intact. An old Ecuadoran saying has it that Independence Day is observed as the anniversary of the "last day of despotism and the first day of the same thing." [14]

Basically, the typical Ecuadoran revolution springs from two major considerations. The first relates to the nature of the country's written constitutions. Fundamentally, these revolutions are violations of constitutions; in Ecuador, these documents are peculiarly susceptible of defiance. Their texts tend to be normative or anticipatory—expressions of what constitution-writers hope will eventually come to pass rather than of what is or can be in actuality. The typical revolution is often merely a statement that tomorrow's ideals have not yet been achieved.

Secondly, constitutional fragility is aggravated by such diverse forces among the whites as *personalismo* and family rivalries, regionalism, and other conflicts of intraclass interests, sometimes translated into doctrinal and ideological terms. These conflicts are frequently sufficiently disruptive to give the *coup de grâce* to a weak and unworkable constitution.[15] They are normally followed by the promulgation of a new—and equally weak and unworkable—constitution, with the political system, fundamentally unchanged, settling down to await its next "revolution."

Governmental Institutions

One consequence of Ecuador's chronic political instability is the fact that the country has had no fewer than fifteen written constitutions since 1830. Despite this great number, the basic structure of government has remained relatively constant. On the national level, Ecuador has clung to the presidential system of government, characterized by the division of powers among the executive, legislative, and judicial branches of government familiar in the United States.

The executive branch is headed by an officer called the President of the Republic. Under the Constitution of 1946, currently in force but due to be replaced in 1965 by a new constitution written under the auspices of the junta emanating from the military seizure of power of July 1963, the president is popularly elected for a four-year term of office. Owing to problems of political instability, most presidents are unable to remain in office for the entire four years; indeed, the average Ecuadoran president serves for 2.74 years. Presidents are ineligible for immediate re-election. Should a president desire to occupy office for another term, the constitution requires that he spend at least one four-year period out of office before he is eligible to present himself for re-election. According to the constitution, the powers of the president of Ecuador are similar to those of the president of the United States.

A vice-president is popularly elected at the same time, and for the same term of office, as the president. The vice-president presides over the senate, voting only in case of a tie. Theoretically, the vice-president succeeds the president if the latter is unable to finish his term, but this has actually happened only twice in the history of the republic. Curiously enough, the same president, Dr. José María Velasco Ibarra, was involved in both instances. Vice-President Mariano Suárez Veintimilla replaced him in 1947, and Vice-President Carlos Julio Arosemena succeeded him in 1961 (see Recent Ecuadoran Politics, below).

The President of the Republic is assisted by a group of eight ministers, appointed by him, through whom the executive powers and duties are administered. Each of the ministers is the chief of an executive agency of government called a ministry. These government agencies are the ministries of government, foreign relations, public education, national defense, public works and communications, social welfare, national economy, and the treasury. Together these eight ministries employ approximately 50,000 government workers.

The legislative branch of the national government is bicameral, being composed of a senate and a chamber of deputies. Senators are elected for four-year terms, and implement two principles of representation in the senate. First, there are "provincial" senators, with a territorial basis for representation; in addition to these, there are a number of "functional" senators, representing the major economic, professional, and occupational groups of Ecuador. So far as the other house is concerned, members of the chamber of deputies are elected for two-year terms on a more simple distribution-by-population basis. "Each Province will elect one Deputy for every 50,000 inhabitants, and, if there remains an excess of 25,000 or more, it will elect another Deputy," the Constitution declares. "Every Province, except the Archipelago of Columbus [Galápagos Islands], will elect at least two Deputies, even though it may not have 50,000 inhabitants." [16] The constitutional powers of the Ecuadoran congress are roughly similar to those of the congress of the United States. However, in actual practice there are many differences between the two bicameral legislatures, owing principally to the weaker legislative organization of Ecuadoran political parties and the stronger role in Ecuador of the executive vis-à-vis the other two branches of national government.

The judicial branch of government in Ecuador is composed of four levels of courts. These are the fifteen-man supreme court; eight superior courts, each located in a judicial district; fifteen provincial courts, that is, one in each of the provinces of the Sierra and the Coast; and about eighty cantonal courts existing on local levels of government. The court system of Ecuador administers code, or "Roman", law rather than common law. Accordingly, the function of the judiciary is to find and apply law rather than to create it. Ecuadoran courts thus have a more passive role in the constitutional system than courts in the United States, where the common-law tradition assigns a more active and creative part to the judiciary in the maintenance of the overall constitutional system.

Constitutionally speaking, governments may be internally organized in any of three theoretically possible ways. The national or central government may have unlimited legal power over all territory within the state, in which case it is said that the organization is unitary; political authority may be divided by the constitution between self-governing parts and the central whole, when the state is federal; or legal power may belong to parts which are loosely associated through a weak central organ, in which case the arrangement is called confederate. Like most of the Latin American countries, Ecuador is a unitary state. The national government, according to the constitution, virtually exercises the power of life and death over the regional and local units of government.

The continental territory of Ecuador is divided into eighteen provinces.* Each of these is administered by a governor who is appointed by the President of the Republic and represents national rather than provincial interests. Each governor is aided—or harassed, as the case may be—by a popularly elected provincial council, which protects regional and local, rather than

* There are ten Provinces (Carchi, Imbabura, Pichincha, Cotopaxi, Tungurahua, Chimborazo, Bolívar, Cañar, Azuay, and Loja) in the Sierra; five (Esmeraldas, Manabí, Los Ríos, Guayas, and El Oro) in the Coast; and three (Napo-Pastaza, Morona-Santiago, and Zamora-Chinchipe in the Oriente. The Galápagos Islands do not have provincial status. Rather, they are governed through the ministry of national defense.

national concerns. For its internal government, each province is divided into a number of cantons, each canton being headed by a political chief appointed by the national president on the recommendation of the appropriate provincial governor. Cantons are in turn divided into parishes, each governed by a political lieutenant, also appointed by the president with the collaboration of the appropriate governor and political chief. The national government's control of the provinces and their subdivisions is fairly complete, being administered through the ministry of the interior.

Municipalities have been established in cantons which contain urban communities. Every municipality which is not a Sierra or Coastal provincial capital has an elected seven-man municipal council functioning without a mayor, the ceremonial head of the municipality being the presiding officer of the council. In twelve of the fifteen Sierra and Coastal provincial capitals there are nine-man councils and separately elected mayors [*alcaldes*] who are not members of the councils. Each of the three largest cities of the Republic—Guayaquil, the nation's chief port; Quito, the national capital; and Cuenca, the "Athens of the South"—has an eleven-man council and a separately elected mayor who may not participate or vote in meetings of the council. The members of all municipal councils are popularly elected by a variation of the list system of proportional representation for two-year terms. The fifteen mayors have two-year terms and are popularly elected at the same time as the councils.

The constitutional and political position of the Ecuadoran municipality is anomalous. In the unitary organization of the Republic the municipality is in a sense an agent or tool of the national government; yet a considerable degree of autonomy rests with the municipality. Municipal autonomy is an Ecuadoran reality. Its roots are deeply embedded in the history of the country and have become interwoven with problems of regionalism and particularism.

Recent Ecuadoran Politics

The contemporary Ecuadoran political pattern dates from the Revolution of 1944, when the government of President Carlos Alberto Arroyo del Río was overthrown by a rebellion which placed Dr. José María Velasco Ibarra in the presidency. This revolution, as we have seen, dealt a serious blow to the Radical-Liberal Party, which has not yet recovered its pre-1944 place in Ecuadoran national politics (see Radical-Liberal Era, and The Radical Liberals, above).

Ad hoc political parties and organizations have played a remarkably significant role in post-1944 affairs. Of initial importance among these was the Ecuadoran Democratic Alliance (ADE, for Alianza Democrática Ecuatoriana), an *ad hoc* coalition of largely leftist parties—the Socialist, Independent Liberal, Democratic, Communist, and Conservative Parties, and the Socialist Revolutionary Vanguard—which delivered the presidency to

Velasco Ibarra in 1944. This second Velasco Ibarra administration (he had also been president from 1934 to 1935) was marked by the inability of the president to come to terms with any of the political parties and by excessive political instability. Declaring that "I am a man of the left, but as a governor I must place myself in the center," [17] Velasco Ibarra performed the remarkable feat of alienating himself from virtually all of the country's political parties. He broke with the ADE a year after it had installed him in the presidency. The Radical Liberals considered him their sworn enemy, since it had been his revolution that had removed them from power. Only the Conservatives offered him their support, but Velasco Ibarra rejected this, insisting that "between Conservatism and my manner of thinking, there are momentous divergences and fundamental discrepancies." [18]

ECUADORAN CHIEF EXECUTIVES SINCE 1944 [a]

CHIEF EXECUTIVE	IN OFFICE	
	FROM	TO
José María Velasco Ibarra	1944	1947
Colonel Carlos Mancheno	1947	1947
Mariano Suárez Veintimilla	1947	1947
Carlos Julio Arosemena (father)	1947	1948
Galo Plaza Lasso	1948	1952
José María Velasco Ibarra	1952	1956
Camilo Ponce Enríquez	1956	1960
José María Velasco Ibarra	1960	1961
Carlos Julio Arosemena (son)	1961	1963

[a] See Blanksten, *Ecuador*, especially pp. 10-11, and Carlos A. Rolando, "Los Presidentes del Ecuador," *Boletín del Centro de Investigaciones Históricas* (Guayaquil), vol. IV, nos. 4-6 (1946), pp. 234-246.

Thus there was little support for President Velasco Ibarra when a *coup d'état* was launched against him in August of 1947. The rebellion was led by Colonel Carlos Mancheno, who had been minister of national defense in Velasco Ibarra's cabinet. Although Macheno was able to obtain the president's resignation, he failed in his attempt to secure support for his own intentions to occupy the presidential office. Accordingly, Mariano Suárez Veintimilla, who had been vice-president under Velasco Ibarra, assumed the presidency early in September of 1947 on an interim basis. He held office for only two weeks, that is, until a legislative committee was able to persuade Carlos Julio Arosemena, a Guayaquil banker and philanthropist, to serve as acting president until a new presidential election could be held.

The presidential election of 1948 took place under these auspices. The election campaign itself reflected the growing influence exercised by *ad hoc* political organizations. Fearing that Velasco Ibarra's crushing blow against the Radical Liberals might result in the Conservatives' return to power, a group of anti-Conservatives banded together to form the *ad hoc* National Civic Democratic Movement (MCDN, after the initial letters of Movimiento Cívico Democrático Nacional). With anti-Conservatism as its basic tenet, the MCDN was a largely moderate organization, although it enjoyed the support of some leftist elements. The MCDN nominated Galo Plaza Lasso for the presidency in 1948. The son of former president Leónidas Plaza Gutiérrez, Galo Plaza was a professed admirer of the United States, where he had been educated.

Elected president in 1948, Galo Plaza organized an administration characterized by marked trends toward economic development and political stability. Partially in consequence of his friendliness toward the United States, his government was among the first in Latin America to respond in a large-scale manner to programs of technical assistance and other forms of foreign aid offered by the North Americans. An early participant in programs of technical cooperation in agriculture, education, industrial productivity, and health and sanitation, Ecuador took remarkable strides toward economic growth during the Plaza administration. Trends toward political and constitutional stability were also noteworthy. Remaining in office until 1952, Plaza became the first Ecuadoran president since José Luis Tamayo (1920-1924) to occupy the presidency for the full four-year term for which he had been elected, without "revolutionary" interruptions. Moreover, this constitutional stability, launched so auspiciously in 1948, endured in Ecuador until 1961.

A new anti-Conservative *ad hoc* organization went into the field for the presidential campaign of 1952 and succeeded in securing the re-election of ex-President Velasco Ibarra. By now known as *el loco*, Velasco Ibarra presided over an administration characterized by a number of his earlier practices. The various political parties and organizations were again alienated from the president, and many of his actions and policies seemed irresponsible. A remarkable orator, Velasco Ibarra made effective appeals to the growing class of urban workers, however. Despite a number of political crises and mounting hostility toward his administration, Velasco Ibarra was also able to serve out his full four-year constitutional term without interruption. He drew no comfort from the tendency of analytical observers to assign the credit for this feat not to Velasco Ibarra himself but rather to the continuing influence of his political rival, ex-President Galo Plaza, who had demanded that political opposition be conducted in a peaceful and constitutional fashion.

The long-expected resumption of Conservative power at last came in consequence of the presidential election of 1956. Camilo Ponce Enríquez, the Conservative candidate, defeated his *ad hoc* opposition and was named president for the four-year period ending in 1960. Despite the dire predictions of the anticlericals, the Ponce administration proved to be relatively peaceful. A moderate Conservative, President Ponce did what he could to make his party's return to power as painless as possible for its opponents. Some measure of Ponce's success is to be found in the fact that he, like Presidents Plaza and Velasco Ibarra before him, was able to serve out the full four-year term without a break in the constitutional fabric.

This magic spell was at length broken with the re-election, once more with *ad hoc* support, of ex-President Velasco Ibarra for another presidential term to begin in 1960. With strong political opposition characteristically stiffening against him within a year of his inauguration, President Velasco Ibarra, deserted by his *ad hoc* organization, defied and baited the hostile political parties. At length, reluctant to wait for the constitutional expiration of Velasco Ibarra's term, his opponents, with the aid of the newly politicized air force, staged a *coup d'état* which overthrew his government in 1961.

Vice-President Carlos Julio Arosemena thereupon assumed the presidential office. The son of the Guayaquil banker and philanthropist who had served briefly as interim president in 1947-1948, President Arosemena also depended upon *ad hoc* organizations for his political support. Although it was primarily moderate in nature, his backing also drew initially from rightist and leftist sectors in sufficient substance to render prediction of his government's policies difficult. On the one hand, his administration, in the interests of more conservative groups, resisted tax reforms and leaned heavily upon the conservative air force for support; on the other, Arosemena's Ecuador was among the few Latin American governments conspicuously championing a conciliatory inter-American attitude toward the Castro regime in Cuba.

Under unremitting pressure from interests of all descriptions, and lacking a firm basis of popular support in its own right, Arosemena's government subsequently modified both of these earlier policies, embarking on a modest program of tax reform and severing relations with Cuba under palpable military pressure. For a time the president was able to conduct a holding operation, barely surmounting a succession of both direct and legislative attacks (including a motion of impeachment) from all points of the political spectrum. Some lukewarm support from moderate center elements, especially on the Coast, enabled him to survive successive crises until he was finally overthrown by a military coup in July of 1963.

The coup had the support of the top leadership of all three services, and the military junta which assumed the executive functions was headed by a naval captain, Ramón Castro Jijón. It was not clear whether the military leaders objected more to Arosemena's ineffectualness in office, to his supposed pro-Communist sympathies, or to his alleged habitual drunkenness. The *junta* pledged itself to draw up a new fundamental law and return the country to civilian rule.

On balance, the contemporary Ecuadoran scene exhibits a number of characteristics. For one thing—and perhaps most important—this is a time of pronounced economic development in the country. Although Ecuador's standard of living is still among the lowest in the Western Hemisphere,[19] the growth rate of the national economy is accelerating sharply, and the symptoms of development have been much in evidence since the Galo Plaza administration.

Dating from about this time, the production of bananas has grown from virtually nothing to become Ecuador's leading export activity. United States owned fruit companies led the way by transferring their activities to the Ecuadoran coast as a consequence of the losses suffered in their Central American operations from banana diseases. Profiting from their experience in Central America, the foreign companies have limited their own growing activities, preferring to concentrate on shipping and marketing the stems, most of which are bought from small local growers.

On the Coast export-oriented agriculture is thus characterized by some small and medium holdings, together with efficiently farmed larger-scale properties often owned by recent immigrants from Europe. In the Sierra the dominant holding is still the traditional estate which produces principally basic food crops for its own and for local consumption by dint of centuries-old methods used by an Indian work force of virtual serfs.

Contemporary Ecuadoran politics exhibits a growing trend toward increased political and constitutional stability. As of only a little more than a decade ago, it could be pointed out that Ecuador had had no fewer than fifteen written constitutions; presidents remained in office for an average of only a little more than 2.5 years; less than 25 percent of the country's presidents had been able to serve out their full constitutional terms; the nation had no fewer than fourteen presidents during the nine-year period ending in 1940; twenty-seven different ministers occupied eight cabinet posts during the three-year period ending in 1947; and twelve foreign ministers attempted to administer Ecuadoran foreign policy during the *two months* between August and October of 1933. Contemporary data reflect much greater stability. Only two presidential administrations have been interrupted since 1947 by so-called revolutions, and constitutional completion of presidential terms appears to be coming to be the rule rather than the rare exception.

Moreover, *personalismo*—adherence to a leader through personal and individual motivations rather than because of common support of an idea or political program—is dramatically on the wane in contemporary Ecuador. It is true that Velasco Ibarra once described a revolution that brought him to power thus: "The people expressed confidence in *me*, in *me* principally. Human waves acclaimed *me* and urged *me* to be their leader and president. . . . It is certain that *I* was the center of popular gravitation." [20] Yet the significance of Velasco Ibarra today may well be that he has become a museum piece, a reminder of the Ecuadoran political style of earlier times. In a contemporary setting his brand of political behavior is unusual rather than typical.

Finally, the country's political party system appears to be changing. The rise of *ad hoc* movements to supplant the ailing Radical-Liberal Party, coupled with the slow renaissance of a moderate Conservative Party, suggests that a long-range change may be at work. It would be foolhardly to describe or predict the change at this stage in time. The trend appears to be toward the moderation and the modernization of the political parties of Ecuador, but time for greater perspective is needed before this—or many another—general proposition about contemporary political change in Ecuador can be made with confidence.

NOTES FOR CHAPTER XIII

1. José María Velasco Ibarra, quoted in George I. Blanksten, *Ecuador: Constitutions and Caudillos*, University of California Press, Berkeley, 1951, p. v.
2. Alfredo Pérez Guerrero, *Ecuador*, Casa de la Cultura Ecuatoriana, Quito, 1948, pp. 62-63.
3. *Ibid.*, p. 62.
4. Moisés Sáenz, *Sobre el Indio Ecuatoriano*, Secretaría de Educación Pública, Mexico City, 1933, p. 103.
5. Federico González Suárez, *Historia General de la República del Ecuador*, Imprenta del Clero, Quito, 1890, Vol. II, p. 224.
6. *Manifesto No. 6* (Lima, 1844), quoted in Blanksten, *Ecuador*, p. 11.
7. Albert B. Franklin, *Ecuador: Portrait of a People*, Doubleday Doran, New York, 1944, pp. 272-273.
8. Jacinto Jijón y Caamaño, *Política Conservadora*, La Buena Prensa de Chimborazo, Riobamba, 1934, Vol. I, pp. 26, 32.
9. Luis Terán Gómez, *Los Partidos Políticos y su Acción Democrática*, Editorial La Paz, La Paz, 1942, pp. 60-61.
10. This discussion of Ecuadoran interest groups in general adheres to the scheme of analysis advanced in George I. Blanksten, "Political Groups in Latin America," *American Political Science Review*, LIII, No. 1, March 1959, pp. 106-127. See also Gabriel A. Almond and James S. Coleman (Eds.), *Politics of the Developing Areas*, Princeton University Press, Princeton, 1960, especially pp. 479-531.
11. Quoted in Blanksten, *Ecuador*, p. 36.
12. Edwin Lieuwen, *Arms and Politics in Latin America*, Praeger, New York, 1960, especially pp. 82-84 and 165-166.
13. Harold E. Davis (Ed.), *Government and Politics in Latin America*, Ronald Press, New York, 1958, pp. 477-495.
14. Pío Jaramillo Alvarado, *El Régimen Totalitario en América*, Editora Noticia, Guayaquil, 1940, p. 73.
15. See Russell H. Fitzgibbon, "Constitutional Development in Latin America: A Synthesis," *American Political Science Review*, XXXIX, No. 3, June 1945, pp. 517-518.
16. *Constitución Política de la República del Ecuador* (Quito, 1946), Art. 47. See also Blanksten, *Ecuador*, pp. 100-119.
17. Velasco Ibarra, *Mensaje Presentado a la Honorable Asamblea Nacional Constituyente, . . . 10 de Agosto de 1944* (Quito, 1944), p. 3.
18. Quoted in *El Comercio*, Quito, May 22, 1946.
19. See Robert N. Burr (Ed.), "Latin America's Nationalistic Revolutions," *Annals of the American Academy of Political and Social Science*, March 1961, pp. 10-19, especially p. 11.
20. Velasco Ibarra, *Mensaje Presentado a la Honorable Asamblea Nacional Constituyente, . . . 6 de Febrero de 1945* (Quito, 1945), p. 5. Italics added.

SELECTED BIBLIOGRAPHY

George I. Blanksten, *Ecuador: Constitutions and Caudillos*, University of California Press, Berkeley, 1951.

Aníbal Buitrón and John Collier, *The Awakening Valley*, University of Chicago Press, Chicago, 1950.

Helen Claggett, *Guide to the Law and Legal Literature of Ecuador*, Library of Congress, Washington, 1947.

Albert B. Franklin, *Ecuador: Portrait of a People*, Doubleday Doran, New York, 1944.

Rafael V. Lasso, *The Wonderland Ecuador*, Alpha-Ecuador Publications, New York, 1944.

Martin C. Needler, *Anatomy of a Coup d'Etat: Ecuador, 1963*, Institute for the Comparative Study of Political Systems, Washington, 1964.

W. Stanley Rycroft (Ed.), *Indians of the High Andes*, Committee on Cooperation in Latin America, New York, 1946.

Moisés Sáenz, *Sobre el Indio Ecuatoriano*, Secretaría de Educación Pública, Mexico City, 1933.

XIV

Rosendo A. Gomez

PERU

THE POLITICS OF MILITARY GUARDIANSHIP

IN RECENT decades Peru has moved rapidly from an oligarchic system which allowed little meaningful participation of the people to a transitional system which promises a fulfillment of constitutional ideals but at the same time impedes rapid movement to any wholesale assumption of the characteristics of modern societies. Yet those who control the society are not motivated by the uncompromising attitudes of traditional oligarchs. An understanding of Peruvian politics involves an appreciation of the motivations and transitional techniques of military guardianship.

Geographic, Economic and Social Background

Three Geographical Divisions

Few nations in the world have been as harshly endowed, geographically, as Peru. There are three distinct geographical areas and each presents tremendous obstacles to the development of the country's natural and human resources. One of the world's greatest oddities is the Peruvian *costa*, the arid coastal strip: narrow, cut by approximately fifty river valleys which carry water only during the summer rains in the Andes, throughout its length it presents on the whole the sparsely vegetated appearance of the desert. Contributing significantly to the phenomenon is the Humboldt Current whose cold waters sweep up parallel to the coast and supply incredibly rich fishing waters but which also creates the peculiar effect of humidity without rain. By means of irrigation a number of the river valleys have become highly productive cotton and sugar areas, however, contributing significantly to Peruvian income. The coast is also the location of much of the industrial output; Lima and Callao, Trujillo, Chimbote, Pisco, Ica, Piura, and other cities are located in irrigated river valleys.

At great altitudes above the *costa*, at times quite close to the Pacific Ocean, rise the Andes, the *sierra*, ranging the entire length of the country and composing 30 percent of its total area. This was the physical setting for most of the Inca Empire and is today the home of a large and poor Indian population. Life in the *sierra* is centered on agricultural labor, much of it in the cold air of altitudes over 10,000 feet; the region also yields considerable mineral wealth. The *sierra* presents considerable economic potential. Some of this is now being exploited, and the possibilities of hydroelectric power in some of the great river systems are now being surveyed. Communications and transportation present staggering difficulties, especially for industrial and marketing efficiency. One recalls Víctor Andres Belaúnde, in his *Peruanidad*, suggesting to fellow Peruvians that it is their patriotic calling "to excel in aviation." [1] Travel from the coast to cities in the *sierra* has indeed been increasing in recent years, thanks to air transport. Railroads and highways have been constructed under the most difficult conditions but are still in only the pioneering stage.

Falling away to the east of the *sierra* is the *selva* (or *montaña*): in large part a lush jungle through which rush a number of great rivers, whose waters empty eventually into the upper Amazon system. Sparsely populated and quite isolated, the *selva* represents nevertheless 60 percent of the total area of Peru. Only a few roads connect the *selva* with the *sierra* and the *costa*. Until the advent of air travel, Iquitos, the capital of the Department of Loreto, located in Peruvian Amazonia, was best approached from the coast by ocean voyage around the continent (or by the Panama Canal) and then up the whole length of the Amazon River.

Thus, throughout all of Peru, it would be difficult to find any spacious area wherein nature has made development of resources anything but a severe hardship and an extremely costly venture. The difficulties in integrating these three geographical divisions into a social and economic whole could hardly have been made more staggering.

Population

According to estimates based on the census of 1961, the population of Peru in 1963 was approximately eleven million. This represents an increase of nearly 50 percent since 1942. The average annual increase of population over the period has been approximately 2.1 percent with the increase during the last decade of the period perhaps exceeding 3 percent. This fact typifies the general population experience throughout Latin America (which is the fastest growing area in the world). And as is typical of many developing areas, Peru's population increase is taking its toll of economic gains.

Population figures for 1960 show that the Peruvian population is strikingly young: about 45 percent were below the age of 15 (compared to roughly 30 percent in the United States). Approximately 58 percent of the people were located on the *sierra*, 29 percent on the *costa*, and 13 percent in the *selva*. Although the figures are not reliable, perhaps 55 percent may be classified as European and *mestizo*, about 44 percent as Indians, and the remaining 1 percent divided among other categories such as Orientals and Negroes. (During the Colonial period the Spaniards brought in a large number of Negroes; in the 19th century approximately 90,000 Chinese were brought in to build the railroads; and later, a smaller number of Japanese moved into the country.) Nearly all immigrants, of whatever origin, are to be found on the coast. As of 1959, official figures show that 58 percent of the economically active population were employed in agricultural pursuits.

The Peruvian population is subject to considerable internal migration from rural to urban areas. Most migration is to the capital city of Lima although other coastal and Andean cities also receive it. Lima, with its nearly 1½ million people, is increasing annually at about 5 percent, as against the national average annual population increase of somewhat more than 3 percent. It has been estimated that 35,000 *provincianos* drifted into Greater Lima during 1961, for example, large numbers of whom were Indians, still in highland costume, living in desperate circumstances on the streets. Around the city are mushrooming slums (*barriadas*) which have taken the brunt of this migration.

The Economy

Measured by the standards of developing countries, the Peruvian economy has been progressing satisfactorily. Peru is one of the very few Latin American countries to present appreciable diversification, thus not falling prey to the ills characteristic of the monocultural economies. In the twenty-year period from 1942 through 1961, the gross national product rose 112 percent. By 1962 the various segments of the economy contributed the following percentages of the gross national product: agricultural activities, 24; mining, 14; industry, 18; commercial, 17; government, 13; services, 7; as a mark of development on a broader base, it was noticeable that over the twenty-year period, industry has increased along with commercial activity while the agricultural contribution had decreased. In 1961, reported new industries numbered 473, most of them established in the Lima area.

Peru's major exports in 1961, in order of their importance, were cotton, fish products, copper, and sugar. Fish products have come into the economy very significantly in the last few years. The rich fishing off the coast has been exploited to meet demands for fish meal to such an extent that it was estimated that by 1962 Peru led the world in the production of this fish product. In addition to these major export items, note should be taken of a very promising petroleum industry and the manufacture of household products, both of which have largely been developed to meet internal consumer demands.

Promising though economic progress has been, a number of observations should be made to put it into proper perspective.

(1) The Indians of the *sierra* stand outside the area of economic improvement. Although technically included in the statistics as agriculturalists, they have little impact on the marketing picture; and, in general, they are not incorporated into the social and economic life of Peru.

(2) The regional distribution of economic change indicates that an over-

whelming proportion of economic activity is still to be found on the coast, and particularly in Lima. Only in mining does one find any substantial contribution to the national economy from the *sierra*. As already noted, this imbalance has brought large numbers of Indians down to the coast, where they aggravate the unemployment situation.

(3) The Peruvian economy is being strained by the rate of population growth, a fact noted increasingly in developing areas. National income has increased in recent years at about 4.5 percent annually, but the per capita income has averaged only 2.4 percent increase.

(4) The economy is still dependent on the United States for the marketing of much of its exports and also for the capitalization of further ventures. Copper, cotton, and sugar are very sensitive to movements in the United States market and all are subject ultimately to the whims of the United States Congress and to subsequent executive action. A decision on the part of the United States to sell its cotton surplus abroad, assisted by a subsidy, spells disaster for the marketing of Peruvian cotton. A lowering of the Peruvian quota of sugar exported to the United States (which has, indeed, taken place recently), or a decision to pay only the world market price rather than the premium price allowed in the United States for "quota sugar," would mean a crisis of serious proportions to a significant segment of the Peruvian economy.

The Standard of Living

As observed above, Peruvian economic development, while promising, has not as yet substantially altered the lives of a very high percentage of the population. There is a great need for accelerated programs in health, education, and housing. Without citing Peruvian statistics (which a rector of the University of San Marcos once characterized as "poetry"), it can be safely estimated that at least two-thirds of the Peruvian people are very poorly provided with necessities and cannot look forward to the improvement of their lot through their own initiative. In addition to the tremendous economic obstacles, cultural obstacles are invariably substantial with respect to the Indians of the *sierra*, who are only with long and patient supervision led to adopt changes and to acquire new skills.

Improvements in living conditions rarely penetrate beyond a few cities. Lima has realized most of the improvements and is in every respect the dominating population center of Peruvian life. In the years 1960-62, approximately 170,000 television sets were sold in Lima; television broadcasting reaches perhaps 800,000 people. In no clearer way can one indicate the great range of living conditions in Peru today.

The appropriate national ministries have, of course, laid plans for the improvement of the social and economic situations. Technical and financial assistance from the United States and from the various agencies and credit institutions of the hemisphere and the United Nations have contributed to some progress on these problems.

Political History

Peruvian political experience has not, until recently, favored substantial progress toward an effective and orderly system. As Emilio Romero puts it, "creole political fanaticism" had made it difficult to find ground for compromise.[2] The power-seeking leader, military or civilian, usually without strong regard for issues, dominated political action. The system of "democratic caesarism" appears to have dominated for most of the time—a system variously described throughout Latin America, but always implying as a minimum a certain powerless equality existing below the level of the strong leader. Nevertheless, Peruvian political history has furnished periods of enlightenment and progress, and indeed a certain current of benevolence appears in evidence. That is to say, Peru's leaders ordinarily have not fallen into the viciousness and the unrelenting whip-cracking generated by class hatred. On the other hand, as the eminent historian of Peru, Jorge Basadre, has pointed out, a responsible elite in the years of Peruvian development might have greatly changed the picture.[3] A dominant viewpoint in between these alternatives, one which tended to see Peru either as an administrative plaything or as an economic arrangement, featuring *personalismo*, resulted.

From Independence to 1845

The early period of Peruvian political history was associated with the pangs of birth and the desperate attempt to find some national identity. From 1821 to 1845 the political scene was dominated by the generals of the Independence wars. Indeed, Peru has an extraordinary place in the arena of the revolution, in that this part of South America was the meeting ground for the military titans Bolívar and San Martín. It was Bolívar who influenced early Peruvian organizational efforts, although his personal constitutional prescription was watered down by the constitutions beginning with those of 1823, 1828, and 1834, the last two featuring a system modeled after that of the United States. The period is best described merely by reference to the succession of generals who were the dominant political figures, beginning with San Martín and Bolívar and followed by men such as Santa Cruz.

From 1845 to 1895

The fifty years from 1845 to 1895 featured the resolution of fundamental problems of organization, such as the provision of a basic code of laws, one which strongly reflected the Napoleonic Code. The Constitution of 1860, which remained the fundamental law until 1920, was also the product of this organizational creativity. Strong leadership prevailed, but appeared now, at least, to have a Peruvian identity and to exhibit less of the power-for-power's-sake motivation. From 1845 to 1862 the dominant figure was Ramón Castilla, who held the presidency during 1845-51 and again during 1858-62, playing also a transitional dictatorial role during 1855-58. He is generally regarded as a leader who contributed greatly to internal progress.

The creativity and greater stability of the period is partly attributable to the extraordinary financial success realized by the marketing of guano, bird deposits of high nitrogen content which for many decades were dug from off-shore islands and shipped to agricultural areas around the world. Handled as a government monopoly (which is still operating), the revenues were sufficiently handsome that Peruvian governments hardly needed any other source of reveune. Many of Peru's modern drawbacks are often attributed to the wealth provided by guano. Suitable progress in a broad economic sense suffered as long as profits from guano could pay the trade balances; also, middle-class energies during this vital formative period were channeled into bureaucratic ambitions rather than into the development of the country's resources.

The 1850's mark the beginning of the hegemony of what are often termed the "forty families." Gaining control of large tracts of land and benefiting from the general prosperity, a limited group held key footholds in the economy and, as a result, became a ruling elite. To be sure, some families in this group had been prominent from an earlier time, but in a more modern framework (for example, within the new basic code of laws), the forty families began their reign in the mid-nineteenth century.

Later in the period (1879-83) came war with Chile, ending in defeat for Peru with the loss of territory and with considerable damage to national pride as well. This event undoubtedly contributed to the continuation of generals in power to a date later than might otherwise have been the case. In any event, the military leader was dominant. Manuel Pardo (1872-76) was a prominent exception. He was distinguished as the first president to be elected by popular vote, and as a reformer of appreciable stature.

In the last years of the period a few political parties were organized, the first worthy of the name. Although they were associated with certain personalities, the Civil Party (Pardo), the Constitution Party (General Cáceres), and the Democratic Party (Piérola) showed some evidence of group identity beyond the ephemeral personalist type. Small but largely sentimental versions of the Civil and Democratic Parties still exist. These years are also noted for the beginning of radical sentiment through the pen of Manuel González Prada, who was so affected by the weaknesses brought out by the war with Chile that he began writing sharply critical pieces on Peruvian society.

The Constitution of 1860 served as a monument to the fact that certain political institutions were now fundamentally accepted in theory: separation of powers, the elective presidency, the bicameral congress, and a council of ministers characterized by some Continental touches.

From 1895 to 1930

Beginning with the Piérola government in 1895-99, there were signs that the distress of the war with Chile was subsiding. Military leadership soon gave way to personalism of the nonmilitary type. Economic improvements were realized. The first stage of substantial foreign investment was begun.

Dominating during the last eleven years of the period was the regime of Augusto B. Leguía (1919-1930). During the Leguía years there occurred circumstances that led to the exile of a young man named Víctor Raúl Haya de la Torre who, living abroad between 1923 and 1930, traveled widely and conceived the idea for the Alianza Popular Revolucionaria Americana (APRA), which has become of crucial significance to Peruvian politics. Haya and other intellectuals at the University of San Marcos in Lima and also at the University of Cuzco had unleashed a movement that brought about university reforms; they made common cause with workers for the betterment of their conditions and soon found themselves a source of annoyance to the Leguía dictatorship. Young Haya was jailed and later deported in 1923.

By 1930 the full spectrum of present Peruvian political ideologies was complete, although not active in every case. A small Communist group had been organized; various socialist groups were on the scene; the *apristas* had made a profound impact among intellectuals and workers; and, as always, large conservative groups could be organized to promote the fortunes of candidates dedicated to the preservation of the status quo.

In 1920 a constitution was fashioned as a setting for Leguía, but which at the same time carried forward the constitutional pattern already established. It was noticeable, however, that a number of social and economic provisions like those already introduced by the Mexican Constitution of 1917 had been added. A startling innovation was the establishment of three regional legislatures (already decreed by Leguía in 1919) in answer to a long-entertained demand by the provinces that centralization in Lima worked injustices. These legislative bodies, however, were soon failures and went out of use by 1926.

Since 1930

The years since 1930 have been especially characterized by political struggles in which the growing popular *aprista* movement, one of the most spectacular party developments in all Latin American experience, has been central. Whether suppressed or allowed to operate freely, APRA has been a controlling force at the polls. The party's discipline, forged to hardness during years of adversity, has no equal in Peruvian politics. Haya de la Torre, although in exile many years, along with other titans of the party, has retained the massive loyalty of the movement through several decades. Haya himself has been presidential candidate in three elections, the first two separated by thirty years, in 1931, 1962, and 1963.

Essentially the elections from 1931 to 1962 featured the forces of traditionalism in many combinations, occasionally making use of *aprista* strength, with the object of keeping *aprismo* out of the top power positions. Standing by, watchfully, the military has felt compelled to perform its protective function directly when ordinary political combinations have failed. In the

background, a force of increasing restlessness which many woo but which
few really want to unleash on the system, stand the millions of unassimilated
Indians who may soon have to be reckoned with.

Speaking in very broad terms, the period from 1931 to 1962 featured two
patterns closely related to each other. For twelve years of the period, Manuel
Prado, a member of the forty-family complex, served as president (1939-45
and 1956-62). The Prado administrations were conservative and not perhaps
sufficiently alert to the great problems of Peruvian progress; on the other
hand, Prado in his second term was not a strong proponent of traditionalism.
The first term of office was perhaps a continuation of the old pattern, but
the second term (1956-62), referred to as the *convivencia*, was an agreement with the *apristas*, probably conceived as a transitional arrangement to
make the *apristas* respectable. In return for power, Prado was, apparently, to
try to bring the *apristas* forward in 1962 with their own candidate. The second pattern has been that of military guardianship in an active role in the
presidency, most recently through General Odría, who held power from
1948 to 1956, during which period *aprismo* was stoutly oppressed and declared illegal. Again in 1962, and continuing into 1963, came military intervention in order to prevent the fulfillment of *aprista* hopes as a result of the
election of 1962.

The Election of 1962

The election for president, two vice-presidents, and both houses of Congress in June 1962 provided a spectacular climax to the patterns just described
—the *convivencia* between traditionalism and *aprismo* attempting to put forward a supposedly mellowed *aprismo* but eventually bringing on military
intervention.

The way had been cleared for a full and free competitive electoral struggle. General Odría, seizing power in 1948 and putting down *aprismo* for
eight years, left office apparently without prejudicing the electoral process
for 1956. Manuel Prado, desirous of another term, made arrangements for
aprista support, apparently promising free operation of the party, some bureaucratic positions, and also support for an *aprista* candidate in 1962 for the
presidency. Thus the *convivencia* succeeded although factors in both *aprista*
and conservative elements felt that a dangerous alliance had been made. Prado
was opposed in 1956 by a supposedly Odría-supported candidate, Hernán
de Lavalle, who ran a weak third; Fernando Belaúnde ran a strong second at
the head of an unexpectedly potent Popular Action movement. The Prado
administration, ending in 1962, had not especially distinguished itself and
there were signs that the coming election in 1962 was to be a very decisive
election which might awaken emotions that had in the past motivated military intervention.

The partisan teams formed for the 1962 election did, indeed, bring forward the promise of some uneasiness. The presidential candidacy of Haya
de la Torre formed at the head of a fully operating *aprista* organization (by

this time technically entitled Peruvian Aprista Party, or PAP). After thirty years, the *jefe* of the party was once again a candidate. The MDP, Prado's party, supported this candidacy along with other small groups; the combined force of these, including *apristas*, presented congressional lists under the title of Alianza Democrática in the various departments. The momentous decision was now to be made: whether, assuming sufficient electoral support, the military could accept *aprismo* in positions at the summit, including perhaps the presidency. Had its clearly moderate behavior in the *convivencia* removed the fears of radicalism that the *aprista* movement had always symbolized to the guardians of the system?

In opposition two major and four lesser candidates came forward. Ex-president Odría entered his candidacy at the head of the Odriist National Union (UNO). Fernando Belaúnde came forward again with Popular Action. Thus from the first it was obvious that a clear decision would be most difficult, since Haya, Odría and Belaúnde could each command massive support. Since the constitution provides that the winner must receive at least one-third of the popular votes cast for the office and, failing this, a decision would be made in the newly elected congress, it was strongly felt that two of the three candidates would find some basis for combining their forces. No arrangement was made, however, although there were apparently many attempts. In the meantime, throughout the campaign both Odría and Belaúnde (and especially the latter) declared that the electoral process was being fraudulently handled in favor of Haya by the electoral machinery which was allegedly subject to the imposition of the *convivencia*. The military made arrangements not only to police the process carefully but also to provide some additional safeguards.

Excitement mounted as the ballots were counted. The National Election Jury, under whose direction the final canvassing of the presidential ballots took place, was constantly subjected to charges of overlooking evidence of fraud. After days during which the lead changed back and forth between Haya and Belaúnde, it became clear that although Haya might win the highest number of votes, this number would fail of one-third and that the congress would be compelled to make the choice. This eventually pointed favorably to the *apristas*, who were winning a large number of congressional posts; however, some deal would have to be made, since the *aprista* number would not constitute a majority. Spectacular attempts were made to secure some kind of alliance of interests among the three candidates, although the details of these conferences are not known. The military, after apparently vetoing Haya as any part of the process and after the refusal of the *apristas* to withdraw Haya's name, intervened and annulled the entire electoral process, including the congressional lists. At this moment, there was some evidence that Haya might withdraw in favor of General Odría, but this outcome was apparently not satisfactory to the military leaders.

After some hesitation and the removal from office of its senior officer, the junta fulfilled its promise of holding elections one year later, in June of 1963.

The results of the voting, extremely close to results of the preceding year, seemed to refute military and Belaundist charges that there had been large-scale fraud in 1962.

The situation was changed in a major respect, however. Although the leading candidates—Haya, Belaúnde, and Odría—were the same in both years, several minor candidates who had run in 1962 did not run in 1963. The organizations of the two most important of these, the Christian Democratic Party and the pro-Communist Front of National Liberation, endorsed Belaúnde, the Christian Democrats providing the candidate for second vice-president on his ticket and pledging themselves to collaborate in his government if elected. The handfuls of votes thus added to Belaúnde's total proved sufficient to elect the young architect, even though the APRA vote increased slightly between the two elections.

What the policies would be of a president who was a member of one of the nation's leading families, who spoke of reform within a democratic context, and who seemed to be favored simultaneously by military leaders, pro-Communists, and Christian Democrats, could only be a matter for speculation. Belaúnde's first acts on taking office betokened a vigorous reformism. How much could be accomplished in the face of a congress dominated by his opponents, and in view of the heterogeneous nature of the new president's own following, remained doubtful.

The Dynamics of the Peruvian Political Process

Of the developing countries of the world, Peru would be placed somewhere above the middle point of the range. As already indicated, the Peruvian economy is of sufficient diversification and development that it is in a far better position than those of most other Latin American republics, and indeed, at the moment, if one considers a stable currency as a promising indication, it promises better than one or two of the most productive economies of the area. In Almond and Coleman's *Politics of the Developing Areas* Peru is grouped with the "semi-competitive" (between "competitive" and "authoritarian") and on the scale of political modernity, as "mixed" (between "modern" and "traditional"),[4] with Colombia, Ecuador, Mexico, and Panama.

This classification is a reasonable one. Peru's location on the scale clearly indicates a transitional status in which the forty families are waging a defensive battle against the pressure of mass expectations. The term "forty families" has become embedded in usage and probably the number of families in this category is much larger now. This is the environment that brings forward military guardianship, a special subclassification that might be subsumed under the broad heading of "semi-competitive, mixed, developing country." Peru's military guardianship is not irresponsible and does not employ the full awesomeness of traditional oppression. It might best be described as a defensive and delaying tactic which realistically has estimated the possibilities of defeat of the traditional ways but wishes to soften its impact. In the 1948-56 regime of General Odría such a function was performed, and between July 1962 and July 1963 a similar set of forces was active in the form of a military junta.

Urbanized Politics

Although Peru can be described as a rural nation in many respects, political activity is centered in the cities. Very few Indians are recruited into political organizations; indeed, few of them are qualified to vote. The registered voters are in cities and towns for the most part. Approximately 35 percent of the registered voters are to be found in the area of Greater Lima. Arequipa, Callao, Chiclayo, Cuzco, Huancayo, Ica, Piura, and Trujillo account for another 25 percent. A large number of smaller cities and towns add to this pattern, although it is not as easy in those cases to make a rural-urban distinction. Until very recently campaigning did not go much beyond the cities mentioned. However, Fernando Belaúnde carried out an extensive campaign over the entire country in 1962, penetrating much of the rural area.

Political recruitment of the Indian occurs first by way of his movement to a city, particularly to a coastal city. If he is recruited in his original environment it will usually be by arbitrary impressment at the hands of local political chieftains. Indeed the traditional methods of intimidation cling to the smaller cities and towns and the rural areas. In the cities there is much greater freedom of choice and competition for votes. Some cities show a tendency to certain movements: Trujillo to the *apristas*, Arequipa to Popular Action, for example. Lima, in the intervened election of 1962, apparently divided into three great blocks of support for the three major presidential candidates, with Odría gaining a plurality.

In Lima, of course, one finds the greatest activity by far. Here the presidential candidates put on massive *manifestaciones* calculated to attract the largest group of uncommitted voters in the country. Newspapers debate at great length the question of the true number of *manifestantes* gathered to hear a presidential candidate. Lima, as the greatest metropolitan area, is the residence of great numbers of middle-class, organized workers, students, and an increasing number of poor slum-dwellers. The combined impact of newspapers, magazines, radio, and television makes a quite impressive assault on the voter.

The Military Guardians

It would appear fitting to consider the armed forces before going on to other groups active in the political process. Peruvian politics has not yet moved out of the position of "military guardianship." It is perhaps unnecessary to explore here the cultural basis for this—that is, the importance of the military in Iberian and Latin American societies.

The Peruvian armed forces consist of army, navy, and air branches. In the Latin American context the Peruvian military ranks high in training programs, and general professional orientation. It has undoubtedly moved far in these respects in recent decades. However, it has clung to its guardian-ship role, upholding what it believes to be its constitutional mission. The plain fact seems to be that the military in its many clashes with *aprismo* dreads the prospect of an *aprista* president not only ideologically but also because it fears reprisals for the past. The generals appear willing to accept a *convivencia* but not *apristas* in complete command of high places. Pre-sumably the apparent moderation of *aprismo* while in the Prado *convivencia* did not calm their uneasiness. Accordingly in 1962 they brought up charges of fraud in the registration of voters and also the balloting process and, when not supported by the National Electoral Jury, they intervened completely and annulled the entire election. It would be impossible of course to deter-mine the justification for their charges but widely held sentiment indicates that fraud, while perhaps involved to some extent, was not perpetrated sufficiently to have substantially altered the results.

There are two provisions in the constitution relating to the role of the military. There is the typical provision placing the armed forces at the command of the president. However there is also a provision which states: "The purpose of the armed force is to assure the laws of the Republic, com-pliance with the Constitution and laws, and the conservation of public order." This provision has served as constitutional support for the military to initiate action without presidential support.

The 1962 election provided an interesting example of military supervision of the electoral process. Before the election date, announcements were made by the armed forces that the military would carefully guard the electoral process all the way. In fact, the military carried out a complete paralleling of the regular election machinery, including, in some places at least, provid-ing its own indelible ink of a different color for the finger-dipping process.

Political Parties

The Peruvian party system, when operating freely, is a multiparty system. At the time of the elections of 1962, there were at least thirteen parties. The electoral law requires that the National Electoral Jury officially recognize a party that is supported by a list of at least 20,000 qualified voters. A con-centration or alliance of parties, when consisting of parties not inscribed, must consist of 40,000 voters' signatures. Parties of international character are banned, which has meant that the Communists have had to place their activists in groups by other names. This has touched the *apristas* as well, since the party's original title had a faint suggestion of international con-nections.

Peruvian parties usually arise as personalistic ventures. Many are small and ephemeral and manage to survive only one election. Some arise as the vehicles for certain personalities but survive to continue as organizations dissociated from the original personality (although some sentimentality may still invoke his name). By and large, however, Peru's continuing parties narrow down to the *apristas* and a few small parties, most of which are of the far left. There are some signs that the Popular Action and Christian Democratic Parties may also outlive their present personalistic stamp. The political scene at the moment appears to provide some settled doctrinal parties on the left and center but none on the right. Rather than a continuing Conservative Party, such as is found in Colombia and Chile, one finds a succession of personalist parties like those that formed around Prado and Odría. To some extent this is due to inability to cement a lasting relationship among various elements—the old and new rich, warring social cliques, and the occasional distribution of those in higher military ranks among such divisions.

(1) *Partido Aprista Peruano* (PAP). The *apristas*, or Party of the People, as it is called by its supporters, form the largest continuing group of political activists in the country. For thirty years they have maintained a disciplined organization and, for much of the time were compelled to survive as an underground movement. If they had been allowed freedom, there was a high degree of likelihood that the *apristas* could have won power in the 1930's. In 1962 the party apparently polled the highest number of votes but it was a number insufficient to gain the presidency outright, and in the 1963 elections it was the largest single party, Belaúnde Terry being elected by a coalition. APRA has suffered to some extent from the tendency to make common cause with conservatism, such as the *convivencia* with Prado (1956-62) which has led some to conclude that the aging leadership of the *apristas* is now settling for power short of the summit and thus compromising the traditionally reformist aims of the movement. On the other hand, *aprismo* has not yet won the confidence of the great bulk of moderate forces.

APRA was organized by Victor Raúl Haya de la Torre with a view to bringing reform not only to Peru but to "Indo-America" as a whole.[5] Conceived in continental terms, it stood against imperialism, advocated inter-American control of the Panama Canal, and emphasized general reforms designed to improve the lot of the Indians. Through the years, parties in other Latin American countries cast in this mold, although never externally managed by Haya or his group, have been referred to as *aprista* parties. Thus *aprismo* has given a generic term to the terminology of political parties. Haya's intellectual gifts have always given a great boost to the party's fortunes. He has written voluminously and often brilliantly on history and politics. These gifts plus enforced exile placed Haya in a circle of international character that has helped greatly to elevate *aprismo*'s fortunes from a merely Peruvian setting.

With the return of Haya de la Torre from exile just before the 1931 election in Peru, the *apristas* began attracting thousands of followers, chiefly from organized labor and intellectuals, a combination that dates from Haya's crusading university years. Hardened by years of underground life, the *apristas* have come to be the largest voting bloc in Peru. In addition to Haya (who is Chief of the Party) the party has been led for many years by Ramiro Prialé (secretary-general) and the late Manuel Seoane (who during the *convivencia* with Prado served as Peruvian ambassador to Chile).

The *apristas* have been for some time a strong anti-Communist ,force. This has contributed undoubtedly to Peruvian solidity against recent Communist threats. In the 1962 election, the far left of pro-Communist bent polled only about 3 percent of the popular vote.

Aprista strength is based largely in the cities of the coast where labor unions are organized. Lima, Callao, and Trujillo are especially strong *aprista* cities. During the 1962 campaign enormous *manifestaciones* were held in Lima, one of these attracting more than 250,000 people.

The disciplined ranks of the *apristas* have on occasion met the military in combat in the streets. One of the most emotional issues in Peruvian politics of the past thirty years involves charges of massacre on both sides. Annually, high-ranking military officers hold ceremonies on the anniversary of the so-called Trujillo massacre of 1932, when a number of officers were killed by *apristas*. It is one of the more common observations in Peruvian politics that the army and the *apristas* have great distaste for each other. The Lima newspaper *El Comercio* is especially anti-*aprista* and is likely to emphasize what it considers thuggery on the part of the young *apristas* (whom it invariably calls "buffaloes" i.e., gangsters).

One of the fundamental techniques of Peruvian politics involves getting *aprista* support without granting the party power at the summit. It is difficult to succeed at the polls without such support. The *apristas* have apparently never thought highly of a strategem of frustration often used elsewhere—the boycotting of an election. Every election between 1931 and 1962 (with the exception of 1950, when General Odría saw to it that he ran unopposed) has involved some arrangements with *aprista* voting power. The *aprista* leaders, becoming great realists with the passage of time, began to trade their support for survival of the party and for minor posts, doubtless waiting for the time they could win acceptability of the guardians of the system. In 1962 and 1963, however, Haya and the *apristas* stood for office in their own right. It was noticeable during the 1962 campaign that many Peruvians persisted in their view that Haya would really withdraw after making a deal with one of the other major candidates.

After the 1963 elections the APRA reached a working arrangement for cooperation in the congress with the *odriístas*. In view of the persecution of the *apristas* conducted during Odría's presidency, and the bitterness of Odría's attacks on the APRA during the 1962 campaign, this alliance seemed an extraordinary about-face for both groups. It certainly marked an extreme point in the evolution of the APRA, either towards the right or towards pure opportunism or towards the mirage of acceptance by respectable elements. Manuel Seoane retired from active politics over the decision to cooperate with the UNO, preferring an alliance with the AP.

(2) *Acción Popular* (AP). Popular Action came forward with massive national support under the leadership of Fernando Belaúnde Terry, a

prominent architect and professor. Belaúnde became active in the election of 1956 against the wishes of President Odría, who upon retiring from office favored the candidacy of Hernán Lavalle. Belaúnde and Popular Action persevered and caught up a good deal of underdog sentiment and also a traditional Peruvian reaction against government candidates, finally losing to the *aprista*-supported Prado. Belaúnde remained very active during the Prado years, working for an even greater and better-prepared assault on the presidency in 1962. By the final moments of the 1962 campaign, Belaúnde had covered all of Peru, a campaign technique not before considered seriously by presidential candidates. Throughout the campaign, Belaúnde charged fraudulent practices on the part of the government in support of Haya de la Torre. When, at the end, he was convinced that the *apristas* were going to win, he dramatically retired to Arequipa, his native city and also a traditional spawning ground for revolt. Opinion in Peru was widespread that the military intervention was in part a pro-Belaúnde move.

Popular Action is a strongly reformist movement making a broad appeal to all but the most conservative elements. It enjoys much middle-class support strongly based on professional people; this portion of the middle class is apparently thereby expressing weariness with all the old arrangements. It is strongly affected by suspicion of, or recent loss of respect for, the *apristas*. The AP has also attracted considerable leftist support and has been stoutly challenged on this score. Belaúnde took stands—for example on the nationalization-of-petroleum issue—that appealed to all leftist support (including Communists). Along with strong support in Lima (greater, apparently, than that of the *apristas*) and Arequipa, Belaúnde also drew on a heavy and widely distributed vote from the provinces of the *sierra*.

(3) *Unión Nacional Odriísta* (UNO). The impact of General Odría (president from 1948-56) is still a powerful one. The ultimate achievement in Peruvian politics is to be president for two full terms. Since a president may not legally succeed himself, the technique involves a return after at least a six-year absence. The Odriist National Union stayed alive during Odría's period out of power with a few congressional seats. The General returned to Peru about one year before the elections of 1962 and explored the possibilities of re-election, apparently finding that the attempt was promising.

The *odriístas* conducted their campaign almost entirely in Lima and a few other cities, carefully avoiding cities where *aprista* strength was most in evidence. General Odría's severe confinement of *aprismo* during his *ochenio* (eight-year period) was remembered with bitterness in certain *aprista* strongholds. It appeared that Odría's strategy was to let *apristas* and *acciopopulistas* hammer each other while a possible ensuing stalemate might favor a deal with the Odría forces. In the meantime two strange bedfellows rallied strongly to Odría's support, each with an enormous following in Lima. A large number of middle-class and upper-class elements, interested in order, fearful of both the *apristas* and the *acciopopulistas*, and mindful of the prosperous years under Odría's government, looked to another Odría administration as an anchor. In addition, the desperately poor of Lima and environs whose lot had improved during the Odría administration, an improvement which had not been as evident during the Prado-*aprista* years, thronged to the polls in support of the general.

Odría ran third to Haya and Belaúnde, but his strategy was well-conceived. Indeed, at the moment the military intervened, an announcement was made that the *apristas* had agreed to support Odría during the congressional election of the president, a constitutional alternative that appeared necessary since no candidate had one-third of the popular votes.

(4) *Movimiento Democrático Peruano* (MDP). The Peruvian Democratic Movement is the vehicle created to put forward the Prado candidacy in 1956, the supporters of the movement being popularly known as the *pradistas*. It brought together conservative elements in support of Prado in the traditional form for conservative impact on the system. It was supported by the *apristas*, however, although this came by way of a last-minute arrangement which brought out the previously uncommitted *aprista* voting strength; the *apristas* had their own congressional list called the Frente Parlamentaria Democrática Independiente. Thus the MDP carries the label of the *convivencia* with *aprismo*. It apparently agreed, in return for *aprista* support, to back an *aprista* presidential candidate in 1962. The MDP may now disappear or become a continuing vehicle for later candidacies. The chances are strong that it will disappear in favor of a similar organization under a different name and in support of a new personality, particularly since the MDP has felt some embarrassment on all sides because of the alliance with *aprismo* and the subsequent annulment of the 1962 election.

(5) *Partido Demócrata-Cristiano* (DC). The Christian Democrats are a small but probably continuing party of the center. The PDC is the Peruvian version of the present trend toward Christian Democracy in Western Europe of post-World War II. Stressing the Catholic liberalism of the latter-day papal encyclicals on social justice and moderate economic reform, it has attracted a small urban following, particularly in Lima and Arequipa. Its leader, Hector Cornejo Chávez, is a prominent professor of law who, as presidential candidate in 1962, emphasized that he came forward with *manos limpias* (clean hands). But the *democristianos*, if they are to swell their numbers, must attract a following from the segments of society now substantially committed to APRA or Popular Action. The movement does not appear to have substantial support of the Church in spite of its Christian Democratic foundation. Its 1963 coalition with the victorious Belaúnde has provided the movement access to the seats of power, however.

(6) *Small Leftist Movements*. A number of small leftist movements are quite active. Because of the powerful *aprista* movement, committed to anti-Communism, with strong support from labor unions, the ultra-left has not had a strong base from which to operate. There are three active groups, each putting forward presidential candidates in 1962: the Frente de Libe-

ración Nacional (FLN), the Movimiento Social Progresista (MSP) and the Partido Socialista del Perú. The most active of these and the most militant has been the FLN. It was organized in an attempt to create an organization to which all the ultra-left might repair. It has become the chief organ of Fidelo-Communism. It has crusaded very strongly against the United States, with particularly emotional appeals against foreign imperialism. Its presidential candidate in 1962, General Pando, is the extraordinary combination of radical and military officer. In addition to Pando, the FLN has been led by a rabid young priest, Father Bolo, who has been suspended from parish duties and is now a full-time pro-Communist agitator. This movement is concentrating on the Indians of the *sierra* to an alarming degree. A number of violent peasant movements, somewhat suggestive of Maoism, have been attributed to FLN leadership. Leaders of the movement were jailed by the military junta in 1962 on charges of subversive activities.

One other leftist movement is worthy of mention, not because of its activity up to the moment but because of its origin and its possibilities: APRA Rebelde, which broke away from the *apristas* in objection to the alliance with conservative Prado. It is reported to have reorganized as the Movement of the Revolutionary Left (MIR), and to be making common cause with the FLN. It is primarily a student movement.

The Church

The Roman Catholic Church is, as nearly everywhere in Latin America, a deeply rooted institutional force in Peruvian life. The constitution declares that the state "protects" the Church but that religious freedom is extended to other sects. The state exercises national patronage (*patronato nacional*) which, by concordat, extends to the internal political leadership the power of nominating the Church leaders, who, also by constitutional provision, must be native Peruvians.

As is now a tendency throughout Latin America, the Church has of late become more and more a voice of moderation, speaking for economic and social progress, and no longer presents the old image of uncompromising alliance with traditionalist sentiment. If one were audacious enough to risk classification in such a matter, probably the Church in Peru would be placed somewhere in the middle area representing transition from traditionalism to modernism. The Church has made its peace with the changing scene in a reasonably flexible manner. During the electoral excitement of July 1962, the newly-elevated Cardinal Landázuri, the primate of the Church in Peru, called for resolution of the affair by constitutional means. Although linked by long friendship from boyhood with Fernando Belaúnde, the Cardinal did not, openly at least, indicate any bias.

Students

The university students of Peru are exceedingly active in national politics. The university is a training ground for a career in politics, and most national political figures first won their spurs in university politics. Indeed, the university is not merely a training ground; it is a branch of national political activity. The "students" may actually, in many cases, be older men in their forties doing actually little or no college work. The faculty members are also quite active; in the 1962 elections at least three presidential candidates and a large number of congressional candidates came from faculty ranks.

The students are organized into federations, representatives of which participate on councils important to university policy-making. Student Federation offices are eagerly sought by the politically ambitious. The elections will invariably be a reflection of the existing national political scene, and the participants are very much emotionally involved with foreign affairs and internal socio-economic matters. At the University of San Marcos in Lima (part of the national university system) one finds a most active student federation. Until 1960 the federation had been dominated by *apristas* for some time; in that year, however, fired by the recent Castro affair in Cuba, a strong *fidelista* movement swept the offices and in more recent elections this trend has continued.

Students are readily available demonstrators and are likely to be revolutionary by persuasion. Of late the demonstrations at San Marcos have been militantly anti-United States in character, as the students' addiction to *fidelismo* suggests. The Peruvian situation indicates that student movements are not as intimidating as in some other places in Latin America, thanks to very alert policing methods. During the 1962 elections, the former president of the federation at San Marcos was arrested and, although released shortly afterward, the reaction was not as violent as might have been expected.

Interest Groups

Interest groups in Peru present the usual variety but their techniques are limited by the political culture, which favors executive domination rather than the independent legislature. They are further limited by the confinement of "influencing public opinion" to the same narrow channel. Nevertheless, many groups are actively calling attention to their interests by whatever means available.

The seats of power are easily accessible to the rich on a social plane. The "oligarchs" (the "forty families") have never encountered difficulty being heard and, indeed, their interests have often been directly represented by the occupant of the Presidential Palace. The "oligarchy" no longer suggests the unanimity that once existed in the Peruvian upper class; it now appears to be divided not only by differing economic views but also by certain social cliques whose enmities sometimes override political and economic motivations.

Labor unions have been organized in great numbers in recent years. They have not been reckonable political forces until recently when, under *aprista* leadership and benefiting from the *convivencia* with Prado, they have apparently had the ears of the highly placed. The movement is largely under the leadership of the Confederación de Trabajadores Peruanos (CTP) which is especially *aprista*-oriented. But, as elsewhere in Latin America, the labor unions are ultimately dependent on a benevolent president and cannot be said to have carved out a continuing and independently powerful position.

A large number of business organizations are actively attempting to influence the policy of the government. Associations of sugar growers, cotton growers, and other agricultural interests are especially in evidence. During the early months of 1962, for example, many sugar growers' associations were disturbed by the possibility of a cut in the quota to be exported to the United States at the premium price in that market. Full-page advertisements in Lima newspapers were used to petition the government to take immediate steps to contact appropriate officialdom in the United States.

Governmental Machinery

The Peruvian governmental structure falls into the Latin American pattern, without major departures. It is the typical presidential system, with a more powerful president than the prototype in the United States, combined with some European ministerial, administrative, and judicial touches. The fundamental law at present in force, together with many amendments, is the Constitution of 1933. That document in its first article describes the system as a "democratic republic" featuring popular sovereignty and government limited by the constitution and laws.

The Electorate and the Electoral Process

Peru has arrived at adult suffrage with a literacy requirement: men and women at least twenty-one (eighteen, if married) who can read and write may vote. Voting is compulsory up to age sixty. An electoral registry is provided, with offices in all the provinces. Every voter is issued an electoral credential (*libreta electoral*) which carries a considerable amount of identification data. The *libreta* is a very important personal possession since it is necessary to present it to enjoy any privilege or service which the government controls: employment, travel, public documents, marriage, admission to a university, professional license, and so forth. It is in this way that the compulsory feature of the voting law is actually made effective.

The electoral process in general (including the official inscription of candidates, parties and alliances, the handling of balloting, and the canvassing of ballots) is the responsibility of the National Electoral Jury (Jurado Nacional de Elecciones) which consists of seven men appointed by various means who sit atop a hierarchy of juries at the departmental level. The counting of ballots for congressional posts is handled finally at the departmental level.

Balloting supposedly takes place in secret although it is possible that in some areas a certain degree of intimidation still exists. Ballots (*cédulas de sufragio*) are provided by the parties. These must be of white paper on which candidates' names are printed in black. Candidates for president and vice-president appear on one ballot; candidates for departmental congressional lists on another. The voter marks the ballots of his choice in secret and then deposits all ballots in an envelope supplied by the government. This envelope is deposited by the voter in a box at the voting table. Then one of the voter's fingers is dipped into indelible ink in order to make it difficult to vote more than once.

For the selection of the members of the senate and chamber of deputies the "incomplete list" type of proportional representation is employed. The precise number of senators and deputies for each department is fixed by law. If one votes in Lima, where the total number of deputies is twenty, the voter is limted to voting for fifteen.

The President

The president of Peru is the overpowering institution of the system. The constitution appears to establish this office as confined by ministerial and congressional power, but in practice these do not substantially limit presidential action. V. A. Belaúnde describes the system as "presidential absolutism" involving, as a result, "parliamentary anarchy." [6] The president not only is free of any real legislative obstacle but he usually chooses, or approves, the congressional candidates to run on his party label. This will not always give him a majority but, on the other hand, usually a majority cannot be mustered against him. The unusual occurred as a result of the 1963 election, however, as the governing coalition of Popular Action and the Christian Democrats was outnumbered in the congress by an opposition coalition of *apristas* and *odriístas*.

The president is elected popularly for a six-year term. He must be a native Peruvian and at least thirty-five years of age and have resided at least ten consecutive years in the Republic. People in a number of categories are ruled ineligible for candidacy, such as ministers of state and members of the armed forces, but a resignation a year before an election removes this limitation. The president may not be immediately re-elected. This means that a term must intervene before he may seek the office once more. He is provided with an official residence of spectacular proportions called the Presidential Palace (often referred to as the Palace of Pizarro), located on the Plaza de Armas in Lima.

First and second vice-presidents are also elected and are intended to stand in line of succession to the presidency. They are not given any constitutional duties to perform.

The powers of the president hardly need detailed enumeration. Let it suffice to say that as *jefe de estado* he is almost omnipotent in internal and external affairs.

The Council of Ministers

The Peruvian constitution provides for the machinery of a certain degree of ministerial responsibility to the congress. The ministers of state (eleven in number, covering the usual functional areas) are, collectively, known as the Council of Ministers. A president of the council is provided for; he is popularly referred to as the premier, but in practice he is more of an administrative convenience than the location of real power. The president of the council may assume one of the ministries; Pedro Beltrán, appointed halfway through the Prado administration (1959), in the midst of economic decline, took the ministry of the treasury as well as the presiding responsibility. Under ordinary circumstances, the president will not appoint (or nominate, technically) a premier whose personality and ability might make the premier's position competitive with his own.

Although the congress can force resignations of ministers, collectively as well as individually, the existence of this power has never seriously undermined the position of the president, who, after all, can simply nominate others to replace them.

The President of the Republic meets with the council as a whole perhaps twice a month but he is constantly conferring with individual ministers and directing their efforts. Although the signatures of appropriate ministers are necessary to public enactments, this has not served to create any departure from the dominance of the president.

The Congress

The Peruvian congress is bicameral, consisting of a senate of 55 members and a chamber of deputies of 186. In each case the number for each department is fixed by law and departmental party lists are used (with the "incomplete list" voting system used as described above). In each house the term of office is six years, which coincides with the presidential term. The senate is designed by the Constitution of 1933 to be a functionally representative body—that is, representing "functional" economic groups, rather than population districts—but this provision has never been implemented. The qualifications are the same for each house except that the senators must be thirty-five years of age as against twenty-five for deputies.

Congressional sessions are held annually for 120 days beginning in July. Special sessions may be called. Each house selects a president who is likely to be the top man on the ticket of the party represented in the Presidential Palace. However, rarely does the president enjoy a majority of his own party in either house. In the congress of 1956-62 the *pradistas* in the chamber of deputies held 80 out of 182 seats and relied on the 31 seats of the Independent Parliamentary Front (largely *apristas*) to complete the majority. Nine other parties held seats in that body.

The congress may find itself carrying out a most critical electoral function, the election of the president, should any candidate not receive one-third of the popular votes cast. This was to have occurred following the election of 1962 but the military intervention prevented it. The congress attempted to meet and organize itself but was prevented by the military from accomplishing this.

The Judiciary

The Peruvian judicial system consists of four levels of courts. At the national level stands the supreme court of justice whose judges are selected by the congress for life terms from a list supplied by the president. It has sweeping jurisdiction of both original and appellate nature. At the departmental level are superior courts whose judges are appointed by the president from lists supplied by the supreme court. At the local level, in larger communities, judges of first instance are appointed, the number varying with the volume of work. Finally, in smaller communities, justices of the peace are found.

The Peruvian legal system is based largely on the Napoleonic Code and Spanish law that had been applied by the Viceroyalty of Peru. It is a codified system in the European tradition. There does not appear to be any use of judicial review, such as has developed in the United States and which has affected the legal systems of a few other Latin American republics.

The Peruvian Administrative System

Peru has one of the most highly centralized administrative systems in Latin America. It is a unitary system consisting of 24 departments which vary from heavily populated Lima with approximately 2½ million people to isolated Madre de Dios with only 15,000. Departments are divided into provinces, provinces into districts and, in some cases, districts into subdistricts. The administrators respectively are prefects, subprefects, governors, and lieutenant governors. The mode of selection is such as to be entirely controlled by the President of the Republic: that is, by appointment. Nearly all public policy is handled by this centralized scheme. The prefects and underlings have traditionally provided loyalty to the president, extending even to practical political affairs, and have many times, particularly in the past, run their jurisdictions with such heavy hands as to be able to intimidate the citizenry in favor of the government, especially in the more remote provincial centers. The prospect of opposing leaders who wield such power can be faced only by the most courageous.

Some minor responsibilities are carried out by elective departmental councils but, except in the larger cities, these do not become posts of great power. Elective municipal councils are provided for, but these had fallen into disuse until revived by President Belaúnde.

With respect to the ranks of public administrators everywhere in Peru, the usual problems attached to public employment in nearly all parts of Latin America apply: there are large, inexpert, and underpaid groups of employees who face the greater complications of progress without the possibility of coping with them efficiently. The spoils system is not widely followed in the lower ranks of the bureaucrats. The prevailing policy seems to be to add positions to accommodate a swelling group of middle-class worthies who cannot be assimilated by industry.

The Great Policy Problems of Peruvian Politics

The great issues of all developing countries have to do with the pressing problems of socio-economic character. These problems have been magnified by the impact of expectations that have outstripped the ability to produce and distribute goods. In Peru increasing numbers of people in miserable circumstances have their faces pressed to the windows. They cannot be ignored much longer.

To create an equitable socio-economic balance under these circumstances is one of the baffling problems of our time. For the race against time is frantic. Too much time without improvements means at least two crises: the unleashing of the wrath of deprived peoples (perhaps accelerated by ultra-leftist agitators), which could solve nothing, and a spectacular increase in population which can easily outstrip any gains.

Yet decades of time are needed. It cannot be overlooked that the abundant economies of the western industrial societies took generations to create. Furthermore, even more often overlooked, these economies were built on social situations and working conditions that were not acceptable by modern standards. The great accomplishment of our time will be the creation of healthy economies in the face of modern impatience and social unrest.

Development of Natural Resources, Industry, and Agriculture

The great problems confronting Peruvian economic progress are the construction of transportation systems, the amassing of capital, and the development of industrial and agricultural skills. A start has been made in all of these. Among all the republics of Latin America, Peru has presented one of the most promising, but also most challenging, environments for progress in these directions.

A great wealth of petroleum is available for exploitation. The International Petroleum Company (a subsidiary of Standard Oil of New Jersey) has extensive works at Talara in the northern coastal department of Piura. One of the issues of Peruvian politics has involved recently the nationalization of the foreign-owned oil industry. The outcome of this problem, of course, will be critical for future development of Peruvian industry, since foreign capital will be required in considerable amounts.

As an inducement to capital ventures the Prado government offered certain tax concessions for the development of industries outside of the Lima area. This seems to be sound policy, but not much development of this sort has begun.

Agricultural output must be increased with a view to development of new products for internal consumption, in order to cut down on the imports for this purpose. Government and private ventures have begun surveys for vast hydroelectric and irrigation projects to incréase the agricultural acreage. In part this is tied to the possibilities of land reform.

Great regional projects are under way, although still largely in the planning phase. One of these, called the Peruvía Plan, begun under President Prado, involves the reclamation of 40,000 square miles of forest and river country centered in the great Apurímac and Urubamba river valleys (sources of tremendous hydroelectric potential). The area lies largely in the *sierra* east and south of Lima. A number of foreign technical missions, international agencies, and the government of the United States have shown great interest in it. Arthur D. Little, Incorporated, economic consultants from Cambridge, Massachusetts, have delivered a very favorable report on the prospects.

A favorite project of President Belaúnde is a scheme for the construction of an international highway on the eastern side of the Andes to link Bolivia, Peru, Ecuador, and Colombia. International financing under the Alliance for Progress is becoming available for this ambitious project.

Housing, Education, and Health

Of basic importance to the development of a nation's standard of living are the provisions for housing, education and health. Peru has a great challenge with respect to all of these. Educational and health facilities are all but nonexistent in most of the country, and even in the cities population pressure has far outstripped their capacity. Teachers, doctors, and associated professional categories are in short supply.

Through the effort of the Instituto Nacional de Vivienda (National Housing Institute) and some private ventures, low-cost housing projects have begun, especially in the Lima area. Associated with this, there have developed, with governmental support, a housing co-operative movement and savings-and-loan associations. A Maryknoll priest, Father Daniel B. McLellan, is credited with having originated much of this. Volunteers from the United States Peace Corps are involved in some of the ventures in this category.

The Indians

Few programs have been set in motion that have affected the poor circumstances of the millions of Indians in the highlands. A governmental ministry—Labor and Indigenous Affairs—has undertaken surveys of the problems but no substantial inroads have been made. The possibility of resettlement down into the *selva* has so far shown little prospect of success.

The monumental proportions of this task have been amply demonstrated by the so-called Vicos experiment conducted by a group of Cornell University anthropologists.[7] Although successfully bringing amazing changes, full of implications for the future, this project has been operating over ten years and results have been accomplished only by the most patient, skilled, and sympathetic approaches.

Indians by the thousands are drifting into urban areas and are gradually taking on Western culture. A political socialization process of the greatest importance is at work in this cultural change.[8] In the meantime, it is to be hoped that future decentralization of industry to provincial centers and the improvement of agricultural methods can keep pace with the problem.

Agrarian Reform

The old and knotty problem of land distribution is an acute one in Peru. The proper solution to this may well be not so much distribution as the rapid assimilation of Indian population surplus into nonagricultural pursuits and the creation of new lands. In some agricultural pursuits, it appears preferable to maintain large-scale methods and large plots. In order to tackle the titanic problem there was created a Commission for Agrarian Reform and Housing which reported to President Prado in 1960. A master plan was set up involving a statement of objectives and a survey of the very complicated problems involved. A proposed law was drafted which provided the machinery for action centering on an Institute for Agrarian Reform and Colonization which would co-ordinate its efforts with other appropriate agencies such as those involved in Indigenous Affairs.

It can be expected that the emphasis will be on the opening up of new lands and colonization, rather than on the expropriation of the large landed estates. Nevertheless, there continue to take place invasions of estates by Indian squatters, especially in Cuzco province, the invaders having to be driven off by troops, often with attendant loss of life.

The Alliance for Progress

As must be concluded from the rapid survey above of socio-economic problems, Peru furnishes a most interesting prospect for the Alliance for Progress. The Peruvians are already well along into the planning that will be necessary to draw up an integrated plan. Already oriented to the problem of creating a developed economy, the Peruvians greeted the idea of a massive assault on such problems with enthusiasm.

A number of problems must be expected before the Alliance can be effectively in operation in Peru, however.

(1) The integrated plan required to qualify for funds will be delayed by the present political circumstances and also by lack of sufficient numbers of trained personnel to accomplish such a plan.

(2) The Peruvians will express impatience with the Alliance if existing economic relationships are altered. During 1962, for example, the Peruvians were greatly disturbed by the possibility of a reduction in the sugar quota to the United States (which since 1960 and the division of the old Cuban quotas has added millions of dollars to annual dollar revenues and has helped

place Peru in a very favorable balance-of-trade situation). The reaction to this was, in effect, that the Alliance for Progress would be rendered meaningless if existing revenues were damaged by the action of the United States.

(3) Although Peruvians will undoubtedly produce acceptable legislation for agrarian reform, it will certainly be a long time before the implementation of such legislation will be satisfactory.

NOTES FOR CHAPTER XIV

1. Víctor Andres Belaúnde, *Peruanidad*, 2d ed., Lima, 1957, p. 24.
2. Emilio Romero, "La política del Perú en la República" in *Cuadernos Americanos*, XXXIV, No. 4, July-Aug. 1947, p. 35.
3. Jorge Basadre, *Meditaciones sobre el destino histórico del Perú*, Lima, 1947, pp. 83 ff.
4. Almond and Coleman, *Politics of Developing Areas*, Princeton, 1960, p. 534.
5. Harry Kantor, *Ideology and Program of the Peruvian Aprista Party*, University of California Press, Los Angeles, 1953.
6. Belaúnde, *Peruanidad*, p. 445.
7. See Allan R. Holmberg, "Changing Community Attitudes and Values in Peru: A Case Study in Guided Change" in *Social Change in Latin America Today*, New York, 1961, Chapter 2, pp. 63-107.
8. See Richard W. Patch, *The Role of a Coastal Hacienda in the Hispanization of Andean Indians*, American Universities Field Staff correspondence, 1959.

SELECTED BIBLIOGRAPHY

Richard Adams, *A Community in the Andes*, University of Washington Press, Seattle, 1959.

Food and Agriculture Organization and International Bank for Reconstruction and Development, *The Agricultural Development of Peru*, Washington, 1959.

Thomas R. Ford, *Man and Land in Peru*, University of Florida Press, Gainesville, 1955.

Allan R. Holmberg, "Changing Community Attitudes and Values in Peru" in *Social Change in Latin America Today*, Vintage Books, New York, 1961.

Harry Kantor, *Ideology and Program of the Peruvian Aprista Party*, University of California Press, Los Angeles, 1953.

Arthur D. Little, Inc., *A Program for the Industrial and Regional Development of Peru: A Report to the Government of Peru*, 1960.

Pan American Union, *The Peruvian Economy*, Washington, D.C., 1950.

Richard W. Patch, various letters and reports since 1958, American Universities Field Staff.

Graham H. Stuart, *The Governmental System of Peru*, Carnegie Institution of Washington, Washington, 1925.

United Nations, Economic Commission for Latin America, *The Industrial Development of Peru*, Mexico City, 1959.

Arthur P. Whitaker, *The United States and South America: The Northern Republics*, Harvard University Press, Cambridge, 1948.

XV

Robert J. Alexander

BOLIVIA

THE NATIONAL REVOLUTION

FOR MORE than a decade Bolivia has been undergoing one of the most fundamental revolutions to take place in any Latin American nation during the twentieth century. This revolution has changed but little the formal structure of government in the republic, but it has completely changed the economic, social, and political bases upon which this structure rests.

Pre-Revolutionary Bolivia

For all practical purposes, Bolivia before 1952 consisted of two nations. One of these was pre-Columbian Indian, rural, and almost out of touch with Western civilization. The other was urban, more or less European in ancestry, and definitely a branch of the civilization of Europe.

The Indian peasants, who made up 85 to 90 percent of the population, lived on subsistence agriculture. Although their work on their landlords' acres grew the foodstuffs which were sold to the cities, they themselves received very little money income—so little, in fact, that only about 600,000 of the 3½ million Bolivians, it is estimated, were in the market for any appreciable amount of goods during any year. They grew their own food, built their own houses, made their own clothes. The few necessities which they could not make for themselves they bartered for in public markets in the villages or smaller cities.

The Indians cultivated the land of the great proprietors under a system comparable to the manorial system of medieval Europe. The great majority of them owned no land of their own, but were granted small plots on the large haciendas, where they could build their huts and grow sufficient crops to keep them and their families alive. In return for the use of these small portions of land, the peasants were required to labor on the part of the haciendas reserved by the owners to grow products for sale in the cities. Until the mid-1930's they were supposed to work six days a week for the landlord, although subsequently this time was reduced by half. In addition, each adult male Indian tenant was required to render *pongaje* or personal service to the landlord for a week at a time. This obligation rotated among the peasants on an hacienda. During the period of *pongaje* an Indian might be used by his landlord for some special project on the hacienda, he might be used as a house servant either on the hacienda or in the owner's town house, or if there was nothing for him to do, he might be rented out to someone else who could use his services.

Most of the Indians remained culturally pre-Columbian. They were pagans, although in many cases their paganism wore a thin veneer of Christianity. The great majority spoke only their own language—Quechua or Aymará —and knew little or no Spanish. Their women dressed in clothes which had been typical from at least the early days of the Spanish Conquest. They received no formal education.

In contrast to the rural Indian was the population of the cities and major towns. This was more heterogeneous than the people of the countryside. Most agricultural landlords possessed city houses where they spent most of their time. The urban upper classes included the small class of industrialists and the larger group of more or less well-to-do merchants and bankers, as well as higher government officials and military men. The upper classes generally tended to be of European or near-European descent.

The urban petty bourgeoisie were more numerous. They consisted of small merchants and craftsmen, as well as white collar workers in private and public employment. Women constituted a very important part of the small trader group in La Paz and other urban centers. A large percentage of this lower middle class were of pure Indian blood, and the market women in particular continued to wear the same clothing as the Indians. But they spoke Spanish and were more or less good Catholics, and so considered themselves *cholos*, or people of mixed blood.

Another large urban group consisted of wage workers in the country's few factories and in workshops, public utilities, and transportation. Like much of the petty bourgeoisie, this urban lower class consisted largely of people of Indian ancestry who had assimilated European cultural patterns.

Thus the urban population consisted in part of people of largely European ancestry and in part of people of mixed blood or of pure Indian ancestry who had to a greater or lesser degree absorbed European culture. They were generally Christians, and most of their children received at least some formal education. They also enjoyed medical facilities and other amenities which were not generally available to the majority of the population.

A third major element in Bolivian society consisted of people in the mining camps. Here, too, aside from the small managerial and technical group in charge, the majority of the population consisted of people of Indian ancestry who had to some degree learned Spanish and become assimilated to urban ways and ideas. But their contacts with their relatives in the rural areas remained close.

Until a decade and a half before the National Revolution the tin miners had enjoyed protection by neither labor legislation nor trade unions. Their living and working conditions were exceedingly primitive. However, during the years before 1952 the miners had been organized and had become highly militant. They played a vital role in bringing about the Revolution.

The mining industry was of peculiar importance to Bolivia. It provided most of the country's foreign exchange. But although it had been in existence for half a century by the time of the National Revolution, the tin-mining industry had provided relatively little return to Bolivia. Most of the industry was in the hands of three large companies, the Patiño, Aramayo, and Hochschild enterprises, which were owned largely by foreigners and Bolivians who spent most of their time abroad. Thus most of the profits from mining had gone abroad. Furthermore, throughout most of its history the tin-mining industry had paid only a very small amount in taxes, and wages and other domestic payments of the industry had been kept very low.

The Realities of Bolivian Politics Before 1952

In the light of the economic and social structure of pre-Revolutionary Bolivia it is not surprising that political power was a monopoly of a very small element in the population. This was reflected in the fact that only about 200,000 citizens, or about 7 percent of the population, had the right to vote. The illiterate Indian rural masses, as well as those in the cities who did not know how to read and write, were excluded from the franchise.

The government on both national and local levels served the interests of the dominant economic and social classes and groups. The Indian peasants not only were deprived of the vote but had little chance in the courts if they were pitted against members of the upper classes. National government policies were generally patterned to the needs of the agricultural landlords and the mining interests.

The owners of the mining industry played a large role in the country's politics. They were generally credited with the ability to make and unmake governments at will. Although this may be something of an exaggeration of the actual state of affairs, there is little doubt but that the tin-mining companies intervened openly and frequently in the country's political affairs.

The military also played a crucial role in government and politics. This is reflected in the fact that six of the nine men who served as president between 1936 and 1952 were military men; altogether, they served eleven of these sixteen years. During this period every administration either began or ended with a military *coup d'état*. There was no civilian group which could effectively challenge the army leaders when they made up their minds to overthrow the regime in power.

In the years just preceding the National Revolution, the trade union movement had begun to play an increasingly larger role in political life. It supported the regime in power between 1943 and 1946 and tried on various occasions to overthrow the governments which ruled during the succeeding six years. Finally, it played a key role in the installation of the revolutionary regime in 1952.

Bolivian History

Political History Before the Chaco War

During the nineteenth century, Bolivian history consisted of a succession of *coups d'état*, dictatorships, and civil wars, punctuated by international wars which the Bolivian armed forces consistently lost. However, the first twenty years of the present century were marked by the advent of the Liberal Party to power, and the beginning of a period of relative political calm. These were the years of the first rapid development of the tin-mining industry, which brought with it the establishment of three railway lines linking Bolivia with the outside world. A modest petroleum industry also developed in the southeastern part of the country, in the hands of the Standard Oil Company of New Jersey, after World War I. The major cities assumed new importance, and the economic prosperity which these events brought undoubtedly is a partial explanation of the country's comparative political stability.

The period of apparently normal constitutional government was marred only once, in 1920, when the Liberal Party was overthrown by a revolution and the rival Republican Party took power. The Republicans remained in office until the end of the Chaco War with Paraguay early in 1936. The armed forces generally remained in the background during this period, insofar as political affairs were concerned, and most of the presidents between 1900 and 1936 were civilians.

Harold Osborne has summed up the situation during the first third of the century as follows: "The revised Constitution, promulgated in 1880, lasted until 1931, lawless dictatorship came to seem like a nightmare from the past and by the twenties of the present century comparative political tranquillity and evidences of increased material prosperity had won for Bolivia the reputation of being one of the more stable and reliable of the Latin American republics." [1]

Although there was some small development of manufacturing in the decades following World War I, the fundamental balance of power within Bolivian society and politics remained undisturbed. Through the first century or more of Independence, the landed aristocracy remained largely in control of the government and politics of Bolivia, although after 1900 they shared this control with the tin interests.

During this whole period the process of despoliation of the Indian went forward apace. Although the country had emerged from the Colonial period with many of the self-governing Indian agrarian communities intact, the enactment of Manchester-Liberal legislation against communal property in the middle of the nineteenth century facilitated their destruction. By 1920 most of the Indian communities had been destroyed and their land had been seized by force or guile by white or *mestizo* landlords. The Indians had absolutely no share in the government of their country, in which they were virtual pariahs.

Impact of the Chaco War

The disastrous war with Paraguay over the desert area of the Chaco began the process of disintegration of the traditional economic, social, and political system of Bolivia. The war itself was a drastic defeat for the Bolivian army, which previous to its outbreak had been regarded as one of the strongest and best-organized of South America. The war also put a tremendous strain on the country's economic and financial resources and constituted a traumatic shock to important elements of the Bolivian community.

Many of the younger officers of the Bolivian army became convinced that the war was lost through the incapacity and cupidity of their superiors and of the civilian government which had presided over the conflict. They were very much impressed and moved by the suffering of the Indian conscripts who had been brought down from their 15,000-foot plateau to fight in the tropical jungles and deserts and died in great numbers of disease and snakebite. These young officers began to question the whole economic and social system dominant in the nation.

The effect of the war on the Indians was also notable. Thousands of them were impressed into the army and were taken for the first time out of their home localities. They saw cities and large towns such as they had hardly known to exist; they were taught habits and forms of behavior which were strikingly different from those that they and their ancestors knew. The upshot was a restlessness and dissatisfaction with the *status quo* which has only become fully evident since the beginning of the National Revolution.

The Toro and Busch Regimes

The first evidence of widespread dissatisfaction with the *status quo* was the overthrow of the government of President Tejada Sorzano in May 1936 by a group of military men led by Colonel David Toro. They proclaimed Bolivia to be a "Socialist Republic." During the year and a half that the Toro regime remained in power its principal accomplishments were the establishment of a ministry of labor, the encouragement of trade union organization, and the expropriation of the holdings of the Standard Oil Company.

Colonel Toro was overthrown by a second *coup d'état*, headed by Colonel Germán Busch, one of the heroes of the Chaco War. Busch's regime was a good deal more radical than that of Toro, and for the first time steps were taken to make the tin-mining companies answerable to the national government. Shortly before his death, President Busch decreed that the tin firms must sell all the foreign exchange they earned to the government. Busch also issued the country's first Labor Code and encouraged organization of the tin miners, with the result that the first Mine Workers' Federation was established.

The Busch regime aroused very strong opposition from the more conservative interests, particularly the tin companies. As a result, when Busch died in the middle of 1939 it was widely rumored that he had been murdered, although his death was officially called a suicide. Whatever the cause of death, Busch's disappearance resulted in a turn back towards the right on the part of the government. His successors during the following four and a half years presided over conservative regimes which did not try to disturb the *status quo*.

The Birth of New Parties

The discontent arising from the debacle of the Chaco War resulted in the establishment of several new political parties of considerable importance. These included the Partido Socialista Obrero Boliviano, the Partido de Izquierda Revolucionaria, the Partido Obrero Revolucionario, the Falange Socialista Boliviano, and the Movimiento Nacionalista Revolucionario.

The first of these, the Partido Socialista Obrero Boliviano, was established under the leadership of a colorful journalist and politician Gustavo Navarro, who was more commonly known by his pen name Tristan Marof. He had attempted in the middle 1920's to organize a Socialist Party and had for some years been a sympathizer with the Communists, although subsequently siding with Trotsky in his great struggle with Stalin. He had been in exile during the Chaco War and returned to Bolivia early in the Busch regime.

Soon after his return home, Marof had an interview with President Busch and subsequently became one of Busch's principal advisers. Political friends of Marof took the lead in organizing the first Miners' Federation, which they largely controlled. With the death of Busch, Marof and his followers established the PSOB, which for half a dozen years thereafter played an important role in the labor movement and in politics generally. It disappeared in the late 1940's as a result of the discrediting of Marof when he assumed a post of importance in the conservative regimes of that period.

The Partido de Izquierda Revolucionaria was founded in 1940 under the leadership of the country's foremost sociologist, José Antonio Arze. It claimed to be "independent Marxist" in ideology, although it undoubtedly contained in its ranks the country's small cadre of Stalinist Communists. Arze ran for president as candidate of the opposition in 1940 and polled a surprisingly large vote in several of the major cities. During most of the 1940's, the PIR controlled a sizable segment of the labor movement, including the organization of artisans, factory workers, railroad workers, and white-collar employees. After the outbreak of the National Revolution the party split and virtually disappeared, as a result of the close collaboration it had afforded the conservative regimes in the years before 1952.

The Partido Obrero Revolucionario was the Trotskyite party of Bolivia. First organized by a group of exiles, it began activities in Bolivia in the early 1940's. It remained a small group until the mid-1940's when, as a result of close personal association with the leader of the Miners' Federation, Juan Lechín (not himself a Trotskyite), it skyrocketed to influence in the labor movement for about half a dozen years. Afterward it declined to little more than a sect and became split into several quarreling groups.

The Falange Socialista Boliviana was very different from any of the other parties. It was also established by a group of exiles at the end of the Chaco War, but was patterned in ideas after the Falange of Franco Spain. It remained small until after the beginning of the National Revolution in 1952, when it became the principal group around which the right-wing opposition to the Revolution congregated.

Finally, there was the Movimiento Nacionalista Revolucionario. Established soon after the fall of the Busch regime under the leadership of Víctor Paz Estenssoro, who had been an economic adviser of Busch, the MNR was a nationalist party with a socialistic tendency. It was accused in its early days of being pro-Nazi, but there seems to be little substance to this charge.

The MNR was pro-Indian from the outset. Although it did not in the beginning advocate a thoroughgoing agrarian reform, it did favor abolition of the semifeudal conditions under which the Indian peasants lived. It was also strongly opposed to the economic and political influence of the tin-mining companies. Paz Estenssoro had been largely responsible for President Busch's establishing government control over foreign exchange earned by the mining firms. During 1942 the MNR gained considerable influence in the tin miners' unions, a position which it was to solidify in the following years.

The Villarroel Regime

In December 1943 a military coup brought to power a radical nationalist regime headed by Major Gualberto Villarroel in which younger military leaders and the Movimiento Nacionalista Revolucionario shared political responsibility and power. The Villarroel administration is important in retrospect mainly because it gave the MNR leaders their first experience in government and because it consolidated the MNR position in the labor movement.

The Villarroel government actively fostered formation of a strong federation among the tin miners. The MNR was the leading political force in this federation, which after 1945 was headed by Juan Lechín, one of the early members of the party. Although Lechín was a *movimientista*, he had relatively little political sophistication at this time and relied heavily on the Trotskyites of the Partido Obrero Revolucionario for preparing public documents setting forth the supposed ideological position of the Federación Sindical de Trabajadores Mineros. As might have been expected, these documents read like orthodox Trotskyite treatises. Juan Lechín has yet to live down the reputation for being an extreme leftist which these early Miners Federation pronouncements earned him.

The Villarroel government also took a hesitatingly pro-Indian attitude. It reiterated the abolition of *pongaje* which the Busch government had originally decreed, and reduced the number of days per week Indian tenants had to work for the landlords. Finally, President Villarroel summoned the First

Congress of Indians, which he himself attended shortly before his death and in which the Indians informed him and other government leaders of their complaints and aspirations.

The MNR was in the government during most of the two and a half years that Villarroel was president. In the early months of the regime, the Partido de Izquierda Revolucionaria also sought to join the government. However, negotiations among the PIR, the MNR, and Villarroel broke down over the excessive price the PIR demanded for its participation. Thereafter the PIR went into opposition and suddenly discovered that the Villarroel government was "pro-Nazi." It participated fully in the overthrow of Villarroel and in the governments which immediately succeeded him.

The Six Years

Major Villarroel's government was overthrown by a street uprising in La Paz in July 1946, and the Major and several of his closest associates were hanged on lampposts in front of the Presidential Palace. After a short period of provisional government, elections were held early in 1947, with rival lists of candidates backed by the Liberal Party and the PIR, on the one hand, and the Partido de Unificación Republicana Socialista (the last reincarnation of the old Republican Party) on the other. The nominee of the PURS, Dr. Enrique Hertzog, was victorious, but he organized a coalition government in which the Liberals, the PURS, and the PIR all participated. The PIR finally withdrew from the government in 1950, but not before its reputation among the workers had been largely destroyed because of its collaboration with the regime.

The MNR remained illegal between 1946 and 1952. However, in the 1946 election it backed a so-called Miners Bloc, consisting of members of the MNR and of the Trotskyite Partido Obrero Revolucionario, which elected two senators and several members of the chamber of deputies.

The MNR attempted several times to overthrow the regime, the most notable instance being in 1950, when a month-long civil war gave the *movimientistas* control of Santa Cruz, Cochabamba, and several towns in the highlands, though they finally lost. In spite of these defeats the MNR remained very strong and in fact gained ground, particularly in the organized labor movement.

During the Villarroel regime the only important labor group controlled by the MNR was the Miners Federation. However, during its period of illegality the party won over most of the leaders of the railroad workers and factory workers who had hitherto belonged to the PIR. Meanwhile, the Trotskyites, who continued to be allied with the MNR, gained considerable influence among white-collar workers and some hold among factory workers.

President Hertzog resigned because of ill health halfway through his administration and was succeeded by Vice-President Mamerto Urriolagoitia. When the latter's term was drawing to a close in 1951, presidential elections were held. The anti-MNR forces were split, the Liberals and PURS each having a nominee, and there were several less important candidates who also had been associated with regimes since 1946. The MNR, whose principal leaders were in exile, nominated Víctor Paz Estenssoro for president and Hernán Siles for vice-president.

When the votes were counted, Paz Estenssoro and Siles ran far ahead of all their rivals. Although the government maintained that the MNR had not received the required 51 percent of the vote, President Urriolagoitia chose not to follow the procedure which was constitutionally provided for under the circumstances, of submitting the final decision to the congress which had been elected at the same time. Rather, he resigned, turning power over to a military junta headed by General Ballivian.

The *junta militar* government lasted eleven months, from May 1951 to April 1952. Although it had promised to hold new elections, few steps were taken in this direction. Meanwhile, the MNR maintained that it had been robbed of a clear victory, and its leaders were busy conspiring to make their victory effective through force.

The Beginning of the National Revolution

On April 9, 1952, an uprising began in La Paz and other cities and in the mining camps. It was under the joint leadership of General Antonio Seleme, commander of the *carabineros* or national military police, and the Movimiento Nacionalista Revolucionario. But on the second day of fighting General Seleme took refuge in a foreign embassy in fear that the movement was being defeated, and full leadership fell to Hernán Siles and Juan Lechín, who were the principal MNR chiefs on the spot.

After three days of fighting the Revolution was victorious. Army units fought a losing battle in La Paz against the *carabineros* and armed civilian workers recruited by the MNR. In the meantime the tin miners, also under MNR direction, had succeeded in capturing the other principal towns and cities of the plateau, and a number of them joined the fray in the capital. By nightfall on April 11 the victory of the revolutionary forces was all but complete.

With their triumph Hernán Siles and Juan Lechín openly took charge of affairs. Siles was proclaimed vice-president of the Republic, in conformity with the MNR version of the results of the 1951 election. It was immediately announced that Víctor Paz Estenssoro, then in Buenos Aires, would be invited to return to head the government as constitutional president. He arrived about two weeks later.

Fundamental Reforms of the Revolution

During its six years in the political wilderness, the Movimiento Nacionalista Revolucionario had become considerably more radical. It had become committed to a thoroughgoing land reform, to nationalization of the Big Three tin-mining companies, and to a series of other proposals to alter fundamentally the economic, social, and political structure of the nation. Soon after taking power, the MNR chiefs began to put this program into execution.

The fundamental tasks of the National Revolution can be listed under three headings: incorporation of the Indian into full citizenship, bringing under national control the principal elements of the economy, and developing the national economy so as to provide a basis for raising living standards of the great mass of the people.

Basic to incorporation of the Indian fully into the life of the community has been the granting to him of three things: the vote, land, and arms. The first step was taken soon after the return of Paz Estenssoro, when a decree was issued establishing universal adult suffrage. Thus in one move the vote was given to all illiterates, which in large measure meant the Indian peasantry. Universal suffrage has been one of the keys to governmental stability since 1952.

The second move was to give the Indian organization and arms to enable him to make his newly acquired citizenship effective. Much of the effort of the Movimiento Nacionalista Revolucionario and of the government during the first year of the Revolution was taken up in this activity. Peasant unions were organized on virtually every hacienda in the country. At the same time, the MNR established local units of the party throughout the Indian areas. Finally, the members of the peasant unions were organized into militia companies, which were issued arms that had formerly been in the hands of the army, which was dissolved. A new regular army was not organized until a year after the victory of the Revolution.

Finally, the MNR regime gave the Indian land. Soon after assuming office, President Paz Estenssoro established an Agrarian Reform Commission to study the problem and draw up an appropriate land redistribution law. The commission was headed by Vice-President Siles and contained members of various political parties, as well as of the newly established Central Obrera Boliviana, the country's central labor organization.

The project of the agrarian reform law drawn up by the commission was revised by the cabinet, and finally, on August 2, 1953, the process of redistributing the country's land got formally under way in a ceremony in the village of Ucureña in the Department of Cochabamba. This law declared that the small plots of land which the landlords had allowed the tenants to use for their own sustenance became the property of the tenants as of the day of the law. The rest of the landowners' holdings were to be redistributed among the tenants as soon as the technical facilities available and the procedures established under the law could bring this about.

The agrarian reform was supposed to apply principally to land which had until then been cultivated by semifeudal methods. For land cultivated by modern methods and wage labor, the law limited itself to setting a maximum number of hectares which a proprietor might possess, only land in excess of that amount being subject to redistribution.

The ex-landlords were to be compensated for the land they lost, in government bonds. As a result of the tremendous inflation since the Revolution, this method of payment has meant virtual confiscation of the land. In many cases the landlords have not even received the bonds.

The Revolutionary government left the decision of how they would cultivate the land up to the Indian peasants. Those who wished to till it as individual private proprietors were free to do so, although the government offered certain incentives to peasants who would agree to work their land co-operatively. In fact, most of the land has been tilled individually.

During the first ten years of the National Revolution about 30 percent of the land likely to be subject to redistribution had been given to the peasants. The principal factor accounting for the slow progress in redistribution was the lack of sufficient surveyors and other technicians to do the job of dividing up the haciendas.

The agrarian reform has created difficulties for the cities. Many of the Indians were unused to a money economy, and rather than continuing to grow crops for sale to the cities, they contented themselves with cultivating enough to meet the needs of their families and no more. Opinion in Bolivia and among foreigners who have studied the problem is divided as to whether the new peasant proprietors are growing more for their own use than they did before they received the land. What is certain is that less is being produced for the cities.

It is unlikely that these economic drawbacks of the agrarian reform will be overcome until the Indian peasant has become fully convinced of the advantages to be gained by growing products for commercial purposes. This will involve a long job of education, in which not only the government but also people in the cities who have things to sell which the Indians might like to buy, will have to participate. Only in the region near La Paz has any significant effort in this direction so far been made, but it has resulted in a considerable increase in the Indian's interest in buying goods from the city and a consequent desire to grow products which can provide him with the necessary cash.

Whatever the economic results of agrarian reform, its political impact has been highly significant. It has been largely responsible for the fact that the Indians have been overwhelmingly in favor of the Revolutionary regime, and upon various occasions when it has been threatened have rallied to its defense. The result has been that Bolivia since 1952 has enjoyed the most stable government in a very long time, one of the most stable in the hemisphere.

The Nationalization of the Tin Mines

The most controversial aspect of the revolutionary government's program has been the nationalization of the Patiño, Aramayo, and Hochschild mining interests. This was carried out in October 1952 and was applauded by nearly all political groups in Bolivia. Economically, the effects of nationalization have not been particularly brilliant. Until 1961 there was a steady decline in production in the nationalized mines, and it was exceedingly hard to maintain labor discipline among the miners, who felt that they were now owners of the mines. Finally, there was a serious problem of overemployment in the mines, which also defied solution until nine years after the beginning of the Revolution.

The principal reasons for declining production of the tin-mining industry were the fall in the metal content of the ore, something which had been going on for several decades before the National Revolution, and the antiquated nature of the equipment used. By the late 1950's many mines were producing less than 1 percent tin in the ore being excavated, whereas before 1930 the percentage had run as high as 20 percent. Subsequent to the Great Depression there had been virtually no prospecting for new mines by the Big Three, and the government did very little exploring either, after it took over the industry.

However, there is little doubt but that labor conditions in the mines contributed to low productivity and high cost. All workers who had been dismissed between 1946 and 1952 for political or trade-union reasons were reinstated in their jobs after the victory of the MNR, while no other workers were dismissed to make room for them. The result was that the mines were considerably overstaffed.

A complicating factor in the mining problem was the inability of the government to make a final settlement with the old mining enterprises of the amount of compensation which it owed them. Although a provisional agreement establishing a basis for compensation was reached in 1953, no determination was made as to how much had to be paid. In the face of this, it was impossible for the government's Corporación Minera de Bolivia to obtain any private financing for its program for re-equipping the existing mines and seeking out sites for new ones.

In 1961 a partial solution to many of the country's mining problems was reached in the so-called Operación Triangular. An agreement among the Inter-American Bank, West German private interests, and the United States Government with the Corporación Minera provided for considerable financing for re-equipment and exploration. In return the Corporación agreed to allow a German firm to reorganize its administration and also agreed to lay off excess workers. By the middle of 1962 this agreement had begun to pay dividends in terms of a reduced work force and an improvement in production.

Economic Development Programs

The revolutionary government has also sought to develop and diversify the country's economy. With this in mind, it spurred the operations of the official petroleum firm, Yacimientos Petrolíferos Fiscales Bolivianos, and during the first three years of the Revolution made the country virtually self-sufficient in oil. Subsequently, it opened up the country to exploration and exploitation by private firms, and by 1962 one of these, Gulf de Bolivia, had discovered and begun to exploit a rich new field. A decade after the beginning of the Revolution it began to appear as if oil might become an important supplement to mineral products among Bolivia's exports.

Much government attention has been centered on opening up and developing the Oriente or eastern part of the country. This region includes about two-thirds of the land area of the republic and is largely tropical in climate, most of it lying only a few hundred feet above sea level. Although there has been some grazing and collection of raw rubber and other wild products of the area, it has been very sparsely populated. The Indians from the highlands have been exceedingly hesitant to go into a region which was so strikingly different from the cold semiarid plateaus to which they were accustomed.

The first move to open up the region was completion by the Revolutionary government of a road from Cochabamba in the eastern foothills of the Andes to Santa Cruz, the main urban center of the Oriente. This road was finished about two years after the Revolutionary regime came to power. Subsequently the government built a large sugar mill in the Santa Cruz area and also encouraged the growing of cotton in an area to the east of Santa Cruz.

Extensive efforts have been made to colonize the Oriente, particularly along the Cochabamba-Santa Cruz highway. Several groups of foreigners, including Japanese, Okinawans, Mennonites, and Italians, have been settled in the region, and most of their colonies are now prospering. In addition, the government used a unit of the reconstituted army to open up areas along the highway, building offshoot roads, clearing land, and constructing houses and other buildings. The discharged Indian draftees were then offered land in the areas which they had helped to prepare.

Until very recent years the Indians remained reluctant to move into the Oriente. However, by the tenth anniversary of the National Revolution, there had begun a sizable trickle of settlers from the highlands and from the foothills. It appeared that the migration the government had hoped for for so long was actually beginning. By 1963 it was estimated that 200,000 Indian settlers had moved into the Oriente.

The Revolutionary regime's development efforts were hampered principally by lack of resources. However, it did engage in modest programs of electric power expansion and road construction and with its own resources built a few new industrial establishments.

The Problem of Inflation

The National Revolution has brought an exaggerated inflation in its train, in large part due to the government's attempt to spend more than its resources would allow. Other causes include a considerable fall in the price of tin and other mineral products and a large decline in output of the mining industry. Of importance, too, has undoubtedly been the fall in the amount of agricultural products available to the cities.

Some measure of the severity of the inflation is offered by what has happened to the international exchange value of the national currency, the boliviano. In 1952 the boliviano was worth about 220 to the United States dollar. By the end of 1956 it was exchanging for 15,000 to the dollar. It has since been stabilized at about 12,000 to the dollar.

A number of programs have been carried out by the government, under prodding from the International Monetary Fund and the United States, to stabilize prices. These programs have more or less stabilized the international exchange rate of the boliviano and have slowed down the internal rise of prices. But they have also caused hardship to the urban workers, whose real wages have fallen, and have brought the closing of several of the already limited number of factories, due to a drying up of markets. In part, this latter phenomenon has been the result, also, of the failure of the industrialists to make sufficient efforts to develop markets among the Indian peasants who have received the land.

The Political Process of Revolutionary Bolivia

Both the formal structure of government and the political groups and pressures operating behind it in Bolivia must be looked at in the light of the revolutionary experience which began in 1952. Since this process has vastly changed the country's social and economic institutions, it has also had a sharp impact upon the nation's government and politics.

Fundamentally, Bolivia has been transformed from a country in which only a small elite had any real participation in government and political activity into a nation in which the masses play the fundamental role through a variety of organizations. It has also been changed from a land in which the military had the last word in political decisions, regardless of the formal strictures of the constitution, into an essentially civilian republic.

All of this has gone far towards establishing a framework within which stable and constitutional political democracy can become a reality. Although, as we shall see, the succeeding Revolutionary administrations have not always behaved in a completely democratic manner, this fact has been largely a reflection of the attitudes of the opposition rather than of the ideology of those in power. Certainly, a fundamental objective of the National Revolution has been the establishment of political democracy on a sound and permanent basis.

The Movimiento Nacionalista Revolucionario

Overwhelmingly the largest and most important political party of contemporary Bolivia is the Movimiento Nacionalista Revolucionario. By the end of a dozen years in power, it still showed little evidence of having worn itself out in office.

The local units of the party are known as *comandos*, and these are to be found throughout the country. They are grouped together in municipal and regional subdivisions of the party, which on a national scale is administered by the Comando Político Nacional.

The top leadership of the government and the MNR party have been undergoing important changes in recent years. Many of those who founded the party or rose to influence in its ranks during the period before the National Revolution remain important. The outstanding figures in this group include Víctor Paz Estenssoro, the undisputed top man in the party, who has twice been president (1952-56 and 1960 to the present), and Hernán Siles, who was vice-president from 1952 to 1956, was president in the succeeding term, and became ambassador to Uruguay when he retired as chief executive. Also of prominence is Luis Penaloza, who served as president of the Central Bank and in several other posts.

However, a number of the older generation of MNR leaders broke away from the party during its first dozen years in power. The first to do so was Walter Guevara Arce, who had served in several cabinet posts during the first two administrations, as well as being executive secretary of the party, and was a leading figure in the MNR right wing. In 1960, when he failed to get the nomination for the presidency, he and his followers withdrew from the MNR and established a rival group which ultimately took the name Partido Revolucionario Auténtico.

During the second administration of Paz Estenssoro, splits to the left occurred in the MNR. Nuflo Chávez, who had been the first Minister of Peasant Affairs and was vice-president for a short while in 1956-57, split with the MNR to establish his own pro-Castro Frente de Liberación Nacional. Late in 1963, when it became clear that Juan Lechín would not receive the MNR nomination for president, he and his personal followers withdrew from the party and established the Partido Revolucionario Nacionalista.

However, to a considerable degree the position of those older leaders who abandoned the MNR was taken by younger men who rose to prominence after 1952. One secret of the strength of the MNR has been its ability to bring bright young men into important and sometimes top positions. These have included Alfredo Franco Guachalla, who served as Minister of Labor in the second Paz Estenssoro administration; Mario Guzmán Galarza, Minister of Education in the same period; Guillermo Bedregal, President of the Corporación Minera de Bolivia after 1961; and José Fellman Velarde, Paz Estenssoro's Minister of Foreign Affairs.

A dozen years after the beginning of the National Revolution, which has as its basic objective the integration of the Indian into full membership in the nation, the leadership of the MNR continued to be drawn principally from the white or *mestizo* urban middle and working classes, particularly from the former. Although some Indian leaders have begun to emerge on a local level, it is too early for any of them to have obtained national prominence.

MNR party membership is hard to define. Although hundreds of thousands of Indians undoubtedly regard themselves, and are regarded by party leaders, as members of the MNR, it is doubtful if more than a handful of these pay dues. The peasants undoubtedly constitute the largest element, though probably the least vocal, in the party's ranks. The party continues to have a large membership also among urban workers and miners, as well as a much smaller group of the middle and upper classes of the cities. Bolivia being a country in which civil service rules are virtually nonexistent, most government employees undoubtedly belong to the party, and they probably make a larger financial contribution to it than do many other groups.

The Left-Wing Opposition Parties

The Revolution has its opponents on the left and on the right. On the left stand two principal groups: the Stalinist Communists and the Trotskyites.

With the advent of the National Revolution, the Partido de Izquierda Revolucionaria fell apart. Most of its trade-union leaders had joined the MNR by 1952. In the first months of the Revolution, the PIR youth movement split with the party and formed the Partido Comunista de Bolivia. At the end of 1952 the PIR held a national convention which decided to dissolve the party. Some of the delegates thereupon organized a second Partido Comunista de Bolivia. After a few months these two Communist parties merged to form a single organization.

From the beginning of the Revolution, the Communists were hostile to the MNR. They opposed it in the unions, and were exceedingly critical of the MNR's conduct of the government. But they remained a small group, with little more than nuisance value, for several years. Then in the late 1950's the PCB began to acquire some influence in the miners' unions, particularly in the Oruro area.

Shortly before the 1956 election, a number of intellectuals who had previously belonged to the PIR reorganized the party. The reconstituted Partido de Izquierda Revolucionaria joined with the PCB to name a joint ticket for the elections of that year. They repeated the procedure in the 1960 election. In neither case did the Communist-PIR ticket receive more than a small fraction of the total vote.

Efforts by the Communists to thwart the government's reorganization of the mining industry in 1961 led to the arrest of a number of Communist miners' union officials. The president refused to bend before the Communists' threats of a general strike and for the time being at least was able to reduce their influence in the Mine Workers Federation. However, the Communists allied themselves closely to Juan Lechín, supporting him in the Miners Federation and in his 1964 campaign for the presidency.

The Trotskyite Partido Obrero Revolucionario achieved a political importance during the first few months of the National Revolution which the Communists were never able to acquire during the first dozen years of the Revolution. Because they had been allied with the MNR in the underground between 1946 and 1952, the Trotskyites had been able to gain considerable influence in the labor movement, particularly among the miners and factory workers. However, the national leadership of the Trotskyites was exceedingly sectarian and doctrinaire. They insisted upon seeing a kind of parallel between the Bolivian National Revolution and the Russia of 1917 which in fact did not exist and were convinced that Paz Estenssoro and the MNR would soon fall, leaving the field to them. Thus they became increasingly critical of MNR leadership, an attitude which alienated Juan Lechín and other MNR leaders who had formerly been very friendly towards them and also drove a wedge between the intellectual leaders of the POR and their followers in the labor movement. In 1954 most of the Trotskyite trade-union leaders joined the MNR. Thereafter, the POR split into two warring factions, each claiming to be the true Partido Obrero Revolucionario, and each having its own mimeographed newspaper.

Even within the MNR the trade-union leaders who had formerly belonged to the PIR and POR continued to be on opposite sides. Generally, the ex-Trotskyites were aligned with the so-called left wing of the MNR, whereas the ex-*PIRistas* were with the right wing.

The Rightist Opposition Parties

After April 1952 the principal right-wing parties of pre-Revolutionary Bolivia, the Partido Liberal and the Partido de Unificación Republicana Socialista, virtually ceased to function. Although they were never formally dissolved, they had been thoroughly discredited in the years 1946 to 1952 and made no serious efforts to reorganize and continue the fight against the MNR and its government.

The principal focus of the right-wing opposition to the Revolution, therefore, tended to be the Falange Socialista Boliviana. It had had no part in the governments from 1946 to 1952 and therefore did not arouse the popular ill will associated with the parties sharing the administration during that period. So after April 1952 the Falange was quickly transformed from a relatively unimportant fringe group into one of the major contenders for power.

Although the leaders of the Falange insisted after 1952 that they no longer held the fascist beliefs which they had quite frankly espoused before and during World War II, there is considerable reason to doubt this assertion. Much of their emphasis was an insistence that the country needed to be restored to "order" and "discipline," and although they were rather vague about how this was to be achieved, dictatorial methods were certainly implied.

The Falange supplemented open political opposition with conspiratorial activity. Sometimes the two were combined, as early in 1957, when the party issued an open proclamation urging the armed forces to overthrow President Siles. Certainly, it had not foregone the hope that the MNR regime could be overthrown by the traditional method of *coup d'état*.

In the 1956 election, the Falange had candidates for president and the congress. It carried most of the middle-class and upper-class wards of the major cities and elected the only opposition members of the chamber of deputies. But it got virtually no support among the urban workers and none at all among the miners and the peasantry. The Falange maintained that it had not been given equal opportunity with the MNR to campaign in the rural areas. Yet it is doubtful whether a party which did not endorse the agrarian reform—as was the case with the Falange—would have gotten any sizable peasant vote, so that the Falangists' small poll in the rural areas is no indication of the validity of their charge. What is certainly true is that the Falange, as well as the left-wing opposition parties, campaigned very vigorously in the cities and towns in both the 1956 and the 1960 elections.

In the 1960 election, the Falange Socialista Boliviana had a serious rival as a center of right-wing opposition to the regime in the Partido Revolucionario Auténtico of Walter Guevara Arce. The two groups split the right-wing vote, which was somewhat larger than it had been in previous elections, about evenly. Then in 1962 a pact of joint action was signed between the two parties.

Previously the Falange had made alliances with two smaller right-wing opposition parties, the Partido Social Democrático and the Partido Social Cristiano. The first of these had been organized as a Christian Democratic party in the years before the National Revolution. Though it claimed to be a party of the moderate left, the PSD took a strong stand against the MNR in power. Its leaders, who wanted a still more drastic tone of opposition, withdrew to form the Partido Social Cristiano. In the elections from 1956 on, both parties supported the Falange.

The Future of the MNR and the Opposition

A dozen years after the National Revolution began none of the opposition parties of right or left had more than a small fraction of the popular influence and support possessed by the Movimiento Nacionalista Revolucionario. It seemed unlikely that in the proximate future any of these, or all of them together, would be able to win sufficient popular backing to oust the MNR from power.

Thus Bolivia seems likely for some time to come to have a party system comparable to that produced by the Mexican Revolution. The MNR is likely to remain overwhelmingly the majority party and to remain in control of the government, though opposition parties will continue to function. Major struggles for power are likely to take place within the MNR rather than between it and the other parties. Such was the case during the first dozen years of the Revolution, and the fate of Walter Guevara Arce and Juan Lechín and those who followed them out of the MNR in 1960 indicates that whoever attempts to split away from the government party will be unable to take any sizable group out with him.

Yet there is a major difference between the position of the Mexican

Partido Revolucionario Institucional and the Bolivian MNR. As yet, the institutional framework of the MNR and the Revolutionary regime is not sufficiently solidified to prevent the party from running a major risk of division each time the presidential succession is at issue. The party has always been divided into somewhat vague left and right wings, and many individual party leaders have gathered around themselves coteries of personal followers.

The 1960 and 1964 elections both provoked splits in the MNR. In the first case, a part of the right wing broke away, in the second some of the left wing withdrew. Neither of these splits resulted in mass desertions from the party, nor affected fundamentally its hold on the electorate. Nevertheless, the possibility of more basic divisions in the future still remains.

The Press

Some opponents of the Revolutionary regime, as well as some outside observers, have insisted that there is no freedom of the press in Bolivia. This claim is based largely on the fact that two pre-Revolutionary newspapers, *La Razón* of La Paz and *Los Tiempos* of Cochabamba, were forced out of existence soon after the MNR came to power. In the first case, elements of the MNR threatened to storm the newspaper's building if it was allowed to publish; in the second, such an attack actually took place. Under these circumstances, the MNR government refused to afford the two papers the police or military protection which would have been necessary to assure publication.

These events are lamentable and undoubtedly reflect upon the democratic *bona fides* of the MNR government. However, they are only part of the picture. Aside from these two papers, there has been a wide degree of freedom of the press, particularly since 1956. Only one newspaper is frankly the organ of the government, *La Nación*. Its principal rival, *El Diario*, is strongly and constantly critical of the government. It regularly publishes statements by leaders of the opposition parties, including those of people who played leading roles in pre-1952 governments. In addition, virtually every opposition political group has its own weekly or monthly publication which is sold freely in the streets of La Paz and other cities. The writer has bought copies of these periodicals whenever he has been in Bolivia since the Revolution. On balance, it is fair to say that the opposition has had since 1956 very extensive facilities for getting its point of view before those who are able to read.

Yet the press does not have in Bolivia the importance it has in many other countries, since a very large part of the population, including most of the peasantry, is still illiterate. Thus the political impact of newspapers is of secondary importance.

The Role of Organized Labor

Much more important than the press as forums for conflicting political currents are various kinds of organization which meet with regularity and provide a platform for the presentation of different points of view. One of the most important of these is the organized labor movement.

It was the trade unionists of La Paz and the mining centers who fought in the streets in April 1952 to put the MNR in power. During the first half-dozen years of the Revolutionary regime the government was officially a coalition or "co-government" of the MNR and the Central Obrera Boliviana. The COB had the right to pick four of the members of the President's cabinet.

One of the effects of the split between President Paz Estenssoro and Vice-President Juan Lechín in the year preceding the 1964 election was the formal ending of the co-government system. However, the support of a sizable segment of the labor movement is still an essential element in the stability of the regime, although the relative influence of organized labor within the MNR has undoubtedly declined greatly.

The MNR is the dominant political force in the labor movement. It still controls the sizable majority of the miners' unions, the oil workers, the industrial and white-collar workers. The influence which the Trotskyites had in the ranks of the industrial and white-collar workers' groups disappeared when the leaders of those organizations joined the MNR in 1954. In recent years the Partido Comunista has gained a foothold in the miners' organizations, particularly in the Oruro area. But they received a serious setback after 1961 when President Víctor Paz Estenssoro stood up to them and refused to accept their demands.

The labor movement has played an important role in the internal feuds within the MNR. This was particularly noticeable in 1956-57 when President Hernán Siles was faced with a showdown with the left wing, headed by Lechín. The left wing attempted to thwart Siles' program of price stabilization and for a few months the whole labor movement was aligned behind Lechín. However, when he attempted to organize a general strike on July 1, 1957, he was deserted by unions controlled by former members of the Partido de Izquierda Revolucionaria, notably the railroad workers and factory workers. Subsequently, Siles carried his fight to the minefields and convinced most local union leaders there not to participate in the walkout, which Lechín was then forced to call off.

Although at that time President Siles was in a position to destroy the influence of Lechín in the labor movement, he failed to take the steps necessary to do so. Some anti-Lechín elements in the Miners Federation were urging the president to sponsor the establishment of a new federation, while a majority of the labor leaders of all groups would probably have supported a move by the president to reorganize the Central Obrera Boliviana. When Siles failed to take the lead in these moves, Lechín was able to reassert his influence in the labor movement.

When President Paz Estenssoro broke with Juan Lechín late in 1963, he moved swiftly to undermine Lechín's position in the labor movement. A rival COB was organized by anti-Lechín forces in the trade unions, and it was quickly given legal recognition by the Ministry of Labor. At the same time, a move was made with President Paz Estenssoro's backing to establish a rival Miners Federation to that controlled by Lechín.

The Peasants' Organizations

Of growing importance in the Bolivian power complex are the peasants' organizations. During the first year of the Revolution, the Indians, who had possessed virtually no organizations previously, were brought into local *sindicatos campesinos* or peasant unions. In the beginning there was great enthusiasm in these groups, but with the passage of time this has decreased. Nevertheless, the mere weight of numbers has given the peasant organizations increasing importance within the MNR and within the general political structure of Bolivia.

Most of the peasant organizations are under the control of the MNR. However, in the Cochabamba region the Trotskyites have had some influence, and in some other areas the Communists have been able to control a few of these organizations. The only group in the right-wing opposition to the government with any peasant following is the Partido Revolucionario Auténtico, which has influence in some Cochabamba peasant unions.

Within the MNR the peasant bloc tends to support Víctor Paz Estenssoro and Hernán Siles, whom they regard as the fathers of the agrarian reform. However, in the Department of La Paz there are some peasant unions whose chiefs are allied with Juan Lechín.

The peasants now have arms and the vote as well as organization. The weight of the peasants at the ballot box is a very strong asset for the MNR since they vote overwhelmingly for the government party. It seems likely that they will continue to do so for the foreseeable future, since the MNR has given them land and other benefits.

The fact that the peasants are armed has also been of key importance to the regime. The arming of the rural and urban workers means that the old pattern of seizure of government by *coup d'état* has been broken. Although it might still be possible for military units in the capital to depose and even kill the president, it is no longer true that such action would give them control of the government. The peasant and working-class supporters of the regime could be counted upon to descend upon La Paz and wrest power from any military usurpers.

The voting and military power of the peasantry brought about a subtle shift of power within the government during the first ten years of the Revolution. Although the regime lost the backing it had had in April 1952 among the middle-class elements of the cities and was probably weaker among the urban proletariat than it had been in 1952, it remained overwhelmingly strong in the countryside. As a result, the government came to rely more on the peasantry, and the influence of peasants within the regime grew, principally at the expense of the urban workers and their leaders.

The Role of the University

University students have played a much less significant role in Bolivian politics since the Revolution than is normal in most Latin American countries, and than they did in pre-Revolutionary Bolivia. During much of the first decade of the Revolution, the university student organizations were dominated by elements of the left-wing opposition to the MNR, while the right-wingers, particularly the Catholic opponents of the regime, also had a considerable following. This fact has not noticeably weakened the MNR government.

This phenomenon is not difficult to explain. So long as politics was the preoccupation of only a small elite group, of which the university students constituted a highly vocal segment, their voice was considerably more powerful than their numbers justify. But in a situation in which the organized labor group is a very active and vocal participant in government and in which the peasants loom as the single most powerful element (though not highly vocal), the relative weight of the students declines.

The MNR has upon various occasions gained control of the student organizations, sometimes by methods which are questionable, but it has not been able to hold on to them for long. By the time of the tenth anniversary of the Revolution, the government party had apparently all but given up hope of maintaining a firm grasp on the student groups.

The Role of the Economic Groups

Another factor in the political structure of the country consists of organizations which represent the economically powerful and more well-to-do elements of the society. There are organizations of small private mining firms, chambers of commerce, and chambers of industry. Generally, these organizations have been aligned with the right-wing opposition to the regime. From time to time they have sought to conspire against it, but with little success. With the disappearance of the Big Three mining companies and of the large private landowners, the remaining upper-class economic groups have had relatively little weight in the country's power system.

One might have expected that the industrialists in particular would have had certain sympathies for the Revolution. They stood to gain by the possibility which the agrarian reform presents them of extending their markets to include the great majority of the population instead of only a small fraction. However, this fact does not seem to have notably influenced their thinking. As a group, the industrialists remain violent opponents of the Revolutionary regime. They protest bitterly against the government's sympathies for the organized workers and demand that the government save them from the consequences of its stabilization program. There seems to be little initiative upon the part of the industrialists to develop the potential markets which the agrarian reform laid open to them.

The Position of the Church

The Church, which in some Latin American countries is a major force in politics, has been of distinctly secondary importance in recent Bolivian history. The Church was not strong in pre-Revolutionary Bolivia, and its power has not been noticeably changed since 1952. Although the Church hierarchy has not taken a position in outright support of the Revolution, and although some laymen have organized parties in the name of Social Catholicism which have been in the opposition, the Catholic Church as such has not quarreled with the Revolutionary government—nor it with the Church. As was the case in previous regimes, ecclesiastical dignitaries share the platform with government, political, and military officials upon most public occasions, including those commemorating aspects of the National Revolution.

The only major formal alteration in Church-State relations arising from the Revolution has been an amendment inserted in the constitution in 1961. This clause provided for the abolition of the so-called *patronato*, under which the President of the Republic had nominated all candidates for positions in the Church hierarchy in Bolivia. The change was agreed to both by government leaders and Church officials. However, Bolivia remains officially a Catholic country.

The Role of the Military

The position of the military within the power structure of Bolivia has been fundamentally altered by the Revolution. Instead of being the final arbiters of power, they have been largely removed from active participation in the political struggle. However, they have constituted an important passive force in support of the National Revolution.

After the victory of the MNR in April 1952, the new government dissolved the national army, retiring its officers and dismissing its enlisted men. The military academy, the cadets of which had fought valiantly for the old regime, was closed down. For a year after the accession of the MNR to power, there was vigorous discussion in governmental ranks as to whether the army should be reconstituted. It was finally decided to reestablish it, but upon a new basis. The officer corps was very carefully selected from military men who had either belonged to the MNR before April 1952 or had worked closely with it in that period. Cadets for the reopened military academy were chosen on a basis which gave preference to sons of workers and to offspring of members and friends of the MNR. The loyalty of the leaders of the armed forces to the new regime was thereby assured, insofar as this was possible given the traditions of the Bolivian military.

Other measures were taken to assure that the army would not again attempt to make and unmake governments. It was kept small. Most of the troops were kept as far away from the capital as possible. Sizable elements of the army were used in economically productive projects such as road-building, opening up new agricultural areas in the Oriente, and so on, projects which also contributed to the government's economic development program.

As a result of all of these steps, the armed forces have not been a cause of concern to the government of the MNR. There has been no serious attempt by any military leader to overthrow the regime. The army and air force officers regard themselves as loyal servants not only of the civilian government of the republic, but of the National Revolution as well.

In 1964 the MNR nominated General René Barrientos, chief of the air force and leader of the MNR Comando in the military, as candidate for vice-president, on the ticket headed by President Paz Estenssoro. Some MNR members and outside observers were somewhat worried by this move, fearing that it signaled the return to the military to active interference in politics. However, it seems clear to the writer that General Barrientos was named more in his capacity as a leading MNR figure than in his capacity as a general.

Stability of the Regime

In spite of the fundamental economic and social changes undertaken by the government since 1952, Bolivia, in the period since the National Revolution began, has enjoyed one of the most stable regimes in its history. Essentially the same regime has been in power for more than a dozen years. Three consecutive presidential elections have been held, as well as two mid-term congressional elections. The traditional system of government change by *coup d'état* has been supplanted by a system of change by constitutional processes of election.

The stability of the MNR regime must of course be gauged in terms of the country's own history, not in terms of the situation in solidly established democratic republics. The continuance of the MNR in power for more than a decade has not been achieved without a great deal of vigilance. The regime has been constantly in danger of conspiracies by elements of both left and right to oust it by force. At least three such plots were uncovered in 1961, for example.

However, the essential fact about the situation since 1952 has been that the traditional ingredients of unstable government were eliminated, and new factors have come into existence which help to assure the continuance of the regime in power. The military was taken out of its traditional role of president-maker. Instead of being based on a segment of a small elite, the Revolutionary government has been based upon the support of the broad masses of the population, particularly in the rural areas. Strong organizations, including the Movimiento Nacionalista Revolucionario, the urban workers' unions, and the peasant organizations, stood ready to defend the regime.

Governmental Institutions

As we have already noted, the National Revolution brought little alteration of the formal structure of government. During the first four years of the regime, there was a *de facto* change of the system established in the constitution, since President Paz Estenssoro governed without a congress. However, since 1956 all three major powers of government have been functioning more or less normally.

In August 1961 a joint session of the congress revised the constitution, incorporating in it the fundamental changes which the Revolution had brought about during the preceding nine years. The agrarian reform, nationalization of the tin mines, and universal adult suffrage were incorporated in the constitution. The workers' and peasants' militia was also declared to be a regular part of the national army. Aside from these alterations, the two most important modifications in the constitution were a clause permitting the re-election of the president, and one which we have already noted ending the *patronato* of the Church.

However, in spite of this revision of the constitution, the framework of the Bolivian government remains essentially similar to what it was before 1952. The country continues to be a centralized republic, with a separation of powers among the three traditional branches of government, the executive, judicial, and legislative. The last consists of two houses, a senate and a chamber of deputies, which under the new constitution are chosen by universal adult suffrage and meet in regular annual sessions.

Bolivia continues also to have a presidential form of government rather than a parliamentary one. Members of the cabinet serve at the pleasure of the president and are named by him. They do not have to be members of congress, and usually are not. As under virtually all Latin American constitutions, the Bolivian president has the right, under certain conditions and for a limited period of time, to suspend certain civil liberties guaranteed in the constitution. He also has powers of legislation by decree, and the ability to issue "regulations" governing the administration of laws passed by Congress, which makes it possible to modify statute law considerably.

The situation of the Bolivian judiciary is weak, as is true in most other Latin American governments. The Bolivian supreme court, which resides in the city of Sucre (the legislative and administrative powers are in La Paz) has rarely caviled at recognizing any new regime which has seized power by force. However, it is notable that in spite of its belief in the urgency of agrarian reform, the MNR government since 1953 has honored the power of the special agrarian courts to study, hold up for a considerable period of time, and even modify the process of land redistribution. Nevertheless, it is perhaps typical that this whole process is outside of the purview of the regular civil courts.

Bolivia is divided for administrative purposes into a number of "departments." There is no pretense that there exists a federal form of government: the governors of the departments are named from La Paz, and there are no regional legislatures, although there are city and town councils.

Since the Revolution there has been much controversy over this aspect of governmental structure. Particularly in the Department of Santa Cruz there has been some agitation for the establishment of regional autonomy. The MNR government has rejected this demand, and in 1961 President Paz Estenssoro declared martial law in Santa Cruz in the face of a movement to obtain autonomy by force. There is reason to believe that this movement has more to do with the quarrels of various factions within the Movimiento Nacionalista Revolucionario than with any widespread desire for any type of federalism. However, it remains a constitutional issue of some importance. It is unlikely that Bolivia will adopt the federal form of government.

Principal Issues of National Policy

Domestic Policy

The National Revolution itself is the basic question of public policy so far as domestic Bolivian affairs are concerned. Much of the right-wing opposition is fundamentally opposed to the Revolution and all of its works. The left-wing opposition has not been opposed to the Revolution, but rather to its nature. The Bolivian National Revolution has not conformed to the preconceived patterns of the Communists, either Stalinist or Trotskyite. They are therefore against it as it now exists.

Although the Revolution itself will undoubtedly remain for some time to come the principal subject of dispute in Bolivian politics, there are special aspects of it which are only a little less bitterly controversial. The rapidity of the agrarian reform, for instance, is the subject of much dispute. The Communists and Trotskyites are especially critical of the slowness of the land redistribution process.

The right-wing opposition is particularly inclined to criticize the role of the labor movement in the regime. They pile upon its leaders much of the blame for the difficulties of the mining industry, the corruption which has been widely prevalent, the crisis in manufacturing, and most of the rest of the country's critical problems. The Falange, for instance, assures the public that it will restore discipline both to industry and to the countryside, by destroying the position of the labor movement. On the other hand, the left-wing opposition accuses the Movimiento Nacionalista Revolucionario of betraying the labor movement.

The right-wing parties have also bitterly accused the government of undemocratic behavior towards them. They center much criticism on the alleged unwillingness of the government to permit them full freedom to criticize and organize opposition. For its part, the government accuses the opposition of continuing to try to overthrow the regime by force rather than through constitutional means.

Inflation is also a major subject of dispute between government and opposition. Both right- and left-wing opponents agree that the government's efforts to control inflation have been insufficiently effective. The left-wingers are particularly insistent that the government is making the workers bear the brunt of the anti-inflationary program.

Issues disputed between the MNR and the opposition parties are also the subject of controversy within the government party itself. The left elements in the MNR tend to agree with the detailed criticisms of the Stalinists and Trotskyites, although they do not question the nature of the National Revolution itself. For their part, the rightists in the MNR criticize their leftist opponents within the MNR on roughly the same basis that the right-wing parties outside of the government attack the MNR regime as a whole.

Foreign Policy

The foreign policy of the revolutionary government has also been the subject of much dispute throughout the existence of the National Revolution. Most of the government's opponents, whether on the left or on the right, generally accuse the regime of being subservient to the United States. The leftist opponents in particular accuse the government of adopting its monetary stabilization policies as the price of continuing aid from the United States.

Generally, the four administrations of the Movimiento Nacionalista Revolucionario have maintained friendly relations with the United States, in spite of the fact that the party had been exceedingly critical of that country when it was in the opposition. For its part, the United States through four different administrations has been friendly towards the Bolivian National Revolution. Starting in 1953, the United States undertook an extensive program of economic and technical aid to Bolivia. This has included the sending of large quantities of foodstuffs and raw materials, underpinning the general budget for several years, granting loans for specific projects such as the Cochabamba–Santa Cruz road, and making available technical assistance in agriculture, education, health, and road construction and repair.

Although the MNR government has in general been friendly towards the United States, it has by no means been uncritical of this country. It has upon numerous occasions followed different policies from those of the United States, both in the United Nations and in the Organization of American States. A notable example occurred early in 1962, when Bolivia sided against the United States at the second Punta del Este Conference, where the United States was seeking the expulsion of the Castro regime from the OAS. Through early 1964, Bolivia remained one of four Latin American governments which continued to maintain diplomatic relations with the Castro regime.

Both the Communists and Trotskyites have violently criticized the friend-ship of the MNR government towards the United States and have argued that the United States was trying to "prevent the economic development" of Bolivia. They have urged that the country "trade with the whole world," meaning particularly the Soviet Union. The USSR has given an assist to the Communists' agitation by offering to build a tin smelter in Bolivia. But the Siles and Paz Estenssoro governments were both very cautious about ac-cepting such a proposal, and a dozen years after the Revolution there had been no official negotiations conducted on the matter.

The advent of the Castro regime presented a new range of problems in foreign affairs. The *fidelistas* found few recruits in Bolivia—aside from the Communists and Trotskyites, who were already opposed to the government in any case. Cuban diplomats in Bolivia adopted a disparaging attitude towards the Bolivian National Revolution, arguing that it was a failure and urging the Bolivians to follow the Cuban model. In 1961 President Paz Estenssoro declared two successive Cuban *chargés d'affaires* to be *persona non grata*.

In its general relations with the rest of Latin America, the MNR gov-ernment adopts a somewhat isolationist attitude, due in part to the country's physical isolation, in part to peculiar difficulties which Bolivia has tradition-ally had with several of its neighbors.

Relations with Chile have been bumpy since 1952. There was an acrimoni-ous dispute between the two countries whether the free exit and entrance through the Chilean ports of Arica and Antofagasta which are assured by treaty to Bolivia included the right to build an oil pipeline to one of these ports. Chile finally conceded the point. Subsequently, early in 1962 a more serious dispute arose when Chile began a project to divert water from a river rising in Bolivia without agreement upon the part of the Bolivian government. As these words are written, this dispute is still raging.

Relations have been reserved with Argentina and Brazil. No love was lost between MNR leaders and the regime of Juan Perón, and upon several occasions before Perón was overthrown, the Argentine government closed the frontier with Bolivia to bring pressure upon the Bolivian government.

With regard to Brazil, the MNR government, like most of its immediate predecessors, harbored misgivings concerning the designs which Brazil might have on certain Bolivian areas near the Brazilian frontier. In long negotiations the MNR regime refused to allow the Brazilian government oil firm Petrobras to develop certain concessions which previous Bolivian gov-ernments had conceded to be in an area to be explored and developed by Brazilians. The concessions were finally made available to a privately financed Brazilian firm.

The MNR government also sought to develop other resources in the frontier area as a means of fending off Brazilian desire to do so. It authorized several United States firms, for instance, to explore for iron ore in the region and to develop plans for its exploitation.

Finally, the Revolutionary government of Bolivia adopted a reserved attitude towards the Latin American Free Trade Area, which was established in 1960. Although participating in the first negotiations over LAFTA, Bolivia did not ratify the agreement setting up the Free Trade Area, because it was unable to get the concessions which the Paz Estenssoro government felt were necessary to protect the very weak manufacturing industries of Bolivia from competition.

Except for Cuba, Bolivian relations with other Latin American nations have not been the cause of particularly bitter disputes in domestic politics. In view of the widespread nationalist feelings of virtually all political elements, it was difficult for any part of the opposition to be violently critical of efforts designed to protect Bolivian national sovereignty and interests.

Summary and Conclusion

The National Revolution has changed the social and economic face of Bolivia, through the agrarian reform, the nationalization of the mining industry, and the beginning of the opening up of the Oriente. It has also wrought deep changes in the real political structure of the country, transferring power from the small landed aristocracy, the tin-mining concerns, and the army to the peasants and the urban workers. The Revolution has been led by a single political party, the Movimiento Nacionalista Revolucionario, which since 1952 has had the backing of the overwhelming majority of the peasantry and a less decisive majority of the urban working class, but has lost most of the middle-class support which it possessed when it came to power. Other parties to both the right and the left of the MNR have continued to exist, and function as the opposition.

In spite of the changes which it has brought about in most aspects of the life of the country, the National Revolution has changed only moderately the formal structure of government. The constitution has been revised to include within it the principal economic and social reforms brought about by the Revolution. However, the fundamental structure of the state as a centralized, presidential republic has been preserved. Agitation for a modification in the direction of federalism has borne little fruit.

In post-Revolutionary Bolivia important political roles are played by various nonpolitical organizations. The labor and peasant movements and the reconstituted army are strong supporters of the new regime. The organizations of the commercial and managerial classes are generally aligned with the right-wing opposition.

The fundamental purposes of the Revolution are to integrate the Indians into full citizenship, to create conditions which will permit raising the living standards of the masses of the people, and to solidify the bases of democracy in the process of achieving these objectives. Bolivia is a case study on whether it is possible to achieve the economic and social transformation which is so widely demanded in Latin America through democracy. It is thus a reply to the totalitarian challenge which emanates from Castro's Cuba.

NOTE FOR CHAPTER XV

1. Harold Osborne, *Bolivia: A Land Divided*, Royal Institute of International Affairs, London, 1954, p. 61.

SELECTED BIBLIOGRAPHY

Robert J. Alexander, *The Bolivian National Revolution*, Rutgers University Press, New Brunswick, 1958.

Charles W. Arnade, "Bolivia's Social Revolution, 1952-59," *Journal of Inter-American Studies*, July 1959.

————, *The Emergence of the Republic of Bolivia*, University of Florida Press, Gainesville, 1957.

Dwight B. Heath, "Land Reform in Bolivia," *Inter-American Economic Affairs*, Spring 1959.

Harold Osborne, *Bolivia: A Land Divided*, Royal Institute of International Affairs, London, 1954.

Richard W. Patch, "Bolivia: U.S. Assistance in a Revolutionary Setting" in Richard N. Adams et al., *Social Change in Latin America Today*, Random House, New York, 1960.

————, "Peasantry and National Revolution: Bolivia" in K. H. Silvert (Ed.), *Expectant Peoples*, Random House, New York, 1963.

Iquique

Antofagasta

CHILE

Santiago

Concepción

XVI   *Federico G. Gil*

CHILE

SOCIETY IN TRANSITION

A COUNTRY of extravagant shape, Chile is located at the southern end of the Andean range, the dominant physical feature of the South American continent. Chile's fantastic length (2,600 miles) contrasts with its width (110 miles). This narrow strip of land, running between formidable mountain heights and abysmal ocean depths, extends over an area of 286,000 square miles, greater than that of any European country except Russia. This republic pressed between the ocean and the mountains presents many physiographic and climatic contrasts. Traveling south from Arica, one crosses first a white desert, with rich nitrate deposits and other mineral resources, followed by a transitional zone, mining and agricultural, set in an austere and sober landscape. Continuing southward, one comes upon the beautiful and fertile central valley with its green vineyards and orchards and its dry stimulating air. Next, one enters a heavily wooded area, colder, rainy, and of varied topography. Farther south there is an almost uninhabited wilderness of islands, foggy channels, rocks, glaciers, and ice. The climate of Chile is very different at different latitudes, a fact which influences the whole economic life of the country. Physical structural units combine with the transverse climatic zones to form the nation's environmental patterns.[1]

Socio-Economic Background

Desert Chile, which stretches from the Peruvian frontier to Coquimbo, is one of the most unmitigated deserts of the world. In parts of it no rain falls for years in succession. Two zones can be distinguished in this region: the Norte Grande (Big North) and the Norte Chico (Little North). The Norte Grande is composed of the provinces of Tarapacá and Antofagasta, which were incorporated into Chile after her victory over Peru and Bolivia in the War of the Pacific. These two provinces occupy about 23 percent of the national territory, with 5 percent of the total population, the majority of which lives in urban centers, seaports, or mining towns. Mining is the chief economic activity, the Norte Grande being the chief producing center of natural sodium nitrate and one of the world's greatest sources of iodine. The inhospitable desert combines with mining exploitation to establish hard living conditions. Total dependence on the fluctuations of foreign markets has led to a high degree of insecurity among the population. The typical *nortino* is a rough, frugal, and courageous individual. Being one of the principal nuclei of the early labor movement, the Norte Grande has witnessed the development of a strong, fighting, well-organized proletariat. The two provinces, despite their small population, have about 16 percent of Chile's unionized labor force. It is also in this region that the Communist Party was first organized. Continuous instability and dependence on foreign markets have resulted in a pronounced leftism in the politics of the Norte Grande.

The Norte Chico is the transitional zone between the desert and mediterranean Chile. Although comprising the provinces of Atacama and Coquimbo, which represent 16 percent of the national area, the region has a population that is only 5.6 percent of the total. The chief activities of this population, more evenly spread in urban and rural areas than that of the Norte Grande, are mining and agriculture. The average miner or small farmer is by tradition and socio-economic circumstances an individualist. There are no great and powerful labor organizations. Politically, the influence of a few powerful families with mining interests is significant. One of the strongest nuclei of the Radical Party developed among this group in the nineteenth century.

The central part of the country stretches from Coquimbo to the Bío-Bío River and includes ten provinces (Aconcagua, Valparaíso, Santiago, O'Higgins, Colchagua, Curicó, Talca, Maule, Linares and Ñuble). This region, "the heart of the Chilean nation," is the home of the vast majority of the population. This was the Chile of colonial and early republican days, enclosed by desert, ocean, mountains and forest, fertile and blessed with a mild climate. This Chile grew northward and southward only in the second half of the nineteenth century. (The two extreme ends of the republic were only recently incorporated into the nation.) It is here that the *fundos* (farm-estates) for wheat and other cereals, orchards and vineyards and livestock enterprises are found. These farms for the most part belong to large landed proprietors under a system which developed in colonial days and has survived with minor alterations. The weight of this land-tenure system is oppressive in many ways, among which is the failure on the part of the landowners to use their property to the best productive advantage. In the provinces of Santiago, Valparaíso and Aconcagua, 7 percent of the properties cover 92 percent of the agricultural land, while the smaller holdings making up almost 85 percent of the total number of farms occupy currently 3 percent of the land area. For the country as a whole 9.7 percent of the property units occupy 87 percent of the agricultural land.[2]

As a result of the Chilean hacienda system a strong paternalistic relationship between peasants and owners has developed and is a major factor in the politics of the Chilean valley. The region is also the stage upon which the transition that Chile is undergoing at present stands out most vividly: the change from an agricultural, traditional society dominated by a landowning oligarchy with a semiservile class at its service, into a complex modern industrial society. The restructuring of society seems more evident here as a result of the appearance of new groups which demand participation in the whole realm of public affairs. Agricultural workers in this region have until now participated only slightly in the organized labor movement and have received small benefit from the existing protective legislation. The great political influence of the landlord class has excluded these workers from whatever protection and benefits are normally received by the industrial laborer. The *inquilinos* (tenant farmers) under the paternalistic rule of landowners still labor here under crude conditions.

A section of the central region is formed by the great urban centers of the provinces of Santiago and Valparaíso, which include 42.4 percent of the total Chilean urban population. The trend toward urbanization which has made urban dwellers of 60 percent of all Chileans is accentuated in this region by a corresponding industrial concentration, with consequent problems of food supply, transportation, energy, and housing. According to statistics, about 48 percent of all industrial workers are found in the provinces of Santiago and Valparaíso. The number of office workers is also high and, given the political and administrative centralization, the proportion of government workers is even higher. This serves to remind us that Santiago and Valparaíso, despite the mass of workers that form part of their populations, are also strong middle-class centers. The great proletarian strongholds are to be found in the mining area of the north and the coal zone of Concepción—not in Santiago, where differentiation born of the variety of industrial enterprises has impaired the development of unionism.

The rainy southern region of forests and grazing lands, known as Forest Chile, begins south of the Bío-Bío River along the frontier drawn between the Spaniards and Araucanians in colonial days. The southern extreme consists of many islands, a narrow coastal strip, the Strait of Magellan, and the larger part of Tierra del Fuego. This is essentially backwoods country of a temperate character. It is a frontier region and as such reveals an economic and social pattern quite distinct from that of the rest of the country. It includes eleven provinces (Concepción, Arauco, Bío-Bío, Malleco, Cautín, Valdivia, Osorno, Llanquihue, Chiloé, Aysén, and Magallanes). Among them are some of the provinces with the greatest natural increase in population. Concepción and Arauco are also, next to Santiago and Valparaíso, the largest industrial centers of the country. The area which produces practically all of Chile's coal is south of Concepción, a decided advantage for the development of heavy industry. With the completion of a steel plant and its subsidiary industries the importance of the region is rapidly increasing. Establishment of the steel industry at Huachipato marked a significant milestone in Chile's industrialization.

For three centuries the northern section of this region was the stage for the war against the Araucanian Indians as well as the southern frontier of Chile. In colonial days it was also the only counterweight to Santiago's political and economic predominance, and a very important army center. Economic factors as well as historical considerations have given rise to profound differences from the traditional central region. The coal miners, together with the nitrate workers of the north, were among the pioneers of the Chilean labor movement.

Bío-Bío, Malleco, and Cautín are prosperous agricultural areas. The lake region (Valdivia, Osorno, and Llanquihue) is also a farming area, although with a less diversified agricultural output. The existence of abundant rich pastures has resulted in the development of great cattle farms. This area had neither been colonized nor explored until a century ago, when German colonists began to arrive, sent by colonizing agents or coming on their own initiative. Some 10,000 German immigrants settled from 1846 to 1926 in the territory situated between Valdivia and Puerto Montt. They received plots in the unsettled lands of the state either directly from it or through concessionaires who under certain conditions were in possession of public land. This German colony not only survived times of distress but made a very deep impression on the total culture of the southern region.

Partly because this colonization established the policy of smaller land-holding areas in consonance with the immigrants' European experiences and with the type of crops they were accustomed to, and partly because of its late assimilation to the rest of the country, the land-tenure system in this area contrasts with the large-holding types which are typical of traditional, older Chile. This region supports an agricultural economy different from that of the central valley both in type of products and in land-tenure systems. The different socio-economic basis of Forest Chile has in turn supported political attitudes often in conflict with those of the established interests of central Chile.

The central zone of Chile was occupied by the Araucanians, the most numerous of Chile's native races, who in the fifteenth century were conquered by the Incas from the Andean Highlands or pushed south into Forest Chile. Into this basic Araucanian population came the Basque and Andalusian adventurers and settlers who intermarried with the Indians. The process of racial intermixing took place early and fairly completely, thus originating the nearly homogeneous Chilean racial type of our time. The European population received its greatest increase during the eighteenth century, when a large immigration from the Basque provinces joined the heretofore almost exclusively Castilian elements, principally Andalusians, already established in Chile. The families that they founded came to acquire considerable influence because of their wealth and culture, as witnessed by the great number of Basque names to be found today among Chile's most prominent political and intellectual leaders. Small numbers of other European immigrants, principally Swiss, German, Italian, French, British, and Yugoslav, settled chiefly in the southern region during the nineteenth and twentieth centuries and made additional contributions to Chile's racial make-up.

The Chilean population continues to increase steadily, as shown by recent censuses, and is at the present time approximately 7,500,000, more than double what it was in 1900. Despite the fact that agriculture remains the basic national activity, there has been a significant urbanization, suggesting that the country is emerging from its underdeveloped economic status. The attraction exercised by the cities may be observed particularly in Santiago, Valparaíso, Concepción, Antofagasta, and Valdivia. Demographic trends magnify the dominance of the central region and its cities to the detriment of the rural areas of the country. The characteristic centralization of the unitary state results in an absolute dependence of the geographical ends of the country on the middle zone. Chile's center views the development of natural resources in the extremes, north and south, with what may be termed a colonialist mentality and approach and, in general, contemplates with indifference the problems and aspirations of those areas.

Of Chile's total population, 2,155,293 persons, that is to say 36.3 percent of those over 12 years of age, are considered to be economically active, and three-fourths of these are men. A useful classification of the population given by the 1952 census on the basis of "habitual occupation" is the following:

OCCUPATION	NUMBERS
Professionals, technicians, etc.	92,195
Managers, administrators, directive personnel	137,616
Office workers and the like	160,621
Salesmen and the like	54,801
Farmers, fishermen, hunters, lumbermen, etc.	608,390
Miners, etc.	60,044
Transport workers	52,385
Manual laborers, day laborers, and other similar	40,119
Service workers, etc.	300,068
Unspecified and miscellaneous	136,256

A summary of the figures above provides a glimpse into the social structure. Of the total active population, 10.7 percent could be classified as directive personnel, 7.5 percent as white-collar employees, 2.5 percent as salesmen and the like, and 79.3 percent as manual workers.[3] With respect to occupational position and ownership, figures show that wage laborers form more than half of the total active population (53.1 percent) and self-employed workers come next with 21.6 percent. White-collar employees constitute 19.4 percent, and employers are only 2.1 percent of the total, the remainder (3.8 percent) being unknown.[4]

Statistics concerning the economically active population and its occupational breakdown can be related to the type of educational training available. Analysis of the last census indicates a very high literacy rate in contrast to low secondary school and university populations. Nothing reveals more clearly Chile's intermediate state of development than this contrast.

The Chilean educational system features a high degree of centralization. Government-authorized private schools fill an important place in the national educational scheme. Many of these private institutions are under the control of religious orders, and this has caused educational issues and policies to become often critically involved in politics. The issue of free education versus the "teaching state" (*estado docente*), as Chileans prefer to call the state-controlled system, has been a touchy one in the political battleground for many years and has often embittered party rivalries, particularly between the Conservative and Radical Parties. One of the greatest sources of strength of the Radical Party has lain for many years in its control over the educational system and its bureaucracy.

Strong class divisions and feelings are basic to Chilean society, if for no other reason than because status, prestige, power, and economic differences are always given especial attention by Chileans. The reasons for this sharp class awareness are partly historical. During colonial times and for a long time after independence, Chile was characterized by a fairly rigid two-class society—a landowning aristocracy descended from the original Spanish settlers, and a lower class formed by the large mass of peasants and domestic servants. The Indians lived as a nation apart. As race mixture proceeded, large numbers of *mestizos* appeared, some of whom acquired education and rose to occupy a middle position. In the latter part of the nineteenth century this middle category started to increase. Its ranks swelled from many sources, including the old upper class, some of whose members had lost their estates and were being forced to enter business or the liberal professions, and from newly arrived foreign elements. Stimulated by the growth of the population, accompanied by the trend toward urbanization and by general economic and educational developments, this emerging middle class became in less than a century and a half one of the largest segments of Chilean society, representing roughly one-fifth of the total population. There exist now in Chile three universally recognized categories: an upper class, a middle or "employee" class, and a lower class. These categories are difficult to define precisely and it is also hard to enumerate accurately the components, for another characteristic of Chilean class divisions is their lack of clearly marked boundaries.

The Chilean system is a highly mobile one, upward mobility being perhaps more in evidence than downward, an almost natural phenomenon given the expansive transitional nature of the economic structure. It should be added that Chile has made notable progress in the way of rendering social differences irrelevant to political rights and because of this has gained an enviable reputation on the continent as an effective democracy. Equality before the law and before the ballot box regardless of social status is an important leveling measure now firmly entrenched in Chilean democracy.

Political History[5]

The revolution for independence in Chile was almost accidental in the sense that it was precipitated by the succession of events that occurred in

Spain after 1808. When the struggle ended, Chile found itself free from all political ties to Spain, but its social structure emerged intact—at one end of the social scale a respectable aristocracy united by blood ties and family interests whose political experience was insignificant; at the other end, an ignorant and servile mass incapable of understanding and practicing the rights and duties of a free people.

During the period from 1817 to 1823, Bernardo O'Higgins, the distinguished military hero, headed a government legally constituted under an autocratic institutional system. O'Higgins' resignation in 1823 marked the appearance of two distinct political tendencies which were later to result in the creation of Chile's early parties. One favored a real republic, free and democratic, and the liberalization of social institutions accordingly, regardless of the lack of traditions and political habits; the other demanded a strong centralized government as opposed to the federalization advocated by its opponents and aspired, in general, to a system which would not break completely with colonial traditions, one which would not modify the existing structure of society and which, in short, would not be different from the one maintained under Spanish control. Supporters of the first tendency were known as the *liberales* or *pipiolos* (Liberals or novices) while the group who subscribed to more conservative ideas became known as the *pelucones* (bigwigs). Except for a short period after the fall of O'Higgins, the *pipiolos* were in ascendancy until 1830. A civil war in 1829 brought success to the Conservatives and the inauguration of an "autocratic republic." In the midst of the chaos a new group, the *estanqueros*, made its appearance under the leadership of a remarkable man, Diego Portales, who was to lead Chile out of anarchy and into strong, solid, and orderly government.

The Chilean aristocracy provided the base for the authoritarian structure created by Portales. The legal framework was provided by the Constitution of 1833, which, with some alterations, was to remain in force for almost a century. During the ensuing forty years the powers of the executive were without an effective counterweight. Under that constitution, Chile was to acquire a reputation for stability in striking contrast to the reputations of other Latin American republics, which were periodically rent by revolutions and military dictatorships. For approximately twenty years the oligarchy made no attempt to oppose the presidential absolutism created by Portales. However, after 1849 and up to 1891, in the words of a Chilean writer, "the politics of Chile [were] synthesized principally in the conflict between two organic spiritual elements, both of which belonged to the past: the aristocracy and the monarchy." [6]

It is not possible to speak of well-defined political parties during the early period of Chilean history. Rather than real parties, there were alignments and groupings dictated by the common interests of the restricted circle which constituted the oligarchy and created as instruments to influence the government. As a matter of convenience, the development of political parties in Chile can be divided into four periods. From 1830 to 1860, political organizations participated very little, if at all, in a system in which presidential authority was all-pervasive. From 1860 to 1890, the presidents governed with support of parties, and there existed a sort of unstable equilibrium between executives and the groups which supported them. During the third period, the period of the "parliamentary republic," from 1891 to 1920, presidential influence became almost extinct and parties grew at will. The fourth, beginning in 1920, has been marked by the rebellion of an electorate until then submissive and the appearance of new party types.

The thirty-year period beginning in 1839 witnessed the orderly ten-year "reigns" of three successive presidents. Long before the end of this period, however, divisions began to arise in the Conservative camp. The last decade of the period witnessed remarkable economic progress and with it the development of a new and vigorous group of wealthy mining and merchant families who, rebelling against the existing semifeudal system, began to demand liberal reforms. Economic development had built up new wealth and created new power structures. At the end of the period of the "aristocratic republic" it was clear that questions of moral and constitutional import were determining the delimitation of political camps. The social transformation which was needed to permit the passing from the "autocratic republic" to the "Liberal republic" had occurred. The growth of the new mining and commercial bourgeoisie and the newly acquired consciousness of strength of this class were determining factors in the ensuing era of moderation in which political parties began to take a more active role in the nation's life.

A new political organization, destined to play a great role in Chilean politics, was born in 1861. This new political group, calling itself the Radical Party, was founded by a small group of dissident Liberals and soon grew into a formidable force as lower-middle-class intellectuals, Masons, members of reform clubs, and small merchants began to swell its ranks. In the beginning the Radical Party program included four essential points: constitutional reform, state supervision over education, administrative decentralization, and freedom of suffrage. The Radicals were later to acquire the strong anticlerical tinge which became their distinctive mark. Socially and economically, the Radical Party was at first the expression of the political demands of the new wealthy bourgeoisie produced by the development of mining in the north, subsequently becoming the focus of the resistance by the agricultural provinces of the south to the centralization of power in Santiago. Later it was reinforced by the other social groups which emerged as a middle class began to develop in the cities.

After 1864 the so-called theological questions involving the relationship between Church and State became the crucial issue in Chilean politics. By this time conflict and upheaval were open and common, and the period was to witness a fierce political struggle which ended with victory for the Liberal cause. Chile's victory over Peru and Bolivia in the War of the Pacific brought about the end of what has been called the Golden Era of Liberalism, an era which gave a new veneer to the old authoritarian political system, making it acceptable for a few more years. The War of the Pacific had opened an era of prosperity which radiated to all the social classes but was in particular concentrated in the upper classes of society. With the richness of the public treasury at its disposal (derived from the income of the newly acquired nitrate and copper territories), the government undertook public work programs, opened new roads, promoted immigration, established war pensions, and increased wages of public employees. The cost of living increased and the mass of consumers became the victims of monetary depreciation. Systematic currency depreciation which favored the interest of the great landowners became a habit. Such was the origin of the chronic inflation which has affected Chile to this day. If the mining wealth meant the salvation of the ruling class by assuring its political and economic dominance, it also brought a grave risk—an exaggerated dependence upon foreign markets which was in the future to unbalance Chile's internal economy. In addition, the varied social and economic base of the newly opened Chile in the south, after pacification of the Araucanians, soon supported political attitudes in opposition to those of the traditional interests, resulting in further amplification of political activities, confined until then almost exclusively to the great landowning and commercial class.

With most of the religious issues settled, the Liberal forces, left without the anticlerical banner, began to disintegrate. The historical issue which then divided the ruling elite was whether a strong executive was to control the power of the parliament which represented this aristocracy or whether the power of that parliament was to prevail over presidential power, establishing itself in undisputed predominance. In 1891, during the administration of José Manuel Balmaceda, this split in the Chilean aristocracy culminated in civil war.

No great social issues were involved in this conflict. Neither the congress, which was the focal point of the anti-presidential movement, nor the president spoke for the lower class. Both represented one single economic group which had monopolistic political control.

Balmaceda's suicide marked the end of the old presidential regime and the beginning of another era, the era of the parliamentary republic (1891 to 1925). Between 1891 and 1920 presidential authority was to disappear almost entirely; political parties were to multiply rapidly and the oligarchs in congress were to wield unrestricted power. During the period of Conservative domination, there had existed two parties: the Conservatives and the Liberals. During the Liberal period there had been four: Conservative, Liberal, National, and Radical, to which the Democratic was added in 1887. But after the victory of the Congressionalist forces in the civil war, Chile's political system came to include a total of seven parties.

Government in Chile reached its lowest ebb during the period of parliamentary rule. The degree of ministerial instability is shown by the fact that while from 1831 to 1886, a 55-year period, the Chilean government was headed by 31 cabinets, in the 33-year period of the parliamentary republic there existed 121 different cabinets with a total of 530 ministers. Even worse than irresponsible government was the influence of the parliamentary system upon electoral habits. With the principle of electoral freedom now formally established, bribery and fraud became substitutes for the earlier governmental intervention as the means of influencing the outcome of elections. By 1915, however, a harsh reaction in civic spirit became noticeable and the presidential election of 1920 transcended the old patterns.

The tendencies toward "democratization" and reform of Chilean national institutions that caused the destruction of oligarchical domination developed gradually. Economic changes as well as profound alterations in the social-political complex took place, leading to a great social and economic upheaval. The social restructuring affected all levels. The aristocratic oligarchy transformed itself gradually into a plutocracy, as the commercial and industrial bourgeoisie continued to augment its ranks. This plutocracy developed a new set of values and a new attitude toward politics and life in general. Economic developments gave rise, in turn, to the integration of new and significant groups into the middle class, groups which contributed substance and vigor. The middle class which was growing so rapidly was in a sense a proletarized group quite distinct from the middle class in Europe, since it lacked the economic and social consistency of its counterparts. As economic development and democratization made progress after the Revolution of 1891, the middle class acquired some measure of consciousness of its condition and, abandoning its former timidity and inertia, became the center of political agitation. In 1920 it was the backbone of the "revolt of the electorate," which gave the masses their first electoral victory.

The lower class was not less affected than the others by the restructuring brought about by economic changes. The Chilean workers finally awakened to their plight. Gradually they learned to give the middle class electoral support. The pattern of Chilean society was changing and changing rapidly. It was no longer to be characterized by the existence of a small elite and an amorphous and submissive mass without ideas and aspirations. Now public opinion had been aroused, and new segments were voicing demands for a fundamental redistribution of power.

This process of change had more emphatic effects upon the political scene after 1920. What may be called a right bloc was formed by the Conservative, National, Liberal, and Liberal-Democratic parties. The Conservatives were the defenders of the landowners and of the Church. The Liberal Party represented no particular ideological position, but in practical politics it was the protector of the great grape-growers, the nitrate and industrial interests, and big business in general. The National Party was the political agency of the high bureaucracy. Its members were closely connected with the large private banks and commercial interests. The Liberal-Democratic Party, heir in 1893 to Balmaceda's ideas, had soon become devoid of ideology and engaged only in opportunistic struggles for office. Socially, it was composed of an aristocratic group of well-to-do families plus some upper-middle-class groups in the provinces. The Radical Party had a broader base than any other political organization. It represented the interests of the southern region, but spoke principally for the dissident upper-middle-class and the middle groups. It was only after 1906 that the party's program began to reflect the growing demands for reform which animated its followers among the middle class. The Democratic Party was distinctive in that it was the only organization with a popular base. Its failure, however, to identify itself with the labor movement had serious consequences: the Chilean worker, searching for leadership and not finding it among the established political groups, turned to the Marxists. This explains why in Chile the organized labor movement assumed a totally revolutionary position in which Communism was to have a preponderant influence, as it still does today.

Such were the conditions in Chile in 1920 when oligarchical domination collapsed. Change had come swiftly—an industrial revolution and social upheaval hand in hand—the machine, the proletariat, the metropolis, and the intellectual middle class appearing almost simultaneously on the scene. While these changes were in the making, parties remained alien to the social revolution. The downfall of the system was inevitable. Its demise can be chiefly attributed to the revolt of the middle class supported by the new proletariat, the loss of political prestige by the traditional oligarchy, administrative chaos, a government on the brink of bankruptcy, and the scandal of parliamentary majorities created by bribery and fraud. To these, the impact of the economic crisis was added when the nitrate boom collapsed after 1910 with the development of synthetic production elsewhere.

At this point a new leader emerged to express the general dissatisfaction with this state of affairs and to become the champion of the common man, Arturo Alessandri Palma. It was he who led a party coalition to victory in the elections of 1920. The Radicals and Democrats provided the basis for this coalition, with additional support from a Liberal faction and a few other small groups. Opposing him was a rightist coalition formed of the Conservatives, a majority of the Liberals, and Nationals.

Faced with strong opposition in the senate, Alessandri could not go far along the road of reform, and the resulting stalemate eventually caused the Chilean army to intervene openly in politics for the first time in almost a century. After a five-month period of military rule, Alessandri returned in 1925, with army support and free from political obstructionism, and began to rule by decree. The new constitution promulgated that year provided for a strong executive and put an end to the parliamentary system. Adoption of this constitution marked the official end of the anarchical years of the parliamentary republic and the re-establishment of a presidential regime. This was, however, "purely a structural restoration; it did not carry with it the restoration of the dominance of a given social economic class." [7]

Incidents during the electoral campaign of 1925 resulted in Alessandri's resignation three months before completion of his term. Within a short period Colonel Carlos Ibáñez established a dictatorship which was to last for the next four years. His regime gave emphasis to the reform of public ad-ministration; state intervention and activities began to acquire new dimensions, while a vast plan of public works was completed. Foreign capital poured into Chile and a sense of prosperity pervaded the country. There existed, however, a reverse side to the picture—political repression and arbitrariness.

A sharp economic depression and civil disturbances finally brought the collapse of Ibáñez's dictatorship in 1931. Naturally, this was followed by a period of agitation and social unrest which witnessed the failure of nine governments, two general strikes, and even a naval revolt in the short space of fifteen months. A *coup d'état* of military men and civilians proclaimed a "socialist republic," dismissed congress, and formed a governing junta. These revolutionaries were not able to accomplish much during the brief period of their rule (December 1931 to September 1932), but they did decree some important measures. Some of this reform legislation long survived the government which enacted it. A new military coup put an end to the "socialist republic" in September 1932. In the same month new elections were called.

Forced out of the political arena by the repressive policies of Ibáñez, political parties reached a maximum point of disorganization during the period of the socialist government. The "social question" had now completely displaced all other political issues, and parties, after a decade of disorder and experimentation, were confronted with the necessity of reorganizing themselves before taking their battle positions. In their 1932 convention, the Conservatives reaffirmed their traditional ideological position opposed to liberalism, particularly the socio-economic kind. In practical terms, the Conservatives unmistakably associated themselves with the extreme right. In reality, nothing differentiated the majority of the Liberals from the Conservatives, for beyond the façade of political factionalism there was the fundamental fact that both represented identical economic interests and the same social stratum. Liberals and Conservatives were destined to unite in a powerful bloc of the right. The acuteness of the class struggles during the preceding decade had had great repercussions in the Radical Party, on the other hand. The leftist inclinations of the urban middle class prevailed over other segments of the party in 1931. After that date it became clear that the Radical Party had taken the side of the proletarian class and that it advocated a system in which individualism would be replaced by social solidarity. Having once been the vanguard of the liberal movement, the Radicals were to play a new role, that of the moderating or center force within the ranks of the new social-economic leftism. While the Radicals veered to the left, the first of the populist parties, the Democratic Party, slowly moved away from its proletarian base and became more and more a lower-middle-class organization. Two other populist parties, however, were giving forceful and dramatic presentation of national socio-economic problems. They constituted formidable new forces, and they carried the banners of the newborn Chilean left. Although somewhat weakened by internal divisions, the Communists had continued to grow, devoting all of their energies to the labor movement. The second of the leftist groups, the Socialist Party of Chile, was formed in 1933 by a merger of the small groups which had contributed to the triumph of the Socialist coup. This new party was destined to play a very significant part in Chile's political life. Another group was to build up, in a short time, a new party with a promising future. The activities of Catholic Action organizations and the appearance of the *Quadragesimo Anno* encyclical gave impetus to Christian Socialism. "With its democratic political ideals, its roots in a traditional religion made consistent with the modern atmosphere, and its neo-socialist economic doctrine," the party of the Chilean Christian Socialists, calling itself subsequently the Christian Democratic party, became in later years a major competitor in Chilean politics.[8]

The multiplicity of party organizations which had gradually become characteristic of the Chilean political system was evident in the election of 1932. Five candidates entered the presidential race. Among these, two represented the rightist forces, two the Socialist and Communist left, and the fifth, Arturo Alessandri, the winner, represented the middle class and received the support of most center groups. During his second administration (1932 to 1938) Alessandri, the champion of the people, was to yield more and more to the claims of the rightist parties and to detach himself from leftist support. The Radicals and other "popular" parties began to move together into unified opposition when it became clear that the Lion of Tarapacá, as Alessandri was called, had ceased to roar and was not going to inaugurate a progressive program.

In the 1938 election, for the first time in Chilean political history, a coalition of middle-class and proletarian groups was challenging the traditional parties that had governed the country for more than a century. This was no desperate attempt of the undisciplined masses, but a well-concerted effort of mature, well-organized political forces, pledged to basic ideological principles. It was a close-fought contest because it afforded the electorate the opportunity of choosing between two different conceptions of government and was to a large extent a national trial of the existing political system. The example of several successful Popular Front coalitions in Europe at this time gave impetus to a similar development in Chile, and parties of the center and left rallied together for the presidential election of 1938. The Popular Front's victory in the presidential race was not clear-cut, for both houses of congress were lost to the rightist bloc. But the leftist victory did mean that Chile was to have the first president, Pedro Aguirre Cerda, elected predominantly by the lower and middle groups of society.

Withdrawal of the Socialists from the Popular Front brought the formal dissolution of the alliance early in 1941. The Popular Front had been weakened by an effective campaign of legislative obstructionism conducted by the right and by the intragovernmental rivalry brought about by the contest for control over patronage and policy between the Radicals and the Socialists. Harmony was further threatened by the acrid controversy between Socialists and Communists, arising from early events of the Second World

War and from their natural competition for control of the labor movement. The Communists chose to remain outside the government and made great gains in the struggle for control of the labor unions.

Despite the dissolution of the Popular Front, one or another coalition of the center and left managed to hold power until the end of the decade. After the untimely death in office of Aguirre Cerda, another loose alliance elected Juan Antonio Ríos, a moderate Radical, who also died in office in 1946. Another Radical, Gabriel González Videla, gained office with the support of a "Radical-Communist-Liberal coalition" when the election was thrown into the congress. He remained in office until 1952, having first unburdened himself of the Communists in 1948.

By 1949 the Chilean political scene was characterized by an extraordinary multiplicity of parties. Of the new political forces the most significant was the Agrarian Labor Party, which had apparently absorbed all the pro-Ibáñez votes and those of the defunct "Nazi Party" as well. As the 1952 presidential election approached, ex-dictator Carlos Ibáñez began to acquire great popularity. The forces of *ibañismo*, as it was called, were heterogeneous and included splinters of varied political coloration. Ibáñez's major strength, however, came from the electorate's strong feeling of disillusionment in the existing parties and from the frustrations and hardships arising from the ever-increasing inflation.

After the coalition of left-wing forces grabbed political power from the aristocratic elite in 1938, the Radical Party dominated this coalition for fourteen years, while within the ranks of the party two wings wrestled for supremacy. One of these wings is to this day definitely Marxist in orientation and logically seeks to place the party politically with the left. The other responds to traditional liberalism and rejects any contact with the extreme-leftist parties. The split personality of the Radicals served well to prevent dangerous extremisms, but the effectiveness of the government was also to suffer. A significant development in the years preceding 1952 was the disintegration of the once great Chilean Socialist Party. After victory, the prerogatives of office, petty jealousies, and personal ambitions triumphed over party interests and ideology, corrupting Socialist ranks. But also important in causing the Socialist decline was the tenacious and effective competition of the homogeneous and highly disciplined Communist Party. As regards the forces of the right, both the Conservative and Liberal Parties remained very strong. A key to the power of the rightist parties was the fact that their hold on the rural parts of Chile remained practically untouched. At no time during the years of leftist predominance did the leadership of the temporarily allied government parties attempt any program involving the partition, the expropriation, or even the increased taxation of the landed estates.

Leftist coalition governments failed to bring immediate and basic social changes and always fell short of their campaign pledges. No basic restructuring of society was ever attempted. In its efforts toward economic development and industrialization the center-left coalition achieved its greatest success, however. The crowning achievement was the creation of CORFO (Chilean Development Corporation), which marked the beginning of a state-directed program for economic development. In other fields of governmental authority, the period of leftist coalition politics witnessed the entrenchment and extension of the social welfare structure founded in the early regimes of Alessandri and Ibáñez, a considerable increase in trade union organization, a notable acceleration of educational programs, and tenacious adherence to constitutional procedure.

The presidential election of 1952 resulted in a remarkable victory for Ibáñez, the candidate who accounted himself above politics. The most significant thing about his victory is that for the first time the majority of the rural workers and tenant farmers defied the rightist landowners in order to vote for Ibáñez.

Like his Radical predecessors, Ibáñez began his administration with the support of left-wing parties but ended it with the support of the rightist parties. If in 1952 the Chilean voters had tried to escape their responsibilities by electing a father figure who would take upon himself all their worries, they were soon disappointed, for Ibáñez' administration turned out to be weak and ineffectual. Toward the end of his term, his popularity dwindled, and deserted by all the political groups that had been carried along with him to victory in 1952, he was a lonely figure.

During the Ibáñez administration there were some important party developments. Prior to the 1957 congressional elections, the parties of the left entered into an alliance and called themselves the Popular Action Front (Frente de Acción Popular, or FRAP). Included in this group were two major factions of the Socialists, the Labor Party (Partido del Trabajo) and the Democrats of the People. Also included in the Front were the Communists, prevented as they were then from operating under their own banner. Before long the Socialists were able to bury their differences and to unify their forces into a single well-organized party which soon emerged as a powerful political force.

In the presidential election of 1958, four major groupings became the contenders. The Conservatives and Liberals, having found a strong champion in Jorge Alessandri, another member of the famous family, made what was their strongest bid for the presidency since their defeat in 1938. The Christian Democrats, having in Eduardo Frei a figure of great appeal among intellectuals, technicians, and non-Marxist leftists, as well as Catholics, waged an active campaign. The left, fortified by the unification of the Socialists, assumed an independent position, and rejecting the possibilities of a new Radical-Left coalition, placed its hopes in its leader-candidate, Salvador Allende. As matters turned out, the unified left came close to winning the presidency, missing it only by the roughly 40,000 votes attracted by an independent candidate. The Radicals found themselves isolated for the first time and fought a hopeless battle for their candidate, Luis Bossay. When the returns were counted, Alessandri had won.

During the Alessandri administration, Chile continued to slide backwards, her economy showing little improvement while popular demands became more pressing. In spite of Alessandri's great personal popularity, his administration (probably the last to represent rightist forces) was characterized by irresolution and proved not only unable but unwilling to accomplish the radical alterations demanded by Chilean society.

As the presidential elections of 1964 approached, discontent was general and pressures grew stronger for adjustment in a political system which many had come to consider defective and ineffectual. The 1964 electoral campaign began early. Salvador Allende was again the candidate for the left (FRAP) coalition. Eduardo Frei was the Christian Democratic nominee, and Julio Durán, a member of the Radical Party, was the candidate of the center-right (Radical, Liberal, Conservative) administration coalition. Jorge Prat's independent candidacy was short-lived. A bipolarization of the electorate soon developed as a result of a congressional election in Curicó Province. So complete was the leftist victory over the right-wing coalition candidate in this context that the government coalition disintegrated. Although the Radicals decided to maintain Durán's candidacy in the hope of wielding decisive power if the election were thrown into the congress, Allende and Frei were left as the only serious presidential contenders. The most significant developments of the 1960's were the impressive gains made by the FRAP coalition and the Christian Democrats. The latter, by reason of their success in attracting new voters (particularly female ones) and thereby developing mass support, had become by now the country's largest party. An avowedly reformist party, it had created a "development mystique" of strong appeal as an alternative to the revolutionary program of the Marxist left. Three months before the election, scheduled for September 1964, the outcome of the close race between Allende and Frei still appeared uncertain.

Political Processes and Governmental Institutions

As in all Latin American countries, the Chilean governmental system is based on the classical concept of separation of powers. In practice, however, separation of political powers is not rigidly observed. This fact, added to the ample constitutional authority granted to the president, results in a system chiefly characterized by the dominant role played by the executive branch in all governmental processes.

The Executive

The Constitution of 1925 defines the qualifications of the presidential candidate as being born a Chilean and being over thirty years of age. The president is elected by direct vote for a six-year term and cannot succeed himself for the following term. In case no candidate obtains a majority, the congress in joint session makes its choice by secret ballot between the two candidates obtaining the highest poll. The president nominates a vice-president from among the members of his cabinet to serve in his place when he is ill, absent from the country, or personally in command of the armed forces; but if he dies in office, new elections are to be called within sixty days.

As is the case elsewhere in Latin America, the president has the authority to issue ordinances with the force of law to amplify legislation passed by the congress.

The ordinance power, *potestad reglamentaria*, is the essence of the broad administrative authority of the executive. In practice, however, the president sometimes uses his ordinance powers in such a fashion as to make changes which affect not only the form but the spirit of the laws as well. The president is the administrative chief of the government in law and fact. In a scheme of administration which is highly centralized, he has, as would be expected, unusually ample powers of appointment. In military affairs, however, his authority is somewhat limited by the constitution and by a law of 1953 which regulates in detail all matters concerning recruitment, appointment, and promotion of military personnel.

Unlike other Latin American countries, Chile has not had an abundance of soldier-presidents. The fact that President Ibáñez was a general was only incidental to his political career; of the last six chief executives, he is the only one who has been a military man. Participation of the armed forces in politics is a rare occurrence in the history of the country, although the Chilean army did play an active political role in the early and difficult period of republican organization. However, after that time, only in the civil conflicts of 1851 and 1891 did the armed forces assume any active participation in public affairs. After both of these conflicts, the army returned to its barracks without attempting to keep control of the government. During the period from 1924 to 1932, the military forces again entered the political arena and, sometimes with the support of civilian groups and of public opinion, exercised power in making and unmaking governments.

If we should seek an explanation for the political abstention of the Chilean military, we would find it above all in the lack of social contact between the aristocratic oligarchy and the armed forces, a phenomenon which was already distinguishable in early republican days. The fact is that the Chilean aristocracy has never been able to count on the support of the army during moments of danger. Neither in 1859 nor in 1891 nor in 1920 did the military side with the aristocracy; the army always maintained a loyalty of a traditional and monarchical sort. Military personnel in general are not identified with upper social groups. Although high military rank is the object of considerable prestige and is sometimes an avenue into the social elite, the vast majority of the military men are of middle- or lower-class status. As such, in 1924, seeing their economic condition impaired by the currency depreciation and the rise in the cost of living, they became the interpreters of public sentiment and thus initiated the military movement of 1924. While it is true that there were attempts on the part of the aristocracy to use the movement in order to regain control, it is equally true that action by the military set in motion the economic and social reforms called for by the needs of the country. With the restoration of constitutional government, the military withdrew as an active participant in politics, supporting only its own specialized demands and becoming what may be designated as an important veto group in Chilean politics. The possibility of a *coup d'état* carried out by units of the military in conjunction with some political parties, barring an economic debacle, seems today only remotely possible and fairly unlikely.

A civil service and merit system of sorts exists in Chile under a so-called Estatuto Administrativo provided by constitutional command. The Estatuto is in reality a body of law composed of various decrees and statutes applicable to public servants. Practically every branch of administration has its own Estatuto, covering its personnel.

The president's power to spend money augments and enhances his authority. The process of preparing and adopting the budget is the standard method universally employed, but shifts in funds and extensive use of supplementary appropriation laws have always been characteristic of the Chilean budgetary system. The president may under certain circumstances, with the approval of his cabinet, decree payments not authorized by law.

In the field of public finance a very important agency in the Chilean government and unique on the American continent is the office of the comptroller-general (Contraloría General de la República). This autonomous agency is entrusted with supervision of the fiscal management of the government and is headed by a comptroller appointed by the president with the consent of the senate, who enjoys the same guarantee of tenure as members of the supreme court. This agency, at once an administrative and a judicial body, is not only the custodian of all national property and the supervising agency of the budget, but it also has jurisdiction over cases concerning financial legislation. Above all these functions, the Chilean Contraloría is invested with significant power to make it an effective controlling agent of the executive. It takes cognizance of executive decrees and pronounces upon their constitutionality and legality. Thus, the Chilean comptroller is, in fact, the ultimate guardian of legality whose duty it is to see that the constitution is respected, the laws interpreted as they should be and the Estatuto Administrativo observed. Although the acts of the congress itself are outside the scope of the comptroller-general, he does pass judgment upon the executive decrees issued to implement those acts. In all matters involving management of funds his word is final.

The mere fact that such an institution exists speaks highly for the country's traditional respect for legality. It is worthy of note that the Contraloría General has been successful in a continent so often torn by revolutionary upheavals. Far from resisting its authority, chief executives have increased it with the consent of congress, thereby converting an institution which began simply as a supervisory agency of public accounts into an alert custodian of legality and a vigorous instrument in the Chilean administrative system. Although frequently presidents have been in disagreement with the Contraloría, they have always accepted its judgments and its authority has remained intact to the present day.

With reference to the legislative function of the president, it should be noted that legislation considerable in volume and in importance is proclaimed by presidential decree rather than by the process of congressional enactment. The use of legislative power by the president is associated in Chile with the issuance of two types of decrees: the *decretos-leyes* (decree laws) and the *decretos con fuerza de ley* (decrees having the force of law). The first type is executive enactment of legislation without authorization or delegation and in usurpation of the powers of the congress. Numerous decree laws have been issued by the various *de facto* governments since the adoption of the Constitution of 1925. The *decretos con fuerza de ley*, on the other hand, are presidential decrees issued by virtue of a delegation of powers by the congress. From a strictly legal viewpoint, there seems to be little doubt that the constitution forbids the congress to delegate such powers. In practice, however, cases of delegation of special powers have been numerous since 1925. The political justification for such delegation is always the necessity of meeting some kind of emergency. Thus, practice and custom have given sanction to these decrees, and the courts, by upholding or by refusing to decide on their constitutionality, have recognized them as sources of law. Extraordinary emergency powers have also been used frequently in Chile to meet grave dangers caused by domestic commotion. Although public opinion has favored restriction in the use of these powers, chief executives have frequently employed them in a repressive way. Actually the country has lived for long periods under emergency powers. In the face of some domestic disturbance, the congress has often acted hurriedly and has been too willing at times to grant this authority to the president.

The president has the power to extend the ordinary sessions of the congress as well as issue calls for extraordinary sessions. The part played by the president in the ordinary law-making process is also important, since he is authorized to initiate legislation in the form of messages. He may, of course, veto the laws that the congress submits for his signature. The constitution provides for the item veto, giving the president thirty days in which to veto the bill. This presidential veto is only suspensive, and the congress may enact legislation rejected by the president if a two-thirds majority of the members present approves.

Judicial functions of the president include the duty of watching over the conduct of judges and other members of the judiciary and of requesting the supreme court to initiate proceedings against them in case of misbehavior. There is no presidential interference in matters which are exclusively judicial and the above refers solely to the administrative functions of judicial personnel.

As to presidential responsibility, the chief executive is responsible to the congress for acts or omissions that violate the constitution and the laws or for "seriously endangering the honor or security of the state." He may be accused only during his term of office or within the six months ensuing. The procedure for impeachment is for the lower house, upon the preferring of charges against the president and with a majority vote of its members, to present the case to the senate for trial. A two-thirds vote in the senate is required for conviction.

Members of the cabinet are appointed by the president and have the title of ministers of state. They cannot be members of the congress but are authorized to participate in its sessions, with precedence in debate but no voting rights. Although after 1925 the congress was deprived of the power to depose cabinet members by means of votes of censure, it is still able to force the resignation of a minister in an indirect way. The constitutional authorization given to the lower house to bring before the senate accusations against ministers is frequently used for this purpose by a legislature long accustomed to having an influential voice and anxious to find ways of compensating for the lack of parliamentary responsibility. In contrast with other Latin American countries, cabinet members in Chile frequently attend sessions of the Congress. The legislature, in turn, is always most eager to subject them to long interrogations which, in spite of the heat of partisan controversy, are often fruitful in terms of policy.

The Legislature

The legislative branch is composed of the senate and a chamber of deputies. The senate is made up of 45 members, elected for eight-year terms, and the chamber of 147 deputies, elected for four years. Members of both houses are chosen by direct, secret, popular vote. Senators are elected under a system of constituencies or groups of provinces so arranged as to give representation to the interests of all the different regions, five senators being elected for each of nine regional groupings. Half of the senate membership is renewed every four years. Membership in the senate is restricted to citizens over thirty-five years of age. Deputies are elected by departments or groupings of departments, one deputy for each 30,000 inhabitants or fraction of 15,000 or more. Naturalized citizens can be elected as deputies or senators provided five years have elapsed since the date of their naturalization. Certain persons are ineligible to serve in either branch of the legislature. Cabinet ministers, intendants and governors, members of the judiciary, and citizens who hold contracts with the government are excluded.

Officers of the lower chamber include a president and two vice-presidents, who compose the steering committee known as the Mesa Directiva. The organization of the senate is similar. As in every legislature, there exists in the Chilean congress a number of regular or standing committees created by the rules of the chamber and the senate. The role played by these committees is significant, since as a rule the bulk of legislation originates in them. The annual legislative session lasts from May 21 to September 18. It can be extended by the chief executive, although this is a rare occurrence. Meetings in which both houses of congress sit together are held on specific dates for purposes determined by the constitution. Foreign precedents and customs, especially those from France, have exerted some influence on the development of parliamentary practices.

The Chilean system recognizes in general the inviolability of the legislators for their opinions and votes. As in most Latin American countries, the scope of parliamentary immunity from arrest is very broad. Legislators are immune from arrest from the day of their election until the expiration of their terms unless surprised *flagrante delicto*, without authorization of the court having jurisdiction over the case. Disciplinary powers of both houses include measures ranging from reprimanding or calling a member to order, or censuring him to depriving him of the right to participate in debates for three consecutive sessions.

In the legislative process, bills may be introduced by any member of the legislative chamber or by the executive. The president has the exclusive initiative of certain specific laws. The lower house has exclusive power to initiate legislation raising revenue and concerning military service, as well as the budget laws. Amnesty and general pardoning laws can only be initiated in the senate. In contrast with other Latin American countries, the judiciary in Chile has no authority to originate proposals dealing with justice and judicial proceedings.

In Chile, as in most of Latin America, lawyers have traditionally been predominant in the congress. Among its members there are also physicians, engineers, journalists, university professors, professional politicians, wealthy landowners, and big industrialists. Then there are others who represent economic groups which only recently have become influential, such as labor unions.

Although the constitutional system has entrusted to the legislature the power to enact laws and to determine public policy, the congress is not the center of the political life of Chile. This is so because of the powerful role the legal system and political customs have assigned to the executive branch; it is also the result of such factors as the nature of the class system, defective electoral processes, and the fragmentation and fluidity of organized political groups. In some periods of Chilean history, the congress, because of its factional quibbling and occasional lack of responsibility, was regarded with contempt, causing the people to look to the chief executive for order and leadership and to condone presidential usurpation of authority. Unlike many Latin American legislatures, however, the Chilean congress is not a rubber-stamp body. It is an independent, properly elected, deliberative assembly which often challenges the ascendancy of the executive and takes an active part in policy-making. The pre-eminence acquired by the congress during the period of the parliamentary republic (1891 to 1925) was conducive to the establishment of a tradition of independence.

The Administration of Justice

The highest court is the supreme court (Corte Suprema) composed of thirteen judges (*ministros*) who elect from their membership a president to serve a three-year term. These judges have tenure for life on good behavior and are appointed by the chief executive from a list of five individuals nominated by the supreme court itself. This list must include the two senior members of the Cortes de Apelaciones (courts of appeal). The lower courts vary in number, designation and structure. They are organized on the basis of the political divisions of the country in a pattern corresponding to the districts, subdelegations, departments, and provinces. The local courts, known as *jueces de letras* (with one judge for each court), function in each department seat and have civil and criminal jurisdiction. In the rural districts and subdelegations there exist judges with no legal training who dispense justice over minor cases for no compensation. They are called inferior judges. Next to the *jueces de letras* in sequence are the Cortes de Apelaciones. These are appellate courts but have jurisdiction in certain cases of first instance. There are nine of these courts in Chile, each having jurisdiction over two or more provinces. The Cortes de Apelaciones are generally composed of four judges, each of whom serves as the presiding officer in his turn, the rotation being on the basis of seniority. The court of Santiago has twenty-one judges, however, while the courts of Valparaíso and Concepción have seven.

Jueces de letras are appointed by the chief executive from a list of three names presented to him by the courts of appeals of the districts concerned. This list is made up by the courts afer competitive sifting of candidates— the only requirement being that the name of the judge with ranking seniority at the level immediately inferior to the vacancy to be filled must be included. The nomination of judges for the courts of appeals follows a similar procedure, the judges being subject to appointment by the president from a list of three names submitted to him by the supreme court. As in the former case, this list must contain the name of the ranking judge immediately inferior to the vacancy. This co-optative method of nomination has given the judiciary a decisive vote in the selection of its own personnel.

In general, judges must be lawyers who are Chilean citizens and at least twenty-five years old. The judicial code specifies for how long they must have practiced their profession, thus giving formal assurance of technical competence. For example, departmental judges need to have been lawyers for two years, while to become a member of the supreme court a law practice of fifteen years is required. The independence of the courts is formally recognized in the constitution and the laws. In a practical sense this independence is safeguarded by tenure as well as by the partial removal of the selection of judicial personnel from the power of the executive and the establishment of a merit system. A corollary of judicial independence is the principle that the courts should abstain from the judgment of political matters. The idea that magistrates should not meddle in the affairs of partisan politics has long been accepted in Chile. Chilean courts have always been reluctant to take cognizance of matters exclusively political, and judges in general are careful to abstain from party politics.

The most important function of the Chilean supreme court is to decide on the constitutionality of all laws. This power of interpreting the constitution, however, has only limited effect, since the decision that a statute or executive act is unconstitutional does not nullify it. It is merely a declaration that the act is inapplicable to a case in question on the grounds that it is contrary to the constitution, so that only this particular case is decided. The highest court can make the declaration of inapplicability by its own initiative in cases in which it has exclusive jurisdiction and also in cases of appeal from the lower courts. The majority of constitutional decisions, however, are made as a result of appeals.

There also exist in Chile some functional courts having special jurisdiction (military, lands and waters, food supplies, customs, juvenile, aeronautical, etc.) and their number tends to increase constantly. The proliferation of these special courts might suggest that Chile, with all other Latin American countries, is returning to a modified version of the old Spanish *fuero* system. Such, however, is not the case, since the present aim is not to establish privileges for certain groups but to supply functional service through tribunals composed of experts in a given field of law.

The Chilean court system may be made the object of criticisms also applicable to all Latin American judiciaries. Its main defects are slowness in the administration of justice, the prevalence of written as against oral procedure, and the expense of the legal process. The criticism that the courts are weak is not justified. Those who would wish a judicial branch to act as a curb on the executive may seek to make the courts a political check without giving them political power—which means in the final analysis control of political patronage, command of the army, and leadership in the dominant political group. Such an investing of political power in the courts would be impractical if tried. In spite of the turmoil caused by revolutions during the initial years of operation of the Constitution of 1925, the Chilean courts remained outside factional political struggles, untouched by those extralegal developments, and have preserved their integrity.

Local Government

The political units of local government are provinces, departments, subdelegations (*subdelegaciones*) and districts. The national territory is divided into twenty-five provinces made up of eighty-seven departments. Departments are subdivided into subdelegations and these into districts. Each province is under the authority of an intendant (*intendente*) who is appointed by the president for a three-year term. As the president's "natural and immediate agent," he is entrusted with supervision and direction of all provincial affairs. Each department has as administrative head a governor, also appointed by the president for three years. However, the intendant is also the governor of the department containing the provincial capital. The subdelegations are under "subdelegates," subordinate to the governor of the respective department and appointed by him for one year. The smallest political units, known as districts, are each headed by an "inspector," appointed by the respective subdelegate and responsible to and removable by him.

For administrative purposes provinces are further subdivided into communes (*comunas*). The administration of each commune or group of communes established by law is managed by a municipality (*municipalidad*), presided over by a mayor (*alcalde*). The municipalities have from five to fifteen councilmen (*regidores*) elected by direct vote for a three-year period. These municipal bodies have authority to legislate, with certain limitations, over matters concerning health, educational and recreational facilities, agricultural, industrial, and commercial developments, and roads and public works. They may also impose certain local taxes.

In spite of constitutional principles, decentralization in Chile has never been a fact. This has resulted in a political system which is top-heavy and indifferent to the interests of the locality. Although provincial and municipal home rule is theoretically favored, promises for a greater degree of autonomy have never been redeemed. Legislation and political practice have been vesting more and more powers in the central government and restricting the activities and jurisdiction of municipalities to matters of minor importance.

In recent years strong regionalist feelings have developed anew. Provinces are rising angrily against the long neglect of their problems by the government in Santiago. Even disasters caused by forces of nature and beyond man's control are often blamed on the disregard and negligence of the national authority. Although yet immeasurable and lacking political expression, this regionalism is a dormant force of some significance. Regional divisions are likely to be exploited by ambitious local demagogues who, unable to exert influence through politically organized groups, may choose instead to exacerbate local feelings. After years of absorbing centralization, many outlying regions have become unproductive. To combat this stagnation, the government has resorted to stopgap measures which have not solved the problem but only alleviated it. The establishment of free ports and duty-free frontiers has, in effect, weakened national unity without solving regional problems.

Autonomous and Semifiscal Agencies

The government is very much involved in Chile's efforts for industrialization. It has supplied the necessary stimulus to industrialize, and credit and development agencies created by the government have participated in the planning, establishment, and operation of new industries. A very important part has been played in this economic growth by a number of state-controlled industrial and commercial corporations. Today the government is responsible for a considerable part of all economic endeavors, and for this reason governmental expenditures show a tendency to increase at a faster pace than the national income. Such a remarkable expansion of governmental activities is a result of the need for state intervention to supply services, the reluctance of private capital to invest in certain industries, the reduction of foreign enterprise as an aim of nationalistic policy, and the fact that only the government is financially able to undertake certain economic ventures. A series of developmental and financing agencies has thus been set up, in the form of autonomous entities.

The oldest and most influential of the developmental agencies in Latin America is the Chilean Development Corporation (Corporación de Fomento de la Producción or CORFO), established in 1939. Divided into five departments, CORFO exercises practical supervision over all industry, since no new industrial operation or plant expansion is permitted without its authorization. A basic principle of CORFO policy is to discontinue support and its share of control of an enterprise as soon as it can dispense with CORFO's aid.

The number of other autonomous and semifiscal agencies related to the government through the various ministries is considerable. The structure and operation of these institutions are varied. In general, however, they are administered by autonomous councils of boards, some having a top executive official such as a director-general. The membership of these boards generally includes a number of presidential appointees and representatives of the organizations and segments of the population interested in and affected by the particular type of activity. Often such membership includes representatives of the workers. This increase in the functions of government has given new impetus to the growing power of the presidency by investing that office with authority to manage a substantial part of the economic affairs of the country. Although the congress has played a significant role in the creation of these agencies, it has often been the president's responsibility to initiate and undertake reforms in the administrative system with the result that some important phases of the industrialization program are under control of the executive branch.

Socio-Economic Problems and Public Policy

Among the economic maladjustments that beset Chile and retard its progress, the one which stands out is the system of land ownership. Ownership of land has been in Chile the major economic basis for the exercise of power and one of the basic conditioning factors of government since a good part of the total active population (30 percent) depends for its living directly on agricultural and pastoral pursuits. Monopolization of land, the core of the plantation system, has been and still is an important source of political power as well as a source of semifeudal social relationships. The conditions which characterize the complex agricultural problem of Chile may be summarized as follows. Agricultural production, while still absorbing the largest percentage of the population, is experiencing great difficulty in keeping pace with the growth of the population. The basic feature of Chilean agriculture is its low productivity in comparison with other economic activities. This difference becomes more and more outstanding as the rhythm of industrialization keeps accelerating in the present intermediate stage of the growth of the country's economy. Chilean agriculture is also exceptionally sensitive to fluctuations in production and marketing of a few products owing to the predominance of cereal crops, particularly wheat. The retarded growth of agriculture has seriously damaged Chile's balance of payments. The effect is a two-sided one: exports have diminished and imports have gone up considerably. Despite recent efforts at agrarian reform no substantial alteration can be expected within the present land-tenure system without a drastic restructuring of the political system.

The importance of the mining industry to Chile has diminished as a dynamic force in its economic development. Although it is true that large mining companies have continued to increase their output, there are numerous small and medium-sized mining concerns which, despite a protectionist policy, have proved unable to follow suit. It seems evident that mining in the long run will not be capable of spurring the economic progress of the country unless its productivity increases substantially. Principally in recognition of this fact, government policy towards the large foreign interests involved is now directed toward improving the climate of investment. In social terms, the complete dependence on mining of the desert region and the coal-producing area and the large number of people supported by mining are matters affecting the stability of the whole country.

Chile, with Argentina, Brazil, and Mexico, has made more progress on the road toward industrialization than other nations on the continent. Two chief factors have been the *leitmotif* of Chilean industrialization: the necessity for raising the standard of living and improving the per capita income, and the urge to attenuate the vulnerability of the country's economy to foreign market fluctuations. Like all countries in the early stages of industrialization, Chile has mostly small-scale industry and factories. Consequently, economic productivity has been uneven, some industries having reached a level of efficiency as high as their counterparts in largely industrialized nations and others having lagged far behind this level. A cursory examination would show that industry is being stimulated by a policy directing the country's resources to produce goods and services which will substitute for imports in order to save valuable foreign exchange. Industry is growing faster than any other economic sector, having more than doubled its volume of production in a fifteen-year period.

In general, no fundamental change has taken place in the foreign-trade pattern in Chile for many years. The country is still chiefly an exporter of minerals and some agricultural products and an importer of manufactured goods and agricultural commodities which cannot be grown domestically. Chile's domestic savings have not been sufficient to finance expansion of the productive capacity basic to economic development, with the result that the country continues to depend heavily for this purpose on foreign trade. Chilean exports, however, have not increased appreciably. Thus the country is obliged to depend almost altogether on foreign credit and investment in order to satisfy import needs. With deterioration of the foreign-exchange situation and consequent difficulties in the balance of payments, there has been increasing need for this assistance from abroad in the form of investments and loans.

The Chilean system for the collection of revenue is hardly at all designed to aid in the country's efforts toward economic development but simply to finance government expenditures. Taxes in Chile are mostly regressive in nature and are centered upon consumption levies. There is also a heavy reliance on import and export taxes as principal sources of revenue. Public spending today is, however, directed toward promoting economic development. While in 1940 government expenditures of this nature were less than one-fourth of the total, they are now more than one-third, and developmental activities have become the most important function of government.

In Chile inflation has been a fact of life for over eighty years and an acute and serious problem for the last decade and a half. What inflation is doing to Chilean society will have incalculable effects. The inflationary process is causing important shifts in society. Chilean workers have been the principal victims, but the middle class is also suffering in the backwash of inflation. The healthy development of this class, upon which political and economic stability so heavily depends, has been seriously impaired. In an otherwise dismal picture, the one bright note is the resilience and inherent dynamic quality of the Chilean population, particularly of the middle class, which has learned to live with its problems and simply take them in its stride.

Summary and Conclusions

A typical feature of Chilean life is a lack of socio-economic coalescence, reflected in a great diversity of organized political groups. But in spite of political divisions, there exists a series of accords, particularly in economic policies. As one writer puts it, "Chilean politicians may argue as to which side of the economic street should be occupied, but not whether the route itself is the correct one." [9] All parties agree today on the desirability of economic nationalism and state intervention in varying degrees. Just as consensus was reached previously on the question of political democracy and on the need for governmental programs of social welfare and labor legislation when the conservative forces acquiesced in these programs, consent has been achieved again on state-directed industrialization. Questions of policy today are no longer concerned with the desirability of economic expansion and the state's role in economic development. Present political debate centers on the question of organization and the problem of coping with new changes brought on by economic expansion. The roots of the national economic problem, in the opinion of a noted Chilean economist, lie in the necessity of making the sacrifice of restricting living standards without losing political democracy. Solutions to the basic problems—the high cost of living and inflation—may require profound alterations of the institutional structure. It is conceivable that political consensus may break down over the question of economic democracy. There are many who believe that Chilean society is not sufficiently open to accomplish in democratic fashion the radical alterations now demanded and the Marxist alternative is sure to be vigorously offered to a discontented population.

The economy's structural imbalances and strong social tensions are threatening to destroy the delicately balanced coalition of center and right, which has until now safeguarded the institutional *status quo*. This danger became evident with the near-victory of the FRAP in the 1958 elections and its subsequent impressive gains in popular support. President Alessandri's program failed to attain a viable and dynamic economy, and the future appears uncertain. The only prediction that can be made is that conditions will not remain static and that, regardless of the outcome of the 1964 elections, an even greater readjustment among Chile's power groups is bound to take place.

NOTES FOR CHAPTER XVI

1. Benjamín Subercaseaux, *Chile: A Geographic Extravaganza*, Macmillan, New York, 1943, is a poetic but accurate geographical description of the country. A good geographical treatise is Elías Almeyda Arroyo, *Geografía de Chile*, Santiago, 1955. For an interesting essay on man and environment in Chile, see Mariano Latorre, *El Paisaje y el Hombre*, Buenos Aires, 1941.
2. Instituto de Economía de la Universidad de Chile, *Desarrollo Económico de Chile, 1940-1956*, Santiago, 1956, p. 194.
3. República de Chile, Servicio Nacional de Estadística y Censos, *XII Censo General de Población y I de Vivienda*, Guttemberg Press, Santiago, 1956, Vol. I, "Resumen nacional," p. 253.
4. *Ibid.*, p. 260.
5. This section reproduces in condensed form a substantial portion of my monograph entitled *Genesis and Modernization of Political Parties in Chile*, University of Florida Press, Gainesville, 1962. Used by permission.
6. Alberto Edwards, *La Fronda Aristocrática*, Editorial del Pacífico, Santiago, 1952, p. 51.
7. John Reese Stevenson, *The Chilean Popular Front*, University of Pennsylvania Press, Philadelphia, 1942, p. 40.
8. Kalman H. Silvert, *A Political-Economic Sketch of Chilean History from 1899*, American Universities Field Staff, Santiago, Jan. 27, 1957, p. 4.
9. *Ibid.*, p. 2.

SELECTED BIBLIOGRAPHY

Robert J. Alexander, *Communism in Latin America*, Rutgers University Press, New Brunswick, N.J., 1957, pp. 177-180.

Gilbert J. Butland, *Chile*, Royal Institute of International Affairs, London, 1951.

Alvin Cohen, *Economic Change in Chile, 1929-1959*, Latin American Monographs No. 11, University of Florida Press, Gainesville, 1961.

F. W. Fetter, *Monetary Inflation in Chile*, Princeton University Press, Princeton, 1931.

Luis Galdames, *A History of Chile*, University of North Carolina Press, Chapel Hill, 1941.

Federico G. Gil, *Genesis and Modernization of Political Parties in Chile*, Latin American Monographs, No. 18, University of Florida Press, Gainesville, 1962.

G. M. McBride, *Chile: Land and Society*, American Geographic Society, New York, 1936.

Kalman H. Silvert, *The Conflict Society: Reaction and Revolution in Latin America*, The Hauser Press, New Orleans, 1961, pp. 50-75.

J. R. Stevenson, *The Chilean Popular Front*, University of Pennsylvania Press, Philadelphia, 1942.

B. Subercaseaux, *Chile: A Geographic Extravaganza*, Macmillan, New York, 1943.

XVII   *Leo B. Lott*

PARAGUAY

No NATION in Latin America has suffered a more bizarre, calamitous, and tragic history than Paraguay. Its political development as an independent republic has been marred by two wars, one of them the most disastrous in Latin American history, from which Paraguay emerged a broken, defeated, and depopulated country. The country has endured long tyrannies under the heel of strange despots. Its economic growth has been strangled by the rigid isolationist policies of a Francia, by the senseless and vicious wars of a López, and by the plunder of its wealth by unscrupulous leaders.

An uninterrupted series of misfortunes and civil disturbances has produced a poor, provincial, primitive, and backward country that stands out in sharp contrast to its next-door neighbor, Uruguay. Unlike Uruguay, which abandoned violence and political turmoil early in this century to become one of the most enlightened democratic and progressive countries in the hemisphere, Paraguay remains shackled to the stultifying traditions of its past.

Its destiny has been shaped by forces which have played an important role in the political culture of other Latin American nations (such as the Iberian heritage and a common religion), but these forces, intermingling and interacting with conditions that have little parallel elsewhere in Latin America, have produced in Paraguay a people and a state that are unique.

The four important factors which have conditioned the political, social, and economic culture of Paraguay are (1) its isolated interior geographical position between Argentina and Brazil, (2) the homogeneity of its population and its Indian heritage, (3) its wars, and (4) its leaders.

The Geography of Paraguay

Physical Features

The third smallest country in Latin America, Paraguay has an area of 157,047 square miles and is about the size of California. It is abruptly broken by the Paraguay River into two major unlike areas, the largest of which is the Chaco Boreal, occupying 96,000 square miles of the national domain.

Beginning at the western bank of the Paraguay River and extending to the borders of Argentina and Bolivia, the vast low plain (maximum elevation 784 feet) has the reputation of being one of the most disagreeable regions on the South American continent. With the exception of a few thousand nomadic Indians, the only other permanent residents of the Chaco are the Mennonites, a courageous, hard-working religious sect who have succeeded in establishing three agricultural colonies in the northern portion. Through sheer tenacity they have been able to adapt themselves to environmental conditions which would have defeated less strongly motivated people.

The Chaco is the source of hardwood and quebracho (tannin), both of which Paraguay exports in quantity.

The pleasant, fertile, well-watered eastern portion of Paraguay presents a vivid contrast to the Chaco. It is given over to virgin forests, rich farmland, vast grasslands which support the cattle ranches, and to some low-lying swamp land.

Ninety-five percent of the population of 1,800,000 lives in eastern Paraguay within a well-defined region radiating 120 miles northeast and south of the capital city of Asunción. This region is called the heartland and constitutes the real Paraguay.

The Economic Effects of Geography

Paraguay shares with Bolivia the unhappy distinction of being a landlocked country. Relations between the two states have been greatly affected by the fact that Paraguay blocks Bolivia's access to the Atlantic Ocean, a situation which increasingly became a source of tension between them after 1883, when Bolivia lost her coastal province to Chile in the War of the Pacific. The efforts of Bolivia to secure an unimpeded route to the sea through the Paraguay-Paraná system were partly responsible for the Chaco War (1932-1935) between the two countries.

The economic life of Paraguay has in turn been dominated by Argentina. Asunción, the capital and principal commercial center, is situated a thousand miles from the ocean. Eight hundred miles of its lifeline, the Paraguay-Paraná river system, run through Argentine territory. This fact has made Paraguay unduly dependent on Argentina throughout its history and has presented it with serious problems in the maintenance of social, commercial, economic, and political relations with other countries.

Argentina is the Paraguayans' best customer, buying approximately one-third of their exports each year, principally lumber. A slump in the Argentine demand for Paraguayan lumber can cause a serious dislocation in the domestic economy. The need for friendly relations between the two countries, therefore, has been one of the hard political facts of life for Paraguay.

Economic isolation and dependence on Argentina are not new phenomena. They have their roots in the colonial period, during most of which the disadvantages of physical isolation were compounded by the shortsighted refusal of Spain to permit direct trade between the La Plata region (to which Paraguay belongs) and the mother country.

Political Effects of Geography

The geographic and economic isolation of the Paraguayan province and the indifference of Spain encouraged an independent nationalistic spirit among the people. As early as 1600 the Paraguayans were coming to consider themselves more Paraguayan than Spanish. Because of their remoteness from Spain, they were perhaps freer than most of Spain's subjects to govern themselves. Spanish governors found it difficult to please the inhabitants of Asunción or to impose their authority on them. It is not without significance that the first serious revolt against Spanish authority in the new world took place in Paraguay in the 1720's.

The physical isolation has also made possible in the national period the imposition of long dictatorships, such as those of Dr. Francia and the two Lópezes.

Social Organization

Racial Bases of Paraguayan Culture

The Paraguayans are the most homogeneous people in Latin America. The high degree of ethnic unity may be accounted for in several ways. In the first place, only a few of the early Spaniards settled in Paraguay. Most were attracted to richer and more glamorous regions. The few who did remain were engulfed by the far more numerous Guaraní Indians with whom they willingly intermarried. So rapid was the process of amalgamation that a new *mestizo* breed of men soon appeared, surviving to become the dominant racial group in Paraguay. The Spaniards, unable to preserve their racial identity, failed to evolve into a privileged socio-economic class with a monopoly on the positions of power and influence, as they did in other parts of Latin America. Nor does one find an inferior, exploited, and downtrodden Indian mass. Indeed, there are perhaps no more than 50,000 aboriginal Indians, and most of these live apart from the national culture in remote, inaccessible areas of the Chaco.

A second reason for the remarkable homogeneity of the Paraguayan people is the fact that the country remained for so long outside the stream of European immigration. Most Europeans were in search of more attractive economic opportunities than Paraguay offered them. Throughout the long rule of Dr. Francia (1811-1840) immigration and emigration were forbidden altogether. By preventing the influx of new blood from Europe and by prohibiting intermarriage of the few remaining white persons with any but Indians or *mestizos*, Francia accelerated the process of racial amalgamation.

The immigrants of recent years, particularly those of Latin origin, are as a rule assimilated quickly into the *mestizo* strain. The vast majority of the people, therefore, are of mixed blood in which the Indian element predominates.

Class Structure

In such a society it seems readily understandable that race or color as determinants of class would be of less importance than they would be in societies of a different racial complexion. The social position of the individual in Paraguayan society is determined by such economic and cultural factors as wealth, dress, education, occupation, residence, and language. In the matter of language, for example, in this bilingual country persons who speak only Guaraní are in a lower social category than those who speak Spanish as well. Similarly, those who engage in manual labor are considered lower in the social scale than those who do not.

Paraguay does not have a large middle or upper class. Together these two groups compose less than 10 percent of the total population. The upper class (with the exception of the few great land-owning families) is concentrated in the capital city, residence in which can alone confer status. The upper class embraces high-ranking political, military, and religious officials (many of whom have had humble origins), wealthy merchants and big industrialists, large cattle ranchers and notable intellectuals.

The members of the middle class, also urban, are small merchants (most of whom are foreign immigrants), small industrialists, merchants, and landowners, persons with small independent incomes, and members of the government bureaucracy.

At the bottom of the social scale in the cities are the factory workers and the casually employed. The rural counterpart of the factory worker is the agricultural peon who has nothing but his physical labor to rely on for a source of income. He is employed for fixed terms in such industries as lumber, tea, and quebracho. Between the landowner and the peon in the social hierarchy of the countryside are the squatters, renters, and tenants of the land.

The Typical Paraguayan

The *campesino* (rural inhabitant) is the typical Paraguayan. He is a melancholy man, full of pessimism for the future because the past has dealt him so many reverses. Although he refers to his country as "luckless Paraguay," he is extremely nationalistic and intensely proud of his heritage and his country. His nationalism finds expression in his obsession with the Guaraní aspects of his culture—almost all Paraguayans speak Guaraní at least as a second tongue—and in his suspicion of everything foreign.[1]

The typical Paraguayan is content with a minimum of material comforts. The cruel wars, long tyrannies, and grinding poverty have taught him to be patient and long-suffering. He is an individual who can bear great hardship, a fact amply demonstrated in the Chaco War with Bolivia.

A characteristic commented upon by many students of Paraguayan culture is the willingness of the people to submit to authority. It is a willingness that borders on servility. Historians trace this trait to the influence of the Jesuits, who for over 150 years had a major influence on the basic population foundation of Paraguay, the Indians. The Jesuit insistence on absolute obedience in their regimented Indian charges produced a people inadequately prepared to think or act for themselves when the paternal direction of the Jesuits was eliminated in 1767.

The typical Paraguayan, furthermore, is a peasant farmer, living in or near a small village or hamlet in the heartland of the country. He speaks Guaraní and perhaps some Spanish; he has had only an elementary education (even the most generous estimates list 31 percent as illiterate) and he lives in a one- or two-room hut. He is politically inarticulate, unambitious, not very religious—although he professes the Catholic faith—and he may expect to live to the age of forty-five.

The Effects of Paraguayan Wars on the Population

The two wars of Paraguay left the country with a lopsided population. Only 200,000 of an estimated 560,000 persons survived the Paraguayan War (1864-1870) and of this number only 28,000 were men, most of them old. Just about the time the balance was being redressed, the Chaco War with Bolivia in 1932 eliminated 40,000 more Paraguayan males.

These two catastrophes have had lasting effects upon the Paraguayan social structure, particularly in the rural areas. Great competition among the women for the remaining men resulted in the latter becoming vain, pampered, and promiscuous. Marital unions have been mainly temporary arrangements, unsanctified by church or state. Today about one-half of the children born each year are illegitimate.

In such a situation lower-class familial organization has become a matrifocal one. In their study of a typical Paraguayan town, the Services found that fewer than half of the households included both a man and a woman, and many of the complete households were only temporary.[2] Under the circumstances it was the woman who had to work to support her family—and her man, if she wanted to keep him; for the average Paraguayan male is Hispanicized enough to regard manual labor as degrading. This attitude, plus the paucity of his needs and wants, causes him to be the despair of the employer. When the Paraguayan does accept a job he ordinarily does so for the purpose of satisfying some immediate need. When that has been accomplished he terminates his employment.

Economic Organization

The economy of Paraguay is an agrarian one, for Paraguay is a nation of small, independent, subsistence farmers, most of whom do not own the small plots which they cultivate. They are in fact squatters. They rarely pay the landowners any form of rent for the land they occupy. Cloudy land titles dating from the War of 1864 (when many landowners fled Paraguay never to return), prohibitive court costs, and general humanitarian considerations restrain the legal owners from attempting to evict the squatters, who produce only enough to satisfy their minimal wants. Lacking the necessary implements and livestock, the average peasant can take care of no more than three or four acres a season. And when the soil wears out, as it inevitably does through poor management, he simply moves on until he finds another suitable spot.

Since about 65 percent of all persons engaged in agriculture are squatters, it is clear that the hacienda system, based upon a more formal and feudalistic association between *patrón* and *peón*, is not as important a factor in the economic life of Paraguay as it is in other Latin American countries. Nor are the abuses attendant on latifundia so pronounced in Paraguay. Large estates (mostly of foreign ownership) do exist, of course, but they are mainly devoted to cattle raising and not to cash agricultural crops, and they do not employ large numbers.

The lack of good domestic and external markets for cash crops and a totally inadequate system of farm-to-market roads has kept the *charcas* tied to a subsistence economy. It will take some time before the rural Paraguayan acquires the market orientation necessary to motivate him to produce a surplus.[3]

Agitation for land reform is not a pressing political issue in Paraguay for several reasons. Land *use*, regardless of title, is relatively free. Eastern Paraguay is so richly blessed with uncultivated, fertile land that landowners do not object seriously to squatters. Then too, the somewhat nomadically inclined *campesino* is not particularly interested in acquiring title to a plot of land because it would tend to tie him to one spot and saddle him with responsibilities and obligations he is not willing to undertake. Finally, the ownership of land is not for him an important prestige symbol.

The wealth of Paraguay is controlled largely by foreigners, both resident and absentee. Argentine interests own three-fourths of the industrial establishments, river transportation, and much of the land. The commercial life of the capital is in the hands of foreign-born merchants—Syrian, Lebanese, and Italian. The quebracho, tea, and lumber industries are also owned by aliens or naturalized European immigrants. There are perhaps 60,000 aliens in Paraguay. From their ownership of the land and a high proportion of the means of production and distribution, it is clear that they possess power disproportionate to their numbers.

Political Evolution

The Colonial Period

Because it had neither mineral wealth, nor advanced sedentary Indian civilizations to exploit, Paraguay was treated as a poor relation by Spain during much of its 274-year dependency. As a result of Spain's restrictive economic policies and the detachment of Paraguay from the province of Rio de la Plata in 1620, Paraguay came under the economic domination of its offspring, Buenos Aires. The residents of Asunción resented their subordination to Buenos Aires, all the more because they felt themselves superior to the Argentines. At one time they seriously considered joining Portuguese Brazil to escape the indifference of Spain. Cut off from economic and intellectual contact with the outside world, colonial Paraguay stagnated, becoming in time little more than a defense post against the Portuguese.

Stagnation did not mean tranquillity, however. Considerable friction arose between the privileged Jesuit Order and the commercial interests of Asunción, who resented the concentration of 200,000 Indians living within the Jesuits' missions. Not only were *mestizos* of Paraguay deprived of a cheap source of exploitable labor, but the tax-exempt missions were very successful business ventures which grew prosperous at the expense of less-favored interests.

Repeated difficulties between Asunción and Spain also arose as Spain occasionally sought to reassert its dwindling authority over the increasingly nationalistic Paraguayan people. Spanish rule in the province came to an end altogether on May 14, 1811, when the city council of Asunción deposed its last Spanish governor and transferred his power to a local five-man junta or board. Paraguayan independence, however, came about more as a reaction against an overbearing and ambitious Argentina (which sought vainly to impose its hegemony on an unwilling Paraguay following Argentina's break with Spain) than as a result of the influence of the Enlightenment. In 1813 Paraguay formally declared its independence of all outside powers.

Independence and Francia (1811-1840)

Independence brought no improvement to Paraguay, for it was soon plunged into fifty-nine years of despotic tyranny. The first of the three men in control during this period was Dr. José Gaspar Rodríguez Francia. Enigmatic, morose, cruel, vindictive, yet scrupulously honest, this melancholy man (called El Supremo by his fearful subjects) was voted absolute power for life in 1816. He proceeded to rule with such a tyrannical hand that no one dared speak his name aloud. Fearful of foreign influences which might undermine his power and resentful of Argentine economic domination, Francia resolutely cut off Paraguay from all contact with the rest of the world.

In his hermit state he tolerated no political rivals. He energetically destroyed the existing class structure, taking particular interest in harassing the small Spanish element and eliminating military leaders. He shaped an egalitarian society in which all were reduced to a position of servility to him. He destroyed the power of the Church by nationalizing it and subordinating it to himself; he ignored education, and by severing economic relations with other countries, he allowed the economy to stagnate. Individual liberty was virtually nonexistent and many individuals were summarily executed at his whim.

In spite of his shortcomings, Francia did confer domestic peace and order on Paraguay at a time when other Latin American countries were suffering from anarchy and bloodshed. Today Francia is regarded as a national hero and his picture adorns the 50-guaraní banknote.

Carlos Antonio López (1841-1862)

Juntas, triumvirates, and consulates succeeded one another in the political turmoil and confusion that followed on the death of the omnipotent Francia. It ended with the acquisition of power by Carlos Antonio López, a fairly well-to-do man who had survived the malevolent Francia by prudently moving to the countryside where the dictator would be less likely to notice him.

Although he preferred to govern with a constitution, his powers were as absolute as had been those of his predecessor. During his twenty-one years as "president" López reopened Paraguay to international trade, established somewhat unsatisfactory diplomatic relations with a number of countries, amassed a great personal fortune, and permitted his son, Francisco Solano López, to build up the army. Paraguayans were happier under his more benign despotism than they had been under Francia, but their lot was little improved.

In 1857 López was elected president for life by his congress and was given the right to name his successor. His choice was his son, Francisco Solano.

Francisco Solano López and the Paraguayan War (1862-1870)

Francisco was a vain, capricious, thirty-six-year-old brigadier general when he inherited Paraguay from his father in 1862. His eight-year rule was a national disaster. Obsessed with the idea of making his country a great power in the La Plata region, he plunged Paraguay into a war with Brazil when that country interfered in the affairs of Uruguay. This course of action soon involved him in war with Uruguay and Argentina also. After six years of savage fighting, bereft of half its population and shorn of 50,000 square miles of its territory, Paraguay had to submit to the indignity of six years of occupation by enemy forces. Its economy was a shambles and few educated people capable of leadership survived the war. It took Paraguay over sixty years to recover from the effects of the Paraguayan War.

The Period Between 1870 and 1932

The sixty-two-year period which followed the end of the Paraguayan War and the death of the man who had precipitated it was characterized by political instability, and agitation in which at least fourteen major outbreaks of violence and many more minor skirmishes may be counted. Thirty-two presidents, where there should constitutionally have been fifteen, came and went according to the vagaries of politics and intrigue. The unhappy country was also subject to continued economic backwardness and to pressing financial problems which the governments tried to solve by a massive sale of public lands.

From 1874 to 1904 the Conservative Party, representing such traditional forces in society as landowners, church, and army, maintained exclusive control of the government. Political strife was generated during these years as much by personal ambitions and rivalries between leading families within the party for the control of the presidency, as by violent competition between the Conservatives and the Liberal Party. Seldom did fundamental political, economic, or social issues play an important role in the political process.

Conservative domination ended in 1904, when a Liberal revolution ushered in a thirty-two-year period of Liberal control of the government. The earlier pattern was repeated. Conservative attempts to regain control and personal rivalries among the Liberal leaders kept the country for another decade in constant turmoil which at times bordered on anarchy. After 1914, however, Paraguay entered upon a less violent phase.

The only truly outstanding man during this long period was the Liberal President Eligio Ayala (1925-1928), who reduced the national debt, encouraged education, permitted free elections, and attacked the health problems of his country.

Some note should be taken of the progress achieved during the years preceding the Chaco War. The public school system of Paraguay dates from 1870. A law school was established in 1882 and a national university in Asunción in 1892. The government made efforts to encourage the investment of private capital, banks were established and the population had almost recovered the losses suffered in the Paraguayan War. The interval between the two wars is regarded by some as a golden age in Paraguayan literature.

The Chaco War (1932-35)

As the period drew to a close, Paraguay appeared to be on the threshold of an era of development. Not only did this not materialize, but Paraguay was again set back in development many years when tension with Bolivia over rival claims to territory in the Chaco exploded into war in 1932. The territory in question was largely worthless, but ill-founded rumors of oil heated the controversy. Both countries, smarting under the national humiliation of previous defeats and territorial losses, fought savagely. In the final outcome Paraguay retained control of 20,000 square miles of the disputed land at an average cost of two men per square mile; Bolivia acquired an uneasy right of access to the sea through Paraguayan territory.

The Years 1936-1940

Economic prostration, inflation, high prices, low wages, disillusionment with the long Liberal control of the government, and the general discontent of returning Chaco veterans bred a spirit of revolt which erupted in February 1936, bringing Colonel Rafael Franco to power. He and his followers, known as *febreristas*, were intent on creating a "New Paraguay" along authoritarian lines. They set loose the forces of economic nationalism and state intervention in the economic life of the nation that persist to this day.

Some of his original army supporters, fearful that his socialist program was veering too far to the left, unseated Franco in August 1937. During the two-year tenure of his successor, Felix Pavia, some social legislation along the lines of Franco's program was enacted; for example, his government established a ten-hour maximum work day, set up a system of maternity benefits, and reorganized the ministry of labor.

Pavia was succeeded by General Estigarribia, the hero of the Chaco War. A nominee of the Liberal Party (but not a member of it), he was elected and took office in 1939. Domestic discontent and increasing criticism of his administration led him to proclaim his assumption of dictatorial powers on February 8, 1940. Believing that the liberal, democratic Constitution of 1870 was totally unsuited to Paraguayan realities he fathered the Constitution of 1940, which is still in effect in Paraguay. Estigarribia lost his life in an airplane accident late in 1940, and the presidency was seized by his war minister, Higinio Morínigo, who governed with the dictatorial powers he had inherited from his predecessor.

Higinio Morínigo (1940-1948)

General Morínigo's eight years in power saw the dissolution of the Liberal Party by decree in 1942, improved relations with Bolivia, financial aid from the United States, membership in the United Nations, improvements in agriculture, some land reform, the encouragement of immigration, and the creation of national agricultural colonies.

The Colorado Party (the Conservatives),* out of power since 1904, emerged as the favored party during the latter years of the Morínigo administration. Early in 1947, Morínigo created a new cabinet composed of four Colorados and four military officials who had Conservative connections. Aspiring to full political control of the government and fearful that Morínigo would not transfer power in 1948 to the candidate they hoped to elect that year, the Colorados spearheaded a coup which deposed the dictator.

The Years 1948-1962

After several years of *confusionismo* in which there were five presidents in fifteen months and a struggle for power between opposing wings of the Colorado Party, a relatively peaceful period began with the inauguration of Federico Chaves in 1950. However, Chaves was forced to resign in 1954, when the army, under General Alfredo Stroessner, revolted against him. General Stroessner with the blessing of the Colorado Party had himself elected president on July 11, 1954. He was reelected without opposition for a full five-year term in 1958, and again reelected, with only token opposition, in 1963.

The constitutional barrier to a president's serving more than two consecutive terms was conveniently removed for Stroessner by his controlled congress when it declared that the limitation applied to two full terms and that Stroessner in his first period of office had merely filled the unexpired term of the man he had deposed.

* Not to be confused with the Colorado Party of Uruguay, who are Liberals.

Theories of the State and the Structure of Government

Political Theory

Modern political thought in Paraguay has its roots in the social and economic discontent which prevailed in Paraguay at the end of the Chaco War. Disillusionment with the long-standing ineffectiveness of government stimulated demands among veterans and students for more vigorous policies and more dynamic leadership. Impressed by the success of European totalitarian systems, and discerning the need for basic reforms in Paraguay, Colonel Franco, upon coming to power in 1936, proclaimed the advent of a "New Paraguay" in which the "liberating revolution and the state are now one and the same thing."

Dr. Juan Stefanich, the leading theoretician of Franco's *febreristas*, described the New Paraguay as a representative, functional democracy based upon the solidarity of interests among men. In his summary of Stefanich's thought, Harris Warren writes, "one may say that *Democracia solidarista* seeks to extract all that is good from individualistic democracy, fascism, nazism and communism and to weld them together to form a political philosophy valid for American realities and capable of answering needs created by complex modern societies." [4]

The *febreristas* were not in power long enough to achieve much in the way of basic reforms, but some of their political and economic ideas persisted and eventually found their way into the Constitution of 1940, which is still in effect.

Like Stefanich and Franco, President Estigarribia, the architect of the Constitution of 1940, rejected the individualistic, democratic orientation of the 1870 document and called for a new charter which would "perfect" democracy along new lines. His views are worth considering, for they form an integral part of the fundamental law of Paraguay today.

In Estigarribia's opinion, Paraguay needed a constitutional basis of politics which would take into consideration the basic economic, social, and political realities of the country. In such an underdeveloped and primitive society, the state must be something more than a mere regulatory agency. Not only must it embark upon positive and far-reaching social and economic reforms, but it must also possess the power necessary to deal quickly and effectively with conflicts which would inevitably arise in those areas.

Central to Estigarribia's theory of government was a powerful executive who would "assume responsibility when problems knock at the gates of government demanding solution." Congress, hitherto a "recalcitrant, slow, political forum" would not, in any sense of the word, be a coordinate equal of the executive branch, but would function instead as a collaborator on projects initiated by the president and his advisors.[5]

Estigarribia's successor, Higinio Morínigo, was even more outspoken. He

scathingly denounced "electoral democracy" as a farce in a people not sufficiently educated to vote intelligently. Liberal democracy must be rejected,
said he, because "it does not admit of the positive intervention of the state
in satisfying human needs . . . we propose interventionist methods, above
all in the field of economics and especially in the relations between capital and
labor in order to rectify social injustices. The inertia of the liberal state must
gave way to the dynamism of the state as a protector and leader." [6]

The government of General Alfredo Stroessner has not departed in any
significant way from the political theories of Estigarribia and Morínigo.

Various provisions of the Constitution of 1940 (Paraguay's fourth) reflect
these and other state-oriented concepts. Private interest must always be subordinate to the interest of the nation and all citizens are obliged to collaborate
for the good of the state, as determined by the executive. Laws may even
compel citizens to accept public office for which they are judged to be competent. The state is granted extensive powers to regulate and intervene in the
economic life of the nation. Although none of the ordinary rights of the
workingman is spelled out in the constitution, exploitation of man by man
is forbidden. The state assumes responsibility for the strict supervision of
labor contracts, social insurance, and workers' safety. The constitution enjoins upon all inhabitants of the land the obligation of earning a living by
legitimate work and states the belief that the home of every Paraguayan
should be located on a piece of property owned by him.

The Executive

The ideas of Estigarribia are most clearly reflected in the distribution of
powers within the government. In the first place, the Constitution of 1940 establishes a highly centralized unitary republic, divided into sixteen administrative departments, each of which is governed by a delegate appointed by the
president. There are no institutions of effective local government nor locally
elected officials. All are appointed either by the president or by his agents.

Secondly, the most important powers of the state rest with the president,
who is directly elected by universal compulsory suffrage by citizens over
the age of eighteen. His term is five years.

The powers of the president are impressive. He commands the armed
forces, determines their organization and distribution, enacts all military
regulations, and confers rank and promotion on military officers. He alone
may initiate legislation dealing with recruitment and mobilization of troops.
He may declare war and establish peace with the approval of the chamber
of representatives.

He exercises the right of ecclesiastical patronage over the official Roman
Catholic Church.

His vast powers of appointment extend to diplomatic and administrative
personnel, the members of his cabinet, the council of state, the judges of the
supreme court (with the consent of the council of state), the tribunal of accounts, and all lesser judges with the approval of the supreme court. In the

absence of a tenured civil service his powers of removal are almost unrestricted.

The president participates directly and effectively in the legislative process, and only he may introduce laws relating to financial matters. The national budget, of course, is his responsibility. Almost all of the laws passed by the chamber of representatives (there is no senate) originate with him. The weak position of the chamber *vis-à-vis* the president is revealed in constitutional provisions stipulating that if the chamber does not dispose of presidential bills in the session in which they are introduced they automatically become law. In the very unlikely event that the chamber should pass a law contrary to the wishes of the president he may kill it with a veto until the next session of the chamber. This situation does in fact not arise in Paraguay.

During the period in which the chamber is in recess (September through March) the president may enact decrees having the force of law. Like most other Latin American executives, he is required to submit such decrees to the chamber when it reconvenes. In Paraguay, approval has been automatic. The president may also call special sessions of the chamber and he may dissolve it, in which case he must call new elections within two months.

Finally, he may "adopt plans for the redistribution of present populations for economic or social reasons of public health or national defense." And he possesses that important element of executive power in Latin America, the right to proclaim a state of siege in the event of domestic disorder or external danger. This provision confers upon the president the authority to arrest suspected persons and to remove them from one place to another within the country. The state of siege can be declared for a limited time only, but may be extended as the executive sees fit. He must report his action to the chamber of representatives.

The president is assisted in his executive duties by a ten-man cabinet and by a nineteen-man advisory council of state which includes, besides the members of the cabinet, such eminent personages as the archbishop of Paraguay, the president of the Central Bank of Paraguay, and the rector of the national university. The council of state is authorized to approve or reject the decrees of the president and to rule on financial and economic matters and on international matters submitted to it by the president. Being appointees of the president and serving at his pleasure, neither the council nor the cabinet is an effective check upon the president. The constitutional requirement that executive acts to be valid must carry the signature of the appropriate minister is meaningless.

The Legislature

Enough has already been said about the constitutional position of the Paraguayan congress to indicate that it is not, nor is it intended to be, an effective part of the pattern of power. Only five of the fourteen grants of power to the chamber may be exercised independently of executive initiation.

Legislative power is vested in a unicameral chamber of representatives elected on the basis of one delegate for every 25,000 persons. In the period prior to the elections of 1963 there were sixty delegates, all members of the president's Colorado Party. Twenty "opposition" delegates, of a faction of the Liberal Party "acceptable to General Stroessner, though not to other Liberals, were seated in the legislature after the 1964 election, under a provision of the electoral law which gives one-third of the seats to the runner-up party.

The Judiciary

The judicial system is perhaps one of the simplest in Latin America. There are only two levels of courts: the lower courts, with original jurisdiction, and a three-judge supreme court with both original and appellate jurisdictions, possessing supervisory powers over the rest of the judicial structure. There is, in addition, a tribunal of accounts which hears matters involving administrative litigation and the expenditure of public funds.

Political Processes

The Role of Violence

The most persistent thread of continuity in Paraguayan politics is the acquisition and maintenance of political power through means resting directly or indirectly on force and coercion. Warren puts his finger on the matter precisely when he says that revolutions and uprisings are "not a passing phenomenon. They are a part of the Paraguayan national life, an inalienable right of the people. Revolution in Paraguay, as in all of Latin America, is a social malaria, a fever that strikes almost without warning, subsides and then strikes again. Revolution is also a cure for government longevity and self-perpetuation." [7] Revolts against the established regime thus constitute a normal institutional pattern. President Stroessner has had to quell at least two major revolts a year since he came to power and will undoubtedly face many more before he is finally finished as a political force.

In view of the history of Paraguay it is not too much to say that revolution has proved the only effective way of bringing about a genuine change in political personnel.

The Role of Elections

As would be expected in an environment which condones the violent approach to politics, elections do not confer real authority or power upon an individual. A president who relies solely upon the ballot for his position and on the constitution for his power does not make a vigorous executive. Nor does he last long in office. Nongovernmental bases of power are absolutely necessary for a man to remain in office and to carry out his policies.

Since the Chaco War the strong presidents have been military men who have used the electoral process to legalize the power they bring with them to their high office. Elections are conducted, but the instrumentalities of the state have been employed in such a fashion as to guarantee victory for the forces which support the regime in power. A president may be driven from power in a coup; he is never unseated by the electorate.

The Paraguayan people have almost never had the opportunity of voting for more than one presidential candidate at a time, in spite of the fact that a number of political parties have existed. Paraguay is probably the best example in Latin America of the electoral device known as *candidato único*. During its early period of domination the Colorado Party simply did not tolerate a Liberal candidate, and the Liberals responded in kind during their days in power. Of the twenty-two presidents chosen during their thirty-two-year rule, twenty-one came to office in an "election" which featured only one candidate. Modern Paraguayan politics have not deviated at all from this pattern as a rule, although General Stroessner did prevail upon a member of the opposition to run against him in 1963.

The Role of Political Parties

Paraguay cannot be said to have developed anything like a genuine party basis for politics. The differences between the Colorado Party and the Liberal Party, both organized in 1887, have been largely artificial. The Colorado Party, as we have already pointed out, represents the traditional forces of society. The Liberals advocate administrative decentralization, better education, more political freedom, and separation of Church and State, principles which they themselves largely ignored when they were in power from 1904 to 1936.

Both parties, in spite of doctrinal differences, represent the elite element of Paraguayan society. Politics, therefore, between the two parties, and, more important, *within them*, has involved only a handful of individuals, who have been primarily concerned with personal rather than with national concerns.

Political parties in Paraguay do not educate the public on policy issues, do not present real alternatives to the voters, and do not provide an official political environment within which the government operates. Paraguay today is a praetorian state. The government is firmly in the hands of the military forces, headed by General Stroessner. His preeminence in politics derives from his military position and not from his titular role as head of the Colorado Party, which has been technically in power since the middle 1940's. It is General Stroessner and the army, not the Colorado Party, that formulate and execute policy.

The Status of Political Parties in Mid-1964

The official party is the Colorado Party. For many years it has been plagued by factionalism, and even today it is not a completely unified organization. One wing, for example, favors a more liberal approach to politics and a relaxation of the state of siege, and is troubled by the methods used by police in the treatment of political opponents. The other wing advocates the continuation of strong dictatorship as the only answer to the problems of Paraguay. The latter wing predominates.

The activities of other political groups, such as the Liberals and the *febreristas*, have been greatly restricted for almost a decade. Their leaders lead a hazardous existence and many of them are either in jail or in exile. Strong censorship of the press, government harassment of their newspapers and headquarters, and the curtailment of their rights of assembly under the now almost permanent state of siege have stifled peaceful political party activity and have engendered frustrations that find their outlets in frequent revolts against the government.

Since the Communist Party was outlawed in 1936 and other political organizations are either denied permission or refuse under present circumstances to participate in the government or in elections, Paraguay is for all practical purposes a one-party dictatorial state.

This situation was not changed by the participation of a newly-formed faction of the Liberal party, called Renovación, in the 1963 elections. Because of the police-state atmosphere of the country, it was clear that only a "tame" and well-behaved opposition would be allowed to function, to lend plausibility to the dictator's foreign propaganda. The twenty legislative seats and some patronage appointments given to the Renovación Liberals were accordingly regarded as their rewards for aiding Stroessner's public-relations efforts.

Public Opinion and Pressure Groups

A high illiteracy rate, a controlled press, and frequent suppression by the government of newspapers which dare to criticize it do not provide a climate conducive to the formation of intelligent public opinion. Many of the educated Paraguayans who would normally form the base of an informed electorate are in exile. These individuals actively engage in underground and clandestine operations designed to bring down the government. They are, in effect, a foreign-based pressure group.

Other pressure groups, possessing varying degrees of power and influence, are the military forces, the foreign owners of the industrial and agricultural establishments, labor (to some extent), and university students, who frequently demonstrate against specific actions of the government. Perhaps the most effective pressure group of all is the Argentine government, which in the past has had a great deal to say about Paraguayan problems.

Public Policy

Labor

In the absence of detailed constitutional provisions dealing with labor rights, and with a specific grant of authority to supervise and regulate the organization, functioning, and activities of groups of a public character, the government of Paraguay has had a free hand in formulating labor policy. The policy is one of paternalistic and somewhat benevolent regulation. Labor unions must have the approval of the Department of Labor to become legal entities. There are perhaps ninety unions now functioning, most of them in Asunción and most affiliated with the Paraguayan Federation of Labor.

Labor agitation and discontent, especially since 1936, have resulted in positive gains for the industrial workingman. Most of the provisions of the present labor code (which went into effect in February 1962) were contained in earlier laws and decrees.

The working day is set at eight hours for workers other than those engaged in domestic service or in agriculture (about 75 percent of the working force). A National Minimum Wage Council determines for specific industries the wages necessary to satisfy the normal daily needs of the worker. Workers are entitled to bonuses, profit-sharing in certain instances, annual paid vacations, sick benefits, old age pensions, full maternity benefits, burial expenses, and free medical care for those who are covered. Paraguay does not have unemployment insurance. Workers contribute 6 percent of their wages, employers, 15 percent, and the government $1\frac{1}{2}$ percent to the social security fund. Only a small number of workers are affected by the labor code.

Agriculture

The alienation of nearly half of the national territory of Paraguay in the great public land sales of 1886-1904 resulted in the concentration of land in the hands of a few people, mainly foreigners. No limitations were placed on the amount of land which an individual might purchase, nor was he required to develop his holdings in any way. The sales netted the government the paltry sum of $5 million and when they were over Paraguay had virtually no public land left.

The present agricultural policy of the government began with the Agrarian Statute of 1940 which sought to bring about a wider distribution of land ownership and to increase both production and the number of acres under cultivation.

In 1960 the government enacted a land settlement law for the purpose of accelerating the division of the large landholdings, particularly those not under cultivation. Once the government acquires title to the land it divides it into tracts of 20 to 200 hectares which are then allotted free of charge to those who can qualify under the terms of the statute. The new owner must enclose his land, begin cultivation within two months, build a home, and plant fruit trees. For reasons outlined elsewhere in this chapter the responsibilities of land ownership outweigh the attractions for many *campesinos*.

A most important development, begun in 1942 and continuing to the present, was the creation of the Inter-American Technical and Cooperative Service for Agriculture, a joint venture of the Paraguayan government and the

Institute of Inter-American Affairs in Washington. Led by a team of United States agricultural experts and functioning as a branch of the ministry of agriculture, STICA maintains experimental farms, dairies, and ranches, provides technical assistance and advice, encourages diversification, and helps organize agricultural colonies. Financial aid to the farmer is extended by the Agricultural Credit Bank.

Under the Stroessner administration, the government has on occasion purchased surplus crops and granted important tax and import exemptions to foreign commercial interests to stimulate investment in Paraguay.

Immigration

Paraguay's immigration policy may be stated very simply: to attract as many persons with agricultural skills as possible with as little expenditure as possible. Eighty percent of all persons admitted each year must be farmers. The government has held out the lure of good land, special exemptions of one kind or another, free internal transportation to future homes and eight days of free lodging. Living conditions are so primitive in rural Paraguay, however, that many immigrants have not been able to make the necessary adjustments and have left in disillusionment. In spite of the inducements, immigration has not contributed significantly to population growth. Almost as many persons leave Paraguay each year as enter it. Many are in search of more tranquil political and economic conditions. It is estimated that several hundred thousand Paraguayans, mostly political refugees, are living in Brazil, Uruguay, and Argentina.

Education

The constitution specifies compulsory education for all children between the ages of seven and fourteen. Although statistics relating to Paraguay are difficult to come by (and are often contradictory), an educated guess is that about 35 percent of the children in the compulsory bracket do not attend school. In many rural areas there are simply no schools to attend. Then, too, obligatory uniforms (which parents cannot afford), parental indifference, and economic pressures at home cut down on school attendance. Total school enrollment in 1961 for all levels was 327,000 students. At least 30 percent of the population over the age of ten can neither read nor write. Some improvement in the educational system should be forthcoming under an agreement between the United States and Paraguay in which each will spend about $3 million on the education of Paraguayans.

The Economy

Progress toward a government-controlled economy has been fairly steady since 1940. In 1948 a National Council of Economic Coordination was set up to advise the president on a wide range of subjects, including taxation, budgeting, banking and currency, immigration and colonization, road construction, and international agreements. The council in turn created the Economic Development Planning Commission, which has proved ineffective. A more active government agency has been the Paraguayan Development Corporation, organized in 1956 with a capital of 200 million guaranís (126 Gs = $1) to foster projects which would lead to domestic economic growth, such as petroleum refineries and a Trans-Chaco pipeline.

The government has also authorized a number of quasi-governmental corporations and commissions to oversee such industries as sugar, alcohol, and meat. Meat processing, for example, is under the jurisdiction of the Paraguayan Meat Corporation, which has the power to issue regulatory decrees and fix domestic quotas and prices.

Financial policy is determined by the government-owned Central Bank of Paraguay. The bank has the exclusive power to issue money, fix interest rates, determine the credit structure, and set exchange rates. Another autonomous government-owned bank is the National Development Bank, which functions to encourage agriculture, industry, and commerce through loans.

The government maintains a monopoly of the telecommunications system and owns the electrical power plants and much of the railway mileage. Public works, immigration projects, and similar activities are financed by the Special Investment Budget attached each year to the budget. In normal years this is equal to about 25 percent of the regular budget.

To stimulate international trade the government concluded a treaty of economic union with Argentina in 1953 and a trade treaty with Brazil in 1956 by which each country grants a free port to the other, and in 1961 it signed the Latin American Free Trade Association agreement with six other countries. To reduce its dependence on Argentine shipping facilities, the government has begun to build up its own merchant fleet with the purchase of foreign-built ships. Various international lending agencies have lent funds to improve such things as the transportation system, waterworks, the national airport, river dredging, and housing.

Foreign Policy

Paraguay's foreign policy has always been dictated by the necessity of maintaining friendly relations with its powerful neighbor Argentina. During World War II, President Morínigo was placed in the dilemma of fulfilling his commitments to support the United States without antagonizing pro-Axis Argentina. He resolved this dilemma by breaking ties with the Axis in 1942 under United States pressure, but continuing to permit considerable German activity in his country—as did Argentina also. Following Argentina's example he refrained from declaring war on the Axis until 1945, when it was perfectly clear that the end was in sight. The declaration entitled Paraguay to become a founding member of the United Nations.

In return for this token and dubious support, the United States rewarded Morínigo with substantial lend-lease equipment and financial aid, most of which he promptly used to strengthen his own political power.

Close relations were maintained between Paraguay and Argentina during the authoritarian regimes of Morínigo and Perón. They reached a high point in 1953 when pro-Perón President Federico Chaves concluded an economic union with Argentina. Perón pledged that his government "would work for the greatness of Paraguay and the happiness of its people" through the utilization of all "such resources and means as may help Paraguay to consolidate social justice, economic independence, and political sovereignty"—in other words, to extend his own system of *justicialismo* to his economic vassal.

Since the collapse of *peronismo* in 1955, relations between the more democratically oriented Argentina and dictator-ruled Paraguay have often been strained. Stroessner is now in the seat of the dictator, and Argentina was offended when he afforded asylum to Perón. For his part, Stroessner complains of the laxity of Argentina (and his other neighbors) in preventing Paraguayan exiles from launching revolts against his regime from their soil.

President Stroessner has also maintained a policy of studied friendship with the United States and has consistently voted with her in the United Nations and the Organization of American States. The undemocratic nature of the Paraguayan regime has proved embarrassing to the American government. Through her Alliance for Progress commitments the United States is put in the position of giving aid ($16 million in 1961) to the most thoroughgoing and repressive military dictatorship in Latin America.

There is no evidence to show that Paraguay is making any progress toward the basic goals of the Alliance. Its land reform law is a paper law; its tax structure is totally inadequate; corruption is rife; and the armed forces absorb a high proportion of the budget each year. Paraguayan exiles lament the fact that Alliance funds are being spent on projects which are used by President Stroessner as evidence of the progressive nature of his government.

The dictatorship is alert to any outside influence that might be detrimental to its continued control. The Communist Party has been outlawed for a number of years, and Stroessner, complaining bitterly of Fidel Castro's intervention in the domestic affairs of Paraguay, broke relations with his government in 1961.

In mid-1964, in spite of its support of hemispheric unity, the praetorian government of Paraguay had no real friends in Latin America. At mid-century it was what it had always been: a poverty-stricken, backward, isolated, dictator-controlled country.

NOTES FOR CHAPTER XVII

1. See Philip Raine, *Paraguay* (1956), p. 13. William Schurz argues in *Latin America* (1949) that the Paraguayan is remarkably tolerant of foreigners.
2. Elman R. and Helen S. Service, *Tobatí: Paraguayan Town* (1954), pp. 151 ff.
3. *Ibid.*, p. 54.
4. Warren, *Paraguay* (1949), p. 320.
5. *Ibid.*, p. 328.

6. *Ibid.*, p. 339.
7. *Ibid.*, p. 226.

SELECTED BIBLIOGRAPHY

Pan American Union, *Materials for the Study of the Middle Class in Latin America*, Vol. III, Washington, D.C., 1950.

Pan American Union, *A Statement of the Laws of Paraguay*, 2d ed., Washington, D.C., 1962.

Bailey W. Diffie, *Latin American Civilization, Colonial Period*, Stackpole Sons, Harrisburg, Pa., 1947.

Joseph Winfield Fretz, *Pilgrims in Paraguay*, Herald Press, Scottdale, Pa., 1953.

George Pendle, *Paraguay, A Riverside Nation*, Royal Institute of International Affairs, London, 1954.

Philip Raine, *Paraguay*, Scarecrow Press, New Brunswick, N.J., 1956.

Elman R. and Helen S. Service, *Tobatí: Paraguayan Town*, University of Chicago Press, Chicago, 1954.

U.S. Department of Commerce, *Investment in Paraguay*, Washington, D.C., 1954.

Harris Gaylord Warren, *Paraguay: An Informal History*, University of Oklahoma Press, Norman, 1949.

David H. Zook, Jr., *The Conduct of the Chaco War*, Bookman Associates, New Haven, Conn., 1960.

ARGENTINA

•Córdoba

Rosario •
Buenos Aires •

Bahía Blanca

XVIII   *Joseph R. Barager*

ARGENTINA

A COUNTRY DIVIDED

ARGENTINA, the second largest in area of the twenty Latin American countries (1,072,749 square miles), is about one-third the size of the continental United States or Brazil, its neighbor to the north. Exploration and drilling operations carried out since 1958 have revealed substantial petroleum and gas reserves, but Argentina does not appear to have significant amounts of the strategic minerals and precious stones and metals found in her Andean neighbors and Brazil, though subsequent exploration may reveal them in as yet largely untapped Andean regions. Yet Argentina is already blessed with one resource that is equaled in few other countries of the world. This resource is the rich, black soil of the Argentine *pampa*, stretching fanlike out from the capital city, Buenos Aires, for over 300 miles along the Atlantic Coast and into the interior. Its fertile topsoil is free of stones or even small pebbles, since the bedrock is buried deep below—at Buenos Aires beneath 985 feet of river and wind deposits. The bulk of the country lies in the temperate zone, but its north-south length of over 2100 miles extends from the hot, humid, and subtropical Chaco to the cold, wind-swept, and arid reaches of Patagonia.

The Argentine population of some 21 million is the second of the country's two major assets. Although the population is somewhat less than two-thirds the size of Mexico's and considerably less than one-third the size of Brazil's, Argentina probably has the largest skilled labor force in the Latin American area. This reflects both the literacy rate (86.4 percent, one of the highest in the area) and the general level of public-school education. It may also reflect the fact that Argentina has far more public libraries (over 1300) than Brazil (444), Chile (185), Peru (163), Colombia (116), and even Canada (873).

With the possible exception of Uruguay (which has not had an official population census since 1908), no other Latin American country has received as large a percentage of its total population from western Europe. Over 90 percent of the Argentines are white, with the indigenous and *mestizo* elements mainly concentrated in the northwestern and southwestern regions. The cultural orientation of the Argentines has traditionally been toward western Europe, particularly France, Spain, and Italy, but in the last decade an increasing number of teachers and students have visited and studied in the United States. As a result there is an increasing Argentine awareness of

United States artistic and educational—as well as industrial and scientific—achievements.

Although living conditions, and particularly housing facilities, deteriorate considerably outside of the nation's capital, there are no large concentrations of underfed and ragged people in Argentina. The caloric consumption is high, particularly in meat. In 1961 Argentina's per capita meat consumption of 197 pounds was exceeded only by New Zealand's (223), Australia's (215), and Uruguay's (212); it was appreciably larger than similar consumption in the United States (161) and Canada (139). Per capita gross national product of about $450 is second in Latin America only to Venezuela's (about $1,000), and is much more evenly distributed. The ratio of inhabitants to doctors was the lowest (760) in the Western Hemisphere in the 1953-58 period; only Chile (61 percent) and Uruguay (73 percent) in Latin America have a larger percentage of their economically active inhabitants covered by social security systems than does Argentina (46 percent).

A paradoxical feature of Argentine society is that while agricultural products constitute about 90 percent of the nation's exports, some 70 percent of the population live in communities of 2,000 or more people. The population density per square mile is low, about 20 per square mile, and one-third of the population lives in or around the city of Buenos Aires. In contrast to most of the rest of Latin America, where in some cases the annual population growth rate has increased to well over 3 percent, Argentina's rate has declined from 2.5 percent in the late 1940's to the present rate of 1.7 percent. This decrease reflects both the tendency of the growing middle class toward smaller families and the slackening pace of immigration during the last decade.

Until 1930 the Argentine people were also fortunate in the stability of their political institutions. In the preceding half-century Argentina had made substantial progress in the fields of civil liberties and representative government and was held up as a model for other Latin American nations to emulate. In September 1930, however, that period came to a close. The discredited Irigoyen administration, which had been unable to resolve the problems created by the 1930 economic crisis, was easily toppled by a military coup. The time of troubles initiated in 1930 has been temporarily relieved for short periods but has not yet been definitively resolved.

In June 1943 a military revolution opened the way for Colonel Juan Domingo Perón to start his rapid rise to power. Perón, a career military officer with a flair for politics and a prototype for other charismatic Latin political leaders, triumphed over his military peers by adding labor support to the military units he controlled. The movement that he formed to legitimize his triumph was the first in Argentina to carry out far-reaching social and economic changes. At the same time it brought organized labor into a leading, even a dominant, position in Argentine politics. Peronism survived the fall of Perón, in 1955, and in one form or another will probably survive his complete disappearance from the scene. Indeed the pressing Argentine political problem of the post-1955 period has been how best to reincorporate the Peronists into the body politic of the nation. The solution of that problem is also closely tied to the recovery of the Argentine economy from the disastrous effects of the incredible mismanagement and gross corruption of the Perón regime (1946 to 1955). One government, that of Arturo Frondizi (1958-62), had already failed on the first problem and had only limited success on the second before it was removed by the Argentine military in March 1962. Both problems remain and must be resolved before Argentina can claim again its position as first among Latin American nations. In fact, the proud Argentine Republic remains a nation divided. That division is further exacerbated by the fundamental problem that has disrupted the Argentine society since 1930—the position of the military vis à vis civilian, representative government.

The Historical Background

The Colonial Period

During most of the two and three-quarters centuries of its colonial period (1536-1810), Argentina was a stepchild in the Spanish Empire's family. The Río de la Plata area, despite its name, produced little if any silver or gold, and the Argentine and Uruguayan regions had no tractable Indians to provide a cheap labor force for exploitation. Here, in fact, was the only South American society that did not owe its founding and subsequent development to the *conquistadores'* search for precious metals.

Until 1776 the present territory of Argentina, Uruguay, Paraguay, and part of Bolivia was governed from Lima, the site of the Viceroyalty of Peru. The controls imposed from Spain sought to restrict trade in the area, and production was largely limited to local consumer needs. Those restrictions reflected the influence of the Spanish merchants of Seville at the Spanish court and their ability to convince a succession of rulers that the merchants' interests were identical with those of Spain and her colonies.

A considerable illegal trade did develop in cattle hides and in exchanges with Portuguese Brazil. Similarly, a wine industry flourished in the Andean foothills despite the prohibitions on viticulture imposed to protect the Spanish vintners. Such conditions were not conducive to rapid settlement of a "land of little lure" and the towns grew slowly. In 1778, almost two centuries after its permanent settlement, the population of the city of Buenos Aires had not quite reached 25,000. What prosperity it had achieved was in considerable part due to the trade generated with British merchants whose government had succeeded in breaking the Spanish monopoly in the Treaty of Utrecht (1713).

The establishment of the Viceroyalty of La Plata (1776) was followed by the opening of the port of Buenos Aires to direct and free commerce with Spanish ports. This marked the real beginning of the growth and prosperity of the city as trade to and from the interior was channeled through its port.

An even greater impetus came in the last decade of the century when a further opening up of trade was followed by the wars of the Napoleonic period, which cut both trade and communicaton between Spain and her colonies. Those struggles gave the British a reason for invading the "River Plate," as they called it then and still call it, and thereby set off the Argentine independence movement.

The First Years of Independence

Political independence, declared at Tucumán (July 9, 1816) and confirmed in the battle of Maipú (April 5, 1818), freed the Río de la Plata area from Spanish controls. Even before independence had been won, the latent forces for regionalism had exerted themselves. Up-river in isolated Asunción, José Gaspar Rodríguez Francia rejected the authority of Buenos Aires and framed the "By-laws of Government" adopted for the "Republic of Paraguay" in 1813. Across the river José Artigas, the Uruguayan gaucho leader, also rejected Buenos Aires' attempt to assume leadership and control over the entire viceroyalty. In what is now Bolivia the Spanish troops destroyed the liberating army sent by Buenos Aires, and that region's independence was delayed until over a decade later (1825). As a result of these conflicting political currents the colonial economic pattern was destroyed and has never been more than partially restored.

Within the area that makes up present-day Argentina virtual anarchy followed hard on the heels of political independence. The Argentine Liberator, José de San Martín, refused to exert his influence on the turbulent scene in the Provincias Unidas del Río de la Plata, choosing instead self-exile in France.*

In the less restricted atmosphere of the final years of the colonial period Buenos Aires had already been turning its attention away from the interior towards trade with the outside world. After 1810 that tendency sharply increased as the port of Buenos Aires became the center through which flowed virtually all commerce to and from the Provincias Unidas. Buenos Aires was still the only seaport, as it had been under Spanish rule. Because of the lack of transportation facilities in the interior, French and British products could be more easily and cheaply obtained in Buenos Aires than could those of San Juan, Mendoza, Tucumán, or even Córdoba.

Buenos Aires also adopted the ideas and customs of France and Great Britain while the interior retained its colonial outlook and regarded the *porteños*—as the inhabitants of Buenos Aires were called—as interlopers trying to impose an alien way of life. Local *caudillos*—individuals with an armed following and ready to use any means to seize and hold power—contested first for provincial leadership and then resisted all efforts to create a centralized nation dominated by the *porteños*. In the struggles that followed, communications between the port and the interior were sharply curtailed and

---

* One can only speculate as to the possible results, had San Martín emulated the role George Washington had played in the fledgling United States.

even cut off for extended periods. The existing differences between Buenos
Aires, which was absorbing the political, economic, social and intellectual
ideas of the Atlantic community, and the much more conservative interior
cities were further extended and sharpened.

In the province of Buenos Aires the struggle for leadership by contesting
factions reached the point where on one day, June 20, 1820, the province had
three governors. The presence of Bernardino Rivadavia provided a farsighted
leader in the mid-1820's, but even the province of Buenos Aires was not yet
ready for the policies he proposed—encouragement of foreign investment
and immigration, a distribution of public land on a permanent rental basis, a
centralized government, and a curtailment of clerical influence in the social
and intellectual life of the country.

These policies had supporters in Buenos Aires, but the key proposal in
Rivadavia's program—a bill to make Buenos Aires the national capital and
thereby divert the customs receipts from the provincial to the national treasury—did not. At this stage in the development of the Río de la Plata area the
province of Buenos Aires was stronger than the rest of the country, and
many of the influential large landowners were not ready to make any sacrifice to organize the nation. The issue polarized the province's political forces
into two parties: the Federalists, who preferred a monopoly over the national
revenues to the organization of the nation; and the Unitarians, who wanted
to organize a centralized state directed from Buenos Aires and were willing
to share the customs receipts in the interest of national union. In the other
provinces the Unitarians had the support of Argentines of similar convic-
tions; the Federalists secured the backing of those *caudillos* who valued local
autonomy above national union and either did not realize or were indifferent
to the concentration of economic benefits in the hands of the Buenos Aires
Federalists. Economically the decision of the Federalist *caudillos* was against
the best interests of their own provinces. This was made clear in the decades
that followed as Buenos Aires prospered while the economies of other provinces declined.

In 1831 Juan Manuel de Rosas, who had won control of the Buenos Aires
provincial government, made a pact (Liga del Litoral) with the Federalist
governors of Santa Fe and Entre Ríos. The pact provided for common action
against the situation in the interior where the Unitarian cause was at the time
in the ascendancy. The Federalist forces prevailed over the Unitarians in one
province after another, and the influence of Rosas and Buenos Aires increased,
but the other provinces continued to decline economically as Rosas' monopolistic tactics restricted trade and involved the United Provinces in his struggles with Uruguay, France, and Great Britain.

The Rosas Era

Rosas, an unusual example of the *caudillo* dictator in Latin America, was
one of that area's great entrepreneurs during the first half of the nineteenth

century.* He founded the first *saladero,* or salted beef plant, in the province
of Buenos Aires. Even before Rosas became governor he had established a
prosperous business and was shipping salted beef in his own ships to Rio de
Janeiro and Havana. After 1829 the lands given him by the province and
those seized from his enemies gave him one of the largest landholdings in a
country where estates of over a hundred thousand acres were not unusual.

By one of the ironies of Argentine history, Rosas, the Federalist par excellence, who thundered against the "savage, filthy Unitarians" for their
efforts to establish a strong national government, was the principal agent in
making such a government possible in Argentina. For almost a quarter of a
century (1829-1852) Rosas was the government of Argentina. By one
means or another Rosas' principal Federalist rivals for leadership—the
caudillos Estanislao López and Juan Facundo Quiroga—were removed from
the scene and the lesser *caudillos* brought to heel. The Unitarian military
leader General José María Paz was captured by a Federalist gaucho's skillful
cast of the bolas and languished in Rosas' prison for nearly two decades. As
a result, Rosas, in establishing his domination, sharply reduced the autonomy
of the provincial *caudillos* and accustomed them to look to Buenos Aires for
leadership. He was in many respects the "providential figure" needed in the
transition from an anarchic period in which the values developing in the
modern Atlantic community were accepted by only a small proportion of
the society. Much of the revulsion the Argentine liberals have felt for Rosas
may be an unconscious attempt to make him the scapegoat for what, in many
respects, were the shortcomings not of Rosas but of Argentine society as a
whole in the second quarter of the nineteenth century.

By 1851 one of the more perceptive of Rosas' Federalist lieutenants in the
interior, General Justo José de Urquiza, the *caudillo* governor of Entre Ríos,
revolted. Urquiza realized that under Rosas' policies the interior would continue to be strangled to death economically while Buenos Aires—and particularly Rosas' own economic interests—prospered. Urquiza, reinforced by
Unitarians, anti-Rosas Federalists and troops from his Uruguayan and Brazilian allies, defeated Rosas at Caseros on February 3, 1852. Although the
political and constitutional problems remained to be solved, the removal of
Rosas opened the way both for their solution and for the rest of the country
to share in the prosperity that Buenos Aires had been enjoying at their expense.

Argentine Economy and Society after Rosas

Even after Rosas' defeat the province of Buenos Aires continued to develop
more rapidly than even the wealthier interior provinces such as Santa Fe,
Entre Ríos, Corrientes, Córdoba, and Mendoza. Some of the first important

* Rosas was so successful as an operator of an *estancia* (cattle ranch) that his book of
instructions has been reprinted many times and can still be bought in Buenos Aires
bookstores.

innovations in Argentine agriculture had already been made. In 1825 improved breeds of sheep from Spain and Great Britain had been introduced by Rivadavia with notable results. During the Rosas period two Englishmen played even more important roles as innovators. Richard Newton put up the first iron wire fence, in 1844, and four years later John Miller imported the first Durham bull from his homeland, thereby preparing the way for the development of the cattle industry during the second half of the century. These innovations, significantly, took place in Buenos Aires province, an oasis of law and order in the United Provinces maintained by Rosas, which proved attractive to English investors in land and livestock.

In 1852 there were no railroads in Argentina, and the closest thing to a highway was the ruts cut by the lumbering, two-wheeled oxcarts that carried the bulk of the commerce between Buenos Aires and the interior. There was an excellent network of navigable rivers, but no vessels to use them nor bridges across which commerce could flow. Although the area was sparsely populated (the first national census in 1869 revealed a population of 1,743,353, including 211,993 foreigners), there had been little encouragement of immigration during the long Rosas period (1829-33, 1835-1852).

Despite the struggles between Buenos Aires and the other provinces united in the Argentine Confederation under the leadership of General Urquiza, the decade following Rosas' overthrow (1852-1862) was one of substantial progress. In both of the warring camps there was an acute realization of the need for promoting immigration, constructing railroads and establishing a public school system—all of which had been ignored under the Rosas dictatorship. Buenos Aires, with its greater financial resources, was more successful in its transportation ventures, and the first 10 kilometers of track were opened in 1857. That same year the Confederation's adoption of the postage stamp considerably facilitated communications, and postal service was further improved by opening new routes and improving existing ones. Both factions promoted public school systems, with Urquiza, the former Rosas lieutenant, vying with Domingo F. Sarmiento, the native of San Juan who had been entrusted with the direction of schools in the province of Buenos Aires.

The next two decades brought further innovations to prepare the way for the country's future cattle industry. In 1866 the Sociedad Rural was founded by a small group of cattle raisers and nine years later held its first livestock show to encourage the use of improved cattle breeds. Several years later (1878) the first frozen Argentine beef arrived in Europe (on the steamer *Paraguay*) in excellent condition. "By 1887, 57 refrigerator ships were in regular service between Buenos Aires and English ports. By the end of the century, the number had risen to 278." [1]

The establishment of meat-packing plants in Argentina followed soon after the *Paraguay*'s voyage and made it profitable for *estancieros* to improve their cattle and sheep breeds and to replace the tough, dry native pampa grass with alfalfa as fodder to fatten the expanding herds. Foreign capital, mostly British but some French, extended the railroad network to over 4,000 miles by 1889; by 1914 the present railroad network of over 27,000 miles was substantially completed.

Immigration to settle the *pampa* and the interior provinces grew from a few hundred a year in the late 1850's to 121,000 in 1887 and 261,000 in 1889. At first the immigrants were mainly from Spain, but soon Italians became the most numerous of the new arrivals, followed by Spaniards, French, Belgians, and English-Irish. During the 1880-1886 period alone some 483,000 immigrants entered the country. By 1895 the population had grown to nearly 4 million and included over a million foreigners. They provided both the labor force and the skilled management to expand the production of cane sugar and wheat. The Indian and gaucho hordes had been vanquished and the Europeanization of Argentina substantially completed by the end of the century.

During the last years of the nineteenth century and the first two decades of the twentieth century Argentina continued to enjoy a prosperity probably unprecedented in Latin America and which had few parallels in other parts of the world. The city of Buenos Aires, with its imposing public buildings, elegant mansions, tree-lined streets, plazas, parks, and cosmopolitan outlook, became a New World showcase. Unfortunately, the pace of progress was far from uniform throughout the nation. The paved and brightly lighted streets, modern plumbing, and public utilities available in the metropolitan area were found only in the other principal urban areas, and on a considerably lesser scale there. A few miles outside the Federal District (Capital Federal—the formal title of the city of Buenos Aires) the towns of the nation's most prosperous province presented a striking contrast to conditions in the capital. Instead of paved boulevards, even the main streets were unpaved dusty tracks that became muddy ruts after a heavy rain. Only a comparatively few homes had electricity, running water, or plumbing, and sanitary conditions usually left much to be desired. Few duplicates were to be found of the neat shops and orderly markets of Buenos Aires. A similar disparity obtained in medical and educational facilities, and the literacy rate decreased as the distance from the metropolis lengthened.

Politics in the Late Nineteenth Century

There were also contrasts in the way in which political institutions operated outside of the capital. Argentina, like the rest of Latin America, had had little experience in self-government during the colonial period. Despite the claims of those who would equate the colonial *cabildo* with the New England town meeting, there was almost no way in which the grievances of the general public could find recourse except in revolution. The achievement of Argentine independence, therefore, meant a sharp break with the pattern of authority, particularly in Buenos Aires, the seat of the viceroyalty. The *cabildo* soon outlived its usefulness as an effective institution, in any case, and was abolished by the provincial government a decade after the coming of Independence.

The *cabildos* of other Argentine cities also had brief moments of influence, but not enough to provide the apprenticeship needed for responsible self-government. In much of the interior of the country the colonial upper classes continued to dominate the towns and cities while the gauchos and Indians contested for or shared control of the countryside. The gaucho *caudillos* often became the effective rulers in their areas. Even under Rosas' suzerainty they were allowed considerable local autonomy as long as they did not clash with the interests of "Don Manuel." This pattern of control by local *caudillos* survived Rosas and impeded national union for several decades after Caseros. In isolated areas the influence of the gaucho *caudillos* continued until almost the end of the century. Their successors were the large landowners, who dominated by their economic power as effectively as had the gaucho *caudillos* by their armed prowess. Since in some cases, such as those of Rosas and Urquiza, the *caudillo* and the proprietor *patrón* had been identical, the transition was not a difficult one—particularly where local antipathy for the metropolis, or even the provincial capital, was strong. As a result local politics tended to be dominated by the *patrón*, and provincial politics by arrangements between the *patrones*. The *patrón* led his following to the polls much as earlier the gaucho *caudillo* had led his armed band off to struggles with other bands or against the authority of Buenos Aires. The Spanish and Italian immigrants who came to labor on the great estates fell easily into place in a pattern which had so many similarities to the one they had known in the old country.

By and large, political parties in the provinces were based on local interests. While principles and ideals might find expression in *discursos* and *pronunciamientos*, they exerted little influence. The first leader to bring the provincial interests together in an effective, disciplined, political organization was General Julio Argentino Roca. The "Hero of the Desert" had already achieved renown by driving back the Indians, destroying their ability to harass frontier settlements and thereby opening up vast new areas in the west for settlement. Roca combined his popularity with a high level of political sagacity and brought the provincial interests together in the first real political machine in Argentine history. It carried him to the presidency twice, 1880-1886 and 1898-1904, and made him the most powerful figure in Argentine politics for over a quarter-century. Roca's political astuteness is revealed by the fact that, although he did not come from Buenos Aires and triumphed with the support of the other provinces, Buenos Aires continued to flourish during his administrations. Small wonder that his sobriquet as a politician was *El Zorro* ("the Fox").

In the city of Buenos Aires, the nation's capital—in contrast to Washington, D.C.—citizens voted not only for president and vice-president but also for the senators and deputies who represented them in the national congress. The opportunities offered by the city attracted the better educated and the trained artisans among the immigrants who came through the port of Buenos Aires. In any event the political parties of the capital extended across the political spectrum and the *porteño* voters were considerably more sophisticated politically than the voting public in the provinces. This was a reflection of the port city's contacts with the outside world, the ideas brought by the immigrants, the city's excellent newspapers, and its superior educational facilities, including provisions for adult education not readily available in other parts of the country. The ever-larger proportion of the nation's population living in the metropolitan area made it a center of attention to any group seeking political power.

Although Buenos Aires has been generally more sympathetic to liberal ideas than the more conservative interior, it also has had a rightist tradition. From the early days of the independence movement the two currents have vied for power in Buenos Aires. At first both liberals and conservatives had their roots in the Spanish past. The liberal forces, however, turned increasingly to other sources for ideas and examples to follow as the lamp of Spanish liberalism burned low, flickered, and at times appeared to have been extinguished. Thus Rivadavia turned to France and Great Britain, and the young liberals of the 1830's and 1840's—Esteban Echeverría, and José Mármol, Juan Bautista Alberdi, Bartolomé Mitre, and others—followed a similar orientation; still another great liberal figure, Domingo F. Sarmiento, found his ultimate model in the United States. Cornelio Saavedra's honest conservatism, however, was turned by Juan Manuel de Rosas into a backward and inward looking current, with xenophobic overtones, that survived Rosas' long and repressive dictatorship.

After Rosas' overthrow the lines between liberalism and conservatism weakened, although Buenos Aires continued to be the incubator of liberal movements. The parties of the second half of the nineteenth century were highly personalistic, and much of their success depended upon their leaders' popular appeal. The first four presidents, after the organization of the nation in 1862, were practical men concerned with keeping order so that the nation might progress. [See table below.] Mitre, Sarmiento, Avellaneda, and Roca can all be classified as either liberal or conservative presidents, depending on which aspects of their administrations are kept in view. On balance, however, the trend would appear to have been toward the right, particularly after 1880, as the Roca administration came more and more to represent expanding pastoral interests. This trend was accentuated by the strength of the political machine Roca had assembled in the interior and then combined with similar interests in Buenos Aires province.

In the 1890's a new party made its appearance as a reaction against the domination of national politics by the administration in power. The example set by Mitre in the 1868 election—not using his administration's influence to determine the choice of his successor—unfortunately was not followed by his successors. The hand-picking of successors reached its apogee in 1886 when President Roca secured the election of his brother-in-law, Miguel Juárez Celman, as his successor. By September 1889 a Youth's Civic Union (Unión Cívica de la Juventud) had been formed by a mass public meeting protesting against the Juárez Celman administration, whose partiality for the grazing interests of Buenos Aires province was creating a financial crisis. Within a year the crisis had arrived and Juárez Celman resigned, despite his having survived a revolutionary attempt against his government.

PRESIDENTS OF ARGENTINA

Of the United Provinces		Roque Sáenz Peña	1910-1913
Bernardino Rivadavia	1826-1827	Victorino de la Plaza	1913-1916
Vicente López	1827	Hipólito Irigoyen	1916-1922
Of the Argentine Confeder-		Marcelo T. de Alvear	1922-1928
ation[a]		Hipólito Irigoyen (second	
Justo José de Urquiza	1854-1860	term)	1928-1930
Santiago Derqui	1860-1861	José F. Uriburu	1930-1932
Bartolomé Mitre	1861-1862	Agustín P. Justo	1932-1938
Of the Argentine Republic		Roberto M. Ortiz	1938-1940
Bartolomé Mitre	1862-1868	Ramón S. Castillo	1940-1943
Domingo F. Sarmiento	1868-1874	Arturo Rawson	1943
Nicolás Avellaneda	1874-1880	Pedro B. Ramírez	1943-1944
Julio A. Roca	1880-1886	Edelmiro Farrell	1944-1946
Miguel Juárez Celman	1886-1890	Juan D. Perón	1946-1952
Carlos Pellegrini	1890-1892	Juan D. Perón (second	
Luis Sáenz Peña	1892-1895	term)	1952-1955
José Evaristo Uriburu	1895-1898	Eduardo Lonardi	1955
Julio A. Roca (second		Pedro E. Aramburu	1955-1958
term)	1898-1904	Arturo Frondizi	1958-1962
Manuel Quintana	1904-1906	José María Guido	1962-1963
José Figueroa Alcorta	1906-1910	Arturo Illía	1963-

[a] The Argentine Confederation consisted of the provinces other than Buenos Aires.

In mid-April 1890, under the impetus of the financial crisis, the youth group was transformed into the Unión Cívica (UC), led by Mitre, the elder statesman, as the nominal leader; the real power in the UC was Leandro Alem. The UC platform of free suffrage and honest elections offered a vehicle for the growing middle class to oppose the control of the government by the *estancieros*, the great landowners. Actually, since there was no possibility of honest elections, Alem was preparing to capture power by revolution with the support of dissatisfied elements of the military, particularly among the junior officers. Before the revolutionary movement was ready, however, it was betrayed to the government and, forced to act prematurely, Alem and his supporters failed in their attempt in less than a week in late July of 1890. Nevertheless, as an expression of public dissatisfaction, the revolution exerted such influence on Juárez Celman that he resigned under heavy pressure a few days later.

In the aftermath of the 1890 revolt—a general amnesty for the revolutionists indicates its popularity—the Civic Union nominated the venerable Mitre as its candidate for the March 1892 elections to oppose the Roca machine, the Partido Autonomista Nacional. Mitre, out of the country when nominated, made a political arrangement with Roca to avoid a clash between the two leaders: Mitre would be supported by Roca in return for accepting Roca's candidate for the vice-presidency.

The Civic Union split wide open over the deal. Those who supported Mitre formed the Unión Cívica Nacional. The younger men and those who had supported the 1890 revolution, Alem, Hipólito Irigoyen, and the Civic Union's vice-presidential candidate, Bernardo de Irigoyen, rejected Mitre and founded the Unión Cívica Radical (UCR). Mitre's arrangement with Roca wrecked the Civic Union and his own presidential chances. The public reaction was so strong that Roca and Mitre agreed on another candidate, Luis Sáenz Peña. The latter's chief virtues were that he was manageable and that since he was the father of the outstanding opposition candidate, Roque Sáenz Peña, the son would decline to contest in deference to his father. Their reasoning was correct. Roque Sáenz Peña dutifully withdrew, and his elderly parent was duly elected by the Roca-Mitre forces.

As leader of the new party Alem again reverted to revolutionary tactics when the legal road to power continued to be blocked by the Roca machine. In the next few years revolts broke out in several provinces, including Buenos Aires, where Alem's nephew Hipólito Irigoyen had organized a substantial following. When they failed, Alem felt himself discredited and committed suicide.

Alem's death brought into the open the sharp conflicts that existed among the upper levels of UCR leadership. The brilliant young Dr. Juan B. Justo had already left the party to found the Argentine Socialist Party in 1894. Others were offended by the personality and tactics of Hipólito Irigoyen, Alem's nephew, who had established an effective UCR provincial organization in the province of Buenos Aires. Irigoyen's efforts to assume Alem's mantle were opposed by another young leader, Lisandro de la Torre. De la Torre resigned at the 1897 Radical convention, bitterly attacking Irigoyen in his explanation of his action. (The two men subsequently fought a duel.)

The Irigoyen Era

Under Irigoyen's dictatorial leadership dissent was not permitted within the UCR. The party was repeatedly rent by factionalism, but Irigoyen ruled his following with an iron hand. Under the existing circumstances he refused to participate in elections on the grounds that the regime in power would not permit them to be fairly conducted. Another UCR revolt was suppressed in 1905, but Irigoyen continued his intransigent attitude towards elections and continued plotting.

Finally in 1912, at the insistence of President Roque Sáenz Peña (elected in 1910), an electoral reform law was enacted. It made voting secret and compulsory and provided for a division of the seats in the chamber of deputies on a proportional basis. The party winning the most votes in an electoral district received two-thirds of the district's seats; the party with the next largest number of votes secured the remaining seats being contested. Under these changed conditions Irigoyen reversed his tactics, and became the winning candidate in the first free and representative general election in Argentine history (1916).

The 1912 electoral law, which in honor of the man who made it possible has become known as the Sáenz Peña law, regulated Argentine elections during the next half-century. Under its provisions the opposition was guaranteed a voice in government. As a result the Argentine Socialist Party became an important factor in politics in the congressional elections in the Federal Capital, frequently winning the minority representation and occasionally the majority seats in the chamber of deputies. In 1932, when the Radical candidates were barred, the Socialists succeeded in gaining the majority seats. In the province of Santa Fe, Lisandro de la Torre took advantage of its provisions to form a new party, the Progressive Democratic Party (Partido Demócrata Progresista, or PDP). While the PDP never won much of a following outside Santa Fe, whose politics it completely dominated, the PDP's high ideals and the caliber of its leadership gave it a moral influence out of proportion to its limited numerical membership.

Once in power President Irigoyen was faced with the problem of satisfying those whose opposition to rule by the *estancieros* had put him in power. In Argentina the system of large landholdings (latifundia) was well established, with over half the occupied land held in estates of more than 10,000 acres. According to the 1914 census some 500 owners held a total of over 53,000,000 acres. The great landowners were not inclined to relinquish the considerable political influence they had exercised for nearly half a century.

The UCR could and did obtain majorities in the popularly elected national chamber of deputies, but had more difficulty in obtaining a majority in the national senate. The senate's members were selected by the provincial legislatures, in which the conservative forces of the provinces were still strongly entrenched. While the presidency and the chamber of deputies had been wrested from the *estancieros'* control, the latter could still block national legislation in the senate and in the provincial governments. Under the federal system of the Constitution of 1853, the provinces had powers which could be used to obstruct the efforts of the national government. At this time the national government's principal counterforce was its power of intervention, under which the federal government could set aside a provincial government and, through its appointee, govern the province until new elections for provincial authorities were held under the intervenor's supervision. Although Irigoyen frequently resorted to federal intervention, it could not replace what he really needed—a truly national party able to win elections on all levels. Finally, despite his verbal attacks on the oligarchy of the great landowners, Irigoyen did not make a serious attempt to destroy its political and economic power.

Perhaps because of the strength of the opposition or (as some observers insist) perhaps because Irigoyen never really intended to make any important social or economic changes, his administration focused its attention on political and educational questions. Irigoyen was something of an enigma to even his closest associates. If he had a program for Argentina, he has left no clear picture of what it was. The main achievements of his first administration were the maintenance of the Conservative policy of neutrality in World War I; the University Reform of 1918 which, in reforming an obsolete system, gave the students an influence over the new system that in many respects has been counterproductive; and the establishment of the State Oil Authority (Yacimientos Petrolíferos Fiscales, or YPF) to protect, promote, and improve the petroleum industry in Argentina. The YPF, established by legislation passed in 1922, was a natural reaction to the wartime fuel shortages in Argentina and to a deep-seated Argentine distrust of the great foreign oil companies.

In the field of Argentine foreign relations Irigoyen inherited a policy of neutrality towards World War I, which his Conservative predecessor had tended to interpret to the benefit of the Allies. Although German submarine activities created strong pressure—including a 23-to-1 vote in the senate—for breaking off relations with Germany, Irigoyen insisted on strict neutrality. His repeated efforts to induce other Latin American countries to follow a similar course, after the United States entered the war early in 1917, have been cited as evidence that Irigoyen was pro-German. Irigoyen obviously resented the close relationship between his conservative opponents and Great Britain; there were pro-Germans among the high-ranking army officers; and German scientific, intellectual, and military prowess had many admirers in Argentina. Irigoyen's militant neutralism, however, was probably based on his sincere conviction that the interests of his country were best served by neutrality. Furthermore, his neutralism was in accord with the traditional Argentine policies of settling disputes by arbitration and keeping out of all conflicts between other countries which did not pose a clear and imminent threat to Argentina's vital security interests. His refusal to follow where the United States would lead also accorded with the pattern set by Roque Sáenz Peña over a quarter-century before (1889) at the First Pan American Congress in Washington. At that time the young Argentine delegate had made clear his thesis that Argentina—not the United States—should be the leader of Latin America.

Irigoyen, in his campaign speeches and during the early years of his administration, had been long on assurances to Argentine workers but dilatory in executing his promises. If by January 1919 organized Argentine labor still had any hopes for a new deal under Irigoyen, those hopes were rudely dashed by the events of the Tragic Week (Semana Trágica). Clashes involving striking workers and policemen escorting supplies for a strike-bound plant accelerated into pitched battles between strikers and police, a general strike and widespread rioting. During the week the city's Jewish population became the target of the mobs roaming the streets. Jewish homes were invaded and their occupants, who had become associated in the popular mind with the anarchists and Bolsheviks then featured in news reports of mass murders and class warfare from Europe, were attacked and beaten to death before the military was able to restore order.

The Constitution of 1853 did not permit a president to succeed himself in office. As a result Irigoyen was faced in 1922 with the problem of nominating his successor. His choice, Marcelo T. de Alvear, an aristocrat who had been one of the organizers of the Unión Cívica de la Juventud, appeared to provide a successor who would be both manageable and respectable. Once elected, however, Alvear the president proved to be more respected by Irigoyen's Conservative opponents than manageable by Irigoyen. In less than two years the two men had broken relations and in September 1924 Alvear and his followers formed the UCR Anti-Personalista, in revolt against Irigoyen's dictatorial control of the UCR.

After his break with Irigoyen, Alvear had to turn to the Conservatives for congressional support. Perhaps as a result, during the rest of his administration (1924-28), while Argentina's neighbors Chile and Uruguay were carrying out social reform programs, there were no sustained efforts along those lines in Argentina. In view of the growing corruption and the lack of vigorous, young, reform-minded leaders in the Radical Party, however, there is little reason to believe that such programs would have been undertaken even if there had been no split in the UCR leadership. Consequently, while the nation apparently continued to enjoy a high level of prosperity, the distribution of the national income became increasingly inequitable, and the need for social, economic, and political reform was intensified.

In 1928 Irigoyen easily defeated a Conservative candidate supported by the UCR Anti-Personalist Party. In contrast to the limited successes of his first administration, Irigoyen's second term was a national disaster. Failing physically and mentally and surrounded by corrupt, incompetent Radical politicians, the aged Irigoyen was clearly unequal to the political and economic problems that were intensified by the 1930 world depression. By mid-1930 his resignation was being openly requested. On September 6, 1930, when the troops from nearby Campo de Mayo advanced on the Casa Rosada, scarcely a hand was raised in the defense of the government.

From Irigoyen to Perón

The Revolution of September 6, 1930, provides a bench mark in Argentine political and economic history. It broke a pattern of elected civilian governments that had lasted for over three-quarters of a century, during which the Argentine military had assumed an increasingly apolitical role. In 1930 the Argentine military not only returned to politics; the faction led by General José Felix Uriburu, who had ousted Irigoyen, decided to impose its own ideas upon the Argentine nation. Under the provisional presidency of General Uriburu a mélange of reactionary native (*criollo*) fascism, garnished with the trappings of European totalitarianism, was concocted and imposed on Argentina. Both the Argentine public and the more democratic element of the military, however, refused to acquiesce. By late 1931 Uriburu was forced to hold elections, and in 1932 to turn over power to General Agustín P. Justo, elected by the Concordancia, a conservative coalition of the National Democrats (Partido Demócrata Nacional, or PDN) and the anti-Irigoyen UCR Anti-Personalista.

Under Justo the Conservative oligarchy that had ruled Argentina before 1916 returned to power, but the Argentine military retained an influential voice in government. That influence was obvious in the continuation of the attempts begun under General Uriburu to make Argentina less dependent upon other nations for the sinews of war. While World War I had accelerated the development of light industries to replace consumer goods no longer available from abroad, there was relatively little heavier industry to produce durable goods and war matériel. Under the prodding of its own and civilian advocates of self-sufficiency, the Argentine army began to create factories to produce the supplies its forces needed and to supply certain civilian needs as well. Thus the Argentine army became one of the principal —though still small—domestic producers of iron and steel. During World War II this trend was increased at first by demand and later by the takeover of German and Italian industrial establishments by the state.

During Justo's presidency the Argentine economy recovered from the depths it had touched in 1930 and 1931. The distribution of that prosperity, however, was if anything more inequitable than before, and the increasing need for social welfare measures was ignored. In 1936, when an Anti-Personalist Radical, Roberto M. Ortiz, was elected, it appeared that there would be a change for the better. Although Ortiz had secured his office through some of the most baldly manipulated elections in Argentine history, he was personally honest, highly respected, and known for his liberal views. Unfortunately, illness incapacitated Ortiz to the point that he was unable to serve much of the time before he finally resigned in June, 1942. During Ortiz' absences from office, Vice-President Ramón S. Castillo, an extreme Conservative of the National Democrat Party, served the interests of the oligarchy and made his pro-Axis sentiments clear. In December 1941, for example, Acting President Castillo used the Japanese attack on Pearl Harbor to impose a state of siege under which he could quell the increasingly vociferous opposition to his domestic and foreign policies.

One of the most unpopular of Argentine presidents, Castillo held office with the support of the oligarchy and the military. By mid-1943 he had offended both—the oligarchy by making it clear that he intended to impose his own chosen successor in the elections scheduled for September 1943. He had already antagonized the military by not redressing the imbalance vis à vis Brazilian military strength, created by United States assistance given Brazil before and during World War II. Castillo's selection of a fellow oligarch known to be pro-British and without any popular support provided the incident for the military to act. On June 4, 1943, his regime was easily toppled by an Argentine army still fundamentally divided into authoritarian and moderate factions that were temporarily united in their common distrust for and disgust with Castillo. General Arturo Rawson, commander of the Campo de Mayo Cavalry and leader of the moderate faction, secured the provisional presidency for about forty-eight hours—the time needed by the authoritarian group to muster its forces and replace him. His successor, General Pedro P. Ramírez, who had been Castillo's minister of war, lasted longer (nine months), but in turn was pulled down in the struggle for power set off by Castillo's overthrow. The next occupant, General Edelmiro Farrell, held the title longer (over two years), but much of that time was merely serving as the pliant puppet of Colonel Juan Domingo Perón, who was emerging as the Argentine strong man.

The Perón Era

Perón (born in 1895) was a career army officer who had participated in the 1930 revolution and had served as military attaché in Chile (1936-38) and in Italy (1939-40). He had been ousted from Chile for trying to buy Chilean defense plans; in Italy he became an admirer of Mussolini (who would avoid Il Duce's mistakes). Perón also had an opportunity to visit Hitler's militarized Germany and Franco's Spain. He returned to Argentina in early 1941 convinced that the Axis would win World War II and that Argentina could profit from being the Axis ally in the Western Hemisphere.

By the time of Castillo's ouster Perón was one of a group of pro-Axis army officers, mostly colonels, who called themselves the Group of United Officers (Grupo de Oficiales Unidos), better known as the GOU. Perón, a champion boxer and fencer in the Argentine army, had directed the training of its crack Andean ski troops, had taught in both army and naval war colleges, and was the author of three volumes on military strategy and history. In his late forties at this time, the athletic Perón made a striking physical impression, could be charming, gracious, or imperious as the occasion required, and had a skill as a public speaker that was unusual even in a society which prized oratory. Within the military, however, Perón was one of several officers, each of whom had attracted a coterie of followers and was maneuvering to take advantage of the political vacuum created by Castillo's downfall. His first upward step was his appointment by the minister of war, General Farrell, to head the ministry's secretariat.

Unlike his fellow officers, Perón recognized the political potential in Argentine labor, particularly in the unorganized workers in metropolitan

Buenos Aires. While he used his post at the ministry of war to cultivate a military following, Perón also sought and received another post his competitors for power overlooked—head of the department of labor and social welfare. Although the department was then under the ministry of interior, within a few weeks Perón had it made an independent secretariat, thereby obtaining cabinet rank. Almost immediately Perón set about expanding his labor post's powers and using them to organize Argentine labor in support of the military government and to create his own mass popular following in the key metropolitan area of Buenos Aires. Recalcitrant unions were brought into line by Perón's use of his powers to grant, withhold, or withdraw recognition from unions and to declare strikes legal or illegal. At the same time Argentine labor quickly learned that cooperation with Colonel Perón brought prompt rewards through his direct influence on labor's side in its disputes with employers.

By mid-1944 Perón had added the ministry of war and the vice-presidency of Argentina to his labor command post. He was recognized as the leader of the pro-Axis group that had ousted Ramírez in Februray 1944 and as the real power behind President Farrell. Consequently, Perón became the principal target of civilian and military groups opposed to the regime's pro-Axis policies and seeking a return to civilian government. The Argentine declaration of war on Germany and Japan, on March 27, 1945, did little to allay that opposition. Since the Axis defeat was clearly in sight by that time, the declaration's only practical purpose was to enable the regime to take over German properties in Argentina and to qualify Argentina for participation in the United Nations Organization, then in process of formation. In October 1945 Perón's military opposition finally achieved sufficient force to arrest him and divest him of his three important offices. Perón was then packed off to the same naval prison on Martín García Island to which Irigoyen had been sent in 1930.

Perón's opponents—then as on later occasions—proved unequal to the task confronting them. They conferred and hesitated and then conferred again. Meanwhile Perón's lieutenants, including María Eva Duarte, rallied the labor following he had cultivated. On the morning of October 17, led by *peronista* strong-arm squads, the *descamisados* (ragamuffins) swarmed through Buenos Aires intimidating the anti-Perón demonstrators—while the pro-Perón police looked the other way—and demanding Perón's restoration. It came late that evening as the military gave way before the new force Perón had fashioned and brought into Argentine politics. Perón returned more powerful than ever, so powerful in fact that he did not need to resume his official positions; the military had been brought to heel so completely that he could even resign his colonel's commission. Perón had also gained a new asset, the glamorous, shapely, blonde María Eva Duarte, who had helped restore him to power. Although Señorita Duarte had made no great mark as a bit actress, as Señora Eva Duarte de Perón she became one of the world's most powerful women and more than carried her share in the Perón partnership.

One might reasonably have expected that the opposition to Perón would have profited from the October fiasco. Instead, when the Democratic Union (Unión Democrática or UD) was formed by most of the prominent parties, it wasted several weeks in disputes before reaching agreement on a lackluster candidate and a return-to-normalcy platform. In a quite fairly contested campaign the UD's prospects might have been brighter. In the contest with the dynamic Perón, however, the official candidate received considerable support from his allies in the Farrell administration. The government decreed the substantial bonus for labor which Perón had initiated just before his temporary ousting in October, and employer resistance served to fortify Perón's claims that only his influence was exerted in labor's behalf. The UD's political rallies were given little or no police protection. Consequently they were subjected to attacks by *peronista* hoodlums, and the train carrying the UD candidates on an electoral campaign tour was shot at, stoned, and set afire.

These were handicaps, but the basic weakness of the UD position lay elsewhere. One of the younger, more astute, but less influential UCR leaders singled it out in declaring that the UD appeared to be making the electorate choose between constitutional liberty and social justice, and to be defending a *status quo* that was indefensible.

Perón also received help from other quarters. The Pastoral Letter of the Argentine Roman Catholic hierarchy instructed the nation's Catholics not to vote for any candidate supported by a party advocating separation of Church and State—a basic tenet of the Socialist Party, a member of the UD coalition. From outside the country aid came in the form of the United States' Department of State publication *Blue Book on Argentina*, which by attacking Perón's pro-Axis record enabled him to justify his claim of foreign intervention against him. Perón probably would have been elected without the *Blue Book,* but it clearly hampered his opponents by strengthening his claim to be the nationalist champion in a nation notable for its nationalistic tendencies.

While the election campaign was conducted to favor the official candidate, Perón, the actual balloting on February 24, 1946, and the counting of ballots were above reproach—the first such election in Argentina since 1916. Perón received 56 percent of the popular vote and 304 out of the 376 votes in the electoral college. His supporters won the majority two-thirds of the chamber of deputies and all but two seats in the senate—an oversight soon taken care of by the Peronist senators' refusing to seat the two oppositionists representing Corrientes, the one province which did not elect a Peronist legislature.

Once inaugurated (June 4, 1946) Perón set about consolidating his electoral victory. He used his compliant legislative majorities to destroy the independence of the supreme court and to reduce virtually all holders of judicial posts to little more than puppets of the chief executive. President Perón also used his powers of intervention to purge the nation's six universities of any remaining opposition and to destroy their hard-won academic freedoms. Eventually the entire public education system was converted into a propaganda machine for the indoctrination of the nation's youth in the Peronist ideology. In provinces and municipalities where the local authorities were non-Peronist or did not hasten to carry out Perón's dicta he employed both federal interventors and his fiscal controls to enforce his will.

During the 1948-1951 period Perón reached the high plateau of his political career. Even though the February 1948 purchase of the British-owned railroads, which made up some 70 percent of the nation's total mileage, would prove in the long run to have been a disastrous mistake, it was an immediate political bonanza. Coming just before the March 1948 congressional elections, it helped to swell the Peronist victory total. It also served to substantiate the formal Declaration of Economic Independence which Perón had ostentatiously proclaimed in 1947, on July 9, national Independence Day.

The 1948 congressional victories were followed by an intensive campaign to denigrate the venerable Constitution of 1853 and prepare the ground for changes to make it more suitable for Perón's purposes. Legislation providing for a constitutional convention was promptly steam-rollered through the Congress. The opposition had about as much freedom in the election campaign for members of the constitutional convention as it had had in the 1946 elections, and the Peronist candidates won better than a 2-to-1 margin of the 158 seats contested. The convention met in January 1949 and moved along slowly until the delegates of the UCR—the only other party represented— provoked a Peronist spokesman into admitting that the real purpose of amending the constitution was to remove the constitutional prohibition against a president's serving successive terms. The Radical bloc of delegates walked out of the convention, which proceeded posthaste to do Perón's will.

The Perón constitution was proclaimed on March 16, 1949. While it retained much of the form and language of its predecessor of 1853—the description of the government as federal, republican and representative, the 1853 distribution of powers and threefold separation of powers, as well as many other features of the earlier version—the spirit was far different. The laissez-faire orientation of 1853 was replaced by a statist concept under which the federal government's economic powers were greatly expanded. Peronist propaganda in the form of Perón's social program, including "the Rights of the Worker" (which did not include the right to strike!), the "Rights of the Aged," and other phrases calculated to appeal to labor, was inserted. Not incidentally, the prohibition against successive presidential terms was removed, despite Perón's earlier declaration that this was a matter of little or no importance. The cumbersome electoral college was eliminated, and provision was made for direct election of the president, vice-president, and senators. The presidential powers were also strengthened—at the expense of the congress.

In 1949 Perón also completed the reorganization of his heterogeneous political following into a more efficient single party, the Peronist Party (Partido Peronista, or PP). The labor groups and the dissident Radical faction which had supported him in the 1946 elections had already been consolidated into a single party despite the objections of such labor leaders as Cipriano Reyes, who had led the packinghouse workers in support of Perón during October 1945. The new party was given a detailed organization, which made it even more responsive to its "sole leader" (*jefe único*), when the latter also happened to be president of the Argentine Nation. While in theory membership was restricted and a privilege, in practice government employees were put under considerable pressure to be at least nominal party members.

In 1951 the first serious break in the military-labor base for Perón's regime seemed imminent. His wife's candidacy for the vice-presidential position on the Peronist ticket in the October 1951 Presidential elections was strongly supported by the obedient top leadership and much of the rank and file of the General Confederation of Labor (Confederación General del Trabajo, or CGT), the Peronist labor organization containing virtually all organized labor. Putting a woman—let alone Evita!—in the line of direct succession to the presidency was too much for the professional military to swallow, however. Publicly the CGT was exerting pressure on the First Lady to assume the position from which on Perón's death, incapacity, or absence from the country she would become commander-in-chief of the Argentine armed forces. Behind the scenes the top military leaders were seething at the prospect they faced and letting Perón know it. Finally, in a dramatic gesture, Señora Perón declined the offer in a typically feminine gesture—she was, she declared, too young to qualify for the office. Actually she was then thirty-two years of age. The minimum age requirement is thirty. It is an open question whether the withdrawal was dictated by military pressure, Evita's declining health, or Perón's second thoughts about having his ambitious spouse in the vice-presidency.

Within the military the unrest created by Señora Perón's candidacy led a group of anti-Peronist officers to think the time was ripe for a coup. Their short-lived attempt, set off in September 1951, aborted a more comprehensive coup that was being formed. Moreover, it provided Perón with an opportunity to oust officers whom he did not trust and to establish the death penalty for military rebellion.

The November 1951 national elections were noteworthy on several counts. There was no coalition against Perón; he had removed that threat with legal prohibitions against electoral coalitions and by controlling the formation of new political parties. Argentine women voted for the first time in national elections; the Argentine Communist Party (Partido Comunista Argentina, or PCA) presented the first female candidate, Alcira de la Peña, actually to secure the vice-presidential nomination of an Argentine party; and the Peronist Party, on Señora Perón's insistence, nominated and elected several female candidates for seats in both houses of the national congress. For the first time also, the president, the vice-president, and the national senators were elected directly, as a result of changes provided for by the Constitution of 1949. During the campaign the opposition candidates were subjected to even more official controls and given even less police protection from Peronist thugs than in 1946. Alfredo L. Palacios, the Socialist Party candidate, had been imprisoned and was so handicapped during the campaign that he withdrew from the race in late October. Rodolfo Ghioldi, the Communist candidate, was also imprisoned, but refused to withdraw. On November 1 he was shot and seriously wounded while conducting an election rally on a tour of the provinces. Official controls enabled virtually all information media to be utilized on behalf of the Peronist candidates, to complete the one-sidedness of the campaign. As in 1946, the Election Day voting and the counting of the ballots were again conducted in an exemplary fashion. Perón's margin of victory was even larger than before, his vote reaching nearly two-thirds of the total.

While Perón's position appeared impregnable, it was already beginning to be undermined. The almost unbelievable Peronist mismanagement, combined with monumental graft and corruption, had already made long strides towards the eventual virtual bankruptcy of one of the world's most richly endowed economies. A substantial portion of the large foreign exchange balance inherited by Perón had been squandered on nationalization of a run-down railroad system whose rate of deterioration increased as a result of inept management and failure to carry out a rehabilitation plan begun with much fanfare. Other state ventures in the transportation and communications fields were equally costly and brought similar deterioration of services for the public, as well as growing deficits to be financed from the national treasury. The Argentine Institute of Production and Exchange (Instituto Argentino de Producción e Intercambio or IAPI), established by the Perón administration in 1946, had been given a virtual monopoly over purchase and sale of the nation's main exports and many of its imports, thereby providing an opportunity for graft on the grand scale.

The agricultural sector of the economy had been saddled with the burden of supporting the ambitious industrialization program that Perón had undertaken to make the nation more self-sufficient and to provide employment for his mass following. The nation's farmers found little reason to grow wheat, corn, linseed, and other cereals for prices which were only a fraction of the prices at which IAPI resold their produce. Furthermore, the Perón regime's industrial program was drawing labor from the countryside without replacing it with standard agricultural equipment, let alone the latest labor-saving machinery being employed by Argentina's principal competitors. As a consequence, the acreage planted in wheat, corn, and other cereals steadily decreased under Perón. Finally, after several years of good weather, the droughts that have regularly devastated Argentine crops every five years on the average struck heavily in 1950 and then returned again during the 1951 and 1952 crop seasons. Previous administrations had planned for such contingencies and maintained adequate reserves to carry them over until the next harvest. The Perón regime had made no such plans, and in 1952-53 Argentines ate black bread—when they could get it—for the first time experienced meatless days, and imported wheat and potatoes from the United States! When the 1952-1953 wheat and corn harvests did come in, and the country was straining to export every possible ton of cereals, the broken-down transportation system and the silted-up ports were inadequate to the task.

One of the most serious blows to the Perón regime also came in 1952 with the death of Eva Perón (July 26, 1952). There have been more controversial figures in recent history, but not a great number. To the *gente bien*, the "right people," she was anathema; to many among the lower classes she was "Evita, our Patroness"; to any who stood in her way she was ruthless, sometimes vengeful, and often cruel; and to those whom she helped, as head of the María Eva Duarte de Perón Welfare Foundation, she was "La Señora," a true-life fairy godmother.

Evita's precise standing vis-à-vis Perón is still not completely clear. Her role in Perón's October 1945 restoration to power has been exaggerated, but it was still an important one. After his elevation to the Casa Rosada she served as his direct contact with the Argentine masses who had placed him there in the 1946 election. Although Evita never held an official post—the Welfare Foundation was her private organization, run as she pleased and accountable to no one else, despite receipt and expenditure of substantial sums from many sources—she took over Perón's role in consolidating the support of the Argentine masses and controlling the Peronist labor movement, which claimed a membership of six million. During the 1946-1952 period she made and unseated ministers of labor and the top leadership of the General Confederation of Labor (CGT). Other cabinet ministers, including Minister of Foreign Affairs Juan A. Bramuglia, found that establishment and maintenance of rapport with Señora de Perón was essential to their survival in office. Not the least of her roles was that of serving as the target for hostility that would otherwise have been directed at Perón. To no small part of the opposition "that woman" was the unacceptable partner of the Perón team, the source of the regime's extremism. While Evita was still active these dissidents could retain their illusions that, but for her, they could "live with Perón."

After the death of Evita a change did take place in the Perón regime's orientation. Although the political restraints were maintained as effectively as before, a noticeable loosening of economic controls took place as Perón sought to entice foreign investment capital into the country. In view of his former diatribes against foreign capitalists and claims that he was the country's economic liberator, this appeared to be a veritable about-face. The fact of the matter was that the economy, plundered and misdirected by Perón and his train, desperately needed new capital investment, and Perón had at hand the ideological justification for the new tack. The Peronist creed, *justicialismo*, did not designate any specific location for its vaunted Third Position. As defined by Perón it was the opportunist's credo par excellence: "an ideological position which is in the center, on the right or on the left, according to specific circumstances." [2]

The new orientation emerged clearly in the Second Five-Year Plan passed by the congress in December 1952. The First Five-Year Plan (1947-1951) had concentrated on an extensive program of state-executed public works— useful as propaganda even when only started (with much attendant publicity) and then quietly abandoned. In the Second Five-Year Plan (1953-1957), state-executed public works accounted for only a small portion of the planned expenditures. Instead it was intended that private initiative would construct public works, the state supplying funds on credit. Perón went even further: as soon as the industries it created were economically productive, the state would turn them over to private enterprise.

By mid-1953 Perón was becoming increasingly more cooperative with employers and less helpful to labor in its disputes with capital, whether domestic or foreign. Then in August 1953 Perón's still pliant legislative majorities provided legislation to attract the foreign capital needed to establish automotive and tractor factories and in particular to develop Argentina's retarded petroleum industry.

By the last quarter of 1954 Perón appeared to have brought off an about-face in his relations with foreign and domestic capital and with his own labor supporters. In February 1954 his hand-picked candidate for the vice-presidency (vacated by Vice-President Quijano's death in 1953) won by about two-thirds of the total vote, suggesting the durability of Perón's rule. In November 1954, however, Perón brought out into the open a conflict with the Roman Catholic Church that had been going on behind the scenes for some time. Within a year this conflict played an important role in the forcible overthrow of the apparently strongly entrenched Perón dictatorship.

At first Perón's relations with the Church had been friendly and cooperative. The Argentine hierarchy's pastoral letter had helped Perón's candidacy in the 1946 election; the Perón administration secured legislative sanction for the executive decree of December 1943, which had restored instruction in the Roman Catholic religion to the Argentine public schools, where it had been prohibited since 1883. A secular Catholic priest, Padre Virgilio Filippo, was elected to the chamber of deputies as a *peronista* candidate. The political tone in Filippo's sermons (which disturbed his parishioners in suburban Belgrano), his presence and that of other priests at *peronista* political and labor rallies, and the restraints placed by the hierarchy on anti-Peronist priests were indicative of the early amicable relationship between Perón and the Church hierarchy.

That relationship gradually deteriorated as Señora de Perón expanded the charitable activities of her Social Aid Foundation, which took over a field the Church had dominated since the colonial period. And even more serious irritant was the official support for the cult of the Peróns, which, besides fostering the myth of Perón's own infallibility, designated Evita as the "Spiritual Leader of Argentina"—a designation customarily reserved for the Archbishop of Buenos Aires, the Primate of Argentina.

The death of Evita (July 1952) seemed to remove a major irritant in Church-State relations, but instead it provoked new strains when overzealous Peronists urged her immediate beatification. Thereafter the Peronist canonization of the Peróns was accelerated as their busts and portraits replaced religious symbols in the textbooks approved for the public school system and in Peronist meeting-places.

Members of the Argentine clergy and of the men's, women's, and younger people's branches of Argentine Catholic Action (Acción Católica Argentina, or ACA) were also alienated by Perón's indecorous personal conduct and the unsavory character of his close associates. Their efforts to dissociate the Church from any connection with the regime appears to have been part of a general reassessment of the Church's relationship with dictatorial governments that has had important consequences in other parts of Latin America as well. At any rate, Perón's overt attacks on the Church reflected his sensitivity to any movement that threatened to erode his popular support. Despite the resignations of some Peronist legislators, the still docile Peronist congressional majorities provided legislation ending Roman Catholic religious instruction in the public schools, legalizing divorce, permitting the return of legalized prostitution, and providing for a constitutional convention to separate Church and State. The conflict was highlighted in June 1955 by the seizure and expulsion from the country of two native-born members of the Argentine hierarchy and the subsequent Vatican announcement of excommunication of Perón and other officials responsible.

While embroiled in his conflict with the Catholic Church, Perón agreed to a petroleum contract with the subsidiary of a United States oil company. This was another important factor in his downfall. Although the YPF, the state petroleum agency, was not providing the crude oil needed by the Argentine market, there was a strong nationalist resistance to any proposals for seeking the assistance of foreign oil companies. The development contract accepted by Perón provided for final arbitration by an international oil expert of any unresolved disputes between the company and the Argentine government. This provision was unacceptable to Argentine nationalists. Even the heretofore obedient Peronist Party leadership was still debating its approval when elements of the Argentine navy launched an abortive revolt on June 16, 1955. As in 1951, a more extensive revolt was being prepared, and Perón again had an opportunity to contain the larger conspiracy.

This time, however, the opposition was too widespread and too determined to be contained. The Argentine people have a long tradition of anticlericalism but not of antireligious actions. The attacks on the Church gave the heterogeneous groups of the opposition a common meeting ground and a respectability that Perón's opposition had heretofore lacked. The petroleum contract particularly antagonized nationalist elements, including those in the armed forces, who previously had supported the regime. Perón sought to divide his opposition by a policy of moderation, as he had in the past, but to no avail. Finally, on August 31, Perón abandoned all pretense of moderation in addressing a mass meeting of his *descamisado* followers. Calling upon them to annihilate and crush the opposition, he laid down the rules of the conflict.

> From now on let us establish as permanent conduct for our movement that he who in any place tries to disturb order in opposition to constituted authorities or contrary to the law or the constitution may be slain by any Argentine. . . . And when one of our people falls, five of them will fall! [3]

Perón's inflammatory speech and the offer on September 7 by the General Confederation of Labor of its 6,000,000 members to the army as a "civil militia" tipped the scales for members of the military still hesitant to come out in opposition. The threat of class warfare contained in both the speech and the CGT offer brought the initiation of the final revolt on September 16. It began in conservative, Catholic Córdoba and in the naval base at Río Santiago and was strengthened by the defection of the Army of the Andes in western Argentina, of most of the air force, and all of the navy.

The army forces around Buenos Aires remained faithful to Perón, and the land forces were thus not unevenly matched for a long and bloody civil war. A new element was introduced, however, as for the first time the Argentine navy held the balance of power. The rebel naval command, under Admiral Isaac Rojas, warned that it would bombard the city of Buenos Aires if Perón's generals did not surrender. It provided an example of its firepower by bombarding the Buenos Aires provincial capital, La Plata (renamed Eva Perón), then drew up in formation before the capital. On September 19 Perón's offer to resign was accepted by his generals. Three days later the government was turned over to the rebel leaders representing the chief of the revolutionary forces, General Eduardo Lonardi, who had been retired by Perón for his involvement in the 1951 plotting against the regime.

The Period Since Perón

The caretaker government, headed by General Lonardi, restored the freedoms circumscribed under Perón and his predecessors; appointed civilians to most of the cabinet posts; and promised free elections as soon as possible. However, Lonardi's policy of reconciliation towards the Peronists angered the military on one hand, while the influence of rightist Catholics in his administration alienated anticlerical civilian forces on the other. On November 13, 1955 he was replaced as provisional president by the leader of a peaceful coup, General Pedro Aramburu.

General Aramburu's de-Peronization program, including proscription of the Peronist Party, brought a violent reaction from the Peronists that included strikes, sabotage, and in June 1956, a military revolt. The revolt was quickly crushed, and for the first time in over a century of Argentine history the leaders of a revolt were court-martialed and executed by firing squads. (The Constitution of 1853, which had been reinstated in May 1956, had abolished the death penalty "forever.")

The provisional government made virtually no progress in its avowed campaign to de-Peronize Argentina. If anything, its attempts to keep in political limbo those who had supported Perón served to strengthen Perón's ability to control his mass following, since under such conditions it had nowhere else to go. General Aramburu had at least temporary success in his other campaign—to return the military to its barracks and restore civilian government. He had promised that elections would be held, that the members of his government would not be eligible for election, and that he would turn the government over to the successful candidate, regardless of his identity. Whatever may have been the shortcomings of his performance otherwise, Argentina, and the rest of Latin America as well, are in Aramburu's debt for the example he set in fulfilling that promise.

Both of the principal contestants in the bitterly fought elections of February 23, 1958, had long records of opposition to Perón as leaders of the Radical Civic Union. The UCR, however, had split wide open over the questions of the party's presidential candidate and its attitude towards the Peronists. The split resulted in the formation of two parties, each headed by one of the UCR's two top candidates in the 1951 elections.

Arturo Frondizi, who had been the vice-presidential candidate in 1951, was the uncontested leader and presidential candidate of the Intransigent Radical Civic Union (Unión Cívica Radical Intransigente, or UCRI). The UCRI was made up largely of the younger UCR leaders and membership who had belonged to the Intransigent faction that had taken over control of the UCR in 1948, after the party's setbacks in the elections of 1946 and 1948.

Ricardo Balbín, UCR presidential candidate in 1951, emerged as the compromise leader and presidential candidate of the People's Radical Civic Union (Unión Cívica Radical del Pueblo, or UCRP). The UCRP was a catch-all of old-line UCR leaders and members who had sponsored the ill-fated Democratic Union in 1946 and various factions and individuals opposed to Frondizi and his advocacy of the reintegration into Argentine politics of the Peronist masses.

The 1958 election—except that the Peronist Party was barred, although the Communist Party was not—carried out Aramburu's promise of free elections. Frondizi, the lawyer son of immigrant Italian parents, received some 4.1 million votes to about 2.6 million for Balbín. His victory was made possible by Peronist support, apparently on the orders of Perón. Consequently Buenos Aires was flooded with rumors that the presidency would not be handed over to the Peronist-supported victor. Aramburu, however, carried out his promise, and Frondizi was inaugurated on May 1, 1958.

President Frondizi assumed leadership of a country whose economy needed rehabilitation but whose political problems were even greater than its economic. There appeared to be an unbridgeable gap between the followers of Perón and the leadership of the armed forces that had overthrown the dictator.

The new president defied the country's xenophobic nationalists when he sought outside aid on the economic problem. He accepted the recommendations of the International Monetary Fund (IMF) as to the economic measures needed and put them into effect with the aid of credits totaling over $325 million, provided by the International Monetary Fund (IMF), the United States government, and private banks in the United States. Frondizi personally inaugurated what many observers consider the most important single move that had yet been taken towards solving the country's economic difficulties. This was the decision, announced in July 1958, that Argentina could no longer afford to spend about $300 million annually on petroleum imports, and that he was negotiating contracts with foreign oil companies to help Argentina become self-sufficient in petroleum production. (Frondizi's announcement signaled a sharp change in his tactical approach to the politically sensitive question of how Argentine petroleum reserves were to be developed. Previously he had espoused the traditional nationalistic shibboleths regarding foreign participation in their development.) By 1961, as a result of Frondizi's decision, Argentina not only had reached a position of being able to discontinue imports of crude petroleum, but also to begin exporting finished petroleum products to Uruguay. Imports of fuel and lubricants (including coal as well as specialty lubricants), which constituted 24 percent of Argentina's imports by value in 1957, were reduced to 12 percent by 1960 and 9 percent by 1961.

President Frondizi also introduced important innovations in his conduct of his country's foreign relations. He was the first Argentine chief executive to visit the United States while in office and made state visits to many of the other Latin American countries, to Europe, and to Asia in his efforts to improve Argentina's diplomatic and economic relations with the countries visited.

Although President Frondizi's economic policies achieved some success in strengthening private enterprise, reduced the sizable deficits incurred by state enterprises, and won applause from abroad, they were politically unpopular at home. His party, the UCRI, fared poorly in April 1960 in the general elections to renew the congress, and in February 1961 in congressional elections in the Federal Capital and in Mendoza. He had no success whatever in his efforts to arrange a *modus operandi* with the Argentine military under which the Peronists could be reincorporated into the normal political life of the nation.

After the defeats of February 1961, Frondizi's party won several provincial elections, and Frondizi permitted the Peronists to run candidates in the gubernatorial and congressional elections of March 18, 1962. When the Peronists won control of ten provinces, including the most important one (Buenos

Aires), and 44 seats in the chamber of deputies, the end was in sight for Frondizi, who had already survived countless political crises. When the other political parties refused to support him in his attempts to form a coalition government, Frondizi was ousted by the military on March 29, 1962. He refused to resign and was seized and removed by the military to confinement on Martín García Island in the Río de la Plata, where Perón and Irigoyen had been taken by the military in 1945 and 1930 respectively.

After Frondizi's removal the curious law of 1868 governing the presidential succession was combined with the constitutional prohibition against the president's leaving the territory of the capital without permission of the congress (Article 86, Sec. 21) to place the president of the senate, José María Guido, in the presidency. This law (*Ley de Acefalía*) provided that when the office of the presidency is not occupied, the next in line of succession—in this case the president of the senate, since the vice-presidency was vacant—becomes president.

The state of affairs under which a constitutional president is declared to have forfeited his office for not having asked permission of the congress to leave the capital—while being forcibly carried off by his military captors—is curious enough. Sanction by the supreme court of the Argentine nation for this interpretation added the final touch to a situation which should provide interesting material for several generations of students of Argentine constitutional law—and of power politics.

After Frondizi's ouster Argentina went from one political crisis to another as the military control behind the civilian façade shifted from one group in the armed forces to another. As a consequence of the political instability, recurrent cabinet changes, and general lack of confidence, economic conditions deteriorated rapidly, and most of the earlier gains were lost. National, provincial, and municipal elections to provide a complete renewal of officials on all three levels were scheduled and then rescheduled.

National elections were finally held in July of 1963. Military prohibitions on candidates with Peronist associations limited the major presidential candidates to three: Arturo Illía for the UCRP, Oscar Alende for the UCRI, and General Aramburu, supported by an *ad hoc* personalist grouping.

Several parties engaged in imaginative maneuvers to attract Peronist votes. The Christian Democrats at first nominated as candidate Dr. Raúl Matera, the former coordinator within Argentina of the Peronist forces. A wing of the UCRI loyal to Frondizi formed an electoral alliance with the Peronists. But the military regime over which President Guido presided vetoed each such attempt, until Perón was reduced to instructing his followers (from his exile in Madrid) to cast blank ballots as a symbol of protest.

Much to the relief of the forces opposed to Peronism, this tactic resulted in a blank vote of only about 18 percent. Leading the poll, with 27 percent of the vote cast, was Arturo Illía, the 63-year-old physician from Córdoba Province nominated by the People's Radicals. The popular verdict was subsequently confirmed by the electoral college. The provincial electoral colleges also gave the UCRP a bare majority of the national senate, 24 of 46 seats, although the party secured only 71 of the 192 seats in the chamber of deputies.

A wave of relief seemed to sweep over the country as it became clear that Argentina was to be returned to constitutional civilian government. President Illía thus began his term of office with a great deal of popular good will, amid a revival of business confidence. It remained to be seen how long the mood of optimism would continue to be warranted.

Political Processes

In 1930 the Argentine military reentered the political arena as an active participant. A sharp disruption of the normal course of political processes immediately ensued. The national congress was dissolved. Since the definitive organization of the Argentine nation (in 1862), the nation's legislative branch had functioned without interference, between May 1 and September 30 of each year, for 68 consecutive years. Unfortunately, this was not the last time the Argentine national congress was to be prorogued.

Fifteen years later, in October 1945, the previously acknowledged role of the Argentine military as the final arbiter of Argentine politics was openly challenged. The challenger was the labor support of Colonel Juan D. Perón, who had been removed from power by his military opponents. The military, however, declined the gauntlet thrown down before them in the streets of Buenos Aires, and restored Perón to power. Until mid-1955—with recurrent but relatively minor defections—the Argentine military performed in its new role as an uneasy partner with the Argentine Labor Confederation (CGT) in support of the Perón dictatorship. Its leaders held government and Peronist party positions, ran as Peronist candidates, and served as elected Peronist officials.

After the Perón regime was overthrown by the Liberating Revolution (Revolución Libertadora) the high expectations of the anti-Perón political parties were brought to earth by the basic reality of Argentine politics—the continued allegiance to the ex-dictator of a large part of the electorate that had supported him in 1946 and 1951. Nearly all of the political parties that opposed Perón have been split by this reality and the attempts of one group or another of the parties' leaders to secure Peronist support.

The Parties

The Peronists have been prevented from forming one united party by official restrictions and by factionalism within their own ranks, which developed as soon as Perón was out of power and in exile. In the elections of March 18, 1962, the Popular Union Party (Unión Popular), which carried the Peronist banner, demonstrated its strength in winning by a sizable margin in the province of Buenos Aires and coming in a close second in the Federal Capital. The Popular Union and other Peronist groups rely heavily on Perón's appeal to labor and stress social legislation and nationalistic slogans.

The two separate Radical Parties, the UCRI and the UCRP, represent in the main the former Radical Civic Union's left (UCRI) and right (UCRP) wings. Since 1958, some of the UCRP leaders had changed their attitude towards the Peronist vote they disdained in 1958. Actually, the combined vote of the two Radical Parties has regularly exceeded the Peronist votes, but the UCRI and the UCRP have continued to go their separate ways. While both parties have adherents in all sectors of Argentine society, they each continue to draw heavily for support on the large Argentine middle class.

The National Democratic Party (Partido Demócrata Nacional, or PDN), the lineal descendant of the Conservative Party defeated by Irigoyen in the 1916 election, was one of the principal victims of Perón's rise to power. The PDN largely disintegrated into provincial parties in Perón's first administration and polled less than 3 percent of the total vote in the 1951 presidential elections. After 1955 the party split, over strategy and tactics. In late 1958 an attempt to regroup the splintered Conservative organizations was started by the National Federation of Parties of the Center (Federación Nacional de Partidos del Centro, or FCPC). In Mendoza the Democratic Party (Partido Demócrata, or PD), adhering to the FNPC, has regained much of its former popularity and scored successive victories in the regular 1960 and 1962 congressional elections, as well as in the 1961 election for governor.

The emergence of Catholic political parties on a nationally organized scale was one result of Perón's struggle with the Catholic Church. The Christian Democratic Party (Partido Demócrata Cristiano, or PDC) appears to represent the liberal elements in the Argentine Catholic Church. The Federal Party (Partido Federal, or PF) contains groups from the opposite side of the political spectrum and has in the main been considerably less successful than the PDC in attracting the support of Argentine voters.

The Argentine Socialist Party (Partido Socialista Argentino, or PSA) had been subject to recurrent defections before the advent of Perón. After World War I an extreme left group of the PSA broke off to form the Communist Party of Argentina (Partido Comunista de Argentina, or PCA). A few years later a conservative faction of the Socialists joined the conservative *concordancia*. Under Perón the PSA suffered more harassment than any other political party because of its long-established influence in the labor movement. A dissident pro-Perón faction tried to take over the PSA leadership with official assistance, but the majority of the party's leaders and members continued to oppose the dictatorship. Once Perón had been overthrown, however, the Socialist leaders split over the party's attitude towards the Peronists. By early 1963 there were four separate Socialist groups. The metropolitan area and the province of Buenos Aires continue to be the principal Socialist centers of influence.

The Argentine Communist Party has never had much success in Argentine elections on the national level, although the party has competed successfully in municipal elections and has won a few seats in the provincial legislatures. In the 1958 elections the PCA supported Frondizi but ran its own candidates for congress. Although the PCA candidates polled over 71,000 votes in the Federal District and some 78,300 in the province of Buenos Aires, the party failed to win a seat due to the Sáenz Peña law, which divided all seats in an electoral district, on a two-to-one basis, between the two parties securing the most votes.

The splintering of political parties resulted in 21 political groups' presenting lists of candidates in the 1958 congressional elections, and 23 parties competing in the Federal District alone in the March 1962 elections to the chamber of deputies. It would appear that, as a result of this political atomization, Argentina is replacing Chile as the France of Latin America. This tendency may also reflect the political demoralization Argentine observers have commented on with increasing frequency since the advent of Perón.

The Interest Groups

The armed forces, particularly the army, are of course among the most important and influential groups in Argentina.

Organized labor, which had usurped the military's position during most of the Perón regime, has been divided into pro-Perón, anti-Perón, independent, and pro-Communist groups. Not until early in 1963 were the two major groups, the Peronist unions and the Independents, able to cooperate in reorganizing the General Confederation of Labor, which had been "intervened" after Perón's overthrow. While the CGT Congress was meeting it was virtually disrupted by the Guido government's decreeing (on January 30, 1963) a State Security Law, which provided penalties ranging from six months' imprisonment for disturbing public order to four to ten years for interrupting or disturbing the normal functioning of transportation, communications, water, light, power, or gas services, or damaging or destroying such services, and life imprisonment for crimes against the national security.

Argentine economic pressure groups are in the main not as varied or as well organized as similar groups in the United States, nor do they provide information services on the same scale. There are Argentine organizations, however, which do resemble their counterparts in the United States to a greater or lesser degree. The Industrial Union (Unión Industrial) might be compared to the National Association of Manufacturers; the Rural Society (Sociedad Rural), The Argentine Wool Producers' Federation (Federación Lanera Argentina), and the Argentine Chamber of Exporters (Cámara Argentina de Exportadores) are three examples of agricultural pressure groups in Argentina. There are also organizations of lawyers, doctors, engineers, and other professionals that more or less correspond to similar interest groups in the United States.

The Roman Catholic Church, on the other hand, has exerted an important influence since the colonial period, though in varying degrees according to the attitude of the administration in power (see below). Since the early 1950's that influence has increasingly been exercised through the several branches of Catholic Action.

Probably the greatest contrast in the respective influence in the United States and Argentina of a particular group is in the role of university students. In Argentina the students play an important role, not only in university affairs but also in national politics.

Until largely destroyed by Perón the Argentine press was among the world's finest. *La Prensa* and *La Nación* of Buenos Aires, founded in 1869 and 1870 respectively, were the two acknowledged leaders, but there were other excellent newspapers in the national capital and in the provincial capitals as well. Since 1955 Argentine newspapers and periodicals have recovered perceptibly; in general, however, they have not yet regained the position they held before the Perón regime destroyed the freedom of the press in Argentina. A notable exception is *Sur*, a review founded (1930) and edited by one of Argentina's outstanding writers, Victoria Ocampo, whose high literary and intellectual standards have earned it an international reputation.

Argentine political parties, interest groups, the press and, in fact, the entire scope of political processes have operated in an abnormal atmosphere since 1930 because of the return of the military to a primary role in politics. In the previous half-century no Argentine president had been overthrown by force, and only one military man, General Roca, had held the presidency. Between January 1, 1930, and January 1, 1963, seven presidents were removed by the military; and only five of the thirteen occupants of the Casa Rosada were civilians, including three overthrown by military revolts.

Since 1955 the attempts of individuals and parties to capture the Peronist vote, and the very presence of a sizable portion of the electorate that continued to look to Perón for leadership, have created so many political crises that observers have noted a public apathy towards politics—with all its demoralizing consequences. The phrase most expressive, perhaps, of the feelings of many Argentines before the elections of July 1963 was the oft-repeated *¡No hay salida!* (There's no way out!)

Governmental Institutions

The Constitution

When the overthrow of Rosas finally came in 1852, the Argentine liberals were prepared to organize the nation under a constitution which contained many of the liberal precepts that had marked the short-lived 1826 Unitarian charter; however, their handiwork, the Constitution of 1853, contained some important points of difference. The federalist form, for example, acknowledged the regional differences that existed, and despite the obvious use of the United States constitution as a model, the Constitution of 1853 was framed in accordance with the political and economic realities of the Argentina it was to serve. As a result, it has survived until the present with only one six-year interlude (1949-1955), when it was replaced by a charter tailored to order to cloak the authoritarian regime of Juan Domingo Perón with the outward forms of legality.

The Constitution of 1853 was in large measure the handiwork of Juan Bautista Alberdi, whose *Bases y puntos de partida para la organización política de la República Argentina* served as a handbook for the members of the constituent congress charged with drawing up the organic law. It reflected the economic liberalism and laissez-faire philosophy of post-Rosas Argentina and of Alberdi, whose motto for Argentine governments was "To govern is to populate" (*Gobernar es poblar*).

The constitution provided that "the Federal Government shall encourage European immigration; and may not restrict, limit, or burden with any tax whatsoever the entrance into Argentine territory of foreigners who arrive for the purpose of tilling the soil, improving industries, and introducing and teaching the arts and sciences" (Article 25 as presently numbered). Foreigners were given all the civil rights of Argentine citizens, and citizenship was made easily obtainable (Article 20). Perhaps the most striking example of the pro-capitalist spirit of the constitution-makers is found in the "general welfare" clause (Article 67, Clause 16) which enjoins the congress to enact legislation to promote "the introduction and establishment of new industries, the importation of foreign capital, . . . by protective laws and by temporary concessions of privileges and the offering of awards."

The Constitution of 1853, after some extensive revisions in 1860 to suit the Province of Buenos Aires, proved sufficiently elastic for the needs of the Argentine Republic. Between 1860 and 1949 it was amended only twice. The 1949 Constitutional Convention made some needed changes but retained much of the form of its predecessor. It did considerably augment the powers of the federal government, particularly those of the executive branch. But the principal purpose of the 1949 Constitutional Convention was to remove the constitutional prohibition against a president's serving successive terms, a provision which of course did not appear in the "Peronista constitution."

While the Aramburu government restored the Constitution of 1853, it nevertheless held elections in 1957 for a Constituent Assembly to consider a limited reform of the venerable charter. The assembly, meeting at Santa Fe, had barely opened when the largest bloc of representatives, those of the UCRI, left, in accordance with the view of Arturo Frondizi that constitutional reform should follow, and not precede, national elections. Other walkouts followed, the discussions became simple partisan disputes, and finally the assembly was left without enough members to form a quorum. At that point it disbanded after having made only slight modifications—insertion of an enumeration of individual rights—in the restored Constitution of 1853.

The National Government

The structure of the Argentine government, as provided by the ruling constitution, follows closely that of its model, the United States. It is a federal system in which the executive power is exercised by a president; the legislative branch consists of a bicameral congress patterned after the United States congress; and the judicial power is wielded by a system of federal courts. The distribution of powers and functions also follows quite closely that of the North American model. There are, however, some significant points of difference.

In Argentina the president and vice-president are required to be members of the Roman Catholic faith, which is the official state-supported religion. Furthermore, the Argentine chief executive has considerably more authority, in actual practice, than does his counterpart in the United States, despite the similarity in the provisions dealing with their powers in the two constitutions. The legislative branch, on the other hand, seldom plays more than a secondary role. The judicial system depends heavily upon continental European theories and practice except in the area of constitutional law, where United States practice is often followed. While the members of the federal courts are appointed by the president ("during their good behavior," that is, normally for life, rather than for fixed terms) with the consent of the senate, the supreme court itself selects its chief justice from among its own members for a three-year term. While the supreme court has declared legislation or acts of the executive branch to be unconstitutional, the practice of judicial review is nowhere near as firmly established as in the United States.

The Argentine chief executive has clearly dominated the legislative and judicial branches of the national government. This is in line with the Spanish tradition of the strong leader (*caudillismo*). The Argentine president, for example, appoints and removes members of his cabinet and other executive assistants at will. The legislative and judicial branches have seldom been able to restrain the authority of a strong chief executive. In fact, under Perón (1946-1955) Argentine legislators and judges were reduced to being little more than his puppets, frequently passing important legislative proposals of the president without reading them—let alone seriously discussing them—and accepting violations of the spirit and letter of the constitution they were sworn to uphold. During the periods when the national congress is either not in session or has been prorogued, decrees issued by the Argentine president have the force of law and are usually confirmed by subsequent congresses.

The national government exerts much closer control over the Argentine provinces and municipalities than does the federal government of the United States over the states and the units of local government. This is a result of several factors, including the dependence of provincial and local governments in Argentina upon the federal authorities for financial aid (since the lower levels of Argentine government have limited taxing powers), the relatively limited experience of the provincial and local authorities in self-government, and the frequent use—or rather misuse—by the national authorities of their constitutional powers to "intervene" the provincial and local governments. Both the Argentine and United States constitutions have provisions for intervention, and these are roughly similar. In the United States, however, the federal government, and particularly the executive branch, has used such powers only on very rare occasions. In Argentina, on the other hand, since 1853 the executive power has decreed over 100 such interventions, not counting those decreed after 1930 by *de facto* regimes.

During the Perón dictatorship his docile legislative majority provided him with extensive new powers, some of which were repealed after Perón's ouster. One law, No. 13,234 of September 1, 1948, however, has not been annulled and has been used by Perón's successors. This law authorized the president, in case of war and during peacetime, to declare "a state of internal disturbance" and impose the *Plan Conintes*, from the Spanish phrase *conmoción interior del estado*. In any area in which the president invokes the *Plan Conintes* the executive authorities are replaced by the president, in his capacity as chief of the armed forces, with military commanders exercising total authority under martial law. Such military governors can override constitutional protections and make disposition of persons over eleven years of age, transferring them to any part of the country and obliging them to provide any services demanded, including the rendering of property, as deemed necessary.

With the reinstatement of the Constitution of 1853, the president and vice-president, who had been chosen in direct elections under the Constitution of 1949, are again selected by an electoral college, as in the United States. They may not serve successive terms, and they continue to be elected for a six-year period. Qualifications for voting in the federal elections are regulated by federal laws and for voting in provincial and municipal elections by provincial election laws. With specified exceptions, such as clergymen, members of the armed forces, convicted criminals, deserters, and the insane, all adult citizens who are eighteen years of age or older are eligible to vote. Unless specifically excepted by advanced years or illness, which must be proved, all eligible citizens are legally obligated to vote or risk application of the penalties provided by law for not voting. Voting is still by paper ballot, with legal safeguards which are adequate when properly enforced. Beginning with the 1946 elections, Argentine elections generally have been as fairly conducted and accurately counted as any in the world. Under the Perón regime, however, the pre-election campaigns were so tightly controlled by the Peronist authorities that the opposition candidates had little opportunity to present their candidates and programs to the electorate.

The Argentine national congress differs from its North American model in certain respects. The members of the senate are chosen by the provincial legislatures, as they originally were in the United States (except in the Federal District where they are chosen by direct elections) for nine-year terms. The seventeen provinces and the Federal District are each represented by two members of the senate, whose membership is normally renewed by one-third every three years. Vacancies caused by death, resignation or removal are filled by special elections, since the system of alternates, found in many other Latin American countries, has never been adopted in Argentina. The members of the chamber of deputies are chosen in direct elections for four-year terms, and one-half the membership is renewed every two years. The number of deputies selected from each province and the Federal District is in proportion to each area's population. The precise provisions of the electoral laws are currently in a state of flux.

The powers of the Argentine congress parallel quite closely those of the United States congress. Both houses share in the traditional legislative powers. The senate confirms or rejects presidential appointments to the federal judiciary and high military and diplomatic posts. Only the chamber of deputies, under the restored Constitution of 1853, may initiate legislation dealing with taxes and the recruitment of troops.

Provincial and Local Government

The organization of Argentine provincial government generally follows the pattern of the national government. In some provinces, however, generally the less populated and poorer ones, the legislative branch may be unicameral, and the number of legislators varies. The provincial governors are indirectly elected by electoral colleges for six-year terms, in most provinces are not permitted to serve successive terms, and usually dominate provincial politics and legislators. Only in the province of Buenos Aires does the legislative branch exert much restraint on the provincial executive. The provinces have judicial systems which vary somewhat from one province to another, and whose members are usually appointed by the governor. The judicial system of the Federal District was absorbed into the federal judiciary during the Perón regime.

During the Perón administration the dictator experimented with new constitutions, for the two new provinces formed from territories in 1951 and 1952, that had certain provisions like those Perón apparently had admired during his tour of duty in Mussolini's Italy. Members of the General Confederation of Labor, in effect, were given a double vote by their right to vote for the public's representatives in the two provincial legislatures, and also for labor's special representatives in those bodies. Whether or not this system would have been developed further and imposed in other provinces—had Evita Perón lived and had Perón not veered to the right after 1952—provides an interesting subject for speculation.

It is in the field of local government that the most striking contrasts with the United States experience appear. Although the venerable institution of the municipal council, or *cabildo*, dates from the Spanish colonial period, local government has no strong roots in Argentina. The famed *cabildos* served mainly as a means of alleviating the absolute rule of the Spanish Crown; although they played an important role in the early independence movement they had little importance after 1820, and disappeared entirely from 1837 to 1853, during the Rosas dictatorship.

The Constitution of 1853 restored municipal government but failed to spell out the form it should take. Article 5 merely instructs each province to adopt a constitution instituting, among other things, a system of municipal government. According to an Argentine authority on the subject the country's supreme court has used this provision as the basis for an opinion that municipalities are mere delegations of provincial powers. At any rate, the Argentine municipalities are subject to intervention by both the federal and provincial governments. Only in one province (Santa Fe), and only from 1932 to 1935, were Argentine cities with the required population of over 25,000 able to adopt their own charters.

Nowhere in Argentina do the municipal governments have adequate economic or judicial powers and financial resources. Unlike cities in the United States, the Argentine cities have almost no control over public education, which is under provincial and national supervision. Another serious handicap is the lack of trained officials and the frequent changes in personnel as a result of political interference in municipal affairs. In Buenos Aires eight municipal executives (*intendentes*) served during the decade between 1947 and 1957.

During certain periods the national capital, Buenos Aires, has come the closest of any Argentine city to approximating the home rule of large cities in the United States. Unlike its counterpart, Washington, D.C., in Buenos Aires resident citizens have long voted in presidential elections and selected their own representatives in both houses of congress. Since 1930, however, and particularly under the Perón regime, the national executive increasingly absorbed functions of the municipal council, which were exercised by puppet *intendentes*. After Perón's overthrow, the Aramburu provisional government decreed the restoration of the city's elected municipal council and returned many of its lost powers. On May 1, 1958, with the return to elected civilian government throughout Argentina, a municipal council elected in February 1958 was installed. At that time the inhabitants of Buenos Aires regained the powers of self-rule that had been lost for almost two decades. But those functions were again interrupted for a period beginning in April 1962.

Outside of the Federal District the development of local government has varied widely within the provinces. In the province of Buenos Aires (which does not include the city of Buenos Aires), the wealthiest and most thickly populated province, local government is relatively well-developed. It is based on the provincial electoral districts (*partidos*), and the local authorities in 114 municipalities are elected directly. The executive power is exercised by an *intendente*, who receives a salary, and the legislative by municipal councilors, who are paid their expenses when the council is in session. The local judicial authorities are usually justices of the peace, appointed by the governor, although in La Pampa province they are elected.

In the other provinces there is no set pattern for municipal government. In some cases local government is organized only in the cities and larger towns, leaving the rest of the province directly under provincial jurisdiction. In some of the less populated areas municipal commissions or development commissions (*comisiones de fomento*) may exercise both executive and legislative functions on the local area. In some provinces, as in Buenos Aires, the local authorities are directly elected. In others, they are appointed by the provincial governor, usually, but not always, with the approval of the provincial legislature.

Between 1930 and 1955 the steady trend toward centralization of power in the national government seriously undermined the limited authority of both provincial and local authorities. Since the overthrow of Perón that trend has slowed down, and public interest in strengthening local government has revived, perhaps in reaction against the centralizing influence of the 1943-1955 period. Unfortunately, the recurrent economic crises which have beset Argentina as a heritage from the Perón decade have seriously impeded such efforts by making the local authorities even more dependent on the national government for the funds needed to maintain essential public services. Nevertheless, on March 18, 1962, Argentines voted in fifteen provinces, the Federal District and the national territory, Tierra del Fuego, for municipal officials to fill 9,291 positions.

Public Policy

Domestic Economic Policy

Until 1930 the laissez-faire philosophy of the Constitution of 1853 dominated Argentine official policy. Although Marxist economic and political theories were current in intellectual circles and openly advocated by Socialist and Communist organizations, they had relatively little impact on official policy, which continued to stress production of agricultural exports that paid for Argentine imports of finished products. Concern over dependence upon imports of petroleum, which might be cut off during wartime, was largely responsible for creation, after World War I, of the State Oilfields (YPF) petroleum monopoly. After 1930 that concern spread to other fields, as Argentine official policies reflected the interests of the military who had assumed direction with the overthrow of Irigoyen.

During the 1890-1930 period industrial development had been taking place, but mainly in light consumer goods industries. When private capital showed little interest in providing the heavier goods desired by military planners who wanted their country to achieve self-sufficiency, the Argentine army attempted to take on the task, founding and operating factories. Their efforts, which continued even though the Roca-Runciman Treaty (1933) maintained the traditional Anglo-Argentine economic relationship, were given urgency by the outbreak of World War II. An important impetus came from the takeover of German properties after Argentina declared war on Germany and Japan on March 27, 1945.

Under Perón (1946-1955) a policy of forced industrialization at the expense of the agrarian sector was followed to the near-bankruptcy of what had been a healthy economy. Argentine agriculture, normally some years behind its competitors because of the margin provided by the unusually fertile soil of the *pampa*, was allowed to fall decades behind as the stepchild drudge that labored to support the favored sister, industrialization, as the queen of the ball. Unfortunately, the drive for industrialization was tragically ill-planned and ill-managed, so that Argentina was soon producing more textiles than even the clothes-conscious *porteños* could use, while still importing a trickle of the agricultural machinery, trucks, and transportation equipment needed in a flood by its hard-pressed farmers. In 1953, while World War II German engineers and Luftwaffe aces were concentrating on producing jet fighter planes in the Córdoba military factories, a sizable portion of the grain crop spoiled for lack of transportation. The extensive intervention of the Perón government in the economy, with its takeover of air, land, and water transportation facilities, as well as telegraph, telephone, and radio communications, had been notably unsuccessful in either maintaining those services or making them pay their own way.

With the advent of the Frondizi administration in 1958 the emphasis upon nationalization was reversed in favor of policies encouraging private enterprise. Ever since Perón's overthrow there have also been repeated gestures indicating that the agrarian sector of the economy was to be given more attention; but official policy has nevertheless continued to respond to the siren call of industrialization.

Church-State Relations

Until the 1954-1955 period the history of Church-State relations in Argentina was marked by an ability on both sides to reconcile differences while not abandoning long-held positions of basic disagreement. The disagreement stems from the Argentine government's assumption of the *patronato real* (the Spanish Crown's right to appoint officials of the Roman Catholic Church) in Argentina, which the authorities in the Vatican have never officially conceded. Since there is no concordat between the papacy and the Argentine government, the informal arrangements had sometimes been strained, before the Perón era, but never had degenerated into open conflict.

In the years before Perón, President Roca had sent an apostolic delegate, Msgr. Matera, out of the country for what he regarded as excessive interference in domestic matters (1884). From 1923 until late in 1926 the archiepiscopal see of Buenos Aires, the principal office in the Argentine hierarchy, remained unfilled when the pope refused to confirm President Alvear's nomination for the office. The principles of both sides were upheld and the impasse was finally resolved by the exercise of sweet reasonableness on both sides.

In 1954-1955, however, Perón was determined to have his way and resorted to foul means as well as fair. The Roman Catholic Church authorities suffered many indignities, but by June 1955, when the Perón regime arrested and expelled two Argentine-born bishops, the point of no return had been reached. The excommunication of Perón and all other officials responsible for the expulsion was followed almost immediately by the June revolt that preceded Perón's final overthrow. Not until March 1963 did the Vatican relax the excommunication of the ex-dictator. In the intervening years Church-State relations in Argentina have resumed their normal pattern of live and let live in a spirit of reasonableness and mutual respect.

Foreign Relations

Argentine foreign policy has been much more consistent than domestic policies have been. The touchstone of foreign policy has been the avoidance of conflicts, particularly between the great world powers, in which Argentina's vital interests were not involved. At times this policy has caused Argentine leaders, such as Irigoyen, to be called isolationists. Such charges, however, are belied by closer examination—which reveals an excess of nationalism, but also an unusually fine record of willingness not only to submit disputes with other nations to international arbitration, but also to abide by adverse decisions.

Argentina traditionally has had a close relationship with Western Europe, the principal source of the Argentine population and its culture, as well as the major purchaser of Argentine exports of agricultural products. The trade relationship with the United Kingdom was particularly close in the century before 1930, and still is important despite the sharp decline in British investments in Argentina consequent on the World War II change in Britain's economic fortunes and on the nationalization of British-owned railroads under the Perón regime. Relations with Spain, on the other hand, have been strained by the asylum given Perón, since his ouster, by General Franco.

Argentina's relations with her immediate neighbors have been complicated by the undemarcated boundaries inherited from the colonial period. Both Argentina and Brazil have tended to regard a predominant influence by the other in either Uruguay or Paraguay as posing a threat to the balance of power between the largest South American powers. Chile and Argentina share a heritage of joint effort in their struggle for independence but have also come to the edge of war over their conflicting boundary claims.

In general, Argentina's relations with her neighbors and with other Latin American states, have varied according to the types of government in power at any time. For example, when Argentina has had a dictatorial regime, relations with the democratic government in Uruguay have frequently been tense as a result of the hospitable asylum Argentine rebels have been given across the Río de la Plata. When President Frondizi was ousted by the military in March 1962, the governments of Costa Rica and Venezuela refused to recognize the successor Guido administration.

Argentine relations with the United States were friendly but not particularly close before the First Pan American Conference, held in Washington in 1889-1890. At that conference and at many of the succeeding ones, Argentina showed a tendency to lead the opposition to the policies advocated by the United States delegations, indicating that Argentina had come of age and considered herself the natural leader of the Latin American nations. Tensions were also created by the pro-Axis tendencies of Argentine governments during World War II and by the dictatorial methods of the Perón regime. Since Perón's overthrow, United States–Argentine relations have become increasingly friendly as the United States has aided in attempts to repair the damage done to the Argentine economy under Perón. In fact, the close and immediate support given the United States by Argentina during the Cuban missile-base crisis of October 1962 appeared to be opening up a new era in United States-Argentine relations.

NOTES FOR CHAPTER XVIII

1. Ysabel F. Rennie, *The Argentine Republic*, Macmillan, New York, 1945, p. 146.
2. Quoted in George Blanksten, *Perón's Argentina*, University of Chicago Press, Chicago, 1953, p. 292. Blanksten's discussion of *justicialismo* is highly recommended as an objective analysis of its major points.
3. From the text of Perón's speech reproduced in the appendix to Comisión Nacional de Investigaciones, *Libro Negro de la Segunda Tiranía*, Buenos Aires, 1958.

SELECTED BIBLIOGRAPHY

Robert J. Alexander, *The Perón Era*, Columbia University Press, New York, 1951.
Joseph R. Barager, "The Historiography of the Río de la Plata Area Since 1830," *Hispanic American Historical Review*, XXXIX, No. 4, Nov. 1959, pp. 588-642.
George I. Blanksten, *Perón's Argentina*, University of Chicago Press, Chicago, 1953.
John J. Kennedy, *Catholicism, Nationalism, and Democracy in Argentina*, University of Notre Dame Press, Notre Dame, Ind., 1958.
Thomas F. McGann, *Argentina, the United States, and the Inter-American System, 1880-1914*, Harvard University Press, Cambridge, Mass., 1957.
George Pendle, *Argentina*, 2d ed., Oxford University Press, New York, 1961.
Ysabel F. Rennie, *The Argentine Republic*, Macmillan, New York, 1945.
Carl C. Taylor, *Rural Life in Argentina*, Louisiana State University Press, Baton Rouge, 1948.
Arthur P. Whitaker, *Argentine Upheaval: Perón's Fall and the New Regime*, Praeger, New York, 1956.
———, *The United States and Argentina*, Harvard University Press, Cambridge, 1954.

URU-
GUAY

Montevideo

XIX   *Göran G. Lindahl*

URUGUAY

GOVERNMENT BY INSTITUTIONS

URUGUAY is anything but a typical Latin American state. A land virtually without inhabitants of indigenous Indian ancestry, it lacks the fabulous mineral wealth that the Spanish conquerors found elsewhere in the hemisphere and is likewise bereft of the mountains, deserts, and jungles which add to the scenery of other states while making their communications difficult.

The country has a population almost entirely literate, chiefly of European ancestry, who live at an average standard above that in perhaps every Latin American republic except Argentina. Close to a third of the over three million Uruguayans live in or around the capital, Montevideo.

Despite the growth of manufacturing and commerce, especially in textiles, the country continues to depend for its livelihood principally on the export of animal products—meat and wool.

Today Uruguay is noted for its political stability and its democratic ways and has a reputation as a country of advanced social legislation. All is not well with the Uruguayan welfare state today, however. Economic conditions have deteriorated, and this is perhaps the main reason why the constitutional debate has once again started in Uruguay.

Even if the present constitution is amended or replaced, it will continue to have a greater theoretical interest than the constitutions of most of Uruguay's Latin American neighbors. Uruguay's modern political history has been non-revolutionary and mainly constitutional, in spite of two *coups d'état*, in 1933 and 1942. In fact, the debate on constitutional problems which has attended changes of constitution has been of positive value for the country's political stability and democratic traditions.

The current constitution, which dates from 1952, is distinctive in three respects, which have all developed slowly during decades, none being a complete innovation: (1) the *colegiado* or pluri-personal executive, (2) *coparticipación*, institutionalized sharing in power by the second largest party, and (3) the election system, especially the *lema* law, which makes possible technical cooperation between parties during elections and serves the interests of the two traditional forces, the Colorados and the Blancos. We will return to a consideration of these features in detail after a glance at Uruguayan history.

447

Political History

Uruguay did not become an independent country until 1830. It is hardly too much to say that independence came as the result of the wish of the English to make this part of the world safe for commerce by creating a buffer state between Spanish-speaking Argentina and Portuguese-speaking Brazil, which had long disputed control of the territory.

For some decades after the achievement of political independence, the political "parties" which have dominated Uruguay's political life ever since were intimately allied to foreign interests. Political events in Uruguay were closely related to what happened in the region of the River Plate: the so-called Colorado ("red") Party was dominated by newly arrived immigrants and supported by European powers and Brazil, while the Blanco ("white") Party, or Nationalist Party as it was later called, pretended to be more nationalist and America-minded—but it was often supported by neighboring states, primarily Argentina.

During the nineteenth century Uruguay was thus one of the centers of unrest in Latin America, nearly always sundered by civil wars. Its present reputation of political and (until recently) economic stability dates from the beginning of this century. When Uruguay's great statesman José Batlle y Ordóñez became president for the first time, in 1903, a turning point in the history of the country was reached: the year following, as he won an undisputed victory in a civil war against his enemies of the Nationalist Party, an end was put to the civil strife which had been virtually continuous during the previous century.

After his presidency of four years, Batlle went to Europe, where he was much impressed by the functioning of the Swiss democracy, in particular its pluripersonal executive, the Federal Council (*Bundesrat*).

In his absence Batlle was again elected president by parliament; back in Uruguay in 1911, Batlle embarked on the policies which made him a famous and controversial statesman, in Uruguay and in the rest of Latin America, in his own time and since. Batlle worked for social legislation which was astonishingly modern and radical, and large parts of this program were carried into effect during the late 1910's and the 1920's. He also worked for a policy of nationalizations which, while not derived from doctrinaire socialist premises, was certainly far-reaching, especially in view of the fact that it was conceived in the beginning of this century by a man who was almost fifty years old when he first reached the presidency.

There is, however, a fact that has often been overlooked in this connection. The principal aim of Batlle's ideas was political rather than economic. He wanted to make Uruguay safe for democracy. His main concern was to give peace to his compatriots. He took the view that it was not worth while making radical reforms if all progressive work could be overthrown by a successor who had seized dictatorial powers. After 1913, when Batlle had published his *apuntes*, his notes on how to change the constitution, he was much more concerned about reconstructing Uruguay politically than socially and economically.

But Batlle and his followers among the Colorados lost the campaign for a new constitution by a small margin in the referendum of 1916. His enemies thought he was now finished politically. But they were mistaken.

A Cycle of Constitutions

By dint of complicated political maneuvers Batlle succeeded in arriving at a compromise with the Nationalists. Uruguay got a new constitution, embodying a *colegiado*, a national council of the Swiss type. But at the same time the Nationalists, as the minority party, were assigned powers which gave them the ability to block much of the majority party's program. The presidency was not abolished as Batlle had wished, but the president could not easily enforce his will and was no longer the pivot of political life in Uruguay. Most of the important executive authorities were transferred to the nine-man *colegiado*, the National Council of Administration, where the opposition was guaranteed at least one third of the seats.

Uruguay's first constitution had nominally been in force for nearly ninety years. Its second constitution was respected during its fourteen years of existence, although the parliamentary and political situation during these years was unclear. No party commanded a working majority; in the council there was one majority, in the senate another, and in the chamber of deputies still another.

Batlle died in 1929, shortly before the world economic crises began to be felt in Uruguay. The president elected in 1930, Gabriel Terra, a Colorado *batllista*, succeeded in making many people believe that the economic difficulties had been caused by the constitution. He made a pact with the leader of the majority of the Nationalists, Luis Alberto de Herrera, and annulled the constitution, after staging a bloodless *coup d'état*. A new constitution was approved by a referendum, after elections whose honesty is disputed.

The Constitution of 1934 was much more of an artificial construction than even the rather original compromise product of 1918. The *colegiado* was abolished, but the president was to function only as the chairman of the council of ministers, the cabinet, where both the majority party and the second largest party were to be represented in about the same proportions as they had been on the national council. At the same time the powers of parliament were increased. The terms of the constitution were such that it has been described both as providing for a presidential system and a parliamentary system, and even as retaining the *colegiado*. From a pragmatic point of view it is perhaps most reasonable to say that it created a presidential government, but one modified by the fact that Terra needed Herrera's assistance in order to govern, which he secured by placing Herrera's followers in positions in the public service.

The constitution was not long in force. Terra's successor as president ignored the rule that the second largest party should be represented in the government, perhaps because this would have compromised the country, since Herrera and his supporters avoided making a stand against the Nazis. By means of a new *coup d'état* and a new referendum, Uruguay got, in 1942, its fourth constitution. This one was more of the presidential type common in Latin America and of no particular interest in this connection.

The present constitution, which came into force in 1952 following its adoption in a referendum the year before, was the result of a compromise among most of the political parties. No *coup d'état* preceded it. According to the new constitution the presidency was abolished and the *colegiado* idea was completely victorious for the first time.

Political Processes and Governmental Institutions

Political Parties

Most of what has been written on Uruguay's political life fails to give a genuine picture of the peculiarities of the country, because the term "political party" is used in an imprecise way. In the nineteenth century the Colorados fought the Blancos or Nationalists. Although these parties had little in common with modern parties, it was at least true that there was a two-party political system in Uruguay. These parties were rarely united and had often two sections each, one dominated by the regional *caudillos*, the other by the "doctors" or intellectuals in Montevideo. But during most of the present century there have been several traditional parties, and besides them, so-called ideological parties, one Catholic, one Socialist, and one Communist.

Let us look at the ideological parties first. The Catholic party, the Unión Cívica, has never gained much support, not only because Uruguay is probably the most atheistic country in Latin America, but possibly also because Batlle was strongly anti-Catholic: he said that the Catholic religion, like all other religions, was filthy. Today Batlle's son, who runs his old newspaper, *El Día,* goes on writing "god" without a capital letter. The Unión Cívica has not even been able to gather many of the Catholic voters, most of whom seem to vote for the Nationalists.

The Socialist Party, for long one of the few really social-democratic parties in Latin America and belonging to the Second International, has recently changed its policy. Leaving the international, taking on the whole a pro-Castro position, it has at the same time cooperated with certain left-wing groups within the Nationalist Party—and has been badly cheated. It even makes it a point to stress nationalist themes in the party's propaganda. The last elections, anticipated by the party with great hope, showed instead a marked decline in the party's support. Today it is a party in disintegration.

Uruguay is one of the few Latin American countries where a Communist

Party has been able to operate with hardly any trouble. It is a sign of the relative political stability of the country that this party has generally got as little support from the voters as have the corresponding parties in Scandinavia.

The political life of Uruguay is still dominated by the traditional parties as, in a way, has been the case since the 1830's. The modern parties, sometimes well organized, with their conventions, party steering committees, caucuses, and the rest, differ vastly from the armed bands of the past century in many ways. There are no longer merely two traditional parties: there are generally at least two bearing each traditional label, and for a time there were four distinct Colorado parties.

Batlle played a very important role in the institutionalization of the political parties. He wrote and worked constantly with the aim of having parties that were permanently in activity, not only during election campaigns but also between them, in order to exert pressure on the members of parliament to act in common in the legislature, to vote according to the party program, to what had been agreed upon in the caucus, and to what they had promised their voters.

At the same time Batlle was, to understate it, a dominating personality who had commanding influence over his party up to his death in 1929. This caused the more independent and ambitious politicians of his party to leave it. The first split in the party occurred in the 1910's, when a small group of the more conservative leaders broke away because they did not like Batlle's propaganda for the *colegiado*. There followed three or four more splits in the 1920's, perhaps rather because of personal quarrels between political leaders than because of principles.

To describe these parties as fractions of the same party is not only incorrect, it is highly misleading. The different parties had their own programs and their own party organs, which met and deliberated continuously, not only just before the elections. In part this was due to the great number of elections held in Uruguay under the second constitution. It was a consequence that had been anticipated by Batlle and was considered one of the gains of the compromise that had been reached on the constitutional question. The situation was changed in 1933, however, when it was decided that elections were not to be held more than every fourth year. This caused party activities between elections to diminish, but not to disappear altogether.

The number of parties of traditional origin has also decreased. But Uruguay is still very far from having a two-party system.

After the coup of 1942, the followers of Batlle have again become the most numerous of the Colorados, but there is still a party of "independent" Colorados. Today, after the presidency of Luis Batlle, 1947-1951, and the elections of 1950, the most important split in the Colorado rank and file has been within the Batllist party, where Batlle's nephew Luis Batlle is supported by the mass of the voters and Batlle's son, Cesar Batlle, by a decreasing troop of mostly older members of the party. Apart from personal differences, Luis Batlle's "List 15" faction differs from the "List 14" group led by his cousin in being oriented to organized labor.

While the Colorados are approaching a nominal unity, the Nationalists are still divided. The Nationalists guarded their unity somewhat longer than the Colorados did, but a small group had already broken away from the Nationalist Party in the early 1920's and formed a party of their own, called the Radicalismo Blanco. This party never succeeded in getting much support from the voters, but it had a separate organization with a program of its own and was already large enough to prevent the Nationalists from gaining the majority during the 1920's.

In the beginning of the 1930's the party was subject to even worse misfortunes. Its most popular leader, Luis Alberto de Herrera, broke party unity and quarreled with the majority of the party's representatives in parliament. It is a matter of taste who broke away from whom; in any case the split was definitive and two different parties were formed. The two groups were so opposed to each other that there was no chance of arriving at any sort of technical cooperation during elections. The ideological gulf was too great, especially during the Second World War.

The divergence between the *herrerista* Nationalists and the others, who first called themselves the Independent Nationalist Party and later the Unión Blanca Democrática, continued until the elections of 1958. In that year it was possible for the first time to arrive at a coalition for electoral purposes between the two parties. The so-called *ruralistas*, essentially a farmers' pressure group which converted itself into a political party, also took part in the coalition and actually decided the outcome of the election, since their votes provided the additional support necessary to bring victory to the Nationalists, and within the Nationalist coalition gave the majority to the *herreristas*. In the elections held in 1962, the *ruralistas* again voted Nationalist, and once more decided the conflict between the Nationalists of *herrerista* origin and the Unión Blanca Democrática in favor of the *herreristas*. The *ruralista* group has avoided calling itself a political party, preferring to consider itself a movement. The Ruralists were once regarded as a danger to democracy, as fascists; but now they are on the verge of dissolution as Benito Nardone (popularly called "Chicotazo"), who was their completely dominating leader, died in 1964.

For the moment there are no definite signs of a reunion of all the various groups who collaborate in voting for the Nationalist ticket. Herrera died in 1959. This event made the chances for a reunion of the party seem brighter, since there had been a great deal of personal rivalry between him and the leaders of the independents. But this reunion still seems far from imminent. There are two parties and one movement, and the parties in their turn are divided into different groups, each of whose leaders are trying hard to inherit the late Herrera's many voters.

The Lema Law

The blame for the very unsatisfactory situation described above is partly to be put on the constitution and on the laws governing elections. Since 1910 there has been a "law of the *lema*," which is interesting from a theoretical point of view and important in its political implications. It has excited the envy of the Argentines, who do not otherwise admire or even like Uruguay. The *lema* is the party label or title; the two most important *lemas* have always been Partido Colorado and Partido Nacional. This fact has evidently given rise to the misconception that there are only two parties in the country.

According to the *lema* law, two or more political parties could agree to use the same *lema* during elections. In the case of elections of presidents of the nation, in the days before the *colegiado*, this meant that the adherents of one presidential candidate could use the same *lema* as the followers of another presidential candidate. With their united votes they could beat another candidate who alone had more adherents than either of the two. If this law had existed in the United States, it would have meant that Wilson would never have become President in 1912—if Taft and Roosevelt had used a right laid down in a *lema* law to unite their votes under the same *lema* and let the fight between them be decided by the number of votes cast for either *sublema*. It is almost as if the primary election were combined with the general election. Thus, let us say, if all the Blanco parties together get more votes than all the Colorado parties together the Blanco candidate with more votes than his rivals becomes president, even if one of the Colorado candidates has more individual votes. For example, let us suppose that there are five presidential candidates, representing what have been the five major *sublemas* in recent years, who secure the following percentages of the popular vote:

BLANCOS
Unión Blanca Democrática	20
Herreristas	18
Ruralistas	17
Total	55

COLORADOS
List 14	23
List 15	22
Total	45

The candidate of the Unión Blanca Democrática is thus elected, as the most-voted candidate within the most-voted *lema*, even though each of the two Colorado candidates has more votes than he does. The *lema* law continues to apply today, with modifications, even though elections under the *colegiado* system are choices among slates of candidates for the national council, and not among presidential hopefuls.

From the point of view of doctrine the law can easily be defended. Two or more parties with many interests in common are offered an opportunity to work together against a political enemy whom they are too weak to vanquish alone but strong enough to beat if they cooperate.

The law of the *lema* and corresponding articles in the constitution have been amended several times—for instance, in order to regulate to whom the *lema* belongs. Especially at the writing of the last constitution, provisions were made which gave advantages to the traditional parties to which the two most important *lemas* belong. It was no coincidence that the ideological, or nontraditional, parties were opposed to the last constitution.

What nowadays makes the *lema* law a doubtful asset to Uruguay is the fact that the different traditional parties, to which this law is an advantage, are so split by personal rivalries that the groups which can cooperate under a single *lema* to win the election cannot cooperate either in the national council or in parliament after the election. As a result there is no majority behind any particular policy. This is why it has been said in Uruguay, with typical Latin eloquence, that no matter who wins the election, the country loses.

This disunity has had drastic and astonishing consequences; for instance it has happened not infrequently that the council cannot decide whom to nominate to important posts, which have for that reason been left vacant for long periods of time. More important is perhaps that because of this disunity no coherent financial policy can be pursued, despite the steady deterioration of the country's financial position.

Coparticipación

This brings us to the subject of *coparticipación*. In order to counteract the difficulties arising from the fact that there is no majority for any long-term policy, the party representatives have to resort to the methods of patronage and to distribute posts in the public service in order to get a workable majority. This is true not only for the parties of the "opposition" but also for parties which have voted for the same *lema*.

Let us look in greater detail at the institution of *coparticipación*, which is a distinctive Uruguayan conception and has long been central to an understanding of the constitutional life of the country. The very word is typically Uruguayan, although it has been used and is known in other parts of the continent, especially in Argentina. *Coparticipación* has had a very positive meaning for the Nationalists, and just as negative a one for the majority of the Colorados. At least this was the case until the Nationalists came into power in 1959 after almost a century in opposition. On the other hand the meaning of the word has undergone many a change during the years in which it has been used.

During the nineteenth century the choice of a president was by far the most important election to be held in Uruguay. It was only natural that the Nationalists, almost continuously in opposition, should ask for an effective voice in this particular election. They took the view that the president should be elected by both Colorado and Nationalist votes and by a consensus of both parties—and they called this *coparticipación*.

This demand could be satisfied in many different ways. At first it seemed most important that the president should not choose ministers of state who were party bosses, especially in the case of the secretary of the interior. The secretary of the interior would thus be able to guarantee that the chiefs of police of each department (that is, province), who were at this time—and not without good reason—called *jefes políticos*, should not coerce the will of the people at elections. As a matter of fact it happened many times that the chiefs of police, obeying the wish of the president, were the real electors, and thus the president was by himself the Great Elector of parliament.

After two of the many civil wars which occurred during the nineteenth century, a peace treaty was agreed upon to the effect that the opposition should administer some of the departments and that the chiefs of police there should belong to the opposition party. Thus, in view of the tradition of the country that the police decided the elections, the opposition was to be represented in parliament. If the Colorados were to be split at the time of the presidential election, the Nationalists would thus have a chance to see to it that they got a president who did not act exclusively along party lines. But conceding the administration of whole departments to the opposition was a primitive way of *coparticipación*, and indeed left Uruguay on the verge of disintegration.

Towards the end of the past century the opposition managed to make their opponents accept explicitly the idea of guaranteed minority representation in parliament. In each of the departments, which functioned as electoral units, one-third or one-fourth of the mandates of the department were to be reserved for the opposition party. This meant that the opposition would normally get a substantial number of seats in the chamber.

The compromise on the Constitution of 1918 included explicit establishment of proportional representation in the elections to the chamber. There was no reform in the way in which senators were elected—by majority vote. This later turned out to the advantage of the Nationalists, since they were in the majority in most interior departments, being outnumbered by the Colorados nationally only by virtue of the Colorados' strength in Montevideo and its populous surrounding departments. This meant that the Nationalists were able to win a majority of the seats in parliament without an increase in the size of their popular vote.

This was not as important as it would have been before, however, since the president was no longer elected by the parliament. There was no longer any question of *coparticipación* in the election of the president; but in any case the powers of the president were drastically reduced, authority being now shared between the president and the national council.

The debate on *coparticipación* went on. Many Nationalists thought they had achieved their goal: every second year the council was renewed by one-third, three members, one of whom belonged to the second largest party, being elected for a six-year term. This meant that at least one-third of the councilors were always from the opposition. On one occasion the Nationalists were victorious in the council election and the council thus consisted of four Nationalists and five Colorados for a six-year period. On the other hand, this kind of arrangement in the council had its disadvantages for the adherents of *coparticipación*. If a disciplined majority in the council decided all questions, the minority would be regarded as co-responsible for the policies pursued without having been able to exercise any real influence. The principal constitutional expert of the Nationalists was thus of the opinion that the Nationalists should not bother to take part in the government of the country at all but should be present in the council only in order to exercise surveillance and to see to it that the majority governed within the limits of the constitution.

This was also Batlle's opinion: he believed that *coparticipación* was possible within the framework of the constitution but not that the composition of the council implied a regime of *coparticipación*. To Batlle, *coparticipación*, which he staunchly opposed, meant that the majority bought political peace with the taxpayers' money by giving positions in the public service and other advantages to a largely spurious opposition. Such treason to the electors could more easily be committed in a presidential regime, Batlle thought.

After the *coup d'état* of 1933, which had nominally been made against *coparticipación*, Terra and Herrera agreed upon a constitution which provided that the ministers of state were to be taken from both of the two biggest parties. This was a new kind of *coparticipación*, which resembled what had existed before 1903. But of course it was not only ministerial posts that went to the Nationalists; Terra would not have dared to make his coup unless he had had the tacit support of Herrera, and to placate him Terra had of course to place Herrera's friends and followers in government jobs at all levels.

Since then, the debate on *coparticipación* has been even more intense and obscured by arbitrary definitions. According to the present Constitution minorities are represented in the council, which has replaced the president. But at the same time the Nationalists, now in the majority, have come to the conclusion that the majority should govern. On the other hand, a peak has been reached in the distribution, on a bipartisan basis in the proportion of three to the majority and two to the minority of positions in the governing bodies of the state-owned industries and other jobs. Thus not only are superfluous state employees not dismissed, their number continues to increase under the pressure to find more jobs for Uruguay's special kind of spoils system.

The Colegiado

The pluripersonal executive, Batlle's most original innovation, has functioned on the whole as Batlle hoped. His main objective, after all, was to prevent anyone from seizing full powers and becoming a dictator, as had happened in Uruguay so many times in the past century or in other Latin American countries more recently.

When Batlle first proposed the *colegiado* the Nationalists believed or pretended to believe that this proposal was made in order to facilitate his own lingering in power, a sort of *porfirismo* or *continuismo* in disguise. But Batlle declared that he was not interested in being elected to the council; and in fact he was a councilor for only short periods and had no chance of attaining any decisive influence in this nine-member body. According to his views, the members of the majority party within the council were to act and vote along party lines. But the majority of the council was by no means homogeneous, and fewer than one-third of the members of the council were prepared to follow Batlle's lead.

In the Constitution of 1952 measures have been taken to prevent the splintering of the majority in the council. Today all six of the majority seats on the national council go to the list within the *lema* coalition which gains more of the votes than its partners; the other lists within the *lema* are not represented. The three seats assigned to the minority *lema*, on the other hand, are divided, two and one, between the two leading *sublema* lists. Thus after the elections of 1954, for example, it was quite obvious that one man commanded a majority within the council. This man was Batlle's nephew, Luis Batlle, who is much more a politician than a statesman. Still, Luis Batlle was very far from having absolute powers or even a chance of getting them if he had wanted to.

It has transpired, however, that the constitution's intent of creating a homogeneous majority has been subverted in the following manner. *Sublemas* within what hopes to become the majority *lema* run the risk of finding themselves in the unenviable position of having their votes counted towards electing a national council majority of candidates from another list within the *lema* coalition, while they themselves secure no representation on the council at all. Accordingly the tendency has grown for individual lists within the *lema* themselves to represent a coalition of different forces. If such a list is victorious, it receives the majority's six seats on the council, but remains divided within itself and unable to agree on a common policy.

This is in fact what has occurred. The Nationalist lists which were victorious in 1958 and again by a slim margin in 1962 were themselves coalitions unable to give a clear policy lead. Thus, despite the fact that the individual political parties show a high degree of party discipline in parliament, comparable to that which prevails in England or in the Scandinavian countries rather than in the United States, the country has once more arrived at about the same situation that Batlle once tried to avoid by attacking *coparticipación*. Since there is no real majority party to govern, almost any kind of decision has to be bought by distributing government jobs.

Uruguay's difficulties are thus of about the same nature as those in a country with a parliamentary system where there is no stable majority in parliament. Because of proportional representation, parliament is very much divided. The national council, perhaps intended to be a strong executive, cannot take the lead in policy because it is split, despite the provision that a relative majority of the electorate receives an absolute majority of the seats in the council. Thus the protracted interparty negotiations before the elections, and the elaborate agreements arrived at, completely falsify the intentions of those who conceived the constitution.

The Economy and Public Policy

Economic Conditions

As has been mentioned above, there have already been cries to amend or abolish the constitution. That is only natural. Internal peace seems, at least partly, to have been the result of constitutional reforms. So why should not economic readjustment be possible thanks to an inventive brand-new constitution? But Uruguay's present problems lie much deeper—in economic realities.

Uruguay has escaped such political upheavals as those in her neighbor Argentina, although economic conditions are or have been much the same in the two countries. It is not easy to explain why, nor is it easy to understand why Uruguay has been able to raise the standard of living of her population to a level that is very high for a Latin American country. Unfortunately, any statistical figures are misleading since statistics are so defective in this country that it is not even possible to tell how many inhabitants there are, the last census having been held in 1908.

Immediately after World War II, Uruguay's currency was perhaps its main asset, and the country served as sort of a Switzerland to the capitalists of large parts of the continent. However, the strength of the currency was at the same time a liability; it destroyed the tourist trade as Uruguay became far too expensive for ordinary people from Argentina. Bankers had good days, however, and the country profited from the situation.

Since World War II there has been some diversification of crops and development of industries, but after the Korean War inflationary tendencies set in which continue—nothing in comparison with the inflations of Argentina, Brazil, or Chile, but quite sufficient to make everything much more expensive, especially imported goods.

Uruguay has resisted all attempts, United States-inspired or not, to make her break diplomatic relations with the Soviet Union and has not abstained from exporting wool, almost her sole export article, to the Eastern European countries. But wool as a staple commodity and the textile industry in general have not offered very good prospects lately. Uruguay has not escaped the fate of most Latin American countries, a decline in demand for their products relative to supply. This and the deterioration of the terms of trade (the prices the country receives for its exports compared to the prices it must pay for imports), together with the fact that Uruguay is too small a country to offer a substantial domestic market for new industries in the age of large-scale production, have contributed to the discouraging slowness of recent economic progress.

These economic facts are the main cause of the present discontent in the country. The critics should also mention, however, the inconsistent economic policies which have been pursued. An attempt was made by the Nationalist parties, after they secured a majority in the national council in 1959, to start a new economic policy. Although the politicians of the traditional parties do not offer markedly differing alternatives for the solution of current economic and political problems, the Nationalists can be said on the whole to protect agrarian interests, ranchers and sheepherders, while the Colorados perhaps try mainly to appeal to small businessmen and tradesmen—and of course to state employees, lately protégés also of the Nationalists since the latter have been in power. The Nationalists attempted to change economic policy so as to stop inflation and attain monetary stability. But the measures taken were too drastic and gave rise to an increase in unemployment. On top of that, the inflation started up again, partly because the Nationalists had to resort to the give-away policy of the Colorados in order to win the election of 1962.

Uruguayans would probably be prone to attribute the country's economic difficulties, in addition, to the mismanagement of public money, and the increase in the bureaucracy and in its demands. For instance, the handling of the pensions program has been very much criticized.

Social Legislation

Although it has been much criticized, the system of pensions is a matter of pride, and rightly so. As early as the 1920's Uruguay passed laws on compulsory pensions for large groups of people which made the country a pioneer in this field. It had certainly no reason to envy the Scandinavian welfare states, which until very recently did not in fact have a counterpart to the Uruguayan pensions system. Though the system was well conceived in principle, the laws governing it were not well written. The administration of the pensions program was also extremely bad and has remained so. Employers have often succeeded in avoiding paying their assessments, and the employees or former employees have often experienced great difficulty in getting the payments due them. In fact they have been forced to seek political help to secure their rights, which has frequently meant that they have been obliged to make payoffs to petty politicians. Lately, inflation has also created new problems for retired people who have not benefited as much as they had hoped from their allotments.

One often hears criticism of the liberal rules governing pension rights. Foreigners are often surprised and indeed shocked by the great number of fairly young people who are allowed a pension: it is possible to get this token of old age at fifty or even earlier. But this system is not quite as blameworthy as it seems. When someone retires he leaves a place in production for a younger person, after all—a still younger person, if one likes. It might be said that the pension system has helped the country to come closer to a society where unemployment, until recently, has not been very great. Of course there are other explanations of this, for instance the fact that, according to official statistics, the Uruguayan birthrate is perhaps the lowest in the world. This fact, although it must be partly discounted owing to the inadequate reporting of new births, has saved Uruguay from many of the problems that have afflicted the prolific countries of the rest of Latin America.

Uruguayans have justly been proud of their record of "advanced" social legislation. The drive for this radical legislation during Batlle's lifetime— Uruguay passed the law on the eight-hour working day as early as 1915—has misled Uruguayans into believing that the country is still ahead of all other nations in this respect. As a matter of fact, only the pension system, criticized as it may be from economic and administrative standpoints, is still to be looked upon as advanced legislation. The rest of Uruguay's social legislation has become commonplace in most other countries.

The same judgment can be applied to nationalization in Uruguay. Uruguay could once be regarded as a pioneer in the field of public ownership of industry, too. This was also Batlle's achievement in the main. He was much more a liberal of the old school than a real socialist, but he did not shrink from radical solutions—especially when they were directed against foreign economic interests.

Today the field of action of the state is not overwhelming in Uruguay, as compared with other Latin American countries. Elsewhere on the continent the state has often entered upon industrial activities much more important than those in which it is involved in Uruguay.

Government corporations are to be found today in public utilities and transport, fishing, meat-packing, and banking. Government has also been responsible for promoting the development of industry, especially in the Montevideo area, and for subsidizing the living standards of urban workers by means of various programs financed ultimately by a manipulation of exchange rates which amounts to an export tax on agricultural products. In effect, dwellers in the city were benefited at the expense of those in the countryside. This direction in national policy was partly reversed following the Blanco success in the elections of 1958.

The public service and the public corporations are on the whole unsatisfactory in their operation today, largely because of their politicization. Leaders in other Latin American countries may still consider the nationalization of businesses as offering a solution to their economic difficulties, and the possibility of emancipation from foreign economic domination. Uruguay has never attracted industrial capital from abroad, and has felt little economic influence from outside. But it has had some unfortunate experiences with its own attempts at a nondoctrinaire socialist policy. These are perhaps important explanations of the fact that the Social Democratic and Communist parties have had little success in Uruguay.

In Conclusion

The mediocre success of the Socialist and Communist parties in Uruguay does not mean that there is no radical opposition, nor that there is not in Uruguay, as elsewhere on the continent, widespread anti-United States feeling. Today, also, many admirers of Castro are to be found, even among fervent anti-Communists. The socialists of democratic persuasion seem to be eradicating themselves by trying the impossible balance-step of applauding Castro and criticizing him at the same time. This will probably mean a strengthening of Communism, still of very little importance in this country. The undisputed domination of the traditional parties has so far been a bar to extremism. For the moment, however, these parties are led mostly by petty politicians unable to look farther than the next election and without much more in mind than getting their party's adherents jobs on the public payroll.

Unless the political parties can attract people of higher stature, intellectually and morally, of the type they attracted only four or five decades ago, there is a risk that the political parties of traditional origin will wear themselves out and leave the country in chaos and misery.

Both the political and the economic trends look dark. Yet the political maturity of the country's inhabitants, the long tradition of democratic government, the almost unbroken respect for the freedom of the press, and the absence of powerful and ambitious officeholders contribute to affording Uruguay a good chance of avoiding the calamities of her sister republics in Latin America. Uruguay is spiraling down, but is far from the bottom. More than half a century of government by institutions is still an asset.

SELECTED BIBLIOGRAPHY

Russell Fitzgibbon, *Uruguay: Portrait of a Democracy*, Rutgers University Press, New Brunswick, N.J., 1954.

John O. Hall, *La Administración Pública en el Uruguay*, Instituto de Asuntos Interamericanos, Montevideo, 1954.

Simon G. Hanson, *Utopia in Uruguay: Chapters in the Economic History of Uruguay*, Oxford University Press, New York, 1938.

John J. Johnson, *Political Change in Latin America: The Emergence of the Middle Sectors*, Stanford University Press, Stanford, Calif., 1958.

Göran G. Lindahl, *Uruguay's New Path: A Study in Politics During the First Colegiado, 1919-1933*, Stockholm, 1962.

George Pendle, *Uruguay: South America's First Welfare State*, Royal Institute of International Affairs, London, 1952.

Philip B. Taylor, Jr., *Government and Politics of Uruguay*, Tulane University Press, New Orleans, 1960.

Milton I. Vanger, *José Batlle y Ordóñez: Creator of His Times*, Vol. I, Harvard University Press, Cambridge, 1963.

BRAZIL

Manaus Belém

Recife

Brasília

São
Paulo Rio de Janeiro

Porto Alegre

           Phyllis Peterson

BRAZIL

INSTITUTIONALIZED CONFUSION

Social and Economic Background

Brazil is a land traditionally described with superlatives. It covers a vast territory, larger than the continental United States excluding Alaska—nearly half of the South American continent, encompassing some 3,286,169 square miles stretching from the tropical rain forests of the Amazon region in the north to the prairies of the southernmost regions of the country. Its mineral resources are extensive; significant deposits of iron and manganese, and lesser but important deposits of other minerals and gem stones, are available for present and future exploitation. With the exception of fuels, a deficiency which may be remedied by future development of atomic energy resources, the mineral base of the nation appears to be sufficient to sustain a considerable industrial complex. The vastness of the territory, the abundance of mineral resources, the empty spaces available for population expansion, the beginnings of industrialization, already pushing past the take-off point in some areas of the nation—all cause Brazil to be commonly described as a land of the future, even a potential world power in an undetermined number of years hence.

But potential alone is not sufficient. Before the many glowing predictions concerning the future of the nation will be able to take on any color of reality, problems as superlative in their scope as the land's undeniable potential will have to be met and solved. In spite of its area and resources, Brazil has as yet not much more than entered the transitional stage of economic and social development. Industrial progress in recent years has been significant, but it has been confined to a relatively small area of the nation. Urbanization has been proceeding apace, but the majority of the Brazilians still live in the rural areas. By far the majority of the population still live the tradition-bound, semifeudal life of the rural peasantry, or they have traded it for the desperate desolation of the city slum-dweller who daily views the wealth of his neighbors but who has not yet found the key to a more abundant life for himself and his family. Transformation of these sectors and their incorporation into a growing, modern industrial society is a process that Brazil as a nation has barely begun.

Economic Factors

Until recent years agriculture and mining dominated Brazilian economic life. The economic pattern of Brazilian history traditionally followed a boom and bust cycle, the booms being based upon the rapid development of a given crop or mineral, usually in the absence of competition from the rest of the world, and the bust coming when the inefficient production techniques of the early period were preserved in the face of growing competition from producers in other countries.

During the seventeenth century the predominant crop was sugar, which flourished in the northeastern region of the country. Brazil was almost the sole supplier of this product to Europe for a time. The eighteenth century brought a gold rush and diamond boom in the Minas Gerais region. Between 1900 and 1913 rubber production had a spectacular boom and an equally spectacular bust in the Amazon region of the north. From the turn of the twentieth century onward, coffee has been the key element in the Brazilian economy, revenues from the crop providing the nation with its major source of foreign exchange, especially dollars, and the government with a large percentage of its funds.

Coffee is one Brazilian boom product that, although it has receded from the peak of its importance, is still a major factor in the economic life and planning of the country. But in recent years coffee revenues have not provided a stable base for the development of the Brazilian economy. Wide fluctuations in the world prices of the commodity and growing international competition have taken a serious toll. One result has been that by the 1950's Brazil had seriously committed herself to a program of industrial expansion and diversification aimed at breaking the stranglehold of coffee on the economy and providing the basis for a general improvement in the standard of living.

The economic cycles of the past and today's program of rapid industrial development have left their mark upon the land, the main result being the existence of extreme regional variations in the standard and style of living and in the problems posed by any demand for significant change in either in the near future. Five major geographic zones are recognized in Brazil: (1) the North or Amazon region, including the states of Amazonas, Pará, Maranhão, Acre, and the territories of Rondônia, Rio Branco, and Amapá; (2) the Northeast, including the states of Piauí, Ceará, Rio Grande do Norte, Paraíba, Pernambuco, Alagoas, Sergipe, and most of Bahia; (3) the Central region, including the rest of Bahia, Espírito Santo, Minas Gerais, Rio de Janeiro, and Guanabara; (4) the West, including Mato Grosso and Goiás; and (5) the South, including the states of São Paulo, Paraná, Santa Catarina, and Rio Grande do Sul. Some authorities classify São Paulo as a separate region.

The North or Amazon region is today almost totally unpopulated and undeveloped, the rubber boom having been the only major economic adventure of the area—an outburst of activity that left but few traces visible today. The region is basically inhospitable to man, and its resources do not lend themselves to easy development. Man may some day be forced to tap the resources of this vast region, but its development on any major scale appears to lie relatively far in the future.

The Northeast is also a region of poverty, although one of considerable population. Approximately 28 percent of the nation's people live in its states. The pattern of large landholding of the sugar and cotton plantations of the coastal zone and the vast cattle ranches of the interior have produced wealth, or at least social position, for the few and a subsistence living or less for the remainder. The economic problems of the area are heightened by the irregular recurrence of the *seca*, the droughts of indeterminable length that come to the interior sections (*os sertões*) of this region from time to time. Social and economic unrest are increasing in this area as its inhabitants compare their relatively unfavorable position with that of their countrymen in the central and especially the southern zones of the nation.

The West is an almost untapped area of sparse population and uncertain potential. Most Brazilians live in a relatively narrow band of territory along the coast and have never shown any great propensity to move into the western interior plateau region. The movement in 1960 of the national capital from the coastal city of Rio de Janeiro to Brasília far in the hinterland of the central plateau some 600 miles from the coast was and continues to be a dramatic attempt to focus attention upon the developmental possibilities of the practically empty interior of the nation. Brasília is intended to be the center of a new population cluster in the heart of the nation, a cluster that will grow and stimulate the eventual occupation of the intervening spaces. The transportation network being built to link Brasília with the existing population centers—Belém, Belo Horizonte, and São Paulo especially—will, it is hoped, provide impetus for the settlement of farmers and ranchers along the various routes, since one of the major impediments to development of the area in the past has been the inaccessibility of markets. Whether this experiment can bring about the major population shift that has been resisted by the nation's inhabitants for centuries is a question that will not be answered immediately, possibly not for several generations. The construction of Brasília most certainly has contributed to the country's rampant inflation, a chronic national economic problem. But Brasília is a significant developmental experiment, the success or failure of which may prove to be of utmost importance to the future of the nation.

The heartland of the nation today is found in the central and southern regions, which have exhibited the greatest change in recent years. In them industrialization has been proceeding most rapidly—in and around the cities of São Paulo and Rio de Janeiro, in the Paraíba Valley which connects the two metropolises, and to a lesser extent in Pôrto Alegre, capital of the state of Rio Grande do Sul, the southernmost state of the nation. The city of São

Paulo and its environs have far outstripped the rest of the nation in both industrial and population growth. The city and the state have become the dynamic centers of the new Brazil.

Social Factors

The Portuguese colonizers brought and implanted in Brazil during the colonial period a patriarchal social system. Social, economic, and political power were all in the hands of the owners of large landed properties—the sugar plantations of the northeast and later the coffee plantations and ranches of the southern and central areas. A two-class society developed. The estate owner and his extended family formed the basis of the upper class. Small tradesmen, servants, peasants, and slaves—all dependent upon the major patriarchs of their locality—formed the basis of the lower class. Merchants and other small businessmen and minor bureaucrats who could legitimately claim middle-class status were very few and wielded little power of any type. As long as the nation remained overwhelmingly agricultural and rural, the patriarchs dominated not only the dependent lower class resident in their areas but their entire extended families as well.

The twin tides of urbanization and industrialization since World War I have brought important social as well as economic changes. The current century has seen the movement of vast numbers of people from the rural areas to the cities. Brazil is still a predominantly rural nation, but during the last forty years the city of São Paulo has grown from 579,033 inhabitants in 1920 to 3,825,351 in 1960; the city of Rio de Janeiro from 1,157,873 in 1920 to 3,307,163 in 1960. The trend has not been confined to these two major metropolitan centers, however: the percentage of the Brazilian population classified as urban dwellers grew in twenty years from 31.2 percent in 1940 to 36.2 percent in 1960.[1]

This movement to the cities has contributed to the weakening of the power of the rural patriarchs on at least two fronts. First, it has freed many of the members of the lower class from dependence upon the estate owner. As city dwellers many have found jobs in which the power of the employer is limited to primarily economic matters. Others not so fortunate have come to the cities and not found any employment, but rather have added to the growing number of slum dwellers, more and more discontented and disillusioned, who up to now have been largely apolitical but who present a potentially explosive force that will have to be dealt with in the very near future. Second, as the sons and daughters and other relatives of the patriarchs have moved to the cities, they too have gained a relative independence from patriarchal dominance, even though family ties have traditionally remained strong in Brazil. As the ranks of urban doctors, lawyers, and commercial men have swelled, they have become an important force, able either to complement or to oppose the rural interests as they see fit in pursuit of their own interests. Although they are as yet no more than a potential split within the upper class rather than a new class, they represent interests often at variance with those of the rural sectors.

In addition, at least two major social effects have resulted from the industrial development that has taken place. (1) Developing industry has created a growing new elite whose power and prestige is based upon industrial, financial, or managerial positions. Many of those attaining these positions are members of the old patriarchal elite class, but many others are not, especially those of foreign origin who emigrated to Brazil during the last three or four decades. Thus the resultant urban elite group has become a combination of elements reflecting both traditional and modern industrial origins. (2) The incipient middle class of the major urban areas has greatly expanded. The rural areas and small towns still embody a predominantly two-class social pattern, but the introduction of a sizable wage-earning class in the cities, both blue- and white-collar, and the growth in size of the minor bureaucracy which has developed to serve the needs of the expanding industrial society, has created a middle class between the professional, commercial, and industrial upper class and the unemployed or partially employed slum dwellers. This middle class is a growing force which up to now has predominantly identified itself with the upper class, but it represents a second at least potentially powerful force for change.

Summary

On both economic and social fronts the Brazilian nation is today in a state of turmoil. Rapid change in both economic and social patterns brought on by a deliberate program of fostering industrialization and economic diversification is characteristic of a portion of the nation. São Paulo, city and state, is the dynamic center of this area, with radii extending to the other major urban centers of the south and central sections of the nation. The rest of the country, however, has been touched but slightly by this wave of modernization. Much of it is uninhabited—especially in the North and West—and the Northeast is largely stagnant, economically and socially.* The land transportation and communication network between regions is poor and in some areas nonexistent.

Awareness of the very visible differences in standards of living between the regions has brought forth increasingly insistent demands for change. Appeals for land reform, industrialization, higher governmental expenditures on public works and development programs, and the like, are frequently made by inhabitants of the less favored areas of the nation—especially those of the Northeast. Both the disruptions caused by rapid change in the already modernizing areas and the resentments and frustrations caused by the wide

* Stefan H. Robock, *Brazil's Developing Northeast: A Study of Regional Planning and Foreign Aid*, Brookings Institution, Washington, D.C., 1963, presents an optimistic view of both the developmental potential and the developmental progress of the Northeast in recent years, challenging the usual "pessimistic and alarmist" picture of this region.

disparity in wealth between the regions have resulted in high instability on almost all fronts. This instability marks the current Brazilian political system as it copes with the problems of becoming a modern industrial society while utilizing democratic political mechanisms.

Political History

Colony and Empire (1500-1889)

In its early political development, Brazil differed from other nations of Latin America in two principal features: (1) the land was discovered, claimed, and settled by the Portuguese rather than by the Spanish, and (2) for the sixty-seven years after the gaining of independence from Portugal, Brazil was an empire governed by a hereditary constitutional monarchy.

Discovered in 1500 and claimed for Portugal by Pedro Alvarez Cabral, Brazil for several years attracted little attention from the Portuguese crown, since the land lacked easily accessible riches and important Indian civilizations such as were encountered in Mexico and Peru. Early colonization and development were carried on by men (*donatários*) who were given almost complete control over designated sections (*capitanias*) of the new land. The system did not work particularly well and was in the course of time discarded in favor of more centralized administration controlled by representatives of the Portuguese crown; but these early geographic divisions did provide the basic boundaries of several of the states of the federal system adopted years later by the nation and still in existence today.

Contrary to the pattern in most of the rest of Latin America, independence from Portugal was achieved without warfare. In 1808 the fall of Portugal to the forces of Napoleon caused the Portuguese court to flee to the New World and establish temporary residence in Brazil. In 1821, following the defeat of Napoleon, the court returned to Portugal, but Dom Pedro I, son of the Portuguese king Dom João VI, remained in Brazil. The following year, when he too was ordered to return to Portugal, he refused. Joining those favoring Brazilian independence, he became the first emperor of Brazil upon the nation's declaration of independence on September 7, 1822.

General dissatisfaction with Dom Pedro I's rule developed within a few years, and on April 7, 1831, he abdicated in favor of his son, Dom Pedro II, who at that time was but five years old. A regency ruled from April 7, 1831, to July 23, 1840, when the majority of Dom Pedro II was declared even though he was not yet fifteen years old. He ruled as emperor of Brazil for forty-nine years until the nation officially became a republic on November 15, 1889.

During the years of the empire Brazil developed a political system that on the surface resembled the British parliamentary system, with ministerial responsibility and two political parties contending for power and alternating in office. But in reality the political battle of that period was not fought in this manner. The two Brazilian political parties of the empire, classically labeled Liberals and Conservatives, were not true political parties. They were simply national groupings of the representatives of patriarchal or semipatriarchal clans contesting for power within the semifeudal milieu of local political life. Real power rested in the hands of the rural landowners and in those of Dom Pedro II.

The landowners and their followers banded together at the local level and formed competing groups bearing Conservative and Liberal labels, and the emperor forced their alternation in office at all levels through use of his constitutionally assigned "moderating power." [2] This power, among other things, gave the emperor the authority to dissolve the national chamber of deputies in cases where the "salvation of the empire demanded it" and to appoint and dismiss freely all ministers of state. Instead of following the pattern of a democratically operated parliamentary system and changing ministerial leadership in accordance with popular election results, Dom Pedro II throughout the years of his reign freely used his "moderating power" to change ministries at the national level—not in response to political crises or election results, but wholly at his own discretion. The new prime minister, once appointed, had the power to name not only his own cabinet but also new provincial (state) governors belonging to his own party. The provincial governors in turn, through having power to make certain key municipal appointments, controlled not only the provincial administrative machinery but also the election machinery and election results.

Thus once Dom Pedro II decreed a change in party control at the top ministerial level, the result was a change in control in almost every corner of the nation. Appointments of provincial and local leaders favorable to the national groupings were made, their power consolidated, and then elections were held which inevitably provided the new ministry with a favorable parliamentary majority at both national and provincial levels, or even a unanimous body if that was the desire. If Dom Pedro II had not enforced alternation of the political groupings in office through picking ministers of first one party and then the other, once in control any group could have perpetuated its power indefinitely. As a result of Dom Pedro's actions, however, at least two political groupings were permitted to exist at all levels of organization. The group out of power had only to wait. It knew that its turn to rule would come. The resultant groupings were not, however, true political parties but rather collections of representatives of the same dominant class—the rural patriarchy. Combinations at the local level were based predominantly upon ties of family. Cooperation at the provincial and national levels was based primarily upon expediency.

To the nation as a whole Dom Pedro II's long and relatively peaceful tutelary rule brought many benefits. Commerce was expanded, railroads and telegraph lines constructed, the coffee industry started. Dom Pedro II himself was a dignified personality who exhibited great interest in the welfare of his nation. He was an intellectual rather than a military figure, more interested in education than in warfare. Under his leadership Brazil was spared much of the turbulence of the caudillistic rule which characterized most of its neighbors. Perhaps most important, in spite of many powerful centrifugal forces national unity was preserved.

The Republic (1889-1930)

Dom Pedro II's age, his lack of a male heir, the dissatisfaction of the landowners following the freeing of the slaves in 1888, the disaffection of elements of the military and the Church, and a variety of other factors promoted sufficient discontent with the monarchical system of government that it was finally overthrown by a military *coup d'état* on November 15, 1889. A short period of military dictatorship followed, but constitutional government was restored by February 1891. Drawing heavily upon the United States constitution as a model, the new republican system featured a popularly elected president, a bicameral national legislature, and federalism.

In actuality, aside from the alteration in external political forms, the main change that resulted from the demise of the monarchy and the substitution of a republican form of government was that the "moderating power" was gone. No way remained to force the alternation of competing political groups in office. Thus there developed during the years of the republic what became known as the "politics of the governors."

The political parties of the monarchy were too closely associated with that regime to survive the transition to the new governmental form. The strongest factions of the rural patriarchy in each state, abandoning the monarchical parties, banded together with the strongest elements of the original supporters of the republican movement to form—in most states—a single statewide oligarchy that controlled, through force if necessary, all the local and state political machinery and offices. Once the oligarchy consolidated its position, there was no way short of force to divest it of power in the state. Each of these state groups adopted the name Republican Party, adding at the end the name of their state, but there was no national Republican Party organization.

The chief spokesman for each state oligarchy was usually the state governor, who, as official representative of his state, could speak and bargain for his state at the national level. The governors of the economically and politically most important states came together to bargain and to select the official candidate for president of the nation. Two states stood out above all others in strength throughout almost all the years of the Republic—São Paulo and Minas Gerais—and together they contrived to control the selection of the president of the republic. Working together they could control the election. The result was that they rotated the office of president of the republic between their outgoing governors during most of the years of the republic.

The fall of the republic came about when other states, particularly the state of Rio Grande do Sul, became strong enough to demand a share in this alternation of power.

The Vargas Era (1930-1945)

The downfall of the republic came as an after-effect of the presidential election campaign of 1930. In choosing the official candidate that year, the outgoing president, Washington Luis of São Paulo, broke the tacit agreement with Minas Gerais and selected the outgoing governor of his own state of São Paulo, Júlio Prestes, as his successor. The leaders of Minas Gerais refused to accept this imposition and banded together with the states of Rio Grande do Sul and Paraíba, forming the Aliança Liberal (Liberal Alliance) to contest the São Paulo candidate's election. When Júlio Prestes won the election as expected, the losers did not accept the electoral verdict.

On July 26, 1930, João Pessôa, governor of Paraíba and vice-presidential candidate of the Aliança Liberal, was assassinated. This provided the catalyst, and a revolt was launched against the government on October 3, 1930. By October 24, 1930, President Washington Luis was forced to resign, and on November 3, 1930, Getúlio Vargas of Rio Grande do Sul, defeated presidential candidate of the Aliança Liberal, assumed the presidency. This successful revolt became known as the Revolution of '30.

In reality the Revolution of '30 was neither directed at nor did it achieve basic changes in the social structure of the nation. The principal cry for reform heard in connection with the movement concerned a demand for the achievement of real political democracy through truly free, fair, and representative elections that would utilize the secret ballot. The movement also reflected the desire of the state of Rio Grande do Sul for a more prominent place in the national political power structure. Such social undercurrents as were present were largely contributed by a group of young army officers known as the *tenentes* (lieutenants). Although many of the group became leaders of the Revolution of '30 and the subsequent Vargas administration—several still being active in politics today—the *tenentes*, individually and collectively, never formulated any real social or political ideology or program.[3] The most they achieved was an expression of a vague desire for social reform. The Revolution of '30 produced no significant immediate demand for social change.

Getúlio Vargas ruled by decree as provisional president from November 3, 1930, to July 16, 1934. On the latter date a new constitution, drawn up by a popularly elected constituent assembly, was promulgated which provided for the continuance of essentially the same type of presidential, federalist system operative during the republic. The secret ballot, proportional representation in the legislative assemblies, a special electoral court to supervise and conduct elections, and other safeguards aimed at ensuring free and fair elections and representation of the minority were included, however, in an attempt to perfect the functioning of a democratic electoral and legislative process. The constituent assembly elected Vargas to continue to serve as president until 1938, when a new president was to be elected by direct popular vote.

These elections were never held. On November 10, 1937, Vargas, with the aid of the army, staged a bloodless *coup d'état*, taking over the government "to preserve the internal order of the country." Congress was dissolved, most of the state governors were ousted and replaced by Vargas-appointed interventors, and a new constitution was decreed which gave Vargas complete discretionary power to rule by decree until a national plebiscite could be held in which the voters would be given a chance to accept or reject the new order. The plebiscite never took place.

Vargas christened his discretionary regime the Estado Novo (New State).[4] The constitution under which he supposedly governed was influenced greatly by Italian fascism, but in reality Vargas ignored the constitution. His regime was a highly personalistic dictatorship rather than a New World variety of European totalitarianism. Through placing those favorable to him in control of the administrative machinery in each state and by winning over and incorporating into that machinery at either the state or national level enough of the key members of the old dominant oligarchy of each state, Vargas managed to control the political situation without the aid of any set political organization or political party. Since the political organizations of the republic had not been actual political parties but state-wide oligarchic combinations dedicated to one principal aim—control of the administrative machinery of government for the benefits to be derived from such control—Vargas, essentially, simply stepped in, added some elements loyal to him not theretofore part of the oligarchic combination, and so turned the existing political pattern to his own ends. He buttressed this administrative control with two other prongs of support—the military and popular adulation. In consolidating his position, Vargas increasingly centralized power, taking away most of what remained of the relative autonomy that the states had enjoyed under the republic. Many of his actions also had the result of increasing the people's feeling of national unity. Both of these factors had an important effect upon the type of governmental system adopted after the termination of the Estado Novo.

The Democracy (1945– ?)

The Estado Novo came to an end on October 25, 1945, when the armed forces quietly deposed Vargas without violence and transferred power to the president of the supreme court, José Linhares. Vargas' fall came as the result of mounting pressures from various sectors of the nation, but the military—the same groups that had aided him in establishing the Estado Novo—were the principal architects of the demise of the dictatorship. The imposition of the dictatorial Estado Novo had taken place during the period of the rise of totalitarian governments in Europe; its downfall came soon after the final military defeat of those regimes. Brazil—following the dictates of economy, geography, tradition, and other forces—had entered World War II on the side of the United States and the Allies; Brazilian troops fought in Italy in the war "to preserve democracy." As the war ended with the democracies victorious, pressures mounted in Brazil demanding the end of discretionary rule and the institution of a democratic form of government at home as well as abroad. By the end of 1944 Vargas had acceded to these demands and had scheduled presidential elections for 1945. As the date approached, however, various elements feared that Vargas would again repeat his maneuver of 1937 and attempt to annul the elections. He was forced to resign in order to eliminate that possibility.

Presidential and congressional elections were held on schedule on December 2, 1945. The major presidential contenders were General Eurico Dutra, candidate of the Partido Social Democratico (PSD), a party organized with Vargas' backing and composed initially of the pro-Vargas state administrators and their state administrative organizations, and Air Brigadier Eduardo Gomes, candidate of the anti-Vargas União Democratica Nacional (UDN), the principal party in the opposition coalition. Surprising many, the election was won by Dutra. Last-minute backing of the PSD candidate by the still-popular Vargas was credited by some observers with tipping the scales in Dutra's favor. The senate and chamber of deputies elected at the same time served first as a constituent assembly to formulate a new constitution for the nation, then, that job done, they became the two houses of the new national legislature, serving through 1950. The PSD won an absolute majority of the seats of both houses of the constituent assembly, the UDN emerging as the second-largest party but gaining only slightly over half as many seats as the PSD. Getúlio Vargas, rather than being repudiated in the election, won senatorial or federal deputy seats in several states, choosing to take office as a senator from his home state of Rio Grande do Sul.

The new constitution was promulgated on September 18, 1946, and once more established a presidential, federalist system. By 1950, when national elections were again scheduled, Getúlio Vargas, the former discretionary ruler, came forth as the leading presidential candidate in the democratic elections. The principal opposition candidate was, as in 1945, Eduardo Gomes of the UDN.

In 1945 Vargas had been the prime mover in the organization of two political parties, one the victorious PSD, a party that gained its principal support from the state administrative organizations and elements of the rural oligarchy; the second the Partido Trabalhista Brasileiro (PTB), a party at first composed primarily of labor union leaders. In the 1950 election period Vargas deserted the PSD, which ran its own candidate, and chose to utilize the PTB as the vehicle to bring him electoral victory. Through the PTB Vargas finally sought to organize and institutionalize the popular adulation of the masses that had been one of the prongs of his support during the Estado Novo. Vargas triumphed easily at the polls, winning 48.7 percent of the presidential vote in a four-candidate race.

After the election the PSD joined the PTB in support of the Vargas administration, thus assuring the president a majority in the national legislature. During Vargas' term in office, political tensions mounted as his administration failed to find entirely successful answers to the nation's growing economic problems. The mounting pressures erupted in volcanic form following an unsuccessful attempt on the life of opposition journalist Carlos Lacerda. The instigation of the attempt was traced to the head of Vargas' own personal protective police force. Lacerda used the forum of his own newspaper and the radio to demand Vargas' ouster, although Vargas himself was never proved to be personally involved in the assassination attempt. Faced with an ultimatum by the military demanding his resignation, and apparently fearing that his acquiescence would connote guilt or at least implication in the attempt against Lacerda, Getúlio Vargas committed suicide on August 24, 1954, rather than resign or once again submit to military ouster.

Vice President José Café Filho assumed the presidency, and a period of considerable turmoil followed. Presidential elections were held October 3, 1955, in which Juscelino Kubitschek of Minas Gerais, backed by the PSD and PTB, campaigned against Juárez Távora, one-time *tenente*, candidate of the UDN and several smaller parties. Also in the race was Adhemar de Barros of São Paulo, personalist leader of his own political party, the Partido Social Progressista (PSP), who unsuccessfully tried to don Vargas' mantle of popular adulation. The vote between these candidates was relatively close with no candidate receiving a majority. Kubitschek won with 35.7 percent of the vote, followed by Távora with 30.2 percent and De Barros with 25.8 percent.

The winning ticket of PSD Kubitschek for president and PTB João Goulart for vice-president was backed in the campaign by the outlawed Communist Party, and both men were attacked subsequent to the election by elements who labeled them dangerous leftists. A movement grew, at least vocally, to prohibit Kubitschek and Goulart from taking office. There were rumors that President Café Filho was going to cooperate in a coup to prevent the Kubitschek inauguration. Café Filho then suffered a heart attack and had to take a leave of absence, turning the presidency over to the president of the chamber of deputies, Carlos Luz, who was rumored to be involved in the plot. The military, headed by Marshal Henrique Teixeira Lott, stepped in at that point and deposed Carlos Luz, replacing him with the man next in the line of presidential succession, the president of the senate, Nereu Ramos. This caretaker government ruled until Kubitschek and Goulart were at last peacefully inaugurated in January 1956. The PSD, PTB, and PSP joined to back the Kubitschek administration.

In the presidential election of 1960 all three of Brazil's major political parties supported candidates not directly associated with their ranks. Army Marshal Henrique Teixeira Lott, former minister of war and principal military leader of the countercoup that ensured the inauguration of Kubitschek and Goulart in 1955, was chosen as the candidate of the PSD-PTB coalition. João Goulart, incumbent vice-president and successor to Vargas as leader of the PTB, was picked to run for reelection to the vice-presidency.

The other major presidential candidate in 1960 was Jânio Quadros, former governor of the state of São Paulo and member of no political party. Quadros, a charismatic figure who had great personal electoral popularity but a mercurial temperament, was backed by the UDN and a variety of minor parties. The principal opposition party chose Quadros rather than a candidate from its own ranks because, hungry for the presidential victory that had eluded them since 1945, Quadros appeared to many to have the qualities of a sure winner. Two vice-presidential candidates sprang from the Quadros coalition—Milton Campos of the UDN and Fernando Ferrari, an electorally popular federal deputy from Rio Grande do Sul who had quit the PTB following a dispute with João Goulart concerning the vice-presidential nomination.

Jânio Quadros won an easy victory in the presidential race, but the split in his backers in the vice-presidential contest permitted João Goulart of the opposition coalition to win reelection to the vice-presidency.

Although swept into office by a large electoral plurality, the unpredictable Quadros served only seven months of his five-year term before he shocked the nation by resigning the office and sailing for Europe in August 1961. His announced reason for leaving was that "reactionary forces" were preventing his reform measures from being adopted. Apparently he was especially piqued at the foot-dragging, opposition-controlled congress—the congress serving in 1961 had been elected in 1958 and was dominated by the PSD-PTB coalition.

Quadros' resignation threw the nation into momentarily acute political turmoil. Part of the military did not want to see Vice-President João Goulart take over the presidency because of the support given him in his election campaigns by the Communists and his supposed leftist leanings. This part of the military threatened that it would launch a coup rather than allow Goulart to take office. The military was divided on the issue, however, as the very important garrison of Goulart's home state, Rio Grande do Sul, came out in support of Goulart. As civil war threatened, political leaders sought a compromise that would preserve order and the democratic institutions that had been functioning in the country since 1945—and their own power position.

The compromise finally adopted was the institution by constitutional amendment of a form of parliamentary rule under which the presidency was retained but the powers of the office curtailed. The new post of prime minister was created, and this office was endowed with part of the powers that had formerly been exercised by the president. The president was given the authority to name the prime minister and the members of the council of ministers, but his appointments had to be approved by the chamber of deputies and his appointees could serve only so long as they maintained the confidence of that body. A plebiscite was scheduled for April 1965—presidential elections being constitutionally scheduled for October 1965—in which the voters would decide whether to continue the parliamentary system or to abolish it and return to the old presidential system.

With the powers of his office thus restricted, João Goulart was finally permitted to assume the presidency. During the months that followed, the economic ills of the nation grew worse, particularly the now practically epidemic problem of rampant inflation. Instead of providing leadership to meet the nation's growing problems, the parliamentary system appeared to provide only divided authority, inaction, and drift. President Goulart took advantage of the increasing dissatisfaction with the regime to consolidate his power and to push for an earlier date for the plebiscite to determine the fate of the system. The national legislature finally acquiesced, and the national plebiscite was held January 6, 1963. In an election characterized by a small turnout, the voters, by an overwhelming margin—approximately five to one—decided to end the parliamentary experiment. The full powers accorded to the president by the Constitution of 1946 were restored.

The restoration of full presidential powers did not save the Goulart regime. An announced vigorous three-year program aimed at abating the nation's economic problems while promoting rapid economic development was never put into operation. Instead of slowing down, the pace of inflation quickened. Goulart did not show himself to be an able administrator capable of using the powers of the presidency to guide the nation out of its increasingly chaotic economic state. His position was neither clear nor consistent. In trying to please all, he pleased none.

Early in April 1964, Goulart was ousted from the presidency as the military once again intervened in the nation's internal politics. A coalition of the military and the governors of several states, including UDN Carlos Lacerda of Guanabara, UDN José de Magalhães Pinto of Minas Gerais, and PSP Adhemar de Barros of São Paulo, joined forces against Goulart, forcing him to flee. This time the garrison of his home state, Rio Grande do Sul, did not come to his assistance. President of the Chamber of Deputies Ranieri Mazzilli served temporarily as his legal successor until the congress elected military-backed General Humberto Castello Branco to fill out the remainder of the term lasting through 1965.

Prior to the General's election to the presidency, the military leadership decreed an "Institutional Act," amending the Constitution of 1946. This act provided that the commanders-in-chief of the three armed services could oust any federal, state, or municipal official, including elected members of the legislatures, whom they considered to be an "extremist"; suspend for ten years the political rights, including the right to vote or to be elected to any office, of any "extremist" citizen; and suspend the immunity of any judge, professor, or other officeholder for six months so that he too could be purged. The president was given the power to send any desired legislation to the national congress where it would have to be acted upon within thirty days;

if the congress did not act within that time the legislation would be considered approved. The remainder of the Constitution of 1946 was to remain in effect.

Under this authorization several thousand Communists, leftists, and "extremists" were rounded up in various parts of the country and jailed. Most were held only temporarily, but by military order many had their political rights suspended. The list of those thus affected included such figures as Juscelino Kubitschek, João Goulart, and Jânio Quadros, former presidents of the nation, Celso Furtado, internationally known economist, and Luis Carlos Prestes, head of the Brazilian Communist Party. In addition, some forty-four members of the national congress were expelled from that body and their political rights also suspended. Although this number included representatives from several parties, the PTB was by far the hardest hit.

The military and their civilian backers claimed that Goulart and those around him were planning a Communist take-over of the country in the near future; their own actions, therefore, were taken only to save the nation from this fate. But the list of those who were ousted from the congress and/or whose political rights were taken away contains the names of many persons who were not Communists. The categories of "leftists" and "extremists" were made very broad indeed.

The nation stands, then, at a political crossroads. The near future may bring a return to democratic processes, or it may bring continued rightist military dictatorship. If the latter is the case, an eventual violent reaction from the now disorganized left may follow. The presidential elections scheduled for October 1965 loom as a potential major political turning point. Whatever the short-run course, political stability does not appear to be a likelihood in Brazil for some time to come.

The Political Process

In a nation larger than the continental United States, beset with the myriad difficulties and tensions that accompany the transition from a semi-feudal, agricultural society to a modern industrial state, the political system, whatever its form, must contend with the problems of integrating highly disparate geographic sectors into a national whole while at the same time responding to the demands of diverse and rapidly changing social, economic, and cultural interests. The longevity of any given governmental system will depend largely upon its success in meeting the needs of the changing society and in integrating into its processes the newly articulate or newly powerful groups that arise as a result of the changed social and economic conditions. In 1945 and 1946 Brazil adopted (as part of the formal machinery through which it intended to try to cope with such problems) (1) democratic governmental mechanisms, including free and fair elections, representative legislative chambers, protections for freedom of dissent and organization, etc., (2) federalism, and (3) a strong presidency (operative except during the recent brief parliamentary interlude). There also developed a multiparty system composed on the average of twelve or thirteen at least nominally national political parties. The question whether this particular governmental form is going to survive is still largely unanswerable.

During the years of the republic the real battle for political power in Brazil took place at the state and municipal level. The struggle for political power revolved around factions or individuals within each state oligarchy as they strove for preeminence within the state. The presidency of the nation was a position possessing sufficient power to provide an element of unification, but, through the operation of the "politics of the governors," throughout most of the years of the republic even the president was principally responsible to the two most powerful state organizations—those of São Paulo and Minas Gerais.

The major contributions of the Vargas years, 1930-1945, were the increasing centralization of power and authority that the dictator effectuated during the Estado Novo and the conscious program of building the psychological feeling of national unity among the masses of the people that Vargas pursued. Among the consequences of the increased centralization of the Vargas period were provisions in the Constitution of 1946 which increased the powers of the national government over the states beyond those held before 1937, although the federal system was maintained. The Constitution of 1946 also attempted to legislate into existence nationally organized and operative political parties. In practice since 1945, while the presidency, the national bureaucracy, and the military have in general appeared to have served primarily as nationally unifying agents, the political parties have taken a rather anomalous position with regard to increasing national unification of power. While there has been greater nationalization of power within the political party organizations than existed before 1937, in general the major sources of power and influence within the party organizations have remained local and individual in origin.

Two significantly different patterns of political activity have developed in the nation which reflect the extreme variations in social and economic development that separate the growing urban and industrial regions from the more tradition-bound rural areas.

Politicking in Rural Areas

Political activity in many of the rural areas of the nation still preserves elements of a system known as *coronelismo* that developed during the period of the empire and which was maintained and even strengthened during the years of the republic. Under the empire and the republic the strongest local patriarchal chieftain—through influencing the votes of his family, controlling the votes of most of those dependent upon him for a livelihood who were permitted to vote, manipulating the electoral machinery, and placing those faithful to him in all local appointive positions—frequently could dominate an entire *município*,* sometimes more than one, or even an entire section of a state. Often under the empire the provincial governor would appoint the political chieftain of a *município* to the post of local commander of the national guard, frequently with the title of "colonel" or "lieutenant-colonel." In time most rural chieftains came to be called *coronel* whether they officially held such a position or not, and the political system they represented thus became known as *coronelismo*.

The phenomenon of the "controlled" vote, representing votes that a *coronel* can deliver to the candidate of his choice regardless of the individual's party affiliation, is still prevalent in some areas of Brazil. The creation of national political parties and the relative centralization of power has not seriously affected the political patterns of the interior and plantation areas of much of the west, central, northeast, and north of the nation. The system has changed somewhat over time, however, as today the *coronel* capable of controlling the votes of a large area—perhaps several *municípios* or an entire section of a state—appears to be rapidly disappearing. In his place have arisen the *chefe político* and the *cabo eleitoral*, the former capable of controlling perhaps 200 to 1,000 votes, the latter being able to deliver perhaps 50 votes to any given candidate. Money also appears to be replacing family ties as the key to controlling votes in many areas, although family influence is still often an important consideration.

The methods of controlling votes in the various sections of the country vary considerably, but a few techniques have general application. Voter registration is vital. Brazilian electoral law requires literacy as a qualification for voter registration. As of 1950 it was estimated that 50.5 percent of all Brazilians over fifteen years of age were illiterate, and the percentage of illiteracy is generally much higher in the rural areas and in the states of the west, north, and northeast. Voting, with some exceptions, is compulsory, but the prospective voters must themselves come forward to effect their initial registration. The local political chiefs are vitally concerned with the registration process, attempting to get as many eligible voters as possible registered in their area—particularly those who can be counted upon to follow the chieftain's directions. The result in some areas has been the registration of many manipulable semiliterates obligated to the local *chefe político*.

Voting under Brazilian electoral law is conducted only at a few central locations in a given *município*. Therefore, transportation of the potential voters to the polling places on or before Election Day becomes a major problem, given the rudimentary character of the Brazilian transportation system throughout most of the interior areas. As a result, one of the most

* The *município* is roughly comparable to the United States county, although it performs for the most part the combined functions of both city and county government. It is today—and has been since colonial times—the basic administrative subdivision of the state. Each state is divided into *municípios*; each *município* contains a principal city or town which is designated as the seat of government, rural areas, and perhaps additional urban concentrations—cities, towns, or villages.

effective means of controlling votes is to have control of any and all transportation facilities on Election Day and the day before. Trucks and buses
bring voters into the town where the balloting is to take place. Some voters
are even provided overnight lodging of a sort so that they can be present on
Election Day. The local political leader may also prepare a *churrasco*—a
feed of beef roasted on a spit—for the benefit of his voters. Election Day
becomes a sort of festival, for which the voters pay by casting their ballots
for the proper candidates. Sometimes the voter is also given a small monetary
reward for proper performance in the voting booth.

Candidates with money to spend or favors to dispense are thus at a
considerable advantage in gaining legislative office in the rural states where
traditional patterns are still predominant. Money buys the means of transportation; and frequently the loyalty and services of the *chefe político* or
cabo eleitoral can also be purchased by the highest bidder among the candidates. A common procedure is for a candidate for the office of federal
deputy to work together with one or more candidates for state deputy
and the latter to work with the local political chieftains. The money is
frequently provided by the federal deputy candidate and is passed down the
line until the local figure's services—and deliverable votes—are purchased.

In the tradition-bound and predominantly rural states the men who are
most likely to possess such monetary resources are usually part of or closely
associated with the rural oligarchy. In some of the states of the north and
northeast, politics is still largely a family matter, the names of members of
a few large, wealthy, and socially prominent families of the old rural
oligarchy cropping up again and again in the lists of candidates and holders
of elective and appointive office.

Politicking in the City

Political activity in the urban areas of the country usually follows quite
a different pattern from that of the predominantly rural areas. The difference
holds true for all urban areas—those of the northeast as well as the major
centers of the south and central sections. Higher rates of literacy, the
accessibility of almost all urban dwellers to some form of the mass media
of communication, the lesser importance of family ties, stemming from
such influences as distance or economic independence, and many other
factors work together to make the urban voter much harder to control in
the manner that a portion of the rural vote is controlled.

In some interior areas, once the local *chefes políticos* are openly committed
to a given candidate, many other candidates will not attempt to campaign
actively in the area, given the distances, the costs, and frequently the futility
of such activity. In the major urban areas, however, with their greater
concentration of voters and the possibility of attracting a greater number
of votes for the money spent in publicity, a much larger number of politicians is enticed to campaign in the area and to engage more or less
continuously in political activity there. The voter is thus exposed to a

wider range of political propaganda and is presented with a much wider choice of legislative candidates. Almost all of the thirteen nationally registered political parties will normally be found to be active in any one of the nation's larger cities.

Given the large number of candidates who regularly campaign for national and state legislative office in the urban areas, well-known political personalities or those with sufficient financial resources to make widespread use of the mass media are favored in election campaigns. Those who operate social service centers such as medical clinics, schools, and other businesses that bring the operator into direct contact with large numbers of people are also favored. So too is the demagogue, the crowd-pleaser, the arouser of the masses.

The popular, opportunistic vote-getter often finds the city to be an excellent nurturing agent for his personal political ambitions whatever political party label he may wear, or even if he wears none. The source of political power in the cities is frequently found in individual electoral popularity and not in the backing of organized political groups. Money, because it buys the use of the communications media, is as important to success as it is in the rural areas, but the urban-based successful politician may manage to get his start in spite of limited financial resources. He may parlay an early success won on the basis of demagogic campaigning into both fame and fortune. Following an initial success, elements flocking to his side to trade upon his popularity frequently provide the ambitious newcomer with the financial resources necessary to expand his audience. As long as his vote-getting ability is sustained there are few limits to the heights to which he may rise. The one sin that is not permitted is electoral failure. The rapid ascent of Jânio Quadros from São Paulo city councilman to São Paulo city mayor to governor of São Paulo state to president of the nation is a case in point. He achieved all this in spite of modest financial beginnings and in spite of the fact that except for a short period early in his political career he belonged to and associated himself with no single political party.

In general, therefore, although the successful urban-based politician may come from one of the traditional families, there are many who do not. Although the wealthy are still favored, the popular can succeed in spite of not initially possessing substantial personal wealth, not belonging to the upper class, and not maintaining close association with one of the national political organizations. The demagogue and the charismatic personality are notably favored in the political climate of the urban areas.

The Electoral System

All elective offices in Brazil today are filled by direct popular election, but two types of electoral contest exist under current electoral law. Elections for the offices of president, vice-president, governor, senator, and prefect (mayor) are all decided according to the plurality principle—the candidate with the most votes wins, even if his total does not represent an absolute majority of the votes cast. Elections for federal deputy, state deputy, and municipal councilman (*vereador*), on the other hand, are all decided according to the principle of proportional representation.

In operation both plurality and proportional-representation contests are carried on in most states in a manner which tends to blur party identification and emphasize the individuality of the candidates. In the proportional-representation contests each political party that has gained official recognition both nationally and in the state in which the election is being held may register a list of candidates equal in number to the number of legislative seats at stake plus one-third. Coalitions in which two or more parties join together to present a single list of candidates are permissible.

In most of the elections since 1945 this has meant that either twelve or thirteen nationally registered parties were eligible to present a separate list of candidates in elections for federal and state deputy, although in 1950 fifteen parties were eligible to do so. In practice in states such as São Paulo and Guanabara all registered parties do present candidates, frequently presenting coalition slates in federal deputy contests, but almost invariably each presenting separate slates for state deputy races. This has resulted, for example, in a total of 253 candidates registered on 8 slates contesting for 44 federal deputy seats, and 895 candidates registered on 12 slates contesting for 75 state deputy seats, in São Paulo in 1958. In Guanabara in the same election 108 candidates registered on 6 slates ran for 17 federal deputy seats, and 733 candidates registered on 12 slates ran for the 50 seats on what was then the city council, since the capital had not yet been moved to Brasília.* Normally, fewer parties present full slates of candidates in the smaller states.

The party list system is not utilized. From the multitude of candidates each voter may cast a ballot for not more than one candidate for federal deputy and one candidate for state deputy, the candidate's name and identification number being written in by the voter on an officially provided ballot. Before the 1962 election each federal and state deputy candidate had to print and distribute his own ballots to the voters.

The votes for all the candidates running on a single slate are tallied, and the party or coalition total is ascertained. The seats are then allocated to the various parties or coalitions according to the principle of proportional representation. The seats won by each party or coalition go to the candidates on their respective slates personally receiving the most votes, seats being assigned according to the descending order of the individual vote until the party or coalition assignment is exhausted. The remaining candidates on the slate become official substitutes for those in office, being called to fill vacancies caused by death, illness, leave of absence, or any other inability to serve on the part of the elected representatives from their party or

---

* The capital of Brazil was officially moved from Rio de Janeiro to Brasília in 1960. The area that had formerly been the Federal District became the state of Guanabara, Rio de Janeiro becoming its capital city. A new Federal District was created around Brasília in the state of Goiás.

coalition. These substitutes are also called according to their individual vote, the candidate with the most votes being called first to fill any vacancy and so on down the list. Thus the need for special elections to fill vacancies is eliminated.

The result of this system is that each candidate for offices filled in this manner finds himself in competition not only with all the candidates of all of the opposition slates, but also with all the others on his own party's slate. The voter can cast but one vote for each office. The candidate's party slate must receive enough votes to share in the proportional distribution of seats, but he must have more votes than other candidates on his party's list if he wishes to secure a seat for himself. The system roughly combines primary and final election in one balloting.

Each state constitutes a separate multimember district for both federal and state deputy elections. Each candidate is at liberty to campaign throughout the state, though his resources may not permit him to do so. The concentration of eligible voters makes the city a prime campaign area for most candidates. In the largest cities the campaign period is one of chaos. Each candidate for federal or state deputy conducts his own campaign and runs to all intents and purposes independent of party. The political organizations rarely assist a candidate for offices filled by proportional representation in any but the most general manner and provide no financial assistance. The candidate must sell his name and himself in any way that he can. With several hundred candidates bombarding the voter with their individual propaganda, attempting in every way possible to get their names before the public, political party identification and party programmatic orientation are often lost in the utter confusion.

Thus the way is paved in the cities for the demagogue—the campaigner who because of voice, mannerisms, special techniques, or special promises and favors stands out from the crowd. Or the voter turns to the man he knows, even slightly, or to the one who has done him some kind of favor during the preceding year, or perhaps to one who is related to him in some manner. Even if the voter wishes to be faithful to a particular political party, he may have to choose one name from among seventy-five candidates put up by that party. Confusion is endemic to the system.

The elections for offices decided according to the plurality principle somewhat counteract the strong centrifugal forces at work in the proportional-representation elections, but centralizing influences do not all redound to the benefit of the political parties. It is very rare for any single political party to capture over 50 percent of the vote in any given state or in the presidential election. Thus a premium is placed upon the formation of coalitions in elections decided according to the plurality principle.

In seeking a gubernatorial candidate, the major parties of a state search, almost from the day an incumbent governor is inaugurated, for a personality of sufficient prominence and vote-getting ability that he can unite perhaps two of the major parties behind him and attract a number of the minor parties as well. Prominent party leaders who are strongly identified in the public mind with one particular party are often at a disadvantage in this selection because other party leaders fear that victory by such a candidate might be looked upon as predominantly a victory for the candidate's party, the contributions of the other parties in the coalition being overlooked to their future disadvantage. In order to unite two relatively strong parties in a state behind a single gubernatorial candidate it has often been found necessary to turn to a well-known individual—e.g., an army general—who is not strongly identified with any particular party, but who leans or tends toward one of the major parties. The gubernatorial race in most states frequently ends up being a contest between an administration-backed candidate and a candidate of the "outs," each supported by at least one major party and a number of minor parties.

If more than one plurality-election office is being contested in the same election, designation of candidates for the posts is often a matter of bargaining within the coalition. The strongest party within the coalition will normally name the gubernatorial candidate, even if the nominee is in actuality a nonparty figure. The next-strongest party will name the candidate for the national senate seat, other parties perhaps indicating the coalition nominee for vice-governor and senatorial substitute (*suplente*).

Candidates may soft-pedal their own party label and campaign in the name of the coalition backing them—a name especially created for the campaign. This is frequently essential because the parties united to back a candidate at the state level may be highly competitive against each other in many *municípios* throughout the state. Mention of the candidate's own party rather than the coalition name in such areas could lose many votes.

The political parties are thus intensely active in the selection of candidates for the offices filled according to the plurality principle, but party affiliation of the candidates is often hidden or minimized in the actual campaigning. Much the same procedure has frequently been followed at the national level in the selection of candidates for president of the republic.

Political Parties

With party lines so frequently blurred in election campaigns, what role is played by the Brazilian political parties? What functions do they perform within the nation's political system? National election results suggest a fairly stable group of political parties contesting national elections and controlling national political activities. But this is only part of the picture.

The post-1945 Brazilian multiparty system has been composed on the average of twelve nationally registered political organizations, although fifteen participated in the 1950 elections and thirteen maintain registration today. Three of these parties can be classified as major parties on the national scene, the remainder being medium-sized and minor parties which may have considerable strength in specific states, but not at the national level.

Two of the major parties—the Partido Social Democrático (PSD) and the União Democrática Nacional (UDN)—arose as the principal contenders in the 1945 elections. The PSD was originally formed by a combination of the Vargas-appointed state interventors and their state and local administrative bureaucracies. Since these administrative organizations of the Estado Novo had in many states incorporated within their ranks most of the leaders of the controlling state oligarchies of the period of the Republic, the new party in several states was in effect dominated by the traditional rural oligarchy. Getúlio Vargas was originally named national president of this party, but he chose not to accept the office. The PSD supported the winning presidential candidate in 1945 and captured or participated in the winning coalition in a majority of the state gubernatorial races in 1947. Since that time the overall national strength of the PSD has declined considerably, but it is still the largest and strongest single political party in the nation.

In the later years of the Estado Novo the opposition to the Vargas regime organized itself into a loose coalition of forces under the title União Democrática Nacional (National Democratic Union). The principal—it may be said the only—uniting tie in this organization was the desire to see Vargas ousted and a liberal democratic governmental system adopted in the nation. The bulk of this group, maintaining the same name, organized itself into the principal opposition party in 1945. Although losing out in the 1945 presidential election, the UDN emerged as the second-largest party in the nation and the predominant party in several states. The UDN has found its most ardent and faithful supporters among the nation's intellectual and professional groups and others of the middle and upper middle classes, although a substantial number of rural landowners and industrialists of upper-class status also adhere to its ranks. The UDN has adopted a liberal democratic posture embracing programs of political reform aimed at perfecting the operation of political democracy in the nation, but it has been more cautious and conservative in its pronouncements concerning social and economic reform. As a result the UDN has found it somewhat difficult to appeal to the urban working class and by 1958 the party had lost its position as second-largest party in the nation to the rapidly growing Partido Trabalhista Brasileiro (PTB), the third of the major parties.

In 1945 Getúlio Vargas, besides sponsoring the formation of the PSD, gave his blessing to the foundation of the PTB, a political party initially organized by a group of labor union leaders. The PTB did not fare exceptionally well in the 1945 contest. Vargas was its principal candidate and he won federal deputy seats for the party in several states.* He chose to occupy none of these seats, however, opting instead to be sworn in as senator from his home state of Rio Grande do Sul as a member of the PSD.

* The Electoral Code of 1945 permitted an individual to be a candidate for office in as many different states as he wished, although he could fill only one seat in Congress. Vargas was a senatorial candidate in at least five states and a candidate for federal deputy in at least nine states. The Electoral Code of 1950 forbade this practice. An individual is still permitted to run for more than one office in a single state, but he is prohibited from running in two or more states simultaneously.

Two events changed the fortunes of the PTB. In 1948 Getúlio Vargas officially took over leadership of the party. He attempted to utilize the PTB as the vehicle to institutionalize the adulation of the masses that had been one of his major prongs of support during the Estado Novo. The PTB became inextricably intertwined with Vargas' image, and the party gained greatly from his victory in the presidential elections of 1950. Following Vargas' suicide in 1954, the reins of party leadership passed to his hand-picked successor, João Goulart. The PTB joined with the PSD to back the successful candidacy of PSD Juscelino Kubitschek for president of the republic in 1955, PTB leader Goulart winning the vice-presidential post. This victory abetted the fortunes of the party because it brought to the PTB, as payment for its support of the administration, continued control over the labor ministry and most of the national social-welfare agencies. Again in 1960 the PSD and PTB joined together to back a PSD-selected presidential candidate. Although losing to Jânio Quadros in the presidential race, the PTB came out of the contest victorious, since João Goulart gained reelection to the vice-presidency when the Quadros forces split their vote between two candidates for the office. This victory became one of extreme importance when, upon Jânio Quadros' unexpected resignation from the presidency, João Goulart became the legal successor to the office.

The other event which enhanced the fortunes of the PTB was the outlawing of the Communist Party in 1947. Vargas utilized nationalistic appeals in seeking to gain and maintain the affections of the masses and of organized labor, and Goulart continued to make nationalism a major appeal of the PTB. With the Brazilian Communist Party no longer able to run candidates under its own party label, the field was largely left clear for the PTB to become the principal popular party of the nation and the most ardent spokesman for nationalistic causes. The Communists, able to maintain their organization openly even though not able to register as a political party, have frequently chosen to give their support to PTB candidates—although they have at different times supported candidates from all the parties, as their interests dictated.

In contrast to the PSD and UDN, both of which have found their strongest support among the upper and middle classes, the PTB has thus in part at least become the major party appealing to the urban working class. Especially in the states of Guanabara, Rio de Janeiro, Rio Grande do Sul, and Pernambuco the PTB has been the vehicle through which many of the newly articulate lower groups have been incorporated into the political process. The preponderance of state over national organization within the political parties and the federal system of representation in the national congress has meant, however, that the PTB has included within its ranks some members of the rural oligarchy and opportunistic industrialists as well as labor union leaders and others who appeal to the lower class. It has thus become the broadest-based party in the nation. While the PSD and UDN have been gradually declining in strength since 1945, the PTB has been consistently growing. However, the purges of 1964 suspended the political rights of most of the PTB leadership. The effect that this may have on the future of the party cannot at this time be foreseen.

While the PSD, PTB, and UDN dominate the national political scene, the multitude of minor parties are not without importance in the Brazilian political process. Almost all the minor parties nationally fit roughly into one of two categories: ideological and programmatic parties, or personalist parties.

The only legal Brazilian political party that can legitimately be dubbed ideologically oriented is the extremely small Partido de Representacão Popular (PRP), led by Plínio Salgado. This organization is the "democratic" descendant of the Integralistas or Green Shirts, a fascist-modeled movement which Salgado headed in Brazil in the 1930's during the time of the Nazi-Fascist rise to power in Europe. The party has but a very small popular following today.

The Brazilian Socialist Party (Partido Socialista Brasileiro, or PSB) and the Christian Democratic Party (Partido Democrata Cristão, or PDC) are distinguished by their formal commitment to international socialist and Christian democratic ideas respectively, but neither party has been consistently successful in translating these broad doctrines into effective action on the Brazilian scene. The Partido Libertador (PL), which has its strength in the state of Rio Grande do Sul, is distinguished by its espousal of the adoption of a parliamentary system in Brazil. Beyond this one plank the PL is hardly distinguishable from the UDN.

The remaining minor parties are personalist parties. Each is led nationally by a prominent figure who possesses either considerable personal electoral popularity or wealth or both. For one reason or another the leading personality has preferred to remain independent of the major parties, finding greater success or satisfaction in conducting an organization of his own. The other members of such an organization are attracted to it either by ties of personal loyalty to the leader or by the hope of greater personal gain to be obtained through riding on his coattails. These organizations usually have little interest in program or principle; instead, expediency and opportunism are the party by-words. The Partido Social Progressista (PSP), led by Adhemar de Barros, twice governor of São Paulo, has been the most successful of the personalist parties to date.

The national picture does not indicate the full importance of the minor parties within the Brazilian political party system. It is on the state level that these parties have their greatest importance—an importance that far exceeds their numerical strength at the polls or the numbers of their representatives in the various legislatures.

In order to run candidates in an election a political party in Brazil must not only gain registration at the national level but must also register its leadership group in each state. National registration, once achieved, remains in effect indefinitely unless a political party violates the principles of democratic government, fails to elect at least one representative to the national congress, or receives less than 50,000 votes in national legislative elections. Once national registration is obtained, state party officers may be registered in the various states at almost any time prior to the deadline for registering candidates for an election. An officially recognized state party directorate must be in existence before a party can register candidates in a given state.

Not all of the nationally registered political parties have legally recognized and actually operative directorates in existence in most states at any given time, especially in between-election periods. Several of the minor parties are thus able to lend their party labels to *ad hoc* groups that form within the state with the sole purpose of registering a slate of candidates. These groups form just prior to the election, normally have little success in gaining office, and disappear the day after the election is over.

What is more important, dissatisfied or dissident members of the major parties of the state often use minor parties to further their own political careers when they are passed over by their own party as nominees for major office or key party leadership posts. The national leadership of several minor parties—especially personalist parties—is often willing to lend its party registration to dissident members of the major parties who wish to run for office in spite of an adverse decision on their candidacy by their own party leadership. Dissident factions frequently borrow the party label of a minor party which either does not have a directorate registered in the state or which is so weak that it is willing to go along in return for promises of jobs, favors, etc., in case of victory. The dissidents may then run a candidate against their own party, sometimes in coalition with the major opposition parties of the state. If the dissident candidates are victorious, they often return to their original party, resuming leadership positions within it. On occasion the dissident wing may retain its independence, becoming the state organization of the minor party. This is most frequently the case if the dissident faction is headed by a politician of considerable personal electoral popularity within the state who feels that his personal fortunes will be consistently thwarted by the major-party leadership.

The net result of this type of maneuvering is that the minor parties provide a convenient haven for major party malcontents; they thus make effective party discipline within the major parties impossible to achieve. They also serve to confuse the voters, through abetting the proliferation of candidates for legislative office, and make party affiliation less meaningful, since individuals freely change party to gain personal advantage.

The present Brazilian political party system does not appear to be performing with any notable success two functions which political parties in a democratic system are expected to perform: controlling nomination and simplifying alternatives for the voter. The confusion of the campaigns for legislative office, the frequent necessity of looking outside of party ranks for major candidates for executive office, the disruptive effect on party discipline produced by the plethora of minor parties, all have contributed to the growth of the feeling in Brazil that the political parties stand for little or nothing, that all is confusion, and that if faith is to be placed anywhere it must be in the individual politician and not in the political party he supposedly represents.

Yet the political parties are not entirely without meaning. The leadership groups of the major parties have exhibited considerable stability throughout the period since 1945. The two more traditionally oriented major parties—the PSD and UDN—have both lost ground nationally, but they still remain major forces to be considered on the national political scene. The three major parties dominate the national congress, and the three together hold the vast majority of seats in almost all state legislatures. All but a handful of state governors have been affiliated with one of the three parties, or if not affiliated at the beginning of the campaign, have worked closely with the leadership groups of one or more of them once elected. True, under the present system it is possible for a popular figure to be politically successful without major party ties, and a charismatic figure like Jânio Quadros can ascend all the way to the presidency of the nation without giving allegiance to any political party. Yet in the total national picture it is still much more likely that success will come to those who do affiliate themselves with one of the major party organizations than to those who do not.

Prior to the events of April 1964, perhaps the greatest advantage of the loose-knit, relatively undisciplined organizational structure of the political parties was that it permitted easy entry into the political process by newly articulate groups. Even important leadership positions were open to members of these groups if they had sufficient appeal. The "extremists" purged in 1964 were primarily the politicians who had become spokesmen for the lower classes; nationalism and basic reforms of the nation's social and economic structure had been their major appeals.

The more traditionally oriented PSD and UDN could together have controlled a majority in nearly all state legislatures and in both houses of the national congress. But the specter of Getúlio Vargas had kept them apart. Instead of cooperating in most states and at the national level they opposed each other. The PSD allied most often with the PTB, both parties having originally been Vargas creations. The policy orientations of the leadership groups of these two parties grew farther and farther apart, until by the end of 1963 their coalition was an extremely tenuous one. A PTB leader in the presidency at the same time as the PTB became the largest single party in the chamber of deputies apparently aroused fears among the traditional groups that they might lose control of the situation. April 1964 brought the ouster of Goulart and the installation of a military president and a cabinet made up primarily of persons affiliated with the UDN and PSD. Most of the PTB leaders lost their political rights in the purge. The traditionally oriented groups took full command; the urban laboring groups lost, for the time being at least, most of their major spokesmen.

The question now arises, Will the system remain closed, as the rural landowning and urban upper and middle classes attempt to keep the urban lower-class groups from effective participation in the political process, with the attendant danger of revolutionary eruption by the disaffected groups? Or will the system be opened once again, perhaps with a new alignment of the conservative groups that, having at last buried Vargas, will work together to oppose within the confines of democratic elections the threat posed by the reform-minded PTB?

The Communist Party

In a system as unstable as that of Brazil today, the position of the Communist Party (the Partido Comunista do Brasil, or PCB) assumes great significance. Founded in the early 1920's, the Communists did not achieve real importance within the nation until the late 1930's when Luis Carlos Prestes took over the leadership of the party. Prestes is an almost legendary figure. He was one of the original *tenentes*. When a revolt in which he participated failed in 1924, he joined a column of insurgents who retreated to the hinterland of the nation and continued their fight against the government of the republic. This column of rebels, known as the Prestes Column in honor of its leader, marched thousands of miles throughout Brazil sowing the seeds of discontent against the government, gaining nationwide fame for its quixotic battle against the whole Brazilian army. The army never did defeat the column, but, weakened by disease and the physical toll of their long march, the rebels finally interned themselves in Bolivia in 1927.

During the following years, while in exile, Prestes became a Communist, spending some time studying and working in the Soviet Union. In 1934 he returned to Brazil from the USSR and joined the PCB, soon becoming its leader. In 1935 the Communists were prime movers in an unsuccessful revolt against the Vargas regime. This defeat resulted in the outlawing of the PCB and the imprisonment of Prestes and other party leaders. Prestes remained in jail throughout World War II, finally gaining release in 1945 when Vargas granted a general amnesty.

The PCB gained legal recognition in 1945 and participated as a political party in the elections of 1945 and 1947. In total votes cast for its candidates throughout the nation the PCB emerged from these elections as the fourth largest party in the nation. In the latter part of 1947, however, the national electoral court reconsidered its grant of legal recognition to the PCB and subsequently withdrew it on the grounds that the Marxist-Leninist principles of the PCB violated the provisions of the Constitution of 1946 requiring political parties to adhere to "the principles of democracy" and "the fundamental rights of man."

This withdrawal of recognition meant that after 1947 the PCB was not able to run candidates in elections under its own party label, nor were those who were its candidates in 1945 and 1947 permitted to run again —including Prestes. The party was not driven underground; it instead retreated to a position of semilegality. It openly endorsed candidates of other parties for executive office, and its own members—those who were not candidates during the brief period of legality—were frequently accommodated on other party slates. However after the success of the revolt of 1964, known Communists were once again deprived of all elective and appointive offices, individual political rights were suspended, and many party members were jailed.

The strength and popularity of the PCB today are difficult to assess for several reasons. It is impossible to ascertain definitely how much of the party's electoral success in 1945 and 1947 was occasioned by voter adherence to the party and how much was due to the great personal prestige and fame of PCB leader Luis Carlos Prestes. In recent years the PCB has wrapped itself in the mantle of Brazilian nationalism, and the nationalists in turn have adopted a variety of Communist-inspired slogans as their own. By no means are all Brazilian nationalists also Communists. Yet the Communists have done everything possible to foster this identification in order to turn the real and potent force of Brazilian nationalism to their own ends. The resultant confusion of the two movements has caused many to view the size of the Brazilian Communist force with great alarm. The calculated intertwining of nationalism and Communism, however, makes it very hard to assess the actual size and influence of the PCB in Brazil today.

Of those deprived of office and political rights in 1964, only a small percentage were actually members of the PCB. However, the avowed PCB leaders were part of that percentage, and the party must again operate underground. The party's future is uncertain, but should the urban and rural masses not find effective representation within the future political system and an attempt be made to turn from evolution to revolution, the PCB will undoubtedly be standing ready to play a leading and perhaps a dominant role in such a movement.

Interest Groups

So few investigations have been made and so very little written about interest groups and how they gain governmental assistance in meeting their needs and desires that little can be said with any certainty concerning their role and importance within the Brazilian political system. Contrary to the general pattern in the United States, the Brazilians are not a nation of joiners who formally organize, with constitution and officers, at every turn. The family, rather than outside groups, has been the principal institution in Brazilian social life. It is true that in recent years there has been a gradual breaking down of the patriarchal tradition and with it some loosening of family ties. But the family still provides for many social and economic needs which are satisfied for residents of the United States through community or interest-group action. Brazilian society is not without a large variety of interests that make claims on the government, but they are less likely to be formally organized and are therefore less easily identifiable and their methods of exerting pressure and their points of access to the political process less easily ascertained.

During the Estado Novo Getúlio Vargas did attempt to organize both business and labor interests, with the aim of tying the resultant organizations closely to the government.[5] In tune with the corporate-state theories of the period, Vargas sponsored the formation of both employers' and workers' organizations in various trades and industries; these subgroups were then to be tied together in separate state confederations of workers and employers. The workers' organizations were very closely controlled by the ministry of labor, but such employers' organizations as were formed were given more independence.

At the end of the Estado Novo these organizations did not disband; most continued in existence and some new groups formed. The labor unions gained more freedom from government control and the employers' organizations became more popular with the entrepreneurial groups as instruments for carrying on relations with the workers and with government.[6]

Organizations that have been set up to promote employers' interests include the National Confederation of Commerce, the National Confederation of Industry, and the Brazilian Rural Confederation, the latter representing farm and plantation owners, cattle ranchers, and those owning rural industries. Each of these confederations has divisions in almost all of the states and territories. Members of the leadership bodies of these organizations are frequently very active in politics; the names of some federal or state deputies or of members of state or national party directorates can nearly always be identified in the lists of confederation officers.

The federal government has since 1945 established a series of "autarchies" (*autarquias*) to deal with the problems of the development and sale of various commodities. There are such organizations as the Instituto Brasileiro do Café, the Instituto do Açúcar e do Alcool (Institute of Sugar and Alcohol), and the Instituto Nacional do Mate, among others. These autarchies exist outside of the regular governmental departments and are headed by representatives of both the government and the industry involved. They deal with such problems as promotion of research to lower the price, increase production, and better the quality of the product; protection of the price of the crop on the market to ensure the producer a just return; perfecting the distribution of the product; study of the consumers' market to find out how to sustain sales and conquer new markets. In carrying out these duties they establish production quotas, set the qualifications for different grades of the product, regulate the amounts permitted to be sold in foreign trade and within the nation, and exercise a number of other controls over the production and distribution of the product. The powers of these organizations over the production of the products concerned are very great, but the fact that representatives of the industry are permitted to sit on the leadership bodies means that there is a direct institutionalized channel available to the producers to make their claims upon the governmental regulators of their industry—a channel which bypasses the legislative arm of the government.

Labor unions were initially organized in Brazil by immigrant workers in the 1890's, but when Getúlio Vargas came to power in 1930, the labor union movement was still very weak.[7] Vargas' subsequent promotion of unionization increased the numbers of labor union members, but he tied the labor organizations so closely to the ministry of labor that they had little opportunity for independent political action. Since 1945, governmental control over labor has gradually been relaxed, but significant areas of dependence still exist. The government levies a "trade union tax" upon the workers and turns over a large percentage of this money to the unions. These funds are used by the unions to provide welfare services to their members. Furthermore, the practice of collective bargaining is not yet well established, and many disputes that in other nations would be settled in this manner are dealt with in Brazil in the nation's labor courts, where the government thus becomes the final arbiter of the dispute.[8]

Labor union leaders, like their business confederation counterparts, have been active in politics. Most union leaders have been affiliated with the PTB or the Communists, sometimes both at the same time, although a few are found in other parties. It is not unusual for a labor union leader to be a federal or state deputy. Some of these, however, lost their positions and their political rights in April 1964.

The pattern of interest group activity in Brazil suggests that most groups make their demands directly upon the administrative branch of government rather than channeling them through the political party system and the legislature. Access to the administrative branch for both business and labor has been institutionalized through the autarchies, the labor ministry, the labor courts, etc., in a manner that bypasses the legislative branch.

Furthermore, the national legislature is not organized in a manner that permits easy, formalized channels for interest groups to use to make their claims. Committees in the national legislature do not as a matter of course call for or receive statements by interest group representatives when holding hearings on bills. Direct lobbying is unusual. Groups do from time to time come to the congress to demonstrate, but this is a rather sporadic type of pressure. Many legislators look upon interest group demands as being somehow a subversion of democratic principles. Representation of interests is thought to be sufficiently provided for by the individual congressmen themselves as they are spokesmen for the business confederations, labor unions, etc., of which they are members and leaders. Many of these congressmen, however, spend more of their time in the capital calling upon administrative officials than they do in the halls of congress. The organs of popular representation—political parties and the legislature—are not yet well enough developed in Brazil to serve successfully as the principal aggregators and sanctioners of interest-group demands.

The Military, the Bureaucracy, and the Church

Three institutions of Brazilian society that frequently function as very potent pressure groups in their relations with the government of the nation are the military, the bureaucracy, and the Roman Catholic Church.

Brazilian independence was won from Portugal without warfare. The transitions between the reign of Dom Pedro I, the Regency, and the personal reign of Dom Pedro II were all effectuated without bloodshed. Throughout the long years of his rule Emperor Dom Pedro II projected the image of the scholar and the man of peace rather than that of the militaristic *caudillo* so common in many of the other Latin American countries of the period. The first real intervention of the military into the national politics of Brazil came with the ouster of Dom Pedro II in 1889. The army forced his abdication, and a short period of military dictatorship inaugurated the republic. It was relatively short-lived, however, and by 1891 a new constitution was in force. The government was in civilian hands throughout most of the years of the republic; on occasion during that period men who had been military officers held the office of president, but they gained it because of other circumstances and not solely because they were military men.

The activities of the *tenentes* in the early 1920's and the army's role in the Revolution of '30 brought the Brazilian military into an active and important role on the political scene, a position they have maintained ever since. The military helped to make the Revolution of '30 successful; they helped Vargas institute the Estado Novo; they also cooperated with democratic elements in ousting him in 1945. Both of the major presidential candidates in 1945 were military men, and at least one major candidate in each succeeding presidential election has had a military background. Military intervention asking Vargas' resignation in 1954 precipitated his suicide, and military intervention again in 1955 protected the inauguration in 1956 of the legally elected president, Juscelino Kubitschek. The military again was active in 1961 following Jânio Quadros' resignation, attempting to prevent João Goulart from assuming the presidency. Another segment of the military—the large garrison stationed in the state of Rio Grande do Sul—by threatening civil war if Goulart was not permitted to take office forced the compromise that brought Goulart to power, with his presidential powers temporarily restricted by the adoption of the parliamentary system. And finally, in 1964 the armed forces ousted Goulart and imposed temporary military rule.

The military thus serves as the arbiter of the Brazilian presidential system. Without at least tacit military consent no man can obtain and retain the presidency. However, the views of the officer corps have not always been monolithic. There have been ardent nationalists and reformers conflicting with supporters of the dominant groups within the post-1945 constitutional system; there have also been some who have felt that professional concerns should predominate, and that the armed forces should not be directly involved in politics. The meeting rooms of the Clube Militar and the Clube Naval have often been forums where conflicting viewpoints could be expressed without openly violating military discipline. Elections of the officers of these clubs have served as indicators as to which groups hold the preponderant position at any given time.

Noncommissioned officers and enlisted men have also organized into clubs which serve political as well as social purposes. A sergeants' revolt was put down in Brasília in 1963, and a demonstration by marine enlisted men, members of the Sailors and Marines Association, was apparently a major factor in triggering Goulart's ouster. A group of rebellious marines barricaded themselves in a downtown Rio de Janeiro building, shouting not only for reforms within the nation but also for reforms of naval regulations. When the mutineers finally surrendered to the army, they were with Goulart's backing granted an amnesty and freed. They held a parade in downtown Rio the next day to celebrate their victory. This open support for insubordination in the ranks apparently provided the catalyst for military action against Goulart; he was deposed during the following week.

The powers conferred by the "Institutional Act"—which passed from the commanders-in-chief of the armed forces to President Castello Branco—mean that while Branco serves through the remainder of Goulart's term, Brazil has a thinly veiled military dictatorship. Even if the military subsequently returns to the barracks and civilian rule is resumed following the 1965 presidential elections, the military veto power will remain. Military interest will have to be served as well as national interest, whether or not the two coincide. Professionalization is not yet the dominant characteristic of the Brazilian military establishment.

The bureaucracy is also a potent political force in the present political system of the nation. In an effort to keep the support of the masses during the Estado Novo, Vargas fostered the initiation of a great deal of social welfare legislation. Not all of the legislated benefits were put into practice, but enough were for Brazil to develop a sizable bureaucratic machine charged with administering social welfare and other governmental programs which touch almost every aspect of human affairs—which affect so large a segment of Brazilian economic and social life, in fact, that many of the demands of the society are apparently channeled through the bureaucracy to the executive rather than through the political parties and the legislative branch. A citizen is more apt to feel that a matter in which the government is in some way concerned can be more successfully expedited through contact with the "right" members of the administrative branch than through contact with political party leaders or legislators. Thus several of the functions found usually to be performed by the political parties in a democratic system—aggregation of demands, simplification of alternatives, and so on—are instead apparently part of the functions of the bureaucracy and the executive in the Brazilian political system today, although evidence on this point is not as yet conclusive.

The bureaucracy also serves as a potent institutional interest group capable of exerting significant pressure on the other arms of government in its own cause. Brazilian administrative departments are generally overstaffed; it is considerably easier to hire than to fire public servants. Thus many government workers are only part-time employees who also hold private jobs or have private law or medical practices. The bureaucracy as a whole forms such a large and influential group that reforms in the area of public administration have been difficult to achieve, especially those which would reduce the number or increase the efficiency of government employees at any level —national, state, or local.

The Roman Catholic Church, although influential, has never had the preeminence in Brazilian political life that it has had in some other Latin American countries. Historically, the Church in many areas of the nation was dependent upon and therefore relatively subservient to the will of the rural patriarchs. It never developed the type of national cohesion in the early years that would have made it a potent political force. Furthermore, in its efforts to hold the allegiance of the masses—particularly descendants of the Negro slaves brought to Brazil from Africa—the Church has had to compete in popularity with the spiritualist sects, a competition in which the Church has not always been victorious.

Today the Church speaks out on political matters—particularly against Communism—but it is only one voice among many. As such it is undoubtedly an influential voice, but by no means a dominant one.

However, the Church has also recently begun to take a vocal position on some of the nation's social problems. The papal encyclicals "Rerum Novarum," "Quadragesimo Anno," and the more recent "Mater et Magistra" have been publicized and interpreted by various clerics to provide the basis for a social doctrine aimed at the reform of some of the basic elements of Brazilian society. Agrarian reform has come in for special consideration, and the Church in the Northeast has begun to be active in forming peasant unions to counteract the influence of *fidelista* Francisco Julião's Peasant Leagues. On these subjects, however, the Brazilian clergy does not always speak with one voice.

The Communications Media

With but few exceptions, freedom of speech and of the press have been maintained in Brazil since the inception of the democracy in 1945.

Each newspaper of the nation is characteristically controlled by a single political party or an influential—and perhaps ambitious—individual. Major cities such as Rio de Janeiro and São Paulo have a multitude of newspapers, each having a relatively small circulation. No newspaper in the country has a truly national distribution. The news coverage of the papers is narrowly concerned with matters of particular interest to the party or individual controlling the paper, and news is regularly slanted to promote such interests. In order to achieve anything resembling a balanced picture of an event or controversy it is often necessary to read a minimum of five or six newspapers. A number of papers deal only in sensationalism. The press in Brazil generally is utilized more as a propaganda medium than as an outlet for unbiased news.

The low rate of literacy, particularly in the interior regions, and the nation's embryonic transportation network make the radio a most important medium of information and influence in the country. The impact of television is as yet minor on the national scene. Only the major cities have television stations, there is as yet no national television network, and the price of television sets is so high as to keep them from mass consumption. Radio, on the other hand, penetrates to almost every village of the nation. In small and remote towns where many families may not have radios of their own, people gather at local stores to hear programs of general interest.

Because of the influence of radio in political communication, the Brazilian government has been more active in regulating the use of the airwaves for political purposes than the use of the press. Such regulation has sometimes provoked complaints that the government is suppressing the opposition. For instance, UDN journalist Carlos Lacerda of Guanabara was for a time banned from speaking on the radio because he was accused of using that medium to incite revolt against the government. At the same time he continued to publish his newspaper, the *Tribuna da Imprensa* of Rio de Janeiro.

Since radio is by all indications a far more effective means of political communication in Brazil than the press, it is likely that its use for political purposes and governmental control of such use will continue to be a source of controversy in the nation. As the availability and use of television increases that medium will undoubtedly join the radio as an important source of political communication and influence.

The Political Culture of Brazil

Like its economic and social life, the political culture of Brazil today is in a transitional stage. The nation was attempting to deal with complex problems of economic development and general national growth within the confines of democratic governmental mechanisms. Such mechanisms by their very nature frequently slow down the decision-making process and thus make it unlikely that rapid, forthright solutions will be applied to pressing national problems. Since representatives of the traditional sector of society are still permitted to grasp and maintain key positions in governmental institutions, changes desired by large and growing sectors of the society are stifled or slowed down at the cost of rising frustration among the affected groups.

Since the present Brazilian political party system—a key element in the operation of any democratic system of government—is not performing well such vital functions as control of the nomination process and simplification of policy alternatives, the Brazilian populace has evidenced considerable disenchantment with the party system, expressed in the popular image of the parties and of the average politician. One result has been continued reliance upon the executive as the principal agent in the political sphere. The executive must set policy, solve problems, be the chief national decision-maker.

The tradition of the strong executive has had a long life and great vitality in Brazilian politics. Its roots are deep in the paternalistic social, economic, and political orientation of the old patriarchal clans. Dom Pedro II served for decades as a benevolent national father figure. During the period of the republic, when political power had its base in the state oligarchies, the president of the nation served as the only figure of real national power, the one element capable of uniting disparate state political machines into some semblance of national action and accord. Getúlio Vargas during the Estado Novo epitomized—and assiduously cultivated—the image of paternalism.

The post-1945 system has not changed this pattern of executive predominance. The political parties have not as yet provided a meaningful alternative to exclusive presidential proposal of solutions for major policy problems. The charismatic personality who promises rapid instead of interminable solutions to pressing national problems, who promises action instead of endless bickering and shifting of position for personal advantage, is in an extremely advantageous position in the current Brazilian political system. Since no really meaningful alternatives to dynamic executive action are at present perceived, the man who gives promise of being capable of performing as the desired national superman may be catapulted to national power without ever stepping outside the bounds of the legal electoral system. The meteoric rise of Jânio Quadros is illustrative of the ease with which an individual possessing the requisite popular appeal can ascend to the most powerful office in the nation. Only his own erratic temperament, which can be credited with his resignation, sidetracked Jânio Quadros from presenting a challenge to the present major political parties in the congressional elections of 1962. These could have shaken the entire basis of the present party system and therefore the present *modus vivendi* of political life in the nation.

In a political system so dependent upon executive leadership and possessing political parties structured to be so little capable of providing leadership, the parliamentary experiment embarked upon following Quadros' resignation had little prospect of success. With the return to the strong-president system, the future of Brazilian political life again turned upon the question, Who occupies the presidential chair? João Goulart was ousted from the presidency with no force of any consequence rising to his defense, not even the bulk of his own party. In the presidency Goulart had not proved himself to be an able administrator. His constant shifting of position alienated even many of his friends. He did not provide the kind of positive leadership the Brazilian political system demanded. This far more than any real or imagined menace of Communist take-over was the likely cause of his downfall.

President Castello Branco, with almost unlimited powers granted him as long as he does not seriously displease the military, has stepped forth as the new leader. He has promised to put aside partisan bickering in order to carry through the reforms of the economic and political system needed to return Brazil to the path of relative stability and continued economic development. The power of the military stands ready to back him up in the accomplishment of these not entirely compatible goals. His success or failure and in all likelihood that of his successors for some time to come will depend primarily on their personal ability to utilize the vast powers of the presidential office to give national policy purpose and direction.

The Brazilian traditional groups have shown thus far a willingness to compromise with modernity—to accept it and even to promote it so long as they do not entirely lose their upper-class status and are not forced completely from the seats of power. Most of them have embraced, not rejected, economic development as a national goal. The pace, however, will likely be set by the national president. Until the organs and institutions of popular control develop greater ability to respond with coherence and dispatch to the demands of the populace, the executive will remain the dominant figure in the Brazilian political process. The method of his anointment will in all likelihood remain less important to the people as a whole than the effectiveness of his performance.

Governmental Institutions

Adopted on September 18, 1946, the present constitution of Brazil provides the nation with a presidential system, a bicameral national legislature, an independent judiciary, and a federal relationship between Brazil's twenty-two states and the national government.

The National Congress

The national congress of Brazil consists of two houses, a senate and a chamber of deputies. The senate is composed of three members elected from each of the twenty-two states—a total of sixty-six members. Senators are elected for eight-year terms, elections being held every four years; one-third of the seats are renewed in one election and two-thirds in the next. Substitutes (*suplentes*) are elected simultaneously with the senator they are to replace. These replacements are called to fill vacancies caused by death, illness, or other inability to serve. If no legally elected substitute is available, special elections are called to fill the vacancy, provided more than nine months remain in the senator's term. To be a candidate for the senate one must be a native-born Brazilian citizen over thirty-five years of age. The vice-president of the nation presides over the senate, but he may vote only in case of a tie.

The chamber of deputies is composed of members from each state and territory elected according to the principle of proportional representation. The number of members is fixed by law, each state being assigned one deputy for each 150,000 inhabitants until the total reaches twenty deputies; above that one seat is assigned for each 250,000 inhabitants. Each state, however, is guaranteed a minimum of seven seats and each territory is guaranteed one. The 1962 chamber of deputies had 409 members. Vacancies are filled by calling, according to the descending order of votes received, the remaining members of the party or coalition slates of candidates who did not initially gain seats. To be a candidate for federal deputy one must be a native-born Brazilian citizen over twenty-one years of age. The chamber elects its own presiding officer.

The national congress meets according to constitutional requirement from March 15 to December 15 each year. The president of the republic or one-third of the members of either house may call a special session. Proposed legislation may be initiated by any individual legislator, by a committee of either house, or by the president of the republic. Seats on committees, committee chairmanships, and positions on the chambers' official directive body, are assigned insofar as possible according to proportional representation of the national political parties holding seats in the house. The senate has the authority to approve or veto the appointments of certain presidential nominees, including judges and ambassadors. Both the senate and the chamber of deputies must approve treaties. Acts of the national congress can be vetoed wholly or in part by the president if he considers them to be unconstitutional or against the national interest. A two-thirds vote of the national congress meeting in joint session is necessary to override a presidential veto.

The President

The president and the vice-president of the republic are elected simultaneously, but in separate elections, for five-year terms. Candidates must be native-born Brazilian citizens of at least thirty-five years of age. In case of vacancy in the presidency the line of succession is the vice-president, the president of the chamber of deputies, the president of the senate, and the president of the federal supreme court. If both the presidency and the vice-presidency become vacant during the first three years of the term, special elections are called within sixty days to fill the vacancies for the remainder of the term. If the vacancies occur during the last two years of the term, the national congress elects someone to serve as president for the remainder of the term. Among his many powers, the president has the power to appoint and dismiss ministers of state, has general authority over foreign affairs, and serves as commander-in-chief of the armed forces.

The Administration

Ministers of state are appointed by and responsible to the president, but either house of the national congress or any committee may request a minister to appear before it to give information on a previously designated subject, and may compel his appearance if necessary. The number of departments and ministries is fixed by acts of the national congress.

Members of the federal civil service are granted many protections by the constitution itself. Civil servants are granted tenure after two years of service if they gained their positions through competitive examination and after five years of service if they were appointed without competitive examination. They may then be dismissed only in consequence of the ruling of an administrative trial in which they are assured of an adequate defense. If a civil servant having tenure finds his job legislated out of existence, he must be paid full salary until another job is found for him equal in nature and in salary to the one lost. Retirement is compulsory at seventy years of age and voluntary after thirty-five years of service. Those with thirty or more years of service are retired at full pay. The Departamento Administrativo do Servico Publico is charged with the administration of the career civil service.

The Judiciary

The Brazilian judiciary is made up of federal and state courts of general jurisdiction and a series of special courts that deal with specific subjects.

At the apex of the system is the federal supreme court (Supremo Tribunal Federal) which sits in the capital of the nation. This is primarily a court of appellate jurisdiction, hearing cases coming from other federal or state courts in which a lower court's decision is claimed to be contrary to the federal constitution or to the literal reading of a treaty or federal law, a federal law is declared unconstitutional, or any of a variety of other federal questions is involved. The supreme court also has original jurisdiction in certain types of cases, such as cases involving the president, ministers of state, ambassadors, or certain other public officials; disputes between states or between states and the national government; and conflicts of jurisdiction between lower courts. The constitution specifically gives the federal supreme court the power to declare acts or parts of acts of the national congress unconstitutional.

The supreme court is composed of a minimum of eleven justices with others added by law if desired. Justices are nominated by the president, and their appointment must be approved by the senate. They must be native-born Brazilian citizens of at least thirty-five years of age. Appointments are for life. Retirement is compulsory at seventy or for proved disability; voluntary retirement at full pay is permissible after thirty years of service.

Below the federal supreme court is an appellate court (Tribunal Federal de Recursos) that also sits in the federal capital. The national congress has the authority to create additional appellate courts if the appellate court itself requests it and the federal supreme court approves. The congress sets the territorial jurisdiction of such courts.

Each state has its own system of courts and judges. These courts have original jurisdiction over cases arising under federal as well as under state law. The national constitution sets the minimum requirements for the appointees to these judicial posts.

In addition to the hierarchy of state and federal courts, three special court systems are provided for by the constitution to deal with disputes involving the military, elections, and labor respectively.

The military court system consists of a Superior Tribunal Militar and such regional tribunals and judgeships as the law specifies. These courts hear all cases arising under military law and involving military personnel or others attached to the military services. Civilians may also be tried by the military courts if they are accused of crimes against the external security of the nation or its military institutions.

The electoral courts consist of a Tribunal Superior Eleitoral, regional electoral tribunals located in each state and in the Federal District, and subsidiary electoral boards and judges. The supreme electoral court is composed of judges chosen by the federal supreme court from among its members, others from the federal appellate court and the highest court of the Federal District, and some members appointed by the president from a list of names submitted by the federal supreme court. The supreme electoral court accords legal recognition to national political parties and their leadership bodies, certifies the election of the president and vice-president of the republic, and hears disputes concerning elections and the electoral law arising in the lower electoral courts. The regional electoral courts register the state leadership bodies and all candidates in state elections. They handle the administration and supervision of all elections in their state. They hear cases arising from complaints against decisions or actions of the electoral boards and judges located throughout the state who are in charge of registering voters, manning polling places on election days, and counting the ballots. When appeals are made to the supreme electoral court, decisions of that body are final unless a law has been declared contrary to the federal constitution. Then appeal to the federal supreme court is possible.

Courts in the final group—the labor courts—are composed of a superior labor court (Tribunal Superior de Trabalho), regional labor courts, and judges or boards of conciliation and judgment. The jurisdiction of these courts extends to all individual and collective disputes between employers and employees and any dispute which arises concerning work regulated by special legislation. Almost every aspect of labor-management relations falls within the jurisdiction of these courts.

Most judicial appointments, once certain conditions have been met, are for life terms. As in other Latin American countries, Roman law rather than English common law is applied throughout the court system, and the jury system is little used.

Federal-State Relations

Although a federal system was not adopted in Brazil until the inception of the republic, the states have considerable vitality and importance in the Brazilian political system today. The amount and nature of the national government's control over state political organization and operation has fluctuated considerably during the nation's history, the greatest amount of centralization being achieved during the Estado Novo. Under the Constitution of 1946 the national government retains considerable power over the states, enough for it and not the states to predominate within the federal relationship.

The national government is empowered by the constitution to act in almost every phase of national life when it so desires. Its powers to act in such areas as economic regulation, social welfare, education, etc., are directly spelled out in the constitution, not implied, as in the constitution of the United States. The states are given specific concurrent powers and, in addition, all powers are reserved to the states which are not implicitly or explicitly denied them by the constitution.

Concerning the vital area of taxation, the constitution provides that there can be no duplication of national, state, and municipal taxes; if the national government imposes taxes of a certain type or if it taxes a specific item, this action automatically excludes the states from levying similar taxes. The national government is empowered to tax imports, consumption, production, income, profits—all of the most lucrative sources of funds. The states may tax such items as sales, inheritance, and export of merchandise from the state to foreign countries up to a maximum of 5 percent *ad valorem*. The *municípios* may tax property, public entertainment, and a limited number of other items. Because the national government is empowered to impose taxes of the types that are the greatest revenue producers, the constitution also stipulates that the naional government must turn a certain percentage of its tax income over to the *municípios*. The dependence of the states upon the federal government for financing most of the governmental projects carried on within them is the most important single source of national governmental control over the states.

The constitution gives the national government power to intervene in the states under certain circumstances. The state government may be temporarily replaced by an "interventor" appointed by the president of the republic. The interventor runs the state government until the "abnormality" which caused the intervention has been corrected and state authorities can safely be returned to power. Intervention is permitted in order to put an end to civil war, assure execution of a judicial order or decision, reorganize the finances of the state, or assure the state a "republican form of government." The power to intervene in the states was used frequently during the years of the republic and constantly during the Estado Novo. After the adoption of the Constitution of 1946 it fell into disuse, until, in the military assumption of power in 1964, the governor of Pernambuco was among those removed from office. The power of intervention remains as a potent threat to state political independence.

The basic vitality of the Brazilian federal system is not to be found in the constitutional delegation of powers—a delegation that ensures national supremacy—but in the psychological attachment and identification of many Brazilian citizens with their states. The present state boundaries can be traced back in many areas to the original *capitanias* set up by the Portuguese crown. The great distances between major population centers have made state capitals attractive as centers of cultural and educational life. The state capital of the most important state of a region characteristically has become the focal point of cultural, educational, and commercial activities for the neighboring smaller states. The extreme variations in regional development have heightened the sense of difference between one region and another—particularly between the northeast and the south. The states, serving as basic units of administrative and, particularly, political organization, have an extremely important place in Brazilian political life in spite of the very definite supremacy of the national government.

State and Local Government

State governments have basically the same organizational structure as the national government. The broad outlines of state organization are set forth in the national constitution, but each state has its own constitution in addition. Each state government is headed by a popularly elected governor who serves either a four-year or a five-year term, depending upon the state. Most states also elect a vice-governor, but a few do not. All have unicameral legislatures; state deputies serve four-year terms, state and national legislative elections being held simultaneously. Each state has an independent judicial branch, with appeal possible from the highest state court to the federal courts.

The states are divided into *municípios,* units roughly equivalent to the United States counties but which combine the functions of both city and county governments and serve as the basic unit of state administration. Each *município* is headed by a popularly elected prefect (mayor), although in certain types of *municípios*—those, for example, where military installations are located—the governor may appoint the prefect. State governors are also empowered by the constitution to appoint the prefect of the *município* designated as the state capital, but in most states today this official is instead popularly elected. Each *município* also elects a council to serve as its legislative body, and maintains an administrative organization.

Public Policy

Economic growth may be considered the principal concern of Brazilian public policy makers today. It lies at the base of almost all national controversies, even those concerning foreign affairs.

The role of the Brazilian national government in stimulating the economic development of the country is a considerable one. The greatest single factor inhibiting growth in the nation is the lack of capital, particularly foreign exchange. Capital is needed not only to start new industries but also to expand and improve power resources, the transportation network, and all of the other complementary facilities without which industry cannot grow. Private capital is either not available for such investment or else is invested in such things as land or urban rental property—property which traditionally has been associated with social prestige and is also more proof against inflation.

The government has stepped in to build power facilities, such as the Paulo Afonso dam on the São Francisco river in the northeast, and basic industries, such as the Volta Redonda steel mill located between Rio de Janeiro and São Paulo. Laws have also been passed to stimulate the development of industry, notably the laws prohibiting the importation of automobiles and automotive parts, which served to stimulate the development of a Brazilian automotive industry. This was part of a governmental drive to promote economic diversification, to lessen the dependence of the nation on the export of raw materials and foodstuffs—particularly coffee. The intervention of the national government in the economy of Brazil is not an area of controversy in the nation today; instead it is seen as a necessity.

On the domestic scene three problem areas stand out as sources of continuing controversy: land reform, inflation, and nationalism.

Land Reform

Controversy generally arises whenever the government seeks to take actions that would have the effect of changing or adversely affecting the fortunes of the traditional sector of the society. The most prominent issue of this type today is the problem of land reform. Since land in Brazil, as in most Latin American countries, has been the symbol of wealth and social prestige, wealthy individuals in the nation have tended to acquire large holdings, not all of which are put into production. Limitation of the amount of land that can be held by any individual or expropriation of lands not in production is frequently suggested as a means of promoting a more equitable distribution of wealth in the nation. Since such programs attack the very core of traditional life and culture, their suggestion inevitably results in heated controversy. Brazil is a nation with an abundance of land, much of it uninhabited, and so the issue of land reform is not so charged emotionally as in some other nations; but it is a continuing and as yet unsolved national problem.

Brazilian politicians speak almost unanimously in favor of instituting an "agrarian reform" program—but their definitions of what constitutes agrarian reform vary widely. Some want extensive, immediate expropriation and redistribution of large landholdings to landless peasants, particularly in the Northeast. An amendment to the constitution is seen as a necessary preliminary to the accomplishment of such a program, since the present constitution authorizes expropriation, but requires immediate payment *in cash* to the owners of the land. Given the state of Brazilian finances, any large-scale program providing cash payments is viewed as an absolute impossibility at the present time. Therefore supporters of rapid and extensive land redistribution programs claim that any proposal that does not provide for change of the constitution to permit payment in long-term bonds is a false program aimed at providing the peasants with a palliative while not accomplishing any meaningful change.

Those who do not wish to go so far or so fast claim that the vast expanse of empty land in the nation obviates the necessity for extensive breaking up of productive large estates. This, they claim, would only destroy the nation's agricultural productivity without providing any real relief to the peasants.

Instead they favor relocation of landless peasants on unused land or the breaking up only of estates not being cultivated, with payment in cash to the owners. They propose that the program be accompanied by extensive technical assistance to the new property-owners plus provision for adequate credit.

The controversy remains unresolved, although at the moment those favoring the second course appear to be in the stronger political position.

Inflation

In the urban areas a most important area of concern is continuing rampant inflation. Governmental investments in such nonproductive facilities as power installations, roads, and the construction of Brasília have poured money into the economy but without a proportional rise in the availability of consumer goods at prices within the range of the average citizen. Governments have issued large amounts of printing-press money to pay for their activities. At the same time, high import taxes have been placed on most consumers' goods in order to promote Brazilian industry and conserve limited foreign exchange, while production costs in new and frequently inefficient Brazilian industries are often higher than comparative costs of imported goods. Moreover, limited transportation and refrigeration or storage facilities often cause food-stuffs to be in limited supply in various areas of the nation. The decline in world prices for Brazil's principal export commodities—particularly coffee—has caused even greater shortages of foreign exchange, especially dollars, just at the time when the demands of the nation's growing industry are increasing the need for greater and greater dollar expenditures for the importation of machinery, parts, and other industrial products. It has also contributed to the continuing devaluation of the *cruzeiro* in relation to the dollar and the concomitant increase in the cost to Brazilians of items which must be purchased with dollars, items which include such absolute necessities as oil and other petroleum products. The rampant inflation that has resulted from these and other factors has made living on a fixed income, installment buying, long-term lending for mortgages, etc., almost impossible.

Control of this inflation, or mitigating its effects on the populace, is a constant concern of Brazilian governments. Many Brazilian economists, however, feel that such inflation is a normal and necessary part of rapid economic development and oppose austerity measures which might be taken by the government to curb it. These economists see the problem as a choice between rapid growth accompanied by inflation, on the one hand, and balanced budgets, a stable currency, and economic stagnation, on the other; they do not believe that fiscal stability and rapid economic growth can be combined. Brazilian governments to date have taken few measures capable of curbing the inflation; instead they have sought to take such measures as seem appropriate to mitigate its effect somewhat on the individual citizen. No real solution to this problem is currently in sight.

Nationalism

Nationalism is a force of continuing importance. Investment of foreign capital in Brazil is acknowledged to be of vital importance if the nations is to continue a program of rapid economic development. Yet nationalistic sentiment identifies foreign capital with foreign control and therefore views it as a threat to national sovereignty. Hence many attempts are led by nationalistic elements to limit the entry of foreign capital, to control the remission of profits, and to regulate strictly the operation of foreign-controlled concerns within the nation. The oil industry and public utilities have been the most frequent targets of nationalistic propaganda.

Getúlio Vargas utilized the spirit of nationalism to advance his own political fortunes. He regularly utilized nationalistic appeals in his campaigning, although his actions in office were normally not as extreme as his words. During Vargas' regime the oil industry became a principal object of nationalistic attack, and the industry was finally nationalized; all exploration, production, and refining of oil was to be carried on by a government corporation called Petrobrás. Foreign firms were permitted to continue to distribute petroleum products imported into the nation, but all other of their properties in Brazil were expropriated and all concessions canceled.

Brazil has however not had sufficient capital to carry on exploration and development on the scale necessary if the nation is ever to become self-sufficient in petroleum. Nationalistic sentiment has prohibited the reentry of foreign oil companies that might today be willing to undertake such activities. The net result is that the nation is still dependent upon imported oil. These imports must be paid for in dollars and these payments constitute a considerable drain on the nation's limited dollar supply. But nationalist sentiment is so strong that no change in policy is in sight.

Foreign-owned utilities, particularly the telephone and the electric light companies, are also objects of nationalistic attack. These industries, for a variety of reasons, have not expanded their facilities rapidly enough to meet the growing needs of the nation. Since their product is one that is utilized daily by the common citizen, failures in service are directly seen and felt by the populace, and nationalistic sentiment is directed particularly against these foreign-owned industries. Part of the facilities of the light and telephone companies have already been expropriated by governments of some of the states. More actions of this type are likely, and within a few years the telephone and electric power industries will probably be entirely government-owned and -operated. These expropriations are not simply domestic issues; since foreign-owned companies are involved, they become international issues.

Foreign Affairs

Relations between the United States and Brazil have traditionally been very friendly. In the years when the United States was intervening frequently in Latin American nations, Brazil, since it was located outside of the Caribbean area in which the interventions took place, was not affected; consequently, some of the extreme antagonisms which were fostered by these actions in other Latin American countries did not develop. Brazil fought on the side of the United States in World War II, actually sending troops to fight in Italy—one of the few Latin American countries which have sent troops outside the hemisphere.

Since the end of World War II, however, the spirit of nationalism has been growing in the nation. The United States, because of its predominant role in Latin American affairs, has been the natural target of nationalist attack. Brazilians, influenced by their location far from the centers of the struggle, often feel themselves very remote from the controversies engendered by the Cold War. A spirit of neutralism has been growing within the nation for at least two reasons: many Brazilians feel that the nation has become a mere pawn between two gigantic forces, neither of which has any real concern for the welfare of Brazil; and the growth of nationalist feeling has been encouraged by the idea that blindly following the lead of the United States in international affairs means demeaning Brazilian sovereignty. The net result has been that in recent years Brazil has become at times a somewhat recalcitrant nation in its dealings with the United States, exhibiting more and more hesitancy in accepting the policy lead of the United States on international and Latin American problems. Brazil still counts itself firmly a Western nation, but its leadership has become less likely to interpret this as meaning that it must accept United States policy orientation on international questions without first considering Brazilian interests.

In his short tenure as president, Jânio Quadros emphasized this trend toward neutralism. Goulart also could not always be counted upon to follow United States policy orientations, particularly in the economic sphere. In recent years Brazil has recognized the Soviet Union, signed trade agreements with the USSR and other Communist nations, opposed overt United States action against Fidel Castro in Cuba, and refused to embark upon the program of fiscal austerity designed to curb inflation which was deemed essential by many United States economists and government officials. The expropriation of foreign-owned utility companies by some of the state governments caused consternation in those United States circles which view any such action as a socialistic prelude to Communist take-over. Fears of expropriation spreading to other areas of business, disputes about compensation for properties already taken, and passage of a law limiting the amount of profit foreign firms could remit to their home countries in any given year caused a decline in the number of United States concerns willing to consider investment in Brazil.

The Castello Branco administration has, temporarily at least, reversed the course of national policy on such matters. Relations have been broken with the Fidel Castro regime in Cuba; Brazil's position as a nation firmly aligned with the West has been reaffirmed; greater cooperation with the

United States in financial matters has been promised. But the underlying causes of the previous swing toward neutralism remain and its spirit will not likely disappear overnight. The Cold War is still seen as but remotely connected with the major problems facing the Brazilian nation today. Prospects still seem to be, accordingly, that as Brazil matures economically and politically, she will take an even more independent stand on foreign policy matters.

In terms of size and resource potential Brazil seems destined to become the major nation of South America. Such a development would in all likelihood strain Brazilian relations with Argentina, its natural competitor for leadership in South American affairs. If the United States is to deal with Brazil on friendly and effective terms in the future, these factors will have to be taken into account. Moreover, there will have to be an increasing recognition on the part of United States governmental officials, Congressmen, and the general public that a policy suitable for United States dealings with the Dominican Republic, Nicaragua, or Paraguay may not be appropriate in United States relations with Brazil.

NOTES FOR CHAPTER XX

1. United Nations, Statistical Office, Department of Economic and Social Affairs, *Demographic Yearbook, 1960*, United Nations, New York, 1961, p. 379.
2. Constitution of the Empire of Brazil, Title V. The entire text of this constitution in English is published in Herman G. James, *The Constitutional System of Brazil*, Carnegie Institution of Washington, Washington, 1923, pp. 237-252.
3. Robert J. Alexander, "Brazilian Tenentismo," *Hispanic American Historical Review*, XXXVI, May 1956, pp. 229-242, examines the phenomenon of the *tenentes*.
4. Karl Lowenstein, *Brazil under Vargas*, Macmillan, New York, 1942, offers the most complete description of the government of Brazil during this period.
5. Robert J. Alexander, *Labor Relations in Argentina, Brazil, and Chile*, McGraw-Hill, New York, 1962, pp. 25-136, discusses these developments and explains in some detail the present relationship between government, business, and organized labor in Brazil.
6. *Ibid.*, p. 65.
7. Robert J. Alexander, "Brazil, Argentina, and Chile," in *Labor in Developing Economies*, Walter Galenson (Ed.), University of California Press, Berkeley and Los Angeles, 1962, p. 155.
8. *Ibid.*, p. 161.

SELECTED BIBLIOGRAPHY

Robert J. Alexander, *Labor Relations in Argentina, Brazil and Chile*, McGraw-Hill, New York, 1962.

Fernando de Azevedo, *Brazilian Culture: An Introduction to the Study of Culture in Brazil*, translated by William Rex Crawford, Macmillan, New York, 1950.

João Panida Calogeras, *A History of Brazil* (*A Formação Historica do Brasil*), translated, edited, and last chapter written by Percy Alvin Martin, University of North Carolina Press, Chapel Hill, 1939.

Euclides de Cunha, *Rebellion in the Backlands* (*Os Sertões*), translated by Samuel Putnam, University of Chicago Press, Chicago, 1957.

Gilberto Freyre, *The Masters and the Slaves: A Study in the Development of Brazilian Culture*, translated by Samuel Putnam, 2d English ed., Alfred A. Knopf, New York, 1956.

——, *The Mansions and the Shanties: The Making of Modern Brazil.* Translated and edited by Harriet de Onís, Knopf, New York, 1963.

——, *New World in the Tropics: the Culture of Modern Brazil*, Alfred A. Knopf, New York, 1959.

Celso Furtado, *The Economic Growth of Brazil: A Survey from Colonial to Modern Times.* Translated by Ricardo W. de Aguiar and Eric C. Drysdale, University of California Press, Berkeley and Los Angeles, 1963.

Marvin Harris, *Town and Country in Brazil*, Columbia University Press, New York, 1956.

Harry W. Hutchinson, *Village and Plantation Life in Northeastern Brazil*, University of Washington Press, Seattle, 1957.

Herman G. James, *The Constitutional System of Brazil*, Carnegie Institution of Washington, Washington, D.C., 1923.

Carolina Maria de Jesús, *Child of the Dark*, Dutton, New York, 1962.

Karl Lowenstein, *Brazil under Vargas.* Macmillan, New York, 1942.

Richard M. Morse, *From Community to Metropolis: A Biography of São Paulo, Brazil*, University of Florida Press, Gainesville, 1958.

João F. Normano, *Brazil: A Study of Economic Types*, University of North Carolina Press, Chapel Hill, 1935.

Stefan H. Robock, *Brazil's Developing Northeast: A Study of Regional Planning and Foreign Aid*, Brookings Institution, Washington, D.C., 1963.

William Lytle Schurz, *Brazil: The Infinite Country*, Dutton, New York, 1961.

T. Lynn Smith, *Brazil: People and Institutions*, 2d ed., Louisiana State University Press, Baton Rouge, 1954.

T. Lynn Smith, and Alexander Marchant (Eds.), *Brazil: Portrait of Half a Continent*, Dryden, New York, 1951.

Charles Wagley, *Amazon Town: A Study of Man in the Tropics*, Macmillan, New York, 1953.

——, *An Introduction to Brazil*, Columbia University Press, New York, 1963.

Mary W. Williams, *Dom Pedro the Magnanimous, Second Emperor of Brazil*, University of North Carolina Press, Chapel Hill, 1937.

George Wythe, Royce A. Wight, and Harold M. Midkiff, *Brazil: An Expanding Economy*, Twentieth Century Fund, New York, 1949.

Martin C. Needler

LATIN AMERICA

DIMENSIONS OF VARIATION

THE TWENTY independent republics referred to as "Latin America" share enough characteristics to make the distortions which are inherent in generalization tolerable for many purposes. They share many cultural attributes —in religion, in the heritage of Roman law, and in subtler questions of attitudes and values; and all except Brazil and Haiti share the more specific cultural complex which is the common property of speakers of Spanish.

The histories of these countries are partly similar and partly identical in the colonial experience common to all of them, and they have all been subject to the same influence in the period since winning independence from the colonial power. In the political realm, the influence of the political institutions of the United States is clearly marked. The republics further share many structural patterns stemming from the fact that most of them have dual economies—one sector dependent on world trade and geared to the revenue from the export of primary commodities, agricultural or mineral, and the other sector a fairly self-contained subsistence producer.

Finally, their commonalty also derives from the feeling of common identity among the twenty states, each country being sensitive to developments in the others. The common features that exist reinforce each other and create new shared experiences as similar problems give rise to similar attempts at solution and to political movements directed at similar ends.

Each of the chapters of this book discusses one of the states of the area, following a basic pattern of the key components of its political system. Let us put the enterprise as a whole in perspective by taking a look at the range of variation within each of these key components.

The Social and Economic Background

The ecological context—the matrix of geographic, economic, and social factors within which the political system operates—is of central importance for the understanding of the basic causative elements. *Geography* determines economic potentialities. The givens of soil, climate, mineral deposits, and barriers to communication set limits to what is economically feasible and desirable. Moreover, geography in a larger sense poses the strategic questions which govern relations with other states; and the local wars which represent the breakdown of normal interstate relations have been critical for the politics of several countries. For instance, everything about Panama, including its very existence as a state, has been determined by its location on the narrowest strip of land separating Atlantic and Pacific in the central portion of the continental land mass.

The importance of *economic factors* for the understanding of politics hardly needs elaboration in our age. Yet the particular modes in which economic factors relate to the political order need more careful examination than they have received hitherto. Charles Anderson's conclusion that Honduras may be in a strong position to evolve in a democratic direction because of its very poverty is a valuable corrective to the current tendency to associate democracy with a high standard of living, and James Busey suggests that a similar comment may be made about Costa Rica. Certainly the major problems which political systems face today are economic ones, and the orientation of major population groups on political questions is determined primarily by economic factors.

Of central significance is the *ethnic composition* of the population of each country. Most of the societies discussed are polyethnic. Their populations are composed of unintegrated strains of diverse origins; and class identification and economic activity are often ethnically determined. The major population elements encountered in the area are (1) the aboriginal inhabitants; (2) the heirs of the Spaniards and Portuguese who settled during the colonial period; (3) the descendants of African slaves brought over during that period and the years immediately succeeding; (4) communities of post-Independence immigrants from Europe and Asia, sometimes unintegrated into the national population and forming separate communities like those of the resident aliens more recently arrived from Europe and the United States; and (5) various mixtures of the above, the most common being the *mestizo*, the descendant of Indian and European ancestors.

Because patterns of settlement, voluntary and forced, differed from one ethnic group to another in relation to climate and topography, the area today shows ecologies or man-milieu complexes of several distinct types. Some prevalent patterns are as follows.

(1) Tropical and subtropical sea-level regions where a population with a heavy Negro admixture is engaged in large-scale primary production for the export market, working on plantations of sugar, cotton, or bananas or in the oilfields, often under overseers who are resident aliens or recent immigrants, sometimes working for foreign companies or individuals. This is a common pattern in the islands and on the coasts of the Caribbean and on the coasts of the northern half of South America.

(2) Temperate to cold regions on the plateaus and in the valleys of the high mountain ranges where heavily Indian populations, using primitive methods, grow food staples in autonomous villages or on

large estates or work in mines. This is a pattern typical of Bolivia, Peru, Ecuador, and to some extent Mexico.

(3) Temperature or semi-arid plains where thinly scattered populations of European and mestizo character grow wheat or herd cattle on large landholding units—Argentina, Uruguay, and parts of Paraguay, Brazil and Central America.

(4) Temperate hilly areas where coffee is picked by individuals of various ethnic backgrounds on small private holdings—in Haiti, Costa Rica, El Salvador, Colombia, Mexico—and on large holdings in Brazil and parts of Colombia.

(5) Large cities where upper and middle classes of European descent engage in commercial, administrative, and professional activities and are heavy consumers of imported goods, lower classes of mestizos or mulattoes are employed primarily in service occupations but also in the manufacturing and processing of raw materials, and resident aliens and recent immigrants are active in trade, representing foreign interests or owning and operating retail stores.

This is a gross classification; refinements of it would yield understanding in greater depth. For example, Indian cultures vary from group to group, variations which today continue to account for some of the differences in national character found among states of the region. Similarly, cultural differences have survived from groups of Spaniards of different origin who emigrated to the various areas of the New World. As James Busey points out, the fact that Costa Rica was settled heavily by Basques and Catalans, accustomed to working on their own small and medium holdings, had its consequence in the landholding structure of the Costa Rica of today; perhaps one ought rather to say that Basques and Catalans came to Costa Rica because their type of landholding was possible there. In his chapter on Colombia, John Martz points out the influence of the variety of origins of the Spanish immigrants in forming the distinctive characters of the regions of that country.

Historical Factors

Given the basic features of the social and physical context of the political system, one has next to take account of another set of autonomous causal forces—the nation's historical tradition. Part of that tradition, to be sure, will consist of themes derivative from the country's geographic and human contexts; but much of it will include "primary" causal factors for whose ultimate origin one must look outside the frame of reference of the ecological givens entirely.

First among these exogenous or accidental influences there might be mentioned the reorientations or mutations induced in national development by *the innovating actions of individual statesmen.* As Dr. Lindahl makes

clear, Uruguay's course of development was radically altered because of the views of José Batlle y Ordóñez. Contrast the divergent paths taken since the second decade of the century by three states that until that time seemed to find themselves in fairly similar situations: Uruguay, Argentina, and Chile. Uruguay has become a peaceful and democratic welfare state; Chile has remained an uneasy oligarchy whose public policy appears ever more inconsistent with modern requirements; Argentine governments tried in vain to hold back the rising tide of working-class expectations, only to have it inundate with that much more power and ruthlessness the structures not only of social feudalism but of constitutional government as well in the rule of Juan D. Perón. Surely one can perceive behind these differences in evolution the differences in personality and policy among the three great Radical-Liberal statesmen who were given the opportunity to renovate their societies: Batlle of Uruguay, who not only brought peace and democracy to his country but laid the groundwork for the solution of problems that had as yet barely shown themselves; Arturo Alessandri of Chile, who was prepared to meet the challenge of the most urgent needs of his time, but stopped short of creative acts of structural change which would have made the way easier for future generations of Chileans; and Hipólito Irigoyen of Argentina, coming to power past his time, in an age he did not understand, prepared only to liquidate the problems that should have been solved a generation before, and refusing to come to terms with the most imperative demands of the moment.

One could multiply examples. If Mexico has managed to break out of the vicious circle in which her politics was trapped for so long and develop into a liberal and peaceable society, this is surely due to a succession of deliberate acts of statesmanship framed to this end, among which was a crucial decision taken by President Plutarco Elías Calles, as the chapter on Mexico endeavors to show. And Robert Alexander has written elsewhere, with his usual insight, of the significance of the fact that Juan Perón *chose* to be a dictator when he could have been instead a great democratic leader.

In this category of factors not included in the human and physical givens of the matrix of explanation there must also be listed *the unpremeditated consequences of wars*. A war is often begun with concrete purposes in view, but has a way of outgrowing the original purposes and imposing its own requirements, plus a set of unanticipated consequences, on the participants. Paraguay is the leading example of a state whose development has been dominated by the unplanned consequences of warfare, as Professor Lott makes clear; and similar influences are visible in the development of Bolivia.

Finally, a leading exogenous influence on national development is *the impact of secular world economic events*, which have led in some countries both to sudden political-economic crises and to long-term reshapings of the socio-economic structure. The deterioration in the terms of trade for most of the area—that is, the tendency of the prices of the things Latin America must import to rise, while the prices of her exports decline—may

prove to be such a change. The economists are not in agreement on all of the factors responsible for this situation, but the fact itself appears incontrovertible; and it presents a major obstacle to the success of programs of economic development in the area.

Similar economic shifts in conditions of world markets have been of importance in the past. The Great Depression ushered in governments of a social-revolutionary orientation; the high level of export prices during the Korean War enabled a generation of dictators to become associated in the popular mind with good times and full employment; and so on.

Besides a set of timeless geographic and social givens and a set of irrationally timed "accidental" historical factors, time itself, in the sense of social time, is a dimension of comparability among the Latin American states. It makes sense to think of the states of the region as standing at different stages of a process of change through time from one situation of equilibrium to another—at different stages of political development. Here we are no longer drawing comparisons in terms of factors which can be used in causal explanation, but have moved on to simpler *descriptive* comparisons.

One has to beware of falling into inviting fallacies here; to speak of a sequence of stages of political development does not mean that any given country cannot be arrested indefinitely at one stage, or that regression to a previous stage is not possible. What it does mean is that the influence of "modern" ideas and practices is steadily encroaching on traditional societies; that modern values and ideas have greater attractive power than traditional ones and, however gradually, eventually win out over them, forcing modification in institutions and informal patterns of behavior; and that the speed of this process varies in accordance with the accessibility of the society to influences from more developed states and with the depth of the roots of traditional behavior.

If such arrest and regression do occur, then many of the elements of difference exhibited by the Latin American republics will derive from the fact that they have arrived at different stages of the process. Ecuador, with a population strongly rooted in Indian ways, with a capital city very much isolated (until the coming of air traffic) high in the Andes, will exhibit in its politics many more features typical of an era of ascribed status—stronger class lines, for example, as Professor Blanksten shows—than Argentina or Uruguay, with European populations of recent arrival and shallow roots, concentrated in seaports, and living in continuing intimate contact with European ideas. Not that Argentina will always be a stable democracy; this has certainly not been the case. But dictatorship in Argentina has been of a very modern variety; Dr. Barager suggests that it has been dictatorship which has proclaimed its goals to be those of democracy, equality, and social progress, even though its attainment of those goals was apparent and not real.

Among the indices of a country's stage of political evolution are such things as the proportion of literates in its population, the circulation of its daily newspapers, the progressiveness of the incidence of its taxes—how closely taxation is related to ability to pay—and the proportion of its population living in cities. The changes associated with modernization may or may not be "good"; that is not the point. They do seem to have greater survival value, however, and so become increasingly predominant.

Political Processes

Two further dimensions of variation among political systems relate to their informal political processes: their party systems and their systems of interest groups. The *interest groups* active in a polity will vary according to the contours of the country's economy. Broadly speaking, the major groups are the same from one country to the next, although the importance of each shows marked variation. Their aims and issue orientations may also differ somewhat. The armed forces, for example, generally the key interest group in any country, may form a group of nonpolitical civil servants performing hardly more than their allotted function—say in Uruguay—or a pressure group concerned primarily with its members' perquisites, or a constitutional arbiter and guardian, or a policy-making elite.

While the role of groups as interests varies with relation to the country's economic and social structure, their role as contenders for power depends principally on its stage of political development. As development takes place, the political importance of the social elite declines rapidly; so does that of the organized students—Professor Alexander makes this point in relation to Bolivian politics, and its validity is clear elsewhere. The political role of the army declines, while the power of organized labor and of the political parties is augmented.

Party systems may be described in terms of several sets of characteristics. One is the number of parties of importance—not simply the number that exist, for parties are likely to be multitudinous, but the number of those which are of account in the securing of positions of public authority. Another is the degree of personalism which the parties embody, the degree to which they are dependent on the will and the popular following of a single leading individual. Personalism stands in inverse relation to permanence of party organization, the extreme case of personalism being found in the party organized solely to support the candidacy of one individual in one election. Parties of this type are not uncommon.

The party's ideological orientation and its position on concrete issues are of course crucial and are related to the range and nature of the groups whose electoral support it commands, and those which provide it with leadership (they are not necessarily the same). Finally, the relative strength of the party's following, that is, how numerous its supporters are, is of key importance.

When one looks at the configuration of parties in each of the political

systems described, one finds correlations among the different characteristics enumerated, so that it is possible to speak of party systems in which
certain typical states of these characteristics coexist in interrelation. Thus
several of the republics—Colombia, Uruguay, Honduras, Nicaragua—have
two-party systems. In each country, these are extremely long-lived parties
boasting over a century of history. The countries' two-partyism is maintained and often recognized and even guaranteed by constitutional and
electoral provisions. Although each of the parties commands loyalty of
great psychological strength vis-à-vis the opposing party in the system, all
are divided among several factions or subparties. Finally, while the Liberal
Party in each system would more often than not win in a free election, the
division of the vote is not very lopsided.

Mexico and Bolivia have what have been called democratic single-party
systems; that is, a single party is so dominant that it invariably wins elections,
no matter how perfectly free and competitive they are. In these systems the
dominant party is the bearer of the ideology of a great national revolution.
This identification of the party with patriotic symbols keeps it in power
(together with the expectation of favors from a sort of permanent spoils
system) despite changes in the party's leadership. While opposition to the
ruling party exists and functions, the more important conflict related to
decision-making occurs among the forces committed to the single party.
These forces embrace a wide range, excluding principally the economic
elite. The leading groups within the party are the organized peasantry, union
labor, and government employees.

The multiparty system is the most common type in the area. The party
system of each country in this category usually embraces a hodgepodge of
groups which vary in size, permanence of organization, degree of personalism, and electoral following, although some systems are markedly more
personalist and impermanent as a whole in the character of their parties than
the systems of other countries.

Thus in Ecuador the old-established Conservatives and Radical-Liberals
can coexist with small but stable ideological parties like the Socialists and
with fluctuating personalist movements like the Velasquistas. In Brazil some
personalist movements become political parties; others attach themselves to
established parties for electoral purposes only; still others originate and develop wholly within the established parties. A higher degree of flux is
characteristic of the Latin American multiparty systems—in the existence
of their parties, in their mutual alliances, and to some extent in the size of
their popular followings—than of the two-party and single-party types.

We have been speaking, of course, of the democratic states here. The
dictatorships may outlaw parties altogether. More often a single legal party
rules; in some cases a tame opposition party is maintained by the regime for
the sake of appearances; in yet others opposition parties are allowed to exist
but their activities are narrowly circumscribed. In any case, the existence of
such parties does not affect how the system actually operates.

Governmental Structure

In the formal institutions of government the similarities among the political systems discussed in this book far outweigh their differences. The features shared in common typically include the separation of powers, national centralization of authority, and the strong president. Yet several of the republics are today dictatorships in which the constitution is suspended (as in Cuba) or honored only nominally (as in Haiti).

Among the interesting variations from the typical pattern, some have remained without noticeable effect. Four states have federal systems—Brazil, Argentina, Mexico, Venezuela—although Venezuela's is clearly federal in name only, as Leo Lott makes clear. The two-chamber legislature prevails except in Paraguay, Guatemala, Honduras, El Salvador, Costa Rica, and Panama, which are unicameral. Only Uruguay and Cuba today lack the strong presidency (Fidel Castro occupies the position of prime minister).

Some ingenuity has been expended in the drafting of constitutional provisions on attempts to limit the president in the interests of avoiding the dictatorship which has been so common in the area. The president is everywhere forbidden indefinite reelection, although the specific rule varies: in Paraguay he may serve two consecutive terms before leaving office; in Mexico he may never again serve after completing a single term; elsewhere the usual rule is that he may be reelected after skipping a term (two terms in Costa Rica and Guatemala). Some agencies are made independent of presidential control, Costa Rica being especially fond of this technique, although the Chilean controller-general exercises formidable powers independent of the president too, as Dr. Gil points out. Occasional attempts have been made to make presidential actions subject to cabinet monitoring, and to make the cabinet itself dependent on the legislature, but without success, as the case of Peru illustrates.

Much creative energy has gone into the drafting of electoral statutes, which are quite various in their content and in their effect. Proportional representation and the single-member district are both encountered with about equal frequency, in the region's legislative election provisions. Several states use the "incomplete list" and other methods of guaranteeing opposition representation in the legislature; among them are Peru, Nicaragua, and now Mexico. Argentina and Cuba employed such methods until very recently. Colombia guarantees the minority party parity of representation in all deliberative bodies, while Uruguay has introduced guaranteed opposition representation (one-third of the total) into the collegial executive itself.

Issues of Public Policy

The variations among the patterns of public policy of the Latin republics are contained within a narrower range than one might think. The policy problems which the different states face today are actually quite similar. The leading issues relate to international orientation, labor and social welfare, land utilization and reform, promotion of investment, monetary stabilization, and the ever-present problem of the degree of freedom to operate to be allowed to opposition groups. The nature of several of these issues has imposed a certain likeness in public policy from one state to another, always with the exception of Cuba, whose present government has chosen a path of policy based on premises different from those generally entertained in the area. Thus the international posture of nearly all the republics is one of friendship for the United States—with reservations; support for international organization and the peaceful settlement of disputes, at least in principle; and concern that economic aid be given by the developed to the underdeveloped economies. In domestic policy the imperatives of economics have forced most states to follow paths aimed at stabilization of the currency (without necessarily reaching the goal) and the encouragement of foreign private investment—again, with reservations, especially in Brazil and Argentina.

An area of policy in which a greater degree of similarity appears than actually exists is land reform. Because of domestic pressure and the urgings of the United States, now formalized in the Charter of Punta del Este, which created the Alliance for Progress, all the governments are on record as undertaking to institute programs of land reform. In some cases the point is moot: Mexico, Bolivia, and now Cuba (which of course is not party to the Alliance) have embarked on some kind of land reform within recent times, and Haiti had a type of land reform a hundred years ago; while land redistribution would hardly make sense in the grazing economies of Argentina and Uruguay. Elsewhere ostensible land-reform programs are being drafted or implemented; but these range from extensive programs of redistribution, as in Venezuela, to mere nominal gestures, as in Chile. One should be placed on notice, therefore, to look beyond the title on the legislation in order to find out what the proposed program actually represents.

The issues which face policy-makers today with greatest urgency and which have led to the adoption of the policies mentioned—the issues, that is, which are most likely to lead to crisis in the system and outbreaks of violence —derive from certain key facts in the present situation. First for several reasons the present is a period of economic deterioration. Among interrelated causes here are the rapid growth in population, the steep drop in the prices of export commodities, and the shortsighted policies of most of the governments in office during the early postwar period, when some surplus in the international balance of payments often existed but was not wisely used.

These factors have contributed in turn to population pressure and heightened dissatisfaction in rural areas. Heavy migration to the cities has resulted in the augmentation of unemployment and the extension of ugly slums. Governments have adopted monetary inflation as a policy. From this situation has grown a massive shift to means of violence on the part of much of the urban and some of the rural poor, living now in desperate straits—and encouraged today by the example of the Castro regime in Cuba.

This development has produced its own reaction. Governmental forces of the center, moderate left, or moderate right have moved increasingly either to acceptance of a demagogic role in the attempt to ally themselves with the masses and direct their resentment against the United States—as in Brazil—or to espouse a policy of repression of discontent and reliance on the armed forces—as in Venezuela. Some states, like Mexico and Bolivia, may have regimes well enough entrenched to ride out the storm; elsewhere the military have seized power from civilian governments which they thought unable or unwilling to keep out of office strong mass movements likely to open the Pandora's box of social change.*

This is the triangle of forces, sometimes coalescing temporarily into unexpected alliances, sometimes struggling bitterly among themselves, which confront each other in the frenetic politics of today's Latin America: the alienated masses, whose allegiance may go to left, right, or center, but who stand ready to do battle in the cause of social revolution; the armed forces' leadership, grim, fearful, sometimes ambitious, committed to the values of order and national power; the well-meaning civilian politicians, hating hard choices but sometimes finding the courage to make them, hoping as an optimum for economic development, stability, democracy, and friendship with the United States but unhappily aware that a compromise on one or more of these values may be unavoidable.

* Between 1962 and 1964, there were at least seven military *coups d'état* of this character.

SCHEDULE OF PRESIDENTIAL ELECTIONS
IN LATIN AMERICA, 1964-70

COUNTRY	LENGTH OF TERM	SCHEDULED DATE
Argentina	6 years	July, 1969
Bolivia	4 years	June, 1968
Brazil	5 years	October, 1965
Chile	6 years	September, 1964
Colombia	4 years	May, 1966
Costa Rica	4 years	February, 1966
Cuba	No elections scheduled	
Dominican Republic	4 years	1965
Ecuador	4 years	1965
El Salvador	5 years	April, 1967
Guatemala	6 years	1965
Haiti	No elections scheduled	
Honduras	6 years	1965
Mexico	6 years	July, 1970
Nicaragua	4 years	February, 1967
Panama	4 years	May, 1968
Paraguay	5 years	February, 1968
Peru	6 years	June, 1969
Uruguay	4 years (National Council, the collegial executive)	November, 1966
Venezuela	5 years	December, 1968

SELECTED GENERAL BIBLIOGRAPHY

Robert J. Alexander, *Prophets of the Revolution*, Macmillan, New York, 1962.

Robert J. Alexander, *Today's Latin America*, Vantage, New York, 1962.

Asher N. Christensen (Ed.), *The Evolution of Latin American Government*, Holt, New York, 1952.

Harold E. Davis (Ed.), *Government and Politics of Latin America*, Ronald, New York, 1956.

Samuel E. Finer, *The Man on Horseback*, Praeger, New York, 1962.

Rosendo A. Gomez, *Latin American Politics and Government*, Random House, New York, 1960.

Lewis Hanke, *Latin America: Continent in Ferment*, Vols. I and II, Van Nostrand, Princeton, 1960.

Austin F. Macdonald, *Latin American Politics and Government*, 2d ed., Crowell, New York, 1954.

Martin C. Needler, *Latin American Politics in Perspective*, Van Nostrand, Princeton, 1963.

William W. Pierson and Federico G. Gil, *Governments and Politics of Latin America*, McGraw-Hill, New York, 1955.

Frank Tannenbaum, *Ten Keys to Latin America*, Knopf, New York, 1962.

INDEX